ENGLISH / ARABIC

انجليزي / عربي

OXFORD PICTURE DICTIONARY

SECOND EDITION

OPD

Jayme Adelson-Goldstein

Norma Shapiro

OXFORD
UNIVERSITY PRESS

198 Madison Avenue
New York, NY 10016 USA

Great Clarendon Street, Oxford OX2 6DP UK

Oxford University Press is a department of the University of Oxford.
It furthers the University's objective of excellence in research, scholarship,
and education by publishing worldwide in

Oxford New York

Auckland Cape Town Dar es Salaam Hong Kong Karachi
Kuala Lumpur Madrid Melbourne Mexico City Nairobi
New Delhi Shanghai Taipei Toronto

With offices in

Argentina Austria Brazil Chile Czech Republic France Greece
Guatemala Hungary Italy Japan Poland Portugal Singapore
South Korea Switzerland Thailand Turkey Ukraine Vietnam

OXFORD and OXFORD ENGLISH are registered trademarks of
Oxford University Press.

© Oxford University Press 2009

Library of Congress Cataloging-in-Publication Data

Adelson-Goldstein, Jayme.
    The Oxford picture dictionary. Monolingual /
Jayme Adelson-Goldstein and Norma Shapiro.– 2nd ed.
        p. cm.
    Includes index.
    ISBN: 978-0-19-474010-4
    1. Picture dictionaries, English. 2. English
language–Textbooks for foreign speakers.
I. Shapiro, Norma. II. Title.
PE1629.S52 2008
423'.1–dc22
                                    2007041017

Database right Oxford University Press (maker)

Executive Publishing Manager: Stephanie Karras
Managing Editor: Sharon Sargent
Development Editors: Glenn Mathes II, Bruce Myint, Katie La Storia
Associate Development Editors: Olga Christopoulos, Hannah Ryu, Meredith Stoll
Design Manager: Maj-Britt Hagsted
Project Manager: Allison Harm
Senior Designers: Stacy Merlin, Michael Steinhofer
Designer: Jaclyn Smith
Senior Production Artist: Julie Armstrong
Production Layout Artist: Colleen Ho
Cover Design: Stacy Merlin
Senior Image Editor: Justine Eun
Image Editors: Robin Fadool, Fran Newman, Jenny Vainisi
Manufacturing Manager: Shanta Persaud
Manufacturing Controller: Eve Wong
Translated by: Techno-Graphics & Translations, Inc.

ISBN: 978 0 19 474010 4

Printed in China

15 14 13 12 11

This book is printed on paper from certified and well-managed sources.

The OPD team thanks the following artists for their storyboarding and sketches:
Cecilia Aranovich, Chris Brandt, Giacomo Ghiazza, Gary Goldstein, Gordan Kljucec,
Vincent Lucido, and Glenn Urieta

Illustrations by: Lori Anzalone: 13, 70-71, 76-77; Joe "Fearless" Arenella/Will Sumpter:
178; Argosy Publishing: 66-67 (call-outs), 98-99, 108-109, 112-113 (call-outs), 152, 178,
193, 194-195, 196, 197, 205; Barbara Bastian: 4, 15, 17, 20-21, 162 (map), 198, 216-217
(map), 220-221; Philip Batini/AA Reps: 50; Thomas Bayley/Sparks Literary Agency:
158-159; Sally Bensusen: 211, 214; Annie Bissett: 112; Peter Bollinger/Shannon
Associates: 14-15; Higgens Bond/Anita Grien: 226; Molly Borman-Pullman: 116, 117;
Jim Fanning/Ravenhill Represents: 80-81; Mike Gardner: 10, 12, 17, 22, 132, 114-115,
142-143, 174, 219, 228-229; Garth Glazier/AA Reps: 106, 118-119; Dennis Godfrey/
Mike Wepplo: 204; Steve Graham: 124-125, 224; Graphic Map & Chart Co.: 200-201,
202-203; Julia Green/Mendola Art: 225; Glenn Gustafson: 9, 27, 48, 76, 100, 101,
117, 132, 133, 136, 155, 161, 179, 196; Barbara Harmon: 212-213, 215; Ben Hasler/
NB Illustration: 94-95, 101, 148-149, 172, 182, 186-187; Betsy Hayes: 134, 138-139;
Matthew Holmes: 75; Stewart Holmes/Illustration Ltd.: 192; Janos Jantner/Beehive
Illustration: 5, 13, 82-83, 122-123, 130-131, 146-147, 164-165, 184, 185; Ken Joudrey/
Munro Campagna: 52, 68-69, 177, 208-209; Bob Kaganich/Deborah Wolfe: 10, 40-41,
121; Steve Karp: 230, 231; Mike Kasun/Munro Campagna: 218; Graham Kennedy:
27; Marcel Laverdet/AA Reps: 23; Jeffrey Lindberg: 33, 42-43, 92-93, 133, 160-161,
170-171, 176; Dennis Lyall/Artworks: 198; Chris Lyons:/Lindgren & Smith: 173, 191;
Alan Male/Artworks: 210, 211; Jeff Mangiat/Mendola Art: 53, 54, 55, 56, 57, 58, 59,
66-67; Adrian Mateescu/The Studio: 188-189, 232-233; Karen Minot: 28-29; Paul
Mirocha/The Wiley Group: 194, 216-217; Peter Miserendino/P.T. Pie Illustrations:
198; Lee Montgomery/Illustration Ltd.: 4; Roger Motzkus: 229; Laurie O'Keefe: 111,
216-217; Daniel O'Leary/Illustration Ltd.: 8-9, 26, 34-35, 78, 135, 136-137, 238; Vilma
Ortiz-Dillon: 16, 20-21, 60, 98-99, 100, 211; Terry Pazcko: 46-47, 144-145, 152, 180,
227; David Preiss/Munro Campagna: 5; Pronk & Associates: 192-193; Tony Randazzo/
AA Reps: 156, 234-235; Mike Renwick/Creative Eye: 126-127; Mark Riedy/Scott Hull
Associates: 48-49, 79, 140, 153; Jon Rogers/AA Reps: 112; Jeff Sanson/Schumann &
Co.: 84-85, 240-241; David Schweitzer/Munro Campagna: 162-163; Ben Shannon/
Magnet Reps: 11, 64-65, 90, 91, 96, 97, 166-167, 168-169, 179, 239; Reed Sprunger/
Jae Wagoner Artists Rep.: 18-19, 232-233; Studio Liddell/AA Reps: 27; Angelo Tillary:
108-109; Ralph Voltz/Deborah Wolfe: 50-51, 128-129, 141, 154, 175, 236-237;
Jeff Wack/Mendola Art: 24, 25, 86-87, 102-103, 134-135, 231; Brad Walker: 104-105,
150-151, 157, 206-207; Wendy Wassink: 110-111; John White/The Neis Group: 199;
Eric Wilkerson: 32, 138; Simon Williams/Illustration Ltd.: 2-3, 6-7, 30-31, 36, 38-39,
44-45, 72-73; Lee Woodgate/Eye Candy Illustration: 222-223; Andy Zito: 62-23; Craig
Zuckerman: 14, 88-89, 112-113, 120-121, 194-195.

Chapter icons designed by Von Glitschka/Scott Hull Associates

Cover Art by CUBE/Illustration Ltd (hummingbird, branch); Paul Mirocha/The Wiley
Group (cherry); Mark Riedy/Scott Hull Associates (stamp); 9 Surf Studios (lettering).

Studio photography for Oxford University Press done by Dennis Kitchen Studio: 37,
61, 72, 73, 74, 75, 95, 96, 100, 180, 181, 183, 226.

Stock Photography: Age FotoStock: 238 (flute; clarinet; bassoon; saxophone; violin; cello;
bass; guitar; trombone; trumpet; xylophone; harmonica); Comstock, 61 (window);
Morales, 221 (bat); Franco Pizzochero, 98 (cashmere); Thinkstock, 61 (sink); Alamy:
Corbis, 61 (table); Gary Crabbe, 220 (park ranger); The Associated Press: 198 (strike;
soldiers in trench); Joe Rosenthal, 198 (Iwo Jima); Neil Armstrong, 198 (Buzz Aldrin
on Moon); CORBIS: Philip Gould, 198 (Civil War); Photo Library, 220 (Yosemite Falls);
Danita Delimont: Greg Johnston, 220 (snorkeling); Jamie & Judy Wild, 220 (El Capitan);
Getty Images: 198 (Martin Luther King, Jr.); Amana Images, 61 (soapy plates), The
Granger Collection: 198 (Jazz Age); The Image Works: Kelly Spranger, 220 (sea turtle);
Inmagine: 238 (oboe; tuba; French horn; piano; drums; tambourine; accordion);
istockphoto: 61 (oven); 98 (silk); 99 (suede; lace; velvet); Jupiter Images: 61 (tiles); 98
(wool); 99 (corduroy); Foodpix, 98 (linen); Rob Melnychuk/Brand X Pictures, 61 (glass
shower door); Jupiter Unlimited: 220 (seagulls); 238 (electric keyboard); Comstock, 99
(denim); Mary Evans Picture Library: 198 (women in factory); NPS Photo: Peter Jones, 221
(Carlsbad Cavern entrance; tour; cavern; spelunker); OceanwideImages.com: Gary Bell,
220 (coral); Photo Edit, Inc: David Young-Wolff, 220 (trail); Picture History: 198 (Hiram
Rhodes); Robertstock: 198 (Great Depression); Punchstock: 98 (t-shirt), Robert Glusic,
31 (Monument Valley); Roland Corporation: 238 (organ); SuperStock: 99 (leather); 198
(Daniel Boone); Shutterstock: Marek Szumlas, 94 (watch); United States Mint: 126;
Veer: Brand X Pictures, 220 (deer); Photodisc, 220 (black bear); Yankee Fleet, Inc.: 220
(Fort Jefferson; Yankee Freedom Ferry), Emil von Maltitz/Lime Photo, 37 (baby carrier).

This second edition of
the Oxford Picture Dictionary
is lovingly dedicated to
the memory of Norma Shapiro.

Her ideas, her pictures, and
her stories continue to teach,
inspire, and delight.

Acknowledgments

The publisher and authors would like to acknowledge the following individuals for their invaluable feedback during the development of this program:

Dr. Macarena Aguilar, Cy-Fair College, Houston, TX

Joseph F. Anselme, Atlantic Technical Center, Coconut Creek, FL

Stacy Antonopoulos, Monterey Trail High School, Elk Grove, CA

Carol Antunano, The English Center, Miami, FL

Irma Arencibia, Thomas A. Edison School, Union City, NJ

Suzi Austin, Alexandria City Public School Adult Program, Alexandria, FL

Patricia S. Bell, Lake Technical Center, Eustis, FL

Jim Brice, San Diego Community College District, San Diego, CA

Phil Cackley, Arlington Education and Employment Program (REEP), Arlington, VA

Frieda Caldwell, Metropolitan Adult Education Program, San Jose, CA

Sandra Cancel, Robert Waters School, Union City, NJ

Anne Marie Caney, Chula Vista Adult School, Chula Vista, CA

Patricia Castro, Harvest English Institute, Newark, NJ

Paohui Lola Chen, Milpitas Adult School, Milpitas, CA

Lori Cisneros, Atlantic Vo-Tech, Ft. Lauderdale, FL

Joyce Clapp, Hayward Adult School, Hayward, CA

Stacy Clark, Arlington Education and Employment Program (REEP), Arlington, VA

Nancy B. Crowell, Southside Programs for Adults in Continuing Education, Prince George, VA

Doroti da Cunha, Hialeah-Miami Lakes Adult Education Center, Miami, FL

Paula Da Silva-Michelin, La Guardia Community College, Long Island City, NY

Cynthia L. Davies, Humble I.S.D., Humble, TX

Christopher Davis, Overfelt Adult Center, San Jose, CA

Beverly De Nicola, Capistrano Unified School District, San Juan Capistrano, CA

Beatriz Diaz, Miami-Dade County Public Schools, Miami, FL

Druci J. Diaz, Hillsborough County Public Schools, Tampa, FL

Marion Donahue, San Dieguito Adult School, Encinitas, CA

Nick Doorn, International Education Services, South Lyon, MI

Mercedes Douglass, Seminole Community College, Sanford, FL

Jenny Elliott, Montgomery College, Rockville, MD

Paige Endo, Mt. Diablo Adult Education, Concord, CA

Megan Ernst, Glendale Community College, Glendale, CA

Elizabeth Escobar, Robert Waters School, Union City, NJ

Joanne Everett, Dave Thomas Education Center, Pompano Beach, FL

Jennifer Fadden, Arlington Education and Employment Program (REEP), Arlington, VA

Judy Farron, Fort Myers Language Center, Fort Myers, FL

Sharyl Ferguson, Montwood High School, El Paso, TX

Dr. Monica Fishkin, University of Central Florida, Orlando, FL

Nancy Frampton, Reedley College, Reedley, CA

Lynn A. Freeland, San Dieguito Union High School District, Encinitas, CA

Cathy Gample, San Leandro Adult School, San Leandro, CA

Hillary Gardner, Center for Immigrant Education and Training, Long Island City, NY

Martha C. Giffen, Alhambra Unified School District, Alhambra, CA

Jill Gluck, Hollywood Community Adult School, Los Angeles, CA

Carolyn Grimaldi, LaGuardia Community College, Long Island City, NY

William Gruenholz, USD Adult School, Concord, CA

Sandra G. Gutierrez, Hialeah-Miami Lakes Adult Education Center, Miami, FL

Conte Gúzman-Hoffman, Triton College, River Grove, IL

Amanda Harllee, Palmetto High School, Palmetto, FL

Mercedes Hearn, Tampa Bay Technical Center, Tampa, FL

Robert Hearst, Truman College, Chicago, IL

Patty Heiser, University of Washington, Seattle, WA

Joyce Hettiger, Metropolitan Education District, San Jose, CA

Karen Hirsimaki, Napa Valley Adult School, Napa, CA

Marvina Hooper, Lake Technical Center, Eustis, FL

Katie Hurter, North Harris College, Houston, TX

Nuchamon James, Miami Dade College, Miami, FL

Linda Jennings, Montgomery College, Rockville, MD

Bonnie Boyd Johnson, Chapman Education Center, Garden Grove, CA

Fayne B. Johnson, Broward County Public Schools, Fort Lauderdale, FL

Stavroula Katseyeanis, Robert Waters School, Union City, NJ

Dale Keith, Broadbase Consulting, Inc. at Kidworks USA, Miami, FL

Blanche Kellawon, Bronx Community College, Bronx, NY

Mary Kernel, Migrant Education Regional Office, Northwest Educational Service District, Anacortes, WA

Karen Kipke, Antioch High School Freshman Academy, Antioch, TN

Jody Kirkwood, ABC Adult School, Cerritos, CA

Matthew Kogan, Evans Community Adult School, Los Angeles, CA

Ineza Kuceba, Renton Technical College, Renton, WA

John Kuntz, California State University, San Bernadino, San Bernadino, CA

Claudia Kupiec, DePaul University, Chicago, IL

E.C. Land, Southside Programs for Adult Continuing Education, Prince George, VA

Betty Lau, Franklin High School, Seattle, WA

Patt Lemonie, Thomas A. Edison School, Union City, NJ

Lia Lerner, Burbank Adult School, Burbank, CA

Krystyna Lett, Metropolitan Education District, San Jose, CA

Renata Lima, TALK International School of Languages, Fort Lauderdale, FL

Luz M. Lopez, Sweetwater Union High School District, Chula Vista, CA

Osmara Lopez, Bronx Community College, Bronx, NY

Heather Lozano, North Lake College, Irving, TX

Betty Lynch, Arlington Education and Employment Program (REEP), Arlington, VA

Meera Madan, REID Park Elementary School, Charlotte, NC

Ivanna Mann Thrower, Charlotte Mecklenburg Schools, Charlotte, NC

Michael R. Mason, Loma Vista Adult Center, Concord, CA

Holley Mayville, Charlotte Mecklenburg Schools, Charlotte, NC

Margaret McCabe, United Methodist Cooperative Ministries, Clearwater, FL

Todd McDonald, Hillsborough Adult Education, Tampa, FL

Nancy A. McKeand, ESL Consultant, St. Benedict, LA

Rebecca L. McLain, Gaston College, Dallas, NC

John M. Mendoza, Redlands Adult School, Redlands, CA

Bet Messmer, Santa Clara Adult Education Center, Santa Clara, CA

Christina Morales, BEGIN Managed Programs, New York, NY

Lisa Munoz, Metropolitan Education District, San Jose, CA

Mary Murphy-Clagett, Sweetwater Union High School District, Chula Vista, CA

Jonetta Myles, Rockdale County High School, Conyers, GA

Marwan Nabi, Troy High School, Fullerton, CA

Dr. Christine L. Nelsen, Salvation Army Community Center, Tampa, FL

Michael W. Newman, Arlington Education and Employment Program (REEP), Arlington, VA

Rehana Nusrat, Huntington Beach Adult School, Huntington Beach, CA

Cindy Oakley-Paulik, Embry-Riddle Aeronautical University, Daytona Beach, FL

Acknowledgments

Janet Ochi-Fontanott, Sweetwater Union High School District, Chula Vista, CA

Lorraine Pedretti, Metropolitan Education District, San Jose, CA

Isabel Pena, BE/ESL Programs, Garland, TX

Margaret Perry, Everett Public Schools, Everett, WA

Dale Pesmen, PhD, Chicago, IL

Cathleen Petersen, Chapman Education Center, Garden Grove, CA

Allison Pickering, Escondido Adult School, Escondido, CA

Ellen Quish, LaGuardia Community College, Long Island City, NY

Teresa Reen, Independence Adult Center, San Jose, CA

Kathleen Reynolds, Albany Park Community Center, Chicago, IL

Melba I. Rillen, Palmetto High School, Palmetto, FL

Lorraine Romero, Houston Community College, Houston, TX

Eric Rosenbaum, BEGIN Managed Programs, New York, NY

Blair Roy, Chapman Education Center, Garden Grove, CA

Arlene R. Schwartz, Broward Community Schools, Fort Lauderdale, FL

Geraldyne Blake Scott, Truman College, Chicago, IL

Sharada Sekar, Antioch High School Freshman Academy, Antioch, TN

Dr. Cheryl J. Serrano, Lynn University, Boca Raton, FL

Janet Setzekorn, United Methodist Cooperative Ministries, Clearwater, FL

Terry Shearer, EDUCALL Learning Services, Houston, TX

Elisabeth Sklar, Township High School District 113, Highland Park, IL

Robert Stein, BEGIN Managed Programs, New York, NY

Ruth Sutton, Township High School District 113, Highland Park, IL

Alisa Takeuchi, Chapman Education Center, Garden Grove, CA

Grace Tanaka, Santa Ana College School of Continuing Education, Santa Ana, CA

Annalisa Te, Overfelt Adult Center, San Jose, CA

Don Torluemke, South Bay Adult School, Redondo Beach, CA

Maliheh Vafai, Overfelt Adult Center, San Jose, CA

Tara Vasquez, Robert Waters School, Union City, NJ

Nina Velasco, Naples Language Center, Naples, FL

Theresa Warren, East Side Adult Center, San Jose, CA

Lucie Gates Watel, Truman College, Chicago, IL

Wendy Weil, Arnold Middle School, Cypress, TX

Patricia Weist, TALK International School of Languages, Fort Lauderdale, FL

Dr. Carole Lynn Weisz, Lehman College, Bronx, NY

Desiree Wesner, Robert Waters School, Union City, NJ

David Wexler, Napa Valley Adult School, Napa, CA

Cynthia Wiseman, Borough of Manhattan Community College, New York, NY

Debbie Cullinane Wood, Lincoln Education Center, Garden Grove, CA

Banu Yaylali, Miami Dade College, Miami, FL

Hongyan Zheng, Milpitas Adult Education, Milpitas, CA

Arlene Zivitz, ESOL Teacher, Jupiter, FL

The publisher, authors, and editors would like to thank the following people for their expertise in reviewing specific content areas:

Ross Feldberg, Tufts University, Medford, MA

William J. Hall, M.D. FACP/FRSM (UK), Cumberland Foreside, ME

Jill A. Horohoe, Arizona State University, Tempe, AZ

Phoebe B. Rouse, Louisiana State University, Baton Rouge, LA

Dr. Susan Rouse, Southern Wesleyan University, Central, SC

Dr. Ira M. Sheskin, University of Miami, Coral Gables, FL

Maiko Tomizawa, D.D.S., New York, NY

The publisher would like to thank the following for their permission to reproduce copyrighted material:

Table of Contents قائمة المحتويات

Introduction مقدمة . . . . ix–xi

1. Everyday Language لغة التحادث اليومية

Meeting and Greeting اللقاء والتحية 2–3
Personal Information معلومات شخصية 4
School المدرسة 5
A Classroom حجرة الصف 6–7
Studying الدراسة 8–9
Succeeding in School النجاح في المدرسة 10
A Day at School اليوم المدرسي 11
Everyday Conversation الحديث اليومي 12
Weather الطقس 13
The Telephone الهاتف / التليفون 14–15
Numbers الأعداد 16
Measurements المقاييس 17
Time الوقت 18–19
The Calendar التقويم 20–21
Calendar Events الأعياد والمناسبات الخاصة 22
Describing Things وصف الأشياء 23
Colors الألوان 24
Prepositions حروف الجر 25
Money النقود 26
Shopping التسوق 27
Same and Different متشابهتان ومختلفتان 28–29

2. People الناس

Adults and Children الكبار والأطفال 30–31
Describing People وصف الناس 32
Describing Hair وصف الشعر 33
Families العائلات 34–35
Childcare and Parenting رعاية الأطفال ودور الوالدين 36–37
Daily Routines الأعمال اليومية الروتينية 38–39
Life Events and Documents الأحداث والوثائق الحياتية 40–41
Feelings أحاسيس 42–43
A Family Reunion اجتماع شمل الأسرة 44–45

3. Housing السكن

The Home المنزل 46–47
Finding a Home البحث عن منزل 48–49
Apartments الشقق 50–51
Different Places to Live أماكن مختلفة للسكن 52
A House and Yard منزل وفناء 53
A Kitchen المطبخ 54
A Dining Area غرفة الطعام 55
A Living Room غرفة الجلوس (الصالة) 56
A Bathroom الحمّام 57
A Bedroom غرفة النوم 58
The Kids' Bedroom غرفة نوم الأطفال 59
Housework الأعمال المنزلية 60
Cleaning Supplies أدوات التنظيف 61
Household Problems and Repairs مشاكل المنزل وإصلاحها 62–63
The Tenant Meeting اجتماع المستأجرين 64–65

4. Food الطعام

Back from the Market العودة من السوق 66–67
Fruit الفاكهة 68
Vegetables الخضروات 69
Meat and Poultry اللحوم والدواجن 70
Seafood and Deli المأكولات البحرية وأطعمة شهية 71
A Grocery Store محل البقالة 72–73
Containers and Packaging حاويات وتعليب 74
Weights and Measurements الأوزان والمقادير 75
Food Preparation and Safety تحضير الطعام وسلامته 76–77
Kitchen Utensils أدوات المطبخ 78
Fast Food Restaurant مطعم الوجبات السريعة 79
A Coffee Shop Menu قائمة الطعام في مقهى 80–81
A Restaurant مطعم 82–83
The Farmers' Market سوق المزارعين 84–85

5. Clothing الملابس

Everyday Clothes الملابس اليومية 86–87
Casual, Work, and Formal Clothes الملابس غير الرسمية والرسمية وملابس العمل 88–89
Seasonal Clothing الملابس الموسمية 90
Underwear and Sleepwear الملابس الداخلية وملابس النوم 91
Workplace Clothing ملابس مكان العمل 92–93
Shoes and Accessories أحذية وإكسسوارات 94–95
Describing Clothes وصف الملابس 96–97
Making Clothes صنع الملابس 98–99
Making Alterations تعديل الثياب 100
Doing the Laundry غسل الملابس 101
A Garage Sale بيع الأشياء الشخصية المستعملة في فناء المنزل 102–103

6. Health الصحة

The Body الجسم 104–105
Inside and Outside the Body أعضاء الجسم الداخلية والخارجية 106–107
Personal Hygiene النظافة الشخصية 108–109
Symptoms and Injuries أعراض مرضية وإصابات 110
Illnesses and Medical Conditions علل وحالات طبية 111
A Pharmacy صيدلية 112–113
Taking Care of Your Health العناية بصحتك 114–115
Medical Emergencies حالات طبية طارئة 116
First Aid إسعافات أولية 117
Medical Care الرعاية الصحية 118
Dental Care رعاية الأسنان 119
Hospital المستشفى 120–121
A Health Fair معرض الصحة 122–123

7. Community المجتمع

Downtown وسط المدينة 124–125

City Streets شوارع المدينة 126–127

An Intersection تقاطع طرق 128–129

A Mall مركز تجاري (مول) 130–131

The Bank البنك / المصرف 132

The Library المكتبة 133

The Post Office مكتب البريد 134–135

Department of Motor Vehicles (DMV) دائرة تسجيل المركبات الآلية . . . 136–137

Government and Military Service الحكومة والخدمة العسكرية 138–139

Civic Rights and Responsibilities الحقوق والواجبات المدنية 140

The Legal System النظام القانوني 141

Crime الجريمة 142

Public Safety السلامة العامة 143

Emergencies and Natural Disasters حالات الطوارئ والكوارث الطبيعية . 144–145

Emergency Procedures الإجراءات المتبعة في حالات الطوارئ 146–147

Community Cleanup المحافظة على نظافة المجتمع 148–149

8. Transportation النقل والمواصلات

Basic Transportation وسائل النقل الأساسية 150–151

Public Transportation النقل العام 152

Prepositions of Motion حروف الجر المتعلقة بالحركة 153

Traffic Signs لافتات المرور 154

Directions and Maps إرشادات وخرائط 155

Cars and Trucks سيارات وشاحنات 156

Buying and Maintaining a Car شراء وصيانة سيارة 157

Parts of a Car قطع غيار سيارة 158–159

An Airport مطار 160–161

Taking a Trip السفر في رحلة 162–163

9. Work العمل

The Workplace مكان العمل 164–165

Jobs and Occupations A-C وظائف ومهن 166

Jobs and Occupations C-H وظائف ومهن 167

Jobs and Occupations H-P وظائف ومهن 168

Jobs and Occupations P-W وظائف ومهن 169

Job Skills مهارات حرفية 170

Office Skills مهارات للعمل في مكتب 171

Career Planning التخطيط لمسار وظيفي 172

Job Search البحث عن وظيفة 173

Interview Skills المهارات المطلوبة للمقابلات الشخصية 174

A Factory مصنع 175

Landscaping and Gardening تنسيق المناظر الطبيعية والبستنة 176

Farming and Ranching الزراعة وتربية المواشي 177

Construction البناء 178

Job Safety السلامة في مكان العمل 179

Tools and Building Supplies أدوات ومواد البناء 180–181

An Office مكتب 182–183

A Hotel فندق 184

Food Service خدمة تقديم طعام 185

A Bad Day at Work يوم سيء في العمل 186–187

Contents المحتويات

10. Areas of Study مجالات الدراسة

Schools and Subjects مدارس ومواد الدراسة. 188–189
English Composition الإنشاء باللغة الإنجليزية. 190–191
Mathematics الرياضيات 192–193
Science العلوم 194–195
Computers الكمبيوتر (الحاسوب) 196
The Internet الإنترنت (شبكة المعلومات العالمية) 197
U.S. History تاريخ الولايات المتحدة الأمريكية 198
World History تاريخ العالم. 199
North America and Central America أمريكا الشمالية والوسطى 200–201
World Map خريطة العالم. 202–203
Geography and Habitats جغرافيا وبيئات طبيعية 204
The Universe الكون 205
A Graduation حفلة التخرُج. 206–207

11. Plants and Animals نباتات وحيوانات

Nature Center مركز الطبيعة 208–209
Trees and Plants أشجار ونباتات 210
Flowers زهور 211
Marine Life, Amphibians, and Reptiles الأحياء البحرية والبرمائيات والزواحف . . . 212–213
Birds, Insects, and Arachnids الطيور والحشرات والعنكبوتيات 214
Domestic Animals and Rodents الحيوانات الأليفة والقوارض 215
Mammals الثدييات 216–217
Energy and Conservation الطاقة وحفظ الموارد الطبيعية 218–219
U.S. National Parks الحدائق والمنتزهات العامة الأمريكية 220–221

12. Recreation الاستجمام

Places to Go أماكن للزيارة 222–223
The Park and Playground الحديقة وملعب الأطفال 224
The Beach الشاطئ 225
Outdoor Recreation وسائل الاستجمام في الطبيعة 226
Winter and Water Sports ألعاب رياضية شتوية ومائية 227
Individual Sports ألعاب رياضية فردية 228
Team Sports ألعاب رياضية جماعية 229
Sports Verbs أفعال متعلقة بالرياضة 230
Sports Equipment معدات رياضية 231
Hobbies and Games هوايات وألعاب 232–233
Electronics and Photography أجهزة إلكترونية وأدوات التصوير 234–235
Entertainment تسلية وترفيه 236–237
Music موسيقى 238
Holidays الأعياد 239
A Birthday Party حفلة عيد ميلاد 240–241

Verb Guide دليل الأفعال 242–244
How to Use the Index كيفية استعمال الفهرس 245
English Index فهرس انجليزي 246–281
Geographical Index فهرس جغرافي 282–284
Arabic Index فهرس عربي 285–304
Research Bibliography مسرد للأبحاث 305

Teaching with the *Oxford Picture Dictionary* Program

The following general guidelines will help you prepare single and multilevel lessons using the OPD program. For step-by-step, topic-specific lesson plans, see *OPD Lesson Plans*.

1. Use Students' Needs to Identify Lesson Objectives

- Create communicative objectives based on your learners' needs assessments (*see OPD 2e Assessment Program*).
- Make sure objectives state what students will be able to do at the end of the lesson. For example: *Students will be able to respond to basic classroom commands and requests for classroom objects.* (pp. 6–7, A Classroom)
- For multilevel classes, identify a low-beginning, high-beginning, and low-intermediate objective for each topic.

2. Preview the Topic

Identify what your students already know about the topic.

- Ask general questions related to the topic.
- Have students list words they know from the topic.
- Ask questions about the picture(s) on the page.

3. Present the New Vocabulary

Research shows that it is best to present no more than 5–7 new words at a time. Here are a few presentation techniques:

- Say each new word and describe it within the context of the picture. Have volunteers act out verbs and verb sequences.
- Use Total Physical Response commands to build vocabulary comprehension.
- For long or unfamiliar word lists, introduce words by categories or select the words your students need most.
- Ask a series of questions to build comprehension and give students an opportunity to say the new words. Begin with *yes/no* questions: *Is #16 chalk?* Progress to *or* questions: *Is #16 chalk or a marker?* Finally, ask *Wh-* questions: *What can I use to write on this paper?*
- Focus on the words that students want to learn. Have them write 3–5 new words from each topic, along with meaning clues such as a drawing, translation, or sentence.

More vocabulary and **Grammar Point** sections provide additional presentation opportunities (see p. 5, School). For multilevel presentation ideas, see *OPD Lesson Plans*.

4. Check Comprehension

Make sure that students understand the target vocabulary. Here are two activities you can try:

- Say vocabulary words, and have students point to the correct items in their books. Walk around the room, checking if students are pointing to the correct pictures.
- Make true/false statements about the target vocabulary. Have students hold up two fingers for true, three for false.

5. Provide Guided and Communicative Practice

The exercise bands at the bottom of the topic pages provide a variety of guided and communicative practice opportunities and engage students' higher-level thinking.

6. Provide More Practice

OPD Second Edition offers a variety of components to facilitate vocabulary acquisition. Each of the print and electronic materials listed below offers suggestions and support for single and multilevel instruction.

OPD Lesson Plans Step-by-step multilevel lesson plans feature 3 CDs with multilevel listening, context-based pronunciation practice, and leveled reading practice. Includes multilevel teaching notes for *The OPD Reading Library*.

OPD Audio CDs or Audio Cassettes Each word in *OPD's* word list is recorded by topic.

Low-Beginning, High-Beginning, and Low-Intermediate Workbooks Guided practice for each page in *OPD* features linked visual contexts, realia, and listening practice.

Classic Classroom Activities A photocopiable resource of interactive multilevel activities, grammar practice, and communicative tasks.

The OPD Reading Library Readers include civics, academic content, and workplace themes.

Overhead Transparencies Vibrant transparencies help to focus students on the lesson.

OPD Presentation Software A multilevel interactive teaching tool using interactive whiteboard and LCD technology. Audio, animation, and video instructional support bring each dictionary topic to life.

The OPD CD-ROM An interactive learning tool featuring four-skill practice based on *OPD* topics.

Bilingual Editions *OPD* is available in numerous bilingual editions including Spanish, Chinese, Vietnamese, Arabic, Korean, and many more.

My hope is that OPD makes it easier for you to take your learners from comprehension to communication. Please share your thoughts with us as you make the book your own.

Jayme Adelson-Goldstein

OPDteam.us@oup.com

Welcome to the
OPD SECOND EDITION

The second edition of the *Oxford Picture Dictionary* expands on the best aspects of the 1998 edition with:

- New artwork presenting words within meaningful, real-life contexts
- An updated word list to meet the needs of today's English language learners
- 4,000 English words and phrases, including 285 verbs
- 40 new topics with 12 intro pages and 12 story pages
- Unparalleled support for vocabulary teaching

Subtopics present the words in easy-to-learn "chunks."

Color coding and icons make it easy to navigate through *OPD*.

New art and rich contexts improve vocabulary acquisition.

Revised practice activities help students from low-beginning through low-intermediate levels.

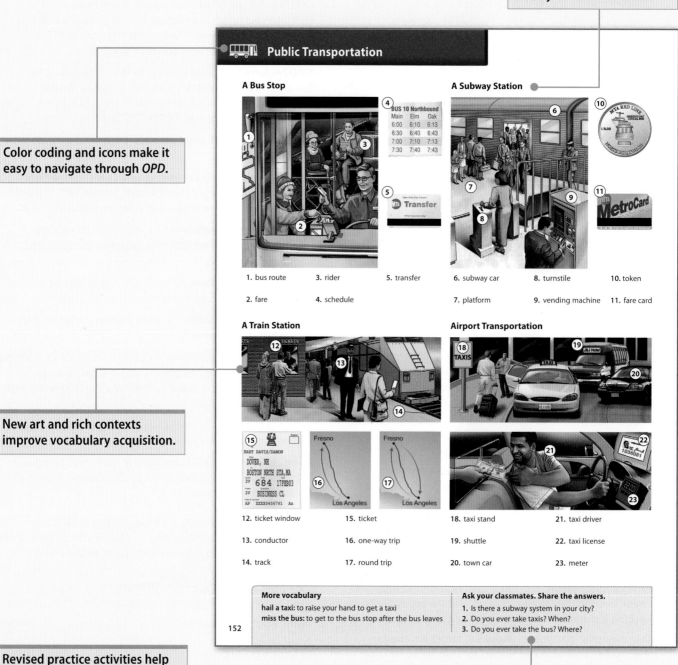

Public Transportation

A Bus Stop

BUS 10 Northbound
Main	Elm	Oak
6:00	6:10	6:13
6:30	6:40	6:43
7:00	7:10	7:13
7:30	7:40	7:43

1. bus route
2. fare
3. rider
4. schedule
5. transfer

A Subway Station

6. subway car
7. platform
8. turnstile
9. vending machine
10. token
11. fare card

A Train Station

12. ticket window
13. conductor
14. track
15. ticket
16. one-way trip
17. round trip

Airport Transportation

18. taxi stand
19. shuttle
20. town car
21. taxi driver
22. taxi license
23. meter

More vocabulary

hail a taxi: to raise your hand to get a taxi
miss the bus: to get to the bus stop after the bus leaves

Ask your classmates. Share the answers.

1. Is there a subway system in your city?
2. Do you ever take taxis? When?
3. Do you ever take the bus? Where?

152

NEW! Intro pages open each unit with key vocabulary related to the unit theme. Clear, engaging artwork promotes questions, conversations, and writing practice for all levels.

Each intro page teaches key vocabulary items within the unit theme.

Practice activities make it easy to manage multilevel classrooms.

NEW! Story pages close each unit with a lively scene for reviewing vocabulary and teaching additional language. Meanwhile, rich visual contexts recycle words from the unit.

Pre-reading questions build students' previewing and predicting skills.

High-interest readings promote literacy skills.

Post-reading questions and role-play activities support critical thinking and encourage students to use the language they have learned.

The thematic word list previews words that students will encounter in the story.

A. **Say**, "Hello."
قل، "أهلا وسهلا."

B. **Ask**, "How are you?"
اسأل، "كيف حالك؟"

C. **Introduce** yourself.
عرّف / قدّم نفسك.

D. **Smile**.
ابتسم.

E. **Hug**.
احضني.

F. **Wave**.
سلّمي وودعي ملوّحة بيدك.

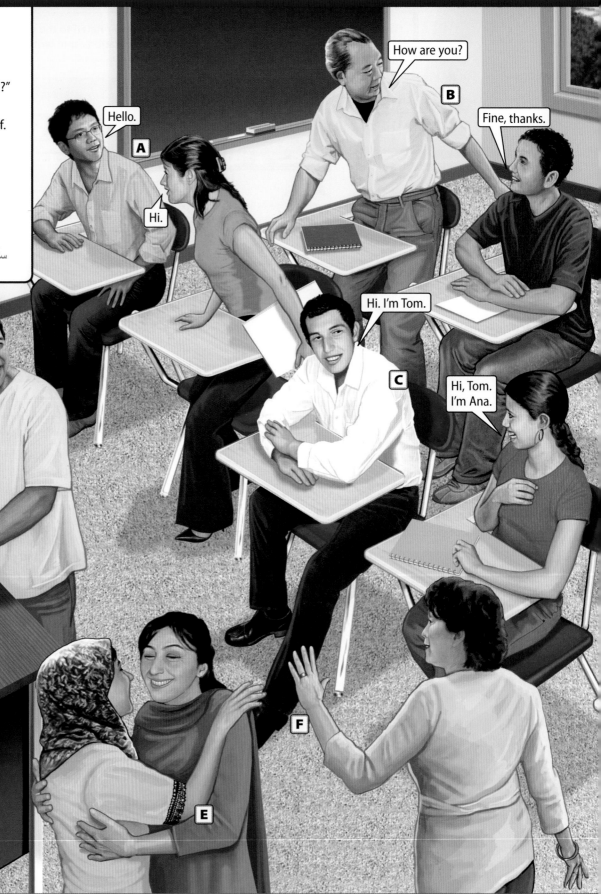

Tell your partner what to do. Take turns.

1. *Say,* "Hello."   4. *Shake hands.*
2. *Bow.*   5. *Wave.*
3. *Smile.*   6. *Say,* "Goodbye."

Dictate to your partner. Take turns.

A: *Write* <u>smile</u>.
B: *Is it spelled* <u>s-m-i-l-e</u>?
A: *Yes, that's right.*

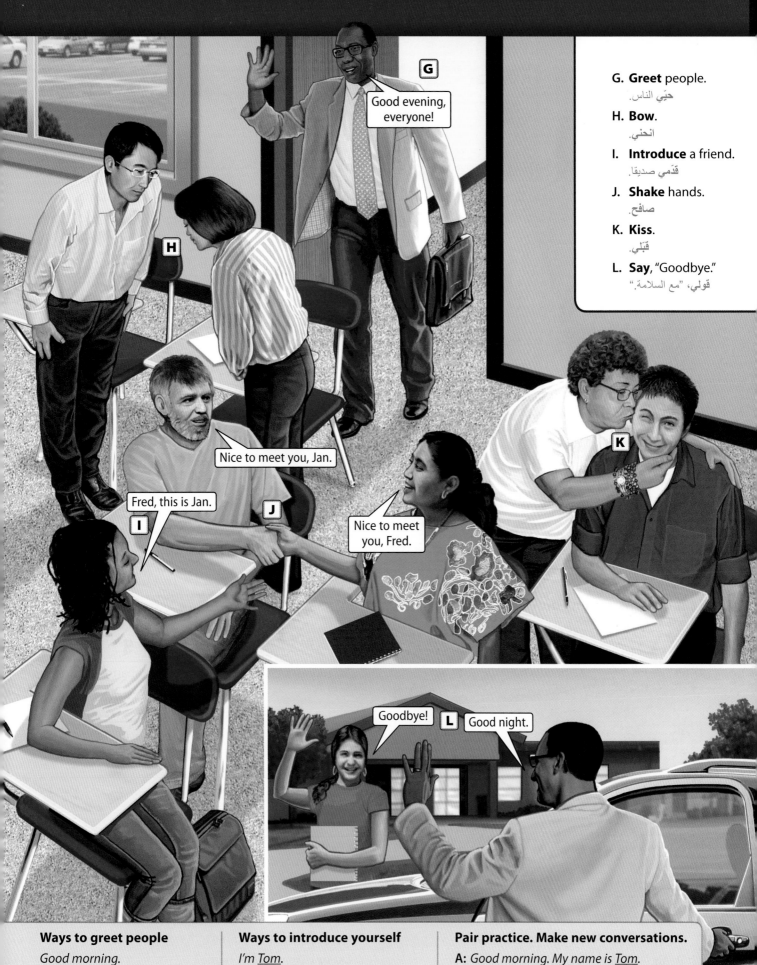

G. **Greet** people.
حَيِّي الناس.

H. **Bow**.
انحني.

I. **Introduce** a friend.
قَدِّمي صديقا.

J. **Shake** hands.
صافح.

K. **Kiss**.
قَبِّلي.

L. **Say**, "Goodbye."
قولي، "مع السلامة."

Ways to greet people

Good morning.
Good afternoon.
Good evening.

Ways to introduce yourself

I'm Tom.
My name is Tom.

Pair practice. Make new conversations.

A: *Good morning. My name is Tom.*
B: *Nice to meet you, Tom. I'm Sara.*
A: *Nice to meet you, Sara.*

3

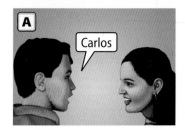

A. Say your name.
قل اسمك.

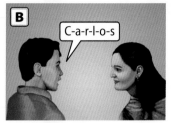

B. Spell your name.
تهجَّ اسمك.

C. Print your name.
اكتب اسمك.

D. Sign your name.
وقِّع اسمك.

Filling Out a Form ملء استمارة

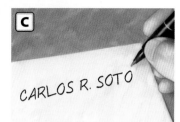

School Registration Form استمارة تسجيل بالمدرسة

1. name:
   الاسم:

_____

2. first name
   الاسم الأول

3. middle initial
   الحرف الأول من اسمك الأوسط

4. last name
   اسم العائلة

5. address
   العنوان

6. apartment number
   رقم الشقة

7. city
   المدينة

8. state
   الولاية

9. ZIP code
   الرمز البريدي

10. area code
    رمز / مفتاح المنطقة

11. phone number
    رقم الهاتف / التليفون

12. cell phone number
    رقم الهاتف / التليفون المحمول (النقال)

13. date of birth (DOB)
    تاريخ الميلاد

14. place of birth
    مكان الميلاد

15. Social Security number
    رقم بطاقة الضمان الاجتماعي

16. sex:
    النوع:

17. male
    ذكر:

18. female
    أنثى:

19. signature
    التوقيع

Pair practice. Make new conversations.

A: *My first name is* <u>Carlos</u>.
B: *Please spell* <u>Carlos</u> *for me.*
A: <u>*C-a-r-l-o-s*</u>

Ask your classmates. Share the answers.

1. Do you like your first name?
2. Is your last name from your mother? father? husband?
3. What is your middle name?

Campus حرم المدرسة

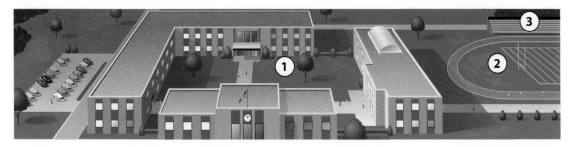

Administrators الإداريون

Around Campus حول الحرم

1. quad
   فناء مربع
2. field
   أرض الملعب
3. bleachers
   مدرجات
4. principal
   ناظر المدرسة / مدير المدرسة
5. assistant principal
   مساعد الناظر
6. counselor
   مشرف
7. classroom
   حجرة صف / فصل دراسي
8. teacher
   معلِّم
9. restrooms
   دورات مياه
10. hallway
    رواق
11. locker
    خزانة
12. main office
    مكتب الإدارة
13. clerk
    موظف/ ـة
14. cafeteria
    كافتيريا
15. computer lab
    مختبر حواسيب
16. teacher's aide
    معاون معلِّم
17. library
    مكتبة
18. auditorium
    قاعة محاضرات
19. gym
    جمنازيوم (قاعة الجمباز)
20. coach
    مدرِّب
21. track
    مضمار الجزْي / السباق

More vocabulary

Students do not pay to go to a **public school**.
Students pay to go to a **private school**.
A church, mosque, or temple school is a **parochial school**.

Grammar Point: contractions of the verb *be*

He + is = He's	*He's a teacher.*
She + is = She's	*She's a counselor.*
They + are = They're	*They're students.*

5

1. chalkboard
سبورة

2. screen
شاشة للعرض

3. whiteboard
سبورة بيضاء

4. teacher / instructor
معلّمة / مدرّسة

5. student
طالبة

6. LCD projector
آلة عرض على شاشة بيلور سائل (إل سي دي)

7. desk
مكتب

8. headphones
سماعات رأس

A. **Raise** your hand.
ارفع يدك.

B. **Talk** to the teacher.
تكلّم مع المعلم.

C. **Listen** to a CD.
استمع إلى قرص مدمج (س دي).

D. **Stand up**.
قف.

E. **Write** on the board.
اكتب على السبورة.

F. **Sit down.** / **Take** a seat.
اجلس. / اقعد على مقعد.

G. **Open** your book.
افتح كتابك.

H. **Close** your book.
أغلق كتابك.

I. **Pick up** the pencil.
التقط القلم الرصاص.

J. **Put down** the pencil.
أنزِل القلم الرصاص.

ABCDEFGHIJKLMNOPQRSTUVWXYZ

9. clock	11. chair	13. alphabet	15. computer
ساعة	كرسي	حروف الهجاء	حاسوب
10. bookcase	12. map	14. bulletin board	16. overhead projector
رف للكتب	خريطة	لوحة منشورات	آلة عرض علوية

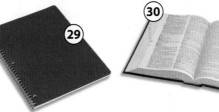

17. dry erase marker	21. (pencil) eraser	25. textbook	29. spiral notebook
قلم جاف للتخطيط قابل للمحو	ممحاة (القلم الرصاص)	كتاب مدرسي	كراسة بسلك
18. chalk	22. pen	26. workbook	30. dictionary
طباشير	قلم حبر	كراسة تمارين	معجم
19. eraser	23. pencil sharpener	27. 3-ring binder / notebook	31. picture dictionary
ممحاة	مبراة الأقلام الرصاص	ملف ذو ثلاث حلقات / كراسة	معجم مصوَّر
20. pencil	24. marker	28. notebook paper	
قلم رصاص	قلم تخطيط	ورق مذكرة	

Look at the picture.
Describe the classroom.

A: There's a chalkboard.
B: There are fifteen students.

Ask your classmates. Share the answers.

1. Do you like to raise your hand in class?
2. Do you like to listen to CDs in class?
3. Do you ever talk to the teacher?

Learning New Words تعلّم كلمات جديدة

A. Look up the word.
ابحثي عن كلمة في المعجم.

B. Read the definition.
اقرئي التعريف.

C. Translate the word.
ترجمي الكلمة.

D. Check the pronunciation.
راجعي النطق.

E. Copy the word.
انسخي الكلمة.

F. Draw a picture.
ارسمي صورة.

Working with Your Classmates العمل مع زملائك في الصف

G. Discuss a problem.
ناقشي مشكلة.

H. Brainstorm solutions / answers.
تبادلوا الأفكار للوصول إلى حلول / أجوبة.

I. Work in a group.
اعمل في مجموعة.

J. Help a classmate.
ساعدي أحد زملائك في الصف.

Working with a Partner العمل مع رفيق

K. Ask a question.
اطرحي سؤالا.

L. Answer a question.
جاوب على السؤال.

M. Share a book.
تقاسما كتابا.

N. Dictate a sentence.
قومي بإملاء جملة.

Following Directions إتباع الإرشادات

O. **Fill in** the blank.
املأ الخانة (الفراغ).

P. **Choose** the correct answer.
اختر الجواب الصحيح.

Q. **Circle** the answer.
ضع **دائرة** حول الجواب.

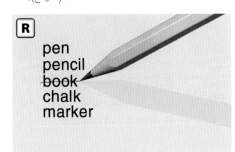

R. **Cross out** the word.
اشطب الكلمة.

Underline the action.
1. Open the book.
2. Close the book.
3. Give me the book.

S. **Underline** the word.
ضع **خطا تحت الكلمة**.

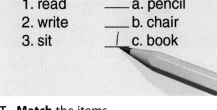

T. **Match** the items.
طابق الكلمات مع بعضها.

Check the box next to each action.
☑ stand   ☑ sit
☐ pen   ☑ write
☐ paper ☐ book

U. **Check** the correct boxes.
ضع **علامة صح** في المربعات الصحيحة.

V. **Label** the picture.
سمِّ الصورة.

1. enp   pen
2. rappe paper
3. okob   book

W. **Unscramble** the words.
حل الكلمات.

X. **Put** the sentences in order.
ضع الجمل في ترتيبها الصحيح.

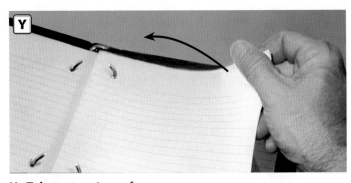

Y. **Take out** a piece of paper.
أخرج قطعة ورق.

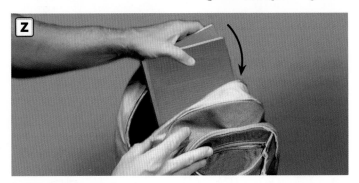

Z. **Put away** your books.
ضع كتبك في مكانها المعتاد.

Ask your classmates. Share the answers.
1. Do you like to work in a group?
2. Do you ever share a book?
3. Do you like to answer questions?

Think about it. Discuss.
1. How can classmates help each other?
2. Why is it important to ask questions in class?
3. How can students check their pronunciation? Explain.

Ways to Succeed وسائل النجاح

A. Set goals.
حدد أهدافا.

B. Participate in class.
شارك في الصف.

C. Take notes.
دوّن مذكرات.

D. Study at home.
ذاكر في المنزل.

E. Pass a test.
انجح في امتحان.

F. Ask for help.
اطلب المساعدة.

G. Make progress.
حقق تقدما.

H. Get good grades.
أحرز درجات جيدة.

Taking a Test التقدم لامتحان

1. test booklet
كتيب الامتحان

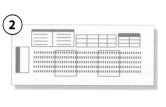
2. answer sheet
ورقة الإجابات

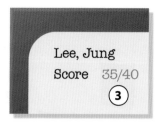
3. score
النتيجة

A	90%-100%	Outstanding
B	80%-89%	Very good
C	70%-79%	Satisfactory
D	60%-69%	Barely passing
F	0%-59%	Fail

4. grades
علامات مدرسية

I. Clear off your desk.
أزل كل شيء من على مكتبك.

J. Work on your own.
اعمل بمفردك.

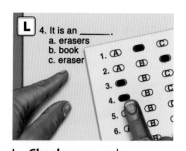
K. Bubble in the answer.
ظلل الإجابة الصحيحة.

L. Check your work.
راجع عملك.

M. Erase the mistake.
أمحُ الخطأ.

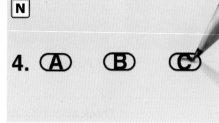
N. Correct the mistake.
صحّح الخطأ.

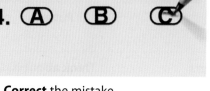
O. Hand in your test.
سلّم ورقة امتحانك.

A. **Enter** the room.
ادخُل الحجرة.

B. **Turn on** the lights.
أشعِل الأنوار.

C. **Walk** to class.
تمشَّ إلى الصف.

D. **Run** to class.
اركض إلى الصف.

E. **Lift / Pick up** the books.
ارفَع / التقِط الكتب.

F. **Carry** the books.
احمِل الكتب.

G. **Deliver** the books.
سلِّم الكتب.

H. **Take** a break.
خُذ استراحة.

I. **Eat**.
كُلي.

J. **Drink**.
اشرب.

K. **Buy** a snack.
اشترِ وجبة خفيفة.

L. **Have** a conversation.
اجرِ محادثة.

M. **Go back** to class.
ارجِعوا إلى الصف.

N. **Throw away** trash.
ألقِ القمامة.

O. **Leave** the room.
اتركوا الحجرة.

P. **Turn off** the lights.
أطفِئ الأنوار.

Grammar Point: present continuous

Use **be** + verb + **ing**
He **is** walk**ing**. They **are** enter**ing**.
Note: He is runn**ing**. They are leav**ing**.

Look at the pictures.
Describe what is happening.

A: They are <u>entering the room</u>.
B: He is <u>walking</u>.

11

A. start a conversation
ابدئي الحديث

B. make small talk
دردش

C. compliment someone
جاملي شخصا

D. offer something
اعرض شيئا

E. thank someone
اشكر شخصا

F. apologize
اعتذر

G. accept an apology
تقبّل الاعتذار

H. invite someone
ادعي أحدا

I. accept an invitation
اقبلي دعوة

J. decline an invitation
ارفض دعوة

K. agree
وافق

L. disagree
اختلف

M. explain something
اشرح شيئا

N. check your understanding
تأكدي من فهمك للكلام

More vocabulary

request: to ask for something

accept a compliment: to thank someone for a compliment

Pair practice. Follow the directions.

1. Start a conversation with your partner.
2. Make small talk with your partner.
3. Compliment each other.

Temperature درجة الحرارة

1. Fahrenheit
درجة فهرنهايت
2. Celsius
درجة مئوية
3. hot
حار
4. warm
دافئ
5. cool
معتدل
6. cold
بارد
7. freezing
بارد جدا
8. degrees
درجات

A Weather Map خريطة أحوال الطقس

9. sunny / clear
مشمس / صافي
10. cloudy
غائم
11. raining
ممطر
12. snowing
يتساقط الثَلج

Weather Conditions أحوال الطقس

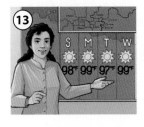

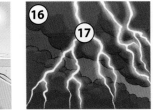

13. heat wave
موجة حارة
14. smoggy
ضباب محمّل بدخان
15. humid
رطب

16. thunderstorm
عاصفة رعدية
17. lightning
برق
18. windy
شديد الرياح

19. dust storm
عاصفة ترابية
20. foggy
ضبابي
21. hailstorm
عاصفة من البَرَد

22. icy
جليدي
23. snowstorm / blizzard
عاصفة ثلجية / عاصفة ثلجية شديدة

Ways to talk about the weather

It's <u>sunny</u> in <u>Dallas</u>.
What's the temperature?
It's <u>108</u>. They're having <u>a heat wave</u>.

Pair practice. Make new conversations.

A: *What's the weather like in <u>Chicago</u>?*
B: *It's <u>raining</u> and it's <u>cold</u>. It's <u>30</u> degrees.*

13

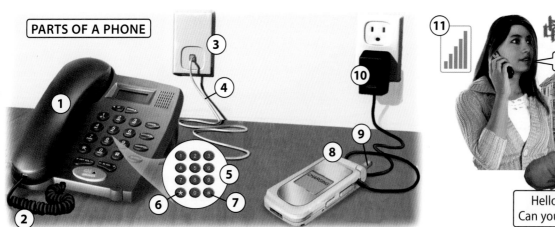

PARTS OF A PHONE

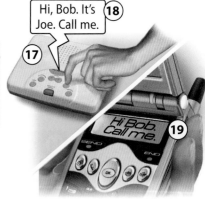

I'll be home by 6:00.

Hello? Hello? Can you hear me?

1. receiver / handset
سماعة الهاتف / التليفون

2. cord
سلك الهاتف / التليفون

3. phone jack
مَقبس الهاتف / التليفون

4. phone line
خط الهاتف / التليفون

5. key pad
لوحة المفاتيح

6. star key
مفتاح النجمة

7. pound key
مفتاح الباوند

8. cellular phone
هاتف / تليفون محمول أو خلوي

9. antenna
هوائي / إيريال

10. charger
شاحن

11. strong signal
إشارة قوية

12. weak signal
إشارة ضعيفة

Hi, Bob. It's Joe. Call me.

Hi Bob. Call me.

13. headset
سماعة رأس بميكروفون

14. wireless headset
سماعة رأس لاسلكية بميكروفون

15. calling card
بطاقة هاتفية / تليفونية (بطاقة مكالمات)

16. access number
رقم الوصول

17. answering machine
جهاز آلي للرد على المكالمات

18. voice message
رسالة صوتية

19. text message
رسالة نصية

Hi, Grandpa.

Hello, Jun.

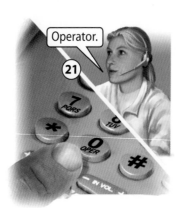

Operator.

City and state, please.

For customer service, please press 2.

20. Internet phone call
مكالمة هاتفية / تليفونية على الإنترنت

21. operator
البدالة / السنترال

22. directory assistance
الاستعلامات

23. automated phone system
نظام الهاتف / التليفون الآلي

24. cordless phone
هاتف / تليفون لاسلكي

25. pay phone
هاتف / تليفون بالأجرة (تليفون عمومي)

26. TDD*
جهاز هاتف / تليفون للمعوقين سمعيا

27. smart phone
هاتف / تليفون ذكي

Reading a Phone Bill قراءة فاتورة الهاتف / التليفون

28. phone bill
فاتورة الهاتف / التليفون

29. area code
رمز / مفتاح المنطقة

30. phone number
رقم الهاتف / التليفون

31. local call
مكالمة محلية

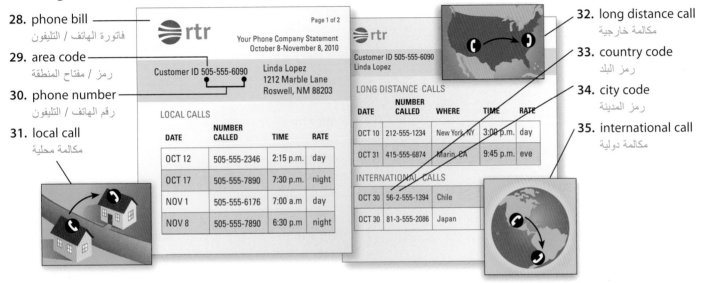

32. long distance call
مكالمة خارجية

33. country code
رمز البلد

34. city code
رمز المدينة

35. international call
مكالمة دولية

Making a Phone Call إجراء مكالمة هاتفية / تليفونية

A. Dial the phone number.
اطلب (اضرب) رقم الهاتف / التليفون.

B. Press "send".
اكبس مفتاح "أرسل."

C. Talk on the phone.
تحدث في الهاتف / التليفون.

D. Hang up. / Press "end".
اقفل السماعة / اكبس مفتاح "انه."

Making an Emergency Call إجراء مكالمة في حالة طارئة

E. Dial 911.
اضرب (اطلب) رقم ٩١١.

This is Roy Chu.

F. Give your name.
أعط/اذكر اسمك.

There's a fire on 5th and Oak.

G. State the emergency.
اذكر الحالة الطارئة.

Please stay on the line.

H. Stay on the line.
انتظر على الخط.

*telecommunication device for the deaf

Cardinal Numbers الأعداد الأصلية

0	zero صفر	20	twenty عشرون
1	one واحد	21	twenty-one واحد وعشرون
2	two اثنان	22	twenty-two اثنان وعشرون
3	three ثلاثة	23	twenty-three ثلاثة وعشرون
4	four أربعة	24	twenty-four أربعة وعشرون
5	five خمسة	25	twenty-five خمسة وعشرون
6	six ستة	30	thirty ثلاثون
7	seven سبعة	40	forty أربعون
8	eight ثمانية	50	fifty خمسون
9	nine تسعة	60	sixty ستون
10	ten عشرة	70	seventy سبعون
11	eleven أحد عشر	80	eighty ثمانون
12	twelve اثنا عشر	90	ninety تسعون
13	thirteen ثلاثة عشر	100	one hundred مائة
14	fourteen أربعة عشر	101	one hundred one مائة وواحد
15	fifteen خمسة عشر	1,000	one thousand ألف
16	sixteen ستة عشر	10,000	ten thousand عشرة آلاف
17	seventeen سبعة عشر	100,000	one hundred thousand مائة ألف
18	eighteen ثمانية عشر	1,000,000	one million مليون
19	nineteen تسعة عشر	1,000,000,000	one billion (مليار) بليون

Ordinal Numbers الأعداد الترتيبية

1st	first الأول	16th	sixteenth السادس عشر
2nd	second الثاني	17th	seventeenth السابع عشر
3rd	third الثالث	18th	eighteenth الثامن عشر
4th	fourth الرابع	19th	nineteenth التاسع عشر
5th	fifth الخامس	20th	twentieth العشرون
6th	sixth السادس	21st	twenty-first الواحد والعشرون
7th	seventh السابع	30th	thirtieth الثلاثون
8th	eighth الثامن	40th	fortieth الأربعون
9th	ninth التاسع	50th	fiftieth الخمسون
10th	tenth العاشر	60th	sixtieth الستون
11th	eleventh الحادي عشر	70th	seventieth السبعون
12th	twelfth الثاني عشر	80th	eightieth الثمانون
13th	thirteenth الثالث عشر	90th	ninetieth التسعون
14th	fourteenth الرابع عشر	100th	one hundredth المئوي
15th	fifteenth الخامس عشر	1,000th	one thousandth الألفي

Roman Numerals الأعداد الرومانية

I = 1	VII = 7	XXX = 30
II = 2	VIII = 8	XL = 40
III = 3	IX = 9	L = 50
IV = 4	X = 10	C = 100
V = 5	XV = 15	D = 500
VI = 6	XX = 20	M = 1,000

A. divide
اقسم

B. calculate
احسبي

C. measure
قِسْ

D. convert
حوّلي

Fractions and Decimals الكسور والكسور العشرية

| 1 | 2 | 3 | 4 | 5 |

1. one whole
1 = 1.00
واحد كامل

2. one half
1/2 = .5
نصف

3. one third
1/3 = .333
ثلث

4. one fourth
1/4 = .25
ربع

5. one eighth
1/8 = .125
ثمن

Percents النسب المئوية

6. calculator
آلة حاسبة

7. decimal point
فاصلة عشرية

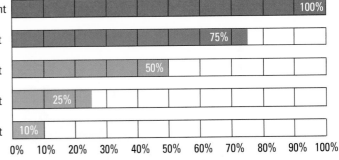

8 100 percent — 100%
9 75 percent — 75%
10 50 percent — 50%
11 25 percent — 25%
12 10 percent — 10%

0% 10% 20% 30% 40% 50% 60% 70% 80% 90% 100%

8. 100 percent
١٠٠ بالمائة

9. 75 percent
٧٥ بالمائة

10. 50 percent
٥٠ بالمائة

11. 25 percent
٢٥ بالمائة

12. 10 percent
١٠ بالمائة

Measurement قياسات

13. ruler
مسطرة

14. centimeter [cm]
سنتيمتر [سم]

15. inch [in.]
بوصة

Dimensions أبعاد

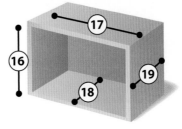

16. height
ارتفاع

17. length
طول

18. depth
عمق

19. width
عرض

Equivalencies

12 inches = 1 foot
3 feet = 1 yard
1,760 yards = 1 mile
1 inch = 2.54 centimeters
1 yard = .91 meters
1 mile = 1.6 kilometers

17

Telling Time قراءة الوقت بالنظر إلى الساعة

1. hour
ساعة

2. minutes
دقائق

3. seconds
ثوانٍ

4. a.m.
ق.ظ. (قبل الظهر)

5. p.m.
ب.ظ. (بعد الظهر)

6. 1:00
one o'clock
الساعة الواحدة

7. 1:05
one-oh-five
five after one
الواحدة وخمس دقائق

8. 1:10
one-ten
ten after one
الواحدة وعشر دقائق

9. 1:15
one-fifteen
a quarter after one
الواحدة وخمسة عشر دقيقة
الواحدة والربع

10. 1:20
one-twenty
twenty after one
الواحد وعشرون دقيقة
الواحدة والثلث

11. 1:30
one-thirty
half past one
الواحدة وثلاثون دقيقة
الواحدة والنصف

12. 1:40
one-forty
twenty to two
الواحدة وأربعون دقيقة
الثانية إلا ثلث

13. 1:45
one-forty-five
a quarter to two
الواحدة وخمسة وأربعون دقيقة
الثانية إلا ربع

Times of Day أوقات النهار

14. sunrise
شروق الشمس

15. morning
الصباح

16. noon
الظهر

17. afternoon
بعد الظهُر (العصر)

18. sunset
غروب الشمس

19. evening
المساء

20. night
الليل

21. midnight
منتصف الليل

Ways to talk about time	Pair practice. Make new conversations.
I wake up at 6:30 a.m.	**A:** *What time do you wake up on weekdays?*
I wake up at 6:30 in the morning.	**B:** *At 6:30 a.m. How about you?*
I wake up at 6:30.	**A:** *I wake up at 7:00.*

22. early
مبكرا

23. on time
في الموعد المحدد

24. late
متأخرا

25. daylight saving time
التوقيت الصيفي

26. standard time
التوقيت القياسي (الشتوي)

Time Zones مناطق التوقيت

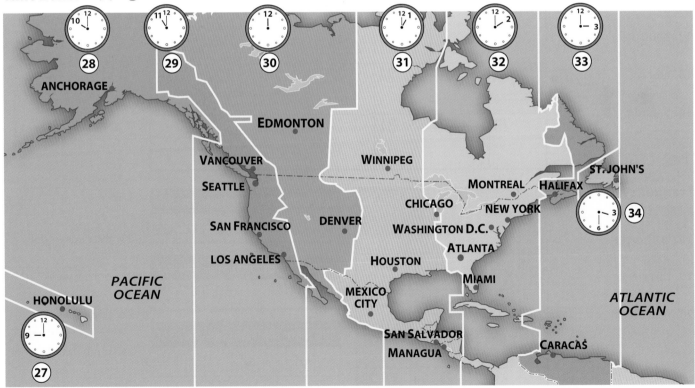

27. Hawaii-Aleutian time
توقيت هاواي - ألوشيان

28. Alaska time
توقيت ألاسكا

29. Pacific time
توقيت المحيط الهادئ (الباسيفيكي)

30. Mountain time
التوقيت الجبلي

31. Central time
توقيت الولايات الوسطى

32. Eastern time
توقيت الولايات الشرقية

33. Atlantic time
التوقيت الأطلنطي

34. Newfoundland time
توقيت نيوفاوندلاند

Ask your classmates. Share the answers.

1. When do you watch television? study? relax?

2. Do you like to stay up after midnight?

3. Do you like to wake up late on weekends?

Think about it. Discuss.

1. What is your favorite time of day? Why?

2. Do you think daylight saving time is a good idea? Why or why not?

1. date
تاريخ

2. day
يوم

3. month
شهر

4. year
سنة

5. today
اليوم

6. tomorrow
الغد (غدا)

7. yesterday
الأمس

Days of the Week
أيام الأسبوع

8. Sunday
الأحد

9. Monday
الاثنين

10. Tuesday
الثلاثاء

11. Wednesday
الأربعاء

12. Thursday
الخميس

13. Friday
الجمعة

14. Saturday
السبت

15. week
أسبوع

16. weekdays
أيام الأسبوع

17. weekend
نهاية الأسبوع (عطلة نهاية الأسبوع)

MAY

SUN	MON	TUE	WED	THU	FRI	SAT
1	2	3	4	5	6	7
8	9	10	11	12	13	14
15	16	17	18	19	20	21
22	23	24	25	26	27	28
29	30	31				

Frequency
التردد

18. last week
الأسبوع الماضي

19. this week
الأسبوع الحالي

20. next week
الأسبوع القادم

MAY

SUN	MON	TUE	WED	THU	FRI	SAT
X1	X2	X3	X4	X5	X6	X7
8	9	10	11	12	13	14
15	16	17	18	19	20	21
22	23	24	25	26	27	28

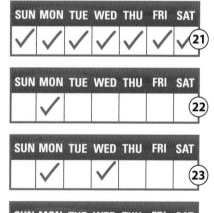

21. every day / daily
كل يوم / يوميا

22. once a week
مرة في الأسبوع

23. twice a week
مرتان في الأسبوع

24. three times a week
ثلاث مرات في الأسبوع

Ways to say the date

Today is <u>May 10th</u>. *It's the* <u>tenth</u>.
Yesterday was <u>May 9th</u>.
The party is on <u>May 21st</u>.

Pair practice. Make new conversations.

A: *The* <u>test</u> *is on* <u>Friday</u>, <u>June 14th</u>.
B: *Did you say* <u>Friday</u>, *the* <u>fourteenth</u>?
A: *Yes, the* <u>fourteenth</u>.

20

25 JAN

SUN	MON	TUE	WED	THU	FRI	SAT
					1	2
3	4	5	6	7	8	9
10	11	12	13	14	15	16
17	18	19	20	21	22	23
24/31	25	26	27	28	29	30

26 FEB

SUN	MON	TUE	WED	THU	FRI	SAT
1	2	3	4	5	6
7	8	9	10	11	12	13
14	15	16	17	18	19	20
21	22	23	24	25	26	27
28						

27 MAR

SUN	MON	TUE	WED	THU	FRI	SAT
1	2	3	4	5	6
7	8	9	10	11	12	13
14	15	16	17	18	19	20
21	22	23	24	25	26	27
28	29	30	31			

28 APR

SUN	MON	TUE	WED	THU	FRI	SAT
				1	2	3
4	5	6	7	8	9	10
11	12	13	14	15	16	17
18	19	20	21	22	23	24
25	26	27	28	29	30	

29 MAY

SUN	MON	TUE	WED	THU	FRI	SAT
						1
2	3	4	5	6	7	8
9	10	11	12	13	14	15
16	17	18	19	20	21	22
23/30	24/31	25	26	27	28	29

30 JUN

SUN	MON	TUE	WED	THU	FRI	SAT
		1	2	3	4	5
6	7	8	9	10	11	12
13	14	15	16	17	18	19
20	21	22	23	24	25	26
27	28	29	30			

31 JUL

SUN	MON	TUE	WED	THU	FRI	SAT
				1	2	3
4	5	6	7	8	9	10
11	12	13	14	15	16	17
18	19	20	21	22	23	24
25	26	27	28	29	30	31

32 AUG

SUN	MON	TUE	WED	THU	FRI	SAT
1	2	3	4	5	6	7
8	9	10	11	12	13	14
15	16	17	18	19	20	21
22	23	24	25	26	27	28
29	30	31				

33 SEP

SUN	MON	TUE	WED	THU	FRI	SAT
			1	2	3	4
5	6	7	8	9	10	11
12	13	14	15	16	17	18
19	20	21	22	23	24	25
26	27	28	29	30		

34 OCT

SUN	MON	TUE	WED	THU	FRI	SAT
					1	2
3	4	5	6	7	8	9
10	11	12	13	14	15	16
17	18	19	20	21	22	23
24/31	25	26	27	28	29	30

35 NOV

SUN	MON	TUE	WED	THU	FRI	SAT
1	2	3	4	5	6
7	8	9	10	11	12	13
14	15	16	17	18	19	20
21	22	23	24	25	26	27
28	29	30				

36 DEC

SUN	MON	TUE	WED	THU	FRI	SAT
			1	2	3	4
5	6	7	8	9	10	11
12	13	14	15	16	17	18
19	20	21	22	23	24	25
26	27	28	29	30	31	

Months of the Year
شهور السنة

25. January
يناير / كانون الثاني

26. February
فبراير / شباط

27. March
مارس / آذار

28. April
إبريل / نيسان

29. May
مايو / أيار

30. June
يونيو / حزيران

31. July
يوليو / تموز

32. August
أغسطس / آب

33. September
سبتمبر / أيلول

34. October
أكتوبر / تشرين الأول

35. November
نوفمبر / تشرين الثاني

36. December
ديسمبر / كانون الأول

Seasons
فصول السنة

37. spring
الربيع

38. summer
الصيف

39. fall / autumn
الخريف

40. winter
الشتاء

Dictate to your partner. Take turns.

A: *Write <u>Monday</u>.*
B: *Is it spelled <u>M-o-n-d-a-y</u>?*
A: *Yes, that's right.*

Ask your classmates. Share the answers.

1. What is your favorite day of the week? Why?
2. What is your busiest day of the week? Why?
3. What is your favorite season of the year? Why?

21

1. birthday
عيد ميلاد

2. wedding
فرح / عرس

3. anniversary
عيد سنوي

4. appointment
موعد

5. parent-teacher conference
اجتماع آباء-معلمين

6. vacation
عطلة / أجازة

7. religious holiday
عيد ديني

8. legal holiday
عيد رسمي

Legal Holidays الأعياد الرسمية

Happy New Year!

I have a dream.

PROUD TO WORK

9. New Year's Day
عيد رأس السنة

10. Martin Luther King Jr. Day
عيد مارتن لوثر كنغ جونيور

11. Presidents' Day
عيد الرؤساء

12. Memorial Day
عيد الذكرى

**13. Fourth of July /
Independence Day**
عيد الرابع من يوليو / عيد الاستقلال

14. Labor Day
عيد العمال

15. Columbus Day
عيد كولومبس

16. Veterans Day
عيد المحاربين القدامى

17. Thanksgiving
عيد الشكر

18. Christmas
أعياد الميلاد (الكريسماس)

Pair practice. Make new conversations.

A: *When is your birthday?*
B: *It's on January 31st. How about you?*
A: *It's on December 22nd.*

Ask your classmates. Share the answers.

1. What are the legal holidays in your native country?
2. When is Labor Day in your native country?
3. When do you celebrate the New Year in your native country?

1. **little** hand
يد صغيرة

2. **big** hand
يد كبيرة

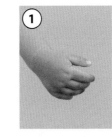 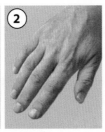

13. **heavy** box
صندوق ثقيل

14. **light** box
صندوق خفيف

3. **fast** driver
سائق مسرع

4. **slow** driver
سائق بطيء

15. **same** color
نفس اللون (ألوان مشابهة)

16. **different** colors
ألوان مختلفة

5. **hard** chair
مقعد جامد (قاسي)

6. **soft** chair
مقعد طري (مريح)

17. **good** dog
كلب مطيع

18. **bad** dog
كلب غير مطيع

7. **thick** book
كتاب سميك (غليظ)

8. **thin** book
كتاب رقيق (رفيع)

19. **expensive** ring
خاتم غالي

20. **cheap** ring
خاتم رخيص

9. **full** glass
كأس ممتلئ

10. **empty** glass
كأس فارغ

21. **beautiful** view
منظر بديع

22. **ugly** view
منظر قبيح

11. **noisy** children /
loud children
أطفال مزعجون

12. **quiet** children
أطفال هادئون

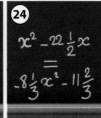 

23. **easy** problem
مسألة سهلة

24. **difficult** problem /
hard problem
مسألة صعبة

Ask your classmates. Share the answers.

1. Are you a slow driver or a fast driver?
2. Do you prefer a hard bed or a soft bed?
3. Do you like loud parties or quiet parties?

Use the new words.
Look at page 150–151. Describe the things you see.

A: _The street_ is _hard_.
B: _The truck_ is _heavy_.

Basic Colors الألوان الأساسية

1. red
   أحمر

2. yellow
   أصفر

3. blue
   أزرق

4. orange
   برتقالي

5. green
   أخضر

6. purple
   أرجواني

7. pink
   وردي

8. violet
   بنفسجي

9. turquoise
   فيروزي / تركواز

10. dark blue
    أزرق غامق

11. light blue
    أزرق فاتح

12. bright blue
    أزرق لامع

Neutral Colors الألوان المحايدة

13. black
    أسود

14. white
    أبيض

15. gray
    رمادي

16. cream / ivory
    أصفر باهت / عاجي

17. brown
    بني

18. beige / tan
    بيج / أسمر مائل إلى الصفرة

Ask your classmates. Share the answers.

1. What colors are you wearing today?
2. What colors do you like?
3. Is there a color you don't like? What is it?

Use the new words. Look at pages 86–87.
Take turns naming the colors you see.

A: *His shirt is blue.*
B: *Her shoes are white.*

1. The yellow sweaters are **on the left**.
البلوفرات (الكنزات) الصفراء **على الجهة اليسرى**.

2. The purple sweaters are **in the middle**.
البلوفرات (الكنزات) الأرجوانية **في الجهة الوسطى**.

3. The brown sweaters are **on the right**.
البلوفرات (الكنزات) البنية **على الجهة اليمنى**.

4. The red sweaters are **above** the blue sweaters.
البلوفرات (الكنزات) الحمراء **فوق** البلوفرات (الكنزات) الزرقاء.

5. The blue sweaters are **below** the red sweaters.
البلوفرات (الكنزات) الزرقاء **تحت/أسفل** البلوفرات (الكنزات) الحمراء.

6. The turquoise sweater is **in** the box.
البلوفر (الكنزة) الفيروزي **في/داخل** الصندوق.

7. The white sweater is **in front of** the black sweater.
البلوفر (الكنزة) الأبيض **أمام** البلوفر (الكنزة) الأسود.

8. The black sweater is **behind** the white sweater.
البلوفر (الكنزة) الأسود **خلف** البلوفر (الكنزة) الأبيض.

9. The orange sweater is **on** the gray sweater.
البلوفر (الكنزة) البرتقالي **فوق/على** البلوفر (الكنزة) الرمادي.

10. The violet sweater is **next to** the gray sweater.
البلوفر (الكنزة) البنفسجي **بجانب** البلوفر (الكنزة) الرمادي.

11. The gray sweater is **under** the orange sweater.
البلوفر (الكنزة) الرمادي **تحت** البلوفر (الكنزة) البرتقالي.

12. The green sweater is **between** the pink sweaters.
البلوفر (الكنزة) الأخضر **بين** البلوفرات (الكنزات) الوردية.

More vocabulary

near: in the same area
far from: not near

Role play. Make new conversations.

A: *Excuse me. Where are the <u>red</u> sweaters?*
B: *They're <u>on the left</u>, <u>above</u> the <u>blue</u> sweaters.*
A: *Thanks very much.*

Coins العملة

1. $.01 = 1¢
a penny / 1 cent
بِني / سنت واحد

2. $.05 = 5¢
a nickel / 5 cents
نِكِل / ٥ سنتات

3. $.10 = 10¢
a dime / 10 cents
دَيْم / ١٠ سنتات

4. $.25 = 25¢
a quarter / 25 cents
كوارتر (ربع دولار) / ٢٥ سنتا

5. $.50 = 50¢
a half dollar
نصف دولار

6. $1.00
a dollar coin
عملة دولار فضي

Bills الورقات

7. $1.00
a dollar
دولار

8. $5.00
five dollars
خمسة دولارات

9. $10.00
ten dollars
عشرة دولارات

10. $20.00
twenty dollars
عشرون دولارا

11. $50.00
fifty dollars
خمسون دولارا

12. $100.00
one hundred dollars
مائة دولار

Do you have change for a dollar?
Yes, I do.
A

A. **Get** change.
فك نقودا.

Can I borrow a dollar?
Sure. Here you go.
B
C

B. **Borrow** money.
اقترض / استلف نقودا.

C. **Lend** money.
اقرض / سلّف نقودا.

Thanks.
D

D. **Pay back** the money.
سدّد النقود.

Pair practice. Make new conversations.

A: *Do you have change for a dollar?*
B: *Sure. How about two quarters and five dimes?*
A: *Perfect!*

Think about it. Discuss.

1. Is it a good idea to lend money to a friend? Why or why not?
2. Is it better to carry a dollar or four quarters? Why?
3. Do you prefer dollar coins or dollar bills? Why?

Ways to Pay طرق الدفع

A. pay cash
يدفع تقدا

B. use a credit card
يستخدم بطاقة انتمان

C. use a debit card
يستخدم بطاقة خصم من الحساب

D. write a (personal) check
يحرر شيكا (شخصيا)

E. use a gift card
يستخدم بطاقة إهداء

F. cash a traveler's check
يصرف شيكا سياحيا

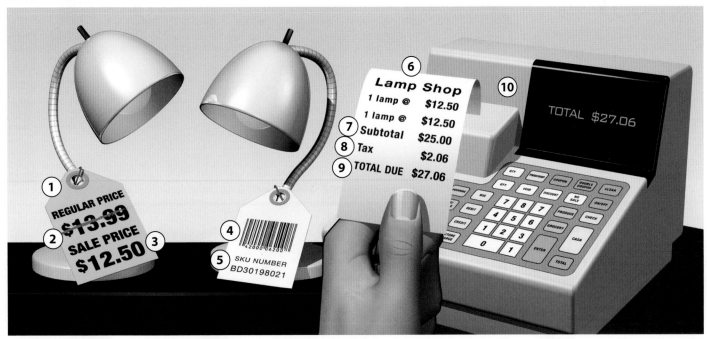

1. price tag بطاقة السعر	**3. sale price** سعر التنزيلات (المخفض)	**5. SKU number** رقم تعريف السلعة (SKU)	**7. price / cost** السعر / التكلفة	**9. total** المجموع / الإجمالي
2. regular price السعر العادي	**4. bar code** شفرة القضبان	**6. receipt** الإيصال / الوصل	**8. sales tax** ضريبة مبيعات	**10. cash register** آلة تسجيل النقود

G. buy / pay for
تشتري / تدفع حساب...

H. return
ترجّع / ترد

I. exchange
يستبدل

1. twins
   توأمان

2. sweater
   بلوفر (كنزة)

3. matching
   مطابقان

4. disappointed
   الشعور بخيبة أمل

5. navy blue
   أزرق كحلي

6. happy
   سعيدتان

A. **shop**
   تتسوّق

B. **keep**
   تحتفظ لنفسها

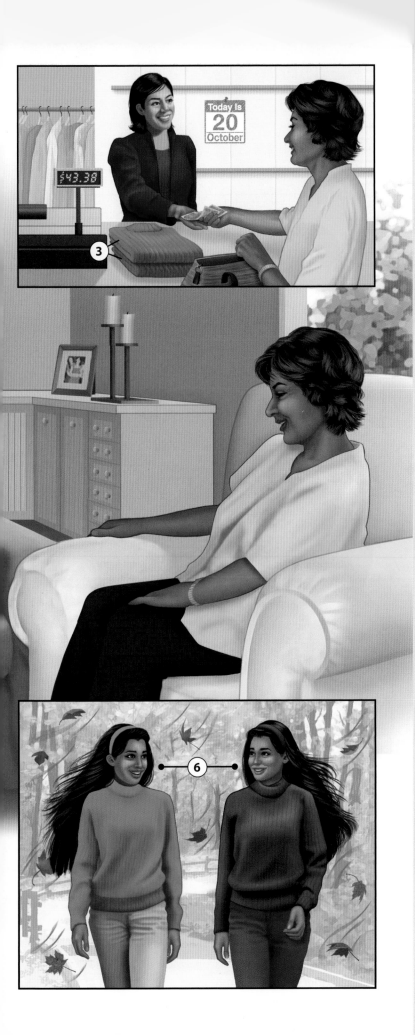

**Look at the pictures.
What do you see?**

Answer the questions.

1. Who is the woman shopping for?

2. Does she buy matching sweaters or different sweaters?

3. How does Anya feel about her green sweater? What does she do?

4. What does Manda do with her sweater?

 **Read the story.**

Same and Different

Mrs. Kumar likes to <u>shop</u> for her <u>twins</u>. Today she's looking at <u>sweaters</u>. There are many different colors on sale. Mrs. Kumar chooses two <u>matching</u> green sweaters.

The next day, Manda and Anya open their gifts. Manda likes the green sweater, but Anya is <u>disappointed</u>. Mrs. Kumar understands the problem. Anya wants to be different.

Manda <u>keeps</u> her sweater. But Anya goes to the store. She exchanges her green sweater for a <u>navy blue</u> sweater. It's an easy answer to Anya's problem. Now the twins can be warm, <u>happy</u>, and different.

Think about it.

1. Do you like to shop for other people? Why or why not?

2. Imagine you are Anya. Would you keep the sweater or exchange it? Why?

1. man
رجل

2. woman
امرأة

3. women
نساء

4. men
رجال

5. senior citizen
مُسِنّة / عجوز

Listen and point. Take turns.

A: *Point to a woman.*

B: *Point to a senior citizen.*

A: *Point to an infant.*

Dictate to your partner. Take turns.

A: *Write woman.*

B: *Is that spelled w-o-m-a-n?*

A: *Yes, that's right, woman.*

6. infant
رضيع

7. baby
طفل

8. toddler
طفل في أول مراحل المشي

9. 6-year-old boy
ولد عمره ٦ سنوات

10. 10-year-old girl
بنت عمرها ١٠ سنوات

11. teenager / teen
مراهق / من ذوي السنوات
بين ١٣ و ١٩ من العمر

Ways to talk about age

1 month – 3 months old = **infant**
18 months – 3 years old = **toddler**
3 years old – 12 years old = **child**

13 – 19 years old = **teenager**
18+ years old = **adult**
62+ years old = **senior citizen**

Pair practice. Make new conversations.

A: *How old is Sandra?*
B: *She's thirteen years old.*
A: *Wow, she's a teenager now!*

31

Age   السن

1. young
   صغير(ة)

2. middle-aged
   متوسط(ة)

3. elderly
   عجوز / مسنّ(ة)

Height   الطول

4. tall
   طويل(ة)

5. average height
   متوسط(ة) الطول

6. short
   قصير(ة)

Weight   الوزن

7. heavy / fat
   بدين(ة)

8. average weight
   متوسط(ة) الوزن

9. thin / slender
   نحيف(ة)

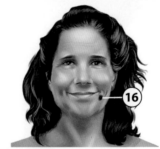

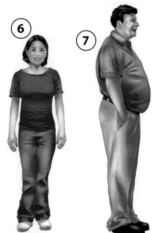

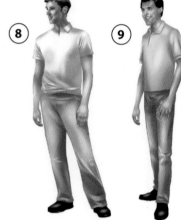

Disabilities   حالات العجز

10. physically challenged
    عاجز(ة)

11. sight impaired / blind
    ضرير(ة)

12. hearing impaired / deaf
    أصمّ / صمّاء

Prepositions of Motion p.153

Appearance   المظهر

13. attractive   14. cute
    وسيم(ة)   جميل(ة)

15. pregnant
    حامل

16. mole
    شامة / خال

17. pierced ear
    أذن مثقوبة

18. tattoo
    وشم

Ways to describe people

He's a <u>heavy</u>, <u>young</u> man.
She's a <u>pregnant</u> woman with <u>a mole</u>.
He's <u>sight impaired</u>.

Use the new words. Look at pages 2–3.
Describe the people and point. Take turns.

A: *He's a <u>tall</u>, <u>thin</u>, <u>middle-aged</u> man.*
B: *She's a <u>short</u>, <u>average-weight</u> <u>young</u> woman.*

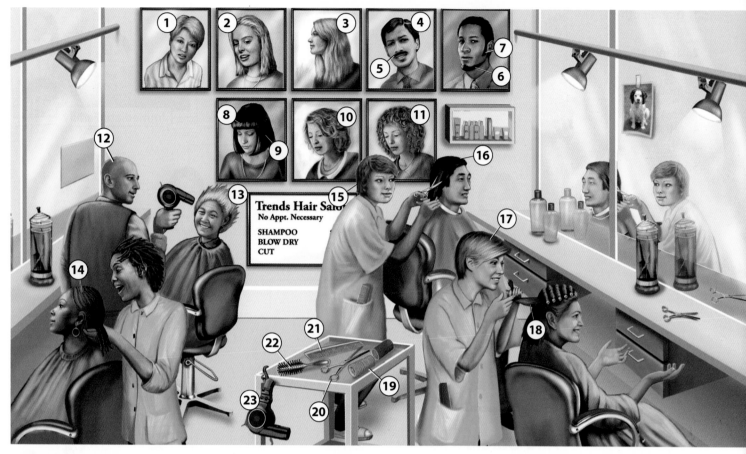

Trends Hair Salon
No Appt. Necessary

SHAMPOO
BLOW DRY
CUT

1. short hair شعر قصير	**6. beard** لحية	**11. curly hair** شعر مجعد	**16. black hair** شعر أسود	**21. comb** مشط
2. shoulder-length hair شعر واصل للكتف	**7. sideburns** السبلة الخدية (سوالف)	**12. bald** أصلع	**17. blond hair** شعر أشقر	**22. brush** فرشاة
3. long hair شعر طويل	**8. bangs** خصلة	**13. gray hair** شعر شائب (أبيض)	**18. brown hair** شعر بني	**23. blow dryer** مجفف شعر بالهواء الساخن (سيشوار)
4. part فرق الشعر	**9. straight hair** شعر ناعم	**14. corn rows** تضفير الشعر على فروة الرأس	**19. rollers** بكرات شعر	
5. mustache شارب / شنب	**10. wavy hair** شعر مموج	**15. red hair** شعر أحمر	**20. scissors** مقص	

Style Hair تصفيف الشعر

A. cut hair
يقص الشعر

B. perm hair
يموّج الشعر

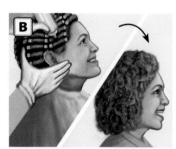

C. set hair
يصفف الشعر

D. color hair / **dye** hair
يلوّن (يصبغ) الشعر

Ways to talk about hair

Describe hair in this order: length, style, and then color.
She has <u>long</u>, <u>straight</u>, <u>brown</u> hair.

Role play. Talk to a stylist.

A: *I need a new hairstyle.*
B: *How about <u>short</u> and <u>straight</u>?*
A: *Great. Do you think I should <u>dye</u> it?*

33

1. grandmother
   جدة

2. grandfather
   جد

3. mother
   أم

4. father
   أب

5. sister
   أخت

6. brother
   أخ

7. aunt
   عمة / خالة

8. uncle
   عم / خال

9. cousin
   بنت/ابن عم(ة)/خال(ة)

10. mother-in-law
    حماة

11. father-in-law
    حمو

12. wife
    زوجة

13. husband
    زوج

14. daughter
    ابنة

15. son
    ابن

16. sister-in-law
    سلفة (أخت الزوج أو الزوجة / زوجة الأخ)

17. brother-in-law
    سلف (أخو الزوج أو الزوجة / زوج الأخت)

18. niece
    ابنة الأخ و الأخت

19. nephew
    ابن الأخ أو الأخت

Tim Lee's Family

GRANDPARENTS

Immediate Family

Min — Lu

PARENTS

Rose — Ken

Lynn — Dan

CHILDREN

Tim — Lily — Alex — Emily

Ana Garcia's Family

Extended Family

Eva — Sam

Ana — Tito

Marta — Carlos

Sara — Felix — Alice — Eddie

More vocabulary

Tim is Min and Lu's **grandson**.
Lily and Emily are Min and Lu's **granddaughters**.
Alex is Min's youngest **grandchild**.

Ana is Tito's **wife**.
Ana is Eva and Sam's **daughter-in-law**.
Carlos is Eva and Sam's **son-in-law**.

Carol, Bruce, and Lisa

Lisa, Age 4

Lisa Green's Family

Rick   Carol   Bruce   Sue

Lisa, Age 7

Lisa, Today

Mary   David   Kim   Bill

20. married couple
شخصان متزوجان

21. divorced couple
شخصان مطلقان

22. single mother
أم عزباء

23. single father
أب أعزب

24. remarried
متزوج للمرة الثانية

25. stepfather
زوج الأم

26. stepmother
زوجة الأب

27. half sister
أخت غير شقيقة

28. half brother
أخ غير شقيق

29. stepsister
أخت من زوجة الأب أو زوج الأم

30. stepbrother
أخ من زوجة الأب أو زوج الأم

More vocabulary

Bruce is Carol's **former husband** or **ex-husband**.
Carol is Bruce's **former wife** or **ex-wife**.
Lisa is the **stepdaughter** of both Rick and Sue.

Look at the pictures.
Name the people.

A: *Who is Lisa's half sister?*
B: *Mary is. Who is Lisa's stepsister?*

35

A. hold
يحمل الطفل

B. nurse
ترضَع

C. feed
يُطعم

D. rock
تهزَّ

E. undress
تخلع ملابسه

F. bathe
تحمّي

G. change a diaper
تغيّر الحفاض

H. dress
تلبّس

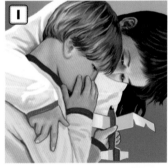

I. comfort
تريّح / تهدئ

Good job!

J. praise
تمدح

No!

K. discipline
تؤدّب

L. buckle up
يحزّم / يربط حزام الأمان

M. play with
تلعب معه

N. read to
يقرأ له

O. sing a lullaby
تغنّي له ترنيمة لتنويمه

P. kiss goodnight
يقبّله متمنيا له نوما مريحا

Look at the pictures.
Describe what is happening.

A: She's <u>changing her baby's diaper</u>.
B: He's <u>kissing his son goodnight</u>.

Ask your classmates. Share the answers.
1. Do you like to take care of children?
2. Do you prefer to read to children or play with them?
3. Can you sing a lullaby? Which one?

1. bottle
زجاجة رضاعة

2. nipple
حلمة زجاجة الرضاعة

3. formula
بديل لبن الأم (حليب مستحضر)

4. baby food
غذاء الأطفال

5. bib
فوطة صدرية

6. high chair
كرسي مرتفع

7. diaper pail
دلو الحفاضات

8. cloth diaper
حفاضات من القماش

9. safety pins
دبابيس أمان

10. disposable diaper
حفاض يلقى بعد الاستعمال

11. training pants
بنطلون أطفال سهل الخلع

12. potty seat
نونية للأطفال

13. baby lotion
غسول أطفال

14. baby powder
بودرة أطفال

15. wipes
مناديل للتنظيف

16. baby bag
حقيبة مستلزمات الطفل

17. baby carrier
حمالة أطفال

18. stroller
عربة أطفال

19. car safety seat
كرسي أمان لسلامة الأطفال بالسيارة

20. carriage
عربة أطفال

21. rocking chair
كرسي هزاز

22. nursery rhymes
أغاني تقليدية للأطفال

23. teddy bear
دبة محشوة

24. pacifier
عضّاضة

25. teething ring
حلقة تسنين

26. rattle
خشخيشة

27. night light
ضوء ليلي (نور سهّاري)

Dictate to your partner. Take turns.

A: *Write pacifier.*
B: *Was that pacifier, p-a-c-i-f-i-e-r?*
A: *Yes, that's right.*

Think about it. Discuss.

1. How can parents discipline toddlers? teens?
2. What are some things you can say to praise a child?
3. Why are nursery rhymes important for young children?

37

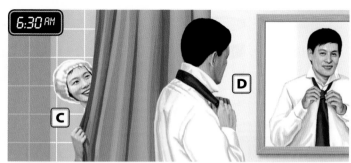

A. wake up
يستيقظ

B. get up
تقوم من السرير

C. take a shower
تستحمَ

D. get dressed
يلبس ثيابه

E. eat breakfast
يتناولون الإفطار

F. make lunch
تحضِّر وجبة الغداء

G. take the children to school / **drop off** the kids
يوصِّل (يأخذ) الأطفال إلى المدرسة / ينزِّل الأطفال عند باب المدرسة

H. take the bus to school
تأخذ (تركب) الأوتوبيس إلى المدرسة

I. drive to work / **go** to work
يقود السيارة إلى مكان العمل / يذهب إلى العمل

J. go to class
تذهب إلى حجرة الصف

K. work
يعمل

L. go to the grocery store
تذهب إلى محل البقالة

M. pick up the kids
تُحضر الأطفال من المدرسة

N. leave work
يغادر العمل

Grammar Point: third person singular

For *he* and *she*, add *-s* or *-es* to the verb:

He wakes up.　　　*He watches TV.*

He gets up.　　　*She goes to the store.*

These verbs are different (irregular):

*Be: She **is** in school at 10:00 a.m.*

*Have: He **has** dinner at 6:30 p.m.*

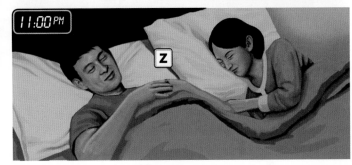

O. clean the house
ينظّفون المنزل

P. exercise
يمارس رياضة

Q. cook dinner / **make** dinner
تطبخ العشاء / تحضّر العشاء

R. come home / **get** home
يرجعِ / يصل إلى المنزل

S. have dinner / **eat** dinner
يتناولون العشاء

T. do homework
يعمل الواجب المدرسي

U. relax
يسترخي

V. read the paper
تقرأ الصحيفة

W. check email
تطلع على البريد الإلكتروني

X. watch TV
يشاهد التلفيزيون

Y. go to bed
يذهب / تذهب للفراش

Z. go to sleep
ينام / تنام

Pair practice. Make new conversations.

A: *When does he go to work?*
B: *He goes to work at 8:00 a.m. When does she go to class?*
A: *She goes to class at 10:00 a.m.*

Ask your classmates. Share the answers.

1. Who cooks dinner in your family?
2. Who goes to the grocery store?
3. Who goes to work?

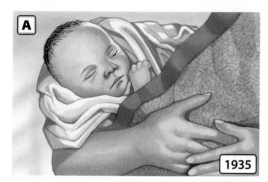

A. be born
يولد
1935

B. start school
يدخل المدرسة
1940

C. immigrate
يهاجر / يهاجرون
1950

D. graduate
يتخرُج
1953

E. learn to drive
يتعلُم قيادة السيارة
1953

F. get a job
يحصل على وظيفة
1954

G. become a citizen
يصبح مواطنا
1954

H. fall in love
يقع في غرام فتاة
1955

1. birth certificate
شهادة ميلاد

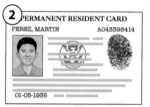

2. Resident Alien card /
green card
بطاقة إقامة دائمة / البطاقة
الخضراء

3. diploma
شهادة دبلوم

4. driver's license
رخصة قيادة سيارة

5. Social Security card
بطاقة ضمان اجتماعي

6. Certificate of Naturalization
شهادة جنسية

Grammar Point: past tense

start		immigrate	retire	
learn	+**ed**	graduate	die	+**d**
travel				

These verbs are different (irregular):

be – was	go – went	buy – bought
get – got	have – had	
become – became	fall – fell	

40

I. **go** to college
يلتحق بالجامعة

J. **get** engaged
يخطب حبيبته

7. college degree
شهادة جامعية

K. **get** married
يتزوّج

L. **have** a baby
تنجب طفلا

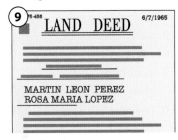

8. marriage license
عقد زواج

M. **buy** a home
يشتري منزلا

N. **become** a grandparent
يصير جدا

9. deed
صك ملكية

O. retire
يتقاعد

P. travel
يسافر

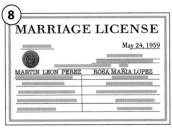

10. passport
جواز سفر

Q. volunteer
يتطوّع

R. die
يتوفّى / يموت

11. death certificate
شهادة وفاة

More vocabulary

When a husband dies, his wife becomes a **widow**.
When a wife dies, her husband becomes a **widower**.

Ask your classmates. Share the answers.

1. When did you start school?
2. When did you get your first job?
3. Do you want to travel?

1. hot
   شاعر بالحَرّ / حرّان

2. thirsty
   ظامئ / عطشان

3. sleepy
   نعسان

4. cold
   شاعر بالبرد / بردان

5. hungry
   جائع / جوعان

6. full / satisfied
   ممتلئ / شبعان

7. disgusted
   مشمئز(ة)

8. calm
   هادئ(ة)

9. uncomfortable
   غير مرتاح

10. nervous
    متوتر(ة)

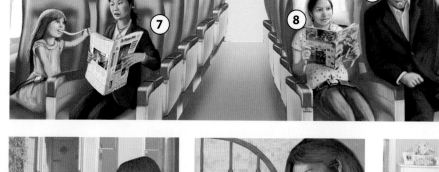

11. in pain
    متألم(ة) / مصاب(ة) بألم

12. sick
    مريض(ة)

13. worried
    قلق(ة)

14. well
    معافى / معافية

15. relieved
    منفرج(ة)

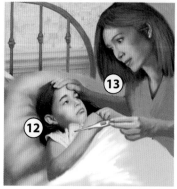

16. hurt
    مكسور الخاطر

17. lonely
    وحيد

18. in love
    محب / عاشق

Pair practice. Make new conversations.

A: *How are you doing?*
B: *I'm <u>hungry</u>. How about you?*
A: *I'm <u>hungry</u> and <u>thirsty</u>, too!*

Use the new words.
Look at pages 40–41. Describe what each person is feeling.

A: *Martin is <u>excited</u>.*
B: *Martin's mother is <u>proud</u>.*

19. **sad**
حزين

20. **homesick**
مشتاق إلى الوطن /
شاعر بالحنين للوطن

21. **proud**
فخور(ة)

22. **excited**
مثار

23. **scared / afraid**
خائف / متخوف

24. **embarrassed**
محرج

25. **bored**
مصاب بالملل / مسئوم

26. **confused**
محتار

27. **frustrated**
محبط

28. **upset**
متضايق / منزعج

29. **angry**
غضبان

30. **surprised**
مندهش

31. **happy**
سعيد / مسرور

32. **tired**
مرهق / تعبان

Ask your classmates. Share the answers.

1. Do you ever feel homesick?
2. What makes you feel frustrated?
3. Describe a time when you were very happy.

More vocabulary

exhausted: very tired
furious: very angry
humiliated: very embarrassed

overjoyed: very happy
starving: very hungry
terrified: very scared

43

A Family Reunion

اجتماع شمل الأسرة

LU FAMILY REUNION

1. banner	3. opinion	5. glad	A. **laugh**
راية	رأي	مسرور	يضحك
2. baseball game	4. balloons	6. relatives	B. **misbehave**
مباراة بيسبول	بالونات	أقارب/أقرباء	تسيء السلوك أو التصرف

44

I think large families are best.

Look at the picture. What do you see?

Answer the questions.

1. How many relatives are there at this reunion?

2. How many children are there? Which children are misbehaving?

3. What are people doing at this reunion?

📖 Read the story.

A Family Reunion

Ben Lu has a lot of <u>relatives</u> and they're all at his house. Today is the Lu family reunion.

There is a lot of good food. There are also <u>balloons</u> and a <u>banner</u>. And this year there are four new babies!

People are having a good time at the reunion. Ben's grandfather and his aunt are talking about the <u>baseball game</u>. His cousins <u>are laughing</u>. His mother-in-law is giving her <u>opinion</u>. And many of the children <u>are misbehaving</u>.

Ben looks at his family and smiles. He loves his relatives, but he's <u>glad</u> the reunion is once a year.

Think about it.

1. Do you like to have large parties? Why or why not?

2. Imagine you see a little girl at a party. She's misbehaving. What do you do? What do you say?

45

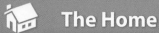

1. roof
   سقف

2. bedroom
   غرفة نوم

3. door
   باب

4. bathroom
   حمّام

5. kitchen
   مطبخ

6. floor
   أرضية

7. dining area
   غرفة الطعام

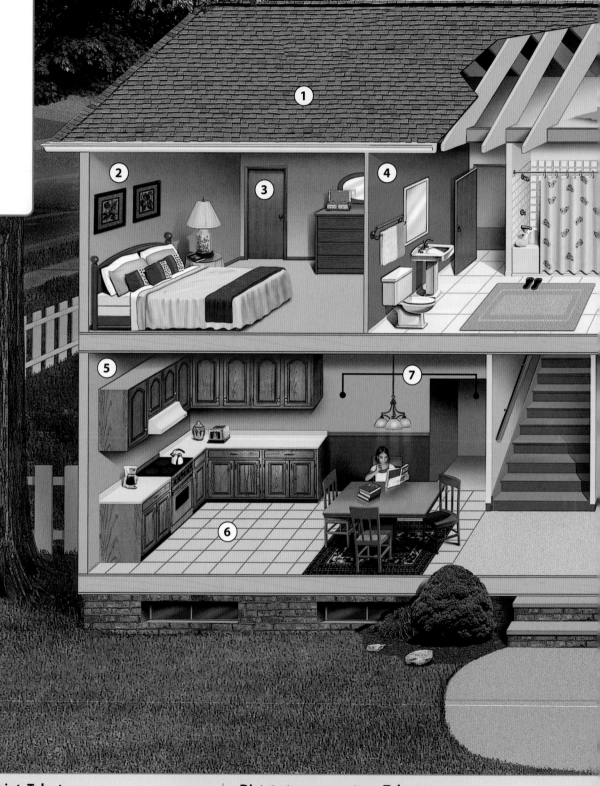

Listen and point. Take turns.

A: *Point to the kitchen*.
B: *Point to the living room*.
A: *Point to the basement*.

Dictate to your partner. Take turns.

A: *Write kitchen*.
B: *Was that k-i-t-c-h-e-n?*
A: *Yes, that's right, kitchen*.

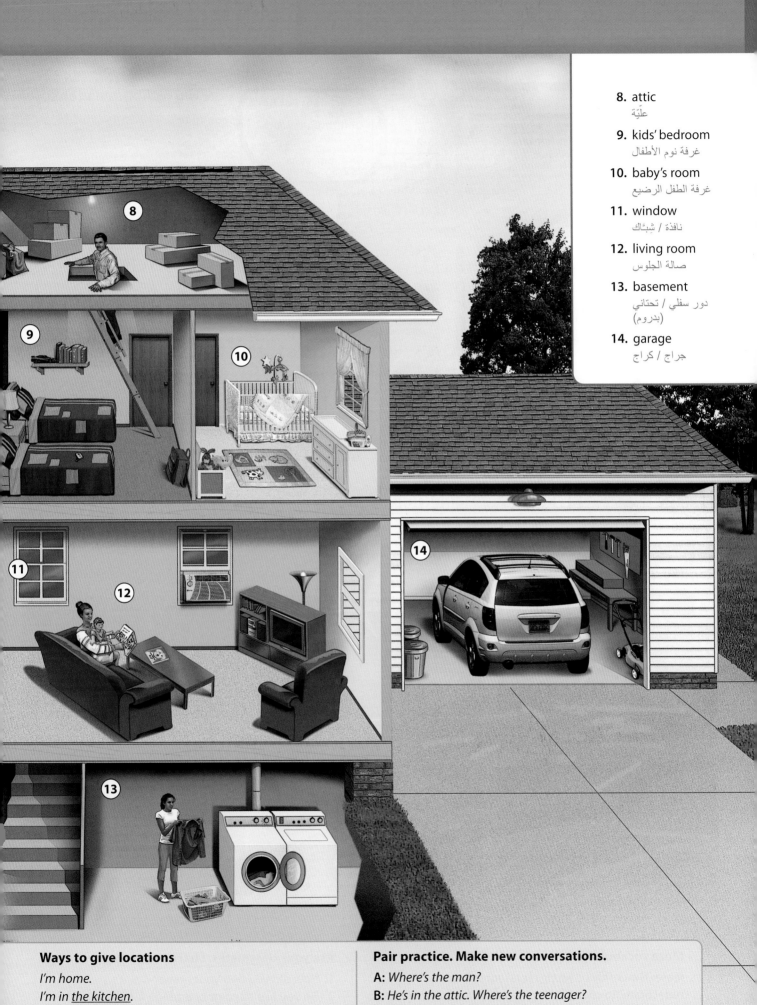

8. **attic**
علّيّة

9. **kids' bedroom**
غرفة نوم الأطفال

10. **baby's room**
غرفة الطفل الرضيع

11. **window**
نافذة / شبّاك

12. **living room**
صالة الجلوس

13. **basement**
دور سفلي / تحتاني
(بدروم)

14. **garage**
جراج / كراج

Ways to give locations

I'm home.
I'm in <u>the kitchen</u>.
I'm on <u>the roof</u>.

Pair practice. Make new conversations.

A: *Where's the man?*
B: *He's in the attic. Where's the teenager?*
A: *She's in the laundry room.*

47

1. Internet listing
عرض المنزل للبيع على الإنترنت

2. classified ad
إعلان مبوب في صحيفة

Abbreviations

apt = apartment

bdrm = bedroom

ba = bathroom

kit = kitchen

yd = yard

util = utilities

incl = included

mo = month

furn = furnished

unfurn = unfurnished

mgr = manager

eves = evenings

3. furnished apartment
شقة مفروشة

4. unfurnished apartment
شقة غير مفروشة

Gas   Water   Electricity   Phone   Cable   DSL

5. utilities
مرافق

Renting an Apartment استئجار شقة

A. Call the manager.
تتصل بالمدير / المشرف.

Are utilities included?

No, they aren't.

B. Ask about the features.
تسأل عن المميزات.

Rental Application
Name: Maya Ramos
Telephone number: 818-555-8407

C. Submit an application.
تقدّم طلبا.

D. Sign the rental agreement.
توقّع عقد الإيجار.

E. Pay the first and last month's rent.
تدفع إيجار الشهرين الأول والأخير.

F. Move in.
تنتقل إلى الشقة.

More vocabulary

lease: a monthly or yearly rental agreement

redecorate: to change the paint and furniture in a home

move out: to pack and leave a home

Ask your classmates. Share the answers.

1. How did you find your home?

2. Do you like to paint or arrange furniture?

3. Does gas or electricity cost more for you?

Buying a House شراء المنزل

G. Meet with a realtor.
يتقابل مع سمسار عقارات.

H. Look at houses.
يتفرّج على بيوت.

$$$$$$

I. Make an offer.
يقدّم عرضا.

Congratulations!

J. Get a loan.
يحصل على قرض.

K. Take ownership.
يتولى / يحصل على الملكية.

Mr. Young Chang
4445 2nd Street
Passville, CA 00543

Pay to the order of _Towne Bank_ $ _2000.00_

Two Thousand and 00/100   Dollars

L. Make a mortgage payment.
يسدد دفعة الرهن العقاري.

Moving In الانتقال إلى المنزل

M. Pack.
تقوم بتعبئة الصناديق.

N. Unpack.
تقوم بتفريغ الصناديق.

We have a new address.

PHONE ✓
DWP ✓
GAS
CABLE ✓

GAS

O. Put the utilities in your name.
يطلب تسجيل المنافع العامة باسمه.

P. Paint.
يدهن / يطلي.

Q. Arrange the furniture.
يرتّب الأثاث.

Welcome!

R. Meet the neighbors.
يقابل / تقابل الجيران.

Ways to ask about a home's features

Are <u>utilities</u> included?
Is <u>the kitchen</u> large and sunny?
Are <u>the neighbors</u> quiet?

Role play. Talk to an apartment manager.

A: *Hi. I'm calling about <u>the apartment</u>.*
B: *OK. It's <u>unfurnished</u> and rent is <u>$800</u> a month.*
A: *Are <u>utilities included</u>?*

Fourth Floor
Third Floor
Second Floor
First Floor

1. apartment building	2. fire escape
بناية شقق /عمارة سكنية	سلّم النجاة من الحريق
3. playground	4. roof garden
ملعب	حديقة على السطح

Entrance المدخل

5. intercom / speaker	7. vacancy sign
نظام اتصال داخلي (إنتركوم)	لافتة شقة خالية
6. tenant	8. manager / superintendent
مستأجر / ساكن	مدير / مشرف

Lobby البهو

9. elevator	11. mailboxes
مصعد	صناديق للبريد
10. stairs / stairway	
سلالم / دَرَج	

Basement الدور السفلي / التحتاني (البدروم)

  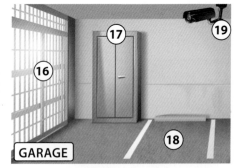

LAUNDRY ROOM   RECREATION ROOM   GARAGE

12. washer	14. big-screen TV	16. security gate	18. parking space
غسالة	تلفزيون بشاشة كبيرة	بوابة أمن	مكان لوقوف السيارة
13. dryer	15. pool table	17. storage locker	19. security camera
مجففة	طاولة بلياردو	مخزن	كاميرا للأمن

Grammar Point: *there is / there are*

singular: there is plural: there are
There is a recreation room in the basement.
There are mailboxes in the lobby.

Look at the pictures.
Describe the apartment building.

A: There's <u>a pool table</u> in the recreation room.
B: There are <u>parking spaces</u> in the garage.

APARTMENT COMPLEX

20. balcony	**22. swimming pool**	**24. alley**
شرفة / بلكونة	مسبح / حمّام سباحة	زقاق
21. courtyard	**23. trash bin**	
حوش / فناء / صحن الدار	وعاء مهملات / صفيحة زبالة	

Hallway الرواق

25. emergency exit	**26. trash chute**
مخرج للطوارئ	فتحة أنبوب النفايات

Rental Office مكتب التأجير

27. landlord	**28. lease / rental agreement**
صاحب الملك	عقد الإيجار

An Apartment Entryway مدخل الشقة

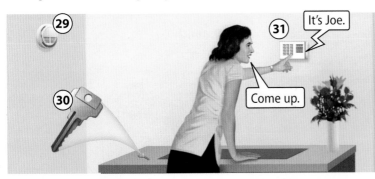

It's Joe.

Come up.

29. smoke detector	**31. buzzer**	**33. door chain**
كاشف أدخنة	رنّان	سلسلة أمان للباب
30. key	**32. peephole**	**34. dead-bolt lock**
مفتاح	ثقب الباب / عين سحرية	قفل بمزلاج ثابت

More vocabulary

upstairs: the floor(s) above you

downstairs: the floor(s) below you

fire exit: another name for emergency exit

Role play. Talk to a landlord.

A: Is there <u>a swimming pool</u> in this <u>complex</u>?

B: Yes, there is. It's near <u>the courtyard</u>.

A: Is there…?

Different Places to Live أماكن مختلفة للسكن

1. the city / an urban area
المدينة / منطقة حضرية

2. the suburbs
الضاحية (الضواحي)

3. a small town / a village
بلدة صغيرة / قرية

4. the country / a rural area
الريف / منطقة ريفية

5. condominium / condo
شقة تمليك

6. townhouse
بيت في مدينة

7. mobile home
بيت متنقل

8. college dormitory / dorm
مساكن الطلاب

9. farm
مزرعة

10. ranch
مزرعة كبيرة

11. senior housing
مساكن المسنين

12. nursing home
بيت للعجزة

13. shelter
ملجأ

More vocabulary

co-op: an apartment building owned by residents
duplex: a house divided into two homes
two-story house: a house with two floors

Think about it. Discuss.

1. What's good and bad about these places to live?
2. How are small towns different from cities?
3. How do shelters help people in need?

A House and Yard

Front Yard and House الفناء الأمامي والمنزل

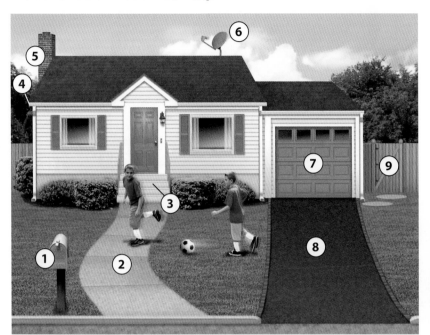

Front Porch الشرفة (الفراندة) الأمامية

1. mailbox صندوق للبريد	**4.** gutter مزراب	**7.** garage door باب الجراج
2. front walk ممر المدخل الرئيسي	**5.** chimney مدخنة	**8.** driveway ممر الجراج
3. steps سلالم / دَرَج	**6.** satellite dish صحن ساتليت	**9.** gate بوابة

10. storm door باب حاجز (مضاد للعواصف)	**13.** porch light مصباح الشرفة (الفراندة)
11. front door باب أمامي	**14.** doorbell جرس الباب
12. doorknob قبضة (أكرة) الباب	**15.** screen door باب منخلي (سلكي)

Backyard الفناء الخلفي

16. patio فناء مرصوف في الهواء الطلق	**19.** patio furniture أثاث للفناء المرصوف	**22.** sprinkler مِرَشّة	**25.** compost pile كومة سماد طبيعي	**A.** **take** a nap تأخذ قيلولة
17. grill شوّاية	**20.** flower bed حوض زهور	**23.** hammock أرجوحة شبكية للنوم	**26.** lawn مَخْضَرة	**B.** **garden** يعمل في الحديقة
18. sliding glass door باب زجاجي منزلق	**21.** hose خرطوم	**24.** garbage can وعاء مهملات	**27.** vegetable garden بستان خضروات	

1. cabinet خزانة	**8.** dishwasher غسالة صحون	**15.** toaster oven فرن لتحميص الخبز	**22.** counter طاولة طويلة / منضدة
2. shelf رف	**9.** refrigerator ثلاجة	**16.** pot قدر طبخ	**23.** drawer دُرج / جارور
3. paper towels مناديل ورق	**10.** freezer حجرة التجميد في الثلاجة / فريزر	**17.** teakettle غلاية / برّاد شاي	**24.** pan طنجرة / مقلاة
4. sink حوض	**11.** coffeemaker صانع قهوة كهربائي	**18.** stove موقد	**25.** electric mixer خلاط كهربائي
5. dish rack رف أو صفاية صحون	**12.** blender خلاط	**19.** burner مضرم	**26.** food processor جهاز تحضير المأكولات
6. toaster محمصة الخبز (توستر)	**13.** microwave فرن ميكروويف	**20.** oven فرن	**27.** cutting board لوحة تقطيع
7. garbage disposal وعاء لتصريف النفايات	**14.** electric can opener فتاحة علب كهربائية	**21.** broiler مشواة	**28.** mixing bowl وعاء / إناء للخلط

Ways to talk about location using *on* and *in*

Use *on* for the counter, shelf, burner, stove, and cutting board. *It's on the counter.* Use *in* for the dishwasher, oven, sink, and drawer. *Put it in the sink.*

Pair practice. Make new conversations.

A: *Please move <u>the blender</u>.*
B: *Sure. Do you want it <u>in the cabinet</u>?*
A: *No, put it <u>on the counter</u>.*

1. dish / plate
طبق / صحن

2. bowl
وعاء / إناء

3. fork
شوكة

4. knife
سكين

5. spoon
ملعقة

6. teacup
فنجان للشاي

7. coffee mug
فنجان قهوة كبير

8. dining room chair
كرسي حجرة الطعام

9. dining room table
طاولة حجرة الطعام / سفرة

10. napkin
منديل مائدة

11. placemat
قطعة قماش مخرمة توضع تحت الطبق

12. tablecloth
مفرش الطاولة

13. salt and pepper shakers
مذرتا الملح والفلفل

14. sugar bowl
إناء للسكر

15. creamer
إناء للحليب

16. teapot
إبريق شاي

17. tray
صينية

18. light fixture
ضوء مثبت / تركيبة إنارة

19. fan
مروحة

20. platter
طبق كبير مسطح

21. serving bowl
إناء تقديم

22. hutch
خزانة البوفيه العلوية

23. vase
زهرية

24. buffet
بوفيه / مقصف

Ways to make requests at the table

May I have the sugar bowl?
Would you pass the creamer, please?
Could I have a coffee mug?

Role play. Request items at the table.

A: *What do you need?*
B: *Could I have a coffee mug?*
A: *Certainly. And would you...*

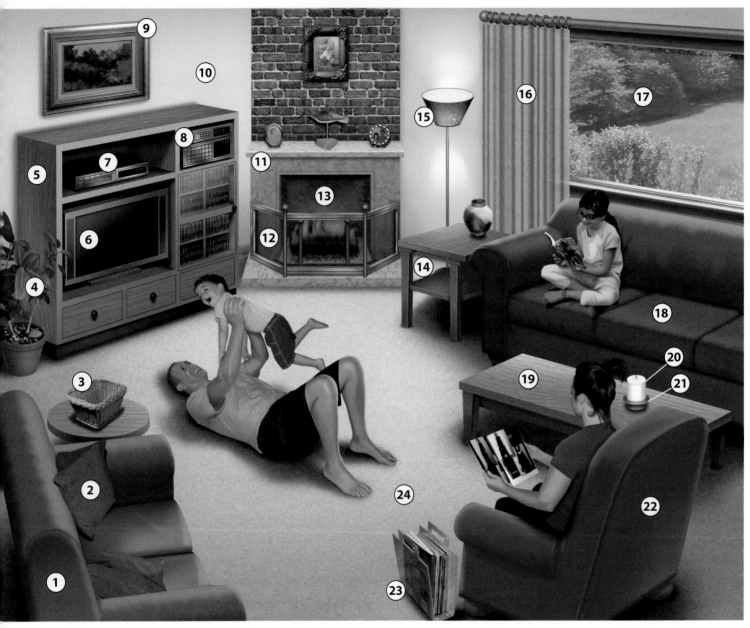

1. love seat أريكة / كنبة مزدوجة	**7. DVD player** جهاز تشغيل أقراص فيديو رقمية (دي في دي)	**13. fireplace** مستوقد / مدفأة	**19. coffee table** طاولة قهوة
2. throw pillow وسادة كنبة للزينة	**8. stereo system** جهاز ستريو	**14. end table** طاولة طرفية أو جانبية	**20. candle** شمعة
3. basket سلة	**9. painting** لوحة فنية	**15. floor lamp** مصباح أرضي	**21. candle holder** قاعدة الشمعة
4. houseplant نبات منزلي	**10. wall** جدار / حائط	**16. drapes** ستائر	**22. armchair / easy chair** كرسي ذو مسندين / فوتيه
5. entertainment center رف الأجهزة الصوتية والمرئية	**11. mantle** رف المستوقد (المدفأة)	**17. window** نافذة / شبّاك	**23. magazine holder** حامل الجرائد ومجلات
6. TV (television) تلفزيون	**12. fire screen** حاجز منخلي للمستوقد (حاجب النار)	**18. sofa / couch** كنبة / أريكة	**24. carpet** سجادة

Use the new words.
Look at pages 44–45. Name the things in the room.

A: *There's a TV.*

B: *There's a carpet.*

More vocabulary

light bulb: the light inside a lamp

lampshade: the part of the lamp that covers the light bulb

sofa cushions: the pillows that are part of the sofa

1. hamper سلة الملابس (سبت للغسيل)	**8. faucet** حنفية	**15. towel rack** حمالة فوط / مناشف	**22. medicine cabinet** دولاب أدوية
2. bathtub حوض الاستحمام (بانيو)	**9. hot water** ماء ساخن	**16. bath towel** منشفة للاستحمام	**23. toothbrush** فرشاة أسنان
3. soap dish صحن صابون	**10. cold water** ماء بارد	**17. hand towel** فوطة يد	**24. toothbrush holder** إناء لفرشاة الأسنان
4. soap صابون	**11. grab bar** قضيب للتمسك	**18. mirror** مرآة	**25. sink** حوض
5. rubber mat بساطة أو حصيرة مطاطية	**12. tile** بلاط / قيشاني	**19. toilet paper** ورق تواليت	**26. wastebasket** سلة مهملات
6. washcloth فوطة / منشفة صغيرة	**13. showerhead** رأس الدش	**20. toilet brush** فرشاة التواليت	**27. scale** ميزان
7. drain مصرف المياه / بلاعة	**14. shower curtain** ستار الدش	**21. toilet** تواليت / مرحاض	**28. bath mat** حصيرة حمام

More vocabulary

stall shower: a shower without a bathtub
half bath: a bathroom with no shower or tub
linen closet: a closet for towels and sheets

Ask your classmates. Share the answers.

1. Is your toothbrush on the sink or in the medicine cabinet?
2. Do you have a bathtub or a shower?
3. Do you have a shower curtain or a shower door?

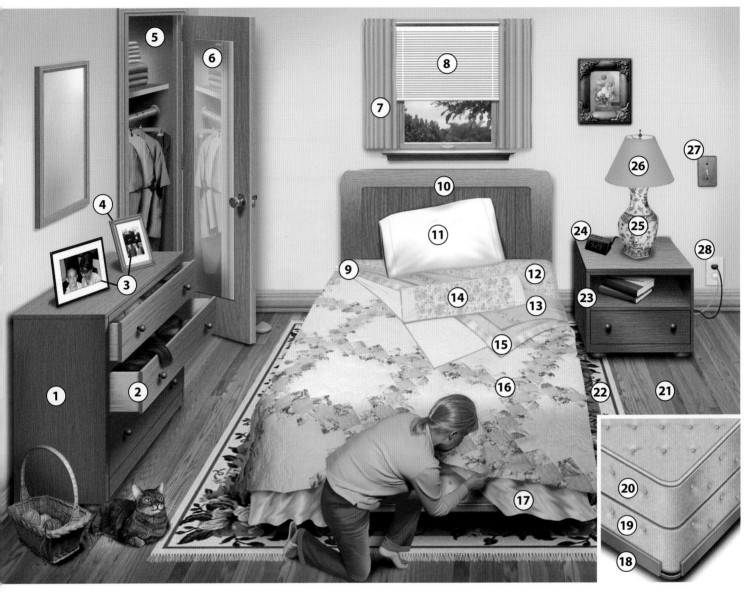

1. dresser / bureau خزانة ملابس بمرآة وأدراج	**8.** mini-blinds ستائر معدنية أو خشبية صغيرة	**15.** blanket بطانية	**22.** rug سجادة
2. drawer دُرج / جارور	**9.** bed سرير / فراش	**16.** quilt لحاف	**23.** night table / nightstand طاولة جانبية / كومودينو
3. photos صور فوتوغرافية	**10.** headboard رأس السرير	**17.** dust ruffle كشكشة مانعة للأتربة	**24.** alarm clock منبّه
4. picture frame إطار للصور / برواز	**11.** pillow وسادة / مخدة	**18.** bed frame قاعدة السرير	**25.** lamp مصباح (أباجورة)
5. closet دولاب / خزانة	**12.** fitted sheet ملاءة مفصلة	**19.** box spring صندوق زنبركي تحت السرير	**26.** lampshade قبعة أو شمسية المصباح
6. full-length mirror مرآة كاملة الطول	**13.** flat sheet ملاءة	**20.** mattress مرتبة / فراش	**27.** light switch مفتاح الضوء
7. curtains ستائر	**14.** pillowcase كيس وسادة / مخدة	**21.** wood floor أرضية خشبية	**28.** outlet مأخذ التيار

Look at the pictures.
Describe the bedroom.

A: *There's a lamp on the nightstand.*
B: *There's a mirror in the closet.*

Ask your classmates. Share the answers.

1. Do you prefer a hard or a soft mattress?
2. Do you prefer mini-blinds or curtains?
3. How many pillows do you like on your bed?

58

The Kids' Bedroom

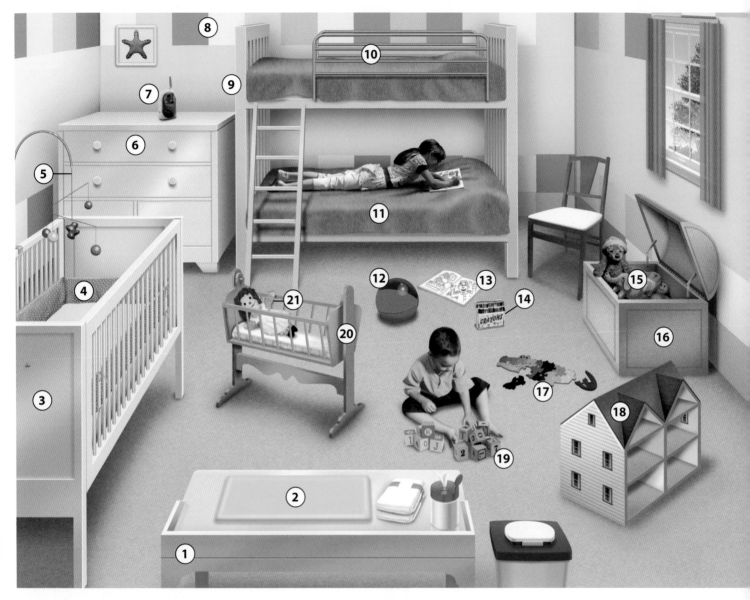

Furniture and Accessories أثاث وإكسسوارات

1. changing table
   طاولة لتغيير ملابس الطفل

2. changing pad
   لبادة لتغيير حفاض الطفل

3. crib
   سرير طفل رضيع

4. bumper pad
   لبادة وقائية للطفل

5. mobile
   لعبة دوارة بزنبرك

6. chest of drawers
   خزانة ذات أدراج

7. baby monitor
   أداة مراقبة الطفل

8. wallpaper
   ورق حائط

9. bunk beds
   كناديس (سرير مزدوج)

10. safety rail
    قضيب أمان

11. bedspread
    مفرش سرير / شرشف

Toys and Games لعب وألعاب

12. ball
    كرة

13. coloring book
    كتاب تلوين

14. crayons
    أقلام ألوان شمعية

15. stuffed animals
    حيوانات محشوة

16. toy chest
    صندوق اللعب

17. puzzle
    لغز

18. dollhouse
    بيت للدمى

19. blocks
    مكعبات

20. cradle
    مهد

21. doll
    دمية

Pair practice. Make conversations.

A: *Where's the changing pad?*
B: *It's on the changing table.*

Think about it. Discuss.

1. Which toys help children learn? How?
2. Which toys are good for older and younger children?
3. What safety features does this room need? Why?

A. **dust** the furniture
تمسح / تزيل التراب عن الأثاث

B. **recycle** the newspapers
يعد الصحف للاستعمال ثانية

C. **clean** the oven
تنظّف الفرن

D. **mop** the floor
يمسح الأرضية

E. **polish** the furniture
تلمّع الأثاث

F. **make** the bed
يرتّب (يسوّي) السرير

G. **put away** the toys
يضع اللعب في مكانها

H. **vacuum** the carpet
يكنس السجاد بالمكنسة الكهربائية

I. **wash** the windows
تغسل النوافذ

J. **sweep** the floor
يكنس الأرضية بالمقشة

K. **scrub** the sink
تنظّف الحوض بالفرشاة

L. **empty** the trash
يفرّغ سلة المهملات

M. **wash** the dishes
يغسل الأطباق أو الصحون

N. **dry** the dishes
تجفف / تنشّف الأطباق

O. **wipe** the counter
تمسح المنضدة

P. **change** the sheets
تغيّر الملاءات

Q. **take out** the garbage
يلقي القمامة

Pair practice. Make new conversations.

A: *Let's clean this place. First, I'll* <u>sweep the floor</u>.

B: *I'll* <u>mop the floor</u> *when you finish.*

Ask your classmates. Share the answers.

1. Who does the housework in your home?
2. How often do you wash the windows?
3. When should kids start to do housework?

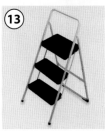     

1. feather duster
   ريشة تنظيف

2. recycling bin
   وعاء للمهملات المعاد تدويرها

3. oven cleaner
   منظف الفرن

4. rubber gloves
   قفازات مطاطية

5. steel-wool soap pads
   قطع سلك للتنظيف

6. sponge mop
   ممسحة إسفنجية

7. bucket / pail
   دلو / جردل

8. furniture polish
   ملمّع الأثاث

9. rags
   خِرَق / أقمشة للتنظيف

10. vacuum cleaner
    مكنسة كهربائية

11. vacuum cleaner attachments
    ملحقات المكنسة الكهربائية

12. vacuum cleaner bag
    كيس المكنسة الكهربائية

13. stepladder
    سلم درجي

14. glass cleaner
    منظف زجاج

15. squeegee
    مسّاحة مطاطية (سكويجي)

16. broom
    مقشة / مكنسة

17. dustpan
    جاروف / لقّاطة الكناسة

18. cleanser
    منظف مطهّر

19. sponge
    إسفنجه

20. scrub brush
    فرشاة مسح وحك

21. dishwashing liquid
    سائل غسل الأطباق

22. dish towel
    فوطة تجفيف الأطباق

23. disinfectant wipes
    مناديل مطهّرة

24. trash bags
    أكياس مهملات

Ways to ask for something

Please hand me <u>the squeegee</u>.
Can you get me <u>the broom</u>?
I need <u>the sponge mop</u>.

Pair practice. Make new conversations.

A: *Please hand me <u>the sponge mop</u>.*
B: *Here you go. Do you need <u>the bucket</u>?*
A: *Yes, please. Can you get me <u>the rubber gloves</u>, too?*

61

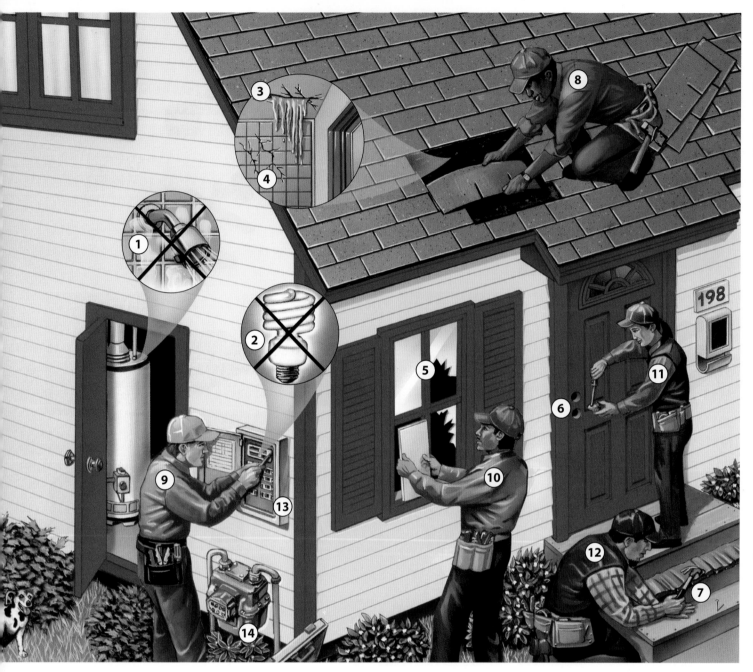

1. The water heater is **not working**.

سخان الماء لا **يعمل**.

2. The power is **out**.

التيار الكهربائي **مقطوع**.

3. The roof is **leaking**.

السقف يسرب / **يرشح**.

4. The tile is **cracked**.

البلاط **مشقوق**.

5. The window is **broken**.

النافذة **مكسورة**.

6. The lock is **broken**.

القفل **مكسور**.

7. The steps are **broken**.

الدرج **مكسور**.

8. roofer

أخصائي تصليح أسقف البيوت

9. electrician

كهربائي

10. repair person

مُصلِّح / عامل تصليح

11. locksmith

مُصلِّح أقفال

12. carpenter

نجّار

13. fuse box

صندوق المصاهر الكهربائية (الفيوزات)

14. gas meter

عداد الغاز

More vocabulary

fix: to repair something that is broken
pests: termites, fleas, rats, etc.
exterminate: to kill household pests

Pair practice. Make new conversations.

A: *The faucet is* <u>*leaking*</u>.
B: *Let's call* <u>*the plumber*</u>. *He can fix it.*

15. The furnace is **broken**.

الفرن/التنور **مُتعطل**.

16. The pipes are **frozen**.

المواسير **مجمدة**.

17. The faucet is **dripping**.

الحنفية **تنقّط / تقطر**.

18. The sink is **overflowing**.

الحوض **طافح / مسدود**.

19. The toilet is **stopped up**.

المرحاض (التواليت) **مسدود**.

20. plumber

سبّاك / سمكري

21. exterminator

شخص متخصص في إبادة الحشرات

22. termites

نملة بيضاء (نمل أبيض)

23. ants

نملة (نمل)

24. bedbugs

بقة (بق)

25. fleas

برغوث (براغيث)

26. cockroaches / roaches

صرصور (صراصير)

27. rats

جرذ (جرذان)

28. mice*

فأر (فئران)

*Note: one mouse, two mice

Ways to ask about repairs

How much will this repair cost?

When can you begin?

How long will the repair take?

Role play. Talk to a repair person.

A: *Can you fix <u>the roof</u>?*

B: *Yes, but it will take <u>two weeks</u>.*

A: *How much will the repair cost?*

THE NEXT DAY...

LATER THAT EVENING...

1. roommates	**3.** music	**5.** noise	**7.** rules	**9.** invitation
رفقاء شقة	موسيقى	الضجيج	قواعد	دعوة / عزومة
2. party	**4.** DJ	**6.** irritated	**8.** mess	**A. dance**
حفلة	مشغّل الأسطوانات (دي جاي)	مهتاج / متهيج	لخبطة / خربطة	يرقصون

THE NEXT SATURDAY...

**Look at the pictures.
What do you see?**

Answer the questions.

1. What happened in apartment 2B?
   How many people were there?

2. How did the neighbor feel? Why?

3. What rules did they write at the
   tenant meeting?

4. What did the roommates do after
   the tenant meeting?

Read the story.

The Tenant Meeting

Sally Lopez and Tina Green are
<u>roommates</u>. They live in apartment 2B.
One night they had a big <u>party</u> with
<u>music</u> and a <u>DJ</u>. There was a <u>mess</u> in the
hallway. Their neighbors were very
unhappy. Mr. Clark in 2A was very
<u>irritated</u>. He hates <u>noise</u>!

The next day there was a tenant
meeting. Everyone wanted <u>rules</u> about
parties and loud music. The girls were
very embarrassed.

After the meeting, the girls cleaned
the mess in the hallway. Then they gave
each neighbor an <u>invitation</u> to a new
party. Everyone had a good time at the
rec room party. Now the tenants have
two new rules and a new place to <u>dance</u>.

Think about it.

1. What are the most important rules in
   an apartment building? Why?

2. Imagine you are the neighbor in 2A.
   What do you say to Tina and Sally?

65

1. fish
سمك

2. meat
لحم

3. chicken
دجاج

4. cheese
جبن

5. milk
حليب

6. butter
زبد

7. eggs
بيض

8. vegetables
خضروات

Listen and point. Take turns.

A: *Point to the vegetables.*
B: *Point to the bread.*
A: *Point to the fruit.*

Pair Dictation

A: *Write vegetables.*
B: *Please spell vegetables for me.*
A: *V-e-g-e-t-a-b-l-e-s.*

9. fruit
فاكهة

10. rice
أرز

11. bread
خبز / عيش

12. pasta
باستا (ضرب من المعكرونة)

13. grocery bag
كيس البقالة

14. shopping list
قائمة التسوق

15. coupons
كوبونات

Ways to talk about food.

Do we need <u>eggs</u>?

Do we have any <u>pasta</u>?

We have some <u>vegetables</u>, but we need <u>fruit</u>.

Role play. Talk about your shopping list.

A: *Do we need eggs?*

B: *No, we have some.*

A: *Do we have any...*

67

1. apples
تفاح

2. bananas
موز

3. grapes
عنب

4. pears
كمثرى

5. oranges
برتقال

6. grapefruit
ليمون الجنة (كريب فروت)

7. lemons
ليمون (ليمون أصفر)

8. limes
ليئم (ليمون أخضر أو حامض)

9. tangerines
يوسفي

10. peaches
خوخ

11. cherries
كرز

12. apricots
مشمش

13. plums
برقوق

14. strawberries
فراولة / فريز

15. raspberries
توت شوكي

16. blueberries
توت العنبية

17. blackberries
توت العلّيق

18. watermelons
بطيخ

19. melons
شمام

20. papayas
ببايا

21. mangoes
مانجو

22. kiwi
كيوي

23. pineapples
أناناس

24. coconuts
جوز الهند

25. raisins
زبيب

26. prunes
قراصيا (برقوق مجفف)

27. figs
تين

28. dates
تمر / بلح

29. a bunch of bananas
حزمة موز

30. **ripe** banana
موز **ناضج**

31. **unripe** banana
موز **عير ناضج (نيئ)**

32. **rotten** banana
موز **عفن**

Pair practice. Make new conversations.

A: *What's your favorite fruit?*
B: *I like <u>apples</u>. Do you?*
A: *I prefer <u>bananas</u>.*

Ask your classmates. Share the answers.

1. Which fruit do you put in a fruit salad?
2. What kinds of fruit are common in your native country?
3. What kinds of fruit are in your kitchen right now?

1. lettuce
خس

2. cabbage
كرنب / ملفوف

3. carrots
جزر

4. radishes
فجل

5. beets
بنجر / شمندر

6. tomatoes
طماطم / قوطة / بندورة

7. bell peppers
فلفل رومي / فلفل حلو

8. string beans
فاصوليا

9. celery
كرفس

10. cucumbers
خيار

11. spinach
سبانخ

12. corn
ذُرة

13. broccoli
بروكلي (نوع من القرنبيط)

14. cauliflower
قرنبيط

15. bok choy
بوك تشوي

16. turnips
لفت

17. potatoes
بطاطا / بطاطس

18. sweet potatoes
بطاطا حلوة

19. onions
بصل

20. green onions / scallions
بصل أخضر / كرّاث أندلسي

21. peas
بسلة (بازلا)

22. artichokes
خرشوف

23. eggplants
باذنجان

24. squash
قرع

25. zucchini
كوسا

26. asparagus
هليون

27. mushrooms
فطر (عيش غراب)

28. parsley
بقدونس

29. chili peppers
فلفل حار

30. garlic
ثوم

31. a **bag of** lettuce
كيس خس

32. a **head of** lettuce
رأس خس

Pair practice. Make new conversations.

A: *Do you eat <u>broccoli</u>?*
B: *Yes. I like most vegetables, but not <u>peppers</u>.*
A: *Really? Well, I don't like <u>cauliflower</u>.*

Ask your classmates. Share the answers.

1. Which vegetables do you eat raw? cooked?
2. Which vegetables do you put in a green salad?
3. Which vegetables are in your refrigerator right now?

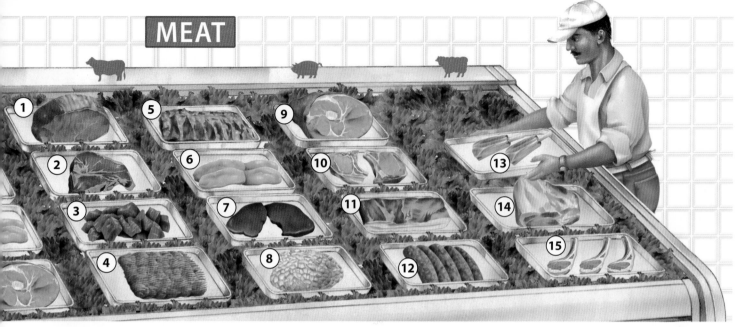

MEAT

Beef لحم بقر

1. roast
لحم معد للشواء (روستو)

2. steak
شريحة لحم (بفتيك)

3. stewing beef
لحم للسلق (لحم معدّ لليخنة)

4. ground beef
لحم مفروم

5. beef ribs
رِيَش (ضلوع) لحم بقري

6. veal cutlets
شرائح لحم عجل (بتلو)

7. liver
كبدة

8. tripe
الكرش (كرشة)

Pork لحم الخنزير

9. ham
لحم فخذ خنزير

10. pork chops
شرائح لحم خنزير

11. bacon
لحم خنزير مملح (بيكون)

12. sausage
سجق / نقانق

Lamb لحم الحمل (الضأن)

13. lamb shanks
ساق حمل

14. leg of lamb
فخذة حمل

15. lamb chops
شرائح لحم حمل

POULTRY

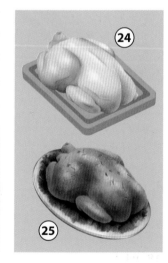

Poultry الدواجن

16. chicken
دجاج

17. turkey
ديك رومي

18. duck
بط

19. breasts
صدور

20. wings
أجنحة

21. legs
أرجل

22. thighs
أفخاذ / أوراك

23. drumsticks
دبابيس (وصلة الفخذ بالكاحل)

24. **raw** chicken
دجاج **نيئ**

25. **cooked** chicken
دجاجة **مطهوة**

More vocabulary

vegetarian: a person who doesn't eat meat
boneless: meat and poultry without bones
skinless: poultry without skin

Ask your classmates. Share the answers.

1. What kind of meat do you eat most often?
2. What kind of meat do you use in soups?
3. What part of the chicken do you like the most?

SEAFOOD

Fish أسماك

1. trout
سمك التروتة المرقّط

2. catfish
سمك الصلور

3. whole salmon
سلمون كامل

4. salmon steak
شريحة (فيليه) سلمون

5. swordfish
سمك أبو سيف

6. halibut steak
شريحة (فيليه) هلبوت

7. tuna
التونة

8. cod
سمك القد (بكلاه)

Shellfish محار

9. crab
سرطان البحر (كابوريا)

10. lobster
جراد البحر (استاكوزة)

11. shrimp
جمبري / ربيان

12. scallops
أسقلوب

13. mussels
بلح البحر

14. oysters
محار رخوي

15. clams
صدف البطلنيوس

16. fresh fish
سمك **طازج**

17. frozen fish
سمك **مجمد**

DELI

18. white bread
خبز أبيض

19. wheat bread
خبز قمحي

20. rye bread
خبز جاوداري

21. roast beef
قطعة لحم بقري مشوي (روزبيف)

22. corned beef
لحم بقري مملح (بلوبيف)

23. pastrami
بسطرمة

24. salami
لانشون السلامي

25. smoked turkey
ديك رومي مدخّن

26. American cheese
جبن أمريكي

27. Swiss cheese
جبن سويسري

28. cheddar cheese
جبن شيدر

29. mozzarella cheese
جبن موتساريلا

Ways to order at the counter

I'd like some <u>roast beef</u>.
I'll have <u>a halibut steak</u> and some <u>shrimp</u>.
Could I get some <u>Swiss cheese</u>?

Pair practice. Make new conversations.

A: *What can I get for you?*
B: *<u>I'd like some roast beef</u>. How about a pound?*
A: *A pound of <u>roast beef</u> coming up!*

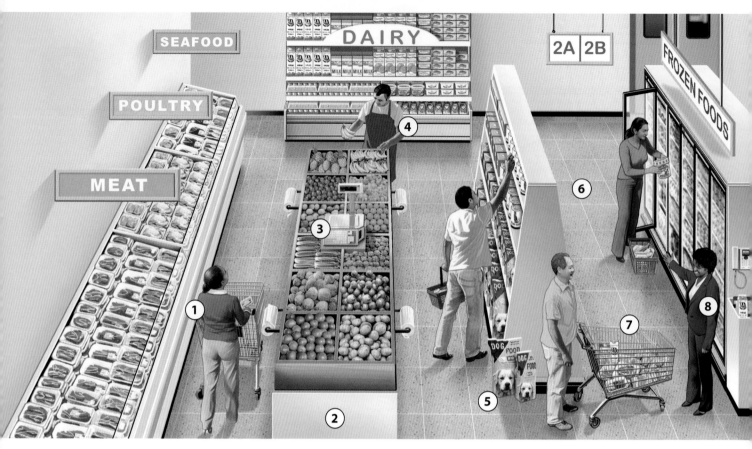

SEAFOOD

POULTRY

MEAT

DAIRY

2A 2B

FROZEN FOODS

1. customer
زبون

2. produce section
قسم المنتجات الزراعية

3. scale
ميزان

4. grocery clerk
بائع في محل البقالة

5. pet food
طعام الحيوانات المنزلية

6. aisle
ممر

7. cart
عربة تسوق

8. manager
مدير

Canned Foods
معلبات

17. beans
فول

18. soup
شوربة / حساء

19. tuna
علبة سمك التونة

Dairy
منتجات الألبان

20. margarine
مرجرين (سمن نباتي)

21. sour cream
قشدة (كريمة) حامضة

22. yogurt
زبادي / لبن

Grocery Products
منتجات بقالة

23. aluminum foil
ورق تغليف ألومنيوم

24. plastic wrap
ورق تغليف بلاستيكي

25. plastic storage bags
أكياس تخزين بلاستيكية

Frozen Foods
مأكولات مجمدة

26. ice cream
آيس كريم / بوظة / جيلاتي

27. frozen vegetables
خضروات مجمدة

28. frozen dinner
وجبة عشاء مجمدة

Ways to ask for information in a grocery store

Excuse me, where are <u>the carrots</u>?

Can you please tell me where to find <u>the dog food</u>?

Do you have any <u>lamb chops</u> today?

Pair practice. Make conversations.

A: <u>*Can you please tell me where to find the dog food*</u>?

B: *Sure. It's in <u>aisle 1B</u>. Do you need anything else?*

A: *Yes, where are <u>the carrots</u>?*

BAKERY

15 items or less

Cash for Bottles

Cash for Bottle

16

15

14

13

Best Baked Goods

3A 3B

SNACKS

12

11

10

9

9. shopping basket	**11. line**	**13. cashier**	**15. cash register**
سلة التسوق	صف / طابور	أمينة صندوق	آلة تسجيل النقود
10. self-checkout	**12. checkstand**	**14. bagger**	**16. bottle return**
دفع الحساب ذاتيا	مركز الدفع	مكيّس / معبّئ أكياس	مكان إعادة الزجاجات الفارغة

WHOLE WHEAT

J&G

Franco's

29 30 31

Italian Roast

Tasty Cola

32 33 34

Baked not Fried!

YUM! CHOCOLATE

35 36 37

38 39 40

Baking Products
منتجات للخبز

29. flour
دقيق

30. sugar
سكر

31. oil
زيت

Beverages
مشروبات

32. apple juice
عصير تفاح

33. coffee
قهوة

34. soda / pop
مشروبات غازية / صودا

Snack Foods
مأكولات خفيفة

35. potato chips
رقائق بطاطس مقلية (شيبس)

36. nuts
مكسرات

37. candy bar
قطعة من الحلوى

Baked Goods
أطعمة مخبوزة

38. cookies
بسكويت (كعك رقيق محلى)

39. cake
كعكة

40. bagels
بيغل (أقراص من الخبز)

Ask your classmates. Share the answers.

1. What is your favorite grocery store?
2. Do you prefer to shop alone or with friends?
3. Which foods from your country are hard to find?

Think about it. Discuss.

1. Is it better to shop every day or once a week? Why?
2. Why do grocery stores put snacks near the checkstands?
3. What's good and what's bad about small grocery stores?

1. bottles
زجاجة

2. jars
برطمان / مرطبان

3. cans
علبة (علب) معدنية

4. cartons
علبة كرتون (كراتين)

5. containers
حاوية / وعاء

6. boxes
علبة / صندوق (صناديق)

7. bags
كيس (أكياس)

8. packages
رزمة (رزم)

9. six-packs
علبة حاوية ست ز جاجات أو علب

10. loaves
رغيف (أرغفة)

11. rolls
لفة (لفافات)

12. tubes
أنبوب (أنابيب)

13. a bottle of water
زجاجة ماء

14. a jar of jam
برطمان مربى

15. a can of beans
علبة فول

16. a carton of eggs
كرتون(ة) بيض

17. a container of cottage cheese
وعاء/حاوية جين حلوم

18. a box of cereal
علبة حبوب (سيريال)

19. a bag of flour
كيس دقيق

20. a package of cookies
رزمة بسكويت

21. a six-pack of soda (pop)
علبة حاوية ست زجاجات صودا

22. a loaf of bread
رغيف خبز

23. a roll of paper towels
لفة مناديل ورقية

24. a tube of toothpaste
أنبوب معجون أسنان

Grammar Point: count and non-count

Some foods can be counted: *an apple, two apples*.

Some foods can't be counted: *some rice, some water*.

For non-count foods, count containers: *two bags of rice*.

Pair practice. Make conversations.

A: *How many <u>boxes of cereal</u> do we need?*

B: *We need <u>two boxes</u>.*

A. **Measure** the ingredients.
تعاير المقادير.

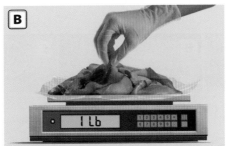

B. **Weigh** the food.
تزِن الطعام.

1 cup = 237 milliliters

C. **Convert** the measurements.
تحوّل المكاييل.

Liquid Measures مقادير السوائل

1 fl. oz.

2

1 c.

3

1 pt.

1 qt.

4

5

1 gal.

Dry Measures مقادير المواد الجافة

6

1 tsp.

7

1 TBS.

8

1/4 c.

9

1/2 c.

10

1 c.

Weight الأوزان

11 0 Lb 1 oz

12 1 Lb

1. a fluid ounce of milk
أونصة سائلية من الحليب

2. a cup of oil
كوب زيت

3. a pint of frozen yogurt
باينت زبادي (لبن) مجمد

4. a quart of milk
كوارت حليب

5. a gallon of water
جالون ماء

6. a teaspoon of salt
ملعقة شاي من الملح

7. a tablespoon of sugar
ملعقة طعام (سفرة) من السكر

8. a quarter cup of brown sugar
ربع كوب من السكر البني

9. a half cup of raisins
نصف كوب من الزبيب

10. a cup of flour
كوب من الدقيق

11. an ounce of cheese
أونصة من الجبن

12. a pound of roast beef
باوند (رطل) من شرائح لحم البقر

Equivalencies	
3 tsp. = 1 TBS.	2 c. = 1 pt.
2 TBS. = 1 fl. oz.	2 pt. = 1 qt.
8 fl. oz. = 1 c.	4 qt. = 1 gal.

Volume
1 fl. oz. = 30 ml
1 c. = 237 ml
1 pt. = .47 L
1 qt. = .95 L
1 gal. = 3.79 L

Weight
1 oz. = 28.35 grams (g)
1 lb. = 453.6 g
2.205 lbs. = 1 kilogram (kg)
1 lb. = 16 oz.

Food Safety سلامة الطعام

A. **clean**
نظّف

B. **separate**
افصل

C. **cook**
اطبخ

D. **chill**
جمّد / برّد

Clean counters!

20 SECONDS

Wash your hands!

Use separate cutting boards for vegetables and meat!

Cook to the right temperature!

Refrigerate leftovers quickly!

Ways to Serve Meat and Poultry طرق لتحضير اللحوم والدواجن

1. fried chicken
دجاج مقلي

2. barbecued / grilled ribs
ريْش (ضلوع) مشوية / مشوية على الفحم

3. broiled steak
شريحة لحم مشوي

4. roasted turkey
ديك رومي مطهو في الفرن

5. boiled ham
لحم فخذ خنزير مسلوق

6. stir-fried beef
لحم بقري مقلي بالتقليب

Ways to Serve Eggs طرق لتحضير البيض

7. scrambled eggs
بيض مفري

8. hardboiled eggs
بيض مسلوق جيدا

9. poached eggs
بيض غير تام السلق

10. eggs sunny-side up
بيض مقلي على شكل عيون

11. eggs over easy
بيض مقلي خفيفا ومقلوب

12. omelet
بيض أومليت (عجة)

Role play. Make new conversations.

A: *How do you like your eggs?*
B: *I like them* scrambled. *And you?*
A: *I like them* hardboiled.

Ask your classmates. Share the answers.

1. Do you use separate cutting boards?
2. What is your favorite way to serve meat? poultry?
3. What are healthy ways of preparing meat? poultry?

Cheesy Tofu Vegetable Casserole كسرولة (طبق) خضار بالتوفو الجبني

A. **Preheat** the oven.
سخّن الفرن مسبقا.

B. **Grease** a baking pan.
شحّم طنجرة / طاسة خبز.

C. **Slice** the tofu.
قطّع التوفو في شرائح.

D. **Steam** the broccoli.
اطهِ البروكولي على البخار.

E. **Saute** the mushrooms.
اقلِ الفطر بسرعة وفي قليل من الدهن.

F. **Spoon** sauce on top.
ضع صلصة بالملعقة على السطح.

G. **Grate** the cheese.
ابشر الجبن.

H. **Bake**.
اخبز في الفرن.

Easy Chicken Soup شوربة دجاج سهلة

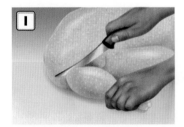

I. **Cut up** the chicken.
قطّع الدجاج إلى قطع صغيرة.

J. **Dice** the celery.
قطّع الكرفس إلى مكعبات.

K. **Peel** the carrots.
قشّر الجزر.

L. **Chop** the onions.
قطّع (قرّط) البصل.

M. **Boil** the chicken.
اسلق الدجاج.

N. **Add** the vegetables.
أضف الخضروات.

O. **Stir**.
قلِّب.

P. **Simmer**.
اطهِ ببطء (على نار هادئة).

Quick and Easy Cake كعكة سريعة وسهلة

Q. **Break** 2 eggs into a microwave-safe bowl.
اكسر بيضتين في سلطانية آمنة الاستعمال في ميكروويف.

R. **Mix** the ingredients.
اخلط المكونات.

S. **Beat** the mixture.
اضرب الخليط.

T. **Microwave** for 5 minutes.
اطهِ في الميكروويف لمدة ٥ دقائق.

Kitchen Utensils

أدوات المطبخ

1. **can opener**
فتّاحة علب

2. **grater**
مبشرة

3. **steamer**
وعاء الطهي بالبخار

4. **plastic storage container**
حاوية تخزين بلاستيكية

5. **frying pan**
طنجرة / مقلاة

6. **pot**
إناء / قِدْرة

7. **ladle**
مغرفة

8. **double boiler**
إناء مزدوج للغلي (غلاية مزدوجة)

9. **wooden spoon**
ملعقة خشبية

10. **casserole dish**
طبق كبير / طبق كسرولة

11. **garlic press**
معصرة ثوم

12. **carving knife**
سكين لتقطيع اللحوم

13. **roasting pan**
طنجرة / إناء للشوي

14. **roasting rack**
شبكة للشوي

15. **vegetable peeler**
قشّارة خضروات

16. **paring knife**
سكين تقشير

17. **colander**
مصفاة

18. **kitchen timer**
ساعة توقيت للمطبخ

19. **spatula**
ملعقة مبسطة

20. **eggbeater**
مخفقة (مضرب) بيض

21. **whisk**
مخفقة

22. **strainer**
مصفاة (للسوائل)

23. **tongs**
ملقطة

24. **lid**
غطاء

25. **saucepan**
قدر صغير

26. **cake pan**
إناء الكعك

27. **cookie sheet**
صينية لخبز الحلوى (البسكويت)

28. **pie pan**
صينية فطائر

29. **pot holders**
ممسكات الآنية الساخنة

30. **rolling pin**
مرقاق العجين / شوبك

31. **mixing bowl**
سلطانية (وعاء) خلط

Pair practice. Make new conversations.

A: *Please hand me <u>the whisk</u>.*
B: *Here's <u>the whisk</u>. Do you need anything else?*
A: *Yes, pass me <u>the casserole dish</u>.*

Use the new words.
Look at page 77. Name the kitchen utensils you see.

A: *Here's <u>a grater</u>.*
B: *This is <u>a mixing bowl</u>.*

Fast Food Restaurant

1. **hamburger**
سندوتش همبورجر (لحم البقر)

2. **french fries**
بطاطس مقلية

3. **cheeseburger**
سندوتش همبورجر مع الجبن

4. **onion rings**
حلقات بصل مقلي

5. **chicken sandwich**
سندوتش دجاج

6. **hot dog**
سجق (هوت دوج)

7. **nachos**
ناتشوز

8. **taco**
تاكو

9. **burrito**
بوريتو

10. **pizza**
بيتزا

11. **soda**
مشروب غازي / صودا

12. **iced tea**
شاي مثلج

13. **ice-cream cone**
آيس كريم في كوز من البسكويت

14. **milkshake**
لبن / حليب مخفوق

15. **donut**
كعكة الدونات

16. **muffin**
فطيرة مدورة (موفينية)

17. **counterperson**
عامل المنضدة (الكاونتر)

18. **straw**
شفّاطة / ماصّة

19. **plastic utensils**
أدوات طعام بلاستيكية

20. **sugar substitute**
بديل السكر

21. **ketchup**
صلصة طماطم (كاتشب)

22. **mustard**
صلصة خردل (موستردة)

23. **mayonnaise**
مايونييز

24. **salad bar**
بوفيه / ركن السلاطات

Grammar Point: yes/no questions (do)

Do you like hamburgers? Yes, I do.
Do you like nachos? No, I don't.

Think about it. Discuss.

1. Do you think that fast food is bad for people? Why or why not?
2. What fast foods do you have in your country?
3. Do you have a favorite fast food restaurant? Which one?

1. bacon
لحم خنزير مملح (بيكون)

2. sausage
سجق (نقانق)

3. hash browns
بطاطس مقلية ومفرومة

4. toast
خبز محمص (توست)

5. English muffin
موفينية إنجليزية

6. biscuits
فطيرة بسكويت

7. pancakes
فطيرة محلاة (بانكيك)

8. waffles
فطير الوافل

9. hot cereal
حبوب (سيريال) ساخنة

10. grilled cheese sandwich
سندوتش جبن مشوي

11. pickle
خيار مخلل

12. club sandwich
سندوتش النادي (كلوب سندوتش)

13. spinach salad
سلاطة سبانخ

14. chef's salad
سلاطة الشيف / سلاطة رئيس الطهاة

15. dinner salad
سلاطة وجبة العشاء

16. soup
شوربة / حساء

17. rolls
أقراص خبز

18. coleslaw
سلاطة كرنب (كولسلو)

19. potato salad
سلاطة بطاطس

20. pasta salad
سلاطة معكرونة (باستا)

21. fruit salad
سلاطة فواكه

BREAKFAST SPECIAL
Served 6 a.m. to 11 a.m.

Two egg omelet with one side

HONEY

JELLY

SYRUP

LUNCH
Served 11 a.m. to 2 p.m.
All sandwiches come with soup or salad

CRACKERS

SIDE SALADS

SALAD DRESSINGS

Thousand Island

Ranch

Italian

Blue Cheese

Ways to order from a menu

I'd like a grilled cheese sandwich.
I'll have a bowl of tomato soup.
Could I get the chef's salad with ranch dressing?

Pair practice. Make conversations.

A: *I'd like a grilled cheese sandwich, please.*
B: *Anything else for you?*
A: *Yes, I'll have a bowl of tomato soup with that.*

A Coffee Shop Menu

قائمة الطعام في مقهى

DINNER

DESSERTS

BEVERAGES

22. roast chicken
دجاج مطهو في الفرن

23. mashed potatoes
بطاطس مهروسة (بوريه)

24. steak
شريحة لحم بقري مشوي (ستيك)

25. baked potato
بطاطس مطهوة في الفرن

26. spaghetti
معكرونة رفيعة وطويلة (اسباجتي)

27. meatballs
كبب لحم (كبيبة)

28. garlic bread
خبز بالثوم

29. grilled fish
سمك مشوي على الفحم

30. rice
أرز

31. meatloaf
لحم مفروم مطبوخ في قالب

32. steamed vegetables
خضروات مطبوخة على البخار

33. layer cake
كعكة من طبقات

34. cheesecake
كعكة جبن

35. pie
فطيرة

36. mixed berries
توت مشكّل

37. coffee
قهوة

38. decaf coffee
قهوة بدون كافيين

39. tea
شاي

40. herbal tea
شاي أعشاب

41. cream
قشدة / قشدة حليب

42. low-fat milk
حليب خفيض الدسم

Ask your classmates. Share the answers.

1. Do you prefer vegetable soup or chicken soup?
2. Do you prefer tea or coffee?
3. Which desserts on the menu do you like?

Role play. Order a dinner from the menu.

A: *Are you ready to order?*
B: *I think so. I'll have <u>the roast chicken</u>.*
A: *Would you also like…?*

81

1. **dining room**
   صالة الطعام

2. **hostess**
   مضيفة

3. **high chair**
   كرسي مرتفع

4. **booth**
   مائدة بين مقعدين طويلين مرتفعي الظهر

5. **to-go box**
   علبة لأخذ الطعام إلى المنزل

6. **patron / diner**
   زبون / شخص يتناول الطعام

7. **menu**
   قائمة الطعام

8. **server / waiter**
   نادل / جرسون

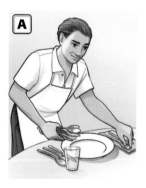    

A. **set** the table
يحضّر الطاولة

B. **seat** the customer
تجلِس الزبون

C. **pour** the water
يسكب الماء

D. **order** from the menu
يطلب من قائمة الطعام

E. **take** the order
يسجّل الطلب

F. **serve** the meal
يقدّم الوجبة

G. **clear / bus** the dishes
يزيل الأطباق من على الطاولة /
ينظّف الطاولة

H. **carry** the tray
يحمل الصينية

I. **pay** the check
يدفع الفاتورة (الحساب)

J. **leave** a tip
يترك بقشيشا

More Vocabulary

eat out: to go to a restaurant to eat

take out: to buy food at a restaurant and take it home to eat

Look at the pictures.
Describe what is happening.

A: She's <u>seating the customer</u>.
B: He's <u>taking the order</u>.

9. server / waitress
نادلة / جرسونة

10. dessert tray
صينية أطباق الحلو

11. bread basket
سلة الخبز

12. busser
مساعد النادل (الجرسون)

13. dish room
غرفة الصحون

14. dishwasher
غسّال الصحون

15. kitchen
مطبخ

16. chef
رئيس الطهاة (شيف)

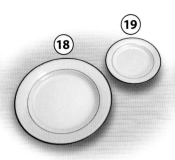
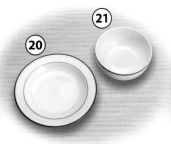

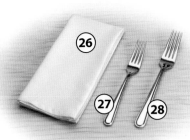

17. place setting
تجهيز سفرة الطعام

18. dinner plate
صحن طعام مفلطح

19. bread-and-butter plate
صحن الخبز والزبدة

20. salad plate
طبق السلاطة

21. soup bowl
سلطانية الشوربة

22. water glass
كأس للماء

23. wine glass
كأس للنبيذ

24. cup
فنجان

25. saucer
صحن للفنجان

26. napkin
منديل قماش للمائدة

27. salad fork
شوكة السلاطة

28. dinner fork
شوكة طعام

29. steak knife
سكين لقطع اللحم

30. knife
سكين

31. teaspoon
ملعقة شاي

32. soupspoon
ملعقة شوربة

Pair practice. Make new conversations.

A: *Excuse me, this <u>spoon</u> is dirty.*

B: *I'm so sorry. I'll get you a clean <u>spoon</u> right away.*

A: *Thanks.*

Role play. Talk to a new busser.

A: *Do the <u>salad forks</u> go on <u>the left</u>?*

B: *Yes. They go <u>next to the dinner forks</u>.*

A: *What about the…?*

The Farmers' Market   سوق المزارعين

1. **live music**
   موسيقى حية

2. **organic**
   منتجات مزروعة بسماد طبيعي

3. **lemonade**
   عصير ليمون (ليموناده)

4. **sour**
   مذاق حمضي / مُر

5. **samples**
   عيّنات

6. **avocados**
   أفوكاته / زُبدية

7. **vendors**
   بائعون

8. **sweets**
   حلويات

9. **herbs**
   أعشاب

A. **count**
   تحصى / تعُدّ

84

CHIVES

DILL

PARSLEY

**Look at the pictures.
What do you see?**

Answer the questions.

1. How many vendors are at the market today?

2. Which vegetables are organic?

3. What are the children eating?

4. What is the woman counting? Why?

 Read the story.

The Farmers' Market

On Saturdays, the Novaks go to the farmers' market. They like to visit the <u>vendors</u>. Alex Novak always goes to the hot food stand for lunch. His children love to eat the fruit <u>samples</u>. Alex's father usually buys some <u>sweets</u> and <u>lemonade</u>. The lemonade is very <u>sour</u>.

Nina Novak likes to buy <u>organic</u> <u>herbs</u> and vegetables. Today, she is buying <u>avocados</u>. The market worker <u>counts</u> eight avocados. She gives Nina one more for free.

There are other things to do at the market. The Novaks like to listen to the <u>live music</u>. Sometimes they meet friends there. The farmers' market is a great place for families on a Saturday afternoon.

Think about it.

1. What's good or bad about shopping at a farmers' market?

2. Imagine you are at the farmers' market. What will you buy?

1. shirt
قميص

2. jeans
بنطلون جينز

3. dress
فستان

4. T-shirt
قميص تي شيرت

5. baseball cap
برنيطة (قبعة) بيسبول

6. socks
جوارب قصيرة

7. athletic shoes
أحذية رياضية

A. **tie**
تربط رباط الحذاء

BEST OF JAZZ CONCERT

TICKETS

BEST OF JAZZ

Listen and point. Take turns.

A: *Point to the dress.*
B: *Point to the T-shirt.*
A: *Point to the baseball cap.*

Dictate to your partner. Take turns.

A: *Write dress.*
B: *Is that spelled d-r-e-s-s?*
A: *Yes. That's right.*

ONE NIGHT ONLY

DOORS OPEN AT 8:00

8. blouse
بلوزة

9. handbag
حقيبة / شنطة يد

10. skirt
تنورة (جونلا)

11. suit
بدلة

12. slacks / pants
بنطلون / سروال

13. shoes
أحذية

14. sweater
بلوفر (كنزة)

B. **put on**
ترتدي البلوفر

Ways to compliment clothes

That's a pretty <u>dress</u>!
Those are great <u>shoes</u>!
I really like your <u>baseball cap</u>!

Role play. Compliment a friend.

A: <u>*That's a pretty dress!*</u> <u>*Green*</u> *is a great color on you.*
B: *Thanks! I really like your…*

87

Casual Clothes الملابس غير الرسمية

1. cap
   قلنسوة / برنيطة

2. cardigan sweater
   بلوفر (كنزة) من صوف محبوك

3. pullover sweater
   بلوفر (كنزة) صوفي يلبس من طريق الرأس

4. sports shirt
   سترة رياضية

5. maternity dress
   فستان للحوامل

6. overalls
   الوزرة (أوفرول)

7. knit top
   سترة صوفية تريكو

8. capris
   بنطلون كابري (بنطلون ضيق مطّاط)

9. sandals
   صندل

Work Clothes ملابس العمل

10. uniform
    زي مُوَحَّد

11. business suit
    بدلة أعمال

12. tie
    رابطة عنق (كرافتة)

13. briefcase
    حقيبة أوراق

More vocabulary

three piece suit: matching jacket, vest, and slacks

outfit: clothes that look nice together

in fashion / in style: clothes that are popular now

Describe the people. Take turns.

A: *She's wearing a maternity dress.*

B: *He's wearing a uniform.*

Formal Clothes الملابس الرسمية

14. sports jacket / sports coat
جاكتة سبور / معطف سبور

15. vest
صدرة

16. bow tie
وردة عنق / بمباغ / بابيون

17. tuxedo
بدلة سهرة رسمية للرجال

18. evening gown
فستان سهرة

19. clutch bag
حقيبة أصابع / شنطة سهرة

20. cocktail dress
فستان شبه رسمي

21. high heels
أحذية ذات كعب عالٍ

Exercise Wear ملابس التمرينات الرياضية

22. sweatshirt / hoodie
كنزة فضفاضة / سترة رياضية بغطاء للرأس

23. sweatpants
سروال فضفاض / بنطلون رياضة

24. tank top
قميص قصير بدون أكمام وبفتحات كبيرة
للذراعين (قميص داخلي)

25. shorts
بنطلون قصير (شورت)

Ask your classmates. Share the answers.

1. What's your favorite outfit?
2. Do you like to wear formal clothes? Why or why not?
3. Do you prefer to exercise in shorts or sweatpants?

Think about it. Discuss.

1. What jobs require formal clothes? Uniforms?
2. What's good and bad about wearing school uniforms?
3. What is your opinion of today's popular clothing?

89

1. hat
قبعة

2. (over)coat
معطف (خارجي) / بلطو (خارجي)

3. headband
شريط للرأس

4. leather jacket
جاكتة (سترة) جلدية

5. winter scarf
وشاح شتوي

6. gloves
قفازات

7. headwrap
ملفوف حول الرأس

8. jacket
جاكتة

9. parka
بَرْكة (سترة فرائية مقلنسة)

10. mittens
قفازات صوفية بلا أصابع

11. ski hat
قبعة التزحلق على الجليد

12. leggings
الطّماق / كساء للساق

13. earmuffs
وقاء للأذن من البرد

14. down vest
صدرة ثقيلة

15. ski mask
قناع التزحلق على الجليد

16. down jacket
جاكتة طويلة من زغب أو وبر

17. umbrella
شمسية

18. raincoat
معطف (بلطو) مطر

19. poncho
البُنْش (معطف شبه عباءة)

20. rain boots
حذاء عالي الساق (جزمة) للمطر

21. trench coat
المِمْطر (معطف واقٍ من المطر)

22. swimming trunks
شورت للسباحة للرجال (مايوه)

23. straw hat
قبعة من القش

24. windbreaker
سترة قصيرة واقية من الرياح

25. cover-up
غطاء خارجي

26. swimsuit / bathing suit
بدلة سباحة / بدلة استحمام للنساء (مايوه)

27. sunglasses
نظارة شمس (واقية من الشمس)

Grammar Point: *should*

*It's raining. You **should** take an umbrella.*
*It's snowing. You **should** wear a scarf.*
*It's sunny. You **should** wear a straw hat.*

Pair practice. Make new conversations.

A: *It's <u>snowing</u>. You should wear <u>a scarf</u>.*
B: *Don't worry. I'm wearing my <u>parka</u>.*
A: *Good, and don't forget your <u>mittens</u>.*

Unisex Underwear
ملابس داخلية لكلا الجنسين

1. undershirt
   قميص داخلي (فانيلا)
2. thermal undershirt
   قميص داخلي حراري
3. long underwear
   ملابس داخلية طويلة

Men's Underwear
ملابس داخلية للرجال

4. boxer shorts
   شورت داخلي (شورت ملاكمين)
5. briefs
   سروال تحتاني قصير
6. athletic supporter /
   jockstrap
   رباط رياضي للجوارب /
   سروال رياضي

Unisex Socks
جوارب قصيرة لكلا الجنسين

7. ankle socks
   جوارب كاحلية
8. crew socks
   جوارب رياضية
9. dress socks
   جوارب رسمية

Women's Socks
جوارب للنساء

10. low-cut socks
    جوارب قصيرة الارتفاع
11. anklets
    جوارب بارتفاع الكاحل
12. knee highs
    جوارب بارتفاع الركبتين

Women's Underwear ملابس داخلية للنساء

13. (bikini) panties
    سروال تحتي قصير نسائي
    / كيلوت بيكيني
14. briefs /
    underpants
    سروال تحتي قصير رجالي
    / سروال تحتي
15. body shaper /
    girdle
    مِشَدّ

16. garter belt
    رباط للجورب
17. stockings
    جورب نسائي فوق الركبة
18. panty hose
    جورب سروالي نسائي
19. tights
    بنطلون ضيق جدا
20. bra
    صديرية للثديين (سوتيان)

21. camisole
    قميصول (سترة
    نسائية قصيرة)
22. full slip
    سترة داخلية
    بطول كامل
23. half slip
    سترة داخلية
    بنصف طول

Sleepwear ملابس النوم

24. pajamas
    بيجاما
25. nightgown
    قميص نوم للنساء
26. slippers
    شبشب / خف

27. blanket sleeper
    مريلة نوم للأطفال / بيجاما
    ذات قدمين
28. nightshirt
    قميص طويل للنوم
29. robe
    ثوب حمام / برنس

More vocabulary

lingerie: underwear or sleepwear for women
loungewear: very casual clothing for relaxing around
the home

Ask your classmates. Share the answers.

1. What kind of socks are you wearing today?
2. What kind of sleepwear do you prefer?
3. Do you wear slippers at home?

Construction Worker

Road Worker

Automotive Painter

Food Processor

1. hard hat
قبعة صلبة

2. work shirt
قميص عمل / قميص شغل

3. tool belt
حزام أدوات

4. Hi-Visibility safety vest
صديرية أمان يمكن رؤيتها عن بعد

5. work pants
بنطلون عمل (شغل)

6. steel toe boots
جزمة عالية الساق ذات مقدَّم
من الفولاذ

7. ventilation mask
قناع تهوية وتنفس

8. coveralls
مئزر(ثوب عمل ذو كمين)

9. bump cap
خوذة واقية

10. safety glasses
نظارات أمان

11. apron
مريلة

Manager

Salesperson

Farmworker

Ranch Hand

12. blazer
جاكتة خفيفة (بليزر)

13. tie
رابطة عنق (كرافتة)

14. polo shirt
فانلا قطن أو تريكو

15. name tag
بطاقة عليها الاسم

16. bandana
منديل رأس مزدان بالرسوم

17. work gloves
قفازات عمل

18. cowboy hat
قبعة راعي البقر

19. jeans
بنطلون جينز

Pair practice. Make new conversations.

A: *What do <u>construction workers</u> wear to work?*
B: *They wear <u>hard hats</u> and <u>tool belts</u>.*
A: *What do <u>road workers</u> wear to work?*

Use the new words.

Look at pages 166–169. Name the workplace clothing you see.

A: *He's wearing <u>a hard hat</u>.*
B: *She's wearing <u>scrubs</u>.*

Security Guard

Emergency Worker

Counterperson

Chef

Line Cook

20. security shirt
قميص خاص لموظف الأمن

21. badge
شارة

22. security pants
بنطلون خاص لموظف الأمن

23. helmet
خوذة

24. jumpsuit
جوبية (سترة يرتديها العمال)

25. hairnet
شبكة للشعر

26. smock
سَمَق

27. disposable gloves
قفازات تلقى بعد الاستعمال

28. chef's hat
قبعة رئيس الطهاة (الشيف)

29. chef's jacket
جاكتة رئيس الطهاة (الشيف)

30. waist apron
مريلة خصرية

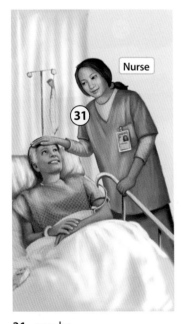

Nurse

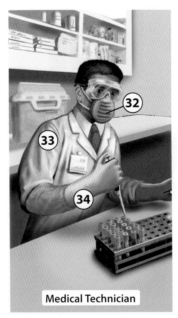

Medical Technician

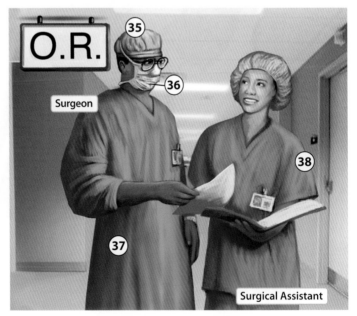

O.R.

Surgeon

Surgical Assistant

31. scrubs
ثياب الجراحون والممرضات

32. face mask
قناع الوجه

33. lab coat
سترة المختبر

34. latex gloves
قفازات من اللثى

35. surgical scrub cap
قبعة الجراح

36. surgical mask
قناع الجراح

37. surgical gown
رداء الجراح

38. surgical scrubs
ثياب غرفة العمليات

Ask your classmates. Share the answers.

1. Which of these outfits would you like to wear?

2. Which of these items are in your closet?

3. Do you wear safety clothing at work? What kinds?

Think about it. Discuss.

1. What other jobs require helmets? disposable gloves?

2. Is it better to have a uniform or wear your own clothes at work? Why?

Shoes and Accessories

أحذية وإكسسوارات

A. purchase تشتري	**1.** suspenders حمالة البنطلون	**3.** salesclerk بائعة أو بائع	**5.** display case صندوق معروضات زجاجي
B. wait in line ينتظر (يقف) في الطابور	**2.** purses / handbags حقائب يد / جزدانات	**4.** customer زبون	**6.** belts أحزمة

13. wallet محفظة	**17.** shoulder bag حقيبة كتف نسائية	**21.** sole نعل الحذاء
14. change purse / coin purse حافظة نقود	**18.** backpack حقيبة تحمل على الظهر	**22.** heel كعب الحذاء
15. cell phone holder حامل الهاتف / التليفون المحمول (النقال)	**19.** tote bag حقيبة نقل	**23.** toe مقدّم (إصبع قدم) الحذاء
16. (wrist)watch ساعة (يد)	**20.** belt buckle إبزيم (مشبك) الحزام	**24.** shoelaces رباط الحذاء

More vocabulary

gift: something you give or receive from friends or family for a special occasion
present: a gift

Grammar Point: object pronouns

My *sister* loves jewelry. I'll buy *her* a necklace.
My *dad* likes belts. I'll buy *him* a belt buckle.
My *friends* love scarves. I'll buy *them* scarves.

94

7. shoe department قسم الأحذية	**9.** bracelets أساور	**11.** hats قبعات	**C. try on** shoes يلبس الحذاء لقياسها
8. jewelry department قسم المجوهرات	**10.** necklaces قلائد / عقود	**12.** scarves أوشحة	**D. assist** a customer يساعد زبونا

25. high heels حذاء ذو كعب عالٍ	**29.** oxfords حذاء أكسفورد	**33.** chain سلسلة	**37.** clip-on earrings حلق بمشبك
26. pumps حذاء نسائي	**30.** loafers حذاء شبيه بالموكاسان	**34.** beads خرز	**38.** pin دبوس
27. flats أحذية نسائية بدون كعب	**31.** hiking boots جزمة (حذاء عالي الساق) للتسلق	**35.** locket مُدَلاة	**39.** string of pearls عقد لؤلؤ
28. boots جزمة (حذاء عالي الساق)	**32.** tennis shoes حذاء تنس (كرة المضرب)	**36.** pierced earrings حلق لأذن مثقوبة	**40.** ring خاتم

Ways to talk about accessories

I need <u>a hat</u> to wear with <u>this scarf</u>.
I'd like <u>earrings</u> to go with <u>the necklace</u>.
Do you have <u>a belt</u> that would go with <u>my shoes</u>?

Role play. Talk to a salesperson.

A: *Do you have <u>boots</u> that would go with <u>this skirt</u>?*
B: *Let me see. How about <u>these brown ones</u>?*
A: *Perfect. I also need…*

Sizes مقاسات

1. extra small	2. small	3. medium	4. large	5. extra large	6. one-size-fits-all
صغير جدا	صغير	متوسط	كبير	كبير جدا	مقاس واحد للجميع

Styles أزياء

7. crewneck sweater
بلوفر (كنزة) ذو رقبة عالية

8. V-neck sweater
بلوفر (كنزة) ذو رقبة على شكل حرف V

9. turtleneck sweater
بلوفر (كنزة) ذو رقبة عالية جدا

10. scoop neck sweater
بلوفر (كنزة) ذو رقبة مقوّرة

11. sleeveless shirt
قميص بدون أكمام

12. short-sleeved shirt
قميص ذو أكمام قصيرة (نصف كم)

13. 3/4-sleeved shirt
قميص ذو 3/4 (ثلاثة أرباع) كم

14. long-sleeved shirt
قميص ذو أكمام طويلة

15. mini-skirt
تنورة قصيرة جدا (ميني)

16. short skirt
تنورة قصيرة

17. mid-length / calf-length skirt
تنورة متوسطة الطول / تنورة بطول بطن الساق

18. long skirt
تنورة طويلة

Patterns تصميمات مرسومة

19. solid
سادة / مصمت

20. striped
مخطط / مقلّم

21. polka-dotted
منقّط

22. plaid
مربعات ملوّنة

23. print
منقوش

24. checked
ذو مربعات

25. floral
مزهر (ذو أشكال وردية)

26. paisley
بيسلي (نسيج مزركش بالرسوم)

Ask your classmates. Share the answers.

1. Do you prefer crewneck or V-neck sweaters?
2. Do you prefer checked or striped shirts?
3. Do you prefer short-sleeved or sleeveless shirts?

Role play. Talk to a salesperson.

A: *Excuse me. I'm looking for this V-neck sweater in large.*
B: *Here's a large. It's on sale for $19.99.*
A: *Wonderful! I'll take it. I'm also looking for…*

Comparing Clothing مقارنة الملبوسات

27. **heavy** jacket
جاكتة ثقيلة

28. **light** jacket
جاكتة خفيفة

29. **tight** pants
بنطلون ضيق

30. **loose / baggy** pants
بنطلون واسع / فضفاض

31. **low** heels
كعب واطئ

32. **high** heels
كعب عالٍ

33. **plain** blouse
بلوزة سادة (بسيطة)

34. **fancy** blouse
بلوزة مُزيّنة (مزركشة)

35. **narrow** tie
رابطة عنق (كرافتة) رفيعة

36. **wide** tie
رابطة عنق (كرافتة) عريضة

Clothing Problems مشاكل خاصة بالملبوسات

37. It's **too small**.
إنه أصغر من اللازم.

38. It's **too big**.
إنه أكبر من اللازم.

39. The zipper is **broken**.
الزمام المنزلق (السوستة) مكسور.

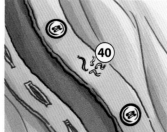

40. A button is **missing**.
هناك زر مفقود.

41. It's **ripped / torn**.
إنه ممزق / مقطوع.

42. It's **stained**.
إنه مبقّع.

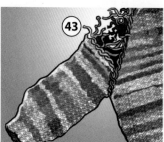

43. It's **unraveling**.
إنه يتمزق / تنحلّ خيوطه.

44. It's **too expensive**.
إنه أغلى من اللازم.

More vocabulary

refund: money you get back when you return an item to the store
complaint: a statement that something is not right
customer service: the place customers go with their complaints

Role play. Return an item to a salesperson.

A: *Welcome to Shopmart. How may I help you?*
B: *This sweater is new, but it's unraveling.*
A: *I'm sorry. Would you like a refund?*

97

Types of Material أنواع الخامات

1. cotton
قطن

2. linen
كتّان

3. wool
صوف

4. cashmere
كشمير

5. silk
حرير

6. leather
جلد

Parts of a Sewing Machine
أجزاء ماكينة الخياطة

A Garment Factory مصنع ملابس

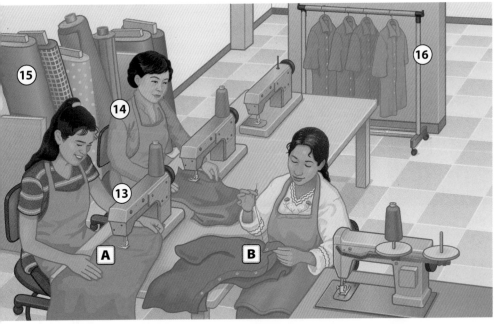

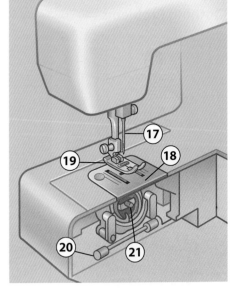

A. **sew** by machine
تخيّط بماكينة الخياطة

B. **sew** by hand
تخيّط باليد

13. sewing machine
ماكينة خياطة

14. sewing machine operator
عامل(ة) ماكينة الخياطة

15. bolt of fabric
ثوب قماش

16. rack
حامل / رف لتعليق الملابس

17. needle
إبرة

18. needle plate
صفيحة معدنية للإبرة

19. presser foot
قدم ضاغط

20. feed dog / feed bar
كلب إمداد / قضيب إمداد

21. bobbin
مكوك / بكرة

More vocabulary

fashion designer: a person who makes original clothes
natural materials: cloth made from things that grow in nature
synthetic materials: cloth made by people, such as nylon

Use the new words.

Look at pages 86–87. Name the materials you see.

A: That's <u>denim</u>.
B: That's <u>leather</u>.

Types of Material أنواع الخامات

7. denim
الدنيم (قماش قطني متين)

8. suede
السويد (جلد أو قماش مزأبر)

9. lace
دنتلة

10. velvet
قطيفة

11. corduroy
قطيفة مضلّعة

12. nylon
نايلون

A Fabric Store محل أقمشة

Closures أدوات للغلق

Trim التزيين

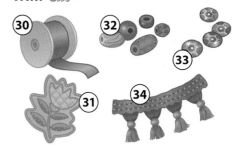

22. pattern
نموذج للتفصيل (باترون)

23. thread
خيط

24. button
زر

25. zipper
زمام منزلق (سوستة)

26. snap
كبسول أو طباقة

27. hook and eye
عقيفة وعروة (مشبك وفتحة)

28. buckle
إبزيم (مشبك)

29. hook and loop fastener
رابط بعقيفة وحلقة

30. ribbon
شريط

31. appliqué
تطريز أبليكيه

32. beads
خرز

33. sequins
ترتر

34. fringe
مزيّن بهداب (شراشيب)

Ask your classmates. Share the answers.

1. Can you sew?
2. What's your favorite type of material?
3. How many types of material are you wearing today?

Think about it. Discuss.

1. Do most people make or buy clothes in your country?
2. Is it better to make or buy clothes? Why?
3. Which materials are best for formal clothes?

An Alterations Shop محل تعديل الثياب

1. dressmaker
خيّاطة

2. dressmaker's dummy
تمثال (مانيكان) الخيّاطة

3. tailor
خياط (ترزي)

4. collar
ياقة

5. waistband
حزام أو نطاق تنورة أو بنطلون

6. sleeve
كُم

7. pocket
جيب

8. hem
حاشية (هدب)

9. cuff
ثنية ساق البنطلون

Sewing Supplies أدوات الخياطة

10. needle
إبرة

11. thread
خيط

12. (straight) pin
دبوس مستقيم

13. pin cushion
مخدة دبابيس / مدبسة

14. safety pin
دبوس بمشبك

15. thimble
كستبان

16. pair of scissors
مقص

17. tape measure
شريط قياس (مازورة)

18. seam ripper
ممزّق الدروز (أداة فك الخياطة)

Alterations تعديل الثياب

A. Lengthen the pants.
يطوّل البنطلون.

B. Shorten the pants.
يقصّر البنطلون.

C. Let out the pants.
يوسّع البنطلون.

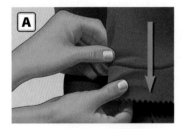

D. Take in the pants.
يضيّق البنطلون.

Pair practice. Make new conversations.

A: *Would you hand me the thread?*
B: *OK. What are you going to do?*
A: *I'm going to take in these pants.*

Ask your classmates. Share the answers.

1. Is there an alterations shop near your home?
2. Do you ever go to a tailor or a dressmaker?
3. What sewing supplies do you have at home?

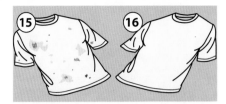

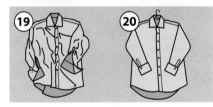

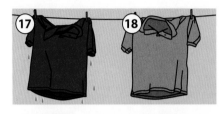

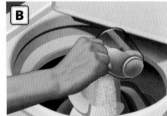

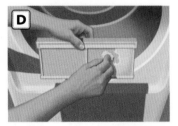

1. laundry
ملابس للغسل

2. laundry basket
سلة ملابس

3. washer
غسالة ملابس

4. dryer
نشافة ملابس

5. dryer sheets
أوراق نشافة

6. fabric softener
مطرّي للنسيج

7. bleach
مسحوق الغسيل

8. laundry detergent
مبيّض

9. clothesline
منشر الغسيل

10. clothespin
مشبك الملابس

11. hanger
حمالة الثياب

12. spray starch
رشاش النشا

13. iron
مكواة

14. ironing board
طاولة الكي

15. dirty T-shirt
تي شيرت **متسخ**

16. clean T-shirt
تي شيرت **نظيف**

17. wet shirt
تي شيرت **مبتلّ**

18. dry shirt
تي شيرت **جاف**

19. wrinkled shirt
قميص **متجعد (متكرمش)**

20. ironed shirt
قميص **مكوي**

A. Sort the laundry.
تفرز الغسيل.

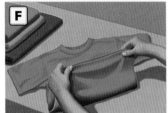

B. Add the detergent.
تضيف مسحوق الغسيل.

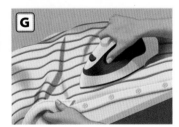

C. Load the washer.
تضع الغسيل في الغسالة.

D. Clean the lint trap.
تُنظّف مكان تجمع النسالة.

E. Unload the dryer.
تفرّغ مجفف الملابس.

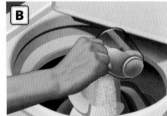

F. Fold the laundry.
تطوي الملابس.

G. Iron the clothes.
تكوي الملابس.

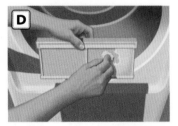

H. Hang up the clothes.
تعلّق الملابس.

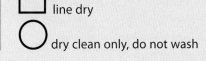

wash in cold water

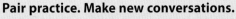

line dry

no bleach

dry clean only, do not wash

Pair practice. Make new conversations.

A: *I have to <u>sort the laundry</u>. Can you help?*
B: *Sure. Here's <u>the laundry basket</u>.*
A: *Thanks a lot!*

1. flyer نشرة إعلانية	**3.** sticker لاصق	**5.** folding chair كرسي قابل للطي	**7.** VCR جهاز فيدي+و	**B. browse** يستعرض السلع المعروضة للبيع.
2. used clothing ملابس مستعملة	**4.** folding card table طاولة قابلة للطي لألعاب الورق أو الشدة	**6.** clock radio راديو بساعة	**A. bargain** تقاول على السعر	

Look at the pictures. What do you see?

Answer the questions.

1. What kind of used clothing do you see?
2. What information is on the flyer?
3. Why are the stickers different colors?
4. How much is the clock radio? the VCR?

 Read the story.

A Garage Sale

Last Sunday, I had a garage sale. At 5:00 a.m., I put up <u>flyers</u> in my neighborhood. Next, I put price <u>stickers</u> on my <u>used clothing</u>, my <u>VCR</u>, and some other old things. At 7:00 a.m., I opened my <u>folding card table</u> and <u>folding chair</u>. Then I waited.

At 7:05 a.m., my first customer arrived. She asked, "How much is the sweatshirt?"

"Two dollars," I said.

She said, "It's stained. I can give you seventy-five cents." We <u>bargained</u> for a minute and she paid $1.00.

All day people came to <u>browse</u>, bargain, and buy. At 7:00 p.m., I had $85.00.

Now I know two things: Garage sales are hard work and nobody wants to buy an old <u>clock radio</u>!

Think about it.

1. Do you like to buy things at garage sales? Why or why not?
2. Imagine you want the VCR. How will you bargain for it?

1. head
   رأس
2. hair
   شعر
3. neck
   رقبة
4. chest
   صدر
5. back
   ظهر
6. nose
   أنف
7. mouth
   فم
8. foot
   قدم

Listen and Point. Take turns.

A: *Point to the chest.*
B: *Point to the neck.*
A: *Point to the mouth.*

Dictate to your partner. Take turns.

A: *Write hair.*
B: *Did you say hair?*
A: *That's right, h-a-i-r.*

9. leg
رجل

10. toe
إصبع قدم

11. eye
عين

12. ear
أذن

13. shoulder
كتف

14. arm
ذراع

15. hand
يد

16. finger
إصبع يد

Grammar Point: imperatives

Please touch your right foot.
Put your hands on your feet.
Don't put your hands on your shoulders.

Pair practice. Take turns giving commands.

A: _Raise_ your _arms_.
B: _Touch_ your _feet_.
A: _Put_ your _hand_ on your _shoulder_.

105

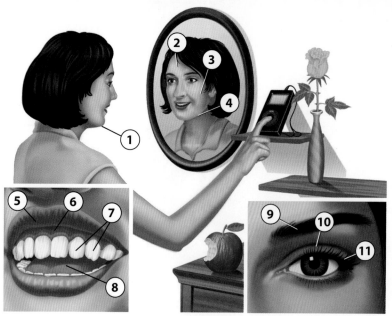
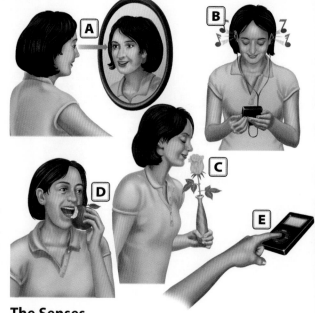

The Face
الوجه

1. chin
   ذقن
2. forehead
   جبهة
3. cheek
   خذ
4. jaw
   فك

The Mouth
الفم

5. lip
   شفة
6. gums
   لثة
7. teeth
   أسنان
8. tongue
   لسان

The Eye
العين

9. eyebrow
   حاجب
10. eyelid
    جفن
11. eyelashes
    رموش

The Senses
الحواس

A. see
   يرى
B. hear
   يسمع
C. smell
   يشم
D. taste
   يتذوق
E. touch
   يلمس (يحس باللمس)

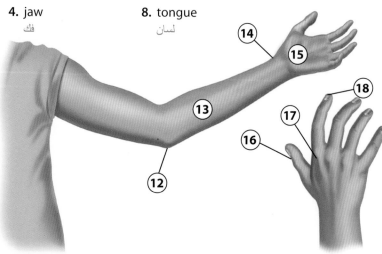
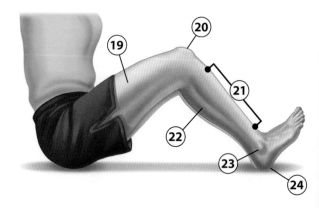

The Arm, Hand, and Fingers   الذراع واليد وأصابع اليد

12. elbow
    كوع
13. forearm
    ساعد
14. wrist
    رسغ
15. palm
    كف
16. thumb
    إبهام
17. knuckle
    برجمة
18. fingernail
    ظفر

The Leg and Foot   الرجل والقدم

19. thigh
    فخذ
20. knee
    ركبة
21. shin
    حرف الظنبوب
22. calf
    ربلة أو بطة الساق
23. ankle
    كاحل
24. heel
    كعب

More vocabulary

torso: the part of the body from the shoulders to the pelvis
limbs: arms and legs
toenail: the nail on your toe

Pair practice. Make new conversations.

A: *Is your <u>arm</u> OK?*
B: *Yes, but now my <u>elbow</u> hurts.*
A: *I'm sorry to hear that.*

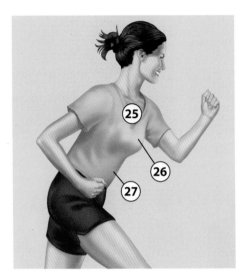

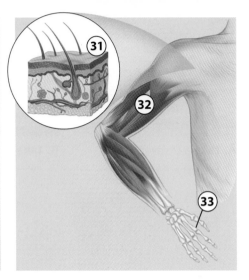

25. chest
صدر

26. breast
ثدي

27. abdomen
بطن

28. shoulder blade
لوح الكتف

29. lower back
الجزء السفلي من الظهر

30. buttocks
مقعدة / أرداف

31. skin
جلد

32. muscle
عضلة

33. bone
عظم

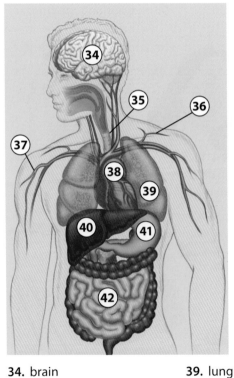

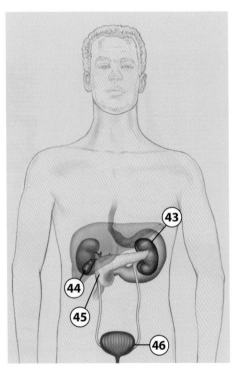

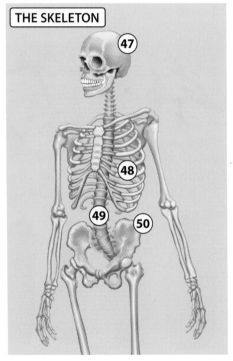

34. brain
مخ

35. throat
حنجرة

36. artery
شريان

37. vein
وريد

38. heart
قلب

39. lung
رئة

40. liver
كبد

41. stomach
معدة

42. intestines
أمعاء

43. kidney
كلية

44. gallbladder
مرارة

45. pancreas
بنكرياس

46. bladder
مثانة

47. skull
جمجمة

48. rib cage
قفص صدري

49. spinal column
عمود فقري

50. pelvis
حوض

A. take a shower

تستحمّ (تأخذ دشا)

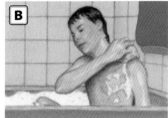

B. take a bath / **bathe**

يأخذ حماما / يستحمّ

C. use deodorant

يستعمل مزيل رائحة العرق

D. put on sunscreen

تضع واقيا من أشعة الشمس

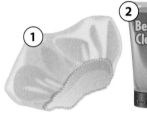     

1. shower cap

غطاء شعر للحمام

2. shower gel

جيل للدش

3. soap

صابون

4. bath powder

بودرة استحمام

5. deodorant / antiperspirant

مزيل رائحة العرق

6. perfume / cologne

كولونيا / عطر

7. sunscreen

واق من أشعة الشمس

8. sunblock

مانع لأشعة الشمس

9. body lotion / moisturizer

كريم للجسم / مرطب للجلد

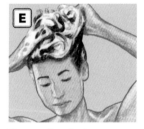 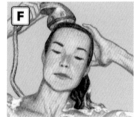 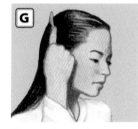 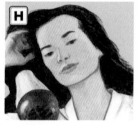 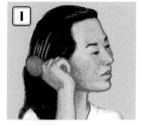

E. wash…hair

تغسل الشعر

F. rinse…hair

تشطف الشعر

G. comb…hair

تمشط (تسرّح) الشعر

H. dry…hair

تجفف الشعر

I. brush…hair

تصفف الشعر بالفرشاة.

10. shampoo

شامبو

11. conditioner

منعّم الشعر

12. hair spray

مثبّت الشعر

13. comb

مشط

14. brush

فرشاة

15. pick

مشط مدبب الأسنان

16. hair gel

جيل للشعر

17. curling iron

مكواة شعر

18. blow dryer

مجفف شعر بالهواء الساخن (سيشوار)

19. hair clip

دبوس شعر

20. barrette

مشبك شعر

21. bobby pins

دبابيس شعر محكمة

More vocabulary

unscented: a product without perfume or scent

hypoallergenic: a product that is better for people with allergies

Think about it. Discuss.

1. Which personal hygiene products should someone use before a job interview?

2. What is the right age to start wearing makeup? Why?

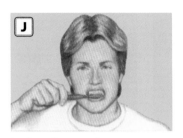 **J. brush**...teeth
يُنْظّف الأسنان بالفرشاة

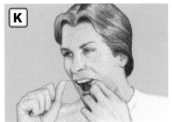 **K. floss**...teeth
يُنْظّف الأسنان بالخيط

 **L. gargle**
يتغرغر

 **M. shave**
يحلق

22. toothbrush
فرشاة أسنان

23. toothpaste
معجون أسنان

24. dental floss
خيط لتنظيف الأسنان

25. mouthwash
مستحضر لغسل الفم

26. electric shaver
ماكينة حلاقة كهربائية

27. razor
ماكينة حلاقة

28. razorblade
موس حلاقة

29. shaving cream
معجون حلاقة

30. aftershave
كولونيا بعد الحلاقة

 **N. cut**...nails
تقلّم الأظافر

 **O. polish**...nails
تطلي الأظافر

 **P. put on / apply**
تضع

 **Q. take off / remove**
تزيل

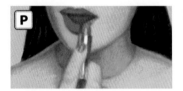

Makeup مكياج

31. nail clipper
مقلمة أظافر

32. emery board
مبرد أظافر

33. nail polish
طلاء الأظافر

34. eyebrow pencil
قلم حواجب

35. eye shadow
قلم كحل

36. eyeliner
قلم تخطيط العين

37. blush
أحمر خدود

38. lipstick
أحمر الشفاء

39. mascara
مَسكرة (مستحضر تجميلي)

40. foundation
كريم أساس

41. face powder
بودرة للوجه

42. makeup remover
مزيل المكياج

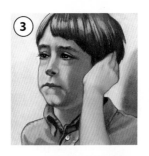

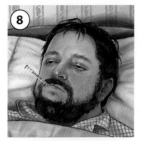

1. headache
صداع

2. toothache
وجع أسنان

3. earache
ألم في الأذن

4. stomachache
ألم في المعدة

5. backache
ألم في الظهر

6. sore throat
التهاب الحنجرة

7. nasal congestion
احتقان في الأنف

8. fever / temperature
حمى / حرارة

9. chills
رعشة

10. rash
طفح جلدي

A. cough
يسعل

B. sneeze
يعطس

C. feel dizzy
يشعر/تشعر بالدوار (دوخة)

D. feel nauseous
تشعر بالغثيان

E. throw up / vomit
تتقيأ / يستفرغ ـ تستفرغ

11. insect bite
لسعة حشرة

12. bruise
كدمة

13. cut
جرح

14. sunburn
سفعة (ضربة) شمس

15. blister
قرحة (كلّو)

16. swollen finger
ورم في الإصبع

17. bloody nose
نزيف في الأنف

18. sprained ankle
التواء الكاحل

Look at the pictures.
Describe the symptoms and injuries.

> A: *He has a backache.*
> B: *She has a toothache.*

Think about it. Discuss.

1. What are some common cold symptoms?
2. What do you recommend for a stomachache?
3. What is the best way to stop a bloody nose?

Illnesses and Medical Conditions

Common Illnesses and Childhood Diseases العلل الشائعة وأمراض الطفولة

1. cold
برد

2. flu
أنفلونزا

3. ear infection
التهاب في الأذن

4. strep throat
التهاب في الحنجرة

5. measles
حصبة

6. chicken pox
جدري الماء (جديري)

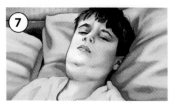

7. mumps
نكاف / أبو كعب

8. allergies
حساسية

Serious Medical Conditions and Diseases حالات طبية وأمراض خطيرة

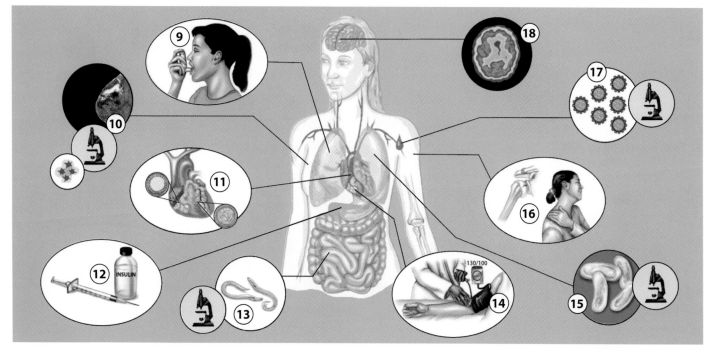

9. asthma
ربو

10. cancer
سرطان

11. heart disease
مرض القلب

12. diabetes
مرض السكري

13. intestinal parasites
دود معوي

14. high blood pressure / hypertension
ضغط دم عالٍ / ارتفاع ضغط الدم

15. TB (tuberculosis)
سل

16. arthritis
التهاب مفاصل

17. HIV (human immunodeficiency virus)
فيروس نقص المناعة البشرية

18. dementia
فقدان القوى العقلية (خبل)

More vocabulary

AIDS (acquired immune deficiency syndrome): a medical condition that results from contracting the HIV virus
Alzheimer's disease: a disease that causes dementia

coronary disease: heart disease
infectious disease: a disease that is spread through air or water
influenza: flu

111

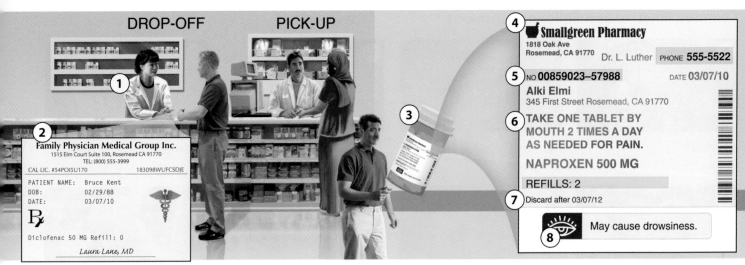

DROP-OFF   PICK-UP

Family Physician Medical Group Inc.
1515 Elm Court Suite 100, Rosemead CA 91770
TEL: (800) 555-3999
CAL LIC. #54POI5U170   183098WUFCSDJE

PATIENT NAME: Bruce Kent
DOB: 02/29/88
DATE: 03/07/10

℞

Diclofenac 50 MG Refill: 0

Laura Lane, MD

Smallgreen Pharmacy
1818 Oak Ave
Rosemead, CA 91770   Dr. L. Luther PHONE **555-5522**
NO **00859023–57988**   DATE 03/07/10
Alki Elmi
345 First Street Rosemead, CA 91770
TAKE ONE TABLET BY MOUTH 2 TIMES A DAY AS NEEDED FOR PAIN.
NAPROXEN 500 MG
REFILLS: 2
Discard after 03/07/12

👁 May cause drowsiness.

1. pharmacist
صيدلي

2. prescription
وصفة طبية (روشتة)

3. prescription medication
دواء موصوف طبيا

4. prescription label
بطاقة الوصفة الطبية

5. prescription number
رقم الوصفة الطبية

6. dosage
جرعة

7. expiration date
تاريخ انتهاء الصلاحية

8. warning label
بطاقة تحذير

Medical Warnings تحذيرات طبية

A. **Take** with food or milk.
تناول مع أكل أو حليب.

B. **Take** one hour before eating.
تناول قبل ساعة من الأكل.

C. **Finish** all medication.
تناول كل الدواء حتى ينتهي.

D. **Do not take** with dairy products.
لا تتناوله مع منتجات ألبان.

E. **Do not drive or operate** heavy machinery.
لا تقود سيارة أو تشغّل آلات ثقيلة.

F. **Do not drink** alcohol.
لا تشرب مشروبات كحولية.

More Vocabulary

prescribe medication: to write a prescription
fill prescriptions: to prepare medication for patients
pick up a prescription: to get prescription medication

Role play. Talk to the pharmacist.

A: Hi. I need to pick up a prescription for <u>Jones</u>.
B: Here's your medication, <u>Mr. Jones</u>. Take these <u>once a day with milk or food</u>.

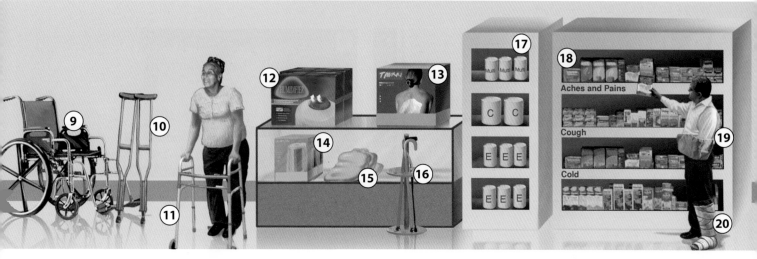

9. wheelchair كرسي بعجلات	**13.** heating pad لبادة تدفئة	**17.** vitamins فيتامينات
10. crutches عكاز	**14.** air purifier منقٍ للهواء	**18.** over-the-counter medication أدوية مباعة بدون وصفة طبية
11. walker ممشاة (مشّاية)	**15.** hot water bottle كيس الماء الساخن	**19.** sling معلاق
12. humidifier مرطب للهواء	**16.** cane عصا	**20.** cast جبيرة / جبص

Types of Medication أنواع الأدوية

21. pill حبة	**22.** tablet قرص	**23.** capsule كبسولة	**24.** ointment مرهم	**25.** cream كريم / معجون

Over-the-Counter Medication الأدوية المباعة بدون وصفة طبية

26. pain reliever مسكّن للآلام	**28.** antacid مضاد للحموضة	**30.** throat lozenges أقراص للمص ملطفة للحنجرة	**32.** nasal spray رشاش للأنف
27. cold tablets أقراص للبرد أو الزكام	**29.** cough syrup شراب للسعال	**31.** eye drops قطرة للعين	**33.** inhaler مِنشَقة

Ways to talk about medication
Use *take* for pills, tablets, capsules, and cough syrup.
Use *apply* for ointments and creams.
Use *use* for drops, nasal sprays, and inhalers.

Ask your classmates. Share the answers.
1. What pharmacy do you go to?
2. Do you ever ask the pharmacist for advice?
3. Do you take any vitamins? Which ones?

113

Ways to Get Well طرق الشفاء

A. Seek medical attention.
اطلب العناية الطبية.

B. Get bed rest.
ألزم الفراش.

C. Drink fluids.
اشرب سوائل.

D. Take medicine.
تعاطَ دواء.

Ways to Stay Well طرق المحافظة على صحتك

E. Stay fit.
حافظ على لياقتك البدنية.

F. Eat a healthy diet.
كُل أطعمة صحية.

G. Don't smoke.
لا تدخّن.

Ms. Jones, you must stop smoking!

H. Have regular checkups.
اطلب إجراء كشوف طبية منتظمة.

I. Get immunized.
اطلب تحصينك بلقاحات ضد الأمراض.

J. Follow medical advice.
اتبع النصيحة الطبية.

More vocabulary

injection: medicine in a syringe that is put into the body

immunization / vaccination: an injection that stops serious diseases

Ask your classmates. Share the answers.

1. How do you stay fit?
2. What do you do when you're sick?
3. Which two foods are a part of your healthy diet?

Types of Health Problems أنواع المشاكل الصحية

1. vision problems
مشاكل في النظر

2. hearing loss
فقدان السمع

3. pain
ألم

4. stress
توتر / إجهاد

5. depression
اكتئاب

Help with Health Problems العون في المشاكل الصحية

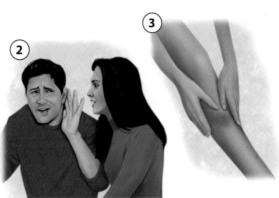

6. optometrist
مصحّح البصر

8. contact lenses
عدسات لاصقة

9. audiologist
أخصائي سمع

10. hearing aid
سماعة أذن

7. glasses
نظارات

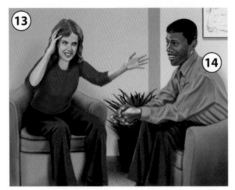

11. physical therapy
علاج طبيعي

13. talk therapy
علاج بالتكلم

15. support group
مجموعة دعم

12. physical therapist
أخصائي علاج طبيعي

14. therapist
معالج

Ways to ask about health problems

Are you <u>in pain</u>?
Are you having <u>vision problems</u>?
Are you experiencing <u>depression</u>?

Pair practice. Make new conversations.

A: Do you know a good <u>optometrist</u>?
B: Why? <u>Are you having vision problems</u>?
A: Yes, I might need <u>glasses</u>.

115

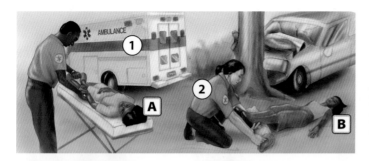

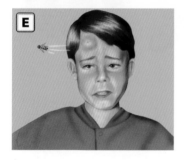

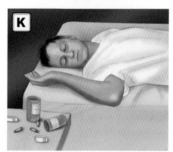

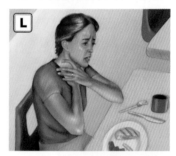

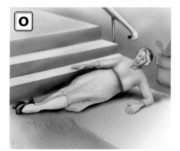

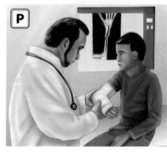

1. ambulance
سيارة إسعاف

2. paramedic
طاقم الإسعاف

A. **be** unconscious
يفقد الوعي

B. **be** in shock
يصاب بصدمة

C. **be** injured / **be** hurt
يصاب بإصابة / يصاب بأذى

D. **have** a heart attack
يصاب بنوبة قلبية

E. **have** an allergic reaction
يعاني من حساسية

F. **get** an electric shock
يصاب بصدمة كهربائية

G. **get** frostbite
يقرسها الصقيع

H. **burn** (your)self
يحرق نفسه

I. **drown**
يغرق

J. **swallow** poison
تبلع مادة سامة

K. **overdose** on drugs
يتناول كمية مفرطة من الدواء

L. **choke**
تختنق

M. **bleed**
ينزف

N. **can't breathe**
لا يستطيع التنفس

O. **fall**
تقع

P. **break** a bone
يكسر عظمة من عظامه

Grammar Point: past tense

For past tense add –ed:
burned, drowned, swallowed,
overdosed, choked

These verbs are different (irregular):

be – was, were	bleed – bled	fall – fell
have – had	can't – couldn't	
get – got	break – broke	

116

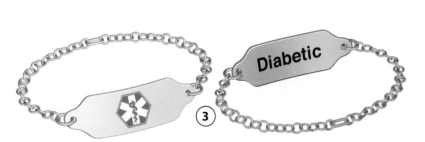
First Aid إسعافات أولية

1. first aid kit
علبة إسعافات أولية

2. first aid manual
كتيب إسعافات أولية

3. medical emergency bracelet
أسورة طوارئ طبية

Inside the Kit داخل العلبة

4. tweezers
ملقاط

8. gauze
شاش

12. elastic bandage
ضمادة مطاطية

5. adhesive bandage
ضمادة لاصقة

9. hydrogen peroxide
بيروكسيد الهيدروجين

13. ice pack
حزمة ثلج

6. sterile pad
لبادة معقمة

10. antihistamine cream
كريم مضاد للهيستامين

14. splint
جبيرة لليد

7. sterile tape
شريط معقم

11. antibacterial ointment
مرهم مضاد للجراثيم

First Aid Procedures إجراءات الإسعافات الأولية

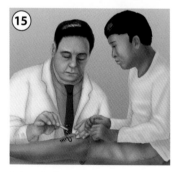
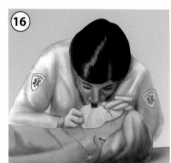
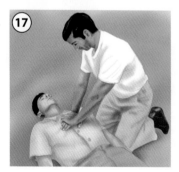
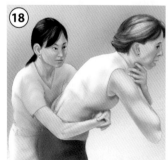

15. stitches
غرز / دروز

16. rescue breathing
تنفس إنقاذي

17. CPR (cardiopulmonary resuscitation)
إنعاش القلب والرئتين

18. Heimlich maneuver
طريقة هيمليك لمعالجة الاختناق

Pair practice. Make new conversations.

A: *What do we need in the first aid kit?*

B: *We need <u>tweezers</u> and <u>gauze</u>.*

A: *I think we need <u>sterile tape</u>, too.*

Think about it. Discuss.

1. What are the three most important first aid items? Why?
2. Which first aid procedures should everyone know? Why?
3. What are some good places to keep a first aid kit?

In the Waiting Room في غرفة الانتظار

Health Form

Name: *Andre Zolmar*
Date of birth: *July 8, 1973*
Current symptoms: *stomachache*

Health History:

Childhood Diseases:
- ☑ chicken pox
- ☑ diphtheria
- ☑ rubella
- ☑ measles
- ☐ mumps
- ☐ other

Description of symptoms:

HEALTH FIRST
Name: Andre Zolmar
Group Number: 98765
Membership Number: 60756789

1. appointment
   موعد

2. receptionist
   موظف استقبال

3. health insurance card
   بطاقة تأمين صحي

4. health history form
   استمارة التاريخ الصحي

In the Examining Room في غرفة الكشف

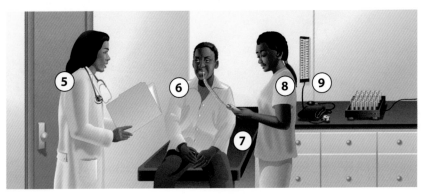

5. doctor
   طبيب

6. patient
   مريض

7. examination table
   طاولة الكشف

8. nurse
   ممرضة

9. blood pressure gauge
   جهاز لقياس ضغط الدم

10. stethoscope
    سماعة طبية

11. thermometer
    مقياس حرارة (ترمومتر)

12. syringe
    إبرة / سرنجة

Medical Procedures إجراءات طبية

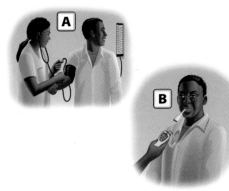

A. **check**...blood pressure
   تفحص ضغط الدم

B. **take**...temperature
   تفحص/تأخذ درجة الحرارة

C. **listen** to...heart
   تستمع إلى نبض القلب

D. **examine**...eyes
   تفحص العينين

E. **examine**...throat
   تفحص الحنجرة

F. **draw**...blood
   تسحب دما

Grammar Point: future tense with *will* + verb

To show a future action, use ***will*** + verb.
The subject pronoun contraction of ***will*** is *-'ll*.
She **will draw** your blood. = She**'ll draw** your blood.

Role play. Talk to a medical receptionist.

A: *Will the nurse <u>examine my eyes</u>?*
B: *No, but she'll <u>draw your blood</u>.*
A: *What will the doctor do?*

Dentistry طب الأسنان

1. dentist
   طبيب/طبيبة أسنان
2. dental assistant
   مساعد طبيب أسنان

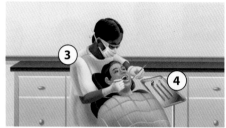

3. dental hygienist
   أخصائي صحة أسنان
4. dental instruments
   أدوات معالجة الأسنان

Orthodontics تقويم الأسنان

5. orthodontist
   طبيب تقويم الأسنان
6. braces
   طوق لتقويم الأسنان

Dental Problems مشاكل الأسنان

 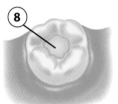  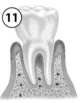

7. cavity / decay
   نخر / بلى
8. filling
   حشو

9. crown
   تاج
10. dentures
    طاقم أسنان اصطناعية

11. gum disease
    مرض اللثة
12. plaque
    لويحات البلاك

An Office Visit زيارة لعيادة أسنان

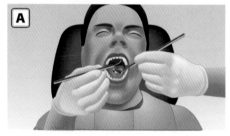

A. **clean**…teeth
   يُنظّف الأسنان

D. **drill** a tooth
   يحفر السن

B. **take** x-rays
   يأخذ أشعة سينية

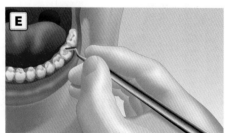

E. **fill** a cavity
   يملأ النخر

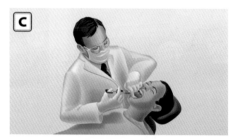

C. **numb** the mouth
   يخدّر الفم

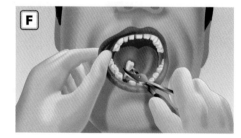

F. **pull** a tooth
   يقتلع (يخلع) السن

Ask your classmates. Share the answers.

1. Do you know someone with braces? Who?
2. Do dentists make you nervous? Why or why not?
3. How often do you go to the dentist?

Role play. Talk to a dentist.

A: *I think I have a cavity.*
B: *Let me take a look.*
A: *Will I need a filling?*

119

Hospital

Medical Specialists أطباء أخصائيون

1. internist
طبيب باطني

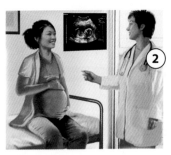

2. obstetrician
طبيب ولادة

3. cardiologist
طبيب قلب

4. pediatrician
طبيب أطفال

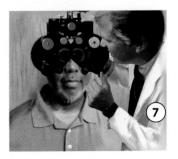

5. oncologist
طبيب أورام

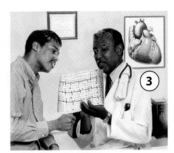

6. radiologist
طبيب أشعة

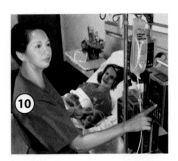

7. ophthalmologist
طبيب عيون

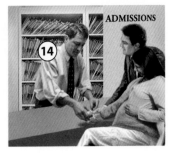

8. psychiatrist
طب أمراض نفسية

Nursing Staff هيئة التمريض

9. surgical nurse
ممرضة جراحة

10. registered nurse (RN)
ممرضة مرخصة

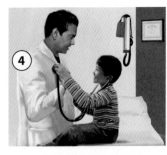

11. licensed practical nurse (LPN)
ممرضة ممارسة مرخصة

12. certified nursing assistant (CNA)
مساعد ممرضة معتمد

Hospital Staff العاملون بالمستشفى

13. administrator
إداري

14. admissions clerk
موظف الإدخال

15. dietician
أخصائي في شؤون التغذية

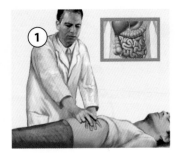

16. orderly
ممرض

More vocabulary

Gynecologists examine and treat women.
Nurse practitioners can give medical exams.
Nurse midwives deliver babies.

Chiropractors move the spine to improve health.
Orthopedists treat bone and joint problems.

120

A Hospital Room غرفة بالمستشفى

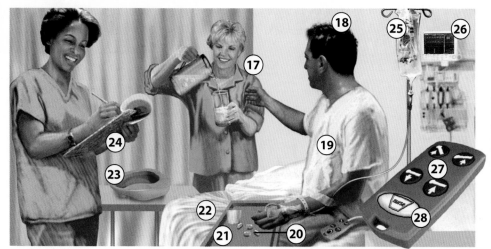

Lab المختبر

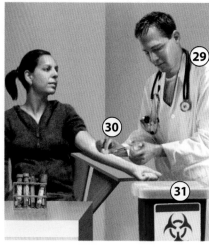

17. volunteer متطوع	**21.** bed table طاولة سرير	**25.** IV (intravenous drip) سائل تغذية يعطى في الوريد
18. patient مريض	**22.** hospital bed سرير مستشفى	**26.** vital signs monitor مرقاب العلامات الحياتية
19. hospital gown رداء مستشفى	**23.** bed pan وعاء للسرير / نونية	**27.** bed control المتحكم في حركة السرير
20. medication دواء	**24.** medical chart ورقة بيانات طبية	**28.** call button جرس الاستدعاء

29. phlebotomist فصّاد
30. blood work / blood test تحليل دم
31. medical waste disposal سلة للمهملات الطبية

Emergency Room Entrance
مدخل غرفة الطوارئ

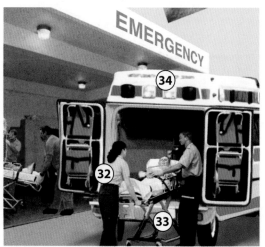

Operating Room
غرفة العمليات

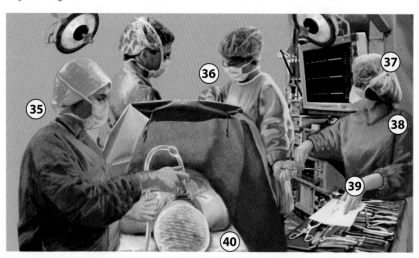

32. emergency medical technician (EMT)
أخصائي طبي لحالات الطوارئ

33. stretcher / gurney
نقالة مرضى

34. ambulance
سيارة إسعاف

35. anesthesiologist طبيب تخدير	**37.** surgical cap قلنسوة غرفة العمليات	**39.** surgical gloves قفازات غرفة العمليات
36. surgeon جراح	**38.** surgical gown رداء غرفة العمليات	**40.** operating table طاولة العملية الجراحية

Dictate to your partner. Take turns.

A: *Write this sentence. She's a volunteer.*

B: *She's a what?*

A: *Volunteer. That's v-o-l-u-n-t-e-e-r.*

Role play. Ask about a doctor.

A: *I need to find a good surgeon.*

B: *Dr. Jones is a great surgeon. You should call him.*

A: *I will! Please give me his number.*

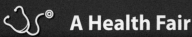
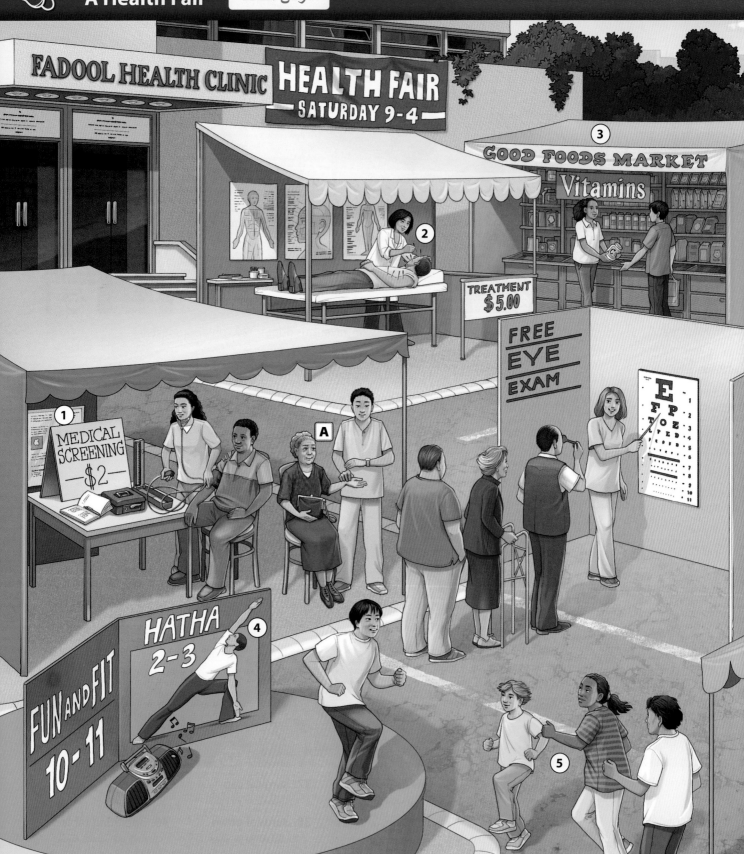

1. low-cost exam كشف قليل التكلفة	**3.** booth جناح	**5.** aerobic exercise تمرين حيهوائي	**7.** sugar-free خالٍ من السكر	**A. check** ... pulse يفحص النبض
2. acupuncture علاج بالإبر الصينية	**4.** yoga اليوجا	**6.** demonstration عرض / تجربة حية	**8.** nutrition label بطاقة بيانات تغذوية	**B. give** a lecture تلقي محاضرة

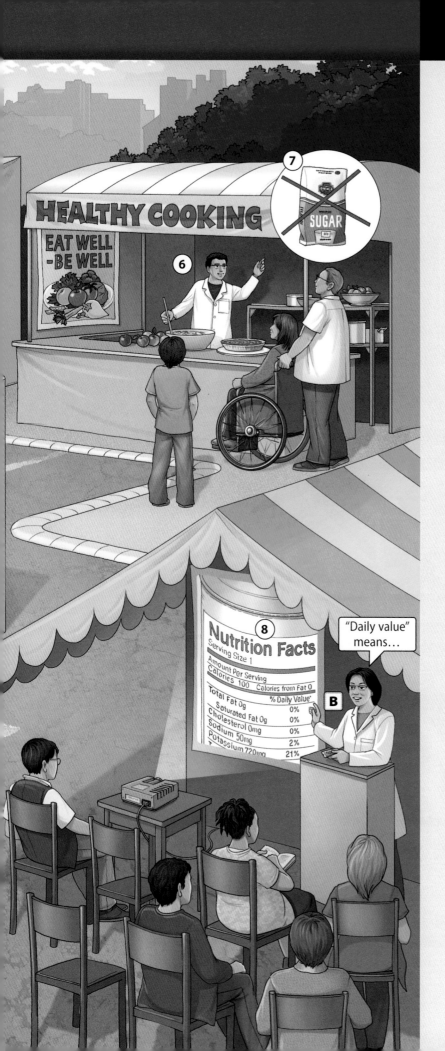

**Look at the picture.
What do you see?**

Answer the questions.

1. How many different booths are there at the health fair?

2. What kinds of exams and treatments can you get at the fair?

3. What kinds of lectures and demonstrations are there?

4. How much is an acupuncture treatment? a medical screening?

📖 **Read the story.**

A Health Fair

Once a month the Fadool Health Clinic has a health fair. You can get a low-cost medical exam at one booth. The nurses check your blood pressure and check your pulse. At another booth you can get a free eye exam. And an acupuncture treatment is only $5.00.

You can learn a lot at the fair. This month a doctor is giving a lecture on nutrition labels. There is also a demonstration on sugar-free cooking. You can learn to do aerobic exercise and yoga, too.

Do you want to get healthy and stay healthy? Then come to the Fadool Clinic Health Fair!

Think about it.

1. Which booths at this fair look interesting to you? Why?

2. Do you read nutrition labels? Why or why not?

1. parking garage
   جراج سيارات /
   موقف سيارات

2. office building
   مبنى خاص للمكاتب

3. hotel
   فندق

4. Department of
   Motor Vehicles
   دائرة تسجيل المركبات الآلية

5. bank
   بنك / مصرف

6. police station
   مخفر الشرطة

7. bus station
   محطة الأوتوبيس

8. city hall
   مبنى البلدية

Listen and point. Take turns.

A: *Point to <u>the bank</u>.*
B: *Point to <u>the hotel</u>.*
A: *Point to <u>the restaurant</u>.*

Dictate to your partner. Take turns.

A: *Write <u>bank</u>.*
B: *Is that spelled <u>b-a-n-k</u>?*
A: *Yes, that's right.*

9. hospital
   مستشفى

10. gas station
    محطة بنزين

11. post office
    مكتب بريد

12. fire station
    إطفائية

13. courthouse
    دار المحكمة

14. restaurant
    مطعم

15. library
    مكتبة

Grammar Point: *in* and *at* with locations

Use *in* when you are inside the building. *I am in (inside) the bank.* Use *at* to describe your general location. *I am at the bank.*

Pair practice. Make new conversations.

A: *I'm in the <u>bank</u>. Where are you?*
B: *I'm at the <u>bank</u>, too, but I'm outside.*
A: *OK. I'll meet you there.*

125

1. stadium
   استاد

2. construction site
   موقع إنشاءات

3. factory
   مصنع

4. car dealership
   معرض سيارات

5. mosque
   مسجد

6. movie theater
   دور عرض / سينما

7. shopping mall
   مركز تسوق

8. furniture store
   محل لبيع الأثاث

9. school
   مدرسة

10. gym
    جمنازيوم (قاعة الجمباز)

11. coffee shop
    مقهى

12. motel
    موتيل (فندق صغير)

Ways to state your destination using *to* and *to the*

Use *to* for schools, churches, and synagogues.
I'm going to school.
Use *to the* for all other locations. *I have to go to the bakery.*

Pair practice. Make new conversations.

A: *Where are you going today?*
B: *I'm going to school. How about you?*
A: *I have to go to the bakery.*

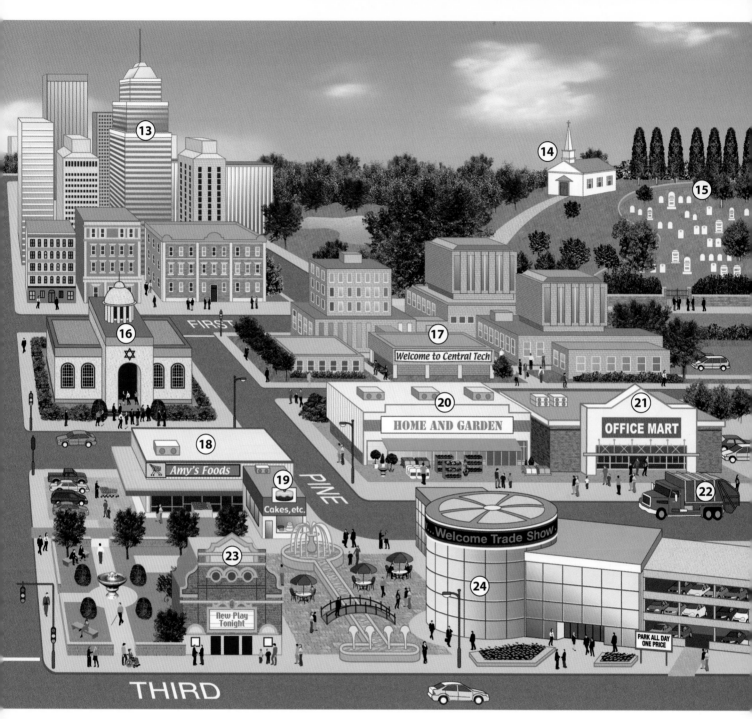

13. skyscraper / high-rise
ناطحة سحاب / بناية عالية الارتفاع

14. church
كنيسة

15. cemetery
مقبرة

16. synagogue
معبد يهودي

17. community college
كلية أهلية

18. supermarket
محل سوبرماركت

19. bakery
مخبز

20. home improvement store
محل أدوات لتحسين المنازل

21. office supply store
محل أدوات مكتبية

22. garbage truck
سيارة النفايات

23. theater
مسرح

24. convention center
مركز مؤتمرات

Ways to give locations

The mall is on 2nd Street.
The mall is on the corner of 2nd and Elm.
The mall is next to the movie theater.

Ask your classmates. Share the answers.

1. Where's your favorite coffee shop?
2. Where's your favorite supermarket?
3. Where's your favorite movie theater?

1. **laundromat**
   مغسلة عامة

2. **dry cleaners**
   مصبغة / تنظيف جاف

3. **convenience store**
   بقالة صغيرة

4. **pharmacy**
   صيدلية

5. **parking space**
   مكان لوقوف السيارة

6. **handicapped parking**
   مكان مخصص للمعوقين لوقوف سياراتهم

7. **corner**
   زاوية / ناصية

8. **traffic light**
   إشارة مرور

9. **bus**
   أوتوبيس / حافلة

10. **fast food restaurant**
    مطعم وجبات سريعة

11. **drive-thru window**
    نافذة تقديم الأطعمة للسيارات

12. **newsstand**
    كشك جرائد

13. **mailbox**
    صندوق البريد

14. **pedestrian**
    مشاة

15. **crosswalk**
    ممر المشاة

A. **cross** the street
   تعبر الشارع

B. **wait for** the light
   ينتظر الإشارة الضوئية

C. **jaywalk**
   يعبر الطريق في غير المكان المخصص لذلك

Pair practice. Make new conversations.

A: *I have a lot of errands to do today.*
B: *Me, too. First, I'm going to* the laundromat.
A: *I'll see you there after I stop at* the copy center.

Think about it. Discuss.

1. Which businesses are good to have in a neighborhood? Why?
2. Would you like to own a small business? If yes, what kind? If no, why not?

16. bus stop موقف أوتوبيس	**22.** bike دراجة	**28.** cart عربة يد
17. donut shop محل لكعك الدونات	**23.** pay phone هاتف / تليفون بالأجرة (تليفون عمومي)	**29.** street vendor بائع متجول
18. copy center مطبعة / محل لتصوير مستندات	**24.** sidewalk رصيف	**30.** childcare center مركز رعاية أطفال
19. barbershop حلاق	**25.** parking meter عداد موقف السيارة	**D. ride** a bike **تركب** دراجة
20. video store محل شرائط فيديو	**26.** street sign لافتة شارع	**E. park** the car **يوقف** سيارة
21. curb حافة رصيف	**27.** fire hydrant مطفئة حريق	**F. walk** a dog **يمشّي** كلبا

More vocabulary

neighborhood: the area close to your home
do errands: to make a short trip from your home to buy or pick up things

Ask your classmates. Share the answers.

1. What errands do you do every week?
2. What stores do you go to in your neighborhood?
3. What things can you buy from a street vendor?

129

1. music store
محل موسيقى

2. jewelry store
محل مجوهرات

3. nail salon
صالون لتجميل الأظافر

4. bookstore
محل بيع كتب

5. toy store
محل لعب

6. pet store
محل منتجات الحيوانات المنزلية

7. card store
محل بطاقات معايدة / محل كروت

8. florist
بائع زهور

9. optician
نظاراتي

10. shoe store
محل أحذية

11. play area
منطقة للعب

12. guest services
خدمات الضيوف

More vocabulary

beauty shop: hair salon
men's store: men's clothing store
gift shop: a store that sells t-shirts, mugs, and other small gifts

Pair practice. Make new conversations.

A: *Where is the florist?*
B: *It's on the first floor, next to the optician.*

13. **department store**
    محل متعدد الأقسام

14. **travel agency**
    مكتب سياحة / وكالة سفر

15. **food court**
    ساحة الطعام

16. **ice cream shop**
    محل أيس كريم

17. **candy store**
    محل بيع الحلوى

18. **hair salon**
    صالون حلاقة

19. **maternity store**
    محل بيع ملابس الحوامل

20. **electronics store**
    محل أجهزة الكترونية

21. **elevator**
    مصعد

22. **cell phone kiosk**
    كشك الهواتف المحمولة (النقالة)

23. **escalator**
    سلم متحرك

24. **directory**
    الدليل

Ways to talk about plans

Let's go to the <u>card store</u>.
I have to go to the <u>card store</u>.
I want to go to the <u>card store</u>.

Role play. Talk to a friend at the mall.

A: *Let's go to the <u>card store</u>. I need to buy <u>a card</u> for <u>Maggie's birthday</u>.*
B: *OK, but can we go to the <u>shoe store</u> next?*

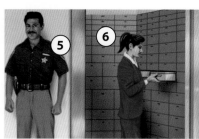

1. teller
أمينة الصندوق

2. customer
زبون / عميل

3. deposit
إيداع

4. deposit slip
بيان الإيداع

5. security guard
حارس أمن

6. vault
خزينة

7. safety deposit box
صندوق حفظ الودائع

8. valuables
نفائس / أشياء ثمينة

Opening an Account فتح حساب

9. account manager
مدير حسابات

10. passbook
دفتر بنكي

11. savings account number
رقم حساب التوفير

12. check book
دفتر شيكات

13. check
شيك

14. checking account number
رقم الحساب الجاري

15. ATM card
بطاقة جهاز الصرف الآلي

16. bank statement
كشف الحساب البنكي

17. balance
الرصيد

A. **Cash** a check.
يصرف شيكا.

B. **Make** a deposit.
يودع نقدا أو شيكا.

C. **Bank** online.
يجري أعمالا بنكية على الإنترنت.

The ATM (Automated Teller Machine) جهاز الصرف الآلي

D. **Insert** your ATM card.
أدخل بطاقة إيه تي أم الخاصة بك.

E. **Enter** your PIN.*
أدخل رقمك السري.

F. **Withdraw** cash.
اسحب النقود.

G. **Remove** your card.
أخرج بطاقة إيه تي أم الخاصة بك.

*PIN = personal identification number

A. get a library card
يحصل على بطاقة مكتبة

B. look for a book
يبحث عن كتاب

C. check out a book
يستعير كتابا

D. return a book
يعيد كتابا

E. pay a late fine
يدفع غرامة تأخير

1. library clerk
كاتب / موظف مكتبة

2. circulation desk
مكتب تداول

3. library patron
مُرتاد مكتبة

4. periodicals
منشورات دورية

5. magazine
مجلة

6. newspaper
صحيفة

7. headline
عنوان رئيسي (مانشت)

8. atlas
أطلس

9. reference librarian
أمين مكتبة للمعلومات المرجعية

10. self-checkout
استعارة كتب ذاتيا

11. online catalog
كتالوج إلكتروني

12. picture book
كتاب مصور

13. biography
سيرة ذاتية

14. title
عنوان

15. author
مؤلف

16. novel
رواية

17. audiobook
كتاب صوتي

18. videocassette
شريط فيديو

19. DVD
قرص فيديو رقمي (دي في دي)

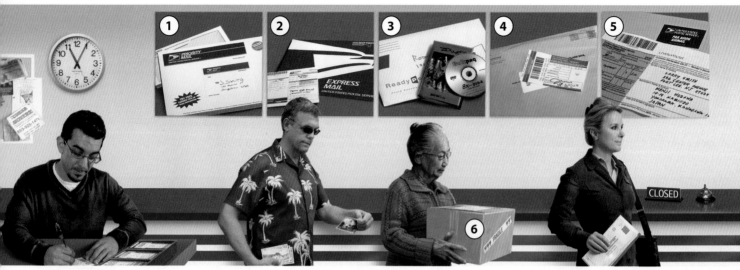

1. Priority Mail®
   بريد مستعجل

2. Express Mail®
   بريد سريع

3. media mail
   بريد إعلامي

4. Certified Mail™
   بريد مسجل

5. airmail
   بريد جوي

6. ground post / parcel post
   بريد برّي

13. letter
    خطاب / جواب

14. envelope
    ظرف / مغلف

15. greeting card
    بطاقة/كارت معايدة

16. post card
    بطاقة بريدية (كارت بوستال)

17. package
    طرد

18. book of stamps
    دفتر طوابع بريدية

19. postal forms
    استمارات بريدية

20. letter carrier
    ساعي البريد / حامل البريد

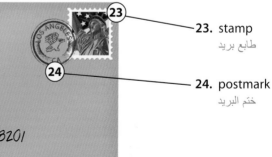

21. return address
    عنوان المرسل

22. mailing address
    عنوان المرسل إليه

Sonya Enriquez
258 Quentin Avenue
Los Angeles, CA 90068-141

Cindy Lin
807 Glenn Drive
Charlotte, NC 28201

23. stamp
    طابع بريد

24. postmark
    ختم البريد

Ways to talk about sending mail

This letter has to get there tomorrow. (Express Mail®)
This letter has to arrive in two days. (Priority Mail®)
This letter can go in regular mail. (First Class)

Pair practice. Make new conversations.

A: *Hi. This letter has to get there tomorrow.*
B: *You can send it by Express Mail®.*
A: *OK. I need a book of stamps, too.*

7. postal clerk
موظف بريد

8. scale
ميزان

9. post office box (PO box)
صندوق بريد (ص. ب.)

10. automated postal center (APC)
مركز بريدي آلي

11. stamp machine
ماكينة طوابع

12. mailbox
صندوق لإلقاء البريد

Sending a Card إرسال بطاقة/كارت

A. Write a note in a card.
تكتب رسالة في الكارت.

B. Address the envelope.
تكتب العنوان على الظرف.

C. Put on a stamp.
تضع طابع البريد.

D. Mail the card.
تلقي الكارت في صندوق البريد.

E. Deliver the card.
يوصّل البريد.

F. Receive the card.
تستلم الكارت.

G. Read the card.
تقرأ الكارت.

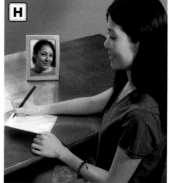

H. Write back.
تكتب إليها ردا على الكارت.

More vocabulary

overnight / next day mail: Express Mail®
postage: the cost to send mail
junk mail: mail you don't want

Think about it. Discuss.

1. What kind of mail do you send overnight?
2. Do you want to be a letter carrier? Why or why not?
3. Do you get junk mail? What do you do with it?

Department of Motor Vehicles (DMV)

دائرة تسجيل المركبات الآلية

No Talking

Quiet Please

BUCKLE UP IT'S THE LAW!

Forms **Handbooks**

Information

California Driver Handbook

CLOSED

Vehicle Registration →

---

1. DMV handbook
كتيب دائرة تسجيل المركبات الآلية

2. testing area
منطقة الامتحان

3. DMV clerk
موظف دائرة تسجيل المركبات الآلية

4. photo
صورة فوتوغرافية

5. fingerprint
بصمة إصبع

6. vision exam
كشف نظر

7. window
نافذة / شِبّاك

Pluto Auto Insurance
Proof of Insurance
Policy Holder: Irene Pena
Policy No: 1119000555
Make: Ford Taurus   Expiration Date: 9/25/12
IMPORTANT: PLEASE PLACE IN DESIGNATED VEHICLE

CALIFORNIA
DRIVERS LICENSE
EXPIRES 07-29-16 N57881049 CLASS
Irene Pena
1313 Balboa Blvd,
Van Nuys, CA 91064
Irene Pena
DONOR DOB 7-29-70

AUG *California* 2012
2OPD OO8

8. proof of insurance
إثبات التأمين

9. driver's license
رخصة قيادة سيارة

10. expiration date
تاريخ الانتهاء

11. driver's license number
رقم رخصة القيادة

12. license plate
لوحة الترخيص المعدنية

13. registration sticker / tag
لاصق / لصيقة التسجيل

More vocabulary

expire: a license is no good, or **expires**, after the expiration date
renew a license: to apply to keep a license before it expires
vanity plate: a more expensive, personal license plate

Ask your classmates. Share the answers.

1. How far is the DMV from your home?
2. Do you have a driver's license? If yes, when does it expire? If not, do you want one?

Getting Your First License الحصول على أول رخصة قيادة لك

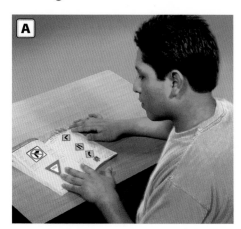

A. **Study** the handbook.
ذاكر الكتيب.

B. **Take** a driver education course.*
التحق بدورة لتعليم قيادة السيارات.

C. **Show** your identification.
أبرز بطاقة هويتك.

D. **Pay** the application fee.
ادفع رسم تقديم الطلب.

E. **Take** a written test.
تقدم للامتحان التحريري.

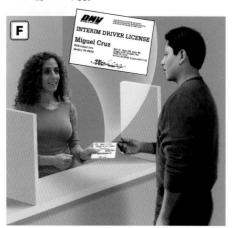

F. **Get** a learner's permit.
احصل على تصريح للمتعلم.

G. **Take** a driver's training course.*
التحق بدورة تدريب السائقين.

H. **Pass** a driving test.
انجح في امتحان قيادة السيارة.

I. **Get** your license.
تسلم رخصة القيادة الخاصة بك.

*Note: This is not required for drivers 18 and older.

Ways to request more information	**Role play. Talk to a DMV clerk.**
What do I do next?	A: *I want to apply for <u>a driver's license</u>.*
What's the next step?	B: *Did you <u>study the handbook</u>?*
Where do I go from here?	A: *Yes, I did. <u>What do I do next</u>?*

Federal Government الحكومة الاتحادية (الفدرالية)

Legislative Branch
السلطة التشريعية

1. U.S. Capitol
الكابيتول (مقر الكونجرس الأمريكي في واشنطن)

2. Congress
الكونجرس

3. House of Representatives
مجلس النواب

4. congressperson
عضو كونجرس

5. Senate
مجلس الشيوخ

6. senator
عضو مجلس شيوخ / سناتور

435   100

Executive Branch
السلطة التنفيذية

7. White House
البيت الأبيض

8. president
الرئيس

9. vice president
نائب الرئيس

10. Cabinet
الوزارة

STATE   DEFENSE   LABOR

Judicial Branch
السلطة القضائية

11. Supreme Court
المحكمة العليا

12. justices
قضاة

13. chief justice
رئيس القضاة / رئيس المحكمة

The Military القوات المسلحة

14. Army
الجيش

15. Navy
البحرية

16. Air Force
القوات الجوية

17. Marines
سلاح مشاة البحرية (المارينز)

18. Coast Guard
خفر السواحل

19. National Guard
الحرس الوطني

State Government حكومة الولاية

20. governor
الحاكم

21. lieutenant governor
نائب الحاكم

22. state capital
عاصمة الولاية

23. Legislature
المجلس التشريعي للولاية

24. assemblyperson
عضو المجلس التشريعي

25. state senator
عضو مجلس شيوخ الولاية

City Government حكومة المدينة

26. mayor
العمدة

27. city council
مجلس المدينة / المجلس البلدي

28. councilperson
عضو مجلس المدينة

An Election انتخابات

A. **run for** office
يرشّح **نفسه** لمنصب عام

29. political campaign
حملة انتخابية سياسية

B. **debate**
يدخل في مناظرة

30. opponent
المنافس / الخصم

CITY TIMES
DAN CHEN WINS!
Chen gets 100,000 votes
Larson gets 65,000

C. **get elected**
يفوز في الانتخابات

31. election results
نتائج الانتخابات

D. **serve**
يتولى منصبه

32. elected official
مسؤول منتخب

More vocabulary

term: the period of time an elected official serves
political party: a group of people with the same
political goals

Think about it. Discuss.

1. Should everyone have to serve in the military? Why or
   why not?
2. Would you prefer to run for city council or mayor? Why?

139

Responsibilities الواجبات

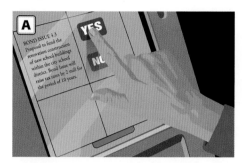

A. vote
يصوت في الانتخابات

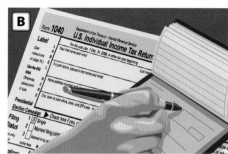

B. pay taxes
يدفع الضرائب

C. obey the law
يطيع القانون

D. register with Selective Service*
يسجل اسمه في الخدمة الانتقائية

E. serve on a jury
يؤدي الخدمة في هيئة محلفين

F. be informed
يبقى على اطلاع بما يجري

Citizenship Requirements متطلبات الحصول على الجنسية

G. be 18 or older
أن يكون عمره ١٨ سنة أو أكبر

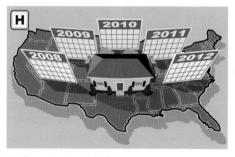

H. live in the U.S. for 5 years
أن يكون مقيما في الولايات المتحدة لفترة ٥ سنوات

I. take a citizenship test
أن يتقدم لامتحان الجنسية

Rights الحقوق

1. peaceful assembly
التجمع السلمي

2. free speech
حرية الكلام

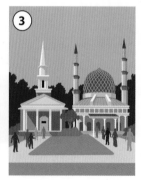

3. freedom of religion
حرية الدين أو العبادة

4. freedom of the press
حرية الصحافة

5. fair trial
المحاكمة العادلة

*Note: All males 18 to 26 who live in the U.S. are required to register with Selective Service.

A. arrest a suspect
يلقي القبض على شخص مشتبه فيه.

1. police officer
ضابط شرطة / شرطي

2. handcuffs
قيود / كلبشات

B. hire a lawyer / **hire** an attorney
يوكّل محاميا

3. guard
حارس

4. defense attorney
محامي دفاع

C. appear in court
يمثل أمام القضاء

5. defendant
متهم / مدعى عليه

6. judge
قاضي

D. stand trial
يحاكم / يخضع للمحاكمة

7. courtroom
قاعة المحكمة

8. jury
هيئة محلفين

9. evidence
دليل / بينة

10. prosecuting attorney
المدعي العام / وكيل النيابة

11. witness
شاهد

12. court reporter
كاتب المحكمة

13. bailiff
حاجب المحكمة

E. convict the defendant
يحكم بإدانة المتهم

14. verdict*
الحكم / القرار

F. sentence the defendant
يصدر الحكم بمعاقبة المتهم

G. go to jail / **go** to prison
يسجن / يودع السجن

15. convict / prisoner
مدان (محكوم عليه) / سجين

H. be released
يفرج عنه / يطلق سراحه

*Note: There are two possible verdicts, "guilty" and "not guilty."

Look at the pictures.
Describe what happened.

A: *The police officer arrested a suspect.*
B: *He put handcuffs on him.*

Think about it. Discuss.

1. Would you want to serve on a jury? Why or why not?
2. Look at the crimes on page 142. What sentence would you give for each crime? Why?

1. vandalism
تخريب متعمد

2. burglary
سطو

3. assault
اعتداء

4. gang violence
عنف عصابات

5. drunk driving
قيادة سيارة تحت تأثير الخمر

6. illegal drugs
مخدرات ممنوعة

7. arson
حرق متعمد

8. shoplifting
سرقة معروضات المتجر

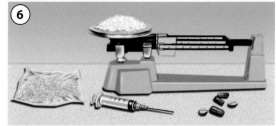

9. identity theft
سرقة هويات الغير

10. victim
ضحية / مجني عليه

11. mugging
اعتداء بهدف السلب

12. murder
جريمة القتل

13. gun
مسدس

More vocabulary

steal: to take money or things from someone illegally
commit a crime: to do something illegal
criminal: someone who does something illegal

Think about it. Discuss.

1. Is there too much crime on TV or in the movies? Explain.

2. How can communities help stop crime?

A. **Walk** with a friend.

امشِ مع صديق أو صديقة.

B. **Stay** on well-lit streets.

ابقَ في شوارع جيدة الإنارة.

C. **Conceal** your PIN number.

اخفِ رقمك السري الذي تستخدمه في جهاز الصرف الآلي.

D. **Protect** your purse or wallet.

حافظ على محفظتك أو حقيبة يدك.

E. **Lock** your doors.

اقفل أبوابك.

F. Don't **open** your door to strangers.

لا **تفتح** بابك للغرباء.

G. Don't **drink** and **drive**.

لا **تشرب** الخمر وتقود سيارة.

H. **Shop** on secure websites.

لا **تتسوّق** إلا على مواقع إنترنت مؤمنة.

I. **Be** aware of your surroundings.

كن على دراية بالبيئة المحيطة بك.

J. **Report** suspicious packages.

بلّغ الشرطة عن أية علب أو طرود مشبوهة.

K. **Report** crimes to the police.

بلّغ الشرطة عن الجرائم.

L. **Join** a Neighborhood Watch.

انضم إلى هيئة أهل الحي لمراقبة الأعمال المشبوهة.

More vocabulary

sober: not drunk

designated drivers: sober drivers who drive drunk people home safely

Ask your classmates. Share the answers.

1. Do you feel safe in your neighborhood?
2. Look at the pictures. Which of these things do you do?
3. What other things do you do to stay safe?

143

1. lost child
   طفل ضائع

2. car accident
   حادث سيارة / حادث طريق

3. airplane crash
   تحطم طائرة

4. explosion
   انفجار

5. earthquake
   زلزال

6. mudslide
   انزلاق الطين

7. forest fire
   حريق غابات

8. fire
   حريق

9. firefighter
   إطفائي / رجل إطفاء

10. fire truck
   سيارة إطفاء

Ways to report an emergency

First, give your name. *My name is <u>Tim Johnson</u>.*
Then, state the emergency and give the address.
There was <u>a car accident</u> at <u>219 Elm Street</u>.

Role play. Call 911.

A: *911 Emergency Operator.*
B: *My name is <u>Lisa Diaz</u>. There is <u>a fire</u> at <u>323 Oak Street</u>. Please hurry!*

11. drought
جفاف / قحط

12. famine
مجاعة

13. blizzard
عاصفة ثلجية شديدة

14. hurricane
إعصار

15. tornado
زوبعة

16. volcanic eruption
انفجار بركاني

17. tidal wave / tsunami
موجة بحرية مدية / تسونامي

18. avalanche
تيهور / جرف ثلجي

19. flood
فيضان

20. search and rescue team
فريق البحث والإنقاذ

Ask your classmates. Share the answers.

1. Which natural disaster worries you the most?
2. Which natural disaster worries you the least?
3. Which disasters are common in your local area?

Think about it. Discuss.

1. What organizations can help you in an emergency?
2. What are some ways to prepare for natural disasters?
3. Where would you go in an emergency?

Before an Emergency قبل حدوث الحالة الطارئة

A. Plan for an emergency.
خطط للحالة الطارئة.

1. meeting place
مكان تجمع

2. out-of-state contact
معارف خارج الولاية

3. escape route
طريق للهرب / مهرب

4. gas shut-off valve
صمام غلق الغاز

5. evacuation route
طريق للإخلاء

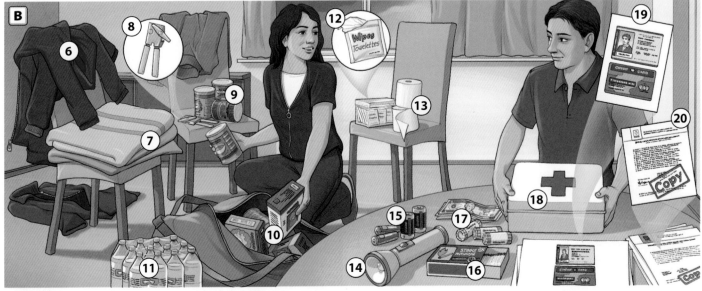

B. Make a disaster kit.
اصنع/جهّز علبة بمستلزمات الكوارث.

6. warm clothes
ملابس ثقيلة للتدفئة

7. blankets
بطاطين

8. can opener
فتاحة علب

9. canned food
مأكولات معلبة

10. packaged food
أطعمة مغلفة

11. bottled water
زجاجات ماء

12. moist towelettes
فوط صغيرة رطبة

13. toilet paper
ورق تواليت

14. flashlight
مصباح بطارية

15. batteries
بطاريات

16. matches
كبريت

17. cash and coins
نقد وعملة

18. first aid kit
علبة إسعافات أولية

19. copies of ID and credit cards
نسخ مصورة من بطاقات الهوية وبطاقات الائتمان

20. copies of important papers
نسخ مصورة من الأوراق المهمة

Pair practice. Make new conversations.

A: *What do we need for our disaster kit?*
B: *We need blankets and matches.*
A: *I think we also need batteries.*

Ask your classmates. Share the answers.

1. Who would you call first after an emergency?
2. Do you have escape and evacuation routes planned?
3. Are you a calm person in case of an emergency?

During an Emergency في أثناء الحالة الطارئة

C. Watch the weather.

راقب حالة الطقس.

Hurricane Watch

D. Pay attention to warnings.

انتبه للتحذيرات العامة.

Hurricane Watch

E. Remain calm.

ابقَ هادئاً.

Go to a shelter.

F. Follow directions.

اتبع الإرشادات.

Shelter

G. Help people with disabilities.

ساعد الناس المعوقين.

Shelter

H. Seek shelter.

ابحث عن مخبأ أو ملجأ.

I. Stay away from windows.

ابتعد عن النوافذ.

J. Take cover.

احتمِ.

K. Evacuate the area.

اخلِ المنطقة.

After an Emergency بعد حدوث الحالة الطارئة

We're OK.

Great.

L. Call out-of-state contacts.

اتصل بمعارفك خارج الولاية.

M. Clean up debris.

نظّف المكان من الأنقاض.

N. Inspect utilities.

فتّش على المرافق.

Ways to say you're OK

I'm fine.
We're OK here.
Everything's under control.

Ways to say you need help

We need help.
Someone is hurt.
I'm injured. Please get help.

Role play. Prepare for an emergency.

A: *They just issued* <u>*a hurricane*</u> *warning.*
B: *OK. We need to stay calm and follow directions.*
A: *What do we need to do first?*

1. graffiti
   رسوم أو نقوش على الجدران

2. litter
   مهملات ملقاة في الطرقات العامة

3. streetlight
   عامود إنارة الشارع

4. hardware store
   محل الأدوات المعدنية / محل أدوات الحدادة

5. petition
   التماس / عريضة رسمية

A. **give** a speech
   تلقي خطابا

B. **applaud**
   تصفيق

C. **change**
   تغيير

Look at the pictures. What do you see?

Answer the questions.

1. What were the problems on Main Street?

2. What was the petition for?

3. Why did the city council applaud?

4. How did the people change the street?

📖 Read the story.

Community Cleanup

Marta Lopez has a donut shop on Main Street. One day she looked at her street and was very upset. She saw graffiti on her donut shop and the other stores. Litter was everywhere. All the streetlights were broken. Marta wanted to fix the lights and clean up the street.

Marta started a petition about the streetlights. Five hundred people signed it. Then she gave a speech to the city council. The council members voted to repair the streetlights. Everyone applauded. Marta was happy, but her work wasn't finished.

Next, Marta asked for volunteers to clean up Main Street. The hardware store manager gave the volunteers free paint. Marta gave them free donuts and coffee. The volunteers painted and cleaned. They changed Main Street. Now Main Street is beautiful and Marta is proud.

Think about it.

1. What are some problems in your community? How can people help?

2. Imagine you are Marta. What do you say in your speech to the city council?

1. car
   سيارة

2. passenger
   راكب

3. taxi
   سيارة أجرة / تاكسي

4. motorcycle
   دراجة بخارية / موتوسيكل

5. street
   شارع

6. truck
   شاحنة / لوري

7. train
   قطار

8. (air)plane
   طائرة

Listen and point. Take turns.

A: *Point to the motorcycle.*
B: *Point to the truck.*
A: *Point to the train.*

Dictate to your partner. Take turns.

A: *Write motorcycle.*
B: *Could you repeat that for me?*
A: *Motorcycle. M-o-t-o-r-c-y-c-l-e.*

9. helicopter
طائرة عمودية /
هليكوبتر

10. airport
مطار

11. subway station
محطة قطار نفقي /
محطة مترو أنفاق

12. subway
قطار نفقي / مترو
أنفاق

13. bus stop
موقف أوتوبيس /
موقف حافلات

14. bus
أوتوبيس / حافلة

15. bicycle
دراجة / بسكيلته

SUBWAY

Mario's ITALIAN DELI

Ways to talk about using transportation
Use **take** for buses, trains, subways, taxis, planes,
and helicopters. Use **drive** for cars and trucks.
Use **ride** for bicycles and motorcycles.

Pair practice. Make new conversations.
A: *How do you get to school?*
B: *I take the bus. How about you?*
A: *I ride a bicycle to school.*

A Bus Stop موقف أوتوبيس

BUS 10 Northbound		
Main	Elm	Oak
6:00	6:10	6:13
6:30	6:40	6:43
7:00	7:10	7:13
7:30	7:40	7:43

New York City Transit
MTA Transfer
◄◄ Going your way

A Subway Station محطة قطار نفقي

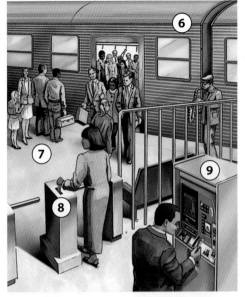

MTA RED LINE
OPENING DAY
JUNE 24, 2000
1 FARE
NORTH HOLLYWOOD

MTA
MetroCard
◄◄ Insert this way/This side facing you

1. bus route
طريق سير الأوتوبيس

2. fare
أجرة / تعريفة

3. rider
راكب

4. schedule
جدول مواعيد

5. transfer
تذكرة تحويل

6. subway car
عربة قطار نفقي

7. platform
رصيف

8. turnstile
حاجز أفقي دوار

9. vending machine
آلة البيع

10. token
عملة رمزية

11. fare card
بطاقة الأجرة المدفوعة

A Train Station محطة قطار

HART DAVIS/DAMON
From
DOVER, NH
To
BOSTON NRTH STA,MA.
2V 684 17FEB03
2V BUSINESS CL
AP XXXX0456791 Ax

Fresno
Los Angeles

Fresno
Los Angeles

Airport Transportation مواصلات إلى المطار

TAXIS

J&J Hotel

TAXI

CCJ 2203

1036081

22.00

12. ticket window
شباك تذاكر

13. conductor
قاطع التذاكر / كمسري

14. track
سكة

15. ticket
تذكرة

16. one-way trip
رحلة ذهاب فقط

17. round trip
ذهاب وعودة

18. taxi stand
موقف سيارات أجرة (تاكسي)

19. shuttle
عربة النقل السريع / مكوك

20. town car
سيارة صالون فاخرة / سيارة ليموزين

21. taxi driver
سائق سيارة أجرة / تاكسي

22. taxi license
رخصة تاكسي

23. meter
عدّاد

More vocabulary

hail a taxi: to raise your hand to get a taxi

miss the bus: to get to the bus stop after the bus leaves

Ask your classmates. Share the answers.

1. Is there a subway system in your city?

2. Do you ever take taxis? When?

3. Do you ever take the bus? Where?

A. go under the bridge
تذهب (تسير) تحت الجسر

B. go over the bridge
يذهب (يسير) فوق الجسر

C. walk up the steps
تطلع/تصعد الدرجات مشيا على قدميها

D. walk down the steps
ينزل/يهبط الدرجات مشيا على قدميه

E. get into the taxi
تدخل إلى سيارة الأجرة (التاكسي)

F. get out of the taxi
يخرج من سيارة الأجرة (التاكسي)

G. run across the street
يركض عبر الشارع

H. run around the corner
تركض حول الزاوية

I. get on the highway
يدخل على الطريق السريع

J. get off the highway
يخرج من الطريق السريع

K. drive through the tunnel
يسوق عبر النفق

Grammar Point: *into, out of, on, off*

Use *get into* for taxis and cars.
Use *get on* for buses, trains, planes, and highways.

Use *get out of* for taxis and cars.
Use *get off* for buses, trains, planes, and highways.

1. stop
قف

2. do not enter / wrong way
ممنوع الدخول / اتجاه خطأ

3. one way
اتجاه واحد

4. speed limit
السرعة القصوى

5. U-turn OK
مسموح الدوران

6. no outlet / dead end
بدون منفذ / طريق مسدود

7. right turn only
الانعطاف إلى اليمين فقط

8. no left turn
ممنوع الانعطاف إلى اليسار

9. yield
انتظر السيارات المارة

10. merge
اندماج

11. no parking
ممنوع الوقوف

12. handicapped parking
موقف للمعاقين

13. pedestrian crossing
عبور المشاة

14. railroad crossing
عبور سكة حديد (مزلقان)

15. school crossing
عبور مدرسة

16. road work
منطقة عمل

17. U.S. route / highway marker
طريق بين ولايات / علامة طريق سريع

18. hospital
مستشفى

Pair practice. Make new conversations.

A: *Watch out! The sign says <u>no left turn</u>.*
B: *Sorry, I was looking at the <u>stop</u> sign.*
A: *That's OK. Just be careful!*

Ask your classmates. Share the answers.

1. How many traffic signs are on your street?
2. What's the speed limit on your street?
3. What traffic signs are the same in your native country?

Directions إرشادات

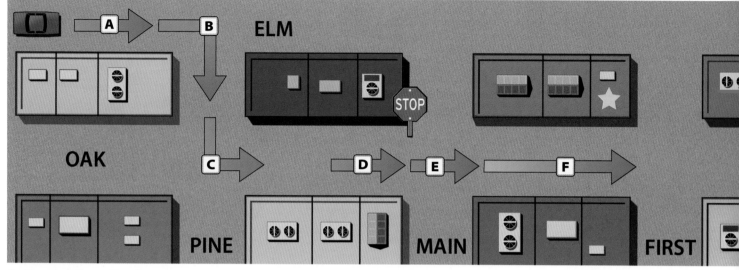

A. Go straight on Elm Street.
سر باتجاه مستقيم على شارع إلم.

B. Turn right on Pine Street.
انعطف يمينا على شارع باين.

C. Turn left on Oak Street.
انعطف يسارا على شارع أوك.

D. Stop at the corner.
قف عند الزاوية/الناصية.

E. Go past Main Street.
اعبر شارع مين.

F. Go one block to First Street.
سر مسافة ناصية إلى شارع فيرست.

Maps خرائط

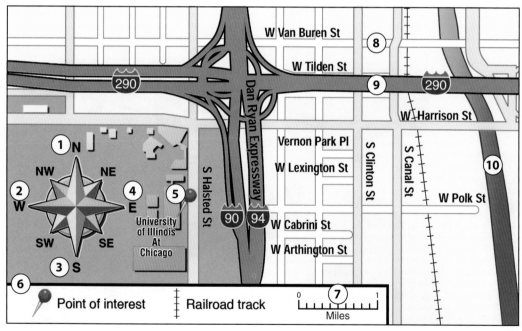

1. north شمال	3. south جنوب	5. symbol رمز	8. street شارع	11. GPS (global positioning system) جي بي إس (نظام تحديد الموضع عالميا)
2. west غرب	4. east شرق	6. key مفتاح	9. highway طريق سريع	12. Internet map خريطة إنترنت
		7. scale مقياس	10. river نهر	

Role play. Ask for directions.

A: *I'm lost. I need to get to Elm and Pine.*

B: *Go straight on Oak and make a right on Pine.*

A: *Thanks so much.*

Ask your classmates. Share the answers.

1. How often do you use Internet maps? GPS? paper maps?

2. What was the last map you used? Why?

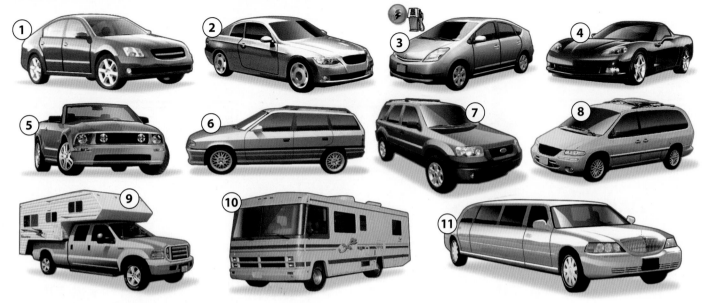

1. **4-door car / sedan**
   سيارة ذات ٤ أبوب / سيارة صالون

2. **2-door car / coupe**
   سيارة ذات بابين / سيارة كوب

3. **hybrid**
   سيارة هيبريد (تعمل بالبنزين والكهرباء)

4. **sports car**
   سيارة سبور (رياضية)

5. **convertible**
   سيارة مكشوفة (كابريوليه)

6. **station wagon**
   سيارة ستايشن

7. **SUV (sport–utility vehicle)**
   سيارة رياضية متعددة الاستعمالات (إس يو في)

8. **minivan**
   سيارة فان صغيرة (ميني فان)

9. **camper**
   كارافان

10. **RV (recreational vehicle)**
    آر في (مركبة ترفيهية)

11. **limousine / limo**
    سيارة ليموزين

12. **pickup truck**
    شاحنة بيك اب

13. **cargo van**
    فان بضائع

14. **tow truck**
    سيارة قطر أو سحب

15. **tractor trailer / semi**
    شاحنة مقطورة

16. **cab**
    كابينة الشاحنة

17. **trailer**
    عربة مقطورة

18. **moving van**
    سيارة فان للنقل

19. **dump truck**
    شاحنة نفايات

20. **tank truck**
    شاحنة صهريجية

21. **school bus**
    أوتوبيس مدرسة

Pair practice. Make new conversations.

A: *I have a new car!*
B: *Did you get a hybrid?*
A: *Yes, but I really wanted a sports car.*

More vocabulary

make: the name of the company that makes the car
model: the style of the car

Buying a Used Car   شراء سيارة مستعملة

A. **Look at** car ads.
انظر في إعلانات السيارات.

B. **Ask** the seller about the car.
اسأل البائع عن السيارة.

C. **Take** the car to a mechanic.
خذ السيارة إلى ميكانيكي.

D. **Negotiate** a price.
فاوض على سعر.

E. **Get** the title from the seller.
احصل على سند الملكية من البائع.

F. **Register** the car.
سجّل السيارة.

Taking Care of Your Car   الاعتناء بسيارتك

G. **Fill** the tank with gas.
عبّئ خزان البنزين.

H. **Check** the oil.
افحص الزيت.

I. **Put in** coolant.
ضع سائل التبريد.

J. **Go** for a smog check.*
اذهب لعمل فحص للغازات الملوثة.

K. **Replace** the windshield wipers.
استبدل المسّاحات.

L. **Fill** the tires with air.
انفخ الإطارات بالهواء.

*smog check = emissions test

Ways to request service

Please check the oil.
Could you fill the tank?
Put in coolant, please.

Think about it. Discuss.

1. What's good and bad about a used car?
2. Do you like to negotiate car prices? Why?
3. Do you know any good mechanics? Why are they good?

157

At the Dealer
عند وكالة السيارات (معرض السيارات)

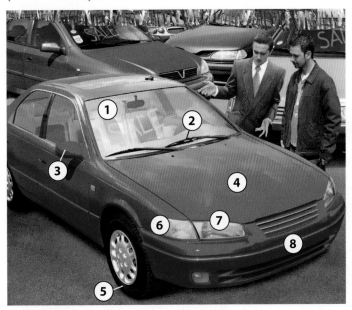

1. windshield
   حاجب الريح الزجاجي

2. windshield wipers
   المسّاحات

3. sideview mirror
   مرآة الرؤية الجانبية

4. hood
   غطاء محرك السيارة (كبّوت)

5. tire
   إطار / عجلة

6. turn signal
   إشارة الانعطاف

7. headlight
   مصباح أمامي

8. bumper
   مخفف الصدمة

At the Mechanic
عند الميكانيكي

9. hubcap / wheel cover
   غطاء محور العجلة

10. gas tank
    خزان البنزين

11. trunk
    صندوق السيارة

12. license plate
    لوحة رقم السيارة

13. tail light
    مصباح خلفي

14. brake light
    مصباح الفرملة

15. tail pipe
    ماسورة العادم

16. muffler
    مخمّد الصوت (شكمان)

Under the Hood
تحت غطاء المحرك (الكبّوت)

17. fuel injection system
    نظام حقن الوقود

18. engine
    محرك / موتور

19. radiator
    راديياتير (مشعاع)

20. battery
    بطارية

Inside the Trunk
داخل صندوق السيارة

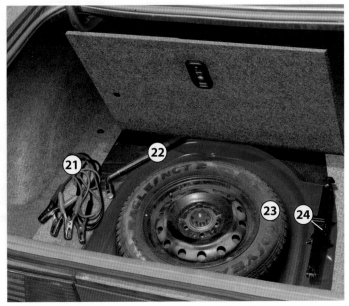

21. jumper cables
    كبل عبور الطاقة

22. lug wrench
    مفتاح ربط

23. spare tire
    إطار احتياطي (استبن)

24. jack
    مرفاع (كوريك)

The Dashboard and Instrument Panel
تابلو السيارة ولوحة العدادات وأجهزة القياس

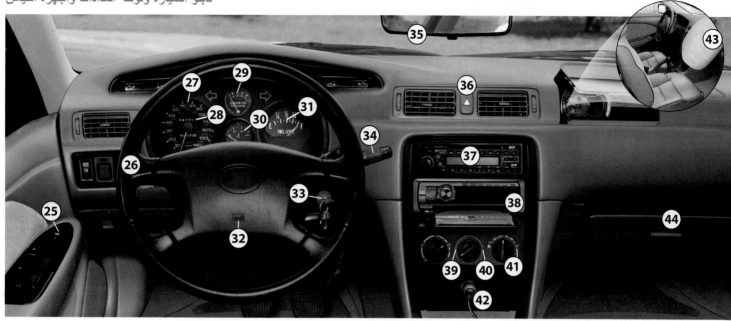

25. door lock قفل الباب	**30.** temperature gauge مقياس الحرارة	**35.** rearview mirror مرآة للرؤية الخلفية	**40.** heater مدفئة
26. steering wheel عجلة القيادة	**31.** gas gauge مقياس البنزين	**36.** hazard lights ضوء الوقوف للطوارئ	**41.** defroster مزيل التجمد
27. speedometer عداد السرعة	**32.** horn بوق (كلاكس)	**37.** radio راديو	**42.** power outlet منفذ طاقة
28. odometer أودومتر (عداد المسافة)	**33.** ignition إشعال	**38.** CD player جهاز تشغيل أقراص مضغوطة (سي دي)	**43.** air bag كيس أمام هوائي
29. oil gauge مقياس الزيت	**34.** turn signal إشارة الانعطاف	**39.** air conditioner مكيف الهواء	**44.** glove compartment صندوق قفازات

An Automatic Transmission
ناقل حركة أوتوماتيكي

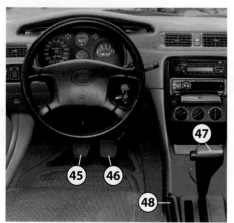

A Manual Transmission
ناقل حركة يدوي

Inside the Car
داخل السيارة

45. brake pedal دواسة الفرملة	**47.** gear shift ناقل التروس	**49.** clutch القابض (الدوبرياج)	**51.** front seat مقعد أمامي	**53.** child safety seat مقعد أمان للطفل
46. gas pedal / accelerator دواسة البنزين	**48.** hand brake فرملة اليد	**50.** stick shift ذراع نقل السرعات (فتيس)	**52.** seat belt حزام أمان بالمقعد	**54.** backseat مقعد خلفي

In the Airline Terminal في صالة المطار

At the Security Checkpoint
عند نقطة تفتيش الأمن

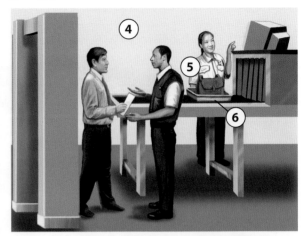

1. skycap
حامل الحقائب

3. ticket agent
وكيل تذاكر

5. TSA* agent / security screener
وكيل تي إس إيه / مفتش أمن

2. check-in kiosk
كشك التسجيل

4. screening area
منطقة فرز وتفتيش

6. bin
حاوية

Taking a Flight السفر في رحلة جوية

A. Check in electronically.
قم بالتسجيل إلكترونيا.

B. Check your bags.
سلّمي الحقائب.

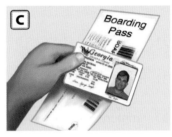

C. Show your boarding pass and ID.
أظهر بطاقة الصعود والهوية.

D. Go through security.
مر عبر نقطة الأمن.

E. Board the plane.
اصعد الطائرة.

F. Find your seat.
أبحث عن مقعدك.

G. Stow your carry-on bag.
خزّن حقيبة اليد الخاصة بك.

H. Fasten your seat belt.
اربط حزام المقعد.

I. Turn off your cell phone.
أغلق هاتفك / تليفونك المحمول.

J. Take off. / Leave.
إقلاع / مغادرة.

K. Land. / Arrive.
هبوط / وصول.

L. Claim your baggage.
استردي أمتعتك.

* Transportation Security Administration

At the Gate عند البوابة

On the Airplane داخل الطائرة

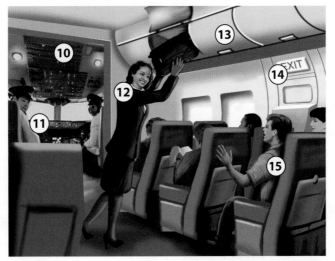

At Customs عند الجمرك

7. **arrival and departure monitors**
شاشات الوصول والمغادرة

8. **gate**
بوابة

9. **boarding area**
منطقة الصعود إلى الطائرة

10. **cockpit**
كابينة الطيارين

11. **pilot**
طيار

12. **flight attendant**
مضيف / مضيفة طائرة

13. **overhead compartment**
حجرة حقائب علوية

14. **emergency exit**
باب خروج في حالات طوارئ

15. **passenger**
راكب

16. **declaration form**
استمارة إقرار جمركي

17. **customs officer**
موظف جمارك

18. **luggage / bag**
أمتعة / حقيبة

19. **e-ticket**
تذكرة إلكترونية

20. **boarding pass**
بطاقة صعود

21. **tray table**
صينية حاملة

22. **turbulence**
مطب هوائي / اضطراب جوي

23. **baggage carousel**
سير الأمتعة المتحرك

24. **oxygen mask**
قناع أكسيجين

25. **life vest**
صديرية النجاة

26. **emergency card**
بطاقة إرشادات للطوارئ

27. **reclined seat**
مقعد مائل الظهر

28. **upright seat**
مقعد مستقيم الظهر

29. **on-time**
في الموعد المحدد

30. **delayed flight**
رحلة متأخرة

More vocabulary

departure time: the time the plane takes off
arrival time: the time the plane lands
direct flight: a trip with no stops

Pair practice. Make new conversations.

A: *Excuse me. Where do I* <u>*check in*</u>?
B: *At the* <u>*check-in kiosk*</u>.
A: *Thanks.*

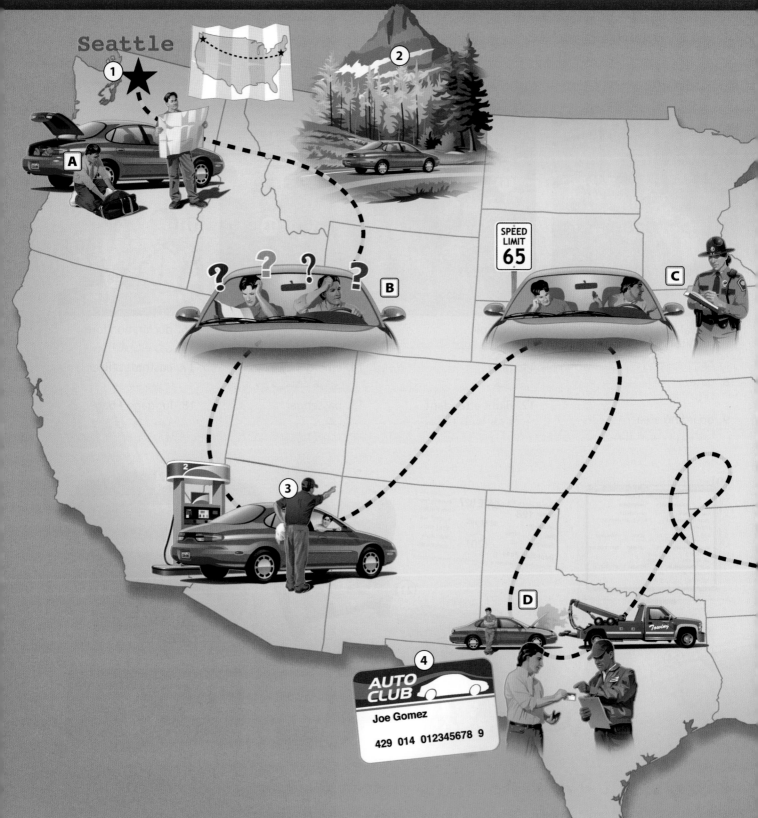

Seattle

SPEED LIMIT 65

AUTO CLUB
Joe Gomez
429 014 012345678 9

1. starting point نقطة البداية	**4.** auto club card بطاقة نادي السيارات	**B. get** lost يضلّ الطريق / يتوه	**E. run out** of gas فرغ البنزين
2. scenery المناظر الخلابة	**5.** destination جهة الوصول	**C. get** a speeding ticket ينول مخالفة لتجاوز السرعة القصوى	**F. have** a flat tire يخلو إطار السيارة من الهواء / تنام العجلة
3. gas station attendant عامل محطة البنزين	**A. pack** حضّر الحقيبة	**D. break down** تتعطل السيارة	

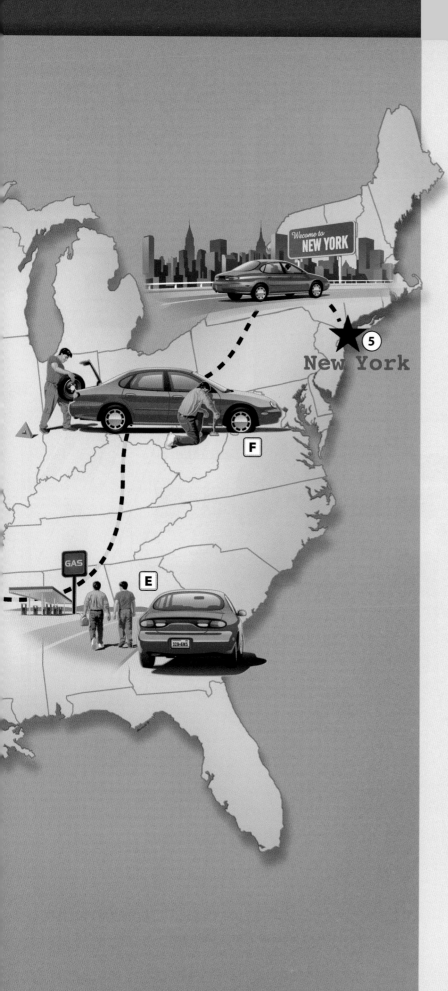

Look at the pictures. What do you see?

Answer the questions.

1. What are the young men's starting point and destination?

2. What do they see on their trip?

3. What kinds of problems do they have?

 Read the story.

A Road Trip

On July 7th Joe and Rob <u>packed</u> their bags for a road trip. Their <u>starting point</u> was Seattle. Their <u>destination</u> was New York City.

The young men saw beautiful <u>scenery</u> on their trip. But there were also problems. They <u>got lost</u>. Then, a <u>gas station attendant</u> gave them bad directions. Next, they <u>got a speeding ticket</u>. Joe was very upset. After that, their car <u>broke down</u>. Joe called a tow truck and used his <u>auto club card</u>.

The end of their trip was difficult, too. They <u>ran out of gas</u> and then they had a <u>flat tire</u>.

After 7,000 miles of problems, Joe and Rob arrived in New York City. They were happy, but tired. Next time, they're going to take the train.

Think about it.

1. What is the best way to travel across the U.S.? by car? by plane? by train? Why?

2. Imagine your car breaks down on the road. Who can you call? What can you do?

1. entrance
   مدخل

2. customer
   زبون

3. office
   مكتب

4. employer /
   boss
   ربة العمل / رئيسة

5. receptionist
   موظفة استقبال

6. safety regulations
   لوائح السلامة

Listen and point. Take turns.

A: Point to <u>the front entrance</u>.
B: Point to <u>the receptionist</u>.
A: Point to <u>the time clock</u>.

Dictate to your partner. Take turns.

A: *Can you spell <u>employer</u>?*
B: *I'm not sure. Is it <u>e-m-p-l-o-y-e-r</u>?*
A: *Yes, that's right.*

7. time clock
ساعة الدوام

8. supervisor
مشرف

9. employee
موظف

10. payroll clerk
موظفة جدول الرواتب

11. pay stub
كعب استلام راتب

12. wages
أجور

13. deductions
خصومات

14. paycheck
شيك الراتب

PLEASE CLOCK IN AND OUT

EMPLOYEES ONLY

Fix this first.

OK.

9:15

10/20   10/23

IRINA'S COMPUTER SERVICE
7000 Main Street
Houston, TX 77031

10/17/11 to 10/23/11

Kate Babic
000-23-4567

Salary   **$ 800.00**
Deductions
Federal   88.00
State   22.40
Social Security   51.00
Medicare   12.00
SDI   7.50
Net   **$ 619.10**

IRINA'S COMPUTER SERVICE   Check number:
7000 Main Street   123456789 999999999 123
Houston, TX 77031

Pay to the order of _____ Kate Babic _____ $ 619.10
Six hundred nineteen and 10/100 dollars

Town Bank   Irina Garkov

Ways to talk about wages

I **earn** $250 a week.
He **makes** $7 an hour.
I'm **paid** $1,000 a month.

Role play. Talk to an employer.

A: *Is everything correct on your paycheck?*
B: *No, it isn't. I make $250 a week, not $200.*
A: *Let's talk to the payroll clerk. Where is she?*

وظائف ومهن

1. accountant
محاسبة

2. actor
ممثل

3. administrative assistant
مساعدة إدارية

4. appliance repair person
أخصائي تصليح أدوات منزلية

5. architect
مهندسة معمارية

6. artist
فنّانة

7. assembler
أخصائي تجميع

8. auto mechanic
ميكانيكي سيارات

9. babysitter
حاضنة أطفال

10. baker
فرّانة / خبّازة

11. business owner
ربة أعمال / صاحبة أعمال

12. businessperson
رجل أعمال / سيدة أعمال

13. butcher
جزّار / لحّام

14. carpenter
نجّار

15. cashier
صرّاف / أمين صندوق

16. childcare worker
أخصائية حضانة أطفال

Ways to ask about someone's job

What's her job?
What does he do?
What kind of work do they do?

Pair practice. Make new conversations.

A: *What kind of work <u>does she</u> do?*
B: *<u>She's an accountant</u>. What <u>do they</u> do?*
A: *<u>They're actors</u>.*

 **17.** commercial fisher
صياد سمك تجاري

 **18.** computer software engineer
مهندسة مبرمجات كمبيوتر (حاسوب)

 **19.** computer technician
فني كمبيوترات (حواسيب)

 We have that shirt in red.
20. customer service representative
مندوب خدمة عملاء

 **21.** delivery person
عامل توصيل

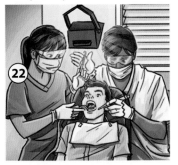 **22.** dental assistant
مساعدة طبيب أسنان

 **23.** dockworker
عامل مراكب

 **24.** electronics repair person
أخصائي تصليح أجهزة إلكترونية

 **25.** engineer
مهندس

 **26.** firefighter
إطفائي

 **27.** florist
بائعة زهور

 **28.** gardener
بستاني / جنايني

 **29.** garment worker
خياطة

 **30.** graphic designer
مصمم فنون تخطيطية

 **31.** hairdresser / hair stylist
مزينة شعر / مصففة شعر

 **32.** home health care aide
مساعدة رعاية صحية منزلية

Ways to talk about jobs and occupations

*Sue's a <u>garment worker</u>. She works **in** a factory.*
*Tom's <u>an engineer</u>. He works **for** <u>a large company</u>.*
*Ann's a <u>dental assistant</u>. She works **with** <u>a dentist</u>.*

Role play. Talk about a friend's new job.

A: *Does your friend like <u>his</u> new job?*
B: *Yes, <u>he</u> does. <u>He's a graphic designer</u>.*
A: *Does <u>he</u> work <u>in an office</u>?*

167

33. homemaker
ربة منزل

34. housekeeper
مدبرة منزل

你好

He says, "Hi."

35. interpreter / translator
مترجم شفهي / مترجم تحريري

36. lawyer
محامي

37. machine operator
عاملة ماكينات

38. manicurist
مزينة أظافر

39. medical records technician
فنية سجلات طبية

40. messenger / courier
مرسال / ساعي

41. model
عارضة أزياء

42. mover
عامل نقليات

43. musician
موسيقي

44. nurse
ممرضة

45. occupational therapist
أخصائية علاج مهني

46. (house) painter
دهّان (منازل)

47. physician assistant
مساعد طبيب

48. police officer
شرطية / ضابطة شرطة

Grammar Point: past tense of be

*I **was** a machine operator for 5 years.*
*She **was** a nurse for a year.*
*They **were** movers from 2003–2007.*

Pair practice. Make new conversations.

A: *What was your first job?*
B: *I was <u>a musician</u>. How about you?*
A: *I was <u>a messenger for a small company</u>.*

49. postal worker
موظف بريد

50. printer
عامل طباعة

51. receptionist
موظفة استقبال

52. reporter
مراسلة صحفية

53. retail clerk
موظف مبيعات

54. sanitation worker
عامل نظافة

55. security guard
حارسة أمن

56. server
نادلة

Here are some programs that will help you.

57. social worker
أخصائية اجتماعية

58. soldier
جندي

59. stock clerk
عامل جرد مخازن

Hello. I'm calling with a very special offer.

60. telemarketer
مسوّق بالهاتف / بالتليفون

61. truck driver
سائق شاحنة

62. veterinarian
طبيبة بيطرية

63. welder
لحّام

Norma's Story

64. writer / author
كاتبة / مؤلفة

Ask your classmates. Share the answers.

1. Which of these jobs could you do now?
2. What is one job you don't want to have?
3. Which jobs do you want to have?

Think about it. Discuss.

1. Which jobs need special training?
2. What kind of person makes a good interpreter? A good nurse? A good reporter? Why?

A. assemble components
يجمع/تجمع القطع

B. assist medical patients
يساعد المرضى

C. cook
يطبخ

D. do manual labor
يقوم بأعمال يدوية

E. drive a truck
يسوق شاحنة

F. fly a plane
يطير طائرة

G. make furniture
يصنع الأثاث

H. operate heavy machinery
يشغّل آلات ثقيلة

I. program computers
يبرمج كمبيوترات

J. repair appliances
يصلح أدوات منزلية

K. sell cars
يبيع سيارات
$4100

L. sew clothes
تخيّط ثيابا

M. solve math problems
تحلّ مسائل رياضيات
4% interest of 5K = x

N. speak another language
يتحدث لغة ثانية
ПРИВЕТ

O. supervise people
تشرف على موظفين

P. take care of children
تعتني بالأطفال

Q. teach
تعلّم / تدرّس

R. type
تطبع

S. use a cash register
تستخدم آلة تسجيل نقود

T. wait on customers
تقوم على خدمة الزبائن

Grammar Point: *can, can't*

I am a chef. I **can** cook.
I'm not a pilot. I **can't** fly a plane.
I **can't** speak French, but I **can** speak Spanish.

Role play. Talk to a job counselor.

A: *Tell me about your skills. Can you* type?
B: *No, I can't, but I* can use a cash register.
A: *OK. What other skills do you have?*

Customers need better service…

Scan Complete

Let's meet at 2:00.
Sure.

Dear Mr. Smith…

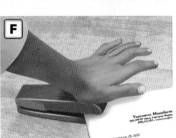
Hello. ABC Company. How may I help you?

Please hold.

Mr. Perez, I'm transferring you.

Hello. This is Sue Jones. Please call me.

Message Pad
Call From Ana Puerta
Tel: 555-1234
Message: Please Call

This is Lee Tran. Please call me back.

Office Skills
مهارات للعمل في مكتب

A. **type** a letter
تطبع رسالة

B. **enter** data
يدخل بيانات

C. **transcribe** notes
يستنسخ ملاحظات

D. **make** copies
يصنع/يعمل نسخا

E. **collate** papers
يرتّب أوراقا

F. **staple**
يخرز/يدبّس

G. **fax** a document
يرسل وثيقة بالفاكس

H. **scan** a document
ينسخ وثيقة بماسحة

I. **print** a document
يطبع وثيقة على طابعة

J. **schedule** a meeting
يحدد موعدا لاجتماع

K. **take** dictation
يأخذ مذكرات بالإملاء

L. **organize** materials
تنظم المواد

Telephone Skills
مهارات هاتفية / تليفونية

M. **greet** the caller
تحيّي الطالب

N. **put** the caller on hold
تحوّل الطالب إلى الانتظار

O. **transfer** the call
تحوّل المكالمة

P. **leave** a message
تترك رسالة

Q. **take** a message
تأخذ رسالة

R. **check** messages
تستمع إلى الرسائل

Career Path المسار الوظيفي

1. entry-level job
وظيفة لمبتدئ

2. training
تدريب

3. new job
وظيفة جديدة

4. promotion
ترقية

Types of Job Training أنواع التدريب الوظيفي

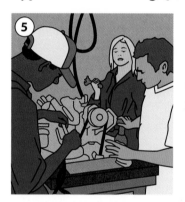

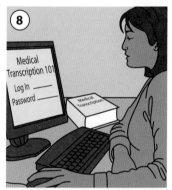

5. vocational training
تدريب حرفي

6. internship
تدريب داخلي

7. on-the-job training
تدريب أثناء أداء الوظيفة

8. online course
دورة مقدمة على الإنترنت

Planning a Career التخطيط لمسار وظيفي

9. resource center
مركز موارد

10. career counselor
استشاري في شؤون المسارات الوظيفية

11. interest inventory
جرد للاهتمامات

12. skill inventory
جرد للمهارات

13. job fair
معرض فرص العمل

14. recruiter
المسؤول عن توظيف موظفين جدد

Ways to talk about job training

I'm looking into an online course.
I'm interested in on-the-job training.
I want to sign up for an internship.

Ask your classmates. Share the answers.

1. What kind of job training are you interested in?
2. Would your rather learn English in an online course or in a classroom?

A. talk to friends / **network**

تحدّث مع أصدقاء / كوّن شبكة من الاتصالات

B. look in the classifieds

راجع الإعلانات المبوبة في الصحف

C. look for help wanted signs

ابحث عن لافتات الوظائف الشاغرة

D. check Internet job sites

راجع مواقع الإنترنت للبحث عن الوظائف الشاغرة

E. go to an employment agency

اذهب إلى مكتب توظيف

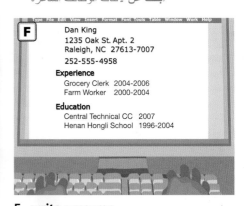

F. write a resume

اكتب خلاصة عن مهاراتك وانجازاتك

G. write a cover letter

اكتب خطابا تقديميا

H. send in your resume and cover letter

أرسل سيرتك الذاتية وخطابك التقديمي

I. set up an interview

حدد موعدا لمقابلة شخصية

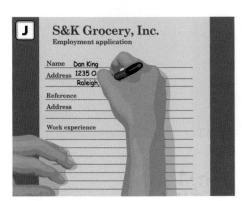

J. fill out an application

املأ طلب التقدم لوظيفة

K. go on an interview

اذهب إلى المقابلة الشخصية

L. get hired

احصل على الوظيفة

A. **Prepare** for the interview.
استعد للمقابلة.

B. **Dress** appropriately.
البس ملابس مناسبة.

C. **Be** neat.
كن مهندما.

D. **Bring** your resume and ID.
أحضر معك سيرتك الذاتية وهويتك.

E. **Don't be** late.
لا تتأخر عن الميعاد.

F. **Be** on time.
صِل في الموعد المحدد.

G. **Turn off** your cell phone.
أغلق هاتفك / تليفونك المحمول.

H. **Greet** the interviewer.
حيّي الشخص القائم بالمقابلة.

I. **Shake** hands.
صافحها باليد.

Hello, I'm Elias Ortiz.

Hello, Mr. Ortiz. I'm Mrs. Perez.

J. **Make** eye contact.
انظر مباشرة في عينيها.

K. **Listen** carefully.
استمع إليها بعناية.

L. **Talk** about your experience.
تحدث عن خبرتك.

Computer skills are important.

I have those skills.

I worked with computers on my last job.

M. **Ask** questions.
اطرح أسئلة.

N. **Thank** the interviewer.
اشكر الشخص القائم بالمقابلة.

O. **Write** a thank-you note.
اكتب رسالة شكر.

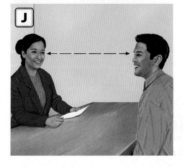

Do you offer training?

Thank you for your time.

Dear Mrs. Perez, Thank you for the opportunity to meet with you.

More vocabulary

benefits: health insurance, vacation pay, or other things the employer can offer an employee
inquire about benefits: ask about benefits

Think about it. Discuss.

1. How can you prepare for an interview?
2. Why is it important to make eye contact?
3. What kinds of questions should you ask?

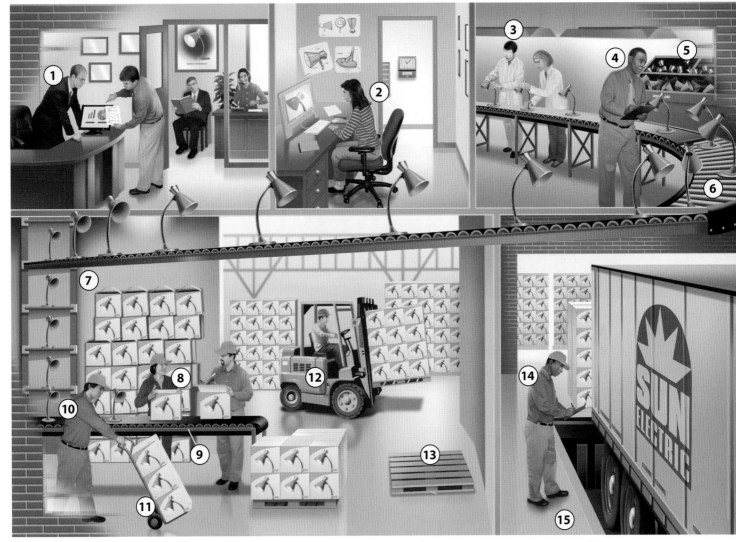

1. factory owner صاحب المصنع	**5. parts** قطع	**9. conveyer belt** سير ناقل	**13. pallet** منصة نقالة
2. designer مصمم	**6. assembly line** خط تجميع	**10. order puller** مسؤول إحضار الطلبات	**14. shipping clerk** موظف مسؤول عن الشحن
3. factory worker عامل بالمصنع	**7. warehouse** مستودع	**11. hand truck** عربة نقل يدوية	**15. loading dock** رصيف تحميل
4. line supervisor مشرف على خط التجميع	**8. packer** عامل تعبئة	**12. forklift** مرفاع شوكي	

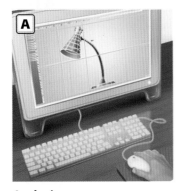

A. design
يصمم

B. manufacture
يصنَع

C. assemble
يجمَع

D. ship
يشحن

Bloom Nursery

1. **gardening crew**
   طاقم البستنة

2. **leaf blower**
   نافخ أوراق الشجر

3. **wheelbarrow**
   عربة يد ذات عجلة واحدة

4. **gardening crew leader**
   ملاحظ طاقم البستنة

5. **landscape designer**
   مصممة تزيين الأراضي

6. **lawn mower**
   جزازة العشب

7. **shovel**
   جاروف

8. **rake** مدمّة / أداة لجمع العشب

9. **pruning shears**
   مجزة تشذيب

10. **trowel**
    مالج

11. **hedge clippers**
    مقلّمة الوشيع (الشجيرات)

12. **weed whacker / weed eater**
    قاطع العشب / آكل العشب

A. **mow** the lawn
يجز المرجة

B. **trim** the hedges
تقلّم الوشيع (الشجيرات)

C. **rake** the leaves
يجمع أوراق الشجر بالمدمّة

D. **fertilize / feed** the plants
يسمّد / يغذّي النباتات

E. **plant** a tree
تزرع شجرة

F. **water** the plants
تسقي الزرع

G. **weed** the flower beds
يقتلع العشب من أحواض الزهور

H. **install** a sprinkler system
يركّب نظاما لرش المياه

Use the new words.
Look at page 53. Name what you can do in the yard.

A: *I can <u>mow the lawn</u>.*
B: *I can <u>weed the flower bed</u>.*

Ask your classmates. Share the answers.

1. Do you know someone who does landscaping? Who?
2. Do you enjoy gardening? Why or why not?
3. Which gardening activity is the hardest to do? Why?

Crops المحاصيل

1. rice	2. wheat	3. soybeans	4. corn	5. alfalfa	6. cotton
أرز	قمح	فول الصويا	ذُرة	فصفصة	قطن

7. field
حقل

12. farm equipment
معدات مزرعة

17. corral
زريبة

22. rancher
مربي مواشي

8. farmworker
عامل مزرعة

13. farmer / grower
مزارع / فلاح

18. hay
قش / برسيم

A. **plant**
يزرع

9. tractor
جرّارة (تراكتور)

14. vegetable garden
حديقة خضروات

19. fence
سياج

B. **harvest**
يحصد

10. orchard
بستان فاكهة

15. livestock
مواشي

20. hired hand
مستخدم مساعد

C. **milk**
يحلب

11. barn
حظيرة

16. vineyard
كرمة

21. cattle
ماشية

D. **feed**
يعلف / يقدم العلف

1. construction worker
عامل بناء

2. ladder
سلم

3. I beam/girder
عارضة

4. scaffolding
سقالة

5. cherry picker
رافعة ذات ذراع طويل

6. bulldozer
جرافة لشق الطرق (بولدوزر)

7. crane
مرفاع (ونش)

8. backhoe
مجرفة خلفية

9. jackhammer / pneumatic drill
ثقّابة آلية / آلة حفر بالهواء المضغوط

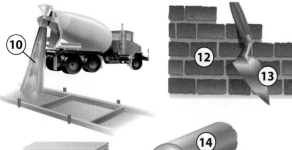

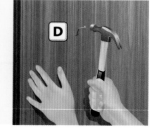

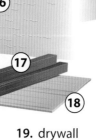

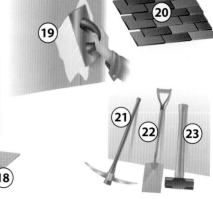

10. concrete
خرسانة

11. tile
بلاط

12. bricks
قرميد / طوب

13. trowel
مالج

14. insulation
مواد عازلة

15. stucco
جص

16. window pane
لوح زجاجي في نافذة

17. wood / lumber
خشب

18. plywood
خشب رقائقي

19. drywall
جدار داخلي

20. shingles
لويحات تسقيف

21. pickax
معول

22. shovel
جاروف

23. sledgehammer
مطرقة ثقيلة / مرزبة

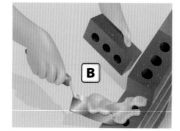

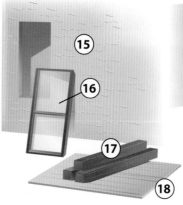

A. paint
يطلي / يدهن

B. lay bricks
يرصد القرميد (الطوب)

C. install tile
يركّب البلاط

D. hammer
يدق بالمطرقة

Safety Hazards and Hazardous Materials الأخطار على السلامة والمواد الخطرة

1. careless worker عامل غير محترس	**3. poisonous fumes** أبخرة سامة	**5. frayed cord** سلك تالف	**7. radioactive materials** مواد مشعة
2. careful worker عامل محترس	**4. broken equipment** معدات مكسورة	**6. slippery floor** أرضية زلقة	**8. flammable liquids** سوائل قابلة للاشتعال

Safety Equipment معدات السلامة

9. hard hat قبعة صلبة	**13. respirator** كمامة ضد الغازات السامة	**17. work gloves** قفازات عمل	**21. fire extinguisher** مطفئة حريق
10. safety glasses نظارات سلامة	**14. particle mask** قناع واقٍ من الجسيمات	**18. back support belt** حزام لدعم الظهر	**22. two-way radio** جهاز لاسلكي مرسل ومستقبل
11. safety goggles منظار واقٍ	**15. ear plugs** سدادة أذن	**19. knee pads** لبادات للركب	
12. safety visor قناع واقٍ	**16. earmuffs** واقية الأذان	**20. safety boots** حذاء وقاية	

HAND TOOLS

HARDWARE

POWER TOOLS

1. hammer	**4.** handsaw	**7.** pliers	**10.** jigsaw
مطرقة	منشار يدوي	زردية	منشار منحنيات
2. mallet	**5.** hacksaw	**8.** electric drill	**11.** power sander
مطرقة خشبية	منشار معادن	مثقاب كهربائي	ماكينة سنفرة للتنعيم
3. ax	**6.** C-clamp	**9.** circular saw	**12.** router
فأس	قامطة تثبيت	منشار دائري	مسحاج تخديد

26. vise	**30.** screwdriver	**34.** nail	**38.** toggle bolt
منجلة / ملزمة	مفك براغي	مسمار	مسمار العقدة
27. blade	**31.** Phillips screwdriver	**35.** bolt	**39.** hook
نصلة / شفرة	مفك براغي مصلّب الرأس	مسمار ملولب	خطّاف / كلاب
28. drill bit	**32.** machine screw	**36.** nut	**40.** eye hook
لقمة ثقب	برغي ربط ملولب	صمولة	خطاف عروة
29. level	**33.** wood screw	**37.** washer	**41.** chain
ميزان بنائين / شلقول	برغي خشب	فلكة	سلسلة

Use the new words.	**Ask your classmates. Share the answers.**
Look at pages 62–63. Name the tools you see.	1. Are you good with tools?
A: *There's a hammer.*	2. Which tools do you have at home?
B: *There's a pipe wrench.*	3. Where can you shop for building supplies?

ELECTRICAL   PLUMBING   LUMBER   PAINT

13. wire
سلك

14. extension cord
سلك تمديد

15. bungee cord
حبل مطاطي

16. yardstick
عصا الياردة

17. pipe
أنبوب / ماسورة

18. fittings
تجهيزات

19. 2 x 4 (two by four)
لوح خشبي مقاس ٢ بوصة
× ٤ بوصة

20. particle board
لوح خشب حبيبي

21. spray gun
مرشة

22. paintbrush
فرشاة طلاء

23. paint roller
فرشاة طلاء أسطوانية

24. wood stain
صبغة للخشب

25. paint
دهان / طلاء

42. wire stripper
مقشرة أسلاك

43. electrical tape
شريط لاصق للأسلاك الكهربائية

44. work light
ضوء عمل (بلادوس)

45. tape measure
شريط قياس

46. outlet cover
غطاء مأخذ التيار الكهربائي

47. pipe wrench
مفتاح أنابيب

48. adjustable wrench
مفتاح ربط قابل للضبط

49. duct tape
شريط شديد اللصق

50. plunger
كباس

51. paint pan
صينية طلاء

52. scraper
مكشطة

53. masking tape
شريط لاصق للتغطية

54. drop cloth
قماش من القنب لوقاية الأثاث والأرضية

55. chisel
إزميل

56. sandpaper
ورق سنفرة

57. plane
مسحاج / فأرة النجار

Role play. Find an item in a building supply store.

A: *Where can I find particle board?*
B: *It's on the back wall, in the lumber section.*
A: *Great. And where are the nails?*

Think about it. Discuss.

1. Which tools are the most important to have? Why?
2. Which tools can be dangerous? Why?
3. Do you borrow tools from friends? Why or why not?

181

GREEN ENERGY CORPORATION

EMPLOYEE SCHEDULE
Ben Hasler 10/11/07
Dan Green 12/11/07

1. supply cabinet خزانة المؤن	**5.** executive مسؤولة تنفيذية	**9.** desk مكتب	**13.** PBX نظام تحويل هاتفي / تليفوني
2. clerk موظف	**6.** presentation عرض	**10.** file clerk موظف تنظيم الملفات	**14.** receptionist موظفة الاستقبال
3. janitor حاجب	**7.** cubicle مقصورة	**11.** file cabinet خزانة ملفات	**15.** reception area منطقة الاستقبال
4. conference room غرفة مؤتمرات	**8.** office manager مدير مكتب	**12.** computer technician فني كمبيوتر (حاسوب)	**16.** waiting area منطقة الانتظار

Ways to greet a receptionist

I'm here for a <u>job interview</u>.
I have a <u>9:00 a.m.</u> appointment with <u>Mr. Lee</u>.
I'd like to leave a message <u>for Mr. Lee</u>.

Role play. Talk to a receptionist.

A: *Hello. How can I help you?*
B: *<u>I'm here for a job interview with Mr. Lee</u>.*
A: *OK. What is your name?*

Office Equipment معدات المكتب

17. computer
كمبيوتر (حاسوب)

18. inkjet printer
طابعة نفاثة للحبر

19. laser printer
طابعة ليزر

20. scanner
ماسحة

21. fax machine
جهاز فاكس

22. paper cutter
قاطعة أوراق

23. photocopier
ماكينة تصوير مستندات

24. paper shredder
آلة تمزيق الورق

25. calculator
آلة حاسبة

26. electric pencil sharpener
مبراة أقلام كهربائية

27. postal scale
ميزان بريدي

Office Supplies مستلزمات المكتب

28. stapler
خرازة / دباسة

29. staples
خرزات / دبابيس من السلك

30. clear tape
شريط لاصق بدون لون

31. paper clip
مشبك ورق

32. packing tape
شريط حزم لاصق

33. glue
صمغ

34. rubber band
طوق (شريط) مطاطي

35. pushpin
دبوس كبسي

36. correction fluid
سائل تصحيح

37. correction tape
شريط تصحيح

38. legal pad
كراسة ورق طويل

39. sticky notes
مذكرات لاصقة

40. mailer
مغلف بريد

41. mailing label
بطاقة تعريف بريدية

42. letterhead / stationery
ورق طبع في رأسه اسم المؤسسة / قرطاسية

43. envelope
ظرف / مغلف

44. rotary card file
ملف بطاقات دوار

45. ink cartridge
خرطوشة حبر

46. ink pad
لبادة تحبير / مختمة

47. stamp
ختم

48. appointment book
دفتر مواعيد

49. organizer
دفتر منظم

50. file folder
حافظة ملفات / دوسيه

183

1. **doorman**
بواب

2. **revolving door**
باب دوار

3. **parking attendant**
خادم لإيقاف السيارات

4. **concierge**
حاجب / ناطور

5. **gift shop**
محل هدايا

6. **bell captain**
رئيس مستخدمي حمل الأمتعة

7. **bellhop**
خادم فندق

8. **luggage cart**
عربة لنقل الأمتعة

9. **elevator**
مصعد

10. **guest**
نزيل

11. **desk clerk**
موظف فندق

12. **front desk**
مكتب الاستقبال والتسجيل

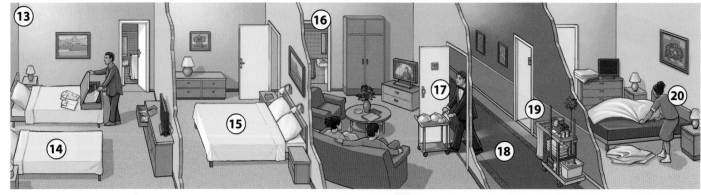

13. **guest room**
غرفة نزيل

14. **double bed**
غرفة بسريرين

15. **king-size bed**
سرير واحد ضخم

16. **suite**
جناح

17. **room service**
خدمة غرف

18. **hallway**
رواق

19. **housekeeping cart**
عربة تجهيز وتنظيف الغرف

20. **housekeeper**
عاملة تجهيز وتنظيف الغرف

21. **pool service**
خدمات المسبح (حمّام السباحة)

22. **pool**
مسبح / حمّام سباحة

23. **maintenance**
صيانة

24. **gym**
مركز جمباز (جمنازيوم)

25. **meeting room**
قاعة اجتماعات

26. **ballroom**
قاعة حفلات

A Restaurant Kitchen المطبخ في مطعم

1. short-order cook
طباخ الطعام السريع

2. dishwasher
غاسل الصحون

3. walk-in freezer
مجمِّد ضخم يمكن السير فيه

4. food preparation worker
عامل تحضير الطعام

5. storeroom
غرفة تخزين

6. sous chef
نائب رئيس الطهاة
(سو شيف)

7. head chef / executive chef
رئيس الطهاة (شيف)

Restaurant Dining تناول الطعام في مطعم

8. server
نادلة / جرسونة

9. diner
زبونة

10. buffet
بوفيه

11. maitre d'
مدير صالة الطعام

12. headwaiter
رئيس الجرسونات / رئيس النوادل

13. bus person
مساعدة النادل

14. banquet room
قاعة الولائم

15. runner
ساعي

16. caterer
ممونة أطعمة

More vocabulary

line cook: short-order cook

wait staff: servers, headwaiters, and runners

Ask your classmates. Share the answers.

1. Have you ever worked in a hotel? What did you do?
2. What is the hardest job in a hotel?
3. Would you prefer to stay at a hotel in the city or in the country?

1. dangerous
   خطير

2. clinic
   عيادة

3. budget
   ميزانية

4. floor plan
   مخطط (تصميم) طابق في مبنى

5. contractor
   مقاول

6. electrical hazard
   خطر كهربائي

7. wiring
   ضفيرة أسلاك

8. bricklayer
   راصد قرميد

A. **call in** sick
   اتصل واطلب أجازة مرضية

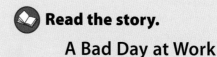

HEALTH CENTER

HARD HAT AREA

Look at the picture. What do you see?

Answer the questions.

1. How many workers are there? How many are working?

2. Why did two workers call in sick?

3. What is dangerous at the construction site?

📖 Read the story.

A Bad Day at Work

Sam Lopez is the <u>contractor</u> for a new building. He makes the schedule and supervises the <u>budget</u>. He also solves problems. Today there are a lot of problems.

Two <u>bricklayers</u> <u>called in sick</u> this morning. Now Sam has only one bricklayer at work. One hour later, a construction worker fell. Now he has to go to the <u>clinic</u>. Sam always tells his workers to be careful. Construction work is <u>dangerous</u>. Sam's also worried because the new <u>wiring</u> is an <u>electrical hazard</u>.

Right now, the building owner is in Sam's office. Her new <u>floor plan</u> has 25 more offices. Sam has a headache. Maybe he needs to call in sick tomorrow.

Think about it.

1. What do you say when you can't come in to work? to school?

2. Imagine you are Sam. What do you tell the building owner? Why?

Schools and Subjects

مدارس ومواد الدراسة

1. preschool / nursery school
حضانة

2. elementary school
مدرسة ابتدائية

3. middle school / junior high school
مدرسة إعدادية

4. high school
مدرسة ثانوية

5. vocational school / technical school
مدرسة حرفية / مدرسة تقنية

6. community college
كلية أهلية

7. college / university
كلية / جامعة

8. adult school
مدرسة للكبار

Listen and point. Take turns.

A: *Point to the preschool.*
B: *Point to the high school.*
A: *Point to the adult school.*

Dictate to your partner. Take turns.

A: *Write preschool.*
B: *Is that p-r-e-s-c-h-o-o-l?*
A: *Yes. That's right.*

188

9. language arts
فنون اللغات

10. math
رياضيات

11. science
علوم

12. history
تاريخ

13. world languages
لغات العالم

14. ESL / ESOL
الإنجليزية كلغة ثانية /
الإنجليزية لمتحدثي
اللغات الأخرى

15. arts
فنون

16. music
موسيقى

17. physical education
تربية بدنية

More vocabulary

core course: a subject students have to take. Math is a core course.

elective: a subject students choose to take. Art is an elective.

Pair practice. Make new conversations.

A: I go to <u>community college</u>.

B: What subjects are you taking?

A: I'm taking <u>history</u> and <u>science</u>.

189

1 factory

2 I worked in a factory.

3 Little by little, work and success came to me. My first job wasn't good. I worked in a small factory. Now, I help manage two factories.

4

1. word
كلمة

2. sentence
جملة

3. paragraph
فقرة

4. essay
مقال

Parts of an Essay
أجزاء المقال

5. title
عنوان

6. introduction
مقدمة

7. body
نص

8. conclusion
ختام

9. quotation
اقتباس

10. footnote
تذييل

Carlos Lopez
Eng. Comp.
10/21/10

5 Success in the U.S.

6 I came to Los Angeles from Mexico in 2006. I had no job, no friends, and no family here. I was homesick and scared, but I did not go home. I took English classes (always at night) and I studied hard. I believed in my future success!

7 More than 400,000 new immigrants come to the U.S every year.[1] Most of us need to find work. During my first year here, my routine was the same: get up; look for work; go to class; go to bed. I had to take jobs with long hours and low pay. Often I had two or three jobs.

Little by little, work and success came to me. My first job wasn't good. I worked in a small factory. Now, I help manage two factories.

8 Hard work makes success possible. Henry David Thoreau said, **9** "Men are born to succeed, not fail." My story shows that he was right.

10 [1] U.S. Census

Punctuation
علامات الوقف والترقيم

11. period
نقطة
.

12. question mark
علامة استفهام
?

13. exclamation mark
علامة تعجب
!

14. comma
فاصلة
,

15. quotation marks
علامات اقتباس
" "

16. apostrophe
فاصلة عليا
'

17. colon
نقطتان
:

18. semicolon
فاصلة منقوطة
;

19. parentheses
قوسان
( )

20. hyphen
شُرطة
-

Writing Rules قواعد الكتابة

A

Carlos
Mexico
Los Angeles

A. Capitalize names.
اكتب الأسماء بحروف كبيرة.

B

Hard work makes success possible.

B. Capitalize the first letter in a sentence.
اكتب الحرف الأول في الجملة بحرف كبير.

C

I was homesick and scared, but I did not go home.

C. Use punctuation.
استخدم علامة الوقف والترقيم.

D

I came to Los Angeles from Mexico in 2006. I had no job, no friends, and no family here. I was homesick and scared, but I did not go home. I took English classes (always at night) and I studied hard. I believed in my future success!

D. Indent the first sentence in a paragraph.
اترك فراغا في سطر أول جملة في فقرة جديدة.

Ways to ask for suggestions on your compositions

What do you think of this title?
Is this paragraph OK? Is the punctuation correct?
Do you have any suggestions for the conclusion?

Pair practice. Make new conversations.

A: *What do you think of this title?*
B: *I think you need to revise it.*
A: *Thanks. Do you have any more suggestions?*

The Writing Process عملية الكتابة

PREWRITING

E. **Think about** the assignment.
فكَّر في المهمة.

F. **Brainstorm** ideas.
اطرح لنفسك أفكارا وتمعن فيها.

G. **Organize** your ideas.
نظم أفكارك.

WRITING AND REVISING

H. **Write** a first draft.
اكتب مسودة أولى.

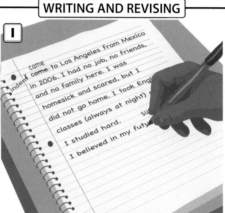

I. **Edit**. / **Proofread**.
نقِّح. / دقِّق.

J. **Revise**. / **Rewrite**.
راجع. / أعد الكتابة.

SHARING AND RESPONDING

K. **Get** feedback.
احصل على رأي شخص آخر.

L. **Write** a final draft.
اكتب مسودة نهائية.

M. **Turn in** your paper.
سلِّم ورقتك.

Ask your classmates. Share the answers.

1. Do you like to write essays?
2. Which part of the writing process do you like best? least?

Think about it. Discuss.

1. In which jobs are writing skills important?
2. What tools can help you edit your writing?
3. What are some good subjects for essays?

Mathematics الرياضيات

Integers الأعداد الصحيحة

...−4 −3 −2 −1 0 1 2 3 4...

(1) (2)

1. negative integers
أعداد صحيحة سالبة

2. positive integers
أعداد صحيحة موجبة

Fractions الكسور

(3) 1, 3, 5, 7, 9, 11...

(4) 2, 4, 6, 8, 10 ...

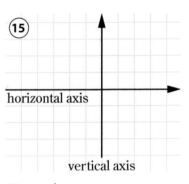

3. odd numbers
أرقام فردية

4. even numbers
أرقام زوجية

5. numerator
البسط

6. denominator
المقام

Math Operations عمليات رياضية

A. **add**
اجمع

B. **subtract**
اطرح

C. **multiply**
اضرب

D. **divide**
اقسم

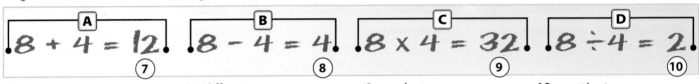

$8 + 4 = 12$ (A) (7)

$8 − 4 = 4$ (B) (8)

$8 × 4 = 32$ (C) (9)

$8 ÷ 4 = 2$ (D) (10)

7. sum
المجموع

8. difference
الفرق

9. product
الحاصل

10. quotient
خارج القسمة

A Math Problem مسألة رياضية

(11)
Tom is 10 years older than Kim. Next year he will be twice as old as Kim. How old is Tom this year?

(12) — x = Kim's age now
$x + 10$ = Tom's age now
$x + 1$ = Kim's age next year
$2(x + 1)$ = Tom's age next year

$x + 10 + 1 = 2(x + 1)$
$x + 11 = 2x + 2$ (13)
$11 − 2 = 2x − x$

$x = 9$, Kim is 9, Tom is 19 (14)

(15)
horizontal axis
vertical axis

11. word problem
مسألة كلامية

12. variable
متغير

13. equation
معادلة

14. solution
حل

15. graph
مخطط بياني

Types of Math أنواع الرياضيات

(16) How much are they?

x = the sale price
x = 79.00 − .40 (79.00)
x = $47.40

16. algebra
الجبر

(17) How many do I need?

area of path = 24 square ft.
area of brick = 2 square ft.
24/2 = 12 bricks

17. geometry
الهندسة

(18) How tall is it?

14 ft.

$\tan 63° = $ height / 14 feet
height = 14 feet $(\tan 63°)$
height $\simeq$ 27.48 feet

18. trigonometry
حساب المثلثات

(19) When will the rocket reach maximum height?

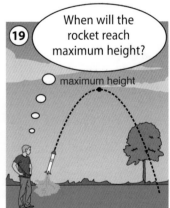

maximum height

$s(t) = -½ gt^2 + V_0 t + h$
$s^I(t) = -gt + V_0 = 0$
$t = V_0 / g$

19. calculus
التفاضل والتكامل

Lines الخطوط

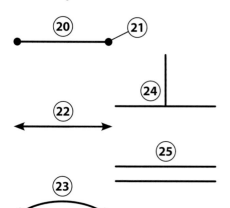

Angles الزوايا

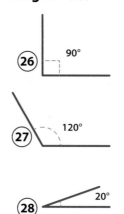

Shapes الأشكال

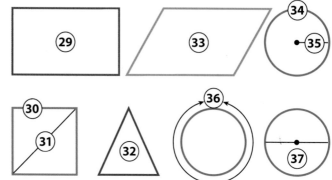

20. line segment
مقطع من خط

21. endpoint
نقطة نهاية

22. straight line
خط مستقيم

23. curved line
خط منحني

24. perpendicular lines
خطوط متعامدة

25. parallel lines
خطوط متوازية

26. right angle / 90° angle
زاوية مستقيمة / زاوية ٩٠°

27. obtuse angle
زاوية منفرجة

28. acute angle
زاوية حادة

29. rectangle
مستطيل

30. square
مربع

31. diagonal
منحرف

32. triangle
مثلث

33. parallelogram
متوازي أضلاع

34. circle
دائرة

35. radius
نصف قطر

36. circumference
محيط

37. diameter
قطر

Geometric Solids
الأشكال الهندسية المجسمة

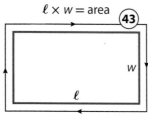

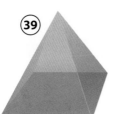

Measuring Area and Volume
قياس المساحة والحجم

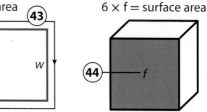

$\ell \times w = area$

$6 \times f = surface\ area$

38. cube
مكعب

39. pyramid
هرم

40. cone
مخروط

43. perimeter
محيط خارجي

44. face
وجه

$\pi \times r^2 \times h = volume$

$\frac{4}{3} \times \pi \times r^3 = volume$

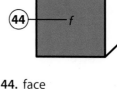

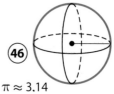

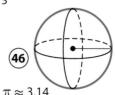

$\pi \approx 3.14$

41. cylinder
أسطوانة

42. sphere
كرة

45. base
قاعدة

46. pi
باي (الرمز الذي يمثل النسبة بين طول
محيط الدائرة وقطرها)

Ask your classmates. Share the answers.

1. Are you good at math?
2. Which types of math are easy for you?
3. Which types of math are difficult for you?

Think about it. Discuss.

1. What's the best way to learn mathematics?
2. How can you find the area of your classroom?
3. Which jobs use math? Which don't?

Biology   علم الأحياء (بيولوجيا)

1. organisms
   كائنات حية
2. biologist
   أحياني (عالم بيولوجيا)
3. slide
   شريحة
4. cell
   خلية
5. cell wall
   جدار الخلية
6. cell membrane
   غشاء الخلية
7. nucleus
   نواة
8. chromosome
   صبغي (كروموسوم)
9. cytoplasm
   هيلولى

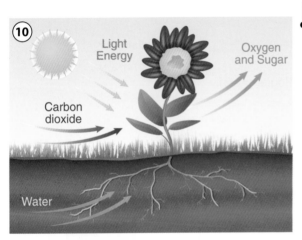

10. photosynthesis
    تخليق ضوئي
11. habitat
    مَوئل
12. vertebrates
    فقاريات
13. invertebrates
    لافقاريات

A Microscope   مجهر (ميكروسكوب)

14. eyepiece
    عَينيّة المِجْهَر
15. revolving nosepiece
    أنْفِيَّة المِجْهَر الدوارة
16. objective
    الشَّيئيَّة (عدسة المجهر)
17. stage
    رف في المجهر
18. diaphragm
    الحجاب
19. light source
    مصدر ضوئي
20. base
    قاعدة
21. stage clips
    مشبك الرف
22. fine adjustment knob
    مقبض تعديل دقيق
23. arm
    ذراع
24. coarse adjustment knob
    مقبض تعديل تقريبي

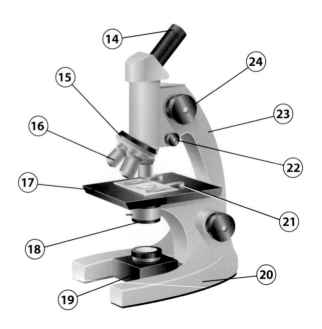

Chemistry الكيمياء

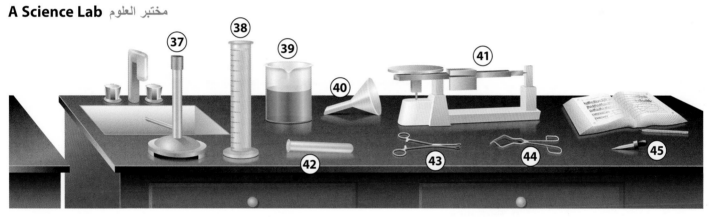

25. chemist
كيميائي (عالم كيمياء)

26. periodic table
الجدول الدوري

27. molecule
جزيء

28. atom
ذَرَّة

29. nucleus
نواة

30. electron
إلكترون

31. proton
بروتون

32. neutron
نيوترون

33. physicist
فيزيائية (عالمة طبيعة)

Physics (الفيزياء) علم الطبيعة

$$c = f\lambda$$

f = frequency
λ = wavelength

34. formula
معادلة / صيغة

35. prism
موشور / منشور زجاجي

36. magnet
مغنطيس

A Science Lab مختبر العلوم

37. Bunsen burner
حاروق/ملهب بنزن

38. graduated cylinder
أنبوب مدرج

39. beaker
كوب صيدلي

40. funnel
قمع

41. balance / scale
ميزان

42. test tube
أنبوب اختبار

43. forceps
كلاّب

44. crucible tongs
ملقط بوتقي

45. dropper
قطّارة

An Experiment تجربة

Salt and sugar crystals will grow the same way.

SALT   SUGAR

SALT   SUGAR

salt crystal

Salt crystals grow faster than sugar crystals.

A. State a hypothesis.
تُبسط / تطرح فرضية.

B. Do an experiment.
تقوم بإجراء تجربة.

C. Observe.
تراقب.

D. Record the results.
تسجل النتائج.

E. Draw a conclusion.
تصل إلى خلاصة.

Desktop Computer الكمبيوتر المكتبي

1. surge protector
جهاز ضد اشتداد التيار

2. power cord
سلك الطاقة

3. tower
صندوق وحدة المعالجة المركزية

4. microprocessor / CPU
معالج صغير (ميكروبروسيسور)
/ وحدة المعالجة المركزية

5. motherboard
اللوح الأم

6. hard drive
محرك القرص الصلب

7. USB port
منفذ الناقل التسلسلي العام (منفذ
يو إس بي)

8. flash drive
محرك أقراص محمول

9. DVD and CD-ROM drive
محرك قرص دي في دي و سي
دي روم

10. software
مبرمجات

11. monitor /screen
شاشة

12. webcam
كاميرا فيديو كمبيوترية

13. cable
كبل

14. keyboard
لوحة مفاتيح

15. mouse
فأرة (ماوس)

16. laptop
كمبيوتر محمول

17. printer
طابعة

Keyboarding الكتابة على لوحة المفاتيح

A. type
يطبع

B. select
ينتقي

C. delete
ينتقي

D. go to the next line
ينتقل إلى السطر التالي

196

Navigating a Webpage تصفُّح موقع على الإنترنت

1. menu bar
   شريط القوائم

2. back button
   زر الرجوع إلى الصفحة السابقة

3. forward button
   زر التقدم إلى الصفحة التالية

4. URL / website address
   محدد موقع المصدر العالمي /
   عنوان موقع الإنترنت

5. search box
   صندوق/خانة البحث

6. search engine
   محرك بحث

7. tab
   تبويب

8. drop-down menu
   قائمة منسدلة

9. pop-up ad
   دعاية منبثقة

10. links
    رابطات / وصلات

11. video player
    مشغّل فيديو

12. pointer
    مؤشر

13. text box
    مربع نصي

14. cursor
    مؤشر

15. scroll bar
    شريط التمرير

Logging on and Sending Email التسجيل وإرسال بريد إلكتروني

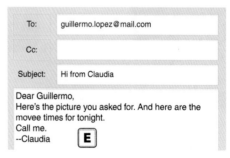

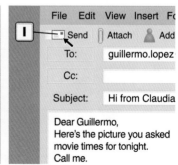

A. **type** your password
   اطبع/أدخل كلمة المرور الخاصة بك

B. **click** "sign in"
   انقر زر "تسجيل" "sign in"

C. **address** the email
   أدخل عنوان البريد الإلكتروني للمرسل إليه

D. **type** the subject
   اطبع/ أدخل موضوع الرسالة

E. **type** the message
   اطبع/ أدخل نص الرسالة

F. **check** your spelling
   راجع هجانك

G. **attach** a picture
   أرفق صورة

H. **attach** a file
   أرفق ملفا

I. **send** the email
   أرسل البريد الإلكتروني

Colonial Period فترة الاستعمار

New Hampshire
Massachusetts
Connecticut
New York
Rhode Island
Pennsylvania
New Jersey
Delaware
Virginia
Maryland
North Carolina
South Carolina
Georgia

1. thirteen colonies
ثلاث عشرة مستعمرة

2. colonists
المستعمرون

3. Native Americans
الأمريكيون الأصليون

4. slave
عبد

5. Declaration of Independence
إعلان الاستقلال

6. First Continental Congress
الكونجرس القاري الأول

7. founders
الآباء المؤسسون

8. Revolutionary War
الحرب الثورية / حرب الاستقلال

9. redcoat
جندي بريطاني

10. minuteman
جندي هوّاري على استعداد للحرب بإنذار دقيقة واحدة

11. first president
أول رئيس

12. Constitution
الدستور

13. Bill of Rights
ميثاق الحقوق

Western Expansion
1803 – 1893

Civil War
1861 – 1865

World War I
1914 – 1918

Jazz Age
1920 – 1929

World War II
1941 – 1945

Civil Rights Movement
1954 – 1972

Information Age
1959 – now

1800   1850   1900   1950   2000 →

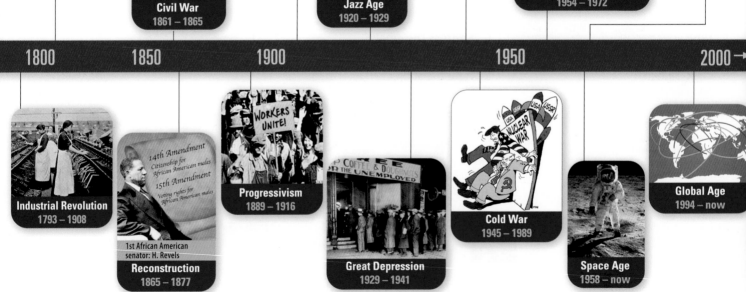

Industrial Revolution
1793 – 1908

14th Amendment
Citizenship for African American males
15th Amendment
Voting rights for African American males
1st African American senator: H. Revels
Reconstruction
1865 – 1877

WORKERS UNITE!
Progressivism
1889 – 1916

COFFEE & DOUGHNUTS
FOR THE UNEMPLOYED
Great Depression
1929 – 1941

NUCLEAR WAR
USA USSR
Cold War
1945 – 1989

Space Age
1958 – now

Global Age
1994 – now

Civilizations الحضارات

Pyramids | Parthenon
(1)
(2)
Times Square

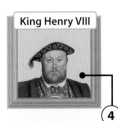
Caesar

King Henry VIII

Qin Shi Huang
(3)

Queen Elizabeth I
(4)

(5)
Juarez

Mussolini
(6)

Churchill
(7)

1. ancient
قديمة

2. modern
حديثة

3. emperor
إمبراطور

4. monarch
ملك

5. president
رئيس

6. dictator
دكتاتور

7. prime minister
رئيس وزراء

Historical Terms مصطلحات تاريخية

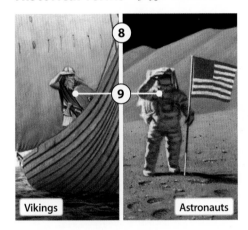
(8)
(9)
Vikings | Astronauts

(10)
(11)

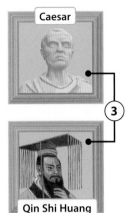
(12)
(13)

8. exploration
استكشاف

9. explorer
مستكشف

10. war
حرب

11. army
جيش

12. immigration
هجرة

13. immigrant
مهاجر

(14)
(15)
Mozart | Duke Ellington

(16)
(17)
Susan B. Anthony | César Chávez

(18)
(19)
Edison | Camarena

14. composer
مؤلف موسيقي / ملحّن

15. composition
تأليف موسيقي / مؤلّفة موسيقية

16. political movement
حركة سياسية

17. activist
ناشط سياسيا

18. inventor
مخترع

19. invention
اختراع

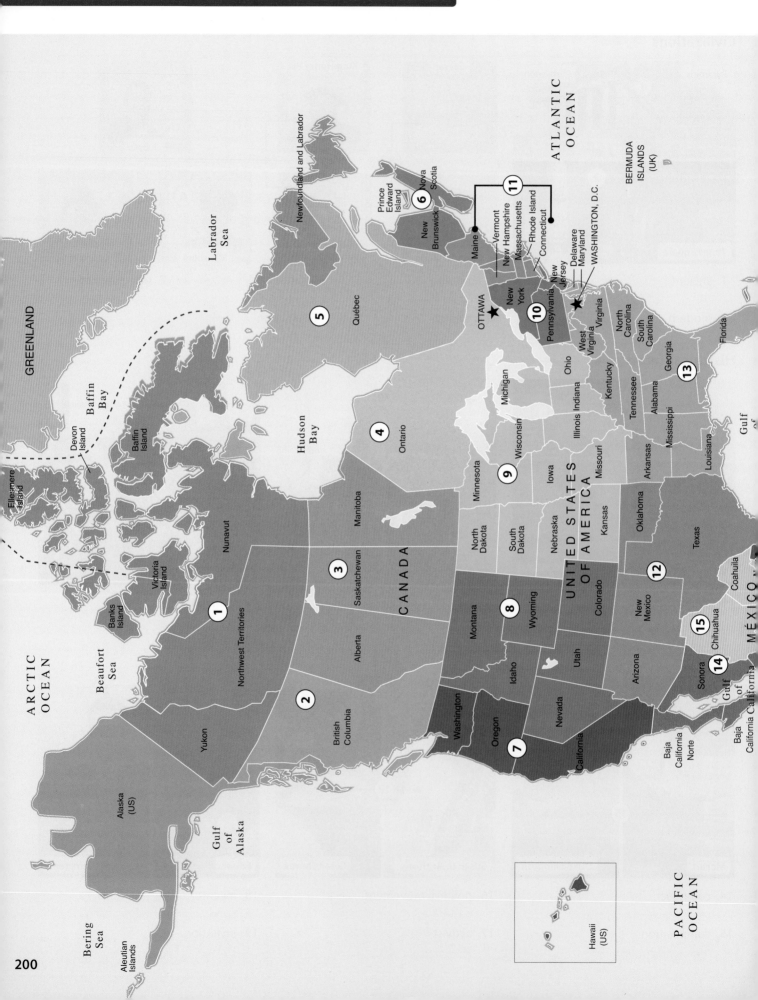

ATLANTIC OCEAN

GREENLAND

BERMUDA ISLANDS (UK)

Labrador Sea

Newfoundland and Labrador

Prince Edward Island

Nova Scotia

New Brunswick

Maine

Vermont
New Hampshire
Massachusetts
Rhode Island
Connecticut

New Jersey

Delaware
Maryland
WASHINGTON, D.C.

Baffin Bay

Québec

New York

Pennsylvania

Virginia

West Virginia

North Carolina

South Carolina

Ellesmere Island

Devon Island

Baffin Island

Hudson Bay

Ontario

Michigan

Ohio

Kentucky

Tennessee

Alabama

Georgia

Florida

Victoria Island

Wisconsin

Illinois Indiana

Missouri

Mississippi

Louisiana

Gulf of

Banks Island

Nunavut

Minnesota

Iowa

Arkansas

Beaufort Sea

ARCTIC OCEAN

Northwest Territories

Saskatchewan

Manitoba

North Dakota

South Dakota

Nebraska

Kansas

Oklahoma

UNITED STATES OF AMERICA

Texas

Coahuila

MÉXICO

Yukon

British Columbia

Alberta

CANADA

Montana

Wyoming

Colorado

New Mexico

Chihuahua

Idaho

Utah

Arizona

Sonora

Washington

Oregon

Nevada

California

Baja California Norte

Baja California

Gulf of California

OTTAWA

Alaska (US)

Gulf of Alaska

Bering Sea

Aleutian Islands

Hawaii (US)

PACIFIC OCEAN

200

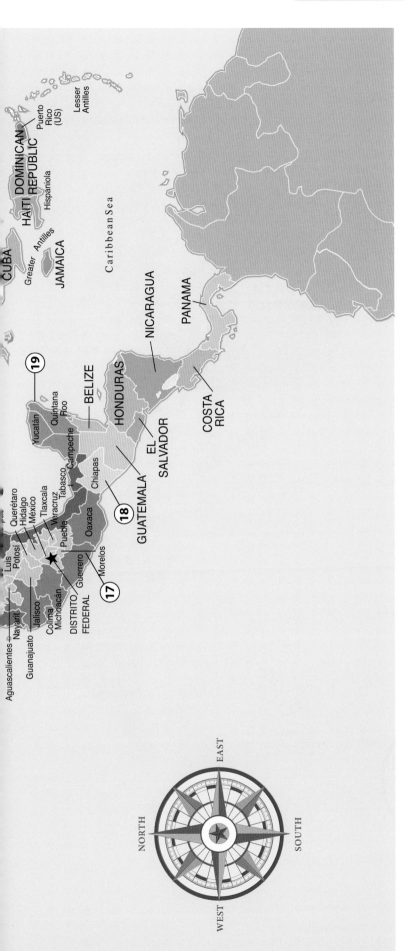

Regions of Mexico
أقاليم المكسيك

14. The Pacific Northwest الشمال الغربي الهادي

15. The Plateau of Mexico هضبة المكسيك

16. The Gulf Coastal Plain سهول ساحل الخليج

17. The Southern Uplands المرتفعات الجنوبية

18. The Chiapas Highlands مرتفعات تشياباس

19. The Yucatan Peninsula شبه جزيرة اليوكاتان

Regions of the United States
أقاليم الولايات المتحدة

7. The Pacific States / the West Coast ولايات المحيط الهادي / الساحل الغربي

8. The Rocky Mountain States ولايات جبال الروكي

9. The Midwest الغرب الأوسط

10. The Mid-Atlantic States ولايات منطقة الأطلنطي الوسطى

11. New England نيو إنغلاند

12. The Southwest الجنوب الغربي

13. The Southeast / the South الجنوب الشرقي / الجنوب

Regions of Canada
أقاليم كندا

1. Northern Canada شمال كندا

2. British Columbia كولومبيا البريطانية

3. The Prairie Provinces مقاطعات البراري (البراري)

4. Ontario أونتاريو

5. Québec كيبك

6. The Maritime Provinces المقاطعات البحرية

Continents

القارات

1. North America
   أمريكا الشمالية

2. South America
   أمريكا الجنوبية

3. Europe
   أوروبا

4. Asia
   آسيا

5. Africa
   إفريقيا

6. Australia
   أستراليا

7. Antarctica
   القارة المتجمدة الجنوبية
   (انتاركتيكا)

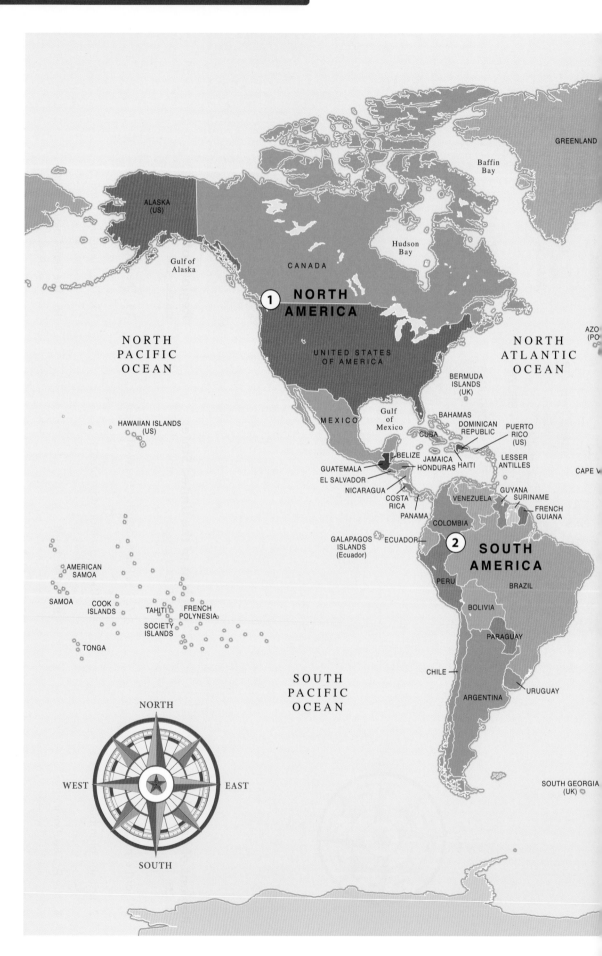

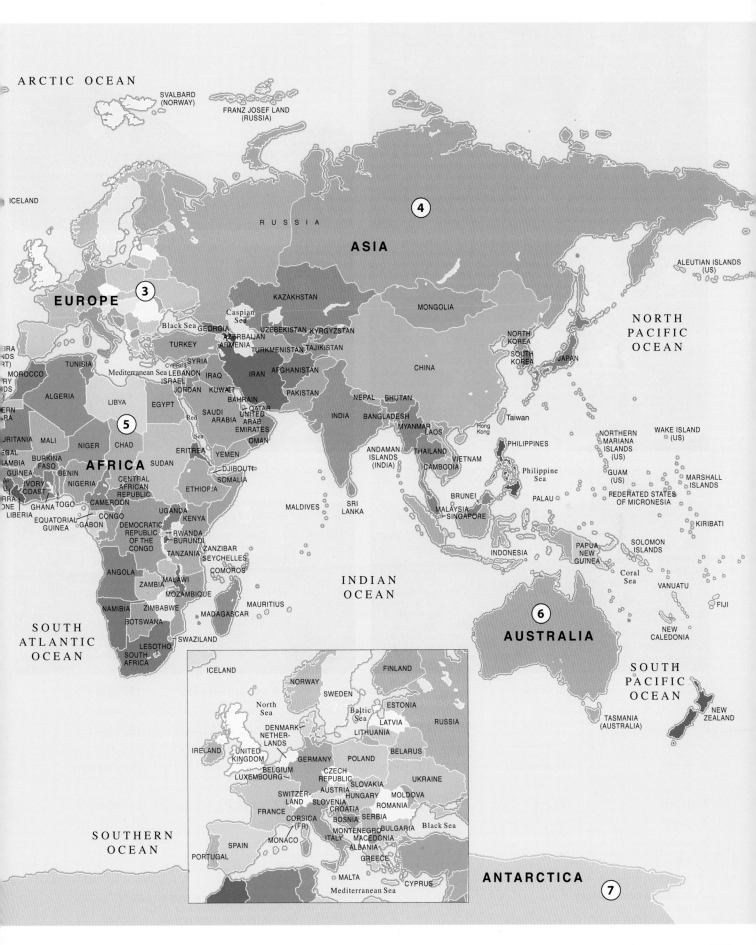

ARCTIC OCEAN

SVALBARD
(NORWAY)

FRANZ JOSEF LAND
(RUSSIA)

ICELAND

RUSSIA

④

ASIA

ALEUTIAN ISLANDS
(US)

③

EUROPE

KAZAKHSTAN

MONGOLIA

NORTH
PACIFIC
OCEAN

Caspian
Sea

Black Sea GEORGIA
AZERBAIJAN
TURKEY ARMENIA
SYRIA
CYPRUS

UZBEKISTAN KYRGYZSTAN

TURKMENISTAN TAJIKISTAN

NORTH
KOREA

SOUTH
KOREA

JAPAN

Mediterranean Sea LEBANON
MOROCCO
ISRAEL
JORDAN

IRAQ IRAN AFGHANISTAN

CHINA

ALGERIA
LIBYA
EGYPT

KUWAIT
BAHRAIN
QATAR
SAUDI UNITED
ARABIA ARAB
EMIRATES
OMAN

PAKISTAN

NEPAL BHUTAN

INDIA BANGLADESH

MYANMAR
LAOS

Taiwan

Hong
Kong

NORTHERN
MARIANA
ISLANDS
(US)

WAKE ISLAND
(US)

⑤

Red

Sea

ERITREA

YEMEN

DJIBOUTI

ANDAMAN
ISLANDS
(INDIA)

THAILAND
CAMBODIA

VIETNAM

PHILIPPINES

Philippine
Sea

GUAM
(US)

MARSHALL
ISLANDS

MAURITANIA MALI
NIGER CHAD

AFRICA SUDAN

GAMBIA BURKINA
FASO
GUINEA BENIN
IVORY NIGERIA
COAST
GHANA TOGO
LIBERIA EQUATORIAL
GUINEA GABON
CONGO

CENTRAL
AFRICAN
REPUBLIC

CAMEROON

UGANDA

DEMOCRATIC
REPUBLIC
OF THE RWANDA
CONGO BURUNDI

ETHIOPIA

SOMALIA

KENYA

MALDIVES

SRI
LANKA

BRUNEI

MALAYSIA
SINGAPORE

PALAU

FEDERATED STATES
OF MICRONESIA

KIRIBATI

SOLOMON
ISLANDS

TANZANIA
ZANZIBAR
SEYCHELLES

INDONESIA

PAPUA
NEW
GUINEA

ANGOLA
ZAMBIA MALAWI
MOZAMBIQUE

COMOROS

INDIAN
OCEAN

Coral
Sea

VANUATU

FIJI

NAMIBIA ZIMBABWE
BOTSWANA

MADAGASCAR

MAURITIUS

⑥

AUSTRALIA

NEW
CALEDONIA

SOUTH
ATLANTIC
OCEAN

SWAZILAND
LESOTHO
SOUTH
AFRICA

SOUTH
PACIFIC
OCEAN

TASMANIA
(AUSTRALIA)

NEW
ZEALAND

ICELAND

NORWAY

FINLAND

North
Sea

SWEDEN

Baltic
Sea

ESTONIA

LATVIA

RUSSIA

IRELAND

UNITED
KINGDOM

DENMARK
NETHER-
LANDS

LITHUANIA

BELGIUM
LUXEMBOURG

GERMANY

POLAND

BELARUS

CZECH
REPUBLIC

UKRAINE

SWITZER-
LAND
FRANCE

AUSTRIA
SLOVENIA

SLOVAKIA
HUNGARY
CROATIA

MOLDOVA
ROMANIA

SERBIA

SOUTHERN
OCEAN

SPAIN

PORTUGAL

CORSICA
(FR)

MONACO

ITALY

BOSNIA
MONTENEGRO
MACEDONIA
ALBANIA
GREECE

BULGARIA

Black Sea

MALTA

CYPRUS

Mediterranean Sea

ANTARCTICA

⑦

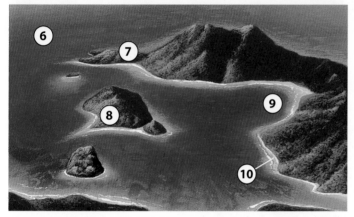

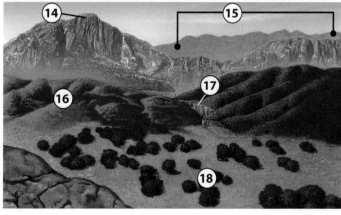

1. **rain forest**
غابات المطر

6. **ocean**
محيط

10. **beach**
شاطئ رملي

14. **mountain peak**
قمة جبل

18. **valley**
وادي

2. **waterfall**
شلال

7. **peninsula**
شبه جزيرة

11. **forest**
غابة

15. **mountain range**
سلسلة جبال

19. **plains**
سهول

3. **river**
نهر

8. **island**
جزيرة

12. **shore**
ساحل

16. **hills**
تلال

20. **meadow**
مَرْج

4. **desert**
صحراء

9. **bay**
خور / شرم

13. **lake**
بحيرة

17. **canyon**
وادي ضيق

21. **pond**
بركة

5. **sand dune**
كثيب

More vocabulary

a body of water: a river, lake, or ocean
stream / creek: a very small river

Ask your classmates. Share the answers.

1. Would you rather live near a river or a lake?
2. Would you rather travel through a forest or a desert?
3. How often do you go to the beach or the shore?

The Solar System and the Planets النظام الشمسي والكواكب

Sun

1 2 3 4

5

6

7

8

Asteroid Belt

Orbit

1. Mercury	**3.** Earth	**5.** Jupiter	**7.** Uranus
عطارد	الأرض	المشتري	أورانوس
2. Venus	**4.** Mars	**6.** Saturn	**8.** Neptune
فينوس	المريخ	زحل	نبتون

PHASES OF THE MOON

9 10 11 12

SPACE

15

14

13

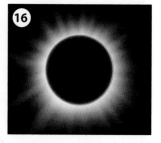

16

9. new moon	**11.** quarter moon	**13.** star	**15.** galaxy
هلال / قمر أول الشهر	ربع قمر	نجم	المجرّة
10. crescent moon	**12.** full moon	**14.** constellation	**16.** solar eclipse
هلال	بدر	مجموعة نجوم متألقة	كسوف الشمس

SPACE EXPLORATION

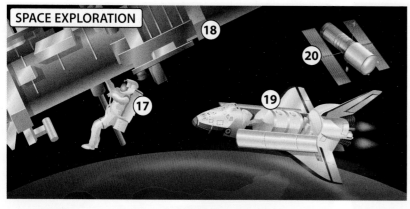

18

20

17

19

ASTRONOMY

21

24

22

23

17. astronaut	**19.** space shuttle	**21.** observatory	**23.** telescope
رائد فضاء	مكوك الفضاء	مرصد	تلسكوب
18. space station	**20.** satellite	**22.** astronomer	**24.** comet
محطة فضاء	قمر صناعي / ساتل	فلكي / عالم فلكي	مذنّب

More vocabulary

solar eclipse: when the moon is between the earth and the sun
Big Dipper: a famous part of the constellation Ursa Major
Sirius: the brightest star in the night sky

Ask your classmates. Share the answers.

1. How do you feel when you look at the night sky?
2. Can you name one or more constellations?
3. Do you want to travel in space?

A Graduation　حفلة التخرُّج

All Adelia's photos

I loved Art History.

My last economics lesson

Marching Band is great!

The photographer was upset.

We look good!

I get my diploma.

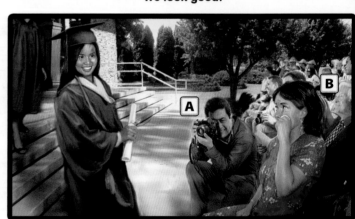
Dad and his digital camera

1. photographer	3. serious photo	5. podium	7. cap	A. **take** a picture	C. **celebrate**
مصور	صورة جادة	منصة	قبعة التخرج	يلتقط صورة فوتوغرافية	تحتفل
2. funny photo	4. guest speaker	6. ceremony	8. gown	B. **cry**	
صورة مضحكة	ضيفة الشرف	احتفال	رداء التخرج	تبكي	

Videos | Music | Classifieds |

People	Comments	
Sara 	June 29th 8:19 p.m. Great pictures! What a day!	Delete
Zannie baby	June 30th 10 a.m. Love the funny photo.	Delete

4
5

I'm behind the mayor.

C

We're all very happy.

**Look at the pictures.
What do you see?**

Answer the questions.

1. How many people are wearing caps and gowns?

2. How many people are being funny? How many are being serious?

3. Who is standing at the podium?

4. Why are the graduates throwing their caps in the air?

 Read the story.

A Graduation

Look at these great photos on my web page! The first three are from my favorite classes, but the other pictures are from graduation day.

There are two pictures of my classmates in <u>caps</u> and <u>gowns</u>. In the first picture, we're laughing and the <u>photographer</u> is upset. In the second photo, we're serious. I like the <u>serious photo</u>, but I love the <u>funny photo</u>!

There's also a picture of our <u>guest speaker</u>, the mayor. She is standing at the <u>podium</u>. Next, you can see me at the graduation <u>ceremony</u>. My dad wanted to <u>take a picture</u> of me with my diploma. That's my mom next to him. She <u>cries</u> when she's happy.

After the ceremony, everyone was happy, but no one cried. We wanted to <u>celebrate</u> and we did!

Think about it.

1. What kinds of ceremonies are important for children? for teens? for adults?

2. Imagine you are the guest speaker at a graduation. What will you say to the graduates?

207

1. trees
   أشجار
2. soil
   تربة
3. path
   مسار
4. bird
   طائر
5. plants
   نباتات
6. rock
   صخرة
7. flowers
   زهور

Listen and point. Take turns.

A: *Point to the trees.*
B: *Point to a bird.*
A: *Point to the flowers.*

Dictate to your partner. Take turns.

A: *Write it's a tree.*
B: *Let me check that. I-t-'s -a- t-r-e-e?*
A: *Yes, that's right.*

208

8. sun
   شمس
9. sky
   سماء
10. mammals
    ثدييات
11. insects
    حشرات
12. nest
    عش
13. water
    ماء
14. fish
    أسماك

Ways to talk about nature

Look at <u>the sky</u>! Isn't it beautiful?
Did you see <u>the fish</u> / <u>insects</u>?
It's / They're so interesting.

Pair practice. Make new conversations.

A: Do you know the name of that <u>yellow flower</u>?
B: I think it's <u>a sunflower</u>.
A: Oh, and what about that <u>blue bird</u>?

Trees and Plants

أشجار ونباتات

PARTS OF A TREE

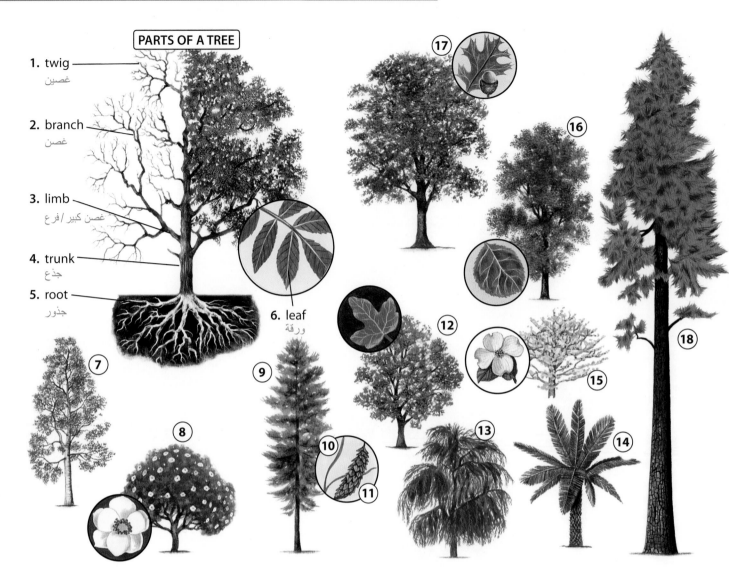

1. twig
غصين

2. branch
غصن

3. limb
غصن كبير / فرع

4. trunk
جذع

5. root
جذور

6. leaf
ورقة

7. birch بتولا (شجر القضبان)	10. needle ورقة إبرية	13. willow صفصاف	16. elm دردار
8. magnolia مغنولية	11. pinecone كوز صنوبر	14. palm نخل	17. oak سنديان
9. pine شجر الصنوبر	12. maple قيقب	15. dogwood قرانيا	18. redwood الشجر الأحمر (صنوبر حرجي)

Plants نباتات

19. holly البهشية	21. cactus صبار	23. poison sumac سماق سام	25. poison ivy لبلاب سام
20. berries توت	22. vine كرمة	24. poison oak بلوط سام	

210

Parts of a Flower أجزاء الزهرة

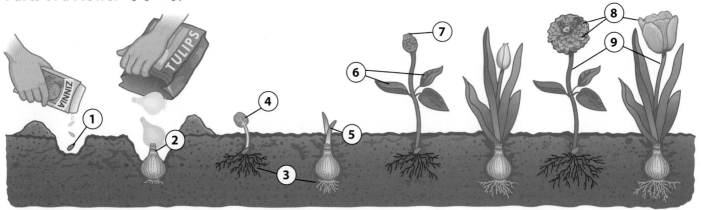

1. seed
   بذرة

2. bulb
   بصلة

3. roots
   جذور

4. seedling
   نبتة صغيرة

5. shoot
   نبتة / فرخ

6. leaves
   ورق

7. bud
   برعم

8. petals
   بتلات (تويجات)

9. stems
   جذوع

10. sunflower
    عباد الشمس

11. tulip
    زنبقة

12. hibiscus
    خبيزة

13. marigold
    قطيفة

14. daisy
    زهرة الربيع

15. rose
    وردة

16. iris
    سوسن

17. crocus
    زعفران

18. gardenia
    غردينيا

19. orchid
    سحلبية

20. carnation
    فُل

21. chrysanthemum
    أقحوان

22. jasmine
    ياسمين

23. violet
    ليلك

24. poinsettia
    بونسيتة

25. daffodil
    نرجس بري

26. lily
    زنبق

27. houseplant
    نبتة منزلية

28. bouquet
    باقة زهور

29. thorn
    شوكة

Sea Animals الحيوانات البحرية

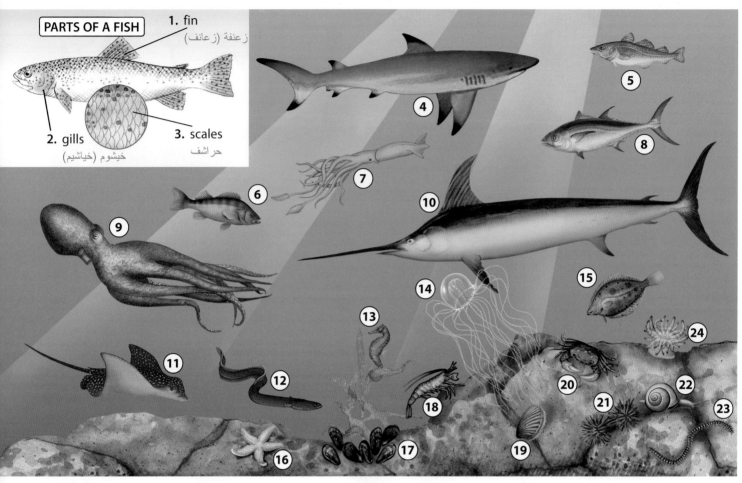

PARTS OF A FISH

1. fin
زعنفة (زعانف)

2. gills
خيشوم (خياشيم)

3. scales
حراشف

4. shark القرش	**9. octopus** أخطبوط	**14. jellyfish** السمك الهلالي (قنديل البحر)	**18. shrimp** الربيان / القريدس (الجمبري)	**22. snail** القوقع
5. cod القد	**10. swordfish** أبو سيف	**15. flounder** السمك المفلطح	**19. scallop** الأسقلوب	**23. worm** دودة
6. bass القاروس	**11. ray** شفنين بحري	**16. starfish** نجم البحر	**20. crab** السلطعون (سرطان البحر)	**24. sea anemone** شقيق البحر
7. squid الحبار	**12. eel** الأنقليس (ثعبان بحري)	**17. mussel** بلح البحر	**21. sea urchin** قنفذ البحر	
8. tuna التونة (سمك التن)	**13. seahorse** فرس البحر			

Amphibians البرمائيات

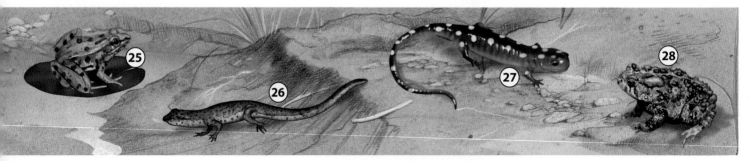

25. frog ضفدع	**26. newt** سمندل الماء	**27. salamander** سمندر	**28. toad** علجوم

Marine Life, Amphibians, and Reptiles

Sea Mammals الثدييات البحرية

29. whale	**31.** dolphin	**33.** sea lion	**35.** sea otter
حوت	دلفين	أسد البحر	قضاعة / قندس (كلب الماء)
30. porpoise	**32.** walrus	**34.** seal	
خنزير البحر	الفظ (فيل البحر)	فقمة	

Reptiles الزواحف

36. alligator	**38.** rattlesnake	**40.** lizard	**42.** tortoise
تمساح	المجلجلة / ذات الأجراس	سحلية	رَق (سلحفاة)
37. crocodile	**39.** garter snake	**41.** cobra	**43.** turtle
قاطور (تمساح أمريكي)	الغرطر	الصل (كوبرا)	سلحفاة

Birds, Insects, and Arachnids

PARTS OF A BIRD

1. wing
جناح

2. claw
مخلب

3. beak / bill
منقار

4. feather
ريشة

5. owl بوم	**8. woodpecker** نقار الخشب	**11. penguin** بطريق	**14. peacock** طاووس
6. blue jay القيق الأزرق / الزرياب	**9. eagle** صقر / نسر	**12. duck** بط	**15. pigeon** حمامة
7. sparrow عصفور / دُوري	**10. hummingbird** الطنان	**13. goose** إوزّة (إوزّ)	**16. robin** أبو الحناء

Insects and Arachnids الحشرات والعنكبوتيات

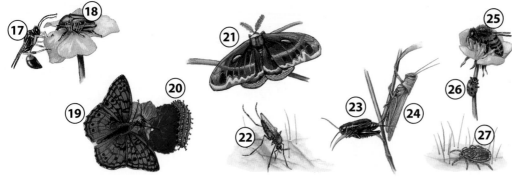

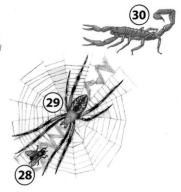

17. wasp زنبور	**21. moth** عثة	**25. honeybee** نحلة عسل	**29. spider** عنكبوت
18. beetle خنفساء	**22. mosquito** بعوضة (ناموسة)	**26. ladybug** دعسوقة	**30. scorpion** عقرب
19. butterfly فراشة	**23. cricket** صرار الليل	**27. tick** قرادة	
20. caterpillar يرقانة	**24. grasshopper** جندب	**28. fly** ذبابة	

Farm Animals حيوانات المزارع

1. cow
بقرة

2. pig
خنزير

3. donkey
حمار

4. horse
حصان

5. goat
عنزة / ماعز

6. sheep
خروف

7. rooster
ديك

8. hen
دجاجة

Pets الحيوانات المنزلية

9. cat
هرة / قطة

10. kitten
هريرة (هرة صغيرة)

11. dog
كلب

12. puppy
جرو

13. rabbit
أرنب

14. guinea pig
خنزير هندي

15. parakeet
درة (ببغاء صغير)

16. goldfish
سمك ذهبي

Rodents القوارض

17. rat
جرذ

18. mouse
فأر

19. gopher
غوفر (سنجاب أمريكي)

20. chipmunk
صيداني (سنجاب أمريكي صغير مخطط)

21. squirrel
سنجاب

22. prairie dog
كلب البراري

More vocabulary

domesticated: animals that work for and / or live with people

wild: animals that live away from people

Ask your classmates. Share the answers.

1. Have you worked with farm animals? Which ones?
2. Are you afraid of rodents? Which ones?
3. Do you have a pet? What kind?

215

1. moose
موظ

2. mountain lion
أسد الجبال (الكوغر)

3. coyote
قيوط (ذئب أمريكي)

4. opossum
أبوسوم

5. wolf
ذئب

6. buffalo / bison
جاموس / بيسون

7. bat
خفاش / وطواط

8. armadillo
المدرع

9. beaver
سمُور

10. porcupine
شيهم / نيص

11. bear
دب

12. skunk
ظربان

13. raccoon
راكون

14. deer
غزال

15. fox
ثعلب

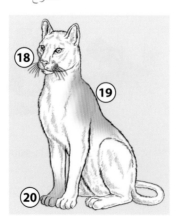

16. antlers
قرون الوعل

17. hooves
حوافر

18. whiskers
سبلات

19. coat / fur
فروة

20. paw
كف الحيوان ذي البراثن

21. horn
قرن

22. tail
ذنب / ذيل

23. quill
أشواك القنفذ

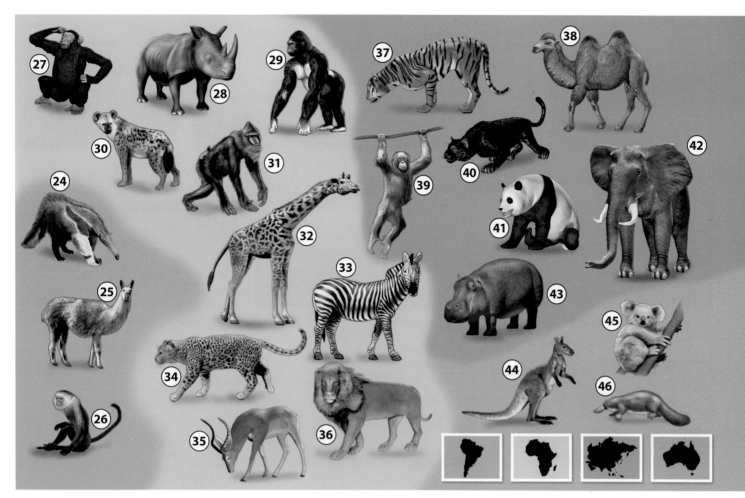

24. anteater	29. gorilla	34. leopard	39. orangutan	44. kangaroo
آكل النمل	غوريلا	فهد	إنسان الغاب	كنغر
25. llama	30. hyena	35. antelope	40. panther	45. koala
لاما	ضبع	ظبي	نمر أمريكي	كوال
26. monkey	31. baboon	36. lion	41. panda	46. platypus
قرد	سعدان إفريقي	أسد / سبع	بندة	بلاتيوس
27. chimpanzee	32. giraffe	37. tiger	42. elephant	
شمبانزي	زرافة	نمر	فيل	
28. rhinoceros	33. zebra	38. camel	43. hippopotamus	
كركدّن (خرتيت)	حمار وحشي	جمل	فرس النهر	

   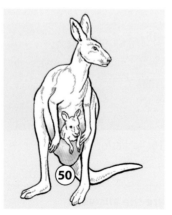 

47. trunk	48. tusk	49. mane	50. pouch	51. hump
خرطوم / زلومة	ناب	عرف	جيب	حدبة

Energy Sources مصادر الطاقة

1. solar energy
الطاقة الشمسية

2. wind power
الطاقة الريحية

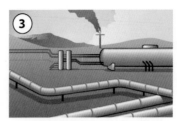

3. natural gas
الغاز الطبيعي

4. coal
فحم

5. hydroelectric power
طاقة كهرمائية

6. oil / petroleum
النفط / البترول

7. geothermal energy
طاقة حرارية أرضية

8. nuclear energy
طاقة نووية

9. biomass / bioenergy
طاقة الكتلة الإحيائية / الطاقة الإحيائية

10. fusion
انصهار

Pollution التَلوُّث

11. air pollution / smog
تلوث الهواء (الجو) / ضباب دخاني

12. hazardous waste
نفايات خطرة

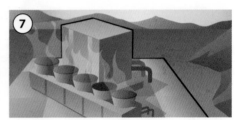

13. acid rain
مطر حمضي

14. water pollution
تلوث المياه

15. radiation
إشعاع

16. pesticide poisoning
تسمم من مبيدات الحشرات

17. oil spill
انسكاب نفطي

Ask your classmates. Share the answers.

1. What types of things do you recycle?
2. What types of energy sources are in your area?
3. What types of pollution do you worry about?

Think about it. Discuss.

1. How can you save energy in the summer? winter?
2. What are some other ways that people can conserve energy or prevent pollution?

Ways to Conserve Energy and Resources وسائل للحفاظ على الطاقة والموارد الطبيعية

A. reduce trash

الحد من القمامة

B. reuse shopping bags

إعادة استعمال أكياس التسوق

C. recycle

إعادة التصنيع أو التدوير

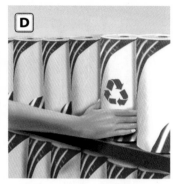

D. buy recycled products

شراء منتجات معاد تصنيعها

E. save water

التوفير في استهلاك الماء

F. fix leaky faucets

إصلاح الحنفيات المتسربة

G. turn off lights

إطفاء الأنوار

H. use energy-efficient bulbs

استعمال لمبات كهربائية خفيضة الطاقة

I. carpool

المشاركة مع آخرين في ركوب سيارة واحدة

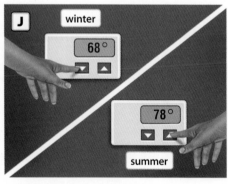

J. adjust the thermostat

ضبط منظّم الحرارة (الترموستات)

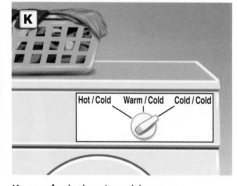

K. wash clothes in cold water

غسل الملابس في ماء بارد

L. don't litter

لا تلق القمامة في غير مكانها

M. compost food scraps

حوّل بقايا الطعام إلى سماد

N. plant a tree

زرع شجرة

Yosemite
NATIONAL PARK

Dry Tortugas
NATIONAL PARK

Half Dome

Fort Jefferson

(1)

(2)

(4)

(3)

(5)

---

1. **landmarks**
معالم

2. **park ranger**
مأمور الحديقة أو المنتزه

3. **wildlife**
الأحياء البرية

4. **ferry**
عَبّارة

5. **coral**
المرجان (الشعب المرجانية)

6. **cave**
غار

7. **caverns**
كهوف

A. **take** a tour
يقومون بجولة سياحية

220

Look at the pictures.
What do you see?

Answer the questions.

1. How many U.S. landmarks are in the pictures?
2. What kinds of wildlife do you see?
3. What can you do at Carlsbad Caverns?

Read the story.

U.S. National Parks

More than 200 million people visit U.S. National Parks every year. These parks protect the <u>wildlife</u> and <u>landmarks</u> of the United States. Each park is different, and each one is beautiful.

At Yosemite, in California, you can take a nature walk with a <u>park ranger</u>. You'll see waterfalls, redwoods, and deer there.

In south Florida, you can take a <u>ferry</u> to Dry Tortugas. It's great to snorkel around the park's <u>coral</u> islands.

There are 113 <u>caves</u> at Carlsbad <u>Caverns</u> in New Mexico. The deepest cave is 830 feet below the desert! You can <u>take a tour</u> of these beautiful caverns.

There are 391 national parks to see. Go online for information about a park near you.

Think about it.

1. Why are national parks important?
2. Imagine you are a park ranger at a national park. Give your classmates a tour of the landmarks and wildlife.

Places to Go أماكن للزيارة

1. zoo
حديقة الحيوانات

2. movies
السينما

3. botanical garden
حديقة النباتات

4. bowling alley
مسرب البولينغ (لعبة الكرة الخشبية)

5. rock concert
حفلة موسيقى الروك آند رول

6. swap meet /
flea market
سوق المقايضة أو الخردوات

7. aquarium
معرض الأحياء المائية

| File | Edit | View | History | Bookmarks | Tools |

Places to Go in Our City

T-SHIRTS $3 2 for $5

SUNGLASSES $10

ANTIQU

Listen and point. Take turns.

A: Point to _the zoo_.
B: Point to _the flea market_.
A: Point to _the rock concert_.

Dictate to your partner. Take turns.

A: Write these words: _zoo, movies, aquarium_.
B: _Zoo, movies_, and what?
A: _Aquarium_.

Search

8. play
   مسرحية

9. art museum
   متحف الفنون

10. amusement park
    مدينة ملاهي

11. opera
    الأوبرا

12. nightclub
    نادي ليلي / ملهى ليلي

13. county fair
    مهرجان ريفي

14. classical concert
    حفلة موسيقى كلاسيكية

Ways to make plans using *Let's go*

Let's go to <u>the amusement park</u> tomorrow.
Let's go to <u>the opera</u> on Saturday.
Let's go to <u>the movies</u> tonight.

Pair practice. Make new conversations.

A: <u>*Let's go to the zoo this afternoon*</u>.
B: *OK. And let's go to* <u>*the movies tonight*</u>.
A: *That sounds like a good plan.*

223

The Park and Playground

الحديقة وملعب الأطفال

1. ball field
ملعب كرة

2. cyclist
راكب دراجة

3. bike path
ممر دراجات

4. jump rope
حبل الوثب

5. fountain
نافورة

6. tennis court
ملعب كرة المضرب (تنس)

7. skateboard
مَزلَق ذو عجلات

8. picnic table
طاولة نزهة

9. water fountain
نافورة مياه للشرب

10. bench
دكة / مقعد طويل

11. swings
مراجيح

12. tricycle
دراجة ثلاثية العجلات

13. slide
زلاقة

14. climbing apparatus
قضبان تسلق

15. sandbox
صندوق رمل

16. seesaw
أرجوحة

A. pull the wagon
تسحب العربة

B. push the swing
تدفع المرجيحة

C. climb the bars
يتسلقان القضبان

D. picnic / have a picnic
تنزه / يقوم (تقوم) بنزهة

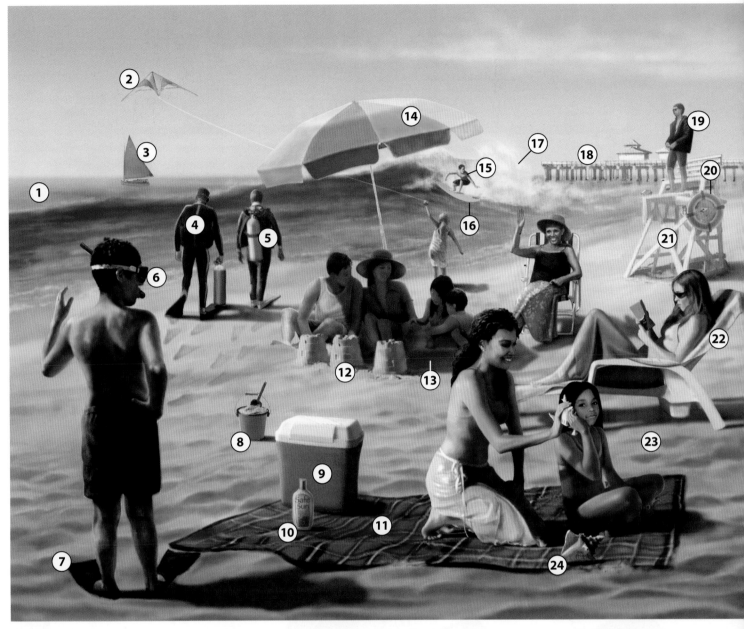

1. ocean / water المحيط / الماء	**7. fins** زعانف	**13. shade** ظل	**19. lifeguard** منقذ / سباح الإنقاذ
2. kite طيارة من الورق والبوص	**8. pail / bucket** دلو / جردل	**14. beach umbrella** مظلة للشاطئ	**20. lifesaving device** أداة إنقاذ
3. sailboat زورق شراعي	**9. cooler** صندوق تبريد	**15. surfer** راكب الأمواج المتكسرة	**21. lifeguard station** مقر سباح الإنقاذ
4. wet suit بدلة غوص	**10. sunscreen / sunblock** مرهم واقٍ من أشعة الشمس	**16. surfboard** لوح خشبي لركوب الأمواج المتكسرة	**22. beach chair** كرسي للشاطئ
5. scuba tank خزان أكسيجين للغوص	**11. blanket** بطَّانية	**17. wave** موجة	**23. sand** رمل
6. diving mask قانع الغطس	**12. sand castle** قلعة من الرمل	**18. pier** رصيف ممتد داخل البحر	**24. seashell** صدفة بحرية

More vocabulary

seaweed: a plant that grows in the ocean

tide: the level of the ocean. The tide goes in and out every 12 hours.

Ask your classmates. Share the answers.

1. Do you like to go to the beach?
2. Are there famous beaches in your native country?
3. Do you prefer to be on the sand or in the water?

1. boating
ركوب الزوارق

2. rafting
رياضة ركوب الرمث

3. canoeing
ركوب الكانو (الصندل)

4. fishing
صيد الأسماك

5. camping
تخييم

6. backpacking
حمل الأمتعة على الظهر

7. hiking
التنزه سيرا على الأقدام

8. mountain biking
ركوب الدراجات على الجبال

9. horseback riding
ركوب الخيل

10. tent
خيمة

11. campfire
نار المخيم

12. sleeping bag
كيس للنوم

13. foam pad
فرشة من الإسفنج

14. life vest
صديرية النجاة

15. backpack
حقيبة تحمل على الظهر

16. camping stove
موقد تخييم

17. fishing net
شبكة صيد أسماك

18. fishing pole
صنارة صيد سمك

19. rope
حبل

20. multi-use knife
سكين متعدد الاستعمالات

21. matches
أعواد ثقاب / كبريت

22. lantern
فانوس

23. insect repellent
مادة طاردة للحشرات

24. canteen
مزادة (قربة ماء)

1. downhill skiing
التزلج على منحدر

2. snowboarding
التزلج على الثلج

3. cross-country skiing
التزلج في الضاحية

4. ice skating
التزلج على الجليد

5. figure skating
التزلج مع القيام بسلسلة من الحركات

6. sledding
ركوب المزلجة

7. waterskiing
التزلج على الماء

8. sailing
الإبحار بمركب شراعي

9. surfing
ركوب الأمواج المتكسرة

10. windsurfing
التزلج على الماء مع استعمال شراع

11. snorkeling
السباحة مع استعمال أنبوب التنفس

12. scuba diving
الغوص مع خزان التنفس

More vocabulary

speed skating: racing while ice skating
windsurfing: sailboarding

Ask your classmates. Share the Answers.

1. Which of these sports do you like?
2. Which of these sports would you like to learn?
3. Which of these sports is the most fun to watch?

1. archery
رماية السهام

2. billiards / pool
بلياردو

3. bowling
بولينغ (لعبة الكرة الخشبية)

4. boxing
ملاكمة

5. cycling / biking
ركوب الدراجة

6. badminton
بادمنتون (لعبة تشبه كرة المضرب)

7. fencing
مبارزة بالسيف

8. golf
جولف

9. gymnastics
الرياضة الجمبازية

10. inline skating
التزلج بمزلج ذي خط دواليب

11. martial arts
الجودو

12. racquetball
راكتبول

13. skateboarding
التزلج على لوح بعجلات

14. table tennis
كرة الطاولة

15. tennis
كرة المضرب (تنس)

16. weightlifting
رفع الأثقال

17. wrestling
مصارعة

18. track and field
سباق المضمار والميدان

19. horse racing
سباق الخيول

Pair practice. Make new conversations.

A: *What sports do you like?*
B: *I like bowling. What do you like?*
A: *I like gymnastics.*

Think about it. Discuss.

1. Why do people like to watch sports?
2. Which sports can be dangerous?
3. Why do people do dangerous sports?

1. score
نتيجة المباراة

2. coach
مدرب

3. team
فريق

4. fan
مشجّع

5. player
لاعب

6. official / referee
حَكَم

7. basketball court
ملعب كرة السلة

8. basketball
كرة السلة

9. baseball
بيسبول

10. softball
صوفتبول (لعبة شبيهة بالبيسبول)

11. football
كرة القدم الأمريكية (الفوتبول)

12. soccer
كرة القدم

13. ice hockey
هوكي الجليد

14. volleyball
الكرة الطائرة

15. water polo
كرة الماء

More Vocabulary

win: to have the best score
lose: the opposite of win
tie: to have the same score

captain: the team leader
umpire: the name of the referee in baseball
Little League: a baseball and softball program for children

A. **pitch**
يرمي

B. **hit**
يضرب

C. **throw**
يلقي

D. **catch**
يلقف

E. **kick**
يركل

F. **tackle**
يمسك بالخصم لإيقافه

G. **pass**
يمرر

H. **shoot**
ترمي الكرة نحو السلة (تقذف الكرة)

I. **jump**
تقفز

J. **dribble**
تنطط الكرة

K. **dive**
يغطس

L. **swim**
يسبح

M. **stretch**
تتمدد

N. **exercise / work out**
تتمرن / تمارس تمرينات رياضية

O. **bend**
تنحني

P. **serve**
يستهل ضرب الكرة

Q. **swing**
توجّه / تصوّب

R. **start**
ينطلق

S. **race**
يسابق

T. **finish**
يصل لخط النهاية

U. **skate**
تتزلج

V. **ski**
يتزلج على الثلج

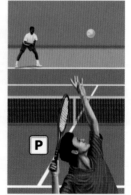

Use the new words.
Look on page 229. Name the actions you see.

A: *He's throwing.*

230

B: *She's jumping.*

Ways to talk about your sports skills

I can throw, but I can't catch.
I swim well, but I don't dive well.
I'm good at skating, but I'm terrible at skiing.

1. golf club	**8.** arrow	**15.** catcher's mask	**22.** weights
هراوة / مضرب جولف	سهم	قناع لاقف الكرة	أثقال
2. tennis racket	**9.** ice skates	**16.** uniform	**23.** snowboard
مضرب تَنس	مزلج جليد	زي مُوَحَّد	لوحة للتزلج على الثلج
3. volleyball	**10.** inline skates	**17.** glove	**24.** skis
كرة الطائرة	مزلج بخط دواليب	قفاز	زلاجة
4. basketball	**11.** hockey stick	**18.** baseball	**25.** ski poles
كرة السلة	عصا هوكي	كرة بيسبول	عصا التزلج على الثلج
5. bowling ball	**12.** soccer ball	**19.** football helmet	**26.** ski boots
كرة البولينغ	كرة قدم	خوذة فوتبول (كرة قدم أمريكية)	حذاء التزلج على الثلج
6. bow	**13.** shin guards	**20.** shoulder pads	**27.** flying disc*
قوس	واقيات قصبة الرجل	لبادة كتف	قرص طائر
7. target	**14.** baseball bat	**21.** football	** **Note:** one brand is
هدف	مضرب بيسبول	كرة الفوتبول	Frisbee®, of Wham-O, Inc.

Use the new words.

Look at pages 228–229. Name the sports equipment you see.

A: *Those are ice skates.*
B: *That's a football.*

Ask your classmates. Share the answers.

1. Do you own any sports equipment? What kind?
2. What do you want to buy at this store?
3. Where is the best place to buy sports equipment?

Hobbies and Games

هوايات وألعاب

A. collect things
تجمع أشياءً

B. play games
تلعب ألعابا

C. quilt
تمارس التضريب

D. do crafts
تمارس أشغالا يدوية

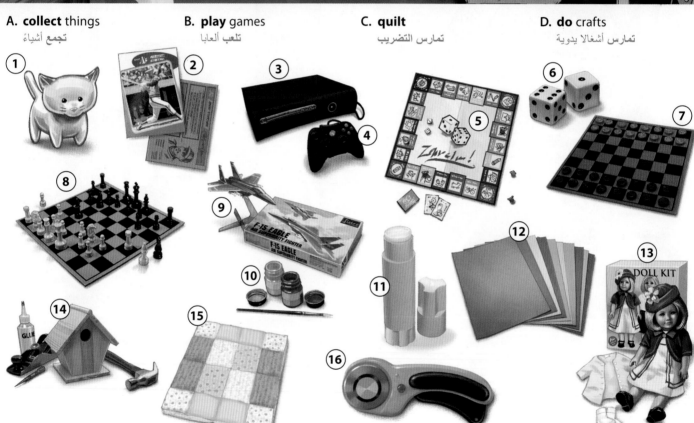

1. figurine
تمثال صغير

2. baseball cards
بطاقات بيسبول

3. video game console
جهاز لألعاب الفيديو

4. video game control
أداة تحكم في ألعاب الفيديو

5. board game
لعبة لوحية

6. dice
زهر الطاولة / النرد

7. checkers
رقعة الداما

8. chess
شطرنج

9. model kit
عدة لتركيب نماذج

10. acrylic paint
دهان أكريليك

11. glue stick
قلم صمغ

12. construction paper
ورق إنشاء

13. doll making kit
عدة لصنع دمية

14. woodworking kit
عدة نجارة

15. quilt block
كتلة تضريب

16. rotary cutter
قاطع دوار

Grammar Point: *How often do you play cards?*

*I play **all the time**. (every day)*

*I play **sometimes**. (once a month)*

*I **never** play. (0 times)*

Pair practice. Make new conversations.

A: *How often do you do your hobbies?*

B: *I <u>play games</u> all the time. I love <u>chess</u>.*

A: *Really? I never play <u>chess</u>.*

E. paint
ترسم بالألوان

F. knit
تحبك بالصنارة

G. pretend
تتظاهر

H. play cards
يلعبان الشدة

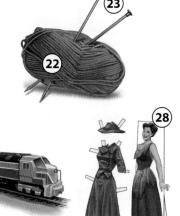

17. canvas
قماش قنب

18. easel
حامل لوحة

19. oil paint
دهان زيتي

20. paintbrush
فرشاة رسم

21. watercolor
لون مائي

22. yarn
لفيفة صوف أو قطن

23. knitting needles
مسلات حياكة

24. embroidery
تطريز

25. crocheting
حبك بصنارة معقوفة (كروشيه)

26. action figure
تماثيل أبطال

27. model trains
قطارات لعب نموذجية

28. paper dolls
دمى ورقية

29. diamonds
الديناري

30. spades
البستوني

31. hearts
الكوبة

32. clubs
الاسباتي

Ways to talk about hobbies and games

*This <u>board game</u> is **interesting**. It makes me think.*
*That <u>video game</u> is **boring**. Nothing happens.*
*I love to <u>play cards</u>. It's **fun** to play with my friends.*

Ask your classmates. Share the answers.

1. Do you collect anything? What?
2. Which games do you like to play?
3. What hobbies did you have as a child?

233

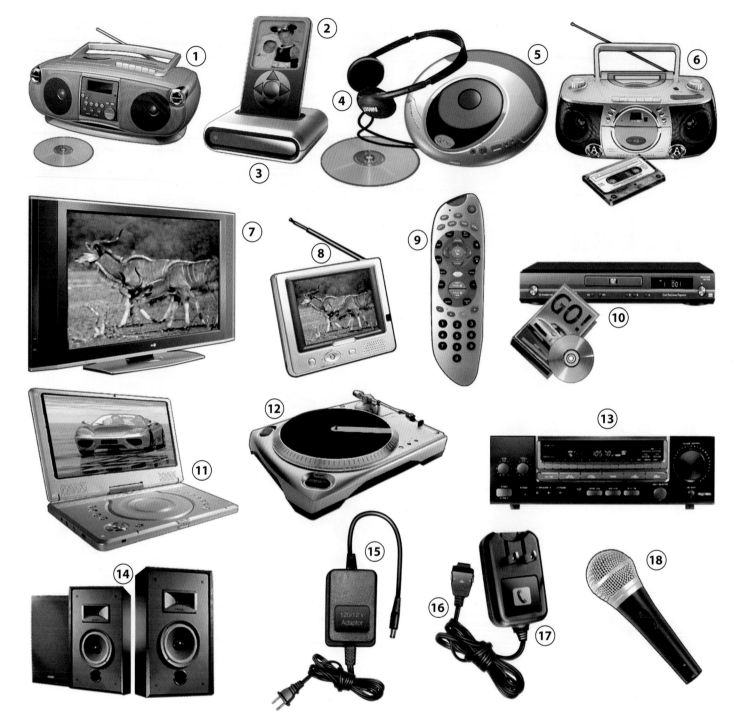

1. CD boombox
   جهاز تشغيل أقراص مضغوطة (سي دي)

2. MP3 player
   جهاز تشغيل ملفات إم بي ٣ الموسيقية (MP3)

3. dock
   قاعدة

4. headphones
   سماعات رأس

5. personal CD player
   جهاز تشغيل س دي شخصي

6. portable cassette player
   آلة كاسيت نقالة

7. flat screen TV / flat panel TV
   تلفزيون ذو شاشة مسطحة

8. portable TV
   تلفزيون نقال

9. universal remote
   جهاز تحكم عن بعد (ريموت) شامل

10. DVD player
    جهاز تشغيل أقراص فيديو رقمية (دي في دي)

11. portable DVD player
    جهاز تشغيل دي في دي نقال

12. turntable
    جهاز تشغيل أسطوانات

13. tuner
    جهاز توليف (أمبليفاير)

14. speakers
    سماعات ستريو

15. adapter
    المهيىء

16. plug
    قابس

17. charger
    شاحن

18. microphone
    ميكروفون

19. digital camera
كاميرا رقمية (ديجيتال)

20. memory card
كارت ذاكرة

21. film camera / 35 mm camera
كاميرا فيلمية / كاميرا ٣٥ مم

22. film
فيلم

23. zoom lens
عدسة مقرّبة (زوم)

24. camcorder
آلة تصوير وفيديو

25. tripod
حامل ثلاثي القوائم

26. battery pack
حزمة بطاريات

27. battery charger
شاحن البطارية

28. camera case
علبة الكاميرا

29. LCD projector
آلة عرض على شاشة ببلور سائل (إل سي دي)

30. screen
شاشة

31. photo album
ألبوم صور

32. digital photo album
ألبوم صور رقمية (ديجيتال)

33. out of focus
صورة غير واضحة

34. overexposed
صورة زائدة التعريض للضوء

35. underexposed
صورة ناقصة التعريض للضوء

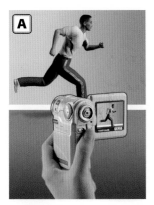
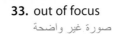
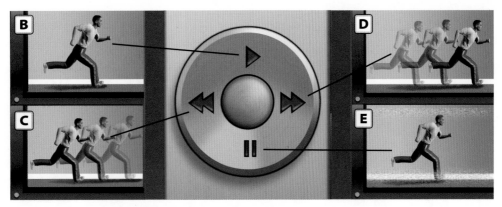

A. record
يسجّل

B. play
يشغّل / يذيع

C. rewind
ترجَع إلى الوراء

D. fast forward
تقدَم إلى الأمام بسرعة

E. pause
يوقف مؤقتا

235

Types of TV Programs أنواع البرامج التليفزيونية

1. news program

برنامج إخباري

2. sitcom (situation comedy)

برنامج كوميدي

3. cartoon

أفلام كارتون (رسوم متحركة)

4. talk show

برنامج مقابلات

5. soap opera

مسلسل تلفيزيوني

6. reality show

برنامج حياة واقعية

7. nature program

برنامج عن الطبيعة

8. game show

برنامج منافسات أو مسابقات

9. children's program

برنامج أطفال

10. shopping program

برنامج تسوق

11. sports program

برنامج رياضي

12. drama

دراما

Types of Movies أنواع الأفلام

13. comedy
هزلي (كوميدي)

14. tragedy
مأسوي (تراجيديا)

15. western
رعاة البقر (كاوبوي)

16. romance
رواية حب (رومانسي)

17. horror story
رواية مرعبة (فيلم رعب)

18. science fiction story
رواية خيال علمي

19. action story / adventure story
رواية إثارة / رواية مغامرات

20. mystery / suspense
رواية بوليسية / تشويق

Types of Music أنواع الموسيقى

21. classical
كلاسيكية

22. blues
موسيقى الكآبة (بلوز)

23. rock
موسيقى صاخبة راقصة (روك أند رول)

24. jazz
جاز

25. pop
بوب (شعبية)

26. hip hop
هيب هوب (راقصة)

27. country
ريفية

28. R&B / soul
إيقاعية حزينة (ريذم أند بلوز) / روحية (صول)

29. folk
شعبية فولكلورية

30. gospel
كنسية

31. reggae
موسيقى الرجي

32. world music
موسيقي عالمية

A. play an instrument
تعزف على آلة

B. sing a song
يغنّي أغنية

C. conduct an orchestra
يقود أوركسترا

D. be in a rock band
يلعب في فرقة روك آند رول

Woodwinds آلات النفخ الخشبية

1. flute
فلوت

2. clarinet
كلارينت

3. oboe
أوبو (مزمار)

4. bassoon
الزمخر (بسون)

5. saxophone
السكسية (ساكسفون)

Strings الآلات الوترية

6. violin
كمان (كمنجة)

7. cello
فيولونسيل (كمنجة كبيرة)

8. bass
كمان أجهر (كونتراباص)

9. guitar
قيثار (جيتار)

Brass آلات النفخ النحاسية

10. trombone
المترددة (ترومبون)

11. trumpet / horn
بوق / نفير (ترومبت)

12. tuba
توبة

13. French horn
بوق فرنسي

Percussion الآلات الإيقاعية

14. piano
بيانو

15. xylophone
الخشبية (زيلوفون)

16. drums
طبل (طبول)

17. tambourine
رق / دف

Other Instruments آلات أخرى

18. electric keyboard
كيبورد (لوحة أصابع) كهربائي

19. accordion
أكورديون

20. organ
أرغن

21. harmonica
هرمونيكا

1. parade
موكب استعراضي

2. float
عربة ذات منصة

3. confetti
قصاصات النثار الورقية

4. couple
زوجان

5. card
كارت / بطاقة

6. heart
قلب

7. fireworks
ألعاب نارية

8. flag
راية / علم

9. mask
قناع

10. jack-o'-lantern
مصباح يصنع من قرعة

11. costume
لباس تنكري

12. candy
حلوى

13. feast
وليمة

14. turkey
ديك رومي

15. ornament
زينة

16. Christmas tree
شجرة أعياد الميلاد (الكريسماس)

17. candy cane
عصا الحلوى

18. string lights
أنوار عقدية (لتزيين الشجر)

*Thanksgiving is on the fourth Thursday in November.

1. decorations
   زينة / زواق

2. deck
   منصة جلوس خارجية

3. present / gift
   هدية

A. **videotape**
   تصوَر بكاميرا فيديو

B. **make** a wish
   يتمنى

C. **blow out**
   يطفئ الشمع

D. **hide**
   يختبئ

E. **bring**
   تُحضِر

F. **wrap**
   تلفَ

Happy Birthday!

Look at the picture. What do you see?

Answer the questions.

1. What kinds of decorations do you see?
2. What are people doing at this birthday party?
3. What wish did the teenager make?
4. How many presents did people bring?

📖 Read the story.

A Birthday Party

Today is Lou and Gani Bombata's birthday barbecue. There are <u>decorations</u> around the backyard, and food and drinks on the <u>deck</u>. There are also <u>presents</u>. Everyone in the Bombata family likes to <u>bring</u> presents.

Right now, it's time for cake. Gani <u>is blowing out</u> the candles, and Lou <u>is making a wish</u>. Lou's mom wants to <u>videotape</u> everyone, but she can't find Lou's brother, Todd. Todd hates to sing, so he always <u>hides</u> for the birthday song.

Lou's sister, Amaka, has to <u>wrap</u> some <u>gifts</u>. She doesn't want Lou to see. Amaka isn't worried. She knows her family loves to sing. She can put her gifts on the present table before they finish the first song.

Think about it.

1. What wish do you think Gani made?
2. What kinds of presents do you give to relatives? What kinds of presents can you give to friends or co-workers?

241

Verb Guide

Verbs in English are either regular or irregular in the past tense and past participle forms.

Regular Verbs

The regular verbs below are marked 1, 2, 3, or 4 according to four different spelling patterns.
(See page 244 for the irregular verbs which do not follow any of these patterns.)

Spelling Patterns for the Past and the Past Participle	Example	
1. Add -ed to the end of the verb.	ASK	ASKED
2. Add -d to the end of the verb.	LIVE	LIVED
3. Double the final consonant and add -ed to the end of the verb.	DROP	DROPPED
4. Drop the final y and add -ied to the end of the verb.	CRY	CRIED

The Oxford Picture Dictionary List of Regular Verbs

accept (1)
add (1)
address (1)
adjust (1)
agree (2)
answer (1)
apologize (2)
appear (1)
applaud (1)
apply (4)
arrange (2)
arrest (1)
arrive (2)
ask (1)
assemble (2)
assist (1)
attach (1)
bake (2)
bank (1)
bargain (1)
bathe (2)
board (1)
boil (1)
borrow (1)
bow (1)
brainstorm (1)
breathe (2)
browse (2)
brush (1)
bubble (2)
buckle (2)
burn (1)
bus (1)
calculate (2)
call (1)
capitalize (2)
carpool (1)

carry (4)
cash (1)
celebrate (2)
change (2)
check (1)
chill (1)
choke (2)
chop (3)
circle (2)
claim (1)
clean (1)
clear (1)
click (1)
climb (1)
close (2)
collate (2)
collect (1)
color (1)
comb (1)
comfort (1)
commit (3)
compliment (1)
compost (1)
conceal (1)
conduct (1)
convert (1)
convict (1)
cook (1)
copy (4)
correct (1)
cough (1)
count (1)
cross (1)
cry (4)
dance (2)
debate (2)
decline (2)

delete (2)
deliver (1)
design (1)
dial (1)
dice (2)
dictate (2)
die (2)
disagree (2)
discipline (2)
discuss (1)
dive (2)
divide (2)
dress (1)
dribble (2)
drill (1)
drop (3)
drown (1)
dry (4)
dust (1)
dye (2)
edit (1)
empty (4)
enter (1)
erase (2)
evacuate (2)
examine (2)
exchange (2)
exercise (2)
expire (2)
explain (1)
exterminate (2)
fasten (1)
fast forward (1)
fax (1)
fertilize (2)
fill (1)
finish (1)

fix (1)
floss (1)
fold (1)
follow (1)
garden (1)
gargle (2)
graduate (2)
grate (2)
grease (2)
greet (1)
hail (1)
hammer (1)
hand (1)
harvest (1)
help (1)
hire (2)
hug (3)
immigrate (2)
indent (1)
inquire (2)
insert (1)
inspect (1)
install (1)
introduce (2)
invite (2)
iron (1)
jaywalk (1)
join (1)
jump (1)
kick (1)
kiss (1)
knit (3)
label (1)
land (1)
laugh (1)
learn (1)
lengthen (1)

lift (1)
listen (1)
litter (1)
live (2)
load (1)
lock (1)
look (1)
mail (1)
manufacture (2)
match (1)
measure (2)
microwave (2)
milk (1)
misbehave (2)
miss (1)
mix (1)
mop (3)
move (2)
mow (1)
multiply (4)
negotiate (2)
network (1)
numb (1)
nurse (2)
obey (1)
observe (2)
offer (1)
open (1)
operate (2)
order (1)
organize (2)
overdose (2)
pack (1)
paint (1)
park (1)
participate (2)
pass (1)
pause (2)
peel (1)
perm (1)
pick (1)

pitch (1)
plan (3)
plant (1)
play (1)
polish (1)
pour (1)
praise (2)
preheat (1)
prepare (2)
prescribe (2)
press (1)
pretend (1)
print (1)
program (3)
protect (1)
pull (1)
purchase (2)
push (1)
quilt (1)
race (2)
raise (2)
rake (2)
receive (2)
record (1)
recycle (2)
redecorate (2)
reduce (2)
register (1)
relax (1)
remain (1)
remove (2)
renew (1)
repair (1)
replace (2)
report (1)
request (1)
retire (2)
return (1)
reuse (2)
revise (2)
rinse (2)

rock (1)
sauté (1)
save (2)
scan (3)
schedule (2)
scrub (3)
seat (1)
select (1)
sentence (2)
separate (2)
serve (2)
share (2)
shave (2)
ship (3)
shop (3)
shorten (1)
sign (1)
simmer (1)
skate (2)
ski (1)
slice (2)
smell (1)
smile (2)
smoke (2)
sneeze (2)
solve (2)
sort (1)
spell (1)
spoon (1)
staple (2)
start (1)
state (2)
stay (1)
steam (1)
stir (3)
stop (3)
stow (1)
stretch (1)
study (4)
submit (3)
subtract (1)

supervise (2)
swallow (1)
tackle (2)
talk (1)
taste (2)
thank (1)
tie (2)
touch (1)
transcribe (2)
transfer (3)
translate (2)
travel (1)
trim (3)
try (4)
turn (1)
type (2)
underline (2)
undress (1)
unload (1)
unpack (1)
unscramble (2)
use (2)
vacuum (1)
videotape (2)
volunteer (1)
vomit (1)
vote (2)
wait (1)
walk (1)
wash (1)
watch (1)
water (1)
wave (2)
weed (1)
weigh (1)
wipe (2)
work (1)
wrap (3)

Verb Guide

Irregular Verbs

These verbs have irregular endings in the past and/or the past participle.

The Oxford Picture Dictionary List of Irregular Verbs

simple	past	past participle	simple	past	past participle
be	was	been	make	made	made
beat	beat	beaten	meet	met	met
become	became	become	pay	paid	paid
bend	bent	bent	picnic	picnicked	picnicked
bleed	bled	bled	proofread	proofread	proofread
blow	blew	blown	put	put	put
break	broke	broken	read	read	read
bring	brought	brought	rewind	rewound	rewound
buy	bought	bought	rewrite	rewrote	rewritten
catch	caught	caught	ride	rode	ridden
choose	chose	chosen	run	ran	run
come	came	come	say	said	said
cut	cut	cut	see	saw	seen
do	did	done	seek	sought	sought
draw	drew	drawn	sell	sold	sold
drink	drank	drunk	send	sent	sent
drive	drove	driven	set	set	set
eat	ate	eaten	sew	sewed	sewn
fall	fell	fallen	shake	shook	shaken
feed	fed	fed	shoot	shot	shot
feel	felt	felt	show	showed	shown
find	found	found	sing	sang	sung
fly	flew	flown	sit	sat	sat
get	got	gotten	speak	spoke	spoken
give	gave	given	stand	stood	stood
go	went	gone	steal	stole	stolen
hang	hung	hung	sweep	swept	swept
have	had	had	swim	swam	swum
hear	heard	heard	swing	swung	swung
hide	hid	hidden	take	took	taken
hit	hit	hit	teach	taught	taught
hold	held	held	think	thought	thought
keep	kept	kept	throw	threw	thrown
lay	laid	laid	wake	woke	woken
leave	left	left	withdraw	withdrew	withdrawn
lend	lent	lent	write	wrote	written
let	let	let			

Index

Index Key

Font

bold type = verbs or verb phrases (example: **catch**)
ordinary type = all other parts of speech (example: baseball)
ALL CAPS = unit titles (example: MATHEMATICS)
Initial caps = subunit titles (example: Equivalencies)

Symbols

✦ = word found in exercise band at bottom of page

Numbers/Letters

first number in **bold** type = page on which word appears
second number, or letter, following number in **bold** type = item number on page
(examples: cool [ko͞ol] **13**-5 means that the word *cool* is item number 5 on page 13;
across [ə krös❘] **153**–G means that the word *across* is item G on page 153).

Pronunciation Guide

The index includes a pronunciation guide for all the words and phrases illustrated in the book. This guide uses symbols commonly found in dictionaries for native speakers. These symbols, unlike those used in pronunciation systems such as the International Phonetic Alphabet, tend to use English spelling patterns and so should help you to become more aware of the connections between written English and spoken English.

Consonants

[b] as in back [băk]	[k] as in key [kē]	[sh] as in shoe [sho͞o]
[ch] as in cheek [chēk]	[l] as in leaf [lēf]	[t] as in tape [tāp]
[d] as in date [dāt]	[m] as in match [măch]	[th] as in three [thrē]
[dh] as in this [dhĭs]	[n] as in neck [nĕk]	[v] as in vine [vīn]
[f] as in face [fās]	[ng] as in ring [rĭng]	[w] as in wait [wāt]
[g] as in gas [găs]	[p] as in park [pärk]	[y] as in yams [yămz]
[h] as in half [hăf]	[r] as in rice [rīs]	[z] as in zoo [zo͞o]
[j] as in jam [jăm]	[s] as in sand [sănd]	[zh] as in measure [mĕzhər]

Vowels

[ā] as in bake [bāk]	[ī] as in line [līn]	[o͝o] as in cook [ko͝ok]
[ă] as in back [băk]	[ĭ] as in lip [lĭp]	[ow] as in cow [kow]
[ä] as in car [kär] or box [bäks]	[ï] as in near [nïr]	[oy] as in boy [boy]
[ē] as in beat [bēt]	[ō] as in cold [kōld]	[ŭ] as in cut [kŭt]
[ĕ] as in bed [bĕd]	[ö] as in short [shört] or claw [klö]	[ü] as in curb [kürb]
[ë] as in bear [bër]	[o͞o] as in cool [ko͞ol]	[ə] as in above [ə bŭv❘]

All the pronunciation symbols used are alphabetical except for the schwa [ə]. The schwa is the most frequent vowel sound in English. If you use the schwa appropriately in unstressed syllables, your pronunciation will sound more natural.

Vowels before [r] are shown with the symbol [¨] to call attention to the special quality that vowels have before [r]. (Note that the symbols [ä] and [ö] are also used for vowels not followed by [r], as in *box* or *claw*.) You should listen carefully to native speakers to discover how these vowels actually sound.

Stress

This index follows the system for marking stress used in many dictionaries for native speakers.

1. Stress is not marked if a word consisting of a single syllable occurs by itself.

2. Where stress is marked, two levels are distinguished:

a bold accent [❘] is placed after each syllable with primary (or strong) stress, a light accent [❘] is placed after each syllable with secondary (or weaker) stress. In phrases and other combinations of words, stress is indicated for each word as it would be pronounced within the whole phrase.

Syllable Boundaries

Syllable boundaries are indicated by a single space or by a stress mark.

Note: The pronunciations shown in this index are based on patterns of American English. There has been no attempt to represent all of the varieties of American English. Students should listen to native speakers to hear how the language actually sounds in a particular region.

Index

Abbreviations [ə brē/vē ā/shənz] **48**
abdomen [ăb/də mən] **107**–27
about [ə bowt/] **48**–B, **174**–L, **191**–E
above [ə bŭv/] **25**–4
accelerator [ĭk sĕl/ə rā/tər] **159**–46
accept [ĭk sĕpt/] **12**–G, **12**–I, **12** ✦
access number [ăk/sĕs/ nŭm/bər] **14**–16
Accessories [ĭk sĕs/ə rēz] **59, 94**–**95**
accident [ăk/sə dənt] **144**–2
accordion [ə kör/dē ən] **238**–19
account [ə kownt/] **132**–11, **132**–14
    account manager [ə kownt/ măn/ə jər] **132**–9
Account [ə kownt/] **132**
accountant [ə kown/tənt] **166**–1
ache [āk]
    backache [băk/āk/] **110**–5
    earache [ir/āk/] **110**–3
    headache [hĕd/āk/] **110**–1
    stomachache [stŭm/ək/ āk/] **110**–4
    toothache [tōōth/āk/] **110**–2
acid rain [ăs/əd rān/] **218**–13
across [ə krös] **153**–G
acrylic paint [ə krĭl/ĭk pānt] **232**–10
action [ăk/shən]
    action figure [ăk/shən fĭg/yər] **233**–26
    action story [ăk/shən stör/ē] **237**–19
activist [ăk/tə vĭst] **199**–17
actor [ăk/tər] **166**–2
acupuncture [ăk/yə pŭngk/chər] **122**–2
acute angle [ə kyōōt/ ăng/gəl] **193**–28
ad [ăd] **48**–2, **197**–9
adapter [ə dăp/tər] **234**–15
add [ăd] **77**–N, **101**–B, **192**–A
address [ə drĕs/, ă/drĕs] **4**–5
    mailing address [mā/lĭng ə drĕs/, –ă/drĕs] **134**–22
    return address [rĭ türn/ ə drĕs/, –ă/drĕs] **134**–21
    website address [wĕb/sīt ə drĕs/, –ă/drĕs] **197**–4
address [ə drĕs/] **135**–B, **197**–C
adhesive bandage [əd hē/sĭv băn/dĭj] **117**–5
adjust [ə jŭst/] **219**–J
    adjustable wrench [ə jŭs/tə bəl rĕnch/] **181**–48
    adjustment [ə jŭst/mənt] **194**–23, **194**–24
administrative assistant
    [əd mĭn/ə strā/tĭv ə sĭs/tənt] **166**–3
administrator [əd mĭn/ə strā/tər] **120**–13
Administrators [əd mĭn/ə strā/tərz] **5**
admissions clerk [əd mĭ/shənz klürk/] **120**–14
ADULTS AND CHILDREN [ə dŭlts/ en chĭl/ drən] **30**–**31**
adult school [ə dŭlt/ skōōl/, ăd/ŭlt–] **188**–8
adventure story [əd vĕn/chər stör/ē] **237**–19
aerobic exercise [ə rō/bĭk ĕk/sər sīz/] **122**–5
afraid [ə frād/] **43**–23
after [ăf/tər]
    afternoon [ăf/tər nōōn/] **18**–17
    aftershave [ăf/tər shāv/] **109**–30
    five after one [fīv/ ăf/tər wŭn/] **18**–7
    quarter after one [kwör/tər ăf/tər wŭn/] **18**–9
    ten after one [tĕn/ ăf/tər wŭn/] **18**–8
    twenty after one [twĕn/tē ăf/tər wŭn/] **18**–10
After an Emergency [ăf/tər ən ĭ mür/jən sē] **147**
Age [āj] **32**
agency [ā/jən sē] **131**–14

agent [ā/jənt] **160**–3, **160**–5
agree [ə grē/] **12**–K
agreement [ə grē/mənt] **51**–28
aid [ād]
    first aid kit [fürst/ ād/ kĭt/] **117**–1, **146**–18
    first aid manual [fürst/ ād/ măn/yōō əl] **117**–2
    hearing aid [hĭr/ĭng ād/] **115**–10
aide [ād] **167**–32
AIDS (acquired immune deficiency syndrome) [ādz] /
    [ə kwī/rd ĭ myōōn/ də fĭ/shən sē sĭn/drōm] **111** ✦
air [ër]
    air bag [ër/ băg/] **159**–43
    air conditioner [ër/ kən dĭsh/ə nər] **159**–39
    Air Force [ër/ förs/] **138**–16
    airmail [ër/māl/] **134**–5
    airplane [ër/plān/] **150**–8
    airplane crash [ër/plān/ krăsh/] **144**–3
    air pollution [ër/ pə lōō/shən] **218**–11
    airport [ër/pört/] **151**–10
    air purifier [ër/ pyōōr/ə fī ər] **113**–14
Airline Terminal [ër/līn/ tür/mə nəl] **160**
Airplane [ër/plān/] **161**
AIRPORT [ër/pört/] **160**–**161**
Airport Transportation
    [ër/pört/ trăns/pər tā/shən] **152**
aisle [īl] **72**–6
alarm clock [ə lärm/ kläk/] **58**–24
Alaska time [ə lăs/kə tīm/] **19**–28
album [ăl/bəm] **235**–31, **235**–32
alfalfa [ăl făl/fə] **177**–5
algebra [ăl/jə brə] **192**–16
allergic reaction [ə lür/jĭk rē ăk/shən] **116**–E
allergies [ăl/ər jēz] **111**–8
alley [ăl/ē] **51**–24, **222**–4
alligator [ăl/ə gā/tər] **213**–36
alphabet [ăl/fə bĕt/] **7**–13
Alterations [öl/tə rā/shənz] **100**
ALTERATIONS [öl/tə rā/shənz] **100**
Alteration Shop [öl/tə rā/shən shäp/] **100**
aluminum foil [ə lōō/mə nəm foyl/] **72**–23
Alzheimer's disease [älts/hī mərz dĭ zēz/, älts–] **111** ✦
a.m. [ā/ĕm/] **18**–4
ambulance [ăm/byə ləns] **116**–1, **121**–34
AMERICA [ə mĕr/ə kə] **200**–**201**
American cheese [ə mĕr/ə kən chēz/] **71**–26
Americans [ə mĕr/ə kənz] **198**–3
Amphibians [ăm fĭb/ē ənz] **212**
AMPHIBIANS [ăm fĭb/ē ənz] **212**–**213**
amusement park [ə myōōz/mənt pärk/] **223**–10
ancient [ān/shənt] **199**–1
anemone [ə nĕ/mə nē] **212**–24
angle [ăng/gəl] **193**–26, **193**–27, **193**–28
Angles [ăng/gəlz] **193**
angry [ăng/grē] **43**–29
animals [ăn/ə məlz] **59**–15
Animals [ăn/ə məlz] **212, 215**
ANIMALS [ăn/ə məlz] **215**
ankle [ăng/kəl] **106**–23, **110**–18
    ankle socks [ăng/kəl säks/] **91**–7
anklets [ăngk/ləts/] **91**–11
anniversary [ăn/ə vür/sə rē] **22**–3

answer [ăn/sər] **8**–L
answering machine [ăn/sə rĭng mə shēn/] **14**–17
answer sheet [ăn/sər shēt/] **10**–2
antacid [ănt ăs/əd] **113**–28
anteater [ănt/ē/tər] **217**–24
antelope [ăn/tə lōp/] **217**–35
antenna [ăn tĕ/nə] **14**–9
antibacterial ointment
    [ăn/tē băk tĭr/ē əl oynt/mənt] **117**–10
antihistamine cream [ăn/tĭ hĭs/tə mēn krēm/] **117**–11
antiperspirant [ăn/tē pürs/pə rənt] **108**–5
antlers [ănt/lərz] **216**–16
ants [ăntz] **63**–23
apartment [ə pärt/mənt] **48**–3, **48**–4
    apartment building [ə pärt/mənt bĭl/dĭng] **50**–1
    apartment number [ə pärt/mənt nüm/bər] **4**–6
Apartment [ə pärt/mənt] **48**
Apartment Complex [ə pärt/mənt käm/plĕx] **51**
Apartment Entryway [ə pärt/mənt ĕn/trē wā/] **51**
APARTMENTS [ə pärt/məntz] **50**–**51**
APC (automated postal center) [ā/pē/sē/] /
    [ö/tə māt ĭd pōs/təl–sĕn/tər] **135**–10
apologize [ə päl/ə jīz/] **12**–F
apostrophe [ə päs/trə fē] **190**–16
apparatus [ăp/ə rä/təs] **224**–14
appear [ə pïr/] **141**–C
Appearance [ə pïr/əns] **32**
applaud [ə plöd/] **148**–B
apples [ăp/əlz] **68**–1
    apple juice [ăp/əl jōōs/] **73**–32
appliance repair person
    [ə plī/əns rĭ për/ pür/sən] **166**–4
appliqué [ăp/lə kā/] **99**–31
apply [ə plī/] **109**–P
appointment [ə poynt/mənt] **22**–4, **118**–1
    appointment book [ə poynt/mənt bŏŏk/] **183**–48
apricots [ăp/rə käts/] **68**–12
April [ā/prəl] **21**–28
apron [ā/prən] **92**–11, **93**–30
aquarium [ə kwër/ē əm] **222**–7
Arachnids [ə răk/nīdz/] **214**
ARACHNIDS [ə răk/nīdz/] **214**
archery [är/chə rē] **228**–1
architect [är/kə tĕkt/] **166**–5
area [ër/ē ə]
    area code [ër/ē ə kōd/] **4**–10, **15**–29
    boarding area [bör/dĭng ër/ē ə] **161**–9
    dining area [dī/nĭng ër/ē ə] **46**–7
    play area [plā/ ër/ē ə] **130**–11
    reception area [rĭ sĕp/shən ër/ē ə] **182**–5
    rural area [rŏŏr/əl ër/ē ə] **52**–4
    screening area [skrē/nĭng ër/ē ə] **160**–4
    testing area [tĕs/tĭng ër/ē ə] **136**–2
    urban area [ür/bən ër/ē ə] **52**–1
AREA [ër/ē ə] **55**
Area and Volume [ër/ē ə ən văl/yəm, –yōōm] **193**
arm [ärm] **105**–14, **194**–15
    armchair [ärm/chër/] **56**–22
armadillo [är/mə dīl/ō] **216**–8
Arm, Hand, and Fingers [ärm/ hănd/ ən fĭng/gərz] **106**
Army [är/mē] **138**–14, **199**–11
around [ə rownd/] **153**–H

Around Campus [ə rownd/ kăm/pəs] 5
arrange [ə rănj/] 49–Q
arrest [ə rĕst/] 141–A
arrival [ə rī/vəl] 161–7, 161 ✦
arrive [ə rīv/] 160–K
arrow [ăr/ō] 231–8
arson [är/sən] 142–7
artery [är/tə rē] 107–36
arthritis [är thrī/təs] 111–16
artichokes [är/tə chōks/] 69–22
artist [är/tĭst] 166–6
arts [ärts] 189–9, 189–15, 228–11
    art museum [ärt/ myōō zē/əm] 223–9
ask [ăsk] 2–B
    ask about [ăsk/ ə bowt/] 48–B, 157–B
    ask for [ăsk/ för/] 10–F
    ask questions [ăsk/ kwĕs/chənz] 8–K, 174–M
asparagus [ə spĕr/ə gəs] 69–26
assault [ə sölt/] 142–3
assemble [ə sĕm/bəl] 170–A, 175–C
assembler [ə sĕm/blər] 166–7
assembly [ə sĕm/blē] 140–1
    assembly line [ə sĕm/blē līn/] 175–6
    assemblyperson [ə sĕm/blē pür/sən] 139–24
assist [ə sĭst/] 95–D, 170–B
assistance [ə sĭs/təns] 14–22
assistant [ə sĭs/tənt]
    administrative assistant
        [əd mĭn/ ə strā/ tĭv ə sĭs/tənt] 166–3
    assistant principal [ə sĭs/tənt prĭn/sə pəl] 5–5
    certified nursing assistant (CNA) [sür/tə fīd/
        nür/sĭng ə sĭs/tənt] / [sē/ĕn/ā/] 120–12
    dental assistant [dĕn/təl ə sĭs/tənt] 119–2, 167–22
    physician assistant [fə zĭ/shən ə sĭs/tənt] 168–47
Assistant [ə sĭs/tənt] 93
asthma [ăz/mə] 111–9
astronaut [ăs/trə nöt/] 205–17
astronomer [ə strä/nə mər] 205–22
Astronomy [ə strä/nə mē] 205
At Customs [ăt/ kŭs/təmz] 161
athletic [ăth lĕt/ĭk]
    athletic shoes [ăth lĕt/ĭk shōōz/] 86–7
    athletic supporter [ăth lĕt/ĭk sə pör/tər] 91–6
Atlantic time [ət lăn/tĭk tīm/] 19–33
atlas [ăt/ləs] 133–8
ATM (Automated Teller Machine) [ā/tē/ĕm/] /
    [ö/tə māt ĭd tĕ/lər mə shēn/] 132
ATM card [ā/tē/ĕm/ kärd/] 132–15
atom [ăt/əm] 195–28
attach [ə tăch/] 197–G, 197–H
attachments [ə tăch/mənts] 61–11
attack [ə tăk/] 116–D
attendant [ə tĕn/dənt] 161–12, 162–3, 184–3
At the Dealer [ăt/ dhə dē/lər] 158
At the Gate [ăt/ dhə gāt/] 161
At the Mechanic [ăt/ dhə mə kăn/ĭk] 158
At the Security Checkpoint
    [ăt/ dhə sə kyōō/ rə tē/ chĕk/ poynt/] 160
attic [ăt/ək] 47–7
attorney [ə tür/nē] 141–4, 141–10
attractive [ə trăk/tĭv] 32–13
audiobook [ö/dē ō bōŏk/] 133–17

audiologist [ö dē ä/lə jĭst] 115–9
auditorium [ö/də tör/ē əm] 5–18
August [ö/gəst] 21–32
aunt [ănt] 34–7
author [ö/thər] 133–15, 169–64
auto [ö/tō]
    auto club card [ö/tō klŭb/ kärd/] 162–4
    auto mechanic [ö/tō mə kăn/ĭk] 166–8
automated [ö/tə māt ĭd]
    automated phone system
        [ö/tə māt ĭd fōn/ sĭs/təm] 14–23
    automated postal center (APC)
        [ö/tə māt ĭd pōs/təl sĕn/tər] / [ā/pē/sē/] 135–10
Automated Teller Machine
    [ö/tə māt ĭd tĕl/ər mə shēn/] 132
Automatic Transmission
    [ö tə māt/ĭk trănz mĭ/shən] 159
Automotive Painter [ö tə mōt/ĭv pān/tər] 92
autumn [ö/təm] 21–39
avalanche [ăv/ə lănch/] 145–18
average [ăv/rĭj]
    average height [ăv/rĭj hīt/] 32–5
    average weight [ăv/rĭj wāt/] 32–8
avocados [ä/və kä/dōz, ăv/ə–] 84–6
ax [ăks] 180–3
baboon [bă bōōn/] 217–31
baby [bā/bē] 31–7
    baby bag [bā/bē băg/] 37–16
    baby carrier [bā/bē kă/rē/ər] 37–17
    baby food [bā/bē fōōd/] 37–4
    baby lotion [bā/bē lō/shən] 37–13
    baby monitor [bā/bē män/ə tər] 59–7
    baby powder [bā/bē pow/dər] 37–14
    babysitter [bā/bē sĭt/ər] 166–9
    baby's room [bā/bēz/ rōōm/] 47–10
back [băk] 104–5
    backache [băk/āk/] 110–5
    back button [băk/ bŭt/n] 197–2
    backhoe [băk/hō/] 178–8
    backpack [băk/păk/] 94–18, 226–15
    backpacking [băk/păk/ĭng] 226–6
    backseat [băk/sēt/] 159–54
    back support belt [băk/ sə pört/ bĕlt/] 179–18
    go back [gō/ băk/] 11–M
    horseback riding [hörs/băk/ rī/dĭng] 226–9
    lower back [lō/ər băk/] 107–29
    pay back [pā/ băk/] 26–D
Backyard [băk/yärd/] 53
BACK FROM THE MARKET
    [băk/ frəm dhə mär/kət] 66–67
bacon [bā/kən] 70–11, 80–1
bad [băd] 23–18
BAD DAY AT WORK [băd/ dā/ ăt würk/] 186–187
badge [băj] 93–21
badminton [băd/mĭn tən] 228–6
bag [băg] 69–31, 74–7, 74–19, 161–18
    air bag [ĕr/ băg/] 159–43
    baby bag [bā/bē băg/] 37–16
    clutch bag [klŭch/ băg/] 89–19
    grocery bag [grōs/rē băg/] 67–13
    handbag [hănd/ băg/] 87–9, 94–2
    plastic storage bags [plăs/tĭk stör/ĭj băgz/] 72–25

    shoulder bag [shōl/dər băg/] 94–17
    sleeping bag [slē/pĭng băg/] 226–12
    totebag [tōt/ băg/] 94–19
    trash bags [trăsh/ băgz/] 61–24
    vacuum cleaner bag
        [văk/yōōm klē/nər băg/] 61–12
bagels [bā/gəlz] 73–40
baggage [băg/ĭj]
    baggage carousel [băg/ĭj kăr/ə sĕl/] 161–23
bagger [băg/ər] 73–14
baggy [băg/ē] 97–30
bailiff [bā/lĭf] 141–13
bake [bāk] 77–H
Baked Goods [bākt/ gōōdz/] 73
baked potato [bākt/ pə tā/tō] 81–25
baker [bā/kər] 166–10
bakery [bā/kə rē] 127–19
Baking Products [bā/kĭng prăd/ŭkts] 73
balance [băl/əns] 132–17, 195–41
balcony [băl/kə nē] 51–20
bald [böld] 33–12
ball [böl] 59–12, 231–5, 231–12
    ball field [böl/ fēld/] 224–1
    ballroom [böl/rōōm/] 184–26
    baseball [bās/böl/] 231–18, 231–14
    basketball [băs/kət böl/] 229–8, 231–4
    basketball court [băs/kət böl/ kört/] 229–7
    football [fōōt/böl/] 229–11, 231–21
    meatballs [mēt/bölz/] 81–27
    racquetball [răk/ət böl/] 228–12
    softball [söft/böl/] 229–10
    volleyball [väl/ē böl/] 229–14, 231–3
balloons [bə lōōnz/] 44–4
bananas [bə năn/əz] 68–2
band [bănd] 183–34
    headband [hĕd/bănd/] 90–3
    waistband [wāst/bănd/] 100–5
bandage [băn/dĭj] 117–5, 117–12
bandana [băn dă/nə] 92–16
bangs [băngz] 33–8
bank [băngk] 124–5
    bank statement [băngk/ stāt/mənt] 132–16
bank online [băngk/ än līn/] 132–C
BANK [băngk] 132
banner [băn/ər] 44–1
banquet room [băng/kwət rōōm/] 185–14
bar [bär]
    bar code [bär/ kōd/] 27–4
    candy bar [kăn/dē bär/] 73–37
    grab bar [grăb/ bär/] 57–9
    menu bar [mĕn/yōō bär/] 197–1
    salad bar [săl/əd bär/] 79–24
    scroll bar [skrōl/ bär/] 197–15
barbecued ribs [bär/bĭ kyōō/d rĭbz/] 76–2
barbershop [bär/bər shäp/] 129–19
bargain [bär/gən] 102–A
barn [bärn] 177–11
barrette [bə rĕt/] 108–20
base [bās] 193–45, 194–20
baseball [bās/böl/] 229–9, 231–18
    baseball bat [bās/böl/ băt/] 231–14
    baseball cap [bās/böl/ kăp/] 86–5

Index

baseball cards [bās/böl/ kärds/] **232**–2
baseball game [bās/böl/ gām/] **44**–2
basement [bās/mənt] **47**–13
Basement [bās/mənt] **50**
Basic Colors [bā/sĭk kŭ/lərz] **24**
BASIC TRANSPORTATION
 [bā/sĭk trănz/pər tā/shən] **150**–151
basket [bās/kət] **56**–3
 basketball [bās/kət böl/] **229**–8, **231**–4
 basketball court [bās/kət böl kört/] **229**–7
 bread basket [brĕd/ bās/kət] **83**–11
 laundry basket [lön/drē bās/kət] **101**–2
 shopping basket [shäp/ĭng bās/kət] **73**–9
 wastebasket [wāst/bās/kət] **57**–26
bass [bās] **212**–6, [bās] **238**–8
bassoon [bə sōōn/] **238**–4
bat [băt] **216**–7, **231**–14
bath [băth]
 bath mat [băth/ măt/] **57**–28
 bath powder [băth/ pow/dər] **108**–4
 bathroom [băth/rōōm/] **46**–4
 bath towel [băth/ tow/əl] **57**–13
 bathtub [băth/tŭb/] **57**–2
 half bath [hăf/ băth/] **57** ✦
bathe [bādh] **36**–F, **108**–B
bathing suit [bā/dhĭng sōōt/] **90**–26
BATHROOM [băth/rōōm/] **57**
battery / batteries [băt/ə rē] / [băt/ə rēz]
 146–15, **158**–20
 battery charger [băt/ə rē chär/jər] **235**–27
 battery pack [băt/ə rē păk/] **235**–26
bay [bā] **204**–9
be [bē]
 be aware [bē ə wër/] **143**–I
 be born [bē börn/] **40**–A
 be 18 or older [bē ā/tēn/ ör ōld/ər] **140**–G
 be hurt [bē hürt/] **116**–C
 be in a rock band [bē ĭn ə räk/ bănd/] **238**–D
 be informed [bē ĭn förmd/] **140**–F
 be injured [bē ĭn/jərd] **116**–C
 be in shock [bē ĭn shäk/] **116**–B
 be neat [bē nēt/] **174**–C
 be on time [bē ön tīm/] **174**–F
 be released [bē rĭ lēst/] **141**–H
 be unconscious [bē ŭn kän/shəs] **116**–A
 don't be late [dōnt/ bē lāt/] **174**–D
beach [bēch] **204**–10
 beach chair [bēch/ chër/] **225**–22
 beach umbrella [bēch/ ŭm brĕl/ə] **225**–14
BEACH [bēch] **225**
beads [bēdz] **95**–34, **99**–32
beak [bēk] **214**–3
beaker [bē/kər] **195**–39
beam [bēm] **178**–3
beans [bēnz] **69**–8, **72**–17
 soybeans [soy/bēnz] **177**–3
bear [bër] **37**–23, **216**–11
beard [bērd] **33**–6
beat [bēt] **77**–S
beater [bē/tər]
 eggbeater [ĕg/bē/tər] **78**–20
beautiful [byōō/tə fəl] **23**–21

beauty shop [byōō/tē shäp/] **130** ✦
beaver [bē/vər] **216**–9
become [bē kŭm/] **40**–G, **41**–N
bed [bĕd] **58**–9
 bedbugs [bĕd/bŭgz/] **63**–24
 bed control [bĕd/ kən trōl/] **121**–27
 bed frame [bĕd/ frām/] **58**–18
 bed pan [bĕd/ păn/] **121**–23
 bedroom [bĕd/rōōm/] **46**–2
 bedspread [bĕd/sprĕd/] **59**–11
 bed table [bĕd/ tā/bəl] **121**–21
 bunk beds [bŭnk/ bĕdz/] **59**–9
 double bed [dŭb/əl bĕd/] **184**–14
 flower bed [flow/ər bĕd/] **53**–20
 hospital bed [häs/pĭ tl bĕd/] **121**–22
 kids' bedroom [kĭdz/ bĕd/rōōm/] **47**–9
 king-size bed [kĭng/sīz/ bĕd/] **184**–15
BEDROOM [bĕd/rōōm/] **58, 59**
bee [bē]
 honeybee [hŭn/ē bē/] **214**–25
beef [bēf]
 beef ribs [bēf/ rĭbz/] **70**–5
 corned beef [körnd/ bēf/] **71**–22
 ground beef [grownd/ bēf/] **70**–4
 roast beef [rōst/ bēf/] **71**–21
 stewing beef [stōō/ĭng bēf/] **70**–3
 stir-fried beef [stür/frīd/ bēf/] **76**–6
Beef [bēf] **70**
beetle [bēt/l] **214**–18
beets [bēts] **69**–5
Before an Emergency [bĭ för/ ən ĭ mür/ jən sē] **146**
behind [bĭ hīnd/] **25**–8
beige [bāzh] **24**–18
bell [bĕl]
 bell captain [bĕl/ kăp/tən] **184**–6
 bellhop [bĕl/häp/] **184**–7
 bell peppers [bĕl/ pĕp/ərz] **69**–7
 doorbell [dör/bĕl/] **53**–14
below [bĭ lō/] **25**–5
belts [bĕlts] **94**–6
 back support belt [băk/ sə pört/ bĕlt/] **179**–18
 belt buckle [bĕlt/ bŭk/əl] **94**–20
 conveyor belt [kən vā/ər bĕlt/] **175**–9
 garter belt [gär/tər bĕlt/] **91**–16
 seat belt [sēt/ bĕlt/] **159**–52
 tool belt [tōōl/ bĕlt/] **92**–3
bench [bĕnch] **224**–10
bend [bĕnd] **230**–O
benefits [bĕn/ə fĭts] **174** ✦
berries [bĕr/ēz] **210**–20
 blackberries [blăk/bĕr/ēz] **68**–17
 blueberries [blōō/bĕr/ēz] **68**–16
 mixed berries [mĭkst/ bĕr/ēz] **81**–36
 raspberries [răz/bĕr/ēz] **68**–15
 strawberries [strö/bĕr/ēz] **68**–14
between [bĭ twēn/] **25**–12
Beverages [bĕv/rə jəz] **73, 81**
bib [bĭb] **37**–5
bicycle / bike [bī/sĭ kəl] / [bīk] **129**–22, **151**–15
big [bĭg] **23**–2, **97**–38
 Big Dipper [bĭg/ dĭ/pər] **205** ✦
 big-screen TV [bĭg/skrēn/ tē/vē/] **50**–15

bike / bicycle [bīk] / [bī/sĭ kəl] **129**–22, **151**–15
 bike path [bīk/ păth/] **224**–3
biking [bī/kĭng] **226**–8, **228**–5
bikini panties [bə kē/nē păn/tēz] **91**–13
bill [bĭl] **214**–3
Bill [bĭl] **15**
billiards [bĭl/yərdz] **228**–2
Bill of Rights [bĭl/ əv rīts/] **198**–10
Bills [bĭlz] **26**
bin [bĭn] **51**–23, **61**–2, **160**–6
bioenergy [bī/ō ĕn/ər jē] **218**–9
biography [bī ä/grə fē] **133**–15
biologist [bī ä/lə jĭst] **194**–2
Biology [bī ä/lə jē] **194**
biomass [bī/ō măs/] **218**–9
birch [bürch] **210**–7
bird [bürd] **208**–4
Bird [bürd] **214**
BIRDS, INSECTS, AND ARACHNIDS
 [bürdz/ ĭn/sĕkts ən ə räk/nĭdz] **214**
birth [bürth]
 birth certificate [bürth/ sər tĭf/ə kət] **40**–1
 birthday [bürth/dā/] **22**–1
BIRTHDAY PARTY [bürth/dā/ pär/tē] **240**–241
biscuits [bĭs/kəts] **80**–6
bison [bī/sən] **216**–6
bit [bĭt] **180**–28
bite [bīt] **110**–11
black [blăk] **24**–13
 blackberries [blăk/bĕr/ēz] **68**–17
 black hair [blăk/ hër/] **33**–16
bladder [blăd/ər] **107**–46
blade [blād] **107**–28, **109**–28, **180**–27
blankets [blăng/kəts] **58**–15, **146**–7, **225**–11
 blanket sleeper [blăng/kət slē/pər] **91**–27
blazer [blā/zər] **92**–12
bleach [blēch] **101**–7
bleachers [blē/chərz] **5**–3
bleed [blēd] **116**–M
blender [blĕn/dər] **54**–12
blind [blīnd] **32**–11
blister [blĭs/tər] **110**–15
blizzard [blĭz/ərd] **13**–23, **145**–13
blocks [bläks] **59**–19
 quilt block [kwĭlt/ bläk/] **232**–15
 sunblock [sŭn/bläk/] **108**–8, **225**–10
blond hair [bländ/ hër/] **33**–17
blood [blŭd] **111**–14
 blood pressure gauge [blŭd/ prĕsh/ər gāj/] **118**–9
 blood test [blŭd/ tĕst/] **121**–30
 blood work [blŭd/ würk/] **121**–30
 bloody nose [blŭd/ē nōz/] **110**–17
blouse [blows] **87**–8
blow dryer [blō/ drī/ər] **33**–23, **108**–18
blower [blō/ər] **176**–2
blow out [blō/ owt/] **240**–C
blue [blōō] **24**–3
 blueberries [blōō/bĕr/ēz] **68**–16
 blue jay [blōō/ jā/] **214**–6
 bright blue [brīt/ blōō/] **24**–12
 dark blue [därk/ blōō/] **24**–10
 light blue [līt/ blōō/] **24**–11
 navy blue [nā/vē blōō/] **28**–5

blues [blōōz] **237**–22
blush [blŭsh] **109**–37
board [bôrd]
    board game [bôrd/ gām/] **232**–5
    bulletin board [bŏŏl/ə tn bôrd/] **7**–14
    chalkboard [chôk/bôrd/] **6**–1
    cutting board [kŭt/ĭng bôrd/] **54**–27
    emery board [ĕm/ə rē bôrd/, ĕm/rē–] **109**–32
    headboard [hĕd/bôrd/] **58**–10
    ironing board [i/ər nĭng bôrd/] **101**–14
    motherboard [mŭdh/ər bôrd/] **196**–5
    particle board [pär/tə kəl bôrd/] **181**–20
    skateboard [skāt/bôrd/] **224**–7
    snowboard [snō/bôrd/] **231**–23
    surfboard [sürf/bôrd/] **225**–16
    whiteboard [wīt/bôrd/] **6**–3
board [bôrd] **160**–E
boarding [bôr/dĭng]
    boarding area [bôr/dĭng ër/ē ə] **161**–9
    boarding pass [bôr/dĭng păs/] **161**–20
    sailboarding [sāl/bôr/dĭng] **227** ✦
    skateboarding [skāt/bôr/dĭng] **228**–13
    snowboarding [snō/bôr/dĭng] **227**–2
boat [bōt]
    sailboat [sāl/bōt/] **225**–3
boating [bō/tĭng] **226**–1
bobbin [bä/bĭn] **98**–21
bobby pins [bäb/ē pĭnz] **108**–21
body [bäd/ē] **190**–7
    body lotion [bäd/ē lō/shən] **108**–9
    body of water [bäd/ē əv wö/tər] **204** ✦
    body shaper [bäd/ē/ shā/pər] **91**–15
BODY [bäd/ē] **104**–**105**, **106**–**107**
boil [boyl] **77**–M
boiled ham [boyld/ hăm/] **76**–5
boiler [boy/lər] **78**–8
bok choy [bäk/ choy/] **69**–15
bolt [bōlt] **51**–34, **180**–35, **180**–38
    bolt of fabric [bōlt/ əv făb/rĭk] **98**–15
bone [bōn] **107**–33, **116**–P
    boneless [bōn/ləs] **70** ✦
book [bŏŏk]
    appointment book [ə poynt/mənt bŏŏk/] **183**–48
    audiobook [ö/dē ō bŏŏk/] **133**–17
    bookkeeper [bŏŏk/ kē/pər] **175**–2
    book of stamps [bŏŏk/ əv stămps/] **134**–18
    bookcase [bŏŏk/ kās/] **7**–10
    bookstore [bŏŏk/ stôr/] **130**–4
    check book [chĕk/ bŏŏk/] **132**–12
    coloring book [kŭl/ə rĭng bŏŏk/] **59**–13
    DMV handbook [dē/ĕm/vē/ hănd/bŏŏk/] **136**–1
    notebook [nōt/bŏŏk/] **7**–27
    passbook [păs/bŏŏk/] **132**–10
    picture book [pĭk/chər bŏŏk/] **133**–12
    spiral notebook [spī/rəl nōt/bŏŏk/] **7**–29
    test booklet [tĕst/ bŏŏk/lət] **10**–1
    textbook [tĕkst/bŏŏk/, tĕks/–] **7**–25
    workbook [würk/bŏŏk/] **7**–26
boombox [bōōm/bäks/] **234**–1
booth [bōōth] **82**–4, **122**–3

boots [bōōts] **95**–28
    hiking boots [hī/kĭng bōōts/] **95**–31
    rain boots [rān/ bōōts/] **90**–20
    safety boots [sāf/tē bōōts/] **179**–20
    ski boots [skē/ bōōts/] **231**–26
    steel toe boots [stēl/ tō/ bōōts/] **92**–6
bored [bôrd] **43**–25
borrow [bär/ō, bör/ō] **26**–B
boss [bäs] **164**–4
botanical garden [bə tăn/ĭ kəl gär/dn] **222**–3
bottle [bät/l] **37**–1, **74**–1, **74**–13
    bottle return [bät/l rĭ türn/] **73**–16
    hot water bottle [hät/ wö/tər bät/l] **113**–15
bottled water [bät/ld wö/tər] **146**–11
bouquet [bō kā/, bōō–] **211**–28
bow [bō] **231**–6
    bow tie [bō/ tī/] **89**–16
bow [bow] **3**–H
bowl [bōl] **55**–2
    mixing bowl [mĭks/ĭng bōl/] **54**–28, **78**–31
    serving bowl [sürv/ĭng bōl/] **55**–21
    soup bowl [sōōp/ bōl/] **83**–21
    sugar bowl [shŏŏg/ər bōl/] **55**–14
bowling [bō/lĭng] **228**–3
    bowling alley [bō/lĭng ăl/ē] **222**–4
    bowling ball [bō/lĭng bōl/] **231**–5
box / boxes [bäks/, bäks/ĭz] **74**–6, **74**–18
    box spring [bäks/ sprĭng/] **58**–19
    CD boombox [sē/dē/ bōōm/bäks/] **234**–1
    fuse box [fyōōz/ bäks/] **62**–13
    mailboxes [māl/bäk/səz] **50**–11, **128**–13
    post office box (PO box)
        [pōst/ ö/fəs bäks/] / [pē/ō bäks/] **135**–9
    safety deposit box [sāf/tē dĭ päz/ət bäks/] **132**–7
    sandbox [sănd/bäks/] **224**–15
    search box [sürch/ bäks/] **197**–5
    text box [tĕkst/ bäks/] **197**–13
    to-go box [tə gō/ bäks/] **82**–5
boxer shorts [bäk/sər shôrts/] **91**–4
boxing [bäks/ĭng] **228**–4
boy [boy] **31**–9
bra [brä] **91**–20
bracelets [brās/ləts] **95**–9, **117**–3
braces [brā/səz] **119**–6
brain [brān] **107**–34
brainstorm [brān/stôrm/] **8**–H, **191**–F
brake [brāk] **159**–48
    brake light [brāk/ līt/] **158**–14
    brake pedal [brāk/ pĕd/l] **159**–45
branch [brănch] **210**–2
Branch [brănch] **138**
Brass [brăs] **238**
bread [brĕd] **67**–11
    bread-and-butter plate [brĕd/ n bŭt/ər plāt/] **83**–19
    bread basket [brĕd/ băs/kət] **83**–11
    garlic bread [gär/lĭk brĕd/] **81**–28
    rye bread [rī/ brĕd/] **71**–20
    wheat bread [wēt/ brĕd/] **71**–19
    white bread [wīt/ brĕd/] **71**–18
break [brāk] **77**–Q, **116**–P
    break down [brāk/ down/] **162**–D

Breakfast Special [brĕk/fəst spē/shəl] **80**
breasts [brĕsts] **70**–19, **107**–26
breathe [brēdh] **116**–N
breathing [brē/dhĭng] **117**–16
bricklayer [brĭk/lā/ər] **186**–8
bricks [brĭks] **178**–12, **178**–B
briefcase [brēf/kās/] **88**–13
briefs [brēfs] **91**–5, **91**–14
bright blue [brīt/ blōō/] **24**–12
bring [brĭng] **174**–D, **240**–E
broccoli [bräk/ə lē] **69**–13
broiled steak [broyld/ stāk/] **76**–3
broiler [broy/lər] **54**–21
broken [brō/kən] **62**–5, **62**–6, **62**–7, **63**–15, **97**–39
    broken equipment [brō/kən ĭ kwĭp/mənt] **179**–4
broom [brōōm] **61**–16
brother [brŭdh/ər] **34**–6, **35**–28
    brother-in-law [brŭdh/ər ĭn lö/] **34**–17
    stepbrother [stĕp/brŭdh/ər] **35**–30
brown [brown] **24**–17
    brown hair [brown/ hër/] **33**–18
    hash browns [hăsh/ brownz/] **80**–3
browse [browz] **102**–B
bruise [brōōz] **110**–12
brush [brŭsh] **33**–22, **108**–14
    paintbrush [pānt/brŭsh/] **181**–22, **233**–20
    scrub brush [skrŭb/ brŭsh/] **61**–20
    toilet brush [toy/lət brŭsh/] **57**–18
    toothbrush [tōōth/brŭsh/] **109**–22
brush [brŭsh] **108**–I, **109**–J
bubble in [bŭ/bəl ĭn/] **10**–K
bucket [bŭk/ət] **61**–7, **225**–8
buckle [bŭk/əl] **94**–20, **99**–28
buckle up [bŭk/əl ŭp/] **36**–L
bud [bŭd] **211**–7
budget [bŭ jĭt/] **186**–3
buffalo [bŭf/ə lō] **216**–6
buffet [bə fā/] **55**–24, **185**–10
bugs [bŭgz]
    bedbugs [bĕd/bŭgz/] **63**–24
building [bĭl/dĭng] **50**–1, **124**–2
BUILDING SUPPLIES [bĭl/dĭng sə plīz/] **180**–**181**
bulb [bŭlb] **56** ✦, **211**–2
bulldozer [bŏŏl/dō/zər] **178**–6
bulletin board [bŏŏl/ə tn bôrd/] **7**–14
bump cap [bŭmp/ kăp/] **92**–9
bumper [bŭm/pər] **158**–8
    bumper pad [bŭm/pər păd/] **59**–4
bunch [bŭnch] **68**–29
bunk beds [bŭngk/ bĕdz/] **59**–9
Bunsen burner [bŭn/sən bür/nər] **195**–37
bureau [byŏŏr/ō] **58**–1
burger [bür/gər]
    cheeseburger [chēz/bür/gər] **79**–3
    hamburger [hăm/bür/gər] **79**–1
burglary [bür/glə rē] **142**–2
burn [bürn]
    sunburn [sŭn/bürn/] **110**–14
burn [bürn] **116**–H
burner [bür/nər] **54**–19, **195**–37
burrito [bə rē/tō] **79**–9

bus [bŭs] **128**–9, **151**–14
   bus person [bŭs/ pür/sən] **185**–13
   bus route [bŭs/ rōōt/, –rowt/] **152**–1
   bus station [bŭs/ stā/shən] **124**–7
   bus stop [bŭs/ stäp/] **129**–16, **151**–13
   miss the bus [mĭs/ dhə bŭs/] **152** ✦
bus [bŭs] **82**–G
business [bĭz/nəs]
   business owner [bĭz/nəs ō/nər] **166**–11
   businessperson [bĭz/nəs pür/sən] **166**–12
   business suit [bĭz/nəs sōōt/] **88**–11
busser [bŭ/sər] **83**–12
Bus Stop [bŭs/ stäp/] **152**
butcher [bōōch/ər] **166**–13
butter [bŭt/ər] **66**–6, **83**–19
butterfly [bŭt/ər flī/] **214**–19
buttocks [bŭt/əks] **107**–30
button [bŭt/n] **99**–24
   back button [băk/ bŭt/n] **197**–2
   call button [köl/ bŭt/n] **121**–28
   forward button [för/wərd bŭt/n] **197**–3
buy [bī] **27**–G
   buy a home [bī/ ə hōm/] **41**–M
   buy a snack [bī/ ə snăk/] **11**–K
   buy recycled products
     [bī/ rē sī/kəld präd/ŭkts] **219**–D
Buying a House [bī/ĭng ə hows/] **49**
BUYING AND MAINTAINING A CAR
   [bī/ĭng ən mān tā/nĭng ə kär/] **157**
Buying a Used Car [bī/ĭng ə yōōzd/ kär/] **157**
buzzer [bŭz/ər] **51**–31
cab [kăb] **156**–16
cabbage [kăb/ĭj] **69**–2
Cabinet [kăb/ə nət] **138**–10
cabinet [kăb/ə nət] **54**–1
   file cabinet [fīl/ kăb/ə nət] **182**–11
   medicine cabinet [mĕd/ə sən kăb/ə nət] **57**–20
   supply cabinet [sə plī/ kăb/ə nət] **182**–1
cables [kā/bəlz] **158**–21, **196**–13
cactus [kăk/təs] **210**–21
cafeteria [kăf/ə tïr/ē ə] **5**–14
cage [kāj] **107**–48
cake [kāk] **73**–39, **81**–33
   cake pan [kāk/ păn/] **78**–26
   cheesecake [chēz/kāk/] **81**–34
   pancakes [păn/kāks/] **80**–7
Cake [kāk] **77**
calculate [kăl/kyə lāt/] **17**–B
calculator [kăl/kyə lā/tər] **17**–6, **183**–25
calculus [kăl/kyə ləs] **192**–19
CALENDAR [kăl/ən dər] **20**–21
CALENDAR EVENTS [kăl/ən dər ĭ vĕnts/] **22**
calf [kăf] **106**–22
   calf-length [kăf/ lĕnth/] **96**–17
call [köl]
   call button [köl/ bŭt/n] **121**–28
   international call [ĭn/tər năsh/ə nəl köl/] **15**–35
   Internet phone call [ĭn/tər nĕt/ fōn/ köl/] **14**–20
   local call [lō/kəl köl/] **15**–31
   long distance call [löng/ dĭs/təns köl/] **15**–32
call [köl] **48**–A, **147**–L
   call in [köl/ ĭn/] **186**–A

calling card [kö/lĭng kärd/] **14**–15
calm [köm] **42**–8
camcorder [kăm/kör dər] **235**–24
camel [kăm/əl] **217**–38
camera [kăm/rə]
   camera case [kăm/rə kās/] **235**–28
   digital camera [dĭ/jə təl kăm/rə] **235**–19
   film camera [fĭlm/ kăm/rə] **235**–21
   security camera [sĭ kyŏŏr/ə tē kăm/rə] **50**–19
   35 mm camera
     [thür/tē fīv/ mĭl/ə mē/tər kăm/rə] **235**–21
camisole [kăm/ə sōl/] **91**–21
campaign [kăm pān/] **139**–29
camper [kăm/pər] **156**–9
campfire [kămp/fïr/] **226**–11
camping [kăm/pĭng] **226**–5
   camping stove [kăm/pĭng stōv/] **226**–16
Campus [kăm/pəs] **5**
can [kăn] **74**–3, **74**–15
   can opener [kăn/ ō/pə nər] **78**–1, **146**–8
   electric can opener [ĭ lĕk/trĭk/ kăn/ ō/pə nər] **54**–14
   garbage can [gär/bĭj kăn/] **53**–24
cancer [kăn/sər] **111**–10
candle [kăn/dl] **56**–20
   candle holder [kăn/dl hōl/dər] **56**–21
candy [kăn/dē] **239**–12
   candy bar [kăn/dē bär/] **73**–37
   candy cane [kăn/dē kān/] **239**–17
   candy store [kăn/dē stör/] **131**–17
cane [kān] **113**–16, **239**–17
canned food [kănd/ fōōd/] **146**–9
Canned Foods [kănd/ fōōdz/] **72**
canoeing [kə nōō/ĭng] **226**–3
can't breathe [kănt/ brēdh/] **116**–N
canteen [kăn tēn/] **226**–24
canvas [kăn/vəs] **233**–17
canyon [kăn/yən] **204**–17
cap [kăp] **88**–1, **206**–7
   baseball cap [bās/böl/ kăp/] **86**–5
   bump cap [bŭmp/ kăp/] **92**–9
   shower cap [show/ər kăp/] **108**–1
   surgical cap [sür/jĭ kəl kăp/] **121**–37
   surgical scrub cap [sür/jĭ kəl skrŭb/ kăp/] **93**–35
capital [kă/pət əl] **139**–22
capitalize [kă/pət əl īz/] **190**–A, **190**–B
Capitol [kă/pət əl] **138**–1
capris [kə prēz/] **88**–8
capsule [kăp/səl] **113**–23
car [kär] **150**–1
   car accident [kär/ ăk/sə dənt] **144**–2
   car dealership [kär/ dē/lər shĭp/] **126**–4
   car safety seat [kär/ sāf/tē sēt/] **37**–19
   4-door car [för/dör/ kär/] **156**–1
   sports car [spörts/kär/] **156**–4
   subway car [sŭb/wā/ kär/] **152**–6
   town car [town/ kär/] **152**–20
   2-door car [tōō/dör/ kär/] **156**–2
Car [kär] **157**, **159**
CAR [kär] **156**, **157**, **158**–159
card [kärd] **239**–5
   ATM card [ā/tē/ĕm/ kärd/] **132**–15
   auto club card [ö tō/ klŭb/ kärd/] **162**–4

baseball cards [bās/böl/ kärdz/] **232**–2
card store [kärd/ stör/] **130**–7
copies of ID and credit cards
   [käp/ēz əv ī/dē/ ən krĕd/ət/ kärdz/] **146**–19
emergency card [ĭ mür/jən sē/ kärd/] **161**–23
fare card [fër/ kärd/] **152**–11
folding card table [fōl/dĭng/ kärd/ tā/bəl] **102**–4
green card [grēn/ kärd/] **40**–2
greeting card [grē/tĭng kärd/] **134**–15
health insurance card
   [hĕlth/ ĭn shŏŏr/əns kärd/] **118**–3
memory card [mĕm/ə rē kärd/] **235**–20
post card [pōst/ kärd/] **134**–16
Resident Alien card [rĕz/ə dənt ā/lē ən kärd/] **40**–2
rotary card file [rō/tə rē kärd/ fīl/] **183**–44
Social Security card
   [sō/shəl sĭ kyŏŏr/ə tē kärd/] **40**–5
Card [kärd] **135**
cardigan sweater [kär/də gən swĕt/ər] **88**–2
Cardinal Numbers [kärd/nəl nŭm/bərz] **16**
cardiologist [kär/dē äl/ə jĭst] **120**–3
cardiopulmonary resuscitation (CPR)
   [kär/dē ō pŏŏl mə nër/ē rĭ sŭs/ə tā/shən] /
   [sē/pē/är/] **117**–17
care [kër] **167**–32
careful worker [kër/fəl wür/kər] **179**–2
careless worker [kër/ləs wür/kər] **179**–1
childcare worker [chīld/kër wür/kər] **166**–16
CARE [kër] **114**–115, **118**, **119**
Care of Your Car [kër/ əv yər kär/] **157**
career counselor [kə rër/ kown/slər] **172**–10
Career Path [kə rër/ păth/] **172**
CAREER PLANNING [kə rër/ plăn/ĭng] **172**
cargo van [kär/gō văn/] **156**–13
carnation [kär nā/shən] **211**–20
carousel [kär/ə sĕl/] **161**–23
carpenter [kär/pən tər] **62**–12, **166**–14
carpet [kär/pət] **56**–24
carpool [kär/pōōl/] **219**–I
carriage [kär/ĭj] **37**–20
carrier [kär/ē ər] **37**–17, **134**–20
carrots [kär/əts] **69**–3
carry [kär/ē] **11**–F, **82**–H
CARS AND TRUCKS [kärz/ ən trŭks/] **156**
cart [kärt] **72**–7, **129**–28
   housekeeping cart [hows/kē/pĭng kärt/] **184**–19
   luggage cart [lŭg/ĭj/ kärt/] **184**–8
carton [kär/tn] **74**–4, **74**–16
cartoon [kär/tōōn] **236**–3
cartridge [kär/trĭj] **183**–45
carving knife [kär/vĭng nīf/] **78**–12
case [kās] **94**–5, **235**–28
cash [kăsh]
   cash and coins [kăsh/ ən koynz/] **146**–17
   cash register [kăsh/ rĕj/ə stər] **27**–10, **73**–15
cash [kăsh] **27**–F, **132**–A
cashier [kă shïr/] **73**–13, **166**–15
cashmere [kăzh/mïr/] **98**–4
Casserole [kăs/ə rōl] **77**
casserole dish [kăs/ə rōl dĭsh/] **78**–10
cassette [kə sĕt/] **234**–6
   videocassette [vĭ/dē ō kə sĕt/] **133**–18

cast [kăst] **113**–20
castle [kă/səl] **225**–12
Casual Clothes [kăzh/ōō əl klōz/] **88**
CASUAL, WORK, AND FORMAL CLOTHES
[kăzh/ōō əl würk/ ən för/ məl klōz/] **88**–**89**
cat [kăt] **215**–9
catfish [kăt/fĭsh/] **71**–2
catalog [kăt ə /lög] **133**–11
catch [kăch] **230**–D
catcher's mask [kăch/ərz măsk/] **231**–15
caterer [kā/tər ər] **185**–16
caterpillar [kăt/ə pĭl/ər, kăt/ər–] **214**–20
cattle [kăt/l] **177**–21
cauliflower [kö/lĭ flow/ər, kä/–] **69**–14
cave [kāv] **220**–6
caverns [că/vərnz] **220**–7
cavity [kăv/ə tē] **119**–7
C-clamp [sē/klămp/] **180**–6
CD [sē/dē/] **196**–9, **234**–5
CD boombox [sē/dē/ bōōm/băks/] **234**–1
CD player [sē/dē/ plā/ər] **159**–38
celebrate [sĕl/ə brāt] **206**–C
celery [sĕl/ə rē] **69**–9
cell [sĕl] **194**–4
cell membrane [sĕl/ mĕm/brān] **194**–6
cell phone holder [sĕl/ fōn/ hōl/dər] **94**–15
cell phone kiosk [sĕl/ fōn/ kē/ösk] **131**–22
cell phone number [sĕl/ fōn/ nŭm/bər] **4**–12
cell wall [sĕl/ wäl/] **194**–5
cello [chĕl/ō] **238**–7
cellular phone [sĕl/yə lər fōn/] **14**–8
Celsius [sĕl/sē əs] **13**–2
cemetery [sĕ/mə tër/ē] **127**–15
cent [sĕnt] **26**–1, **26**–2, **26**–3, **26**–4
center [sĕn/tər]
automated postal center (APC)
[ö/tə māt ĭd pōs/təl sĕn/tər] / [ā/pē/sē/] **135**–10
childcare center [chĭld/kër/ sĕn/tər] **129**–30
convention center [kən vĕn/shən sĕn/tər] **127**–24
copy center [käp/ē sĕn/tər] **129**–18
entertainment center
[ĕn/tər tān/mənt sĕn/tər] **56**–5
resource center [rē/sörs sĕn/tər] **172**–9
CENTER [sĕn/tər] **208**–**209**
centimeter [cm] [sĕn/tə mē/tər] **17**–14
CENTRAL AMERICA [sĕn/trəl ə mĕr/ə kə] **200**–**201**
Central time [sĕn/trəl tīm/] **19**–31
cereal [sïr/ē əl] **80**–9
ceremony [sĕr/ə mō/nē] **206**–6
certificate [sər tĭf/ə kət] **40**–1, **41**–11
Certificate of Naturalization
[sər tĭf/ə kət əv năch/rə lə zā/shən] **40**–6
certified [sür/tə fīd/]
Certified Mail® [sür/tə fīd/ māl] **134**–4
certified nursing assistant (CNA)
[sür/tə fīd/ nür/sĭng ə sĭs/tənt] / [sē/ĕn/ā/]
120–12
chain [chān] **51**–33, **95**–33, **180**–41
chair [chër] **7**–11
armchair [ärm/chër/] **56**–22
beach chair [bēch/ chër/] **225**–22
dining room chair [dī/nĭng rōōm/chër/] **55**–8

easy chair [ē/zē/ chër] **56**–22
folding chair [fōld/ĭng chër/] **102**–5
high chair [hī/ chër/] **37**–6, **82**–3
rocking chair [räk/ĭng chër/] **37**–21
wheelchair [wēl/chër/] **113**–9
chalk [chök] **7**–18
chalkboard [chök/börd/] **6**–1
challenged [chăl/əngd] **32**–10
change [chānj] **36**–G, **60**–P, **148**–C
change purse [chānj/ pürs/] **94**–14
changing [chān/jĭng]
changing pad [chān/jĭng păd/] **59**–2
changing table [chān/jĭng tā/bəl] **59**–1
charger [chär/jər] **14**–10, **234**–17, **235**–27
chart [chärt] **121**–24
cheap [chēp] **23**–20
check [chĕk] **132**–13
check book [chĕk/ bōōk/] **132**–12
check-in kiosk [chĕk/ĭn/ kē/ösk] **160**–2
checkstand [chĕk/stănd/] **73**–12
paycheck [pā/chĕk/] **165**–14
check [chĕk]
check blood pressure [chĕk/ blŭd/ prĕsh/ər] **118**–A
check email [chĕk/ ē/ māl/] **39**–W
check in [chĕk/ ĭn/] **160**–A
check Internet job sites
[chĕk/ ĭn/tər nĕt/ jäb/ sīts/] **173**–D
check messages [chĕk/ mĕs/ə jĭz] **171**–R
check out [chĕk/ owt/] **133**–C
check the correct boxes
[chĕk/ dhə kə rĕkt/ bäk/səz] **9**–U
check the oil [chĕk/ dhə oyl/] **157**–H
check the pronunciation
[chĕk/ dhe prə nən sē ā/ shən] **8**–D
check your bags [chĕk/ yər băgz/] **160**–B
check pulse [chĕk/ pŭls/] **122**–A
check your spelling [chĕk/ yər spĕl/ĭng] **197**–F
check your understanding
[chĕk/ yər ŭn/dər stănd/ĭng] **12**–N
check your work [chĕk/ yər würk/] **10**–L
checked [chĕkt] **96**–24
checkers [chĕk/ərz] **232**–7
checking account number
[chĕk/ĭng ə kownt/ nŭm/bər] **132**–14
checkout [chĕk/owt/] **133**–10
Checkpoint [chĕk/poynt/] **160**
cheddar cheese [chĕd/ər chēz/] **71**–28
cheek [chēk] **106**–3
cheese [chēz] **66**–4
American cheese [ə mĕr/ə kən chēz/] **71**–26
cheddar cheese [chĕd/ər chēz/] **71**–28
cheeseburger [chēz/bür/gər] **79**–3
cheesecake [chēz/kāk/] **81**–34
grilled cheese sandwich
[grĭld/ chēz/ săn/wĭch, –sănd/–] **80**–10
Swiss cheese [swĭs/ chēz/] **71**–27
Cheesy Tofu Vegetable Casserole
[chē/zē tō/fōō vĕj/tə bəl kăs/ə rōl] **77**
chef [shĕf] **83**–16
chef's hat [shĕfs/ hăt/] **93**–28
chef's jacket [shĕfs/ jăk/ət] **93**–29
chef's salad [shĕfs/ săl/ əd] **80**–14

executive chef [ĭg zĕk/yə tĭv shĕf/] **185**–7
head chef [hĕd/ shĕf/] **185**–7
sous chef [sōō/ shĕf/] **185**–6
Chef [shĕf] **93**
chemist [kĕm/ĭst] **195**–25
Chemistry [kĕm/ə strē] **195**
cherries [chĕr/ēz] **68**–11
cherry picker [chĕr/ē pĭk/ər] **178**–5
chess [chĕs] **232**–8
chest [chĕst] **59**–16, **104**–4, **107**–25
chest of drawers [chĕst/ əv drörz/] **59**–6
chicken [chĭk/ən] **66**–3, **70**–16
chicken pox [chĭk/ən päks/] **111**–6
chicken sandwich [chĭk/ən săn/wĭch, –sănd–] **79**–5
fried chicken [frīd/ chĭk/ən] **76**–1
roast chicken [rōst/ chĭk/ən] **81**–22
Chicken [chĭk/ən] **77**
chief justice [chēf/ jŭs/təs] **138**–13
CHILDCARE AND PARENTING
[chīld/kër ən për/ən tĭng] **36**–**37**
child / children [chīld] / [chĭl/ drən]
childcare center [chīld/kër sĕn/tər] **129**–30
childcare worker [chīld/kër wür/kər] **166**–16
children's program [chĭl/drənz prō/grăm] **236**–9
child safety seat [chīld/ săf/tē sēt/] **159**–53
grandchild [grăn/chīld, gränd/–] **34** ◆
lost child [löst/ chīld/] **144**–1
Childhood Diseases [chīld/hōōd dĭ zē/zəz] **111**
chili peppers [chĭl/ē pĕp/ərz] **69**–29
chill [chĭl] **76**–D
chills [chĭlz] **110**–9
chimney [chĭm/nē] **53**–5
chimpanzee [chĭm/păn zē/] **217**–27
chin [chĭn] **106**–1
chipmunk [chĭp/mŭngk] **215**–20
chips [chĭps] **73**–35
chiropractors [kī/rō prăk/tərz] **120**
chisel [chĭz/əl] **181**–55
choke [chōk] **116**–L
choose [chōōz] **9**–P
chop [chäp] **77**–L
chops [chäps] **70**–10, **70**–15
Christmas [krĭs/məs] **22**–18
Christmas tree [krĭs/məs trē/] **239**–16
chromosome [krō/mə zōm/] **194**–8
chrysanthemum [krĭ săn/thə məm] **211**–21
church [chürch] **127**–14
chute [shōōt] **51**–26
circle [sür/ kəl] **193**–34
circle [sür/ kəl] **9**–Q
circular saw [sür/kyə lər sö/] **180**–9
circulation desk [sür/kyə lā/shən dĕsk/] **133**–2
circumference [sər kŭm/frəns] **193**–36
citizen [sĭt/ə zən] **30**–5
Citizenship Requirements
[sĭt/ə zən shĭp/ rĭ kwĭr/mənts] **140**
city [sĭt/ē] **4**–7, **52**–1
city code [sĭt/ē kōd/] **15**–34
city council [sĭt/ē kown/səl] **139**–27
city hall [sĭt/ē häl/] **124**–8
City Government [sĭt/ē gŭ/vərn mənt] **139**
CITY STREETS [sĭt/ē strēts/] **126**–**127**

Index

CIVIC RIGHTS AND RESPONSIBILITIES
[sĭ/vĭk rīts n rĭ spän/sə bĭl/ə tēz] **140**
Civilizations [sĭ/və lə zā/shenz] **199**
claim [klām] **160**–L
clamp [klămp] **180**–6
clams [klămz] **71**–15
clarinet [klăr/ə nĕt/] **238**–2
classical [kla/sĭ kəl] **237**–21
  classical concert [kla/sĭ kəl kän/sərt] **223**–14
classified ad [klăs/e fĭd] **48**–2
Classmates [klăs/māts/] **8**
classroom [klăs/rōōm/] **5**–7
CLASSROOM [klăs/rōōm/] **6–7**
claw [klö] **214**–2
clean [klēn] **101**–16
clean [klēn] **76**–A
  clean teeth [klēn/ tēth/] **119**–A
  clean the house [klēn/ dhə hows/] **39**–O
  clean the lint trap [klēn/ dhə lĭnt/ trăp/] **101**–D
  clean the oven [klēn/ dhə ŭv/ən] **60**–C
  clean up [klēn/ ŭp/] **147**–M
cleaner [klēn/ər]
  dry cleaners [drī/ klēn/ərz] **128**–2
  glass cleaner [glăs/ klēn/ər] **61**–14
  oven cleaner [ŭv/ən klēn/ər] **61**–3
  vacuum cleaner [văk/yōōm klēn/ər] **61**–10
  vacuum cleaner attachments
    [văk/yōōm klēn/ər ə tăch/mənts] **61**–11
  vacuum cleaner bag [văk/yəm klēn/ər băg/] **61**–12
CLEANING SUPPLIES [klē/nĭng sə plīz/] **61**
cleanser [klēn/zər] **61**–18
CLEANUP [klēn/ŭp/] **148–149**
clear [klĭr] **13**–9
  clear tape [klĭr/tāp/] **183**–30
clear [klĭr] **82**–G
  clear off [klĭr/ äf/] **10**–I
clerk [klürk] **5**–13, **182**–2
  admissions clerk [əd mĭsh/ənz klürk/] **120**–14
  desk clerk [dĕsk/ klürk/] **184**–11
  DMV clerk [dē/ĕm/vē/ klürk/] **136**–3
  file clerk [fīl/ klürk/] **182**–10
  grocery clerk [grōs/rē klürk/, grōsh/–, grō/sə–] **72**–4
  library clerk [lī/brĕr ē klürk/] **133**–1
  payroll clerk [pā/rōl/ klürk/] **165**–10
  postal clerk [pō/stəl klürk/] **135**–7
  retail clerk [rē/tāl/ klürk/] **169**–53
  salesclerk [sālz/klürk/] **94**–3
  shipping clerk [shĭp/ĭng klürk/] **175**–16
  stock clerk [stäk/ klürk/] **169**–59
click [klĭk] **197**–B
climb [klīm] **224**–C
climbing apparatus [klĭm/ĭng ă/pə ră/təs] **224**–14
clinic [klĭn/ĭk] **186**–2
clip-on earrings [klĭp/än ĭr/ĭngz, –ön–] **95**–37
clipper [klĭp/ər] **109**–31, **176**–11
clips [klĭps] **108**–19, **183**–31, **194**–24
clock [kläk] **7**–9, **58**–24, **165**–7
  clock radio [kläk/ rā/dē ō] **102**–6
close [klōz] **6**–H
closet [kläz/ət] **57** ✦, **58**–5
Closures [klō/zhərz] **99**

cloth [klöth] **181**–54
  cloth diaper [klöth/ dī/pərz] **37**–8
  tablecloth [tā/bəl klöth/] **55**–12
  washcloth [wäsh/klöth/] **57**–4
clothes [klōz] **146**–6
  clothesline [klōz/līn/] **101**–9
  clothespin [klōz/pĭn/] **101**–10
CLOTHES [klōz] **86–87, 88–89, 96–97, 98–99**
clothing [klō/dhĭng] **102**–2
CLOTHING [klō/dhĭng] **90, 92–93**
Clothing Problems [klō/dhĭng präb/ləmz] **97**
cloudy [klow/dē] **13**–10
club [klŭb] **162**–4, **223**–12, **231**–1
  club sandwich [klŭb săn/wĭch/, –sănd–] **80**–12
clubs [klŭbz] **233**–32
clutch [klŭch] **159**–49
  clutch bag [klŭch/ băg/] **89**–19
CNA (certified nursing assistant) [sē/ĕn/ā/] /
    [sür/tə tə fĭd/ nür/sĭng ə sĭs/tənt] **120**–12
coach [kōch] **5**–20, **229**–2
coal [kōl] **218**–4
coarse adjustment knob
    [körs/ ə jüst/mənt näb/] **194**–22
Coast Guard [kōst/ gärd/] **138**–18
coat [kōt] **90**–2, **216**–19
  lab coat [lăb/ kōt/] **93**–33
  raincoat [rān/ kōt/] **90**–18
  sports coat [spörts/ kōt/] **89**–14
  trench coat [trĕnch/ kōt/] **90**–21
cobra [kō/brə] **213**–41
cockpit [käk/pĭt/] **161**–10
cockroaches [käk/rō/chəz] **63**–26
cocktail dress [käk/tāl/ drĕs/] **89**–20
coconuts [kō/kə nŭts/] **68**–24
cod [käd] **71**–8, **212**–5
code [kōd]
  area code [ĕr/ē ə kōd/] **15**–29
  bar code [bär/ kōd/] **27**–4
  city code [sĭt/ē kōd/] **15**–34
  country code [kŭn/trē kōd/] **15**–33
coffee [kö/fē] **73**–33, **81**–37, **81**–38
  coffeemaker [kö/fē mā/kər] **54**–11
  coffee mug [kö/fē mŭg/] **55**–7
  coffee shop [kö/fē shäp/] **126**–11
  coffee table [kö/fē tā/bəl] **56**–19
COFFEE SHOP MENU [kö/fē shäp/ mĕn/yōō] **80–81**
coins [koynz] **146**–17
  coin purse [koyn/ pürs/] **94**–14
Coins [koynz] **26**
colander [käl/ən dər] **78**–17
cold [kōld] **13**–6, **42**–4, **111**–1
  cold tablets [kōld tăb/ləts] **113**–27
  cold water [kōld wö/tər] **57**–7
coleslaw [kōl/slö/] **80**–18
collar [käl/ər] **100**–4
collate [kō/lāt/, kə lāt/] **171**–E
collect [kə lĕkt/] **232**–A
college [käl/ĭj] **127**–17, **188**–6, **188**–7
  college degree [käl/ĭj də grē/] **41**–7
  college dormitory [käl/ĭj dör/mə tör/ē] **52**–8
cologne [kə lōn/] **108**–6
colon [kō/lən] **190**–17

Colonial Period [kə lō/nē əl pĭr/ē əd] **198**
colonies [kä/lə nēz] **198**–1
colonists [kä/lə nĭsts] **198**–2
color [kŭl/ər]
  watercolor [wö/tər kŭl/ər] **233**–21
color [kŭl/ər] **33**–D
coloring book [kŭl/ə rĭng bŏŏk/] **59**–13
Colors [kŭl/ərs] **24**
COLORS [kŭl/ərs] **24**
Columbus Day [kə lŭm/bəs dā/] **22**–15
column [käl/ŭm] **107**–49
comb [kōm] **33**–21, **108**–13
comb [kōm] **108**–G
come [kŭm] **39**–R
comedy [käm/ə dē] **236**–2, **237**–13
comet [käm/ət] **205**–24
comfort [kŭm/fərt] **36**–I
comma [käm/ə] **190**–14
commercial fisher [kə mür/shəl fĭsh/ər] **167**–17
commit a crime [kə mĭt/ ə krīm/] **142** ✦
Common Illnesses and Childhood Diseases
    [käm/ən ĭl/nə səz ən chīld/hŏŏd-dĭ zē/zəz] **111**
COMMUNITY CLEANUP
    [kə myōō/nə tē klēn/ŭp] **148–149**
community college
    [kə myōō/nə tē käl/ĭj] **127**–17, **188**–6
Comparing Clothing [kəm pĕr/ĭng klō/dhĭng] **97**
compartment [kəm pärt/mənt] **159**–44, **161**–13
complaint [kəm plānt/] **97** ✦
Complex [käm/plĕks] **51**
compliment [käm/plə mĕnt/] **12** ✦
compliment [käm/plə mĕnt/] **12**–C
composer [kəm pō/zər] **199**–15
composition [käm/pə zĭsh/ən] **199**–14
compost [käm/pōst/] **219**–M
compost pile [käm/pōst pīl/] **53**–25
computer [kəm pyōō/tər] **7**–15, **183**–17
  computer lab [kəm pyōō/tər lăb/] **5**–15
  computer software engineer
    [kəm pyōō/tər söft/wĕr/ ĕn/jə nĭr/] **167**–18
  computer technician [kəm pyōō/tər tĕk nĭsh/ən]
    167–19, **182**–12
Computer [kəm pyōō/tər] **196**
COMPUTERS [kəm pyōō/tərz] **196**
conceal [kən sēl/] **143**–C
concert [kän/sərt] **222**–5, **223**–14
concierge [kän/sē ĕrzh/, kōn/–] **184**–4
conclusion [kən klōō/zhən] **190**–8
concrete [käng/krēt, kän krēt/] **178**–10
conditioner [kən dĭsh/ə nər] **108**–11, **159**–39
Conditions [kən dĭsh/ənz] **13, 111**
CONDITIONS [kən dĭsh/ənz] **111**
condominium [kän/də mĭn/ē əm] **52**–5
conduct [kən dŭkt/] **238**–C
conductor [kən dŭk/tər] **152**–13
cone [kōn] **79**–13, **193**–40
  pinecone [pīn/kōn] **210**–11
conference room [kän/frəns rōōm/] **182**–4
confetti [kən fĕt/ē] **239**–3
confused [kən fyōōzd/] **43**–26
congestion [kən jĕs/chən] **110**–7
Congress [käng/grəs] **138**–2, **198**–6

congressperson [kän/grəs pür/sən] **138**–4
CONSERVATION [kän/sər vā/shən] **218**–**219**
Conserve Energy and Resources
  [kən sürv/ ĕn/ər jē ən rē/sörs/əz] **219**
console [kän/söl] **232**–3
constellation [kän/stə lā/shən] **205**–14
Constitution [kän/stə tōō/shən] **198**–19
construction [kən strŭk/shən]
  construction paper [kən strŭk/shən pā/pər] **232**–12
  construction site [kən strŭk/shən sīt/] **126**–2
  construction worker
    [kən strŭk/shən wür/kər] **178**–1
CONSTRUCTION [kən strŭk/shən] **178**
Construction Worker [kən strŭk/shən wür/kər] **92**
contact [kän/tăkt] **146**–2
  contact lenses [kän/tăkt lĕn/zəz] **115**–8
container [kən tā/nər] **74**–5, **74**–17, **78**–4
CONTAINERS AND PACKAGING
  [kən tā/nərz ən păk/ĭ jĭng] **74**
continental [kän/tə nĕnt/əl] **198**–6
contractor [kän/trăk tər] **186**–5
control [kən trōl/] **121**–27, **232**–4
convenience store [kən vēn/yəns stör/] **128**–3
convention center [kən vĕn/shən sĕn/tər] **127**–24
convert [kən vürt/] **17**–D, **75**–C
convertible [kən vür/tə bəl] **156**–5
conveyer belt [kən vā/ər bĕlt/] **175**–16
convict [kän/vĭkt/] **141**–15
convict [kən vĭkt/] **141**–E
cook [kŏŏk] **185**–1, **185** ✦
cook [kŏŏk] **39**–Q, **76**–C, **170**–C
cooked [kŏŏkt] **70**–25
cookies [kŏŏk/ēz] **73**–38
  cookie sheet [kŏŏk/ē shēt/] **78**–27
cool [kōōl] **13**–5
cooler [kōō/lər] **225**–19
co-op [kō/äp/] **52** ✦
copier [kä/pē ər]
  photocopier [fō/tō kä/pē ər]**183**–23
copies / copy [kä/pēz] / [kä/pē]
  copies of ID and credit cards
    [käp/ēz əv ī/dē ən krĕd/ət kärdz/] **146**–19
  copies of important papers
    [käp/ēz əv ĭm pört/ənt pā/pərz] **146**–20
  copy center [käp/ē sĕn/tər] **129**–18
copy [käp/ē] **8**–E
coral [kör/əl] **220**–5
cord [körd] **14**–2
  bungee cord [bŭn/jē körd/] **181**–15
  cordless phone [körd/ləs fōn/] **15**–24
  extension cord [ĭk stĕn/shən körd/] **181**–14
  frayed cord [frād/ körd/] **179**–5
  power cord [pow/ər körd/] **196**–2
corduroy [kör/də roy/] **99**–11
core course [kör/ körs/] **189** ✦
corn [körn] **69**–12, **177**–4
  corn rows [körn/ rōz/] **33**–14
  corned beef [körnd/ bēf/] **71**–22
corner [kör/nər] **128**–7
coronary disease [kör/ə nĕ/rē dĭ zēz/] **111** ✦
corral [kə răl/] **177**–17
correct [kə rĕkt/] **10**–N

correction [kə rĕk/shən]
  correction fluid [kə rĕk/shən flōō/əd] **183**–36
  correction tape [kə rĕk/shən tāp/] **183**–37
cost [köst] **27**–7, **122**–1
costume [käs/tōōm] **239**–11
cotton [kät/n] **98**–1, **177**–6
couch [kowch] **56**–18
cough [köf] **110**–A
cough syrup [köf/ sĭr/əp, –sür/–] **113**–29
council [kown/səl] **139**–27
  councilperson [kown/səl pür/sən] **139**–28
counselor [kown/slər] **5**–6, **172**–10
count [kownt] **84**–A
counter [kown/tər] **54**–22, **113**–18
  counterperson [kown/tər pür/sən] **79**–17
Counterperson [kown/tər pür/sən] **93**
country [kŭn/trē] **52**–4, **227**–3, **237**–27
  country code [kŭn/trē kōd/] **15**–33
county fair [kown/tē fër/] **223**–13
coupe [kōōp] **156**–2
couple [kŭ/pəl] **35**–20, **35**–21, **239**–4
coupons [kōō/pönz/] **67**–15
courier [kür/ē ər, kŏŏr/–] **168**–40
course [körs] **172**–8, **189** ✦
court [kört]
  basketball court [băs/kət böl/ kört/] **229**–7
  courthouse [kört/hows/] **125**–13
  courtroom [kört/rōōm/] **141**–7
  court reporter [kört/ rĭ pör/tər] **141**–12
  courtyard [kört/yärd/] **51**–21
  food court [fōōd/ kört/] **131**–15
  Supreme Court [sə prēm/ kört/] **138**–11
  tennis court [tĕ/nəs kört/] **224**–6
cousin [kŭz/ən] **34**–9
cover [kŭv/ər] **158**–9, **181**–46
  coveralls [kŭv/ər ölz/] **92**–8
  cover-up [kŭv/ər ŭp/] **90**–25
cow [kow] **215**–1
cowboy hat [kow/boy/ hăt/] **92**–18
coyote [kī ō/tē, kī/ōt/] **216**–3
CPR (cardiopulmonary resuscitation) [sē/pē/är/] /
  [kär/dē ō pŏŏl/mə nër/ē–rē sŭs/ə tā/shən] **117**–17
CPU [sē/pē/yōō] **196**–4
crab [krăb] **71**–9, **212**–20
cracked [krăkt] **62**–4
cradle [krād/l] **59**–20
crane [krān] **178**–7
crash [krăsh] **144**–3
crayons [krā/änz] **59**–14
cream [krēm] **24**–16, **81**–41, **113**–25
  antihistamine cream
    [ăn/tĭ hĭs/tə mēn krēm/] **117**–11
  ice-cream [īs/ krēm/] **72**–26
  ice-cream cone [īs/ krēm kōn/] **79**–13
  ice cream shop [īs/ krēm shäp/] **131**–16
  shaving cream [shā/vĭng krēm/] **109**–29
  sour cream [sow/ər krēm/] **72**–21
creamer [krē/mər] **55**–15
credit [krĕd/ət] **146**–19
creek [krēk, krĭk] **204** ✦
crescent moon [krĕs/ənt mōōn/] **205**–10

crew [krōō] **176**–1, **176**–4
  crewneck [krōō/nĕk] **96**–7
  crew socks [krōō/säks/] **91**–8
crib [krĭb] **59**–3
cricket [krĭk/ət] **214**–23
crime [krīm] **142** ✦
CRIME [krīm] **142**
criminal [krĭm/ə nəl] **142** ✦
crocheting [krō shā/ĭng] **233**–25
crocodile [kräk/ə dīl/] **213**–37
crocus [krō/kəs] **211**–17
Crops [kräps] **177**
cross [krös]
  cross-country skiing [krös/kŭn/trē skē/ĭng] **227**–3
  crosswalk [krös/wök/] **128**–15
cross [krös] **128**–A
  cross out [krös/ owt/] **9**–R
crossing [krö/sĭng] **154**–13, **154**–14, **154**–15
crown [krown] **119**–9
crucible tongs [krōō/sə bəl tängz/, –töngz/] **195**–44
crutches [krŭch/əz] **113**–10
cry [krī] **206**–B
cube [kyōōb] **193**–38
cubicle [kyōōb/ə kəl] **182**–7
cucumbers [kyōō/kŭm bərz] **69**–10
cuff [kŭf] **100**–9
cup [kŭp] **75**–2, **75**–10, **83**–24
  1/2 cup [hăf/ kŭp/] **75**–9
  1/4 cup [kwör/tər kŭp/] **75**–8
  teacup [tē/kŭp/] **55**–6
curb [kürb] **129**–21
curling iron [kür/lĭng ī/ərn] **108**–17
curly hair [kür/lē hër/] **33**–11
cursor [kür/sər] **197**–14
curtains [kür/tnz] **57**–12, **58**–7
curved line [kürvd/ līn/] **193**–23
cushion [kŏŏ/shən] **56** ✦, **100**–13
customer [kŭs/tə mər] **72**–1, **94**–4, **132**–2, **164**–2
  customer service [kŭs/tə mər sür/vəs] **97** ✦
  customer service representative
    [kŭs/tə mər-sür/vəs rĕ/prə zĕn/tə tĭv] **167**–20
Customs [kŭs/təmz] **161**
customs officer [kŭs/təmz ö/fə sər] **161**–17
cut [kŭt] **91**–10, **110**–13
cut [kŭt] **33**–A, **109**–N
  cut up [kŭt/ ŭp/] **77**–I
cute [kyōōt] **32**–14
cutlets [kŭt/ləts] **70**–6
cutter [kut/ər] **183**–22, **232**–16
cutting board [kŭt/ĭng börd/] **54**–27
cycling [sī/klĭng] **228**–5
cyclist [sī/klĭst] **224**–2
cylinder [sĭl/ən dər] **193**–41, **195**–38
cytoplasm [sī/tə plăzm] **194**–9
daffodil [dăf/ə dĭl/] **211**–25
daily [dā/lē] **20**–21
DAILY ROUTINES [dā/lē rōō tēnz/] **38**–**39**
Dairy [dër/ē] **72**
daisy [dā/zē] **211**–14
dance [dăns] **64**–A
dangerous [dān/jər əs] **186**–1
dark blue [därk/ blōō/] **24**–10

Index

Dashboard and Instrument Panel
[dăsh/bôrd/ ən ĭn/strə mənt păn/əl] **159**

dates [dāts] **20**–1, **68**–28

  date of birth [dāt əv bûrth/] **4**–13

  expiration date
    [ĕk/spə rā/shən dāt/] **112**–7, **136**–10

daughter [dö/tər] **34**–14

  daughter-in-law [dö/tər ĭn lö/] **34** ✦

  granddaughters [grăn/dö/tərz] **34** ✦

  stepdaughter [stĕp/dö/tər] **35** ✦

day [dā] **20**–2

  birthday [bûrth/dā/] **22**–1

  Columbus Day [kə lŭm/bəs dā/] **22**–15

  daylight saving time [dā/līt/ sā/vĭng tīm/] **19**–25

  every day [ĕv/rē dā/] **20**–21

  Independence Day [ĭn/də pĕn/dəns dā/] **22**–13

  Labor Day [lā/bər dā/] **22**–14

  Martin Luther King Jr. Day
    [mär/tən lōō/thər kĭng/ jōōn/yər-dā/] **22**–10

  Memorial Day [mə mör/ē əl dā/] **22**–12

  New Year's Day [nōō/ yîrz/ dā/] **22**–9

  Presidents' Day [prĕz/ə dənts dā/] **22**–11

  Veterans Day [vĕt/ər ənz dā/] **22**–16

Day [dā] **18**

DAY AT SCHOOL [dā/ ăt skōōl/] **11**

DAY AT WORK [dā/ ăt wûrk/] **186**–**187**

Days of the Week [dāz/ əv dhə wēk/] **20**

dead [dĕd]

  dead-bolt lock [dĕd/bōlt/ läk/] **51**–34

  dead end [dĕd/ĕnd/] **154**–6

deaf [dĕf] **32**–12

Dealer [dē/lər] **158**

dealership [dē/lər shĭp/] **126**–4

death certificate [dĕth/ sər tĭf/ə kət] **41**–11

debate [də bāt/] **139**–B

decaf coffee [dē/kăf/ kö/fē] **81**–38

decay [də kā/] **119**–7

December [dĭ sĕm/bər] **21**–36

decimal point [dĕ/sə məl poynt/] **17**–7

Decimals [dĕ/sə məlz] **17**

deck [dĕk] **240**–2

declaration [dĕk/lə rā/shən]

  declaration form [dĕk/lə rā/shən förm/] **161**–16

  Declaration of Independence
    [dĕk/lə rā/shən əv ĭn/də pĕn/dəns] **198**–5

decline [də klīn/] **12**–J

decorations [dĕk/ə rā/shənz] **240**–1

deductions [də dŭk/shənz] **165**–13

deed [dēd] **41**–9

deer [dîr] **216**–14

defendant [dĭ fĕn/dənt] **141**–5

defense attorney [dĭ fĕns/ ə tür/nē] **141**–4

defroster [də frös/tər] **159**–41

degrees [də grēz/] **13**–8, **193**–26

delete [də lēt/] **196**–C

DELI [dĕl/ē] **71**

deliver [də lĭv/ər] **11**–G, **135**–E

delivery person [də lĭv/ə rē pür/sən] **167**–21

dementia [də mĕn/shə] **111**–18

demonstration [dĕ/mən strā/shən] **122**–6

denim [dĕ/nəm] **99**–7

denominator [də nömə nā/tər] **192**–6

dental [dĕn/təl]

  dental assistant [dĕn/təl ə sĭs/tənt] **119**–2, **167**–22

  dental floss [dĕn/təl flös/, –fläs/] **109**–24

  dental hygienist [dĕn/təl hī jē/nĭst, –jē/nĭst] **119**–3

  dental instruments [dĕn/təl ĭn/strə mənts] **119**–4

DENTAL CARE [dĕn/təl kĕr/] **119**

Dental Problems [dĕn/təl präb/ləmz] **119**

dentist [dĕn/tĭst] **119**–1

Dentistry [dĕn/təs trē/] **119**

dentures [dĕn/chərz] **119**–10

deodorant [dē ō/dər ənt] **108**–5

department [dĭ pärt/mənt] **95**–7, **95**–8

  Department of Motor Vehicles
    [dĭ pärt/mənt əv mō/tər vē/ĭ kəlz] **124**–4

  department store [dĭ pärt/mənt stör/] **131**–13

DEPARTMENT OF MOTOR VEHICLES (DMV)
  [dĭ pärt/mənt əv mō/tər vē/ĭ kəlz] / [dē/ĕm/vē/]
  136–**137**

departure [dĭ pär/chər] **161**–5, **161**–7

deposit [dĭ päz/ət] **132**–3, **132**–7

  deposit slip [dĭ päz/ət slĭp/] **132**–4

depression [də prĕ/shən] **115**–5

depth [dĕpth] **17**–18

DESCRIBING CLOTHES [dĭ skrī/bĭng klōz/] **96**–**97**

DESCRIBING HAIR [dĭ skrī/bĭng hĕr/] **33**

DESCRIBING PEOPLE [dĭ skrī/bĭng pē/pəl] **32**

DESCRIBING THINGS [dĭ skrī/bĭng thĭngz/] **23**

desert [dĕz/ərt] **204**–4

design [dĭ zīn/] **175**–A

designated drivers [dĕz/ĭg nā/təd drī/vərz] **143** ✦

designer [dĭ zī/nər] **98** ✦, **167**–30, **175**–2, **176**–5

desk [dĕsk] **6**–7, **182**–9

  circulation desk [sür/kyə lā/shən dĕsk/] **133**–2

  desk clerk [dĕsk klürk/] **184**–11

  front desk [frŭnt/ dĕsk/] **184**–12

Desktop Computer [dĕsk/täp/ kəm pyōō/tər] **196**

Desserts [dĭ zürts/] **81**

dessert tray [dĭ zürt/ trā/] **83**–10

destination [dĕs/tə nā/shən] **161** ✦

detector [dĭ tĕk/tər] **51**–29

detergent [dĭ tür/jənt] **101**–8

device [də vīs/] **225**–20

diabetes [dī/ə bē/tēz, –təs] **111**–12

diagonal [dī ăg/ə nəl, –ăg/nəl] **193**–31

dial [dī/əl] **15**–A, **15**–E

diameter [dī ăm/ə tər] **193**–37

diamonds [dī/məndz] **233**–29

diaper [dī/pər] **37**–8, **37**–10

  diaper pail [dī/pər pāl/] **37**–7

diaphragm [dī/ə frăm] **194**–19

dice [dīs] **232**–6

dice [dīs] **77**–J

dictate [dĭk/tāt] **8**–N

dictator [dĭk/tā/tər] **199**–6

dictionary [dĭk/shə nĕr/ē] **7**–30, **7**–31

die [dī] **41**–R

dietician [dī/ə tĭsh/ən] **120**–15

difference [dĭf/rəns] **192**–8

different [dĭf/frənt, dĭ/fə rənt] **23**–16

DIFFERENT [dĭ/frənt, dĭ/fə rənt] **28**–29

DIFFERENT PLACES TO LIVE
[dĭ/frənt plā/səz tə lĭv/, dĭ/fə rənt] **52**

difficult [dĭf/ĭ kŭlt/] **23**–24

digital [dĭ/jə təl]

  digital camera [dĭ/jə təl kăm/rə] **235**–19

  digital photo album [dĭ/jə təl fō/tō ăl/bəm] **235**–32

dime [dīm] **26**–3

Dimensions [də mĕn/shənz] **17**

diner [dī/nər] **82**–6, **185**–9

dining [dī/nĭng]

  dining area [dī/nĭng ĕr/ē ə] **46**–7

  dining room [dī/nĭng rōōm/] **82**–1

  dining room chair [dī/nĭng rōōm/ chĕr/] **55**–8

  dining room table [dī/nĭng rōōm/tā/bəl] **55**–9

Dining [dī/nĭng] **185**

DINING AREA [dī/nĭng ĕr/ē ə] **55**

dinner [dĭn/ər] **72**–28

  dinner fork [dĭn/ər förk/] **83**–28

  dinner plate [dĭn/ər plāt/] **83**–18

  dinner salad [dĭn/ər săl/əd] **80**–15

Dinner [dĭn/ər] **81**

diploma [də plō/mə] **40**–3

direct flight [də rĕkt/ flīt/, dī–] **161** ✦

Directions [də rĕk/shənz] **9**, **155**

DIRECTIONS AND MAPS
[də rĕk/shənz ən măps/, dī–] **155**

directory [də rĕk/tə rē, dī–] **131**–24

  directory assistance
    [də rĕk/tə rē ə sĭs/təns, dī–] **14**–22

dirty [dür/tē] **101**–15

Disabilities [dĭ/sə bĭl/ə tēz] **32**

disagree [dĭ/sə grē/] **12**–L

disappointed [dĭ/sə poyn/təd] **28**–4

DISASTERS [dĭ/zăs tərz] **144**–**145**

disc [dĭsk] **231**–27

discipline [dĭs/ə plən] **36**–K

discuss [dĭ skŭs/] **8**–G

disease [dĭ zēz/] **111**–11, **111** ✦, **119**–11

Diseases [dĭ zē/zəz] **111**

disgusted [dĭ skŭs/təd] **42**–7

dish [dĭsh] **55**–1

  casserole dish [kăs/ə rōl dĭsh/] **78**–10

  dish rack [dĭsh/ răk/] **54**–5

  dish room [dĭsh/ rōōm/] **83**–13

  dish towel [dĭsh/ tow/əl] **61**–22

  dishwasher [dĭsh/wä/shər, –wö/–]
    54–8, **83**–14, **185**–2

  dishwashing liquid [dĭsh/wä/shĭng lĭk/wəd] **61**–21

  satellite dish [să/tə lĭt dĭsh/] **53**–6

  soap dish [sōp/ dĭsh/] **57**–25

disinfectant wipes [dĭs/ən fĕk/tənt wīps/] **61**–23

display case [dĭ splā/ kās/] **94**–5

disposable [dĭ spō/zə bəl]

  disposable diaper [dĭ spō/zə bəl dī/pər] **37**–10

  disposable gloves [dĭ spō/zə bəl glŭvz/] **93**–27

disposal [dĭ spō/zəl] **54**–7, **121**–31

dive [dīv] **230**–K

divide [də vīd/] **17**–A, **192**–D

diving [dī/vĭng] **227**–12

  diving mask [dī/vĭng măsk/] **225**–6

divorced couple [də vörst/ kŭ/pəl] **35**–21

DJ [dē/jā/] **64**–4

DMV [dē/ĕm/vē/]
    DMV clerk [dē/ĕm/vē/ klürk/] **136**–3
    DMV handbook [dē/ĕm/vē/ hănd/bŏŏk/] **136**–1
do [dōō] **39**–T
    do an experiment [dōō ən ĭk spër/ə mənt] **195**–B
    do crafts [dōō krăfts/] **232**–D
    do errands [dōō ër/əndz] **128** ✦
    do manual labor [dōō măn/yōō əl lā/bər] **170**–D
    do not drink [dōō nät drĭnk/] **112**–F
    do not enter [dōō nät/ ĕn/tər] **154**–2
    do not operate [dōō nät/ äp/ə rāt/] **112**–E
    do not take [dōō nät/ tāk/] **112**–F
    don't be late [dōnt/ bē/ lāt/] **174**–E
    don't litter [dōnt/ lĭ/tər] **219**–L
    don't smoke [dōnt/ smōk/] **114**–G
dock [däk] **175**–15, **234**–3
    dockworker [däk/wür/kər] **167**–23
doctor [däk/tər] **118**–5
DOCUMENTS [dä/kyə mənts] **40**–41
dog [dög] **79**–6, **215**–11, **215**–22
dogwood [dög/wŏŏd/] **210**–15
DOING THE LAUNDRY [dō/ĭng dhə lön/drē] **101**
doll [däl] **59**–21, **233**–28
    dollhouse [däl/hows/] **59**–16
    doll making kit [däl/ mā/kĭng kĭt/] **232**–13
dollar [däl/ər] **26**–7
    dollar coin [däl/ər koyn/] **26**–6
    fifty dollars [fĭf/tē däl/ərz] **26**–11
    five dollars [fĭv/ däl/ərz] **26**–8
    half dollar [hăf/ däl/ər] **26**–5
    one hundred dollars
        [wŭn/ hŭn/drəd däl/ərz] **26**–12
    ten dollars [tĕn/ däl/ərz] **26**–9
    twenty dollars [twĕn/tē däl/ərz] **26**–10
dolphin [däl/fən, döl/–] **213**–31
domesticated [də mĕs/tə kā/təd] **215** ✦
DOMESTIC ANIMALS AND RODENTS
    [də mĕs/tĭk ăn/ə məlz ən rōd/nts] **215**
donkey [däng/kē, dŭng/–, döng/–] **215**–3
donut [dō/nŭt] **79**–15
    donut shop [dō/nŭt shäp/] **129**–17
door [dör] **46**–3
    doorbell [dör/bĕl/] **53**–14
    door chain [dör/ chān/] **51**–33
    doorknob [dör/näb/] **53**–12
    door lock [dör/ läk/] **159**–25
    doorman [dör/măn/] **184**–1
    4-door car [för/dör kär/] **156**–1
    front door [frŭnt/ dör/] **53**–11
    garage door [gə räj/ dör/] **53**–7
    revolving door [rĭ väl/vĭng dör/] **184**–2
    screen door [skrēn/ dör/] **53**–15
    sliding glass door [slī/dĭng glăs/dör/] **53**–18
    storm door [störm/ dör/] **53**–10
    2-door car [tōō/dör kär/] **156**–2
dorm / dormitory [dörm/] / [dör/mə tör/ē] **52**–8
dosage [dō/sĭj] **112**–6
double [dŭb/əl]
    double bed [dŭb/əl bĕd/] **184**–14
    double boiler [dŭb/əl boy/lər] **78**–8

down [down]
    break down [brāk/ down/] **162**–D
    downhill skiing [down/hĭl/ skē/ĭng] **227**–1
    down jacket [down jăk/ət] **90**–16
    down vest [down vĕst/] **90**–14
    drop-down menu [dräp/ down/ mĕn/yōō/] **197**–8
    put down [pŏŏt/ down/] **6**–J
    sit down [sĭt down/] **6**–F
    walk down [wäk down/] **153**–D
downstairs [down/stërz/] **51** ✦
DOWNTOWN [down/town/] **124**–125
drain [drān] **57**–5
drama [drä/mə] **236**–12
drapes [drāps] **56**–16
draw [drö] **8**–F, **118**–F, **195**–E
drawer [drör] **54**–23, **58**–2, **59**–6
dress [drĕs] **86**–3, **88**–5, **89**–20
    dressmaker [drĕs/mā/kər] **100**–1
    dressmaker's dummy [drĕs/mā/kərz dŭ/mē] **100**–2
    dress socks [drĕs/ säks/] **91**–9
dress [drĕs] **36**–H, **174**–B
dressed [drĕst] **38**–D
dresser [drĕs/ər] **58**–1
Dressings [drĕs/ĭngz] **80**
dribble [drĭb/əl] **230**–J
drill [drĭl] **178**–9, **180**–8
    drill bit [drĭl bĭt/] **180**–28
drill [drĭl] **119**–D
drink [drĭnk] **11**–J
    do not drink alcohol
        [dōō/ nät/ drĭnk/ ăl/kə höl/] **112**–F
    don't drink and **drive** [dōnt/ drĭnk ən drĭv/] **143**–G
    drink fluids [drĭnk flōō/ədz] **114**–C
drip [drĭp] **121**–25
dripping [drĭp/ĭng] **63**–17
drive [drīv] **196**–6, **196**–8, **196**–9
    drive-thru window [drīv/thrōō/ wĭn/dō] **128**–11
    driveway [drīv/wā/] **53**–8
drive [drīv]
    don't drink and **drive** [dōnt/ drĭnk ən drīv/] **143**–G
    drive a truck [drĭv ə trŭk/] **170**–E
    drive through [drĭv/ thrōō] **153**–K
    drive to work [drĭv/ tə würk/] **38**–I
driver [drī/vər] **152**–21, **169**–61
    designated drivers [dĕz/ĭg nā/təd drī/vərz] **143** ✦
    driver's license [drī/vərz lī/səns] **40**–4, **136**–9
    driver's license number
        [drī/vərz lī/səns nŭm/bər] **136**–11
    Phillips screwdriver [fĭl/ĭps skrōō/drī/vər] **180**–31
    screwdriver [skrōō/drī/vər] **180**–30
driving [drī/vĭng] **142**–5
drop [dräp]
    drop cloth [dräp/ klöth/] **181**–54
    drop-down menu [dräp/ down/ mĕn/yōō/] **197**–8
drop off [dräp/ öf/] **38**–G
dropper [dräp/ər] **195**–45
drops [dräps] **113**–31
drought [drowt] **145**–11
drown [drown] **116**–I
drugs [drŭgz] **116**–K, **142**–6
drums [drŭmz] **238**–16
drumsticks [drŭm/stĭks/] **70**–23
drunk driving [drŭngk/ drī/vĭng] **142**–5

dry [drī] **101**–18
    dry cleaners [drī/ klē/nərz] **128**–2
    dry erase marker [drī/ ĭ rās/ mär/kər] **7**–17
    drywall [drī/wöl/] **178**–19
dry [drī] **60**–N, **108**–H
dryer [drī/ər] **50**–13, **101**–4
    blow dryer [blō/ drī/ər] **33**–23, **108**–18
    dryer sheets [drī/ər shēts/] **101**–5
Dry Measures [drī/ mĕzh/ərz] **75**
duck [dŭk] **70**–18, **214**–12
duct tape [dŭkt/ tāp/] **181**–49
dummy [dŭ/mē] **100**–2
dump truck [dŭmp/ trŭk/] **156**–19
dune [dōōn] **204**–5
duplex [dōō/plĕks/] **52** ✦
During an Emergency [dōō/rĭng ən ĭ mür/jən sē] **147**
dust [dŭst]
    dustpan [dŭst/păn/] **61**–17
    dust ruffle [dŭst/ rŭf/əl] **58**–17
    dust storm [dŭst/ störm/] **13**–19
dust [dŭst] **60**–A
duster [dŭs/tər] **61**–1
DVD [dē/vē/dē/] **133**–19, **234**–11
    DVD and CD-ROM drive
        [dē/vē/dē/ ən sē/dē/räm/ drīv/] **196**–9
    DVD player [dē/vē/dē/ plā/ ər] **56**–7, **234**–10
dye [dī] **33**–D
eagle [ē/gəl] **214**–9
ear [ïr] **32**–17, **105**–11
    earache [ïr/āk/] **110**–3
    ear infection [ïr/ ĭn fĕk/shən] **111**–3
    earmuffs [ïr/mŭfs/] **90**–13, **179**–16
    ear plugs [ïr/ plŭgz/] **179**–15
    pierced earrings [pïrst/ ïr/ĭngz] **95**–36
early [ür/lē] **19**–22
Earth [ürth] **205**–3
earthquake [ürth/kwāk/] **144**–5
easel [ē/zəl] **233**–18
east [ēst] **155**–4
Eastern time [ē/stərn tīm/] **19**–32
easy [ē/zē] **23**–23, **76**–11
    easy chair [ē/zē chër/] **56**–22
Easy Chicken Soup [ē/zē chĭk/ən sōōp/] **77**
eat [ēt] **11**–1
    eat a healthy diet [ēt ə hĕl/thē dī/ət] **114**–F
    eat breakfast [ēt brĕk/fəst] **38**–E
    eat dinner [ēt dĭn/ər] **39**–S
    eat out [ēt/ owt/] **82** ✦
eater [ē/tər] **176**–12
eclipse [ĭ klĭps/] **205**–16, **205** ✦
edit [ĕd/ət] **191**–I
education [ĕ jyōō/ kā/shən] **189**–17
eel [ēl] **212**–12
eggplants [ĕg/plănts/] **69**–23
eggs [ĕgz] **66**–7
    eggbeater [ĕg/bē/tər] **78**–20
    eggs over easy [ĕgz ō/vər ē/zē] **76**–11
    eggs sunny-side up [ĕgz sŭn/ē sīd/ ŭp/] **76**–10
    hardboiled eggs [härd/ boyld/ ĕgz/] **76**–8
    poached eggs [pōcht/ ĕgz/] **76**–9
    scrambled eggs [skrăm/bəld ĕgz/] **76**–7
Eggs [ĕgz] **76**

Index

eight [āt] **16**
eighteen [ā/tēn/] **16**
eighteenth [ā/tēnth/] **16**
eighth [ātth, āth] **16**
eightieth [ā/tē/əth] **16**
eighty [ā/tē] **16**
elastic bandage [ĭ lăs/tĭk băn/dĭj] **117**–12
elbow [ĕl/bō] **106**–12
elderly [ĕl/dər lē] **32**–3
elected [ĭ lĕk/təd] **139**–C
elected official [ĭ lĕk/təd ə fĭ/shəl] **139**–32
Election [ĭ lĕk/shən] **139**
election results [ĭ lĕk/shən rĭ zŭltz/] **139**–31
elective [ĭ lĕk/tĭv] **189** ✦
electric [ĭ lĕk/trĭk] **116**–F
electric can opener [ĭ lĕk/trĭk kăn/ ō/pə nər] **54**–14
electric drill [ĭ lĕk/trĭk drĭl/] **180**–8
electric keyboard [ĭ lĕk/trĭk kē/börd/] **238**–18
electric mixer [ĭ lĕk/trĭk mĭk/sər] **54**–25
electric pencil sharpener
[ĭ lĕk/trĭk pĕn/səl shär/pə nər] **183**–26
electric shaver [ĭ lĕk/trĭk shā/vər] **109**–26
electrical [ĭ lĕk/trĭ kəl]
electrical hazard [ĭ lĕk/trĭ kəl hăz/ərd] **186**–6
electrical tape [ĭ lĕk/trĭ kəl tāp/] **181**–43
electrician [ĭ lĕk trĭsh/ən] **62**–9
electron [ĭ lĕk/trän] **195**–30
electronics [ĭ lĕk trän/ĭks]
electronics repair person
[ĭ lĕk trän/ĭks rĭ pĕr/ pŭr/sən] **167**–24
electronics store [ĭ lĕk trän/ĭks stör/] **131**–20
ELECTRONICS AND PHOTOGRAPHY
[ĭ lĕk trän/ĭks ən fə täg/rə fē] **234**–235
elementary school [ĕl/ə mĕn/trē skool/] **188**–2
elephant [ĕl/ə fənt] **217**–42
elevator [ĕl/ə vā/tər] **50**–9, **131**–21, **184**–9
eleven [ĭ lĕv/ən] **16**
eleventh [ĭ lĕv/ənth] **16**
elm [ĕlm] **210**–16
Email [ē/māl/] **197**
embarrassed [ĭm băr/əst] **43**–24
embroidery [ĭm broy/də rē] **233**–24
EMERGENCIES [ĭ mür/jən sēz] **116**
EMERGENCIES AND NATURAL DISASTERS
[ĭ mür/jən sēz ən năch/rəl dĭ zăs/tərz,–năch/ə rəl–]
144–145
emergency [ĭ mür/jən sē] **117**–3
emergency card [ĭ mür/jən sē kärd/] **161**–26
emergency exit
[ĭ mür/jən sē ĕg/zət,–ĕk/sət] **51**–25, **161**–14
emergency medical technician (EMT) [ĭ mür/jən sē
mĕd/ĭ kəl tĕk nĭsh/ən] / [ē/ĕm/tē/] **121**–32
Emergency [ĭ mür/jən sē] **146**–147
Emergency Call [ĭ mür/jən sē köl/] **15**
EMERGENCY PROCEDURES
[ĭ mür/jən sē prə sē/jərz] **146**–147
Emergency Room Entrance
[ĭ mür/jən sē room/ ĕn/trəns] **121**
Emergency Worker [ĭ mür/jən sē wür/kər] **93**
emery board [ĕm/ə rē börd/, ĕm/rē-] **109**–32
emperor [ĕm/pər ər] **199**–3
employee [ĕm ploy/ē] **165**–9

employer [ĕm ploy/ər] **164**–4
empty [ĕmp/tē] **23**–10
empty [ĕmp/tē] **60**–L
EMT (emergency medical technician) [ē/ĕm/tē/] /
[ĭ mür/jən sē mĕd/ĭ kəl tĕk nish/ən] **121**–32
end [ĕnd] **154**–6
endpoint [ĕnd/poynt/] **193**–21
end table [ĕnd/ tā/bəl] **56**–14
energy [ĕn/ər jē] **218**–1, **218**–7, **218**–8
bioenergy [bī/ō ĕn/ər jē] **218**–9
ENERGY AND CONSERVATION
[ĕn/ər jē ən kän/sər vā/shən] **218**–219
Energy and Resources [ĕn/ər jē ən rē/sör/səz] **219**
Energy Sources [ĕn/ər jē sör/səz] **218**
engine [ĕn/jən] **158**–18, **197**–6
engineer [ĕn/jə nïr/] **167**–18, **167**–25
ENGLISH COMPOSITION
[ĭng/glĭsh käm/pə zĭsh/ən] **190**–191
English muffin [ĭng/glĭsh mŭf/ən] **80**–5
enter [ĕn/tər]
do not **enter** [doo/ nät/ ĕn/tər] **154**–2
enter data [ĕn/tər dā/tə] **171**–B
enter the room [ĕn/tər dhe room/] **11**–A
enter your PIN [ĕn/tər yər pĭn/] **132**–E
ENTERTAINMENT [ĕn/tər tān/mənt] **236**–237
entertainment center [ĕn/tər tān/mənt sĕn/tər] **56**–5
entrance [ĕn/trəns] **164**–1
Entrance [ĕn/trəns] **50, 121**
entry-level job [ĕn/trē lĕv/əl jäb/] **172**–1
Entryway [ĕn/trē wā/] **51**
envelope [ĕn/və löp/] **134**–14, **183**–43
equation [ĭ kwā/zhən] **192**–13
equipment [ĭ kwĭp/mənt] **177**–12, **179**–4
Equipment [ĭ kwĭp/mənt] **179, 183**
EQUIPMENT [ĭ kwĭp/mənt] **231**
Equivalencies [ĭ kwĭ/və lən sēz/] **17, 75**
erase [ĭ rās/] **10**–M
eraser [ĭ rā/sər] **7**–19, **7**–21
errands [ĕr/əndz] **128** ✦
eruption [ĭ rŭp/shən] **145**–16
escalator [ĕs/kə lā/tər] **131**–23
escape [ĭs kāp/] **50**–2
escape route [ĭs kāp/ root/, rowt/] **146**–3
ESL [ē/ĕs/ĕl/] **189**–14
ESOL [ē/ĕs/ō/ĕl/] **189**–14
essay [ĕs/ā] **190**–4
Essay [ĕs/ā] **190**
e-ticket [ē/tĭ kət/] **161**–19
evacuate [ĭ văk/yoo/ āt/] **147**–K
evacuation route [ĭ văk/yoo/ā shən root/, rowt/] **146**–5
evening [ēv/nĭng] **18**–19
evening gown [ēv/nĭng gown/] **89**–18
even numbers [ē/vən nŭm/bərz] **192**–4
EVENTS [ĭ vĕnts/] **22, 40**–41
every day [ĕv/rē dā/] **20**–21
EVERYDAY CLOTHES [ĕv/rē dā/ klōz] **86**–87
EVERDAY CONVERSATION
[ĕv/rē dā/ kän/vər sā/shən] **12**
evidence [ĕv/ĭ dəns/] **141**–9
exam [ĭg zăm/] **122**–1, **136**–6
examination table [ĭg zăm/ə nā/shən tā/bəl] **118**–7
examine [ĭg zăm/ən] **118**–D, **118**–E

Examining Room [ĭg zăm/ə nĭng room/] **118**
exchange [ĭks chänj/] **27**–I
excited [ĭk sī/təd] **43**–22
exclamation mark [ĕk/sklə mā/shən märk] **190**–13
executive [ĭg zĕk/yə tĭv] **182**–5
executive chef [ĭg zĕk/yə tĭv shĕf/] **185**–7
Executive Branch [ĭg zĕk/yə tĭv bränch/] **138**
exercise [ĕk/sər sīz/] **122**–4
exercise [ĕk/sər sĭz/] **39**–P, **230**–N
Exercise Wear [ĕk/sər sīz/wër] **89**
exhausted [ĭg zö/stəd] **43** ✦
ex-husband [ĕks/ hŭz/bənd] **35** ✦
exit [eg/zət, ĕk/sət] **51**–25, **51** ✦, **161**–14
expensive [ĭk spĕn/sĭv] **23**–19, **97**–44
Experiment [ĭk spër/ə mənt] **195**
expiration date [ĕk/spə rā/shən dāt/] **112**–7, **136**–10
expire [ĕk/spïr/] **136** ✦
explain [ĭk splān/] **12**–M
exploration [ĕk/splə rā/shən] **199**–8
explorer [ĭk splör/ər] **199**–9
explosion [ĭk splō/zhən] **144**–4
exposed [ĭk spōzd/]
overexposed [ō/vər ĭk spōzd/] **235**–34
underexposed [ŭn/dər ĭk spōzd/] **235**–35
Express Mail® [ĭk sprĕs/ māl/] **134**–2
Extended Family [ĭk stĕn/dəd făm/lē, făm/ə lē] **34**
extension cord [ĭk stĕn/shən körd/] **181**–14
exterminate [ĭk stür/mə nāt/] **62** ✦
exterminator [ĭk stür/mə nā/tər] **63**–21
extinguisher [ĭk stĭn/gwə shər] **179**–21
extra [ĕk/strə]
extra large [ĕk/strə lärj/] **96**–5
extra small [ĕk/strə smöl/] **96**–1
ex-wife [ĕks/ wif/] **35** ✦
eye [ī] **99**–27, **105**–11
eyebrow [ī/brow/] **106**–9
eyebrow pencil [ī/brow/ pĕn/səl] **109**–34
eye drops [ī/dräps/] **113**–31
eye hook [ī/hook/] **180**–40
eyelashes [ī/lăsh/əz] **106**–11
eyelid [ī/lĭd/] **106**–10
eyeliner [ī/li/nər] **109**–36
eyepiece [ī/pēs/] **194**–14
eye shadow [ī/shă/dō] **109**–35
Eye [ī] **106**
fabric [făb/rĭk] **98**–15
fabric softener [făb/rĭk sö/fə nər] **101**–6
Fabric Store [făb/rĭk stör/] **99**
face [fās] **193**–44
face mask [fās măsk/] **93**–32
face powder [fās/ pow/dər] **109**–41
Face [fās] **106**
factory [făk/tə rē, –trē] **126**–3
factory owner [făk/tə rē ō/nər] **175**–1
factory worker [făk/tə rē wür/kər] **175**–3
Factory [făk/tə rē] **98**
FACTORY [făk/tə rē] **175**
Fahrenheit [făr/ən hīt/] **13**–1
fair [fër] **172**–13, **223**–13
fair trial [fër/ trī/əl] **140**–5
FAIR [fër] **122**–123
fall [föl] **21**–39

fall [föl] **40**–H, **116**–O
FAMILIES [făm/lēz, făm/ə lēz] **34**–35
Family [făm/lē, făm/ə lē] **34**
FAMILY REUNION
[făm/lē rē yōōn/yən, făm/ə lē] **44**–45
famine [fă/mĭn] **145**–12
fan [făn] **55**–19, **229**–4
fancy [făn/sē] **97**–34
far from [fär/ frŭm/, –frəm/] **25** ✦
fare [fër] **152**–2
fare card [fër kärd/] **152**–11
farm [färm] **52**–9
farm equipment [färm/ ĭ kwĭp/mənt] **177**–12
farmworker [färm/ wür/kər] **177**–8
Farm Animals [färm/ ăn/ə məlz] **215**
farmer [fär/mər] **177**–13
FARMERS' MARKET [fär/mərz mär/kət] **84**–85
FARMING AND RANCHING
[fär/mĭng ən răn/chĭng] **177**
Farmworker [färm/ wür/kər] **92**
fashion [făsh/ən] **88** ✦
fashion designer [făsh/ən dĭ zī/nər] **98** ✦
fast [făst] **23**–3
fast food restaurant [făst/ fōōd/ rĕs/tə rənt, –ränt]
128–10
fasten [făs/ən] **160**–H
fastener [făs/nər] **99**–29
FAST FOOD RESTAURANT
[făst/ fōōd/ rĕs/tə rənt, –ränt] **79**
fast forward [făst/ för/wərd] **235**–D
fat [făt] **32**–7
father [fä/dhər] **34**–4, **35**–23
father-in-law [fä/dhər ĭn lö/] **34**–11
grandfather [grăn/fä/dhər, grănd/–] **34**–2
stepfather [stĕp/fädhər] **35**–25
faucet [fö/sət] **57**–6
fax [făks] **171**–G
fax machine [făks/ mə shēn/] **183**–21
feast [fēst] **239**–13
feather [fĕdh/ər] **214**–4
feather duster [fĕdh/ər dŭs/tər] **61**–1
February [fĕb/yōō ër/ē, fĕb/rōō–] **21**–26
Federal Government
[fĕ/də rəl gŭ/vərn mənt, fĕ/drəl] **138**
feed [fēd] **36**–C, **176**–D, **177**–D
feed dog / feed bar [fēd/ dög/ / fēd/ bär/] **98**–20
feel [fēl] **110**–C, **110**–D
FEELINGS [fē/lĭngz] **42**–43
female [fē/māl/] **4**–18
fence [fĕns] **177**–19
fencing [fĕn/sĭng] **228**–7
ferry [fër/ē] **220**–4
fertilize [fürt/ əl īz/] **176**–D
fever [fē/vər] **110**–8
fiction [fĭk/shən] **237**–18
field [fēld] **5**–2, **177**–7
ball field [böl/ fēld/] **224**–1
track and field [trăk/ ən fēld/] **228**–18
fifteen [fĭf/tēn/] **16**
fifteenth [fĭf/tēnth/] **16**
fifth [fĭfth] **16**
fiftieth [fĭf/tē əth] **16**

fifty [fĭf/tē] **16**
fifty dollars [fĭf/tē däl/ərz] **26**–11
50 percent [fĭf/tē pər sĕnt/] **17**–10
fighter [fī/tər]
firefighter [fīr/fī/tər] **144**–9, **167**–26
figs [fĭgz] **68**–27
figure [fĭg/yər] **233**–26
figure skating [fĭg/yər skā/tĭng] **227**–5
figurine [fĭg/yə rēn/] **232**–1
file [fīl] **183**–44
file cabinet [fīl kăb/ə nət] **182**–11
file clerk [fīl klürk/] **182**–10
file folder [fīl fōl/dər] **183**–50
fill [fīl]
fill a cavity [fīl/ ə kăv/ə tē] **119**–E
fill prescriptions [fīl/ prĭ skrĭp/shənz] **112** ✦
fill in [fīl/ ĭn] **9**–O
fill out [fīl/ owt/] **173**–J
fill the tank [fīl/ dhe tănk/] **157**–G
fill the tires [fīl/ dhe tīrz/] **157**–L
filling [fĭl/ĭng] **119**–8
Filling Out a Form [fĭl/ĭng owt ə förm/] **4**
film [fĭlm] **235**–22
film camera [fĭlm kăm/rə] **235**–21
find [fīnd] **160**–F
FINDING A HOME [fīn/dĭng ə hōm/] **48**–49
fine adjustment knob [fīn/ ə jŭst/mənt näb/] **194**–23
fingers [fĭng/gərz] **105**–16, **110**–16
fingernail [fĭng/gər nāl/] **106**–18
fingerprint [fĭng/gər prĭnt/] **136**–5
Fingers [fĭng/gərz] **106**
finish [fĭn/ĭsh] **112**–C, **230**–T
fins [fĭnz] **212**–1, **225**–7
fire [fīr] **144**–7, **144**–8
campfire [kămp/fīr/] **226**–11
fire escape [fīr ĭ skāp/] **50**–2
fire exit [fīr/ ĕg/zət, –ĕk/sət] **51** ✦
fire extinguisher [fīr ĭk stĭng/gwĭ shər] **179**–21
firefighter [fīr/fī/tər] **144**–9, **167**–26
fire hydrant [fīr hī/drənt] **129**–27
fireplace [fīr/plās/] **56**–13
fire screen [fīr skrēn/] **56**–12
fire station [fīr stā/shən] **125**–12
fire truck [fīr trŭk/] **144**–10
fireworks [fīr/würks/] **239**–7
first [fürst] **16**
first aid kit [fürst/ ād/ kĭt/] **117**–1, **146**–18
first aid manual [fürst/ ād/ măn/yōō əl] **117**–2
First Continental Congress
[fürst/ kän/tə nĕnt/ əl käng/grəs] **198**–6
first name [fürst/ nām/] **4**–2
first president [fürst/ prĕz/ə dənt] **198**–11
First Aid [fürst/ ād/] **117**
FIRST AID [fürst/ ād/] **117**
First Aid Procedures [fürst/ ād/ prə sē/ jərz] **117**
First Floor [fürst/ flör/] **50**
First License [fürst/ lī/səns] **137**
fish [fĭsh] **66**–1, **81**–29, **209**–14
catfish [kăt/fĭsh/] **71**–2
goldfish [gōld/fĭsh/] **215**–16
jellyfish [jĕ/lē fĭsh/] **212**–14
starfish [stär/fĭsh/] **212**–16
swordfish [sörd/fĭsh/] **71**–5

Fish [fĭsh] **71**, **212**
fisher [fĭsh/ər] **167**–17
fishing [fĭsh/ĭng] **226**–4
fishing net [fĭsh/ĭng nĕt/] **226**–17
fishing pole [fĭsh/ĭng pōl/] **226**–18
fitted sheet [fĭt/əd shēt/] **58**–12
fittings [fĭt/ĭngz] **181**–18
five [fīv] **16**
five after one [fīv ăf/tər wŭn/] **18**–7
five dollars [fīv däl/ərz] **26**–8
fix [fĭks] **62** ✦, **219**–F
fixture [fĭks/chər] **55**–18
flag [flăg] **239**–8
flammable liquids [flăm/ə bəl lĭk/wədz] **179**–8
flashlight [flăsh/līt/] **146**–14
flat [flăt]
flat panel TV [flăt/ păn/əl tē/vē/] **234**–7
flat screen TV [flăt/ skrēn/ tē/vē/] **234**–7
flat sheet [flăt/ shēt/] **58**–13
have a flat tire [hăv/ ə flăt/ tīr/] **162**–F
flats [flăts] **95**–27
fleas [flēz] **63**–25
flea market [flē/ mär/kət] **222**–6
flight [flīt] **161**–30, **161** ✦
flight attendant [flīt/ ə tĕn/dənt] **161**–12
Flight [flīt] **160**
float [flōt] **239**–2
flood [flŭd] **145**–19
floor [flör] **46**–6, **58**–21, **179**–6
floor lamp [flör lămp/] **56**–15
floor plan [flör plăn/] **186**–4
Floor [flör] **50**
floral [flör/əl] **96**–25
florist [flör/ĭst] **130**–8, **167**–27
floss [flös, fläs] **109**–24
floss [flös, fläs] **109**–K
flounder [flown/dər] **212**–15
flour [flow/ər] **73**–29
Flower [flow/ər] **211**
flowers [flow/ərz] **208**–7
flower bed [flow/ər bĕd/] **53**–20
FLOWERS [flow/ərz] **211**
flu [flōō] **111**–2
fluid [flōō/əd] **183**–36
fluid ounce [flōō/əd owns/] **75**–1
flute [flōōt] **238**–1
fly [flī] **214**–28
fly [flī] **170**–F
flyer [flī/ər] **102**–1
flying disc [flī/ĭng dĭsk/] **231**–27
foam pad [fōm/ păd/] **226**–13
focus [fō/kəs] **235**–33
foggy [fö/gē, fäg/ē] **13**–20
foil [foyl] **72**–23
fold [fōld] **101**–F
folder [fōl/dər] **183**–50
folding [fōl/dĭng]
folding card table [fōl/dĭng kärd/ tā/bəl] **102**–4
folding chair [fōl/dĭng chër/] **102**–5
folk [fōk] **237**–29
follow [fäl/ō] **114**–J, **147**–F
Following Directions [fäl/ō də rek/shənz, –dī–] **9**

Index

food [fōōd]
  baby food [bā/bē fōōd/] **37**–4
  canned food [kănd/ fōōd] **146**–9
  fast food restaurant [făst/ fōōd/ rĕs/tə ränt] **128**–10
  food court [fōōd/ kört] **131**–15
  food preparation worker
      [fōōd/ prĕ/pə rā/shən wür/kər] **185**–4
  food processor [fōōd/ prä/sĕ sər] **54**–26
  packaged food [păk/ĭjd fōōd] **146**–10
  pet food [pĕt/ fōōd/] **72**–5
FOOD [fōōd] **79**
FOOD PREPARATION AND SAFETY
    [fōōd/ prĕ/pə rā/shən ən sāf/tē] **76**–77
Food Processor [fōōd/ prä/sĕ sər] **92**
Foods [fōōdz] **72, 73**
Food Safety [fōōd/ sāf/tē] **76**
FOOD SERVICE [fōōd/sür/vəs] **185**
foot [fōōt] **104**–8
  football [fōōt/böl/] **229**–11, **231**–21
  football helmet [fōōt/böl/ hĕl/mət] **231**–19
  footnote [fōōt/nōt/] **190**–10
Foot [fōōt] **106**
for [för] **128**–B, **173**–C
forceps [för/səps, –sĕps] **195**–43
forearm [för/ärm/] **106**–13
forehead [för/əd/, –hĕd, fär/–] **106**–2
forest [för/əst, fär/–] **204**–1, **204**–11
  forest fire [för/əst fir/] **144**–7
fork [förk] **55**–3, **83**–27, **83**–28
  forklift [förk/lĭft/] **175**–12
Form [förm] **4**
Formal Clothes [förm/əl klōz/] **89**
former husband [för/mər hŭz/bənd] **35** ✦
former wife [för/mər wif/] **35** ✦
forms [förmz] **118**–4, **134**–19, **161**–16
formula [för/myə lə] **37**–3, **195**–34
fortieth [för/tē əth] **16**
forty [för/tē] **16**
forward [för/wərd] **235**–D
  forward button [för/wərd bŭt/n] **197**–3
foundation [fown dā/shən] **109**–40
founders [fown/dərz] **198**–7
fountain [fown/tn] **224**–5, **224**–9
four [för] **16**
  4-door car [för/ dör kär/] **156**–1
  2 x 4 (two by four) [tōō/ bī för/] **181**–19
fourteen [för/tēn/] **16**
fourteenth [för/tēnth/] **16**
fourth [förth] **16**
Fourth Floor [förth flör/] **50**
Fourth of July [förth əv jōō lī/] **22**–13
fox [făks] **216**–15
Fractions [frăk/shənz] **192**
Fractions and Decimals [frăk/shənz ən dĕ/sə məlz] **17**
frame [frām] **58**–4, **58**–18
frayed cord [frād/ körd] **179**–5
free [frē] **122**–7
  free speech [frē/ spēch/] **140**–2
freedom [frē/dəm]
  freedom of religion [frē/dəm əv rĭ lĭ/jən] **140**–3
  freedom of the press [frē/dəm əv dhə prĕs/] **140**–4
freezer [frē/zər] **54**–10, **185**–3

freezing [frē/zĭng] **13**–7
French [frĕnch]
  french fries [frĕnch/ friz/] **79**–2
  French horn [frĕnch/ hörn/] **238**–13
Frequency [frē/kwən sē/] **20**
fresh [frĕsh] **71**–16
Friday [frī/dā, –dē] **20**–13
fried [frīd] **76**–6
  fried chicken [frid/ chĭk/ən] **76**–1
fringe [frĭnj] **99**–34
frog [frög, fräg] **212**–25
front [frŭnt] **25**–7
  front desk [frŭnt/ dĕsk/] **184**–12
  front door [frŭnt/ dör/] **53**–11
  front seat [frŭnt/ sēt/] **159**–51
  front walk [frŭnt/ wök/] **53**–2
Front Porch [frŭnt/ pörch/] **53**
Font Yard and House [frŭnt/ yärd/ en hows/] **53**
frostbite [fräst/bit/] **116**–G
frozen [frō/zən] **63**–16, **71**–17
  frozen dinner [frō/zən dĭn/ər] **72**–28
  frozen vegetables [frō/zən vĕj/tə bəlz] **72**–27
Frozen Foods [frō/zən fōōdz/] **72**
fruit [frōōt] **67**–9
  fruit salad [frōōt săl/əd] **80**–21
FRUIT [frōōt] **68**
frustrated [frŭs/trā/təd] **43**–27
frying pan [fri/ĭng păn/] **78**–5
fuel injection system
    [fyōō/əl ĭn jĕk/shən sĭs/təm] **158**–17
full [fōōl] **23**–9, **42**–6
  full-length mirror [fōōl/lĕnth/ mĭr/ər] **58**–6
  full moon [fōōl/ mōōn/] **205**–12
  full slip [fōōl/ slĭp/] **91**–22
fumes [fyōōmz] **179**–3
funnel [fŭn/əl] **195**–40
funny photo [fŭn/ē fō/tō] **206**–2
fur [für] **216**–19
furious [fyōōr/ē əs] **43** ✦
furnished apartment [für/nĭsht ə pärt/mənt] **48**–3
furniture [für/nĭ chər] **53**–19
  furniture polish [für/nĭ chər päl/ĭsh] **61**–8
  furniture store [für/nĭ chər stör/] **126**–8
Furniture and Accessories
    [für/nĭ chər ən ĭk sĕs/ə rēz] **59**
fuse box [fyōōz/ bäks/] **62**–13
fusion [fyōō/zhən] **218**–10
galaxy [găl/ək sē] **205**–15
gallbladder [göl/blăd/ər] **107**–44
gallon [găl/ən] **75**–5
game [gām]
  baseball game [bās/böl gām/] **44**–2
  board game [börd/ gām/] **232**–5
  game show [gām/ shō/] **236**–8
  video game console [vĭd/ē ō gām/ kän/sōl] **232**–3
  video game control [vĭd/ē ō gām kən trōl] **232**–4
Games [gāmz] **59**
GAMES [gāmz] **232**–233
gang violence [găng/ vi/ə ləns] **142**–4
garage [gə räzh/, –räj/] **47**–14, **124**–1
  garage door [gə räzh/ dör/] **53**–7
Garage [gə räzh/, –räj/] **50**

GARAGE SALE [gə räzh/ săl/] **102**–103
garbage [gär/bĭj]
  garbage can [gär/bĭj kăn/] **53**–24
  garbage disposal [gär/bĭj dĭ spō/zəl] **54**–7
  garbage truck [gär/bĭj trŭk/] **127**–22
garden [gär/dn]
  botanical garden [bə tăn/ə kəl gär/dn] **222**–3
  roof garden [rōōf/gär/dn] **50**–4
  vegetable garden [vĕj/tə bəl gär/dn] **53**–27, **177**–14
garden [gär/dn] **53**–B
gardener [gär/dn er, gärd/nər] **167**–28
gardenia [gär dēn/yə] **211**–18
gardening [gärd/nĭng]
  gardening crew [gärd/nĭng krōō/] **176**–1
  gardening crew leader
      [gärd/nĭng krōō lēd/ər] **176**–4
GARDENING [gärd/nĭng] **176**
gargle [gär/gəl] **109**–L
garlic [gär/lĭk] **69**–30
  garlic bread [gär/lĭk brĕd/] **81**–28
  garlic press [gär/lĭk prĕs/] **78**–11
Garment Factory [gär/mənt făk/tə rē, fäk/trē] **98**
garment worker [gär/mənt wür/kər] **167**–29
garter [gär/tər]
  garter belt [gär/tər bĕlt/] **91**–16
  garter snake [gär/tər snāk/] **213**–39
gas [găs] **218**–3
  gas gauge [găs/gāj/] **159**–31
  gas meter [găs mē/tər] **62**–14
  gas pedal [găs pĕd/l] **159**–46
  gas shut-off valve [găs/ shŭt/öf vălv/] **146**–4
  gas station [găs stā/shən] **125**–10
  gas station attendant
      [găs stā/shən ə tĕn/dənt] **162**–3
  gas tank [găs tăngk/] **158**–10
gate [gāt] **50**–16, **53**–9, **161**–8
Gate [gāt] **161**
gauge [gāj]
  blood pressure gauge [blŭd/ prĕsh/ər gāj/] **118**–9
  gas gauge [găs/gāj/] **159**–31
  oil gauge [oyl/gāj/] **159**–29
  temperature gauge [tĕm/prə chər gāj/] **159**–30
gauze [göz] **117**–8
gear shift [gĭr/ shĭft/] **159**–47
gel [jĕl] **108**–2, **108**–16
GEOGRAPHY AND HABITATS
    [jē äg/rə fē ən hă/bə tăts/] **204**
Geometric Solids [jē/ə mĕ/trĭk säl/ədz] **193**
geometry [jē äm/ə trē] **192**–17
geothermal energy [jē/ō thür/məl ĕn/ər jē] **218**–7
get [gĕt]
  get a job [gĕt/ ə jäb/] **40**–F
  get a learner's permit
      [gĕt/ ə lürn/ərz pür/mĭt] **137**–F
  get a library card [gĕt/ ə lī/brĕr ē kärd/] **133**–A
  get a loan [gĕt/ ə lōn/] **49**–J
  get an electric shock [gĕt/ ən ĭ lĕk/trĭk shäk/] **116**–F
  get a speeding ticket [gĕt/ ə spē/dĭng tĭk/ət] **162**–C
  get bed rest [gĕt/ bĕd/ rĕst/] **114**–B
  get change [gĕt/ chănj/] **26**–A
  get dressed [gĕt/ drĕst/] **38**–D
  get elected [gĕt/ ĭ lĕk/təd] **139**–C

get engaged [gĕt/ ĭn gājd/] **41**–J
get feedback [gĕt/ fēd/băk/] **191**–K
get frostbite [gĕt/ fröst/bīt/] **116**–G
get good grades [gĕt/ good/ grādz/] **10**–H
get hired [gĕt/ hīrd/] **173**–L
get home [gĕt/ hōm/] **39**–R
get immunized [gĕt/ ĭm/yə nīzd/] **114**–I
get into [gĕt/ ĭn/tōō] **153**–E
get lost [gĕt/ löst/] **162**–B
get married [gĕt/ măr/ēd] **41**–K
get off [gĕt/ öf/] **153**–J
get on [gĕt/ än/, ön/] **153**–I
get out of [gĕt/ owt/ əv] **153**–F
get the title [gĕt/ dhə tīt/l] **157**–E
get up [gĕt/ ŭp/] **38**–B
get your license [gĕt/ yər lī/səns] **137**–I
Getting Your First License
    [gĕt/ĭng yər fürst/ lī/səns] **137**
Get Well [gĕt/ wĕl/] **114**
gift [gĭft] **94** ✦, **240**–3
gift shop [gĭft/ shäp/] **130** ✦, **184**–5
gills [gĭlz] **212**–2
giraffe [jə răf/] **217**–32
girder [gür/dər] **178**–3
girdle [gür/dl] **91**–15
girl [gürl] **31**–10
give [gĭv] **15**–F, **122**–B, **148**–A,
glad [glăd] **44**–5
glass [glăs] **53**–18, **83**–22, **83**–23
    glass cleaner [glăs klē/nər] **61**–14
glasses [glăs/əz] **92**–10, **115**–7, **179**–10
    sunglasses [sŭn/glăs/əz] **90**–27
global positioning system (GPS) [glō/bəl
    pə zĭ/shə nĭng sĭs/təm] / [jē/pē/ĕs/] **155**–11
gloves [glŭvz] **90**–6, **231**–17
    disposable gloves [dĭ spō/ zə bəl glŭvz/] **93**–27
    glove compartment [glŭv/ kəm pärt/mənt] **159**–44
    latex gloves [lā/tĕks glŭvz/] **93**–34
    rubber gloves [rŭb/ər glŭvz/] **61**–4
    surgical gloves [sür/jĭ kəl glŭvz/] **121**–39
    work gloves [würk/ glŭvz/] **92**–17, **179**–17
glue [glōō] **183**–33
    glue stick [glōō/ stĭk] **232**–11
go [gō]
    go back [gō/ băk/] **11**–M
    go for [gō/ fər] **157**–J
    go on [gō/ än] **173**–K
    go over [gō/ ō/vər] **153**–B
    go past [gō/ păst/] **155**–E
    go straight [gō/ strāt/] **155**–A
    go through [gō/ thrōō/] **160**–D
    go to an employment agency
        [gō/ tə ən ĭm ploy/mənt ā/jən sē] **173**–E
    go to bed [gō/ tə bĕd/] **39**–Y
    go to college [gō/ tə käl/ĭj] **41**–I
    go to jail [gō/ tə jāl/] **141**–G
    go to prison [gō/ tə prĭz/ən] **141**–G
    go to school [gō/ tə skōōl] **38**–J
    go to sleep [gō/ tə slēp/] **39**–Z

go to the grocery store
    [gō/ tə dhə grōs/rē stör/, grōsh/rē] **38**–L
go to the next line [gō/ tə dhə nĕkst/ lĭn] **196**–D
go to work [gō/ tə würk/] **38**–I
go under [gō/ ŭn/dər] **153**–A
to-go box [tə gō/ bäks/] **82**–5
GO [gō] **222**–223
goat [gōt] **215**–5
goggles [gäg/əlz] **179**–11
goldfish [gōld/fĭsh/] **215**–16
golf [gälf, gölf] **228**–8
    golf club [gälf/ klŭb/] **231**–1
good [good] **23**–17
Goods [goodz] **73**
goose [gōōs] **214**–13
gopher [gō/fər] **215**–19
gorilla [gə rĭl/ə] **217**–29
gospel [gäs/pəl] **237**–30
Government [gŭ/ vərn mənt] **138**–139
GOVERNMENT AND MILITARY SERVICE
    [gŭ/ vərn mənt ən mĭ/ lə tër ē sür/vəs] **138**–139
governor [gŭ/ vər nər] **139**–20, **139**–21
gown [gown] **206**–8
    evening gown [ēv/nĭng gown/] **89**–18
    hospital gown [häs/pĭ tl gown/] **121**–19
    nightgown [nīt/gown/] **91**–25
    surgical gown [sür/jə kəl gown/] **93**–37, **121**–38
GPS (global positioning system) [jē/pē/ĕs/] /
    [glō/bəl pə zĭ/shə nĭng sĭs/təm] **155**–11
grab bar [grăb/ bär/] **57**–9
grades [grādz] **10**–4
graduate [grăj/ōō āt/] **40**–D
graduated cylinder [grăj/ōō ā/təd sĭl/ən dər] **195**–38
GRADUATION [grăj/ōō ā/shən] **206**–207
graffiti [grə fēt/tē] **148**–1
grandchild [grăn/chīld/, grănd/–] **34** ✦
granddaughters [grăn/dö/tərz] **34** ✦
grandfather [grăn/fä/dhər, grănd/–] **34**–2
grandmother [grăn/mŭdh/ər, grănd/–] **34**–1
Grandparents [grăn/për/ənts, grănd/–] **34**
grandson [grăn/sŭn/, grănd/–] **34** ✦
grapefruit [grāp/frōōt/] **68**–6
grapes [grāps] **68**–3
graph [grăf] **192**–15
graphic designer [grăf/ĭk dĭ zī/nər] **167**–30
grasshopper [grăs/häp/ər] **214**–24
grate [grāt] **77**–G
grater [grā/tər] **78**–2
gray [grā] **24**–15
    gray hair [grā hër] **33**–13
grease [grēs] **77**–B
green [grēn] **24**–5
    green card [grēn/ kärd/] **40**–2
    green onions [grēn/ ŭn/yənz] **69**–20
greet [grēt] **3**–G, **171**–M, **174**–H
GREETING [grē/tĭng] **2**–3
greeting card [grē/tĭng kärd/] **134**–15
grill [grĭl] **53**–17
grilled [grĭld/]
    grilled cheese sandwich
        [grĭld/ chēz/ săn/wĭch, –sănd/–] **80**–10

grilled fish [grĭld/ fĭsh/] **81**–29
grilled ribs [grĭld/ rĭbz/] **76**–2
grocery [grōs/rē, grōsh/rē]
    grocery bag [grōs/rē băg/] **67**–13
    grocery clerk [grōs/rē klürk/] **72**–4
Grocery Products [grōs/rē präd/ŭkts] **72**
GROCERY STORE [grōs/ rē stör/] **72**–73
ground [grownd]
    ground beef [grownd/ bēf/] **70**–4
    ground post [grownd/ pōst/] **134**–6
    playground [plā/grownd/] **50**–3
group [grōōp] **115**–15
grower [grō/ər] **177**–13
guard [gärd] **141**–3
    Coast Guard [kōst/ gärd/] **138**–18
    lifeguard [līf/gärd] **225**–19
    lifeguard station [līf/gärd/ stā/shən] **225**–21
    National Guard [nă/shə nəl gärd/] **138**–19
    security guard [sĭ kyŏŏr/ə tē gärd/] **132**–5, **169**–55
    shin guards [shĭn/ gärdz/] **231**–13
guest [gĕst] **184**–10
    guest room [gĕst/ rōōm] **184**–13
    guest services [gĕst/ sür/vəs əs] **130**–12
    guest speaker [gĕst/ spē/kər] **206**–4
guinea pig [gĭn/ē pĭg/] **215**–14
guitar [gĭ tär/] **238**–9
gums [gŭmz] **106**–6
    gum disease [gŭm/ dĭ zēz/] **119**–11
gun [gŭn] **142**–13, **181**–21
gurney [gür/nē] **121**–33
gutter [gŭt/ər] **53**–4
gym [jĭm] **5**–19, **126**–10, **184**–24
gymnastics [jĭm năs/tĭks] **228**–9
gynecologists [gī/nə kä/lə jĭsts] **120** ✦
habitat [hă/bə tăt/] **194**–12
HABITATS [hă/bə tăts] **204**
hacksaw [hăk/sö/] **180**–5
hail a taxi [hāl/ ə tăx/ē/]] **152** ✦
hailstorm [hāl/störm] **13**–21
hair [hër] **104**–2
    black hair [blăk/ hër/] **33**–16
    blond hair [bländ/ hër/] **33**–17
    brown hair [brown/ hër/] **33**–18
    curly hair [kür/lē hër/] **33**–11
    gray hair [grā/ hër/] **33**–13
    hair clip [hër klĭp/] **108**–19
    hairdresser [hër/drĕs/ər] **167**–31
    hair gel [hër jĕl/] **108**–16
    hairnet [hër nĕt/] **93**–25
    hair salon [hër sə län/] **131**–18
    hair spray [hër sprā/] **108**–12
    hair stylist [hër stī/lĭst] **167**–31
    long hair [löng/ hër/] **33**–3
    red hair [rĕd/ hër/] **33**–15
    short hair [shört/hër/] **33**–1
    shoulder-length hair [shōl/dər lĕnth/ hër/] **33**–2
    straight hair [strāt/ hër/] **33**–9
    wavy hair [wā/vē hër/] **33**–10
HAIR [hër] **33**

half [hăf]
  half bath [hăf/ băth/] **57** ✦
  half brother [hăf/ brŭdh/ər] **35**–28
  1/2 cup [hăf/ kŭp/] **75**–9
  half dollar [hăf/ däl/ər] **26**–5
  half past one [hăf/ păst/ wŭn/] **18**–11
  half sister [hăf/ sĭs/tər] **35**–27
  half slip [hăf/ slĭp/] **91**–23
halibut steak [hăl/ə bət stāk/] **71**–6
hall [höl] **124**–8
  hallway [höl/wā/] **5**–10, **184**–18
Hallway [höl/wā/] **51**
ham [hăm] **70**–9, **76**–5
hamburger [hăm/bür/gər] **79**–1
hammer [hăm/ər] **180**–1
  jackhammer [jăk/hăm/ər] **178**–9
  sledgehammer [slĕj/ hăm/ər] **178**–23
hammer [hăm/ər] **178**–D
hammock [hăm/ək] **53**–23
hamper [hăm/pər] **57**–1
hand [hănd] **105**–15, **177**–20
  DMV handbook [dē/ĕm/vē/ hănd/book/] **136**–1
  handbag [hănd/băg/] **87**–9, **94**–2
  handbrake [hănd/ brāk/] **59**–48
  handcuffs [hănd/kŭfs/] **141**–2
  handsaw [hănd/sö/] **180**–4
  handset [hănd/sĕt] **14**–1
  hand towel [hănd tow/əl] **57**–15
  hand truck [hănd trŭk/] **175**–11
Hand [hănd] **106**
handicapped parking [hăn/dē kăpt pär/kĭng]
  128–6, **154**–12
hand in [hănd/ ĭn/] **10**–O
hanger [hăng/gər] **101**–11
hang up [hăng/ ŭp/] **15**–D, **101**–H
happy [hăp/ē] **28**–6, **43**–31
hard [härd] **23**–5, **23**–24
  hardboiled eggs [härd/boyld/ ĕgz/] **76**–8
  hard drive [härd/ drīv/] **196**–6
  hard hat [härd/ hăt/] **92**–1, **179**–9
hardware store [härd/wër/ stör/] **148**–4
harmonica [här mä/ nĭ kə] **238**–21
harvest [här/vəst] **177**–B
hash browns [hăsh/ brownz/] **80**–3
hats [hăts] **90**–1, **95**–11
  chef's hat [shĕfs/ hăt/] **93**–28
  cowboy hat [kow/boy/ hăt/] **92**–18
  hard hat [härd/ hăt/] **92**–1, **179**–9
  ski hat [skē/ hăt/] **90**–11
  straw hat [strö/ hăt/] **90**–23
have [hăv]
  have a baby [hăv/ ə bā/bē] **41**–L
  have a conversation [hăv/ ə kän/vər sā/shən] **11**–L
  have a heart attack [hăv/ ə härt/ ə tăk/] **116**–D
  have an allergic reaction
    [hăv/ ən ə lür/jĭk rē ăk/shən] **116**–E
  have a picnic [hăv/ ə pĭk/nĭk] **224**–D
  have dinner [hăv/ dĭn/ər] **39**–S
  have regular checkups
    [hăv/ rĕg/yə lər chĕk/ups] **114**–H
Hawaii-Aleutian time [hə wī/ē ə loo/shən tim/] **19**–27

hay [hā] **177**–18
hazard [hăz/ərd] **186**–6
  hazard lights [hăz/ərd līts/] **159**–36
Hazardous Materials [hăz/ər dəs mə tïr/ē əlz] **179**
  hazardous waste [hăz/ər dəs wäst/] **218**–12
Hazards [hăz/ərdz] **179**
head [hĕd] **69**–32, **104**–1
  headache [hĕd/āk/] **110**–1
  headband [hĕd/bănd/] **90**–3
  headboard [hĕd/börd/] **58**–10
  head chef [hĕd/ shĕf/] **185**–7
  headlight [hĕd/līt/] **158**–7
  headline [hĕd/līn/] **133**–7
  headphones [hĕd/fōnz/] **6**–8, **234**–4
  headset [hĕd/sĕt] **14**–13
  headwaiter [hĕd/wā/tər] **185**–12
  headwrap [hĕd/răp/] **90**–7
  letterhead [lĕt/ər hĕd] **183**–42
  overhead compartment
    [ō/vər hĕd/ kəm pärt/mənt] **161**–13
  overhead projector [ō/vər hĕd/prə jĕk/tər] **7**–16
  wireless headset [wīr/ləs hĕd/sĕt] **14**–14
health [hĕlth] **167**–32
  health history form [hĕlth/ hĭs/tə rē förm/] **118**–4
  health insurance card
    [hĕlth/ ĭn shoor/əns kärd/] **118**–3
HEALTH [hĕlth] **114**–115
HEALTH FAIR [hĕlth/ fër/] **122**–123
Health Problems [hĕlth/ präb/ləmz] **115**
hear [hïr] **106**–B
hearing [hïr/ĭng]
  hearing aid [hïr/ĭng ād/] **115**–10
  hearing impaired [hïr/ĭng ĭm përd/] **32**–12
  hearing loss [hïr/ĭng lös/] **115**–2
heart [härt] **107**–38, **116**–D, **239**–6
  heart disease [härt/ dĭ zēz/] **111**–11
hearts [härts] **233**–31
heater [hē/tər] **159**–40
heating pad [hē/tĭng păd/] **113**–13
heat wave [hēt/ wāv/] **13**–13
heavy [hĕv/ē] **23**–13, **32**–7, **97**–27
hedge clippers [hĕj/ klĭp/ərz] **176**–11
heel [hēl] **94**–22, **106**–24
  high heels [hī/ hēlz/] **89**–21, **95**–25
height [hīt] **17**–16, **32**–5
Height [hīt] **32**
Heimlich maneuver [hīm/lĭk mə noo/vər] **117**–18
helicopter [hĕl/ə käp/tər] **151**–9
helmet [hĕl/mət] **93**–23, **231**–19
help [hĕlp] **8**–J, **147**–G
Help with Health Problems
  [hĕlp/ wĭth/ hĕlth/ präb/ləmz] **115**
hem [hĕm] **100**–8
hen [hĕn] **215**–8
herbal tea [ür/bəl tē/, hür/bəl–] **81**–40
herbs [ürbz, hürbz] **84**–9
hibiscus [hī bĭs/kəs, hĭ–] **211**–12
hide [hīd] **240**–D
high [hī] **91**–12, **97**–32, **188**–3
  high blood pressure [hī/ blŭd/ prĕsh/ər] **111**–14
  high chair [hī/ chër/] **37**–6, **82**–3
  high heels [hī/ hēlz/] **89**–21, **95**–25

high-rise [hī/ rīz/] **127**–13
high school [hī/ skool] **188**–4
highway [hī/wā] **155**–9
  highway marker [hī/wā mär/kər] **154**–17
hiking [hī/kĭng] **226**–7
  hiking boots [hī/kĭng boots/] **95**–31
hills [hĭlz] **204**–16
  downhill skiing [down/hĭl/ skē/ĭng] **227**–1
hip hop [hĭp/häp] **237**–26
hippopotamus [hĭp/ə pät/ə məs] **217**–43
hire [hīr] **141**–B
hired hand [hīrd/ hănd/] **177**–20
Historical Terms [hĭs/tör/ə kəl türmz/] **199**
history [hĭs/tə rē] **118**–4, **189**–12
HISTORY [hĭs/tə rē] **198**–199
hit [hĭt] **230**–B
HIV (human immunodeficiency virus)
  [āch/ī/vē/] / [hyoo/mən ĭm/yə nō
  dĭ fĭsh/ən sē vī/rəs) **111**–17
Hi-Visibility safety vest [hī/vĭ/zə bĭl/ə tē vĕst/] **92**–4
HOBBIES AND GAMES [häb/ēz ən gāmz/] **232**–233
hockey [häk/ē] **229**–13
  hockey stick [häk/ē stĭk/] **231**–11
hold [hōld] **36**–A
holder [hōl/dər]
  candle holder [kăn/dl hōl/dər] **56**–21
  cell phone holder [sĕl/ fōn/ hōld/ər] **94**–15
  magazine holder [măg/ə zēn/ hōld/ər] **56**–23
  pot holders [pät/ hōl/dərz] **78**–29
  toothbrush holder [tooth/brŭsh/ hōld/ər] **57**–22
holiday [häl/ə dā/] **22**–7, **22**–8
Holidays [häl/ə dāz/] **22**
HOLIDAYS [häl/ə dāz/] **239**
holly [häl/ē] **210**–19
home [hōm] **52**–7, **52**–12
  home health care aide [hōm/ hĕlth/ kër ād] **167**–32
  home improvement store
    [hōm/ ĭm proov/mənt stör/] **127**–20
  homemaker [hōm/mā/kər] **168**–33
  homesick [hōm/sĭk/] **43**–20
HOME [hōm] **46**–47, **48**–49
honeybee [hŭn/ē bē/] **214**–25
hood [hood] **158**–4
Hood [hood] **158**
hoof / hooves [hoof/] / [hoovz] **216**–17
hook [hook] **180**–39, **180**–40
  hook and eye [hook/ ən ī/] **99**–27
  hook and loop fastener
    [hook/ ən loop/ fă/sən ər] **99**–29
horn [hörn] **159**–32, **216**–21, **238**–11
  French horn [frĕnch/ hörn] **238**–13
horror story [hör/ər stör/ē, här/–] **237**–17
horse [hörs] **215**–4
  horseback riding [hörs/băk rī/dĭng] **226**–9
  horse racing [hörs/ rā/sĭng] **228**–19
  seahorse [sē/hörs/] **212**–13
hose [hōz] **53**–21, **91**–18
hospital [häs/pĭ tl] **125**–9, **154**–18
  hospital bed [häs/pĭ tl bĕd/] **121**–22
  hospital gown [häs/pĭ tl gown/] **121**–19
HOSPITAL [häs/pĭ tl] **120**–121
Hospital Room [häs/pĭ tl room/] **121**

Hospital Staff [häs/pĭ tl stăf/] **120**
hostess [hō/stəs] **82**–2
hot [hät] **13**–3, **42**–1
   hot cereal [hät sïr/ē əl] **80**–9
   hot dog [hät/ dög/] **79**–6
   hot water [hät/ wö/tər] **57**–8
   hot water bottle [hät/ wö/tər bät/l] **113**–15
hotel [hō tĕl/] **124**–3
A HOTEL [hō tĕl/] **184**
hour [ow/ər] **18**–1
house [hows]
   courthouse [kört/hows/] **125**–13
   dollhouse [däl/hows/] **59**–18
   housekeeper [hows/kē/pər] **168**–34, **184**–20
   housekeeping cart [hows/kē/pĭng kärt/] **184**–19
   House of Representatives
      [hows/ əv rĕp/rĭ zĕn/tə tĭvz] **138**–3
   house painter [hows/ pān/tər] **168**–46
   houseplant [hows/plănt/] **56**–4, **211**–27
   townhouse [town/hows/] **52**–6
   two-story house [tōō/stör/ē hows/] **52** ✦
   warehouse [wĕr/hows/] **175**–7
   White House [wīt/ hows/] **138**–7
House [hows] **49, 53**
A HOUSE AND YARD [hows/ən yärd/] **53**
HOUSEHOLD PROBLEMS AND REPAIRS
   [hows/hōld/ präb/ləmz ən rĭ përz/] **62**–**63**
HOUSEWORK [hows/würk/] **60**
housing [how/zĭng] **52**–11
hubcap [hŭb/kăp/] **158**–9
hug [hŭg] **2**–E
human immunodeficiency virus (HIV)
   [hyōō/mən ĭm/yə nō dĭ fĭsh/ən sē vī/rəs] /
   [āch/ī/vē/] **111**–17
humid [hyōō/məd] **13**–15
humidifier [hyōō mĭd/ə fī/ər] **113**–11
humiliated [hyōō mĭl/ē ā/təd] **43** ✦
hummingbird [hŭm/ĭng bürd/] **214**–10
hump [hŭmp] **217**–51
hungry [hŭng/grē] **42**–5
hurricane [hür/ə kān/] **145**–14
hurt [hürt] **42**–16, **116**–C
husband [hŭz/bənd] **34**–13
   ex-husband [ĕks/ hŭz/bənd] **35** ✦
   former husband [för/mər hŭz/bənd] **35** ✦
hutch [hŭch] **55**–22
hybrid [hy/brĭd] **156**–3
hydrant [hī/drənt] **129**–27
hydroelectric power [hī/drō ĭ lĕk/trĭk pow/ər] **218**–5
hydrogen peroxide [hī/drə jən pə räk/sīd] **117**–9
hyena [hī ē/nə] **217**–30
HYGIENE [hy/jēn] **108**–**109**
hygienist [hī jē/nĭst, –jĕn/ĭst] **119**–3
hypertension [hī/pər tĕn/shən] **111**–14
hyphen [hy/fən] **190**–20
hypoallergenic [hī/pō ăl/ər jĕn/ĭk] **108** ✦
I beam [ī/ bēm/] **178**–3
ice [īs]
   ice cream [īs/ krēm/] **72**–26
   ice-cream cone [īs/ krēm/ kōn] **79**–13
   ice cream shop [īs/ krēm/ shäp/] **131**–16
   ice hockey [īs/ häk/ē] **229**–13

ice pack [īs/ păk/] **117**–13
ice skates [īs/ skāts/] **231**–9
ice skating [īs/ skā/tĭng] **227**–4
iced tea [īst/ tē/] **79**–12
icy [ī/sē] **13**–22
ID [ī/dē/] **146**–19
identity theft [ī dĕn/tə tē thĕft/] **142**–9
ignition [ĭg nĭsh/ən] **159**–33
illegal drugs [ĭ lē/gəl drŭgz/] **142**–6
Illnesses and Childhood Diseases
   [ĭl/nə səz ən chīld/hōōd dĭ zēz/ əz] **111**
ILLNESSES AND MEDICAL CONDITIONS
   [ĭl/nə səz ən mĕd/ĭ kəl kən dĭsh/ənz] **111**
Immediate Family
   [ī mē/ dē ət făm/lē, –fă/məlē] **34**
immigrant [ĭm/ə grənt] **199**–19
immigrate [ĭm/ə grāt/] **40**–C
immigration [ĭm/ə grā/shən] **199**–18
immunization [ĭm/yə nə zā/shən] **114** ✦
immunodeficiency [ĭm/yə nō dĭ fĭsh/ən sē] **111**–17
impaired [ĭm përd/] **32**–11, **32**–12
important [ĭm pört/ənt] **146**–19
improvement [ĭm prōōv/mənt] **127**–20
in [ĭn] **25**–6
   be in shock [bē/ ĭn shäk/] **116**–B
   bubble in [bŭb/l ĭn/] **10**–K
   call in [käl/ ĭn/] **186**–A
   check in [chĕk/ ĭn/] **160**–A
   check-in kiosk [chĕk/ĭn kē/äsk/] **160**–2
   fall in love [fäl/ ĭn lŭv/] **40**–H
   fill in [fĭl/ ĭn/] **9**–O
   hand in [hănd/ĭn/] **10**–O
   in fashion [ĭn făsh/ən] **88** ✦
   in front of [ĭn frŭnt/ əv] **24**–7
   in love [ĭn lŭv/] **42**–18
   in pain [ĭn pān/] **42**–11
   in style [ĭn stīl/] **88** ✦
   in the middle [ĭn dhə mĭd/l] **24**–2
   look in [lōōk/ ĭn] **173**–B
   move in [mōōv/ ĭn/] **48**–F
   send in [sĕnd/ ĭn/] **173**–H
   take in [tāk/ ĭn/] **100**–D
   turn in [türn/ ĭn/] **191**–M
   walk-in freezer [wäk/ĭn frē/zər] **185**–3
inch [ĭnch] **17**–15
indent [ĭn dĕnt/] **190**–D
independence [ĭn/də pĕn/dəns]
   Declaration of Independence
      [dĕk/lə rā/shən əv ĭn/də pĕn/dəns] **198**–5
   Independence Day [ĭn/də pĕn/dəns dā/] **22**–13
INDIVIDUAL SPORTS [ĭn/də vĭj/ōō əl spörts/] **228**
infant [ĭn/fənt] **31**–6
infection [ĭn fĕk/shən] **111**–3
infectious disease [ĭn fĕk/shəs dĭ zēz/] **111** ✦
influenza [ĭn/flōō ĕn/zə] **111** ✦
INFORMATION [ĭn/fər mā/shən] **4**
inhaler [ĭn hā/lər] **113**–33
injection [ĭn jĕk/shən] **114** ✦, **158**–17
injured [ĭn/jərd] **116**–C
INJURIES [ĭn/jə rēz] **110**

ink [ĭnk]
   ink cartridge [ĭnk/ kär/trĭj] **183**–45
   inkjet printer [ĭnk/jĕt prĭn/tər] **183**–18
   ink pad [ĭnk/ păd/] **183**–46
inline [ĭn/līn/]
   inline skates [ĭn/līn/ skāts/] **231**–10
   inline skating [ĭn/līn/ skā/tĭng] **228**–10
inquire about benefits
   [ĭn kwīr/ ə bowt/bĕn/ə fĭts] **174** ✦
insects [ĭn/sĕkts] **209**–11
   insect bite [ĭn/sĕkt bīt/] **110**–11
   insect repellent [ĭn/sĕkt rĭ pĕl/ənt] **226**–23
Insects [ĭn/sĕkts] **214**
INSECTS [ĭn/sĕkts] **214**
insert [ĭn sürt/] **132**–D
INSIDE AND OUTSIDE THE BODY
   [ĭn/sīd/ ən owt/sīd/ dhə băd/ē] **106**–**107**
Inside the Car [ĭn/sīd/ dhə kär/] **159**
Inside the Kit [ĭn/sīd/ dhə kĭt/] **117**
Inside the Trunk [ĭn/sīd/ dhə trŭnk/] **158**
inspect [ĭn spĕkt/] **147**–N
install [ĭn stäl/] **176**–H, **178**–C
instructor [ĭn strŭk/tər] **6**–4
Instrument Panel [ĭn/strə mənt păn/əl] **159**
instruments [ĭn/strə mənts] **119**–4, **238**
insulation [ĭn/sə lā/shən] **178**–14
insurance [ĭn shōōr/əns] **118**–3, **136**–8
integers [ĭn/tə jərz] **192**–1, **192**–2
Integers [ĭn/tə jərz] **192**
intercom [ĭn/tər käm/] **50**–5
interest inventory [ĭn/trəst ĭn/vən tör/ ē] **172**–11
international call [ĭn/tər năsh/ə nəl köl/] **15**–35
Internet [ĭn/tər nĕt/]
   Internet listing [ĭn/tər nĕt/ lĭst/ĭng] **48**–1
   Internet map [ĭn/tər nĕt/ măp/] **155**–12
   Internet phone call [ĭn/tər nĕt/ fōn/ käl] **14**–20
INTERNET [ĭn/tər nĕt/] **197**
internist [ĭn/tür/nĭst] **120**–1
internship [ĭn/türn shĭp/] **172**–6
interpreter [ĭn tür/prə tər] **168**–35
INTERSECTION [ĭn/tər sĕk/shən] **128**–**129**
INTERVIEW SKILLS [ĭn/tər vyōō/ skĭlz/] **174**
intestinal parasites [ĭn tĕs/tə nəl păr/ə sīts/] **111**–13
intestines [ĭn tĕs/tənz] **107**–42
In the Airline Terminal [ĭn dhə ër/līn tür/mə nəl] **160**
In the Examining Room
   [ĭn dhə ĭg zăm/ə nĭng rōōm/] **118**
In the Waiting Room [ĭn dhə wā/tĭng rōōm/] **118**
into [ĭn/tōō, –tə] **153**–E
intravenous drip (IV)
   [ĭn/trə vē/nəs drĭp/] / [ī/vē/] **121**–25
introduce [ĭn/trə dōōs/] **2**–C, **3**–I
introduction [ĭn/trə dŭk/shən] **190**–6
invention [ĭn vĕn/shən] **199**–12
inventor [ĭn vĕn/tər] **199**–13
inventory [ĭn/vən tör/ ē] **172**–11, **172**–12
invertebrates [ĭn vür/ tə brāts/] **194**–13
invitation [ĭn və tā/shən] **12**–I, **12**–J, **64**–9
invite [ĭn vīt/] **12**–H
iris [ī/rəs] **211**–16
iron [ī/ərn] **101**–13, **108**–17
iron [ī/ərn] **101**–G

Index

ironed [ī/ərnd] **101**–20

ironing board [ī/ər nĭng börd/] **101**–14

irritated [ĭr/ə tā/təd] **64**–6

island [ī/lənd] **204**–8

IV (intravenous drip)
[ī/vē/] / [ĭn/trə vē/nəs drĭp/] **121**–25

ivory [ī/vər ē] **24**–16

ivy [ī/vē] **210**–25

jack [jăk] **158**–24

jacket [jăk/ət] **90**–8
    chef's jacket [shĕfs/ jăk/ət] **93**–29
    down jacket [down/ jăk/ət] **90**–16
    leather jacket [lĕdh/ər jăk/ət] **90**–4
    sports jacket [spörts/ jăk/ət] **89**–14

jackhammer [jăk/ hăm/ər] **178**–9

jack-o'-lantern [jăk/ə lăn/tərn] **239**–10

janitor [jăn/ĭ tər] **182**–3

January [jăn/yōō ër/ē] **21**–25

jar [jär] **74**–2, **74**–14

jasmine [jăz/mən] **211**–22

jaw [jö] **106**–4

jay [jā] **214**–6

jaywalk [jā/wäk] **128**–C

jazz [jăz] **237**–24

jeans [jēnz] **86**–2, **92**–19

jellyfish [jĕl/ē fĭsh/] **212**–14

jewelry [jōō/əl rē]
    jewelry department [jōō/əl rē dĭ pärt/mənt] **95**–8
    jewelry store [jōō/əl rē stör/] **130**–2

jigsaw [jĭg/sö/] **180**–10

job [jäb] **172**–1, **172**–3, **172**–7
    job fair [jäb/ fër] **172**–13

JOB SAFETY [jäb/ sāf/tē] **179**

JOBS AND OCCUPATIONS
[jäbz/ ən äk/yə pā/shənz] **166**–**169**

JOB SEARCH [jäb/ sürch/] **173**

JOB SKILLS [jäb/ skĭlz/] **170**

Job Training [jäb/ trān/ĭng] **172**

jockstrap [jäk/străp/] **91**–6

join [joyn] **143**–L

judge [jŭj] **141**–6

Judicial Branch [jōō dĭ/shəl brănch/] **138**

juice [jōōs] **73**–32

July [jōō lī/] **21**–31

jump [jŭmp] **230**–I

jumper cables [jŭm/pər kā/bəlz] **158**–21

jump rope [jŭmp/ rōp/] **224**–4

jumpsuit [jŭmp/sōōt/] **93**–24

June [jōōn] **21**–30

junior high school [jōōn/yər hī/ skōōl] **188**–3

junk mail [jŭnk/ māl/] **135** ✦

Jupiter [jōō/pə tər] **205**–5

jury [jür/ē] **141**–8

justices [jŭs/tə səz] **138**–12, **138**–13

kangaroo [kăng/gə rōō/] **217**–44

keep [kēp] **28**–B

ketchup [kĕch/əp, kăch/–] **79**–21

kettle [kĕt/l] **54**–21

key [kē] **51**–30, **155**–9
    key pad [kē/ păd/] **14**–5
    pound key [pownd/ kē/] **14**–7
    star key [stär/ kē/] **14**–6

keyboard [kē/börd/] **196**–14, **238**–18

Keyboarding [kē/börd/ĭng] **196**

kick [kĭk] **230**–E

kidney [kĭd/nē] **107**–43

kids' bedroom [kĭdz/ bĕd/rōōm/] **47**–9

KIDS' BEDROOM [kĭdz/ bĕd/rōōm/] **59**

king-size bed [kĭng/sīz/ bĕd/] **184**–15

kiosk [kē/äsk/] **131**–22, **160**–2

kiss [kĭs] **3**–K, **36**–P

kit [kĭt]
    doll making kit [däl/ mā/kĭng kĭt/] **232**–13
    first aid kit [fürst/ ād/ kĭt/] **117**–1, **146**–18
    model kit [mäd/l kĭt/] **232**–9
    woodworking kit [wōōd/wür/kĭng kĭt/] **232**–14

Kit [kĭt] **117**

kitchen [kĭch/ən] **46**–5, **83**–15
    kitchen timer [kĭch/ən tī/mər] **78**–18

A KITCHEN [ə kĭch/ən] **54**

Kitchen [kĭch/ən] **185**

KITCHEN UTENSILS [kĭch/ən yōō tĕn/səlz] **78**

kite [kīt] **225**–2

kitten [kĭt/n] **215**–10

kiwi [kē/wē] **68**–22

knee [nē] **106**–20
    knee highs [nē/hīz/] **91**–12
    knee pads [nē/pădz/] **179**–19

knife [nīf] **55**–4, **83**–30
    carving knife [kär/vĭng nīf/] **78**–12
    multi-use knife [mŭl/tē yōōs/nīf/, mŭl/tī–] **226**–20
    paring knife [për/ĭng nīf/] **78**–16
    steak knife [stāk/ nīf/] **83**–29

knit [nĭt] **233**–F

knitting needles [nĭt/ĭng nēd/lz] **233**–23

knit top [nĭt/ täp/] **88**–7

knob [näb] **194**–22, **194**–23
    doorknob [dör/näb/] **53**–12

knuckle [nŭk/l] **106**–17

koala [kō ä/lə] **217**–45

lab [lăb] **5**–15
    lab coat [lăb/ kōt/] **93**–33

Lab [lăb] **195**

label [lā/bəl]
    mailing label [mā/lĭng lā/bəl] **183**–41
    nutrition label [nōō trĭ/shən lā/bəl] **122**–8
    prescription label [prĭ skrĭp/shən lā/bəl] **112**–4
    warning label [wär/nĭng lā/bəl] **112**–8

label [lā/bəl] **9**–V

Labor Day [lā/bər dā/] **22**–14

lace [lās] **99**–9
    shoelaces [shōō/lā səz] **94**–24

ladder [lăd/ər] **178**–2

ladle [lā/dl] **78**–7

ladybug [lā/dē bŭg/] **214**–26

lake [lāk] **204**–13

lamb [lăm] **70**–14
    lamb chops [lăm/ chäps/] **70**–15
    lamb shanks [lăm/ shăngks/] **70**–13

Lamb [lăm] **70**

lamp [lămp] **56**–15, **58**–25
    lampshade [lămp/shād/] **56** ✦, **58**–26

land [lănd] **160**–K

landlord [lănd/lörd/] **51**–27

landmarks [lănd/märks/] **220**–1

landscape designer [lănd/skāp/ dĭ zī/nər] **176**–5

LANDSCAPING AND GARDENING
[lănd/skā/pĭng ən gärd/nĭng] **176**

languages [lăng/gwĭ jəz] **189**–13
    language arts [lăng/gwĭj ärts/] **189**–9

lantern [lăn/tərn] **226**–22, **239**–10

laptop [lăp/täp/] **196**–16

large [lärj] **96**–4, **96**–5

laser printer [lā/zər prĭn/tər] **183**–19

lashes [lăsh/əz]
    eyelashes [ī/lăsh/əz] **106**–11

last [lăst]
    last name [lăst/ nām/] **4**–4
    last week [lăst/wēk/] **20**–18

late [lāt] **19**–24

latex gloves [lā/tĕks glŭvz/] **93**–34

laugh [lăf] **44**–A

laundromat [lön/drə mät/] **128**–1

laundry [lön/drē] **101**–1
    laundry basket [lön/drē băs/kət] **101**–2
    laundry detergent [lön/drē dĭ tür/jənt] **101**–8

LAUNDRY [lön/drē] **101**

Laundry Room [lön/drē rōōm/] **50**

lawn [lön] **53**–26
    lawn mower [lön/ mō/ər] **176**–6

lawyer [lö/yər] **168**–36

lay [lā] **178**–B

layer cake [lā/ər kāk/] **81**–33

LCD projector [ĕl/sē/dē/ prə jĕk/tər] **6**–6, **235**–29

leader [lē/dər] **176**–4

leaf / leaves [lēf] / [lēvz] **210**–6, **211**–6
    leaf blower [lēf/ blō/ər] **176**–2

leaking [lē/kĭng] **62**–3

learn [lürn] **40**–E

Learning New Words [lür/nĭng nōō/ würdz/] **8**

lease [lēs] **48** ✦, **51**–28

leather [lĕdh/ər] **98**–6
    leather jacket [lĕdh/ər jăk/ət] **90**–4

leave [lēv] **11**–O, **38**–N, **82**–J, **160**–J, **171**–P

leaves / leaf [lēvz] / [lēf] **210**–6, **211**–6
    leaf blower [lēf/ blō/ər] **176**–2

lecture [lĕk/chər] **122**–9

left [lĕft] **25**–1, **154**–8, **155**–C

legal [lē/gəl]
    legal holiday [lē/gəl häl/ə dā/] **22**–8
    legal pad [lē/gəl păd/] **183**–38

Legal Holidays [lē/gəl häl/ə dāz/] **22**

LEGAL SYSTEM [lē/gəl sĭs/təm] **141**

Leg and Foot [lĕg/ ən fōōt/] **106**

leggings [lĕg/ĭngz] **90**–12

Legislature [lĕ/jəs lā/chər] **139**–23

legs [lĕgz] **70**–21, **105**–9
    leg of lamb [lĕg/ əv lăm/] **70**–14

lemonade [lĕm/ə nād/] **84**–2

lemons [lĕm/ənz] **68**–7

lend [lĕnd] **26**–C

length [lĕngkth] **17**–17, **96**–17

lengthen [lĕngk/thən] **100**–A

lens / lenses [lĕnz] / [lĕnz/əz] **115**–8, **235**–23

leopard [lĕp/ərd] **217**–34

let out [lĕt/ owt/] **100**–C

letter [lĕt/ər] **134**–13
   letter carrier [lĕt/ər kăr/ē ər] **134**–20
   letterhead [lĕt/ər hĕd/] **183**–42
lettuce [lĕt/əs] **69**–1
level [lĕv/əl] **172**–1, **180**–29
librarian [lī brër/ē ən] **133**–9
library [lī/brër ē] **5**–17, **125**–15
   library clerk [lī/brër ē klürk/] **133**–1
   library patron [lī/brër ē pā/trən] **133**–3
LIBRARY [lī/brër ē] **133**
license [lī/səns]
   driver's license [drī/vərz lī/səns] **40**–4, **136**–9
   driver's license number
     [drī/vərz lī/səns nŭm/bər] **136**–11
   license plate [lī/səns plāt/] **136**–12, **158**–12
   marriage license [măr/ĭj lī/səns] **41**–8
   renew a license [rĭ nōō/ ə lī/səns, –nyōō/–] **136** ✦
   taxi license [tăk/sē lī/səns] **152**–22
License [lī/səns] **137**
licensed practical nurse (LPN)
   [lī/sənst prăk/tə kəl nürs/] / [ĕl/pē/ĕn/] **120**–11
lid [lĭd] **78**–24
lieutenant governor [lōō tĕ/nənt gŭ/ vər nər] **139**–21
life [līf]
   lifeguard [līf/gärd/] **225**–19
   lifeguard station [līf/gärd/ stā/shən] **225**–21
   lifesaving device [līf/sā/vĭng dĭ vīs/] **225**–20
   life vest [līf/ vĕst/] **161**–25, **226**–14
   wildlife [wīld/ līf/] **220**–3
LIFE [līf] **212**–**213**
LIFE EVENTS AND DOCUMENTS
   [līf/ ĭ vĕnts/ ən dä/kyə mənts] **40**–**41**
lift [lĭft] **11**–E
light [līt] **23**–14, **97**–28
   brake light [brāk/ līt/] **158**–14
   daylight saving time [dā/līt/ sā/vĭng tīm/] **19**–25
   flashlight [flăsh/līt/] **146**–14
   hazard lights [hăz/ərd līts/] **159**–36
   headlight [hĕd/ līt/] **158**–7
   light blue [līt/ blōō/] **24**–11
   light bulb [līt/ bŭlb/] **56** ✦
   light fixture [līt/ fĭks/chər] **55**–18
   light source [līt/ sörs/] **194**–21
   light switch [līt/ swĭch] **58**–27
   night light [nīt/ līt/] **37**–27
   porch light [pörch/ līt/] **53**–13
   streetlight [strēt/līt/] **148**–3
   string lights [strĭng/ lītz/] **239**–18
   tail light [tāl/ līt/] **158**–13
   traffic light [trăf/ĭk līt/] **128**–8
   work light [würk/ līt/] **181**–44
lightning [līt/nĭng] **13**–17
lily [lĭl/ē] **211**–26
limbs [lĭmz] **106** ✦, **210**–3
limes [līmz] **68**–8
limit [lĭ/mət] **154**–4
limo / limousine [lĭ/mō] / [lĭ/mə zēn] **156**–11
line [līn] **73**–11
   assembly line [ə sĕm/blē līn] **175**–6
   clothesline [klōz/līn] **101**–9
   curved line [kürvd/ līn/] **193**–23
   headline [hĕd/līn] **133**–7

line cook [līn/ kŏŏk/] **93, 185** ✦
line segment [līn/ sĕg/mənt] **193**–20
line supervisor [līn/ sōō/pər vī zər] **175**–4
   parallel lines [pă/rə lĕl līnz/] **193**–25
   perpendicular lines
     [pür/pən dĭk/yə lər līnz/] **193**–24
   straight line [strāt/ līn/] **193**–22
linen [lĭn/ən] **98**–2
   linen closet [lĭn/ən kläz/ət] **57** ✦
liner [lī/nər]
   eyeliner [ī/lī/nər] **109**–36
Lines [līnz] **193**
lingerie [län/zhə rā/, –jə–] **91** ✦
links [lĭnkz] **197**–10
lion [lī/ən] **213**–33, **216**–2, **217**–36
lip [lĭp] **106**–5
   lipstick [lĭp/stĭk/] **109**–38
Liquid Measures [lĭk/wəd mĕzh/ərz] **75**
liquids [lĭk/wədz] **61**–21, **179**–8
list [lĭst] **67**–14
listen [lĭs/ən] **6**–C, **118**–C, **174**–K
listing [lĭst/ĭng] **48**–1
litter [lĭ/tər] **148**–2
litter [lĭ/tər] **219**–L
little [lĭt/l] **23**–1
Little League [lĭt/l lēg/] **229** ✦
live [lĭv] **140**–H
LIVE [lĭv] **52**
live music [līv/ myōō/zĭk] **84**–1
liver [lĭv/ər] **70**–7, **107**–40
livestock [līv/stäk/] **177**–15
living room [lĭv/ĭng rōōm/] **47**–12
LIVING ROOM [lĭv/ĭng rōōm/] **56**
lizard [lĭz/ərd] **213**–40
llama [lä/mə] **217**–25
load [lōd] **101**–C
loading dock [lō/dĭng däk/] **175**–15
loaf [lōf] **74**–10, **74**–22
   meatloaf [mēt/lōf/] **81**–31
loafers [lō/fərz] **95**–30
Lobby [läb/ē] **50**
lobster [läb/stər] **71**–10
local call [lō/kəl köl/] **15**–31
lock [läk] **51**–34, **159**–25
   locksmith [läk/smĭth/] **62**–11
lock [läk] **143**–E
locker [lä/kər] **5**–11, **50**–17
locket [läk/ət] **95**–35
Logging on and Sending Email
   [lög/ĭng än/ ən sĕnd/ĭng ē/māl, –ön–] **197**
lonely [lōn/lē] **42**–17
long [löng] **96**–18
   long distance call [löng/dĭs/təns köl/] **15**–32
   long hair [löng/ hër/] **33**–3
   long-sleeved [löng/slēvd/] **96**–14
   long underwear [löng/ ŭn/dər wër/] **91**–3
look [lŏŏk]
   look at [lŏŏk/ ăt/, –ət] **49**–H, **157**–A
   look for [lŏŏk/ för/] / [lŏŏk/ fər] **133**–B, **173**–C
   look in [lŏŏk/ ĭn] **173**–B
   look up [lŏŏk/ ŭp] **8**–A
loop [lōōp] **99**–29

loose [lōōs] **97**–30
lose [lōōz] **229** ✦
loss [lös] **115**–2
lost child [löst/ chīld/] **144**–1
lotion [lō/shən] **37**–13, **108**–9
loud [lowd] **23**–11
loungewear [lownj/wër/] **91** ✦
love [lŭv] **40**–H, **42**–18
   love seat [lŭv sēt/] **56**–1
low [lō] **97**–31
   low-cost exam [lō/köst ĭg zăm/] **122**–1
   low-cut socks [lō/kŭt/ säks/] **91**–10
   low-fat milk [lō/făt/ mĭlk/] **81**–42
lower back [lō/ər băk/] **107**–29
lozenges [läz/ən jəz] **113**–30
LPN (licensed practical nurse) [ĕl/pē/ĕn/] /
   [lī/sənst prăk/tə kəl nürs/] **120**–11
luggage [lŭg/ĭj] **161**–18
   luggage cart [lŭg/ĭj kärt/] **184**–8
lug wrench [lŭg/ rĕnch/] **158**–22
lumber [lŭm/bər] **178**–17
Lunch [lŭnch] **80**
lung [lŭng] **107**–39
machine [mə shēn/]
   answering machine [ăn/sər ĭng mə shēn/] **14**–17
   ATM (Automated Teller Machine) [ā/tē/ĕm/] /
     [ö/tə māt ĭd tĕ/lər mə shēn/] **132**
   fax machine [făks/ mə shēn/] **183**–21
   machine operator [mə shēn/ äp/ə rā tər] **168**–37
   machine screw [mə shēn/ skrōō/] **180**–32
   sewing machine [sō/ĭng mə shēn/] **98**–13
   sewing machine operator
     [sō/ĭng mə shēn/ äp/ə rā/tər] **98**–14
   stamp machine [stămp/ mə shēn/] **135**–11
   vending machine [vĕnd/ĭng mə shēn/] **152**–9
Machine [mə shēn/] **98, 132**
magazine [măg/ə zēn/, măg/ə zēn] **133**–5
   magazine holder [măg/ə zēn/ hōl/dər] **56**–23
magnet [măg/nət] **195**–36
magnolia [măg nōl/yə] **210**–8
mail
   airmail [ër/māl/] **134**–5
   Certified Mail® [sür/tə fīd māl/] **134**–4
   Express Mail® [ĭk sprĕs/ māl/] **134**–2
   junk mail [jŭnk/ māl/] **135** ✦
   mailboxes [māl/bäk/səz] **50**–11, **53**–1, **128**–13,
     135–12
   media mail [mē/dē ə māl/] **134**–3
   overnight / next day mail
     [ō/vər nīt/ / nĕkst/ dā/ māl/] **135** ✦
   Priority Mail® [prī/ör ə tē māl/] **134**–1
mail [māl/] **135**–D
mailer [mā/lər] **183**–40
mailing [mā/lĭng]
   mailing address [mā/lĭng ə drĕs/, ă/drĕs] **134**–22
   mailing label [mā/lĭng lā/bəl] **183**–41
main office [mān/ ö/fəs] **5**–12
MAINTAINING A CAR [mān/tā nĭng ə kär/] **157**
maintenance [mān/tn əns] **184**–23
maitre d' [mā/trə dē/] **185**–11
make [māk] **156** ✦

Index

make [māk]
  make a deposit [māk/ ə dǐ pǎz/ət] **132**–B
  make a disaster kit [māk/ ə dǐz/ tər kǐt/] **146**–B
  make a mortgage payment
    [māk/ ə mör/gəj pā/mənt] **49**–L
  make an offer [māk/ ən ö/fər] **49**–I
  make a wish [māk/ ə wǐsh/] **240**–B
  make copies [māk/ käp/ēz] **171**–D
  make dinner [māk/ dǐn/ər] **39**–Q
  make eye contact [māk/ ī/ kän/täkt] **174**–J
  make furniture [māk/ für/nǐ chər] **170**–G
  make lunch [māk/ lŭnch/] **38**–F
  make progress [māk/ prä/grəs] **10**–G
  make small talk [māk/ smöl/tök] **12**–B
  make the bed [māk/dhə bĕd/] **60**–F
maker [mā/kər]
  dressmaker [drĕs/mā/kər] **100**–1
  dressmaker's dummy [drĕs/mā/kərz dŭ/mē] **100**–2
  homemaker [hōm/mā/kər] **168**–33
Makeup [māk/ŭp] **109**
makeup remover [māk/ŭp rǐ mōōv/ər] **109**–42
making [mā/kǐng] **232**–13
MAKING ALTERATIONS [māk/ǐng öl/tə rā/shənz] **100**
MAKING CLOTHES [māk/ǐng klōz/] **98**–**99**
Making an Emergency Call
  [mā/kǐng ən ǐ mür/jən sē köl/] **15**
Making a Phone Call [mā/kǐng ə fōn/ köl/] **15**
male [māl] **4**–17
mall [möl] **126**–7
MALL [möl] **130**–**131**
mallet [māl/ət] **180**–2
mammals [măm/əlz] **209**–10
Mammals [măm/əlz] **213**
MAMMALS [măm/əlz] **216**–**217**
manager [măn/ǐ jər] **50**–8, **72**–8
  account manager [ə kownt/ măn/ǐ jər] **132**–9
  office manager [ö/fəs măn/ǐ jər] **182**–8
Manager [măn/ǐ jər] **92**
mane [mān] **217**–49
maneuver [mə nōō/vər] **117**–18
mangoes [măng/gōz] **68**–21
manicurist [măn/ə kyōō/rǐst] **168**–38
man / men [măn] / [mĕn] **30**–1, **30**–4
  doorman [dör/măn/] **184**–1
mantle [măn/təl] **56**–11
manual [măn/yōō əl] **117**–2
Manual Transmission [măn/yōō əl tränz mǐsh/ən] **159**
manufacture [măn/yə făk/chər] **175**–B
map [măp] **7**–12, **155**–12
Map [măp] **13**
maple [mā/pəl] **210**–12
Maps [măps] **155**
MAPS [măps] **155**
March [märch] **21**–27
margarine [mär/jər ən] **72**–20
marigold [mär/ə gōld/] **211**–13
MARINE LIFE, AMPHIBIANS, AND REPTILES
  [mə rēn/ līf/ ăm fǐb/ē ənz ən rĕp/tǐlz] **212**–**213**
Marines [mə rēnz/] **138**–17
mark [märk] **190**–12, **190**–13, **190**–15
  postmark [pōst/märk/] **134**–24

markers [mär/kərz] **7**–17, **7**–24, **154**–17
market [mär/kət] **222**–6
  supermarket [sōō/pər mar/kət] **127**–18
MARKET [mär/kət] **66**–**67**
marriage license [măr/ǐj lī/səns] **41**–8
married couple [măr/ēd kŭ/pəl] **35**–20
Mars [märz] **205**–4
martial arts [mär/shəl ärts/] **228**–11
Martin Luther King Jr. Day
  [mär/tən lōō/thər-kǐng/ jōōn/yər dā/] **22**–10
mascara [mă skăr/ə] **109**–39
mashed potatoes [măsht/ pə tā/tōz] **81**–23
mask [măsk] **239**–9
  catcher's mask [kăch/ərz măsk/] **231**–15
  diving mask [dī/vǐng măsk/] **225**–6
  face mask [fās/ măsk/] **93**–32
  oxygen mask [äk/sǐ jən măsk/] **161**–24
  particle mask [pär/tǐ kəl măsk/] **179**–14
  ski mask [skē/ măsk/] **90**–15
  surgical mask [sür/jǐ kəl măsk/] **93**–36
  ventilation mask [vĕnt/əl ā/shən măsk/] **92**–7
masking tape [măs/kǐng tāp/] **181**–53
mat [măt] **57**–3, **57**–28
  placemat [plās/măt] **55**–11
match [măch] **9**–T
matches [măch/əz] **146**–16, **226**–21
matching [mă/chǐng] **28**–3
Material [mə tïr/ē əl] **98**
materials [mə tïr/ē əlz] **98** ✦, **179**–7
Materials [mə tïr/ē əlz] **179**
maternity [mə tür/nə tē]
  maternity dress [mə tür/nə tē drĕs/] **88**–5
  maternity store [mə tür/nə tē stör/] **131**–19
math [măth] **189**–10
MATHEMATICS [măth/ə măt/ǐks] **192**–**193**
Math Operations [măth/ äp/ə rā/shənz] **192**
Math Problem [măth/ präb/ləmz] **192**
mattress [mā/trəs] **58**–20
May [mā] **21**–29
mayonnaise [mā/ə nāz/, mā/ə nāz/] **79**–23
mayor [mā/ər] **139**–26
meadow [mĕd/ō] **204**–20
measles [mē/zəlz] **111**–5
measure [mĕzh/ər] **100**–17, **181**–45
measure [mĕzh/ər] **17**–C
Measurement [mĕzh/ər mənt] **17**
MEASUREMENTS [mĕzh/ər mənts] **17**, **75**
Measures [mĕzh/ərz] **75**
Measuring Area and Volume
  [mĕ/zhər ǐng ĕr/ē ə ən văl/yəm, –yōōm] **193**
meat [mēt] **66**–2
  meatballs [mēt/bölz] **81**–27
  meatloaf [mēt/löf/] **81**–31
Meat [mēt] **70**, **76**
MEAT AND POULTRY [mēt/ n pōl/trē] **70**
mechanic [mə kăn/ǐk] **166**–8
Mechanic [mə kăn/ǐk] **158**
media mail [mē/dē ə māl/] **134**–3
medical [mĕd/ǐ kəl] **121**–32
  medical chart [mĕd/ǐ kəl chärt/] **121**–24
  medical emergency bracelet
    [mĕd/ǐ kəl ǐ mür/jən sē brās/lət] **117**–3

medical records technician
  [mĕd/ǐ kəl rĕkərdz tĕk nǐsh/ən] **168**–39
medical waste disposal
  [mĕd/ǐ kəl wāst/ dǐ spō/zəl] **121**–31
MEDICAL CARE [mĕd/ǐ kəl kër/] **118**
MEDICAL CONDITIONS [mĕd/ǐ kəl kən dǐsh/ənz] **111**
MEDICAL EMERGENCIES [mĕd/ǐ kəl ǐ mür/jən sēz] **116**
Medical Procedures [mĕd/ǐ kəl prə se/jərz] **118**
Medical Specialists [mĕd/ǐ kəl spĕ/shə lǐsts] **120**
Medical Technician [mĕd/ǐ kəl tĕk nǐsh/ən] **93**
Medical Warnings [mĕd/ǐ kəl wör/nǐngz] **112**
medication [mĕd/ə kā/shən] **112**–3, **112** ✦,
  113–18, **121**–20
Medication [mĕd/ə kā/shən] **113**
medicine cabinet [mĕd/ə sən kăb/ə nət] **57**–20
medium [mē/dē əm] **96**–3
meet [mēt] **222**–6
meet [mēt] **49**–G, **49**–R
meeting [mē/tǐng]
  meeting place [mē/tǐng plās/] **146**–1
  meeting room [mē/tǐng rōōm/] **184**–25
MEETING AND GREETING [mē/tǐng ən grē/tǐng] **2**–**3**
melons [mĕl/ənz] **68**–19
  watermelons [wö/tər mĕl/ənz] **68**–18
membrane [mĕm/brān] **194**–6
Memorial Day [mə mör/ē əl dā/] **22**–12
memory card [mĕm/ə rē kärd/] **235**–20
men / man [mĕn] / [măn] **30**–1, **30**–4
  doorman [dör/măn/] **184**–1
  men's store [mĕnz/ stör/] **130** ✦
Men's Underwear [mĕnz/ un/dər wër/] **91**
menu [mĕn/yōō] **82**–7, **197**–8
  menu bar [mĕn/yōō bär/] **197**–1
MENU [mĕn/yōō] **80**–**81**
Mercury [mür/kyə rē] **205**–1
merge [mürj] **154**–10
mess [mĕs] **64**–8
message [mĕs/ǐj] **14**–18, **14**–19
messenger [mĕs/ən jər] **168**–40
meter [mē/tər] **62**–14, **129**–25, **152**–23
mice / mouse [mīs] / [mows] **63**–28, **196**–15, **215**–18
microphone [mī/krə fōn/] **234**–18
microprocessor [mī/krō prä/sĕ sər] **196**–4
Microscope [mī/krə skōp/] **194**
microwave [mī/krə wāv/] **77**–T
microwave oven [mī/krə wāv/ ŭv/ən] **54**–13
middle [mǐd/l] **25**–2
  middle-aged [mǐd/l ājd/] **32**–2
  middle initial [mǐd/l ǐ nǐsh/əl] **4**–3
  middle school [mǐd/l skōōl/] **188**–3
mid-length [mǐd/lĕnth] **96**–17
midnight [mǐd/nīt/] **18**–21
Military [mǐ/lə tër ē] **138**
MILITARY SERVICE [mǐ/lə tër ē sür/vəs] **138**–**139**
milk [mǐlk] **66**–5, **81**–42
  milkshake [mǐlk shāk/] **79**–14
milk [mǐlk] **177**–C
mini [mǐn/ē] **96**–15
  mini-blinds [mǐn/ē blindz/] **58**–8
  minivan [mǐn/ē văn/] **156**–8
minister [mǐ/nə stər] **199**–7

minutes [mĭn′əts] **18**–2

mirror [mĭr′ər] **57**–16

full-length mirror [fŏŏl′lĕnth mĭr′ər] **58**–6

rearview mirror [rĭr′vyōō′ mĭr′ər] **159**–35

sideview mirror [sīd′vyōō′ mĭr′ər] **158**–3

misbehave [mĭs′bĭ hāv′] **44**–B

miss the bus [mĭs dhə bŭs′] **152** ✦

missing [mĭs′ĭng] **97**–40

mittens [mĭt′nz] **90**–10

mix [mĭks] **77**–R

mixed berries [mĭkst′ bĕr′ēz] **81**–36

mixer [mĭk′sər] **54**–25

mixing bowl [mĭk′sĭng bōl′] **54**–28, **78**–31

mobile [mō′bēl] **59**–5

mobile home [mō′bəl hōm′] **52**–7

model [mäd′l] **156** ✦, **168**–41

model kit [mäd′l kĭt′] **232**–9

model trains [mäd′l trānz′] **233**–27

modern [mä′dərn] **199**–2

moist towelettes [moyst′ tow′əl ĕts] **146**–12

moisturizer [moys′chə rī′zər] **108**–9

mole [mōl] **32**–16

molecule [mäl′ĭ kyōōl′] **195**–27

monarch [mä′nərk, mä′närk′] **199**–4

Monday [mŭn′dā, –dē] **20**–9

MONEY [mŭn′ē] **26**

monitor [män′ə tər] **196**–11

arrival and departure monitors [ə rī′vəl ən dĭ pär′chər män′ə tərz] **161**–7

baby monitor [bā′bē män′ə tər] **59**–7

vital signs monitor [vī′təl sīnz män′ə tər] **121**–26

monkey [mŭng′kē] **217**–26

month [mŭnth] **20**–3

Months of the Year [mŭnths′ əv dhə yïr′] **21**

moon [mōōn]

crescent moon [krĕs′ənt mōōn′] **205**–10

full moon [fŏŏl′ mōōn′] **205**–12

new moon [nōō′ mōōn′] **205**–9

quarter moon [kwör′tər mōōn′] **205**–11

Moon [mōōn] **205**

moose [mōōs] **216**–1

mop [mäp] **61**–6

mop [mäp] **60**–D

morning [mör′nĭng] **18**–15

mosque [mäsk] **126**–5

mosquito [mə skē′tō] **214**–22

motel [mō tĕl′] **126**–12

moth [möth] **214**–21

mother [mŭdh′ər] **34**–3, **35**–22

grandmother [grăn′mŭdh′ər, gränd′–] **34**–1

motherboard [mŭdh′ər börd′] **196**–5

mother-in-law [mŭdh′ər ĭn lö′] **34**–10

stepmother [stĕp′mŭdh′ər] **35**–26

MOTION [mō′shən] **153**

motor [mō′tər] **124**–4

motorcycle [mō′tər sī′kəl] **150**–4

mountain [mown′tn]

mountain biking [mown′tn bī′kĭng] **226**–8

mountain lion [mown′tn lī′ən] **216**–2

mountain peak [mown′tn pēk′] **204**–14

mountain range [mown′tn rānj′] **204**–15

Mountain time [mown′tn tīm′] **19**–30

mouse / mice [mows] / [mīs] **63**–28, **196**–15, **215**–18

mouth [mowth] **104**–7

mouthwash [mowth′wäsh′, –wösh′] **109**–25

Mouth [mowth] **106**

move in [mōōv′ ĭn′] **48**–F

move out [mōōv′ owt′] **48** ✦

movement [mōōv′mənt] **199**–16

mover [mōō′vər] **168**–42

movies [mōō′vēz] **222**–2

movie theater [mōō′vē thē′ə tər] **126**–6

Movies [mōō′vēz] **237**

Moving In [mōō′vĭng ĭn] **49**

moving van [mōō′vĭng văn′] **156**–18

mow [mō] **176**–A

mower [mō′ər] **176**–6

mozzarella cheese [möts′ə rĕ lə chēz′] **71**–29

MP3 player [ĕm′pē′thrē′ plā′ər] **234**–2

mudslide [mŭd′slīd′] **144**–6

muffin [mŭf′ən] **79**–16, **80**–5

muffler [mŭf′lər] **158**–16

muffs [mŭfs] **179**–16

mug [mŭg] **55**–7

mugging [mŭg′ĭng] **142**–11

multiply [mŭl′tə plī] **192**–C

multi-use knife [mŭl′tē yōōs′ nīf′, mŭl′tī–] **226**–20

mumps [mŭmps] **111**–7

murder [mŭr′dər] **142**–12

muscle [mŭs′əl] **107**–32

mushrooms [mŭsh′rōōmz′] **69**–27

music [myōō′zĭk] **64**–3, **189**–15

live music [līv′ myōō′zĭk] **84**–1

music store [myōō′zĭk stör′] **130**–1

world music [würld′ myōō′zĭk] **237**–32

Music [myōō′zĭk] **237**

MUSIC [myōō′zĭk] **238**

musician [myōō zĭsh′ən] **168**–43

mussels [mŭs′əlz] **71**–13, **212**–17

mustache [mŭs′tăsh] **33**–5

mustard [mŭs′tərd] **79**–22

mystery [mĭs′tə rē] **237**–20

nachos [nä′chōz] **79**–7

nail [nāl] **180**–34

fingernail [fĭng′gər nāl′] **106**–18

nail clipper [nāl klĭp′ər] **109**–31

nail polish [nāl päl′ĭsh] **109**–33

nail salon [nāl sə län′] **130**–3

toenail [tō′nāl′] **106** ✦

name [nām] **4**–1, **4**–2, **4**–4

name tag [nām′ tăg′] **92**–15

napkin [năp′kĭn] **55**–10, **83**–26

narrow [năr′ō] **97**–35

nasal [nā′zəl]

nasal congestion [nā′zəl kən jĕs′chən] **110**–7

nasal spray [nā′zəl sprā′] **113**–32

National Guard [nä′shə nəl gärd′] **138**–19

NATIONAL PARKS [nä′shə nəl pärks′] **220**–221

Native Americans [nā′tĭv ə mĕr′ə kənz] **198**–3

natural [năch′rəl, năch′ər əl′]

natural gas [năch′rəl găs′] **218**–3

natural materials [năch′rəl mə tïr′ē əlz] **98** ✦

NATURE CENTER [nā′chər sĕn′tər] **208**–209

nature program [nā′chər prō′grăm] **236**–7

Navigating a Webpage [nă′və gā′tĭng ə wĕb′pāj] **197**

Navy [nā′vē] **138**–15

navy blue [nā′vē blōō′] **28**–5

near [nïr] **25** ✦

neck [nĕk] **96**–8, **96**–10, **104**–3

crewneck [krōō′nĕk] **96**–7

necklaces [nĕk′lə sĕz] **95**–10

turtleneck [tür′tl nĕk′] **96**–9

needle [nēd′l] **98**–17, **100**–10, **210**–10, **233**–23

needle plate [nēd′l plāt′] **98**–18

negative integers [nĕ′gə tĭv ĭn′tə jərz] **192**–1

negotiate [nĭ gō′shē āt′] **157**–D

neighborhood [nā′bər hŏŏd′] **128** ✦

nephew [nĕf′yōō] **34**–19

Neptune [nĕp′tōōn] **205**–8

nervous [nür′vəs] **42**–10

nest [nĕst] **209**–12

net [nĕt] **226**–17

hairnet [hĕr′nĕt′] **93**–25

network [nĕt′würk′] **173**–A

Neutral Colors [nōō′trəl kŭl′ərz] **24**

neutron [nōō′trän] **195**–32

new [nōō]

new job [nōō′ jäb′] **172**–3

new moon [nōō′ mōōn′] **205**–9

New Year's Day [nōō′ yïrz′ dā′] **22**–9

Newfoundland time [nōō′fən lənd tīm′, –fənd–] **19**–34

news [nōōz]

newspaper [nōōz′pā′pər] **133**–6

news program [nōōz prō′grăm] **236**–1

newsstand [nōōz′stănd′] **128**–12

newt [nōōt] **212**–26

New Words [nōō′ würdz′] **8**

next [nĕkst]

next day mail [nĕkst′ dā′ māl′] **135** ✦

next to [nĕkst′ tōō, –tə] **24**–9

next week [nĕkst′ wēk′] **20**–20

nickel [nĭk′əl] **26**–2

niece [nēs] **34**–18

night [nīt] **18**–20

nightclub [nīt′klŭb′] **223**–12

nightgown [nīt′gown′] **91**–25

night light [nīt′līt′] **37**–27

nightshirt [nīt′shürt′] **91**–28

nightstand [nīt′stănd′] **58**–23

night table [nīt′ tā′bəl] **58**–23

nine [nīn] **16**

nineteen [nīn′tēn′] **16**

nineteenth [nīn′tēnth′] **16**

ninetieth [nīn′tē əth] **16**

ninety [nīn′tē] **16**

90° angle [nīn′tē də grē′ ăng′gəl] **193**–26

ninth [nīnth] **16**

nipple [nĭp′əl] **37**–2

no [nō]

no left turn [nō′ lĕft′ türn′] **154**–8

no outlet [nō′ owt′lĕt, –lət] **154**–6

no parking [nō′ pär′kĭng] **154**–11

noise [noyz] **64**–5

noisy [noy′zē] **23**–11

noon [nōōn] **18**–16

afternoon [ăf′tər nōōn′] **18**–17

Index

north [nörth] **155**–1

NORTH AMERICA AND CENTRAL AMERICA
[nörth/ ə mĕr/ə kə ən sĕn/trəl ə mĕr/ə kə] **200**–**201**

nose [nōz] **104**–6, **110**–17
revolving nosepiece [rə väl/vĭng nōz/pēs] **194**–17

not [nät]
can't breathe [kănt/ brēdh/] **116**–N
do not drink [dōō/ nät/ drĭnk] **112**–F
do not enter [dōō/ nät/ ĕn/tər] **154**–2
do not operate [dōō/ nät/ äp/ər āt/] **112**–E
do not take [dōō nät/ tāk/] **112**–D
don't be late [dōnt/ bē/ lāt/] **174**–E
don't litter [dōnt/ lĭt/ər] **219**–L
don't smoke [dōnt/ smōk/] **114**–G
not working [nät/ wür/kĭng] **62**–1

note [nōt] **183**–39
footnote [fŏŏt/nōt/] **190**–10
notebook [nōt/bŏŏk/] **7**–27
notebook paper [nōt/bŏŏk/ pāp/ər] **7**–28
spiral notebook [spī/rəl nōt/bŏŏk/] **7**–29

novel [nä/vəl] **133**–16
November [nō vĕm/bər] **21**–35
nuclear energy [nōō/klē ər ĕn/ər jē] **218**–8
nucleus [nōō/klē əs] **194**–7, **195**–29
numb [nŭm] **119**–C

number [nŭm/bər]
access number [ăk/sĕs/ nŭm/bər] **14**–16
apartment number [ə pärt/mənt nŭm/bər] **4**–6
cell phone number [sĕl/ fōn/ nŭm/bər] **4**–12
checking account number
[chĕk/ĭng ə kownt/ nŭm/bər] **132**–14
driver's license number
[drī/vərz lī/səns nŭm/bər] **136**–11
even numbers [ēv/ən nŭm/bərz] **192**–4
odd numbers [öd/ nŭm/bərz] **192**–3
phone number [fōn/ nŭm/bər] **4**–11, **15**–30
prescription number
[prĭ skrĭp/shən nŭm/bər] **112**–5
savings account number
[sā/vĭngz ə kownt/ nŭm/bər] **132**–11
SKU number [ĕs/kā/yōō/ nŭm/bər] **27**–5
Social Security number
[sō/shəl sĭ kyŏŏr/ə tē nŭm/bər] **4**–15

Numbers [nŭm/bərz] **16**
NUMBERS [nŭm/bərz] **16**
Numerals [nōō/mər əlz] **16**
numerator [nōō/mər ā/ tər] **192**–5
nurse [nürs] **118**–8, **168**–44
licensed practical nurse (LPN) [lī/sənst
prăk/tə kəl nürs/] / [ĕl/pē/ĕn/] **120**–11
nurse midwives [nürs/ mĭd/wīvz/] **120** ✦
nurse practitioners [nürs/ prăk tĭ/shən ərz] **120** ✦
registered nurse (RN) [rĕj/ə stərd nürs/] / [är/ĕn/]
120–10
surgical nurse [sür/jĭ kəl nürs/] **120**–9
nurse [nürs] **36**–B
Nurse [nürs] **93**
nursery [nür/sə rē]
nursery rhymes [nür/sə rē rīmz/] **37**–22
nursery school [nür/sə rē skōōl/] **188**–1
nursing [nür/sĭng] **120**–12
nursing home [nür/sĭng hōm/] **52**–12

Nursing Staff [nür/sĭng stăf/] **120**
nutrition label [nōō trĭ/shən lā/bəl] **122**–8
nuts [nŭts] **73**–36, **180**–36
nylon [nī/län] **99**–12
oak [ōk] **210**–17, **210**–24
obey [ō bā/] **140**–C
objective [əb jĕk/tĭv] **194**–18
oboe [ō/bō] **238**–3
observatory [əb zür/və tör/ē] **205**–21
observe [əb zürv/] **195**–C
obstetrician [äb/stə trĭsh/ən] **120**–2
obtuse angle [äb/tōōs ăng/gəl] **193**–27
occupational therapist
[äk/yə pā/shən əl thĕr/ə pĭst]**168**–45
OCCUPATIONS [äk/yə pā/shənz] **166**–**169**
ocean [ō/shən] **204**–6, **225**–1
o'clock [ə kläk/] **18**–6
October [äk tō/bər] **21**–34
octopus [äk/tə pəs] **212**–9
odd numbers [öd/ nŭm/bərz] **192**–3
odometer [ō däm/ə tər] **159**–28
off [öf]
clear off [klĭr/ öf/] **10**–I
drop off [dräp/ öf/] **38**–G
gas shut-off valve [găs/ shŭt/öf vălv/] **146**–4
get off [gĕt/ öf/] **153**–J
take off [tāk/ öf/] **109**–Q
turn off [türn/ öf/] **11**–P, **160**–I, **174**–G, **219**–G
offer [ö/fər] **12**–D
office [ö/fəs] **164**–3
main office [mān/ ö/fəs] **5**–12
office building [ö/fəs bĭld/ĭng] **124**–2
office manager [ö/fəs măn/ĭ jər] **182**–8
office supply store [ö/fəs sə plī/ stör/] **127**–21
post office [pōst/ ö/fəs] **125**–11
post office box (PO box) [pōst/ ö/fəs bäks/] /
[pē/ō bäks/] **135**–9
run for office [rŭn/ fər ö/fəs/] **139**–A
Office [ö/fəs] **51**
OFFICE [ö/fəs] **134**–**135**, **182**–**183**
Office Equipment [ö/fəs ĭ kwĭp/mənt] **183**
officer [ö/fə sər] **161**–17, **168**–48
Office Skills [ö/fəs skĭlz/] **171**
OFFICE SKILLS [ö/fəs skĭlz/] **171**
Office Supplies [ö/fəs sə plīz/] **183**
Office Visit [ö/fəs vĭ/zət] **119**
official [ə fĭsh/əl] **139**–32, **229**–6
oil [oyl] **73**–31, **218**–6
oil gauge [oyl/ gāj/] **159**–29
oil paint [oyl/ pānt/] **233**–19
oil spill [oyl/ spĭl/] **218**–17
ointment [oynt/mənt] **113**–24, **117**–10
OK [ō kā/] **154**–5
old [ōld] **31**–9, **31**–10
omelet [äm/lət, ä/mə lət] **76**–12
on [än, ön] **25**–11
get on [gĕt/ än, –ön] **153**–I
go on [gō/ än, –ön] **173**–K
on-the-job training [än dhə jäb/ trā/nĭng, –ön]
172–7
on the left [än dhə lĕft/, –ön] **25**–1
on the right [än dhə rīt/, –ön] **25**–3

on time [än tīm/, –ön] **19**–23, **16**–29
overdose on drugs [ō/vər dōs/ än drŭgz/] **116**–K
put on [pŏŏt/ än/, –ön] **87**–B, **108**–D, **109**–P
try on [trī/ än/, –ön] **95**–C
turn on [türn/ än/, –ön] **11**–B
once a week [wŭns/ə wēk/] **20**–22
oncologist [än/kö lə jĭst/] **120**–5
one [wŭn] **16**
five after one [fīv/ ăf/ tər wŭn/] **18**–7
one billion [wŭn/ bĭl/yən] **16**
one eighth [wŭn/ ātth/, –āth/] **17**–5
one-fifteen [wŭn/fĭf/tēn/] **18**–9
one-forty [wŭn/för/tē] **18**–12
one-forty-five [wŭn/för/tē fīv/] **18**–13
one fourth [wŭn/ förth/] **17**–4
one half [wŭn/ hăf/] **17**–2
one hundred [wŭn/ hŭn/drəd] **16**
one hundred dollars
[wŭn/ hŭn/drəd däl/ərz] **26**–12
one hundred one [wŭn/ hŭn/drəd wŭn/] **16**
100 percent [wŭn/ hŭn/drəd pər sĕnt/] **17**–8
one hundredth [wŭn/ hŭn/drəth] **16**
one hundred thousand
[wŭn/ hŭn/drəd thow/zənd] **16**
one million [wŭn/ mĭl/yən] **16**
one o'clock [wŭn/ ə kläk/] **18**–6
one-oh-five [wŭn/ō fīv/] **18**–7
one-size-fits-all [wŭn/sīz fĭts/äl] **96**–6
one-ten [wŭn/tĕn/] **18**–8
one third [wŭn/ thürd/] **17**–3
one-thirty [wŭn/thür/tē] **18**–11
one thousand [wŭn/ thow/zənd] **16**
one thousandth [wŭn/ thow/zənth] **16**
one-twenty [wŭn/twĕn/tē] **18**–10
one way [wŭn/ wā/] **154**–3
one-way trip [wŭn/wā/ trĭp/] **152**–16
one whole [wŭn/hōl/] **17**–1
quarter after one [kwör/tər ăf/tər wŭn/] **18**–9
ten after one [tĕn/ ăf/tər wŭn/] **18**–8
twenty after one [twĕn/tē ăf/tər wŭn/] **18**–10
onions [ŭn/yənz] **69**–19, **69**–20
onion rings [ŭn/yən rĭngz/] **79**–4
online [än/līn/, ön–]
online catalog [än/līn/ kă/tə lög, ön–] **133**–11
online course [än/līn/ körs/, ön–]**172**–8
only [ōn/lē] **154**–7
On the Airplane [än/ dhe ër/plān/] **161**
open [ō/pən] **6**–G, **143**–F
opener [ō/pən ər] **54**–8, **78**–1, **146**–8
Opening an Account [ō/pə nĭng ən ə kownt/] **132**
opera [äp/rə] **223**–11, **236**–5
operate [äp/ə rāt/] **112**–E, **170**–H
Operating Room [äp/ə rā/tĭng rōōm/] **121**
operating table [äp/ə rā/tĭng tā/bəl] **121**–40
Operations [äp/ə rā/shənz] **192**
operator [äp/ə rā/tər] **14**–21, **98**–14, **168**–37
ophthalmologist
[äf/thəl mäl/ə jĭst, –thə mäl/–, äp/–] **120**–7
opinion [ə pĭn/yən] **44**–3
opossum [ə päs/əm, päs/əm] **216**–4
opponent [ə pō/nənt] **139**–30
optician [äp tĭsh/ən] **130**–9

optometrist [äp täm/ə trĭst] **115**–6
orange [ör/ənj, är/–] **24**–4
oranges [ör/ən jəz, är/–] **68**–5
orangutan [ə răng/ə tăng/, –tăn/] **217**–39
orchard [ör/chərd] **177**–10
orchid [ör/kĭd] **211**–19
order [ör/dər] **185**–1
    order puller [ör/dər pool/ər] **175**–10
order [ör/dər] **82**–D
orderly [ör/dər lē] **120**–16
Ordinal Numbers [ör/dn əl nŭm/bərz] **16**
organ [ör/gən] **238**–20
organic [ör gä/nĭk] **84**–2
organisms [ör/gə nĭzmz] **194**–1
organize [ör/gə nīz/] **171**–L, **191**–G
organizer [ör/gə nī/zər] **183**–49
ornament [ör/nə mənt] **239**–15
Orthodontics [ör/thə dän/tĭks] **119**
orthodontist [ör/thə dän/tĭst] **119**–5
orthopedists [ör/thə pē/dĭsts] **120** ✦
Other Instruments [ŭdh/ər ĭn/strə mənts] **238**
otter [ät/ər] **213**–35
ounce [owns] **75**–1, **75**–11
out [owt] **62**–2
    blow out [blō/ owt/] **240**–C
    check out [chĕk/ owt/] **133**–C
    cross out [krös/ owt/] **9**–R
    eat out [ēt/ owt/] **82** ✦
    fill out [fĭl/ owt/] **173**–J
    get out of [gĕt/ owt/ əv] **153**–F
    let out [lĕt/ owt/] **100**–C
    move out [moov/ owt/] **48** ✦
    outfit [owt/fĭt] **88** ✦
    out of focus [owt/ əv fō/kəs] **235**–33
    out-of-state contact [owt/əv stāt/ kän/täkt] **146**–2
    run out of gas [rŭn/ owt/ əv gäs/] **162**–E
    take out [tāk/ owt/] **9**–Y, **60**–Q, **82** ✦
    work out [würk/ owt/] **230**–N
OUTDOOR RECREATION [owt/dör rĕk/rē ā/shən] **226**
outlet [owt/lĕt, –lət] **58**–28, **154**–6, **159**–42
    outlet cover [owt/lĕt kŭv/ər] **181**–46
OUTSIDE THE BODY [owt/sīd/ dhe bä/dē] **106**–**107**
oven [ŭv/ən] **54**–15, **54**–20
    oven cleaner [ŭv/ən klē/nər] **61**–3
over [ō/vər] **76**–11, **153**–B
    overalls [ō/vər ölz/] **88**–6
    overcoat [ō/vər kōt/] **90**–2
    overexposed [ō/vər ĭk spōzd/] **235**–34
    overflowing [ō/vər flō/ĭng] **63**–17
    overhead compartment
        [ō/vər hĕd/ kəm pärt/mənt] **161**–13
    overhead projector [ō/vər hĕd/ prə jĕk/tər] **7**–16
    overjoyed [ō/vər joyd/] **43** ✦
    overnight mail [ō/vər nīt/ māl/] **135** ✦
    over-the-counter medication
        [ō/vər dhə -kown/tər mĕd/ə kā/shən] **113**–18
overdose [ō/vər dōs/, ō/vər dōs/] **116**–K
Over-the-Counter Medication
    [ō/vər dhə kown/tər mĕd/ə kā/shən] **113**
owl [owl] **214**–5
owner [ō/nər] **166**–11, **175**–1
oxfords [äks/fərdz] **95**–29

oxygen mask [äk/sĭ jən mäsk/] **161**–24
oysters [oy/stərz] **71**–14
Pacific time [pə sĭf/ĭk tīm/] **19**–29
pacifier [päs/ə fī/ər] **37**–24
pack [päk] **74**–9, **117**–13, **235**–26
    backpack [bäk/päk/] **94**–18, **226**–15
pack [päk] **49**–M, **162**–A
package [päk/ĭj] **74**–8, **74**–20, **134**–17
packaged food [päk/ĭjd food/] **146**–10
PACKAGING [päk/ə jĭng] **74**
packer [päk/ər] **175**–18
packing tape [päk/ĭng tāp/] **183**–32
pad [päd]
    bumper pad [bŭm/pər päd/] **59**–4
    changing pad [chānj/ĭng päd/] **59**–2
    foam pad [fōm/ päd/] **226**–13
    heating pad [hē/tĭng päd/] **113**–13
    ink pad [ĭnk/ päd/] **183**–46
    knee pads [nē/ pädz/] **179**–19
    legal pad [lē/gəl päd/] **183**–38
    shoulder pads [shōl/dər pädz/] **231**–20
    steel-wool soap pads [stēl/wool/sōp/ pädz/] **61**–5
    sterile pad [stĕr/əl päd/] **117**–6
pail [pāl] **37**–7, **61**–7, **225**–8
pain [pān] **42**–11, **115**–3
    pain reliever [pān rĭ lē/vər] **113**–26
paint [pānt] **181**–25, **232**–10, **233**–19
    paintbrush [pānt/brŭsh/] **181**–22, **233**–20
    paint pan [pānt/ pän/] **181**–51
    paint roller [pānt/ rō/lər] **181**–23
paint [pānt] **49**–P, **178**–A, **233**–E
painter [pān/tər] **168**–46
Painter [pān/tər] **92**
painting [pān/tĭng] **56**–9
pair of scissors [pĕr/ əv sĭz/ərz] **100**–16
paisley [pāz/lē] **96**–26
pajamas [pə jä/məz, –jä/–] **91**–24
pallet [pä/lət] **175**–13
palm [päm] **106**–15, **210**–14
pan [pän] **54**–24
    bed pan [bĕd/ pän/] **121**–28
    cake pan [kāk/ pän/] **78**–26
    dustpan [dŭst/ pän/] **61**–17
    frying pan [frī/ĭng pän/] **78**–5
    paint pan [pānt/ pän/] **181**–51
    pancakes [pän/kāks/] **80**–7
    pie pan [pī/ pän/] **78**–28
    roasting pan [rō/stĭng pän/] **78**–13
    saucepan [sös/pän/] **78**–25
pancreas [päng/krē əs] **107**–45
panda [pän/də] **217**–41
pane [pān] **178**–16
panel [pän/əl] **234**–7
Panel [pän/əl] **159**
panther [pän/thər] **217**–40
panties [pän/tēz] **91**–13
pants [pänts] **87**–12
    security pants [sĭ kyoor/ə tē pänts/] **93**–22
    training pants [trā/nĭng pänts/] **37**–11
    work pants [würk/ pänts/] **92**–5
panty hose [pän/tē hōz/] **91**–18
papayas [pə pī/əz] **68**–20

paper [pā/pər]
    construction paper [kən strŭk/shən pā/pər] **232**–12
    copies of important papers
        [kä/pēz əv ĭm pört/ənt pā/pərz] **146**–20
    newspaper [nooz/pā/pər] **133**–6
    notebook paper [nōt/book/ pā/pər] **7**–28
    paper clip [pā/pər klĭp/] **183**–31
    paper cutter [pā/pər kŭt/ər] **183**–22
    paper dolls [pā/pər dälz/] **233**–28
    paper shredder [pā/pər shrĕd/ər] **183**–24
    paper towels [pā/pər tow/əlz] **54**–3
    sandpaper [sänd/ pā/pər] **181**–56
    toilet paper [toy/lət pā/pər] **57**–17, **146**–13
    wallpaper [wäl/ pā/pər] **59**–8
parade [pə rād/] **239**–1
paragraph [păr/ə grăf/] **190**–3
parakeet [păr/ə kēt/] **215**–15
parallel lines [păr/ə lĕl/ līnz/] **193**–25
parallelogram [păr/ə lĕl/ə grăm/] **193**–33
paramedic [păr/ə mĕ/dĭk] **116**–2
parasites [păr/ə sīts/] **111**–13
parcel post [pär/səl pōst/] **134**–6
parentheses [pə rĕn/thə sēz/] **190**–19
PARENTING [păr/ən tĭng, pĕr/–] **36**–**37**
Parents [păr/ənts, pĕr/–] **34**
parent-teacher conference
    [păr/ənt tē/chər kän/frəns, pĕr/–] **22**–5
paring knife [pĕr/ĭng nīf/] **78**–16
park [pärk] **223**–10
    park ranger [pärk/ rānj/ər] **220**–2
park [pärk] **129**–E
parka [pär/kə] **90**–9
PARK AND PLAYGROUND [pärk/ ən plā/grownd/] **224**
parking [pär/kĭng] **128**–6, **154**–11, **154**–12
    parking attendant [pär/kĭng ə tĕn/dənt] **184**–3
    parking garage [pär/kĭng gə räzh/, –räj/] **124**–1
    parking meter [pär/kĭng mē/tər] **129**–25
    parking space [pär/kĭng spās/] **50**–18, **128**–5
PARKS [pärks] **220**–**221**
parochial school [pə rō/kē əl skool/] **5** ✦
parsley [pär/slē] **69**–28
part [pärt] **33**–4
participate [pär tĭ/sə pāt/] **10**–B
particle [pär/tĭ kəl]
    particle board [pär/tĭ kəl börd/] **181**–20
    particle mask [pär/tĭ kəl mäsk/] **179**–14
Partner [pärt/nər] **8**
parts [pärts] **175**–5
Parts of a Bird [pärts/ əv ə bürd/] **214**
PARTS OF A CAR [pärts/ əv ə kär/] **158**–**159**
Parts of a Fish [pärts/ əv ə fĭsh/] **212**
Parts of a Flower [pärts/ əv ə flow/ər] **211**
Parts of an Essay [pärts/ əv ən ĕs/ā] **190**
Parts of a Phone [pärts/ əv ə fōn/] **14**
Parts of a Sewing Machine
    [pärts/ əv ə sō/ĭng mə shēn] **98**
Parts of a Tree [pärts/ əv ə trē/] **210**
party [pär/tē] **64**–2
pass [päs] **161**–20
    passbook [päs/book/] **132**–10
    passport [päs/pört/] **41**–10
pass [päs] **10**–E, **137**–H, **230**–G

Index

passenger [păs/ən jər] **150**–2, **161**–15
past [păst] **155**–E
pasta [päs/tə] **67**–12
    pasta salad [päs/tə săl/əd] **80**–20
paste [păst]
    toothpaste [tōōth/păst/] **109**–23
pastrami [pə strä/mē] **71**–23
path [păth] **208**–3, **224**–3
Path [păth] **172**
patient [pā/shənt] **118**–6, **121**–18
patio [păt/ē ō] **53**–16
    patio furniture [păt/ē ō für/nĭ chər] **53**–19
patron [pā/trən] **82**–6, **133**–3
pattern [păt/ərn] **99**–22
PATTERNS [păt/ərnz] **96**
pause [pöz] **235**–E
paw [pö] **216**–20
pay [pā]
    paycheck [pā/chĕk/] **165**–14
    payroll clerk [pā/rōl klürk/] **165**–10
    pay stub [pā/ stŭb/] **165**–11
pay [pā]
    pay a late fine [pā/ ə lāt/ fīn/] **133**–E
    pay attention [pā/ ə tĕn/shən] **147**–D
    pay back [pā/ băk/] **26**–D
    pay cash [pā/ kăsh/] **27**–A
    pay for [pā/ för/, –fər] **27**–G
    pay phone [pā/ fōn/] **15**–25, **129**–23
    pay taxes [pā/ tăks/əz] **140**–B
    pay the application fee
        [pā/ dhe ăp/lə kā/shən fē/] **137**–D
    pay the check [pā/ dhe chĕk/] **82**–I
    pay the rent [pā/ dhe rĕnt/] **48**–E
Pay [pā] **27**
PBX [pē/ bē/ ĕks/] **182**–13
peaceful assembly [pēs/fəl ə sĕm/blē] **140**–1
peaches [pē/chəz] **68**–10
peacock [pē/käk/] **214**–14
peak [pēk] **204**–14
pearls [pürlz] **95**–39
pears [pĕrz] **68**–4
peas [pēz] **69**–21
pedal [pĕd/əl] **159**–45, **159**–46
pedestrian [pə dĕs/trē ən] **128**–14
    pedestrian crossing [pə dĕs/trē ən krö/sĭng] **154**–13
pediatrician [pē/dē ə trĭsh/ən] **120**–4
peel [pēl] **77**–K
peeler [pē/lər] **78**–15
peephole [pēp/hōl/] **51**–32
pelvis [pĕl/vəs] **107**–50
pen [pĕn] **7**–22
pencil [pĕn/səl] **7**–20, **109**–34
    pencil eraser [pĕn/səl ĭ rā/sər] **7**–21
    pencil sharpener [pĕn/səl shär/pə nər] **7**–23, **183**–26
penguin [pĕng/wĭn] **214**–11
peninsula [pə nĭn/sə lə] **204**–7
penny [pĕn/ē] **26**–1
PEOPLE [pē/pəl] **32**
pepper [pĕp/ər] **55**–13, **69**–7, **69**–29
percent [pər sĕnt/]
    50 percent [fĭf/tē pər sĕnt/] **17**–10
    100 percent [wŭn/ hŭn/drəd pər sĕnt/] **17**–8

75 percent [sĕv/ən tē fīv/ pər sĕnt/] **17**–9
10 percent [tĕn/ pər sĕnt/] **17**–12
25 percent [twĕn/tē fīv/ pər sĕnt/] **17**–11
Percents [pər sĕnts/] **17**
Percussion [pər kŭsh/ən] **238**
perfume [pür/fyōōm/, pər fyōōm/] **108**–6
perimeter [pə rĭ/mə tər] **193**–43
period [pïr/ē əd] **190**–11
Period [pïr/ē əd] **198**
periodicals [pïr/ē äd/ĭ kəlz] **133**–4
periodic table [pïr/ē äd/ĭk tā/bəl] **195**–26
perm [pürm] **33**–B
peroxide [pə räk/ sīd] **117**–9
perpendicular lines [pür/pən dĭk/yə lər līnz/] **193**–24
person [pür/sən]
    appliance repair person
        [ə plī/əns rĭ pĕr/ pür/sən] **166**–4
    assemblyperson [ə sĕm/blē pür/sən] **139**–24
    businessperson [bĭz/nəs pür/sən] **166**–12
    bus person [bŭs/ pür/sən] **185**–13
    congressperson [kän/grəs pür/sən] **138**–4
    councilperson [kown/səl pür/sən] **139**–28
    counterperson [kown/tər pür/sən] **79**–17
    delivery person [də lĭv/ə rē pür/sən] **167**–21
    electronics repair person
        [ĭ lĕk trän/ĭks rĭ pĕr/ pür/sən] **167**–24
    repair person [rĭ pĕr/ pür/sən] **62**–10
personal CD player [pür/sə nəl sē/dē/ plā/ər] **234**–5
PERSONAL HYGIENE [pür/sə nəl hī/jēn] **108**–**109**
PERSONAL INFORMATION
    [pür/sə nəl ĭn/fər mā/shən] **4**
pesticide poisoning [pĕs/tə sīd/ poy/zə nĭng] **218**–16
pests [pĕsts] **62** ✦
pet [pĕt]
    pet food [pĕt fōōd/] **72**–5
    pet store [pĕt stör/] **130**–6
petals [pĕt/lz] **211**–8
petition [pə tĭ/shən] **148**–5
petroleum [pə trō/lē əm] **218**–6
Pets [pĕts] **215**
pharmacist [fär/mə sĭst] **112**–1
pharmacy [fär/mə sē] **128**–4
PHARMACY [fär/mə sē] **112**–**113**
Phase of the Moon [fāz/ əf dhə mōōn/] **205**
Phillips screwdriver [fĭl/ĭps skrōō/drī/vər] **180**–31
phlebotomist [flĭ bä/tə mĭst] **121**–29
phone [fōn]
    automated phone system
        [ö/tə măt ĭd fōn/ sĭs/təm] **14**–23
    cell phone holder [sĕl/ fōn/ hōl/dər] **94**–15
    cell phone kiosk [sĕl/ fōn/ kē/ösk] **131**–22
    cell phone number [sĕl/ fōn/ nŭm/bər] **4**–12
    cellular phone [sĕl/yə lər fōn/] **14**–8
    cordless phone [körd/ləs fōn/] **15**–24
    headphones [hĕd/fōnz/] **6**–8, **234**–4
    Internet phone call [ĭn/tər nĕt/ fōn/ käl/] **14**–20
    microphone [mī/krə fōn/] **234**–18
    pay phone [pā/ fōn/] **15**–25, **129**–23
    phone bill [fōn/ bĭl/] **15**–28
    phone jack [fōn/ jăk/] **14**–3
    phone line [fōn/ līn/] **14**–4
    phone number [fōn/ nŭm/bər] **4**–11, **15**–30
    smart phone [smärt/ fōn/] **15**–27

Phone [fōn] **14**
Phone Bill [fōn/ bĭl/] **15**
Phone Call [fōn/ köl/] **15**
photo [fō/tō] **58**–3, **136**–4
    digital photo album [dĭ/jə təl fō/tō ăl/bəm] **235**–32
    funny photo [fŭn/ē fō/tō] **206**–2
    photo album [fō/tō ăl/bəm] **235**–31
    photocopier [fō/tə käp/ē ər] **183**–23
    serious photo [sïr/ē əs fō/tō] **206**–3
photographer [fə täg/rə fər] **206**–1
PHOTOGRAPHY [fə täg/rə fē] **234**–**235**
photosynthesis [fō/tō sĭn/thə səs] **194**–10
physical [fĭz/ĭ kəl]
    physical education [fĭz/ĭ kəl ĕ jə kā/shən] **189**–17
    physical therapist [fĭz/ĭ kəl thĕr/ə pĭst] **115**–12
    physical therapy [fĭz/ĭ kəl thĕr/ə pē] **115**–11
physically challenged [fĭz/ĭ klē chăl/ənjd] **32**–10
physician assistant [fĭz/ĭ shən ə sĭs/tənt] **168**–47
physicist [fĭz/ĭ sĭst/] **195**–33
Physics [fĭz/ĭks] **195**
pi (π) [pī] **193**–46
piano [pē ăn/ō] **238**–14
pick [pĭk] **108**–15
pickax [pĭk/ăks/] **178**–21
picker [pĭ/kər] **178**–5
pickle [pĭk/l] **80**–11
pick up [pĭk/ ŭp/] **6**–I, **11**–E, **38**–M, **112** ✦
pickup truck [pĭk/ŭp trŭk/] **156**–12
picnic [pĭk/nĭk] **224**–D
picnic table [pĭk/nĭk tā/bəl] **224**–8
picture [pĭk/chər]
    picture book [pĭk/chər bŏŏk/] **133**–12
    picture dictionary [pĭk/chər dĭk/shə nër ē] **7**–31
    picture frame [pĭk/chər frām/] **58**–4
pie [pī] **81**–35
    pie pan [pī/ păn/] **78**–28
pier [pïr] **225**–18
pierced [pïrst]
    pierced ear [pïrst/ ïr/] **32**–17
    pierced earrings [pïrst/ ïr/ĭngz] **95**–36
pig [pĭg] **215**–2, **215**–14
pigeon [pĭj/ən] **214**–15
pile [pīl] **53**–25
pill [pĭl] **113**–21
pillow [pĭl/ō] **56**–2, **58**–11
    pillowcase [pĭl/ō kās/] **58**–14
pilot [pī/lət] **161**–11
pin [pĭn] **95**–38
    bobby pins [bäb/ē pĭnz/] **108**–21
    clothespin [klōz/ pĭn/] **101**–10
    pin cushion [pĭn/ kŏŏsh/ən] **100**–13
    pushpin [pŏŏsh/pĭn/] **183**–35
    rolling pin [rō/lĭng pĭn/] **78**–30
    safety pin [sāf/tē pĭn/] **37**–9, **100**–14
    straight pin [strāt pĭn/] **100**–12
pine [pīn] **210**–9
    pinecone [pīn/kōn/] **210**–11
pineapples [pī/năp/əlz] **68**–23
pink [pĭnk] **24**–7
pint [pīnt] **75**–3
pipe [pīp] **158**–15, **181**–17
    pipe wrench [pīp rĕnch/] **181**–47

Index

pitch [pĭch] 230–A
pizza [pēt′sə] 79–10
place [plās] 146–1
  fireplace [fīr′plās/] 56–13
  placemat [plās′ măt/] 55–11
  place of birth [plās/ əv bürth/] 4–14
  place setting [plās/ sĕt′ĭng] 83–17
PLACES TO GO [plā′səz tə gō/] 222–223
PLACES TO LIVE [plā′səz tə lĭv/] 52
plaid [plăd] 96–22
plain [plān] 97–33
plains [plānz] 204–19
plan [plăn] 186–4
plan [plăn] 146–A
plane [plān] 144–3, 150–8, 181–57
Planets [plăn′əts] 205
Planning a Career [plă′nĭng ə kə rēr/] 172
plant [plănt] 176–E, 177–A, 219–N
plants [plănts] 208–5
  houseplant [hows′plănt/] 56–4, 211–27
Plants [plănts] 210
PLANTS [plănts] 210
plaque [plăk] 119–12
plastic [plăs′tĭk]
  plastic storage bags [plăs′tĭk stör′ĭj băgz] 72–25
  plastic storage container
    [plăs′tĭk stör′ĭj kən tā′nər] 78–4
  plastic utensils [plăs′tĭk yōō tĕn′ səlz] 79–19
  plastic wrap [plăs′tĭk răp/] 72–24
plate [plāt] 55–1
  bread-and-butter plate [brĕd/n bŭt′ər plāt/] 83–19
  dinner plate [dĭn′ər plāt/] 83–18
  license plate [lī′səns plāt/] 136–12, 158–12
  salad plate [săl′əd plāt/] 83–20
  vanity plate [vă′nə tē plāt/] 136 ✦
platform [plăt′förm/] 152–7
platter [plăt′ər] 55–20
platypus [plăt′ĭ pəs, –pōōs/] 217–46
play [plā] 223–8
  play area [plā/ ĕr′ē ə] 130–11
  playground [plā/grownd/] 50–3
play [plā] 235–B
  play an instrument [plā/ ən ĭn/strə mənt] 238–A
  play cards [plā/ kärdz/] 233–H
  play games [plā/ gāmz/] 232–B
  play with [plā/ wĭth/] 36–M
player [plā/ər] 229–5
  CD player [sē/dē plā′ər] 159–38
  DVD player [dē/vē/dē/ plā/ər] 56–7, 234–10
  MP3 player [ĕm/pē/thrē/ plā/ər] 234–2
  personal CD player [pür/sə nəl sē/dē plā/ər] 234–5
  portable cassette player
    [pör/tə bəl kə sĕt/ plā/ər] 234–6
  portable DVD player
    [pör/tə bəl dē/vē/dē/ plā/ər] 234–11
  video player [vĭd/ē ō plā/ər] 197–11
PLAYGROUND [plā/grownd/] 224
pliers [plī/ərz] 180–7
plugs [plŭgz] 179–15, 234–16
plumber [plŭm/ər] 63–20
plums [plŭmz] 68–13
plunger [plŭn/jər] 181–50

plywood [pli/wōōd/] 178–18
p.m. [pē/ĕm/] 18–5
pneumatic drill [nōō măt/ĭk drĭl/] 178–9
poached eggs [pōcht/ ĕgz/] 76–9
PO box (post office box) [pē/ō bäks/] /
    [pōst/ ö/fəs bäks/] 135–9
pocket [päk/ət] 100–7
podium [pō/dē əm] 206–5
poinsettia [poyn sĕt/ē ə, –sĕt/ə] 211–24
point [poynt] 17–7,
  endpoint [ĕnd/poynt/] 193–21
pointer [poyn/tər] 197–12
poison [poy/zən] 116–J
  poison ivy [poy/zən ī/vē] 210–25
  poison oak [poy/zən ōk/] 210–24
  poison sumac [poy/zən sōō/măk, –shōō/–] 210–23
poisoning [poy/zən ĭng] 218–16
poisonous fumes [poy/zən əs fyōōmz/] 179–3
poles [pōlz] 226–18, 231–25
police [pə lēs/]
  police officer [pə lēs/ ö/fə sər] 141–1, 168–48
  police station [pə lēs/ stā/shən] 124–6
polish [päl/ĭsh] 61–8, 109–33
polish [päl/ĭsh] 60–E, 109–O
political [pə lĭ/tĭ kəl]
  political campaign [pə lĭ/tĭ kəl kăm pān/] 139–29
  political movement [pə lĭ/tĭ kəl mōōv/mənt] 199–16
  political party [pə lĭ/tĭ kəl pär/tē] 139 ✦
polka-dotted [pō/kə dät/əd] 96–21
pollution [pə lōō/shən] 218–11, 218–14
Pollution [pə lōō/shən] 218
polo [pō/lō] 229–15
  polo shirt [pō/lō shïrt/] 92–14
poncho [pän/chō] 90–19
pond [pänd] 204–21
pool [pōōl] 51–22, 184–22, 228–2
  pool service [pōōl/ sür/vəs] 184–21
  pool table [pōōl/ tā/bəl] 50–14
pop [päp] 73–34, 237–25
  pop-up ad [päp/ŭp/] 197–9
porch light [pörch/ lit/] 53–13
porcupine [pör/kyə pīn/] 216–10
Pork [pörk] 70
pork chops [pörk/ chäps/] 70–10
porpoise [pör/pəs] 213–30
port [pört] 196–7
  airport [ĕr/pört/] 151–10
portable [pör/tə bəl]
  portable cassette player
    [pör/tə bəl kə sĕt/ plā/ər] 234–6
  portable DVD player
    [pör/tə bəl dē/vē/dē/ plā/ər] 234–11
  portable TV [pör/tə bəl tē/ vē/] 234–8
positive integers [pö/zə tĭv ĭn/tə jərz] 192–2
post [pōst] 134–6
  post card [pōst/kärd/] 134–16
  postmark [pōst/märk/] 134–24
  post office [pōst/ ö/fəs] 125–11
  post office box (PO box) [pōst/ ö/fəs bäks/] /
    [pē/ō bäks/] 135 ✦
postage [pō/stĭj] 135 ✦

postal [pō/stəl] 135–10
  postal clerk [pō/stəl klürk/] 135–7
  postal forms [pō/stəl förmz/] 134–19
  postal scale [pō/stəl skāl/] 183–27
  postal worker [pō/stəl wür/kər] 169–49
POST OFFICE [pōst/ ö/fəs] 134–135
pot [pät] 54–16, 78–6
  pot holders [pät hōl/dərz] 78–29
  teapot [tē/pät/] 55–16
potatoes [pə tā/tōz] 69–17
  baked potato [bākt/ pə tā/tō] 81–25
  mashed potatoes [măsht/ pə tā/tōz] 81–23
  potato chips [pə tā/tō chĭps/] 73–35
  potato salad [pə tā/tō săl/əd] 80–19
  sweet potatoes [swēt/ pə tā/tōz] 69–18
potty seat [pät/ē sēt/] 37–12
pouch [powch] 217–50
Poultry [pōl/trē] 70, 76
POULTRY [pōl/trē] 70
pound [pownd] 75–12
  pound key [pownd/ kē/] 14–7
pour [pör] 82–C
powder [pow/dər] 37–14, 108–4, 109–41
power [pow/ər] 218–2, 218–5
  power cord [pow/ər körd/] 196–2
  power outlet [pow/ər owt/lĕt] 159–42
  power sander [pow/ər săn/dər] 180–11
pox [pöks] 111–6
practical [prăk/tə kəl] 120–11
prairie dog [prĕr/ē dög/] 215–22
praise [prāz] 36–J
pregnant [prĕg/nənt] 32–15
preheat [prē/hēt/] 77–A
preparation [prĕ/pə rā/shən] 185–4
PREPARATION [prĕ/pə rā/shən] 76–77
prepare [prĭ/pĕr/] 174–A
PREPOSITIONS [prĕp/ə zĭsh/ənz] 25
PREPOSITIONS OF MOTION
    [prĕp/ə zĭsh/ənz əv mō/shən] 153
preschool [prē/skōōl/] 188–1
prescribe medication [prĭ skrīb/mĕd/ə kā/shən] 112 ✦
prescription [prĭ skrĭp/shən] 112–2
  pick up a prescription
    [pĭk/ ŭp/ə prĭ skrĭp/shən] 112 ✦
  prescription label [prĭ skrĭp/shən lā/bəl] 112–4
  prescription medication
    [prĭ skrĭp/shən mĕd/ə kā/shən] 112–3
  prescription number [prĭ skrĭp/shən nŭm/bər]
    112–5
present [prĕz/ənt] 94 ✦, 240–3
presentation [prĕ/zən tā/shən] 182–6
president [prĕz/ə dənt] 138–8, 199–5
  first president [fürst/ prĕz/ə dənt] 198–11
  Presidents' Day [prĕz/ə dənts dā/] 22–11
  vice president [vis/ prĕz/ə dənt] 138–9
press [prĕs] 78–11, 140–4
press [prĕs] 15–B, 15–D
presser foot [prĕs/ər fōōt/] 98–19
pressure [prĕsh/ər] 111–14, 118–9
pretend [prĭ tĕnd/] 233–G
Prewriting [prē/ri/tĭng] 191

Index

price [prīs] **27**–2, **27**–3, **27**–7
    price tag [prīs tăg/] **27**–1
prime minister [prīm/ mĭn/ə stər] **199**–7
principal [prĭn/sə pəl] **5**–4
print [prĭnt] **96**–23
    fingerprint [fĭng/gər prĭnt/] **136**–5
print [prĭnt] **4**–C, **171**–I
printer [prĭn/tər] **169**–50, **196**–17
    inkjet printer [ĭnk/jĕt prĭn/tər] **183**–18
    laser printer [lā/zər prĭn/tər] **183**–19
Priority Mail® [prī ör/ə tē māl/, –är/–] **134**–1
prism [prĭz/əm] **195**–35
prisoner [prĭz/nər] **141**–15
private school [prī/vət skool/] **5** ✦
Problem [präb/ləm] **192**
problems [präb/ləmz] **115**–1, **192**–11
Problems [präb/ləmz] **115**, **119**
PROBLEMS [präb/ləmz] **62**–**63**
Procedures [prə sē/jərz] **117**, **118**
PROCEDURES [prə sē/jərz] **146**–**147**
Process [prä/sĕs] **191**
processor [prä/sĕ sər] **54**–26
Processor [prä/sĕ sər] **92**
produce section [prō/doos sĕk/shən] **72**–2
product [präd/ŭkt] **192**–9
Products [präd/ŭkts] **72**, **73**
program [prō/grăm]
    children's program [chĭl/drənz prō/grăm] **236**–9
    nature program [nā/chər prō/grăm] **236**–7
    news program [nooz/ prō/grăm] **236**–1
    shopping program [shäp/ĭng prō/grăm] **236**–10
    sports program [spörtz/ prō/grăm] **236**–11
program [prō/grăm] **170**–I
Programs [prō/grămz] **236**
projector [prə jĕk/tər] **6**–6, **7**–16, **235**–29
promotion [prə mō/shən] **172**–4
proof of insurance [proof/ əv/ĭn shoor/əns] **136**–8
proofread [proof/rĕd/] **191**–I
prosecuting attorney
    [präs/ĭ kyoo/tĭng ə tür/nē] **141**–10
protect [prə tĕkt/] **143**–D
protector [prə tĕk/tər] **196**–1
proton [prō/tön] **195**–31
proud [prowd] **43**–21
prunes [proonz] **68**–26
pruning shears [proo/nĭng shĭrz/] **176**–11
psychiatrist [sī kī/ə trĭst, sə–] **120**–8
PUBLIC SAFETY [pŭb/lĭk sāf/tē] **143**
public school [pŭb/lĭk skool/] **5** ✦
PUBLIC TRANSPORTATION
    [pŭb/lĭk trăns/pər tā/shən] **152**
pull [pool] **119**–F, **224**–A
puller [pool/ər] **175**–10
pullover sweater [pool/ō/vər swĕt/ər] **88**–3
pulse [pŭls] **122**–A
pumps [pŭmps] **95**–26
Punctuation [pŭngk/choo ā/shən] **190**
puppy [pŭp/ē] **215**–12
purchase [pür/chəs] **94**–A
purifier [pyoor/ə fī/ ər] **113**–13
purple [pür/pəl] **24**–6
purses [pür/səz] **94**–2, **94**–14

push [poosh] **224**–B
pushpin [poosh/pĭn/] **183**–35
put [poot] **9**–X
put away
    [poot/ə wā/] **9**–Z, **60**–G
    put down [poot/ down/] **6**–J
    put in coolant [poot/ ĭn koo/lənt] **157**–I
    put on [poot/ än/, –ön/] **87**–B, **108**–D, **109**–P, **135**–C
    put on hold [poot/ än hōld/, –ön] **171**–N
    put the utilities in your name
        [poot/ dhe yoo tĭl/ə tēz ĭn yər nām/] **49**–O
puzzle [pŭz/əl] **59**–17
pyramid [pĭr/ə mĭd] **193**–39
quad [kwäd] **5**–1
quart [kwört] **75**–4
quarter [kwör/tər] **26**–4
    quarter after one [kwör/tər ăf/tər wŭn/] **18**–9
    1/4 cup [kwör/tər kŭp/] **75**–8
    quarter moon [kwör/tər moon/] **205**–11
    quarter to two [kwör/tər tə too/] **18**–13
    3/4 sleeved [thrē/ kwör/tər slēvd/] **96**–13
question mark [kwĕs/chən märk/] **190**–12
Quick and Easy Cake [kwĭk/ ən ē/zē kāk/] **77**
quiet [kwī/ət] **23**–12
quill [kwĭl] **216**–23
quilt [kwĭlt] **58**–16
    quilt block [kwĭlt/ bläk/] **232**–15
quilt [kwĭlt] **232**–C
quotation [kwōt tā/shən] **190**–9
    quotation marks [kwō tā/shən märks/] **190**–15
quotient [kwō /shənt] **192**–10
rabbit [răb/ət] **215**–13
raccoon [ră koon/] **216**–13
race [rās] **230**–S
racing [rā/sĭng] **228**–19
rack [răk] **98**–16
    dish rack [dĭsh/ răk/] **54**–5
    roasting rack [rō/stĭng răk/] **78**–14
    towel rack [tow/əl răk/] **57**–13
racket [răk/ət] **231**–2
racquetball [răk/ət böl/] **228**–12
radiation [rā/dē ā/shən] **218**–15
radiator [rā/dē ā/tər] **158**–19
radio [rā/dē ō] **102**–6, **159**–37, **179**–22
radioactive materials
    [rā/dē ō ăk/tĭv mə tïr/ē əlz] **179**–7
radiologist [rā/dē äl/ə jĭst] **120**–6
radishes [răd/ĭ shəz] **69**–4
radius [rā/dē əs] **193**–35
rafting [răf/tĭng] **226**–2
rags [răgz] **61**–9
rail [rāl] **59**–10
railroad crossing [rāl/rōd krö/sĭng] **154**–14
rain [rān] **218**–13
    rain boots [rān/ boots/] **90**–20
    raincoat [rān/kōt/] **90**–18
    rain forest [rān/ för/əst, fär/–] **204**–1
raining [rā/nĭng] **13**–11
raise [rāz] **6**–A
raisins [rā/zənz] **68**–25
rake [rāk] **176**–8
rake [rāk] **176**–C

ranch [rănch] **52**–10
rancher [răn/chər] **177**–22
Ranch Hand [rănch hănd/] **92**
RANCHING [răn/chĭng] **177**
R&B [är/n bē/] **237**–28
range [rānj] **204**–15
ranger [răn/jər] **220**–2
rash [răsh] **110**–10
raspberries [răz/bĕr/ēz] **68**–15
rats [răts] **63**–27, **215**–17
rattle [răt/l] **37**–26
    rattlesnake [răt/l snāk/] **213**–38
raw [rö] **70**–24
ray [rā] **212**–11
razor [rā/zər] **109**–27
    razorblade [rā/zər blād/] **109**–28
reaction [rē/ăk shən] **116**–E
read [rēd]
    proofread [proof/rĕd/] **191**–I
    read the card [rĕd/ dhe kärd/] **135**–G
    read the definition [rĕd/ dhe dĕ/fə nĭ/shən] **8**–B
    read the paper [rĕd/ dhe pā/pər] **39**–V
    read to [rĕd/ too/] **36**–N
Reading a Phone Bill [rē/dĭng ə fōn/ bĭl/] **15**
reality show [rē ă lə tē shō/] **236**–6
rearview mirror [rïr/vyoo/ mïr/ər] **159**–35
receipt [rĭ sēt/] **27**–6
receive [rĭ sēv/] **135**–F
receiver [rĭ sē/vər] **14**–1
reception area [rĭ sĕp/shən ĕr/ē ə] **182**–15
receptionist [rĭ sĕp/shə nĭst] **118**–2, **164**–5, **169**–51, **182**–14
reclined seat [rĭ klīnd/ sēt/] **161**–27
record [rĭ körd/] **195**–D, **235**–A
records [rĕk/ərdz] **168**–39
RECREATION [rĕk/rē ā/shən] **226**
recreational vehicle (RV)
    [rĕk/rē ā/shən əl vē/ə kəl] / [är/vē/] **156**–10
Recreation Room [rĕk/rē ā/shən room/] **50**
recruiter [rə kroo/tər] **172**–14
rectangle [rĕk/tăng/gəl] **193**–29
recycle [rē sī/kəl] **60**–B, **219**–C
recycling bin [rē sī/klĭng bĭn/] **61**–2
red [rĕd] **24**–1
    red hair [rĕd/ hër/] **33**–15
    redwood [rĕd/wood/] **210**–18
redecorate [rē dĕk/ə rāt/] **48** ✦
reduce [rĭ doos/] **219**–A
referee [rĕf/ə rē/] **229**–6
reference librarian [rĕf/rəns lī brër/ē ən] **133**–9
refrigerator [rĭ frĭj/ə rā/tər] **54**–9
refund [rē/fŭnd] **97** ✦
reggae [rĕ gā/] **237**–31
register [rĕj/ə stər] **73**–15
register [rĕj/ə stər] **140**–D, **157**–F
registered nurse (RN)
    [rĕj/ə stərd nürs/] / [är/ĕn/] **120**–10
registration [rĕj/ə strā/shən]
    registration sticker
        [rĕj/ə strā/shən stĭk/ər] **136**–13
    registration tag [rĕj/ə strā/shən tăg/] **136**–13
regular price [rĕg/yə lər prīs/] **27**–2

regulations [rĕ gyə lā/shənz] **164**–6
relatives [rĕ lə tĭvz] **44**–6
relax [rĭ lăks/] **39**–U
relieved [rĭ lēvd/] **42**–15
reliever [rĭ lēv/ər] **113**–26
religious holiday [rĭ lĭj/əs hăl/ə dā/] **22**–7
remain [rĕ/mān] **147**–E
remarried [rē măr/ēd] **35**–24
remote [rĭ mōt/] **234**–9
remove [rĭ mōōv/] **109**–Q, **132**–G
remover [rĭ mōō/vər] **109**–42
renew a license [rĭ nōō/ ə lī/səns, –nyōō/–] **136** ✦
rental agreement [rĕn/təl ə grē/mənt] **51**–28
Rental Office [rĕn/təl ö/fəs] **51**
Renting an Apartment [rĕn/tĭng ən ə pärt/mənt] **48**
repair [rĭ për/] **166**–4, **167**–24
   repair person [rĭ për/ pür/sən] **62**–10
repair [rĭ për/] **170**–J
REPAIRS [rĭ përz/] **62–63**
repellent [rĭ pĕl/ənt] **226**–23
replace [rĭ plās/] **157**–K
report [rĭ pört/] **143**–J, **143**–K
reporter [rĭ pör/tər] **169**–52
representative [rĕ/prĭ zĕn/tə tĭv] **138**–3, **167**–20
Reptiles [rĕp/tīlz] **213**
REPTILES [rĕp/tīlz] **212–213**
request [rĭ kwĕst/] **12** ✦
Requirements [rĭ kwīr/mənts] **140**
rescue [rĕs/kyōō] **145**–20
   rescue breathing [rĕs/kyōō brē/dhĭng] **117**–16
Resident Alien card [rĕz/ə dənt ā/lē ən kärd/] **40**–2
resource center [rē/sörs sĕn/tər] **172**–9
Resources [rē/sörs/səz, rĭ sör/səz] **219**
respirator [rĕs/pə rā/tər] **179**–13
Responding [rĭ spän/dĭng] **191**
Responsibilities [rĭ spän/sə bĭl/ə tēz] **140**
RESPONSIBILITIES [rĭ spän/sə bĭl/ə tēz] **140**
restaurant [rĕs/tə rənt, –ränt/] **125**–14, **128**–10
RESTAURANT [rĕs/tə rənt, –ränt/] **79, 82–83**
Restaurant Dining [rĕs/tə rənt dī/nĭng, –ränt/] **185**
Restaurant Kitchen [rĕs/tə rənt kĭ/chən, –ränt/] **185**
restrooms [rĕst/ rōōmz/] **5**–10
results [rĭ zŭltz/] **139**–31
resuscitation [rĭ sə sə tā/shən] **117**–17
retail clerk [rē/tāl/ klürk/] **169**–53
retire [rĭ tīr/] **41**–O
return [rĭtürn/] **73**–16
   return address [rĭ türn/ ə drĕs/, –ă/drĕs] **134**–21
return [rĭ türn/] **27**–H, **133**–D
REUNION [rē yōōn/yən] **44–45**
reuse [rē yōōz/] **219**–B
revise [rĭ vīz/] **191**–J
Revising [rĭ vī/zĭng] **191**
Revolutionary War [rĕ/və lōō/shə nër ē wör/] **198**–8
revolving [rĭ väl/vĭng]
   revolving door [rĭ väl/vĭng dör/] **184**–2
   revolving nosepiece [rĭ väl/vĭng nōz/pēs/] **194**–17
rewind [rē wīnd/] **235**–C
rewrite [rē rīt/] **191**–J
rhinoceros [rĭ näs/ər əs] **217**–28
ribbon [rĭ/bən] **99**–30

ribs [rĭbz] **70**–5, **76**–2
   rib cage [rĭb/ kāj/] **107**–48
rice [rīs] **67**–10, **81**–30, **177**–1
ride [rīd] **129**–D
rider [rī/dər] **152**–3
riding [rī/dĭng] **226**–9
right [rīt] **25**–3, **155**–B, **198**–10
   right angle [rīt/ ăng/gəl] **193**–26
   right turn only [rīt/ türn/ ōn/lē] **154**–7
Rights [rīts] **140**
RIGHTS AND RESPONSIBILITIES
   [rīts/ ən rĭ spän/sə bĭl/ə tēz] **140**
ring [rĭng] **37**–25, **79**–4, **95**–40
   clip-on earrings [klĭp/än ïr/ĭngz, –ön–] **95**–37
   pierced earrings [pïrst/ ïr/ĭngz] **95**–36
rinse [rĭns] **108**–F
ripe [rīp] **68**–30
ripped [rĭpt] **97**–41
ripper [rĭ/pər] **100**–18
rise [rīz] **127**–13
   sunrise [sŭn/rīz/] **18**–14
river [rĭv/ər] **155**–10, **204**–3
RN (registered nurse) [är/ĕn/] / [rĕj/ə stərd nürs/]
   120–10
road work [rōd/ würk/] **154**–16
Road Worker [rōd/ wür/kər] **92**
roast [rōst] **70**–1
   roast beef [rōst bēf/] **71**–21
   roast chicken [rōst chĭk/ən] **81**–22
   roasted turkey [rō/stəd tür/kē] **76**–4
   roasting pan [rō/stĭng păn/] **78**–13
   roasting rack [rō/stĭng răk/] **78**–14
robe [rōb] **91**–29
robin [räb/ən] **214**–16
rock [räk] **36**–D
rock concert [räk/ kän/sərt] **222**–5
rocking chair [räk/ĭng chër/] **37**–21
rocks [räks] **208**–6, **237**–23
Rodents [rōd/nts] **215**
RODENTS [rōd/nts] **215**
rollers [rō/lərz] **33**–19, **181**–23
rolling pin [rō/lĭng pĭn/] **78**–30
rolls [rōlz] **74**–11, **74**–23, **80**–17
romance [rō măns/, rō/măns] **237**–16
Roman Numerals [rō/mən nōō/mər əlz] **16**
roof [rōōf] **46**–1
roof garden [rōōf/ gär/dn] **50**–4
roofer [rōō/fər] **62**–8
room [rōōm]
   baby's room [bā/bēz rōōm/] **47**–10
   ballroom [böl/ rōōm/] **184**–26
   banquet room [băn/kwət rōōm/] **185**–14
   bathroom [băth/rōōm/] **46**–4
   bedroom [bĕd/rōōm/] **46**–2
   conference room [kän/frəns rōōm/] **182**–4
   dining room [dī/nĭng rōōm/] **82**–1
   dining room chair [dī/nĭng rōōm/ chër/] **55**–8
   dining room table [dī/nĭng rōōm/ tā/bəl] **55**–9
   dish room [dĭsh/ rōōm/] **83**–13
   guest room [gĕst/ rōōm/] **184**–13
   kids' bedroom [kĭdz/ bĕd/rōōm/] **47**–9

living room [lĭv/ĭng rōōm/] **47**–12
meeting room [mē/tĭng rōōm/] **184**–25
roommates [rōōm/māts/] **64**–1
room service [rōōm/ sür/vəs] **184**–17
storeroom [stör/rōōm/] **185**–5
Room [rōōm] **50, 118, 121**
ROOM [rōōm] **56**
rooster [rōō/stər] **215**–7
roots [rōōts] **210**–5, **211**–3
rope [rōp] **224**–4, **226**–19
rose [rōz] **211**–15
rotary [rō/tə rē]
   rotary card file [rō/tə rē kärd/ fīl/] **183**–44
   rotary cutter [rō/tə rē kŭt/ər] **232**–16
rotten [rät/n] **68**–32
round trip [rownd/ trĭp/] **152**–17
route [rōōt] / [rowt]
   bus route [bŭs/ rōōt, –rowt] **152**–1
   escape route [ĕs/kāp rōōt, –rowt] **146**–3
   evacuation route
      [ĭ văk/yōō/ā shən rōōt, –rowt] **146**–5
   U.S. route [yōō/ĕs/ rōōt, –rowt] **154**–17
router [row/tər] **180**–12
ROUTINES [rōō tēnz/] **38–39**
rubber [rŭb/ər]
   rubber band [rŭb/ər bănd/] **183**–34
   rubber gloves [rŭb/ər glŭvz/] **61**–4
   rubber mat [rŭb/ər măt/] **57**–3
ruffle [rŭ/fəl] **58**–17
rug [rŭg] **58**–22
ruler [rōō/lər] **17**–13
rules [rōōlz] **64**–8
Rules [rōōlz] **190**
run [rŭn] **11**–D
   run across [rŭn/ə krös/] **153**–G
   run around [rŭn/ə rownd/] **153**–H
   run for office [rŭn/ fər ö/fəs] **139**–A
   run out [rŭn/owt/] **162**–E
runner [rŭ/nər] **185**–15
rural area [rōor/əl ër/ē ə] **52**–4
RV (recreational vehicle)
   [är/vē/] / [rĕk/rē ā/shən əl vē/ə kəl] **156**–10
rye bread [rī/ brĕd/] **71**–20
sad [săd] **43**–19
safety [sāf/tē] **37**–19, **92**–4, **159**–53
   safety boots [sāf/tē bōōts/] **179**–20
   safety deposit box [sāf/tē dĭ päz/ət bäks/] **132**–7
   safety glasses [sāf/tē glăs/əz] **92**–10, **179**–10
   safety goggles [sāf/tē gäg/əlz] **179**–11
   safety pin [sāf/tē pĭn/] **37**–9, **100**–14
   safety rail [sāf/tē rāl/] **59**–10
   safety regulations [sāf/tē rĕ/gyə lā/shənz] **164**–6
   safety visor [sāf/tē vī/zər] **179**–12
Safety [sāf/tē] **76**
SAFETY [sāf/tē] **76–77, 143, 179**
Safety Equipment [sāf/tē ĭ kwĭp/mənt] **179**
Safety Hazards and Hazardous Materials
   [sāf/tē hăz/ərdz ən hăz/ər dəs-mə tïr/ē əlz] **179**
sailboat [sāl/bōt/] **225**–3
sailing [sā/lĭng] **227**–8

salad [săl/əd]
   chef's salad [shĕfs/ săl/əd] **80**–14
   dinner salad [dĭn/ər săl/əd] **80**–15
   fruit salad [frōōt/ săl/əd] **80**–21
   pasta salad [päs/tə săl/əd] **80**–20
   potato salad [pə tā/tō săl/əd] **80**–19
   salad bar [săl/əd bär/] **79**–24
   salad fork [săl/əd förk/] **83**–27
   salad plate [săl/əd plāt/] **83**–20
   spinach salad [spĭ/nĭch săl/əd] **80**–13
Salad Dressings [săl/əd drĕ/sĭngz] **80**
Salads [săl/ədz] **80**
salamander [săl/ə măn/dər] **212**–27
salami [sə lä/mē] **71**–24
SALE [sāl] **102**–**103**
sales [sālz]
   sale price [sāl/ prīs/] **27**–3
   salesclerk [sālz/klürk/] **94**–3
   sales tax [sālz/ tăks/] **27**–8
Salesperson [sālz/pür/sən] **92**
salmon [săm/ən] **71**–3
   salmon steak [săm/ən stāk/] **71**–4
salon [sə lön/] **130**–3, **131**–18
salt and pepper shakers
   [sölt/ n pĕp/ər shā/kərz] **55**–13
same [sām] **23**–15
SAME AND DIFFERENT
   [sām/ ən dĭ/frənt, –dĭ fə rənt] **28**–**29**
samples [săm/pəlz] **84**–5
sand [sănd] **225**–23
   sandbox [sănd/bäks/] **224**–15
   sand castle [sănd kăs/əl] **225**–12
   sand dune [sănd dōōn/] **204**–5
   sandpaper [sănd/pā/pər] **181**–56
sandals [săn/dlz] **88**–9
sander [săn/dər] **180**–11
sandwich [săn/wĭch, –sănd/–] **79**–5, **80**–10, **80**–12
sanitation worker [săn/ə tā/shən wür/kər] **169**–54
satellite [săt/əl ĭt/] **205**–20
   satellite dish [săt/əl lĭt/ dĭsh/] **53**–6
satisfied [săt/ĭs fīd/] **42**–6
Saturday [săt/ər dā/, –dē] **20**–14
Saturn [săt/ərn] **205**–6
saucepan [sös/păn/] **78**–25
saucer [sö/sər] **83**–25
sausage [sö/sĭj] **70**–12, **80**–2
sauté [sö tā/, sö –] **77**–E
save [sāv] **219**–E
saving [sā/vĭng] **19**–25, **225**–20
savings account number
   [sā/vĭngz ə kownt/ nŭm/bər] **132**–11
saw [sö] **180**–9
   hacksaw [hăk/sö/] **180**–5
   jigsaw [jĭg/sö/] **180**–10
saxophone [săk/sə fōn/] **238**–5
say [sā] **2**–A, **3**–L, **4**–A
scaffolding [skăf/əl dĭng] **178**–4
scales [skālz] **57**–27, **72**–3, **135**–8, **155**–7, **195**–41, **212**–3
   postal scale [pō/stəl skāl/] **183**–27
scallions [skăl/yənz] **69**–20
scallops [skăl/əps, skäl/–] **71**–12, **212**–19

scan [skăn] **171**–H
scanner [skăn/ər] **183**–20
scared [skĕrd] **43**–23
scarf / scarves [skärf] / [skärvz] **95**–12
   winter scarf [wĭn/tər skärf/] **90**–5
scenery [sē/ nə rē/ / sēn/rē] **162**–3
schedule [skĕj/ōōl, –ōō əl] **152**–4
schedule [skĕj/ōōl, –ōō əl] **171**–J
school [skōōl] **126**–9
   adult school [[ə dŭlt/–, ăd/ŭlt skōōl/] **188**–8
   elementary school [ĕl/ə mĕn/trē skōōl/] **188**–2
   high school [hī skōōl/] **188**–4
   junior high school [jōōn/yər hī/ skōōl/] **188**–3
   middle school [mĭd/l skōōl/] **188**–3
   nursery school [nür/sə rē skōōl/] **188**–1
   parochial school [pə rō/kē əl skōōl/] **5** ✦
   preschool [prē/skōōl] **188**–1
   private school [prī/vət skōōl/] **5** ✦
   public school [pŭb/lĭk skōōl/] **5** ✦
   school bus [skōōl/ bŭs/] **156**–21
   school crossing [skōōl/ krö/sĭng] **154**–15
   technical school [tĕk/nĭ kəl skōōl/] **188**–5
   vocational school [vō kā/shə nəl skōōl/] **188**–5
SCHOOL [skōōl] **5, 10, 11**
School Registration Form
   [skōōl/ rĕj/ə strā/shən förm/] **4**
SCHOOLS AND SUBJECTS
   [sklōōz ən sŭb/jĭkts] **188**–**189**
science [sī/əns] **189**–11
SCIENCE [sī/əns] **194**–**195**
Science Lab [sī/əns lăb/] **195**
scissors [sĭz/ərz] **33**–20, **100**–16
scoop neck [skōōp/ nĕk/] **96**–10
score [skör] **10**–3, **229**–1
scorpion [skör/pē ən] **214**–30
scrambled eggs [skrăm/bəld ĕgz/] **76**–7
scraper [skrā/pər] **181**–52
screen [skrēn] **6**–2, **196**–11, **235**–30
   big-screen TV [bĭg/skrēn/ tē/ vē/] **50**–15
   fire screen [fīr/ skrēn/] **56**–12
   flat screen TV [flăt/ skrēn/ tē/vē/] **234**–7
   screen door [skrēn/ dör/] **53**–15
   sunscreen [sŭn/skrēn/] **108**–7, **225**–10
screener [skrēn/ər] **160**–5
screening area [skrē/nĭng ër/ē ə] **160**–4
screw [skrōō] **180**–32, **180**–33
   Phillips screwdriver [fĭl/ĭps skrōō/drī/vər] **180**–31
   screwdriver [skrōō/drī/vər] **180**–30
scroll bar [skrōl/bär/] **197**–15
scrub [skrŭb] **60**–K
scrubs [skrŭbz] **93**–31
   scrub brush [skrŭb/ brŭsh/] **61**–20
   surgical scrub cap [sür/jĭ kəl skrŭb/ kăp/] **93**–35
   surgical scrubs [sür/jĭ kəl skrŭbz/] **93**–38
scuba [skōō/bə]
   scuba diving [skōō/bə dī/vĭng] **227**–12
   scuba tank [skōō/bə tăngk/] **225**–5
sea [sē]
   sea anemone [sē/ ə nĕm/ə nē] **212**–24
   seahorse [sē/ hörs/] **212**–13
   sea lion [sē/ lī/ən] **213**–33
   sea otter [sē/ ät/ər] **213**–35

seashell [sē/ shĕl/] **225**–24
sea urchin [sē/ ür/chən] **212**–21
seaweed [sē/ wēd/] **225** ✦
Sea Animals [sē/ ăn/ə məlz] **212**
SEAFOOD AND DELI [sē/fōōd/ ən dĕ/lī] **71**
seal [sēl] **213**–34
Sea Mammals [sē/ măm/əlz] **213**
seam ripper [sēm/ rĭp/ər] **100**–18
search [sürch]
   search and rescue team
     [sürch/ ən rĕs/kyōō tēm/] **145**–20
   search box [sürch/ bäks/] **197**–5
   search engine [sürch/ ĕn/jən] **197**–6
SEARCH [sürch] **173**
SEASONAL CLOTHING [sē/zə nəl klō/dhĭng] **90**
Seasons [sē/zənz] **21**
seat [sēt]
   backseat [băk/ sēt/] **159**–54
   car safety seat [kär/ sāf/tē sēt/] **37**–19
   child safety seat [chīld/ săf/tē sēt/] **159**–53
   front seat [frŭnt/ sēt/] **159**–51
   love seat [lŭv/ sēt/] **56**–1
   potty seat [pät/ē sēt/] **37**–12
   reclined seat [rĭ klīnd/ sēt/] **161**–27
   seat belt [sēt/ bĕlt/] **159**–52
   upright seat [ŭp/rīt/ sēt/] **161**–28
seat [sēt] **82**–B
second [sĕk/ənd] **16**
Second Floor [sĕk/ənd flör/] **50**
seconds [sĕk/əndz] **18**–3
section [sĕk/shən] **72**–2
security [sĭ kyōōr/ə tē]
   security camera [sĭ kyōōr/ə tē kăm/rə] **50**–19
   security gate [sĭ kyōōr/ə tē gāt/] **50**–16
   security guard [sĭ kyōōr/ə tē gärd/] **132**–5, **169**–55
   security pants [sĭ kyōōr/ə tē pănts/] **93**–22
   security screener [sĭ kyōōr/ə tē skrē/nər] **160**–5
   security shirt [sĭ kyōōr/ə tē shürt] **93**–20
Security Checkpoint [sĭ kyōōr/ə tē chĕk/poynt/] **160**
Security Guard [sĭ kyōōr/ə tē gärd/] **93**
sedan [sə dăn/] **156**–1
see [sē] **106**–A
seed [sēd] **211**–1
   seedling [sēd/lĭng] **211**–4
seek [sēk] **114**–A, **147**–H
seesaw [sē/sö/] **224**–16
select [sə lĕkt/] **196**–B
self-checkout [sĕlf/ chĕk/owt/] **73**–10, **133**–10
sell [sĕl] **170**–K
semi [sĕm/ī] **156**–15
semicolon [sĕm/ē kō/lən] **190**–18
Senate [sĕn/ət] **138**–5
senator [sĕn/ə tər] **138**–6
   state senator [stāt/ sĕn/ə tər] **139**–25
send [sĕnd] **197**–I
   send in [sĕnd/ ĭn] **173**–H
Sending a Card [sĕn/dĭng ə kärd/] **135**
Sending Email [sĕn/dĭng ē/māl/] **197**
senior [sēn/yər]
   senior citizen [sēn/yər sĭt/ə zən] **30**–5
   senior housing [sēn/yər howz/ĭng] **52**–11
Senses [sĕn/səz] **106**

sentence [sĕn′tns] **190**–2
sentence [sĕn′tns] **141**–E
separate [sĕ′pə rāt′] **76**–B
September [sĕp tĕm′bər] **21**–33
sequins [sē′kwĭnz′] **99**–33
Serious Medical Conditions
   [sïr′ē əs mĕd′ĭ kəl dĭsh′ənz] **111**
serious photo [sïr′ē əs fō′tō] **206**–3
serve [sürv] **139**–D, **230**–P
   serve on a jury [sürv′ än ə jŏŏr′ē, –ön–] **140**–E
   serve the meal [sürv′ dhə mēl′] **82**–F
Serve [sürv] **76**
server [sür′vər] **82**–8, **83**–9, **169**–56, **185**–8
service [sür′vəs]
   customer service [kŭs′tə mər sür′vəs] **97** ✦
   customer service representative
      [kŭs′tə mər-sür′vəs rĕ′prə zĕn′tə tĭv] **167**–20
   guest services [gĕst′ sür′vəs əz] **130**–12
   pool service [pōōl′ sür′vəs] **184**–21
   room service [rōōm′ sür′vəs] **184**–17
SERVICE [sür′vəs] **138**–**139**, **185**
serving bowl [sür′vĭng bōl′] **55**–21
set [sĕt] **10**–A, **33**–C, **82**–A
   set up [sĕt′ ŭp′] **173**–I
   sunset [sŭn′sĕt′] **18**–18
setting [sĕ′tĭng] **83**–17
seven [sĕv′ən] **16**
seventeen [sĕv′ən tēn′] **16**
seventeenth [sĕv′ən tēnth′] **16**
seventh [sĕv′ənth] **16**
seventieth [sĕv′ən tē əth] **16**
seventy [sĕv′ən tē] **16**
   75 percent [sĕv′ən tē fīv′ pər sĕnt′] **17**–9
sew [sō] **98**–A, **98**–B, **170**–L
sewing [sō′ĭng]
   sewing machine [sō′ĭng mə shēn′] **98**–13
   sewing machine operator
      [sō′ĭng mə shēn′ äp′ə rā′ tər] **98**–14
Sewing Machine [sō′ĭng mə shēn′] **98**
Sewing Supplies [sō′ĭng sə plīz′] **100**
sex [sĕks] **4**–16
shade [shād] **225**–13
   lampshade [lămp′shād′] **56** ✦, **58**–26
shadow [shă′dō′] **109**–35
shake [shāk]
   milkshake [mĭlk′shāk′] **79**–14
shake [shāk] **3**–J, **174**–I
shakers [shā′kərz] **55**–13
shampoo [shăm pōō′] **108**–10
shanks [shănks] **70**–13
shaper [shā′pər] **91**–15
Shapes [shāps] **193**
share [shĕr] **8**–M
Sharing and Responding
   [shĕr′ĭng ən rĭ spän′dĭng] **191**
shark [shärk] **212**–4
sharpener [shär′pən ər] **183**–26
shave [shāv]
   aftershave [ăf′tər shāv′] **109**–30
shave [shāv] **109**–M
shaver [shā′vər] **109**–26
shaving cream [shā′vĭng krēm′] **109**–29

shears [shïrz] **176**–9
sheep [shēp] **215**–6
sheet [shēt]
   cookie sheet [kŏŏk′ē shēt′] **78**–27
   dryer sheets [drī′ər shēts′] **101**–5
   fitted sheet [fĭt′əd shēt′] **58**–12
   flat sheet [flăt′ shēt′] **58**–13
shelf [shĕlf] **54**–2
shell [shĕl]
   seashell [sē′shĕl′] **225**–24
Shellfish [shĕl′fĭsh′] **71**
shelter [shĕl′tər] **52**–13
shield [shēld]
   windshield [wĭnd′shēld′] **158**–1
   windshield wipers [wĭnd′shēld wī′pərz] **158**–2
shift [shĭft] **159**–49, **159**–50
shin [shĭn] **106**–21
   shin guards [shĭn′ gärdz′] **231**–13
shingles [shĭng′gəlz] **178**–20
ship [shĭp] **175**–D
shipping clerk [shĭp′ĭng klürk′] **175**–14
shirt [shürt] **86**–1
   nightshirt [nīt′shürt′] **91**–28
   polo shirt [pō′lō shürt′] **92**–14
   security shirt [sĭ kyŏŏr′ə tē shürt′] **93**–20
   sports shirt [spörts′ shürt′] **88**–4
   T-shirt [tē′shürt′] **86**–4
   work shirt [würk′ shürt′] **92**–2
shock [shäk] **116**–B, **116**–F
shoes [shōōz] **86**–7, **87**–13, **95**–32
   shoe department [shōō′ dĭ pärt′mənt] **95**–7
   shoelaces [shōō′lās əz] **94**–24
   shoe store [shōō′ stör′] **130**–10
SHOES AND ACCESSORIES
   [shōōz′ ən ĭk sĕs′ə rēz] **94**–**95**
shoot [shōōt] **211**–5
shoot [shōōt] **230**–H
shop [shäp]
   barbershop [bär′bər shäp′] **129**–19
   beauty shop [byōō′tē shäp′] **130** ✦
   coffee shop [kö′fē shäp′] **126**–11
   donut shop [dō′nŭt shäp′] **129**–17
   gift shop [gĭft′ shäp′] **130** ✦, **184**–5
   ice cream shop [īs′ krēm shäp′] **131**–16
shop [shäp] **28**–A, **143**–H
Shop [shäp] **100**
SHOP [shäp] **80**–**81**
shoplifting [shäp′lĭf′tĭng] **142**–8
shopping [shäp′ĭng]
   shopping basket [shäp′ĭng băs′kət] **73**–9
   shopping list [shäp′ĭng lĭst′] **67**–14
   shopping mall [shäp′ĭng mäl′] **126**–7
   shopping program [shäp′ĭng mäl′] **236**–10
SHOPPING [shäp′ĭng] **27**
shore [shör] **204**–12
short [shört] **32**–6, **96**–16
   short hair [shört′ hĕr′] **33**–1
   short-order cook [shört′ör′dər kŏŏk′] **185**–1
   short-sleeved [shört′slēvd′] **96**–12
shorten [shört′ən] **100**–B
shorts [shörts] **89**–25, **91**–4

shoulder [shōl′dər] **105**–13
   shoulder bag [shōl′dər băg′] **94**–17
   shoulder blade [shōl′dər blād′] **107**–28
   shoulder-length hair [shōl′dər lĕngkth′ hĕr′] **33**–2
   shoulder pads [shōl′dər pădz′] **231**–20
shovel [shŭv′əl] **176**–7, **178**–22
show [shō] **236**–4, **236**–6, **236**–8
show [shō] **137**–C, **160**–C
shower [show′ər]
   shower cap [show′ər kăp′] **108**–1
   shower curtain [show′ər kür′tn] **57**–12
   shower gel [show′ər jĕl′] **108**–2
   showerhead [show′ər hĕd′] **57**–11
   stall shower [stöl′ show′ər] **57** ✦
shredder [shrĕ′dər] **183**–24
shrimp [shrĭmp] **71**–11, **212**–18
shut [shŭt] **146**–4
shuttle [shŭt′l] **152**–19, **205**–19
sick [sĭk] **42**–12
   homesick [hōm′sĭk′] **43**–20
side [sīd] **76**–10
   sideburns [sīd′bürnz′] **33**–7
   sideview mirror [sīd′vyōō′ mïr′ər] **158**–3
Side Salads [sīd′ săl′ədz] **80**
sidewalk [sīd′wök′] **129**–24
sight impaired [sīt′ ĭm pērd′] **32**–11
sign [sīn] **4**–D
   street sign [strēt′ sīn′] **129**–26
   vacancy sign [vā′kən sē sīn′] **50**–7
   vital signs monitor [vīt′l sīnz′ män′ə tər] **121**–26
sign [sīn] **48**–D
signal [sĭg′nəl]
   strong signal [ströng′ sĭg′nəl] **14**–11
   turn signal [türn′ sĭg′nəl] **158**–6, **159**–34
   weak signal [wēk′ sĭg′nəl] **14**–12
signature [sĭg′nə chər] **4**–19
SIGNS [sīnz] **154**
silk [sĭlk] **98**–5
simmer [sĭm′ər] **77**–P
sing [sĭng] **36**–O, **238**–B
single [sĭng′gəl]
   single father [sĭng′gəl fä′dhər] **35**–23
   single mother [sĭng′gəl mŭdh′ər] **35**–22
sink [sĭnk] **54**–4, **57**–23
Sirius [sïr′ē əs] **205** ✦
sister [sĭs′tər] **34**–5, **35**–27
   sister-in-law [sĭs′tər ĭn lö′] **34**–16
   stepsister [stĕp′sĭs′tər] **35**–29
sitcom (situation comedy)
   [sĭt′käm′] / [sĭch′ōō ā′shən käm′ə dē] **236**–2
sit down [sĭt′ down′] **6**–F
site [sīt] **126**–2
sitter [sĭt′ər] **166**–9
situation comedy (sitcom)
   [sĭch′ōō ā′shən käm′ə dē] / [sĭt′käm′] **236**–2
six [sĭks] **16**
   six-pack [sĭks′păk′] **74**–9, **74**–21
   6-year-old boy [sĭks′yïr öld′ boy′] **31**–9
sixteen [sĭks′tēn′] **16**
sixteenth [sĭks′tēnth′] **16**
sixth [sĭksth] **16**
sixtieth [sĭks′tē əth] **16**

Index

sixty [sĭks/tē] **16**
Sizes [sī/zəz] **96**
skate [skāt] **230**–U
skates [skāts] **231**–9, **231**–10
  skateboard [skāt/börd/] **224**–7
  skateboarding [skāt/bör/dĭng] **228**–13
skating [skā/tĭng] **227**–4, **227**–5, **227** ✦, **228**–10
ski [skē] **230**–V
skiing [skē/ĭng] **227**–1, **227**–3
  waterskiing [wö/tər skē/ĭng] **227**–7
skill inventory [skĭl/ ĭn/vən tör/ē] **172**–12
Skills [skĭlz] **171**
SKILLS [skĭlz] **170, 171, 174**
skin [skĭn] **107**–31
  skinless [skĭn/ləs] **70** ✦
skirt [skürt] **87**–10
skis [skēz] **231**–24
  ski boots [skē/ bōots] **231**–26
  ski hat [skē/ hăt/] **90**–11
  ski mask [skē/ măsk/] **90**–15
  ski poles [skē/ pölz/] **231**–25
skull [skŭl] **107**–47
skunk [skŭngk] **216**–12
SKU number [ĕs/kā/yōō/ nŭm/bər, skyōō/] **27**–5
sky [skī] **209**–9
  skycap [skē/kăp/] **160**–1
  skyscraper [skī/skrā/pər] **127**–13
slacks [slăks] **87**–12
slaves [slāvz] **198**–4
sledding [slĕd/ĭng] **227**–6
sledgehammer [slĕj/hăm/ər] **178**–23
sleeper [slē/pər] **91**–27
sleeping bag [slē/pĭng băg/] **226**–12
Sleepwear [slēp/wër] **91**
SLEEPWEAR [slēp/wër] **91**
sleepy [slē/pē] **42**–3
sleeve [slēv] **100**–6
  long-sleeved [löng/slēvd/] **96**–14
  short-sleeved [shört/slēvd/] **96**–12
  sleeveless [slēv/ləs] **96**–11
  3/4 sleeved [thrē/kwör/tər slēvd/] **96**–13
slender [slĕn/dər] **32**–9
slice [slīs] **77**–C
slide [slīd] **194**–3, **224**–13
  mudslide [mŭd/slīd/] **144**–6
sliding glass door [slī/dĭng glăs/ dör/] **53**–18
sling [slĭng] **113**–19
slip [slĭp] **91**–22, **91**–23, **132**–4
slippers [slĭp/ərz] **91**–26
slippery floor [slĭ/pər ē flör/] **179**–6
slow [slō] **23**–4
small [smöl] **96**–1, **96**–2, **97**–37
  small town [smöl/ town/] **52**–3
smart phone [smärt/ fōn/] **15**–27
smell [smĕl] **106**–C
smile [smīl] **2**–D
smock [smök] **93**–26
smog [smäg, smög] **218**–11
smoggy [smä/gē, smö/–] **13**–14
smoke [smōk] **114**–G
smoke detector [smōk/ dĭ tĕk/tər] **51**–29
smoked turkey [smōkt/ tür/kē] **71**–25

Snack Foods [snăk/ fōōdz/] **73**
snail [snāl] **212**–22
snake [snāk] **213**–39
  rattlesnake [ră/təl snāk] **213**–38
snap [snăp] **99**–26
sneeze [snēz] **110**–B
snorkeling [snör/kə lĭng] **227**–11
snow [snō]
  snowboard [snō/börd/] **231**–23
  snowboarding [snō/bör/dĭng] **227**–2
  snowstorm [snō/störm/] **13**–23
snowing [snō/ĭng] **13**–12
soap [sōp] **57**–24, **61**–5, **108**–3
  soap dish [sōp/ dĭsh/] **57**–25
  soap opera [sōp/ äp/rə] **236**–5
sober [sō/ bər] **143** ✦
soccer [säk/ər] **229**–12
  soccer ball [säk/ər böl/] **231**–12
social [sō/shəl]
  Social Security card
    [sō/shəl sĭ kyŏŏr/ə tē kärd/] **40**–5
  Social Security number
    [sō/shəl sĭ kyŏŏr/ə tē nŭm/bər] **4**–15
  social worker [sō/shəl wür/kər] **169**–57
socks [säks] **86**–6
  ankle socks [ang/kəl säks/] **91**–7
  crew socks [krōō/ säks/] **91**–8
  dress socks [drĕs/ säks/] **91**–9
  low-cut socks [lō/kŭt säks/] **91**–10
Socks [säks] **91**
soda [sō/də] **73**–34, **79**–11
sofa [sō/fə] **56**–18
  sofa cushions [sō/fə kŏŏ/shənz] **56** ✦
soft [söft] **23**–6
  softball [söft/böl/] **229**–10
softener [sö/fən ər] **101**–6
software [söft/wër/] **167**–18, **196**–10
soil [soyl] **208**–2
solar [sō/lər]
  solar eclipse [sō/lər ĭ klĭps/] **205**–16, **205** ✦
  solar energy [sō/lər ĕn/ər jē] **218**–1
Solar System and the Planets
  [sō/lər sĭs/təm ən dhə plăn/əts] **205**
soldier [sōl/jər] **169**–58
sole [sōl] **94**–21
solid [säl/əd] **96**–19
Solids [säl/ədz] **193**
solution [sə lōō/ shən] **192**–14
solve [sölv] **170**–M
son [sŭn] **34**–15
  grandson [grăn/sŭn/, grănd/–] **34** ✦
  son-in-law [sŭn/ĭn lö/] **34** ✦
sore throat [sör/ thrōt/] **110**–6
sort [sört] **101**–A
soul [sōl] **237**–28
soup [sōōp] **72**–18, **80**–16
  soup bowl [sōōp/ böl/] **83**–21
  soupspoon [sōōp/spōōn/] **83**–32
Soup [sōōp] **77**
sour [sow/ər] **84**–4
  sour cream [sow/ər krēm/] **72**–21
Sources [sör/səz] **218**

sous chef [sōō/ shĕf/] **185**–6
south [sowth] **155**–3
soybeans [soy/bēnz/] **177**–3
space [spās] **50**–18, **128**–5
  space shuttle [spās/ shŭt/əl] **205**–19
  space station [spās/ stā/shən] **205**–18
Space [spās] **205**
Space Exploration [spās/ ĕk/splə rā/shən] **205**
spades [spādz] **233**–30
spaghetti [spə gĕt/ē] **81**–26
spare tire [spër/ tīr/] **158**–23
sparrow [spăr/ō] **214**–7
spatula [spăch/ə lə] **78**–19
speak [spēk] **170**–N
speakers [spē/kərz] **50**–5, **206**–4, **234**–14
Special [spĕ/shəl] **80**
Specialists [spĕsh/ə lĭsts/] **120**
speech [spēch] **140**–2
speed limit [spēd/ lĭm/ət] **154**–4
speedometer [spĭ däm/ə tər] **159**–27
speed skating [spēd/skā/tĭng] **227** ✦
spell [spĕl] **4**–B
sphere [sfïr] **193**–42
spider [spī/dər] **214**–29
spill [spĭl] **218**–17
spinach [spĭn/ĭch] **69**–11
  spinach salad [spĭn/ĭch săl/əd] **80**–13
spinal column [spī/nəl käl/əm] **107**–49
spiral notebook [spī/rəl nōt/bŏŏk/] **7**–29
splint [splĭnt] **117**–14
sponge [spŭnj] **61**–19
  sponge mop [spŭnj/ mäp/] **61**–6
spoon [spōōn] **55**–5, **78**–9
  soupspoon [sōōp/spōōn/] **83**–32
  tablespoon [tā/bəl spōōn/] **75**–7
  teaspoon [tē/spōōn/] **75**–6, **83**–31
spoon [spōōn] **77**–F
sports [spörts]
  sports car [spörts/ kär/] **156**–4
  sports coat [spörts/ kōt/] **89**–14
  sports jacket [spörts/ jăk/ət] **89**–14
  sports program [spörts/ prō/grăm] **236**–11
  sports shirt [spörts/ shürt/] **88**–4
  sport-utility vehicle (SUV) [spört/
    yōō tĭl/ə tē vē/ĭ kəl] / [ĕs/yōō/vē/] **156**–7
SPORTS [spörts] **228, 229, 230, 231**
SPORTS EQUIPMENT [spörts/ ĭ kwĭp/mənt] **231**
SPORTS VERBS [spörts/ vürbz/] **230**
sprained ankle [sprānd/ ăng/kəl] **110**–18
spray [sprā] **108**–12, **113**–32
  spray gun [sprā/ gŭn/] **181**–21
  spray starch [sprā/ stärch/] **101**–12
spread [sprĕd]
  bedspread [bĕd/sprĕd/] **59**–11
spring [sprĭng] **21**–37, **58**–19
sprinkler [sprĭng/klər] **53**–22
square [skwër] **193**–30
squash [skwäsh, skwösh] **69**–24
squeegee [skwē/jē] **61**–15
squid [skwĭd] **212**–7
squirrel [skwür/əl] **215**–21
stadium [stā/dē əm] **126**–1

staff [stăf] **185** ✦
Staff [stăf] **120**
stage [stāj] **194**–16
   stage clips [stāj/ klĭps/] **194**–24
stain [stān] **181**–24
stained [stānd] **97**–42
stairs [stĕrz] **50**–10
stairway [stĕr/wā/] **50**–10
stall shower [stöl/ show/ər] **57** ✦
stamps [stămps] **134**–18, **134**–23, **183**–47
   stamp machine [stămp/ mə shēn/] **135**–11
stand [stănd] **152**–18
   checkstand [chĕk/stănd/] **73**–12
   newsstand [nōōz/stănd/] **128**–12
   nightstand [nīt/stănd/] **58**–23
stand [stănd] **141**–D
   stand up [stănd/ ŭp/] **6**–D
standard time [stăn/dərd tīm/] **19**–26
staple [stā/pəl] **171**–F
stapler [stā/plər] **183**–28
staples [stā/pəlz] **183**–29
star [stär] **205**–13
   starfish [stär/fĭsh/] **212**–16
   star key [stär/ kē/] **14**–6
starch [stärch] **101**–12
start [stärt] **12**–A, **40**–B, **230**–R
starting point [stär/tĭng poynt/] **162**–1
starving [stär/vĭng] **43** ✦
state [stāt] **4**–8, **146**–2
   state capital [stāt kă/pət əl] **139**–22
   state senator [stāt sĕn/ə tər] **139**–25
state [stāt] **15**–G, **195**–A
State Government [stāt gŭ/ vərn mənt] **139**
statement [stāt/mənt] **132**–16
station [stā/shən]
   bus station [bus/ stā/shən] **124**–7
   fire station [fīr/ stā/shən] **125**–12
   gas station [găs/ stā/shən] **125**–10
   gas station attendant
     [găs/ stā/shən ə tĕn/dənt] **162**–3
   lifeguard station [līf/gärd/ stā/shən] **225**–21
   police station [pə lēs/ stā/shən] **124**–6
   space station [spās/ stā/shən] **205**–18
   station wagon [stā/shən wăg/ən] **156**–6
   subway station [sŭb/wā/ stā/shən] **151**–11
Station [stā/shən] **152**
stationery [stā/shə nĕr/ ē] **183**–42
stay [stā]
   stay away [stā ə wā/] **147**–I
   stay fit [stā fĭt/] **114**–E
   stay on the line [stā ön dhə līn/] **15**–H
   stay on well-lit streets [stā ön wĕl lĭt/ strēts/] **143**–B
Stay Well [stā wĕl/] **114**
steak [stāk] **70**–2, **81**–24
   broiled steak [broyld/ stāk/] **76**–3
   halibut steak [hăl/ə bŭt stāk/] **71**–6
   salmon steak [săm/ən stāk/] **71**–4
   steak knife [stāk/ nīf/] **83**–29
steal [stēl] **142** ✦
steam [stēm] **77**–D
steamed vegetables [stēmd/ vĕj/tə bəlz] **81**–32
steamer [stē/mər] **78**–3

steel [stēl]
   steel toe boots [stēl/ tō/ bōōts/] **92**–6
   steel-wool soap pads [stēl/wōōl/ sōp/ pădz/] **61**–5
steering wheel [stïr/ïng wēl/] **159**–26
stems [stĕmz] **211**–9
step [stĕp]
   stepbrother [stĕp/brŭdh/ər] **35**–30
   stepdaughter [stĕp/dö/tər] **35** ✦
   stepfather [stĕp/fä/dhər] **35**–25
   stepladder [stĕp/lăd/ər] **61**–13
   stepmother [stĕp/mŭdh/ər] **35**–26
   steps [stĕps] **53**–3
   stepsister [stĕp/sĭs/tər] **35**–29
stereo system [stĕr/ē ō sĭs/təm] **56**–8
sterile [stĕr/əl]
   sterile pad [stĕr/əl păd/] **117**–6
   sterile tape [stĕr/əl tāp/] **117**–7
stethoscope [stĕth/ə skōp/] **118**–10
stewing beef [stōō/ĭng bēf/] **70**–3
stick [stĭk] **231**–11, **232**–11
   drumsticks [drŭm/stĭks/] **70**–23
   lipstick [lĭp/stĭk/] **109**–38
   stick shift [stĭk/ shĭft/] **159**–50
   yardstick [yärd/stĭk/] **181**–16
sticker [stĭk/ər] **102**–3, **136**–13
sticky notes [stĭk/ē nōts/] **183**–39
stir [stür] **77**–O
   stir-fried beef [stür/frīd/ bēf/] **76**–6
stitches [stĭch/əz] **117**–15
stock clerk [stäk/ klürk/] **169**–59
stockings [stäk/ĭngz] **91**–17
stomach [stŭm/ək] **107**–41
   stomachache [stŭm/ək āk/] **110**–4
stop [stäp] **129**–16, **151**–13, **154**–1
   stopover [stäp/ō/vər] **161** ✦
stop [stäp] **155**–D
Stop [stäp] **152**
stopped up [stäpt/ ŭp/] **63**–19
storage [stör/ĭj] **72**–25, **78**–4
   storage locker [stör/ĭj läk/ər] **50**–17
store [stör]
   bookstore [bŏŏk/stör/] **130**–4
   candy store [kăn/dē stör/] **131**–17
   card store [kärd/stör/] **130**–7
   convenience store [kən vēn/yəns stör/] **128**–3
   department store [dĭ pärt/mənt stör/] **131**–13
   electronics store [ē lĕk trän/ĭks stör/] **131**–20
   furniture store [für/nĭ chər stör/] **126**–8
   hardware store [härd/wër/ stör/] **148**–4
   home improvement store
     [hōm/ ĭm prōōv/mənt stör/] **127**–20
   jewelry store [jōō/əl rē stör/] **130**–2
   maternity store [mə tür/nə tē stör/] **131**–19
   men's store [mĕnz/ stör/] **130** ✦
   music store [myōō/zĭk stör/] **130**–1
   office supply store [ö/fəs sə plī/ stör/] **127**–21
   pet store [pĕt/ stör/] **130**–6
   shoe store [shōō/ stör/] **130**–10
   toy store [toy/ stör/] **130**–5
   video store [vĭd/ē ō stör/] **129**–20
Store [stör] **99**
STORE [stör] **72**–**73**

storeroom [stör/rōōm/] **185**–3
storm [störm] **13**–19
   hailstorm [hāl/störm/] **13**–21
   snowstorm [snō/störm/] **13**–23
   storm door [störm/ dör/] **53**–10
   thunderstorm [thŭn/dər störm/] **13**–16
story [stör/ē]
   action story [ăk/shən stör/ē] **237**–19
   adventure story [ăd vĕn/chər stör/ē] **237**–19
   horror story [hör/ər stör/ē, här/–] **237**–17
   science fiction story [sī/əns fĭk/shən stör/ē] **237**–18
   two-story house [tōō/stör/ē hows/] **52** ✦
stove [stōv] **54**–18, **226**–16
stow [stō] **160**–G
straight [strāt] **155**–A
   straight hair [strāt/ hër/] **33**–9
   straight line [strāt/ līn/] **193**–22
   straight pin [strāt/ pĭn/] **100**–12
strainer [strā/nər] **78**–22
straw [strö] **79**–18
   strawberries [strö/bĕr/ēz] **68**–14
   straw hat [strö/ hăt/] **90**–23
stream [strēm] **204** ✦
street [strēt] **150**–5, **155**–8
   streetlight [strēt/līt/] **148**–3
   street sign [strēt/ sīn] **129**–26
   street vender [strēt/ vĕn/dər] **129**–29
STREETS [strēts] **126**–**127**
strep throat [strĕp/ thrōt/] **111**–4
stress [strĕs] **115**–4
stretch [strĕch] **230**–M
stretcher [strĕch/ər] **121**–33
string [strĭng]
   string beans [strĭng/ bēnz/] **69**–8
   string lights [strĭng/ līts/] **239**–18
   string of pearls [strĭng/ əv pürlz/] **95**–39
Strings [strĭngz] **238**
striped [strīpt] **96**–20
stripper [strĭ/pər] **181**–42
stroller [strō/lər] **37**–18
strong signal [sströng/ sĭg/nəl] **14**–11
stub [stŭb] **165**–11
stucco [stŭk/ō] **178**–15
student [stōōd/nt] **6**–5
study [stŭ/dē] **10**–D, **137**–A
STUDYING [stŭ/dē ĭng] **8**–9
stuffed animals [stŭft/ ăn/ə məlz] **59**–15
style [stīl/] **88** ✦
Styles [stīlz] **96**
STYLES [stīlz] **96**
stylist [stī/lĭst] **167**–31
SUBJECTS [sŭb/jĭkts/] **188**–**189**
submit [səb mĭt/] **48**–C
substitute [sŭb/stə tōōt/] **79**–20
subtract [səb trăkt/] **192**–B
suburbs [sŭb/ürbz] **52**–2
subway [sŭb/wā/] **151**–12
   subway car [sŭb/wā/ kär/] **152**–6
   subway station [sŭb/wā/ stā/shən] **151**–11
Subway Station [sŭb/wā/ stā/shən] **152**
Succeed [sək sēd/] **10**
SUCCEEDING IN SCHOOL [sək sē/dĭng ən skōōl/] **10**

Index

suede [swād] **99**–8
sugar [shŏŏg/ər] **73**–30
    sugar bowl [shŏŏg/ər bōl/] **55**–14
    sugar-free [shŏŏg/ər frē/] **122**–7
    sugar substitute [shŏŏg/ər sŭb/stə tōōt/] **79**–20
suit [sōōt] **87**–11
    bathing suit [bā/dhĭng sōōt/] **90**–26
    business suit [bĭz/nəs sōōt/] **88**–11
    jumpsuit [jŭmp/sōōt/] **93**–24
    three piece suit [thrē/pēs/ sōōt/] **88** ✦
    wet suit [wĕt/ sōōt/] **225**–4
suite [swēt] **184**–16
sum [sŭm] **192**–7
sumac [sōō/măk] **210**–23
summer [sŭm/ər] **21**–38
sun [sŭn] **209**–8
    sunblock [sŭn/blăk/] **108**–8, **225**–0
    sunburn [sŭn/bürn/] **110**–14
    sunflower [sŭn/flow/ər] **211**–10
    sunglasses [sŭn/glăs/əz] **90**–27
    sunrise [sŭn/ rīz] **18**–14
    sunscreen [sŭn/skrēn/] **108**–7, **225**–10
    sunset [sŭn/ sĕt] **18**–19
Sunday [sŭn/dā, –dē] **20**–8
sunny [sŭn/ē] **13**–9, **76**–10
superintendent [sōō/prĭn tĕn/dənt, sōō/pər ĭn–] **50**–8
supermarket [sōō/pər/ mär/kət] **127**–18
supervise [sōō/pər vīz/] **170**–O
supervisor [sōō/pər vī/zər] **165**–8, **175**–4
Supplies [sə plīz/] **100, 183**
SUPPLIES [sə plīz/] **61, 180–181**
supply [sə plī/] **127**–21
    supply cabinet [sə plī/ kăb/ə nət] **182**–1
support [sə pört/] **179**–18
    support group [sə pört/ grōōp/] **115**–15
supporter [sə pör/tər] **91**–6
Supreme Court [sə prēm/ kört/] **138**–11
surfboard [sürf/börd/] **225**–16
surfer [sür/fər] **225**–15
surfing [sür/fĭng] **227**–9, **227**–10, **227** ✦
surgeon [sür/jən] **121**–36
Surgeon [sür/jən] **93**
surge protector [sürj/ prə tĕk/tər] **196**–1
surgical [sür/jĭ kəl]
    surgical cap [sür/jĭ kəl kăp/] **121**–37
    surgical gloves [sür/jĭ kəl glŭvz/] **121**–39
    surgical gown [sür/jĭ kəl gown/] **93**–37, **121**–38
    surgical mask [sür/jĭ kəl măsk/] **93**–36
    surgical nurse [sür/jĭ kəl nürs/] **120**–9
    surgical scrub cap [sür/jĭ kəl skrŭb/ kăp/] **93**–35
    surgical scrubs [sür/jĭ kəl skrŭbz/] **93**–38
Surgical Assistant [sür/jĭ kəl ə sĭs/tənt] **93**
surprised [sər prīzd/, sə–] **43**–30
suspenders [sə spĕn/dərz] **94**–1
suspense [sŭs/pĕns] **237**–20
SUV (sport-utility vehicle) [ĕs/yōō/vē/] / [spört/ yōō tĭl/ə tē vē/ĭ kəl] **156**–7
swallow [swäl/ō] **116**–J
swap meet [swäp/ mēt] **222**–6
sweat [swĕt]
    sweatpants [swĕt/pănts/] **89**–23
    sweatshirt [swĕt/shürt/] **89**–22

sweater [swĕt/ər] **28**–2, **87**–14
    cardigan sweater [kär/də gən swĕt/ər] **88**–2
    pullover sweater [pŏŏl/ō/vər swĕt/ər] **88**–3
sweep [swēp] **60**–J
sweet potatoes [swĕt pə tā/tōz] **69**–18
sweets [swĕts] **84**–9
swim [swĭm] **230**–L
    swimsuit [swĭm/sōōt/] **90**–26
swimming [swĭm/ĭng]
    swimming pool [swĭm/ĭng pōōl/] **51**–22
    swimming trunks [swĭm/ĭng trŭngks/] **90**–22
swing [swĭng] **230**–Q
swings [swĭngz] **224**–11
Swiss cheese [swĭs/ chēz/] **71**–27
switch [swĭch] **58**–27
swollen finger [swō/lən fĭng/gər] **110**–16
swordfish [sörd/fĭsh/] **71**–5, **212**–10
symbol [sĭm/bəl] **155**–8
SYMPTOMS AND INJURIES [sĭmp/təmz ən ĭn/jə rēz] **110**
synagogue [sĭn/ə gäg/] **127**–16
synthetic materials [sĭn thĕ/tĭk mə tïr/ē əlz] **98** ✦
syringe [sə rĭnj/] **118**–12
syrup [sĭr/əp, sür/–] **113**–29
system [sĭs/təm]
    fuel injection system [fyōō/əl ĭn jĕk/shən sĭs/təm] **158**–17
    stereo system [stĕr/ē ō sĭs/təm] **56**–8
SYSTEM [sĭs/təm] **141**
tab [tăb] **197**–7
table [tā/bəl]
    bed table [bĕd/ tā/bəl] **121**–21
    changing table [chān/jĭng tā/bəl] **59**–1
    coffee table [kö/fē tā/bəl] **56**–19
    dining room table [dī/nĭng rōōm/ tā/bəl] **55**–9
    end table [ĕnd/ tā/bəl] **56**–14
    examination table [ĭg zăm/ə nā/shən tā/bəl] **118**–7
    folding card table [fōl/dĭng kärd/ tā/bəl] **102**–4
    night table [nīt/ tā/bəl] **58**–23
    operating table [äp/ə rā/tĭng tā/bəl] **121**–40
    periodic table [pïr/ē äd/ĭk tā/bəl] **195**–26
    picnic table [pĭk/nĭk tā/bəl] **224**–8
    pool table [pōōl/ tā/bəl] **50**–15
    tablecloth [tā/bəl klöth/] **55**–12
    tablespoon [tā/bəl spōōn/] **75**–7
    table tennis [tā/bəl tĕn/əs] **228**–14
    tray table [trā/ tā/bəl] **161**–21
    turntable [türn/tā/bəl] **234**–12
tablet [tăb/lət] **113**–22, **113**–27
tackle [tăk/əl] **230**–F
taco [tä/kō] **79**–8
tags [tăgz] **92**–15, **136**–13
tail [tāl] **216**–22
tail light [tāl/ līt/] **158**–13
tail pipe [tāl/ pīp/] **158**–15
tailor [tā/lər] **100**–3
take [tāk]
    do not take with dairy products [dōō nät/ tāk/ wĭth dër/ē prăd/ŭkts] **112**–A
    take a bath [tāk/ ə băth/] **108**–B
    take a break [tāk/ ə brāk/] **11**–H
    take a citizenship test [tāk/ ə sĭt/ə zən shĭp tĕst/] **140**–I

    take a driver education course [tāk/ ə drī/vərz ĕj/ə kā/shən körs/] **137**–B
    take a driver's training course [tāk/ ə drī/vərz trā/nĭng körs/] **137**–G
    take a message [tāk/ ə mĕs/ĭj] **171**–Q
    take a nap [tāk/ ə năp/] **53**–A
    take a picture [tāk/ ə pĭk/chər] **206**–B
    take a seat [tāk/ ə sēt/] **6**–F
    take a shower [tāk/ ə show/ər] **38**–C, **108**–A
    take a tour [tāk/ ə tōōr/] **220**–A
    take a written test [tāk/ ə rĭt/ən tĕst] **137**–E
    take care of children [tāk/ kër/ əv chĭl/drən] **170**–P
    take cover [tāk/ kŭv/ər] **147**–J
    take dictation [tāk/ dĭk/tā shən] **171**–K
    take in [tāk/ ĭn] **100**–D
    take medicine [tāk/ mĕd/ə sən] **114**–D
    take notes [tāk/ nōts/] **10**–C
    take off [tāk/ öf/] **109**–Q, **160**–J
    take one hour before eating [tāk/ wŭn/ ow/ər bĭ för/ ē/tĭng] **112**–B
    take out [tāk/ owt/] **9**–Y, **60**–Q, **82** ✦
    take ownership [tāk/ ō/nər shĭp/] **49**–K
    take temperature [tāk/ tĕm/prə chər] **118**–B
    take the bus to school [tāk/ dhə bŭs/ tə skōōl/] **38**–H
    take the car to a mechanic [tāk/ dhə kär/ tə dhə mə kăn/ĭk] **157**–C
    take the children to school [tāk/ dhə chĭl/drən tə skōōl/] **38**–G
    take the order [tāk/ dhē ör/dər] **82**–E
    take with food [tāk/ wĭth fōōd/] **112**–A
    take x-rays [tāk/ ĕks/rāz/] **119**–B
Taking a Flight [tā/kĭng ə flīt/] **160**
Taking a Test [tā/kĭng ə tĕst/] **10**
TAKING A TRIP [tā/kĭng ə trĭp/] **162–163**
Taking Care of Your Car [tā/kĭng kër/ əv yər kär/] **157**
TAKING CARE OF YOUR HEALTH [tā/kĭng kër əv yər hĕlth/] **114–115**
talk [tök]
    talk show [tök/ shō/] **236**–4
    talk therapy [tök/ thër/ ə pē] **115**–13
talk [tök]
    talk about [tök ə bowt/] **174**–L
    talk on the phone [tök/ ön dhə fōn/] **15**–C
    talk to friends [tök/ tə frĕndz/] **173**–A
    talk to the teacher [tök/ tə dhə tē/chər] **6**–B
tall [töl] **32**–4
tambourine [tăm/bə rēn/] **238**–17
tan [tăn] **24**–18
tangerines [tăn/jə rēnz/] **68**–9
tank [tăngk] **158**–10, **225**–5
    tank top [tăngk/ täp/] **89**–24
    tank truck [tăngk/ trŭk] **156**–20
tape [tāp]
    clear tape [klēr/ tāp/] **183**–30
    correction tape [kə rĕk/shən tāp/] **183**–37
    duct tape [dŭkt/ tāp/] **181**–49
    electrical tape [ĭ lek/trĭ kəl tāp/] **181**–43
    masking tape [măs/kĭng tāp/] **181**–53
    packing tape [păk/ĭng tāp/] **183**–32
    sterile tape [stĕr/ əl tāp/] **117**–7
    tape measure [tāp mĕzh/ər] **100**–17, **181**–45

target [tär/gət] **231**–7
taste [tāst] **106**–D
tattoo [tă tōō/] **32**–18
tax / taxes [tăks] / [tăks/əz] **27**–8
taxi [tăk/sē] **150**–3
   hail a taxi [hāl/ ə tăk/sē] **152** ✦
   taxi driver [tăk/sē drī/vər] **152**–21
   taxi license [tăk/sē lī/səns] **152**–22
   taxi stand [tăk/sē stănd/] **152**–18
TB (tuberculosis) [tē/bē/] / [tōō bür/kyə lō/səs] **111**–15
TDD [tē/dē/dē/] **15**–26
tea [tē] **79**–12, **81**–39, **81**–40
   teacup [tē/kŭp] **55**–6
   tea kettle [tē/ kĕt/l] **54**–21
   teapot [tē/pät/] **55**–16
   teaspoon [tē/spōōn/] **75**–6, **83**–31
teach [tēch] **170**–Q
teacher [tē/chər] **5**–8, **6**–4, **22**–5
   teacher's aide [tē/chərz ād/] **5**–16
team [tēm] **145**–20, **229**–3
TEAM SPORTS [tēm/ spörts/] **229**
technical school [tĕk/nĭ kəl skōōl/] **188**–5
technician [tĕk nĭsh/ən]
   computer technician
      [kəm pyōō/tər tĕk nĭsh/ən] **167**–19, **182**–12
   emergency medical technician (EMT)
      [ĭ mür/jən sē mĕd/ĭ kəl tĕk nish/ən] / [ē/ĕm/tē]
      121–32
   medical records technician
      [mĕd/ĭ kəl rĕk/ərdz tĕk nish/ən] **168**–39
Technician [tĕk nĭsh/ən] **93**
teddy bear [tĕd/ē bër/] **37**–23
teen / teenager [tēn] / [tē/nā/jər] **31**–11
teething ring [tē/dhĭng rĭng/] **37**–25
teeth / tooth [tēth] / [tōōth] **106**–7
   toothache [tōōth/āk/] **110**–2
   toothbrush [tōōth/brŭsh/] **57**–21, **109**–22
   toothbrush holder [tōōth/brŭsh/ hōl/dər] **57**–22
   toothpaste [tōōth/pāst/] **109**–23
telemarketer [tĕl/ə mär/kə tər] **169**–60
TELEPHONE [tĕl/ə fōn/] **14**–15
Telephone Skills [tĕl/ə fōn/ skĭlz/] **171**
telescope [tĕl/ə skōp/] **205**–23
television / TV [tĕl/ə vĭzh/ən] / [tē/vē/] **56**–6
   big-screen TV [bĭg/skrēn/ tē/vē/] **50**–14
   flat panel TV [flăt/ păn/əl tē/vē/] **234**–7
   flat screen TV [flăt/ skrēn/ tē/vē/] **234**–7
   portable TV [pör/tə bəl tē/vē/] **234**–8
teller [tĕl/ər] **132**–1
Teller [tĕl/ər] **132**
Telling Time [tĕl/ĭng tīm/] **18**
temperature [tĕm/prə chər] **110**–8
   temperature gauge [tĕm/prə chər gāj/] **159**–30
Temperature [tĕm/prə chər] **13**
ten [tĕn] **16**
   ten after one [tĕn/ ăf/tər wŭn/] **18**–8
   ten dollars [tĕn/ däl/ərz] **26**–9
   10 percent [tĕn/ pər sĕnt/] **17**–12
   ten thousand [tĕn/ thow/zənd] **16**
   10-year-old girl [tĕn/yïr ōld/ gürl/] **31**–10
tenant [tĕn/ənt] **50**–6
TENANT MEETING [tĕn/ənt mē/tĭng] **64**–65

tennis [tĕn/əs] **228**–15
   table tennis [tā/bəl tĕn/əs] **228**–14
   tennis court [tĕn/əs kört/] **224**–6
   tennis racket [tĕn/əs răk/ət] **231**–2
   tennis shoes [tĕn/əs shōōz/] **95**–32
tent [tĕnt] **226**–10
tenth [tĕnth] **16**
Terminal [tür/mə nəl] **160**
termites [tür/mīts] **63**–22
term [türm] **139** ✦
Terms [türmz] **199**
terrified [tĕr/ə fīd/] **43** ✦
test [tĕst] **121**–30
   test booklet [tĕst/ bŏŏk/lət] **10**–1
   testing area [tĕs/tĭng ër/ē ə] **136**–2
   test tube [tĕst/ tōōb/] **195**–42
Test [tĕst] **10**
text [tĕkst]
   textbook [tĕkst/bŏŏk/, tĕks/-] **7**–25
   text box [tĕkst/ bäks/, tĕks/-] **197**–13
   text message [tĕkst/ mĕs/ĭj, tĕks/-] **14**–19
thank [thăngk] **12**–E, **174**–N
Thanksgiving [thăngks gĭv/ĭng] **22**–17
theater [thē/ə tər] **126**–6, **127**–23
theft [thĕft] **142**–9
therapist [thĕr/ ə pĭst] **115**–12, **115**–14, **168**–45
therapy [thĕr/ ə pē] **115**–11, **115**–13
thermal undershirt [thür/məl ŭn/dər shürt/] **91**–2
thermometer [thər măm/ə tər] **118**–11
thick [thĭk] **23**–7
thighs [thīz] **70**–22, **106**–19
thimble [thĭm/bəl] **100**–15
thin [thĭn] **23**–8, **32**–9
THINGS [thĭngz] **23**
think [thĭnk] **191**–E
third [thürd] **16**
Third Floor [thürd/ flör/] **50**
thirsty [thür/stē] **42**–2
thirteen [thür/tēn/] **16**
   thirteen colonies [thür/tēn/ kä/lə nēz] **198**–1
thirteenth [thür/tēnth/] **16**
thirtieth [thür/tē əth/] **16**
thirty [thür/tē] **16**
   35 mm camera
      [thür/tē fïv/ mĭl/ə mē/tər kăm/rə] **235**–21
this week [dhĭs/ wēk/] **20**–19
thorn [thörn] **211**–29
thread [thrĕd] **99**–23, **100**–11
three [thrē] **16**
   three piece suit [thrē/pēs/ sōōt/] **88** ✦
   3-ring binder [thrē/ rĭng/ bīn/dər] **7**–27
   3/4 sleeved [thrē/kwör/tər slēv/] **96**–13
   three times a week [thrē/ tīmz/ ə wēk/] **20**–24
throat [thrōt] **107**–35, **110**–6, **111**–4
   throat lozenges [thrōt/ läz/ən jəz] **113**–30
through [thrōō] **153**–K
throw [thrō] **230**–C
   throw away [thrō/ ə wā/] **11**–N
   throw up [thrō/ ŭp/] **110**–E
throw pillow [thrō/ pĭl/ō] **56**–2
thumb [thŭm] **106**–16
thunderstorm [thŭn/dər störm/] **13**–16

Thursday [thürz/dā, –dē] **20**–12
tick [tĭk] **214**–27
ticket [tĭk/ət] **152**–15, **161**–19
   ticket agent [tĭk/ət ā/jənt] **160**–3
   ticket window [tĭk/ət wĭn/dō/] **152**–12
tidal wave [tīd/l wāv/] **145**–17
tide [tīd] **225** ✦
tie [tī] **88**–12, **89**–16, **92**–13, **229** ✦
tie [tī] **86**–A
tiger [tī/gər] **217**–37
tight [tīt] **97**–29
tights [tīts] **91**–19
tile [tīl] **57**–10, **178**–11, **178**–D
time [tīm]
   Alaska time [ə lăs/kə tīm/] **19**–28
   arrival time [ə rī/vəl tīm/] **161** ✦
   Atlantic time [ət lăn/tĭk tīm/] **19**–33
   Central time [sĕn/trəl tīm/] **19**–31
   daylight saving time [dā/līt/ sā/vĭng tīm/] **19**–25
   departure time [dĭ pär/chər tīm/] **161** ✦
   Eastern time [ē/stərn tīm/] **19**–32
   Hawaii-Aleutian time
      [hə wī/ē ə lōō/shən tīm/] **19**–27
   Mountain time [mown/tn tīm/] **19**–30
   Newfoundland time
      [nōō/fən lənd tīm/, –fənd–] **19**–34
   on time [än/ tīm/, ön/ tīm/] **19**–23, **161**–29
   Pacific time [pə sĭf/ĭk tīm/] **19**–29
   standard time [stăn/dərd tīm/] **19**–26
   three times a week [thrē tīmz/ ə wēk/] **20**–24
   time clock [tīm/ kläk/] **165**–7
Time [tīm] **18**
TIME [tīm] **18**–19
timer [tī/mər] **78**–18
Times of Day [tīmz/ əv dā/] **18**
Time Zones [tīm/ zōnz/] **19**
tire [tīr] **158**–5, **158**–23, **162**–F
tired [tīrd] **43**–32
title [tīt/l] **133**–14, **190**–5
toad [tōd] **212**–28
toast [tōst] **80**–4
toaster [tō/stər] **54**–6
   toaster oven [tō/stər ŭv/ən] **54**–15
today [tə dā/] **20**–5
toddler [täd/lər] **31**–8
toe [tō] **92**–6, **94**–23, **105**–10
   toenail [tō/nāl/] **106** ✦
Tofu [tō/fōō/] **77**
toggle bolt [täg/əl bōlt/] **180**–38
to-go box [tə gō/ bäks/] **82**–5
toilet [toy/lət] **57**–19
   toilet brush [toy/lət brŭsh/] **57**–18
   toilet paper [toy/lət pā/pər] **57**–17, **146**–13
token [tō/kən] **152**–10
tomatoes [tə mā/tōz] **69**–6
tomorrow [tə mär/ō, –mör/ō] **20**–6
tongs [tängz, töngz] **78**–23, **195**–44
tongue [tŭng] **106**–8
too [tōō]
   too big [tōō/ bĭg/] **97**–38
   too expensive [tōō/ ĭk spĕn/sĭv/] **97**–44
   too small [tōō/ smöl/] **97**–37

tool belt [tool/ bĕlt/] **92**–3
TOOLS AND BUILDING SUPPLIES
[toolz/ ən bĭl/dĭng sə plīz/] **180**–**181**
tooth / teeth [tooth] / [tēth] **106**–7
toothache [tooth/āk/] **110**–2
toothbrush [tooth/brŭsh/] **57**–21, **109**–22
toothbrush holder [tooth/brŭsh/ hōl/dər] **57**–22
toothpaste [tooth/pāst/] **109**–23
top [täp] **88**–7, **89**–24
torn [törn] **97**–41
tornado [tör nā/dō] **145**–15
torso [tör/sō/] **106** ✦
tortoise [tör/təs] **213**–42
total [tōt/l] **27**–9
totebag [tōt/ băg/] **94**–19
touch [tŭch] **106**–E
towel [tow/əl]
bath towel [băth/ tow/əl] **57**–14
dish towel [dĭsh/ tow/əl] **61**–22
hand towel [hănd/ tow/əl] **57**–15
paper towels [pā/pər tow/əlz] **54**–3
towel rack [tow/əl răk/] **57**–13
towelettes [tow/əl ĕts] **146**–12
tower [tow/ər] **196**–3
town [town] **52**–3
town car [town/ kär/] **152**–20
townhouse [town/hows/] **52**–6
tow truck [tō/ trŭk/] **156**–14
toy [toy]
toy chest [toy/ chĕst/] **59**–16
toy store [toy/ stör/] **130**–5
Toys and Games [toyz/ ən gāmz/] **59**
track [trăk] **5**–21, **152**–14
track and field [trăk/ ən fēld/] **228**–18
tractor [trăk/tər] **177**–9
tractor trailer [trăk/tər trā/lər] **156**–15
traffic light [trăf/ĭk līt/] **128**–8
TRAFFIC SIGNS [trăf/ĭk sīnz/] **154**
tragedy [trăj/ə dē] **237**–14
trailer [trā/lər] **156**–15, **156**–17
train [trān] **150**–7, **233**–27
training [trā/nĭng **172**–2, **172**–5, **172**–7
training pants [trā/nĭng pănts/] **37**–11
Training [trā/nĭng] **172**
Train Station [trān/ stā/shən] **152**
transcribe [trăn skrīb/] **171**–C
transfer [trăns für/, trăns/fər] **152**–5
transfer [trăns für/, trăns/fər] **171**–O
translate [trănz/lāt] **8**–C
translator [trănz/lā/tər, trăns/–] **168**–35
Transmission [trănz mĭsh/ən, trăns–] **159**
Transportation [trăns/pər tā/shən] **152**
TRANSPORTATION [trăns/pər tā/shən] **150**–**151, 152**
trash [trăsh]
trash bags [trăsh/ băgz/] **61**–24
trash bin [trăsh/ bĭn/] **51**–23
trash chute [trăsh/ shoot/] **51**–26
travel [trăv/əl] **41**–P
travel agency [trăv/əl ā/jən sē] **131**–14
tray [trā] **55**–17, **83**–10
tray table [trā tā/bəl] **161**–21
Tree [trē] **210**

trees [trēz] **208**–1, **239**–16
TREES AND PLANTS [trēz/ ən plănts/] **210**
trench coat [trĕnch/ kōt/] **90**–21
trial [trī/əl] **140**–5
triangle [trī/ăng/gəl] **193**–32
tricycle [trī/sī kəl] **224**–12
trigonometry [trĭg/ə năm/ə trē] **192**–18
trim [trĭm] **176**–B
trip [trĭp] **152**–16, **152**–17
tripe [trīp] **70**–8
tripod [trī/päd] **235**–25
trombone [träm bōn/] **238**–10
trout [trowt] **71**–1
trowel [trow/əl] **176**–10, **178**–13
truck [trŭk] **150**–5
dump truck [dŭmp/trŭk/] **156**–19
fire truck [fīr/ trŭk/] **144**–10
garbage truck [gär/bĭj trŭk/] **127**–22
hand truck [hănd/ trŭk/] **175**–11
pickup truck [pĭk/ŭp trŭk/] **156**–12
tank truck [tăngk/ trŭk/] **156**–20
tow truck [tō/ trŭk/] **156**–14
truck driver [trŭk/ drī/vər] **169**–61
TRUCKS [trŭks] **156**
trumpet [trŭm/pət] **238**–11
Trunk [trŭngk] **158**
trunks [trŭngks] **158**–11, **210**–4, **217**–47
swimming trunks [swĭm/ĭng trŭngks/] **90**–22
try on [trī/ön] **95**–C
TSA agent [tē/ĕs/ā/ ā/jənt] **160**–5
T-shirt [tē/shürt/] **86**–4
tsunami [soo nä/ mē/, tsoo–] **145**–17
tub [tŭb]
bathtub [băth/tŭb/] **57**–2
tuba [too/bə] **238**–12
tube [toob] **74**–12, **74**–24, **195**–42
tuberculosis (TB)
[too bür/kyə lō/səs] / [tē/bē/] **111**–15
Tuesday [tooz/dā, –dē] **20**–10
tulip [too/ləp] **211**–11
tuna [too/nə] **71**–7, **72**–19, **212**–8
tuner [too/nər] **234**–13
turbulence [tür/byə ləns] **161**–22
turkey [tür/kē] **70**–17, **239**–14
roasted turkey [rōs/təd tür/kē] **76**–4
smoked turkey [smōkt/ tür/kē] **71**–25
turn [türn] **154**–5, **154**–7, **154**–8
turn signal [türn/ sĭg/nəl] **158**–6, **159**–34
turnstile [türn/stīl/] **152**–8
turntable [türn/tā/bəl] **234**–12
turn [türn]
turn in [türn/ ĭn/] **191**–M
turn left [türn/ lĕft/] **155**–C
turn off [türn/ öf/] **11**–P, **160**–I, **174**–G, **219**–G
turn on [türn/ ön/, –än/] **11**–B
turn right [türn/ rīt/] **155**–B
turnips [tür/nəps] **69**–16
turquoise [tür/koyz, –kwoyz] **24**–9
turtle [tür/tl] **213**–43
turtleneck [tür/tl nĕk/] **96**–9
tusk [tŭsk] **217**–48
tuxedo [tŭk sē/dō] **89**–17

TV Programs [tē/vē/ prō/grămz] **236**
TV / television [tē/vē/] / [tĕl/ə vĭzh/ən] **56**–6
big-screen TV [bĭg/skrēn/ tē/vē/] **50**–14
flat panel TV [flăt/ păn/əl tē/vē] **234**–7
flat screen TV [flăt/ skrēn/ tē/ vē/] **234**–7
portable TV [por/tə bəl tē/vē/] **234**–8
tweezers [twē/zərz] **117**–4
twelfth [twĕlfth] **16**
twelve [twĕlv] **16**
twentieth [twĕn/tē əth] **16**
twenty [twĕn/tē] **16**
twenty after one [twĕn/tē ăf/tər wŭn/] **18**–10
twenty dollars [twĕn/tē däl/ərz] **26**–10
twenty-first [twĕn/tē fürst/] **16**
twenty-five [twĕn/tē fīv/] **16**
25 percent [twĕn/fīv/ pər sĕnt/] **17**–11
twenty-four [twĕn/tē för/] **16**
twenty-one [twĕn/tē wŭn/] **16**
twenty-three [twĕn/tē thrē/] **16**
twenty to two [twĕn/tē tə too/] **18**–12
twenty-two [twĕn/tē too/] **16**
twice a week [twīs/ ə wēk/] **20**–23
twig [twĭg] **210**–1
twins [twĭnz] **28**–1
two [too] **16**
2-door car [too/dör kär/] **156**–2
two-story house [too/stör/ē hows/] **52** ✦
two-way radio [too/wā rā/dē ō] **179**–22
2 x 4 (two by four) [too/ bī/ för/] **181**–19
type [tīp] **170**–R, **196**–A
type a letter [tīp/ə lĕt/ər] **171**–A
type the message [tīp/ dhə mĕs/ĭj] **197**–E
type the subject [tīp/ dhə sŭb/jĭkt] **197**–D
type your password [tīp/ yər păs/würd/] **197**–A
Types of Health Problems
[tīps/ əv hĕlth/ präb/ləmz] **115**
Types of Job Training [tīps/ əv jäb/ trā/nĭng] **172**
Types of Material [tīps/ əv mə tir/ē əl] **99**
Types of Math [tīps/ əv măth/] **192**
Types of Medication [tīps/ əv mĕd/ə kā/shən] **113**
Types of Movies [tīps/ əv moo/vēz] **237**
Types of Music [tīps/ əv myoo/zĭk] **237**
Types of TV Programs [tīps/ əv tē/vē/ prō/grămz] **236**
ugly [ŭg/lē] **23**–22
umbrella [ŭm brĕl/ə] **90**–17, **225**–14
umpire [ŭm/pīr] **229** ✦
uncle [ŭng/kəl] **34**–8
uncomfortable [ŭn kŭmf/tə bəl, –tər–] **42**–9
unconscious [ŭn/kän/shəs] **116**–A
under [ŭn/dər] **25**–10, **153**–A
long underwear [löng/ ŭn/dər wër] **91**–3
thermal undershirt [thür/məl ŭn/dər shürt] **91**–2
underexposed [ŭn/dər ĭk spōzd/] **235**–35
underpants [ŭn/dər pănts/] **91**–14
undershirt [ŭn/dər shürt/] **91**–1
underline [ŭn/dər līn/] **9**–S
Under the Hood [ŭn/dər dhə hood/] **158**
Underwear [ŭn/dər wër/] **91**
UNDERWEAR AND SLEEPWEAR
[ŭn/dər wër/ ən slēp/wër/] **91**
undress [ən drĕs/] **36**–E

unfurnished apartment
[ŭn/für nĭsht ə pärt/ mənt] **48**–4

uniform [yōō/nə förm/] **88**–10, **231**–16

Unisex Socks [yōō/nə sĕks/ säks/] **91**

Unisex Underwear [yōō/nə sĕks/ ŭn/dər wër] **91**

universal remote [yōō/nə vür/səl rĭ mōt/] **234**–9

UNIVERSE [yōō/nə vürs/] **205**

university [yōō/nə vür/sə tē] **188**–7

unload [ŭn lōd/] **101**–E

unpack [ŭn păk/] **49**–N

unraveling [ŭn răv/əl ĭng] **97**–43

unripe [ŭn rīp/] **68**–31

unscented [ŭn sĕn/təd] **108** ✦

unscramble [ŭn skrăm/bəl] **9**–W

up [ŭp]

buckle up [bŭk/əl ŭp/] **36**–L

clean up [klēn/ ŭp/] **147**–M

cut up [kŭt/ ŭp/] **77**–I

eggs sunny-side up [ĕgz/ sŭn/ē sīd ŭp/] **76**–10

get up [gĕt/ ŭp/] **38**–B

hang up [hăng/ ŭp/] **15**–D, **101**–H

look up [lŏŏk/ ŭp/] **8**–A

pick up [pĭk/ ŭp/] **6**–I, **11**–E, **38**–M

pop-up ad [päp/ ŭp ăd/] **197**–9

set up [sĕt/ ŭp/] **173**–I

stand up [stănd/ ŭp/] **6**–D

stopped up [stäpt/ ŭp/] **63**–19

throw up [thrō/ ŭp/] **110**–E

wake up [wāk/ ŭp/] **38**–A

walk up [wök/ ŭp/] **153**–C

upright seat [ŭp/rīt/ sĕt/] **161**–28

upset [ŭp sĕt/] **43**–28

upstairs [ŭp/stërz/] **51** ✦

Uranus [yŏŏr/ə nəs, yŏō rā/nəs] **205**–7

urban area [ür/bən ër/ē ə] **52**–1

urchin [ür/chən] **212**–21

URL [yōō/är/ĕl/] **197**–4

U.S. [yōō/ĕs/]

U.S. Capitol [yōō/ĕs/ kă/pət əl] **138**–1

U.S. route [yōō/ĕs/ rōōt/, –rowt/] **154**–17

USB port [yōō/ĕs/ bē/ pört/] **196**–7

use [yōōz]

use a cash register [yōōz/ə kăsh/ rĕj/ə stər] **170**–S

use a credit card [yōōz/ə krĕ/dət kärd/] **27**–B

use a debit card [yōōz/ə dĕ/bət kärd/] **27**–C

use a gift card [yōōz/ ə gĭft/ kärd/] **27**–E

use deodorant [yōōz/dē ō/dər ənt] **108**–C

use energy-efficient bulbs
[yōōz/ ĕn/ər jē ĭ fĭ/shənt bŭlbz] **219**–H

use punctuation [yōōz/ pŭngk/chōō ā/shən] **190**–C

Used Car [yōōzd/ kär/] **157**

used clothing [yōōzd/ klō/dhĭng] **102**–2

U.S. HISTORY [yōō/ĕs/ hĭs/tə rē] **198**

U.S. NATIONAL PARKS
[yōō/ĕs năsh/ə nəl pärks/] **220**–**221**

utensils [yōō tĕn/səlz] **79**–19

utility / utilities [yōō tĭl/ə tē] / [yōō tĭl/ə tēz]
48–5, **156**–7

U-turn [yōō/türn/] **154**–5

vacancy sign [vā/kən sē sīn/] **50**–7

vacation [vā kā/shən] **22**–6

vaccination [văk/sə nā/shən] **114** ✦

vacuum [văk/yōōm]

vacuum cleaner [văk/yōōm klē/nər] **61**–10

vacuum cleaner attachments
[văk/yōōm klē/nər ə tăch/mənts] **61**–11

vacuum cleaner bag
[văk/yōōm klē/nər băg/] **61**–12

vacuum [văk/yōōm] **60**–H

valley [văl/ē] **204**–17

valuables [văl/yə bəlz, –yə wə–] **132**–8

valve [vălv/] **146**–4

van [văn] **156**–13, **156**–18

vandalism [văn/də lĭz/əm] **142**–1

vanity plate [vă/nə tē plāt/] **136** ✦

variable [vër/ē ə bəl] **192**–12

vase [vās, văz, văz] **55**–23

vault [völt] **132**–6

VCR [vē/sē/är/] **102**–7

veal cutlets [vēl/ kŭt/ləts] **70**–6

Vegetable [vĕj/tə bəl] **77**

vegetables [vĕj/tə bəlz] **66**–8, **72**–27, **81**–32

vegetable garden [vĕj/tə bəl gär/dn] **53**–27, **177**–14

vegetable peeler [vĕj/tə bəl pē/lər] **78**–15

VEGETABLES [vĕj/tə bəlz] **69**

vegetarian [vĕj/ə tër/ē ən] **70** ✦

vehicles [vē/ĭ kəlz] **124**–4, **156**–7, **156**–10

vein [vān] **107**–37

velvet [vĕl/vət] **99**–10

vending machine [vĕn/dĭng mə shēn/] **152**–9

vendors [vĕn/dərz] **84**–7, **129**–29

ventilation mask [vĕnt/əl ā/shən măsk/] **92**–7

Venus [vē/nəs] **205**–2

verdict [vür/dĭkt] **141**–14

vertebrates [vür/ tə brəts] **194**–13

vest [vĕst] **89**–15

down vest [down/ vĕst/] **90**–14

Hi-Visibility safety vest
[hī/vĭz/ə bĭl/ə tē săf/tē vĕst] **92**–6

life vest [līf/ vĕst/] **161**–25, **226**–14

Veterans Day [vĕt/ər ənz dā/] **22**–16

veterinarian [vĕt/ər ə nër/ē ən] **169**–62

vice president [vīs/ prĕz/ə dənt] **138**–9

victim [vĭk/təm] **142**–10

video [vĭd/ē ō]

videocassette [vĭd/ē ō kə sĕt/] **133**–18

video game console [vĭd/ē ō gām/ kän/sōl/] **232**–3

video game control [vĭd/ē ō gām/ kän trōl/] **232**–4

video player [vĭd/ē ō plā ər/] **197**–11

video store [vĭd/ē ō stör/] **129**–20

videotape [vĭd/ē ō tāp/] **240**–A

view [vyōō]

rearview mirror [rïr/vyōō/ mïr/ər] **159**–35

sideview mirror [sīd/vyōō/ mïr/ər] **158**–3

village [vĭ/lĭj] **52**–3

vine [vīn] **210**–22

vineyard [vĭn/yərd] **177**–16

violence [vī/ləns, vī/ə–] **142**–4

violet [vī/ə lət, vī/lət] **24**–8, **211**–23

violin [vī/ə lĭn/] **238**–6

virus [vī/rəs] **111**–17

vise [vīs] **180**–26

vision [vĭ/zhən]

vision exam [vĭ/zhən ĭg zăm/] **136**–6

vision problems [vĭ/zhən präb/ləmz] **115**–1

Visit [vĭ/zət] **119**

visor [vī zər] **179**–12

vital signs monitor [vīt/l sīnz/ män/ə tər] **121**–26

vitamins [vī/tə mənz] **113**–17

v-neck [vē/nĕk/] **96**–8

vocational [vō kā/shə nəl]

vocational school [vō kā/shə nəl skōōl/] **188**–5

vocational training [vō kā/shə nəl trā/nĭng] **172**–5

voice message [voys mĕs/ĭj] **14**–18

volcanic eruption [väl kăn/ĭk ĭ rŭp/shən] **145**–16

volleyball [väl/ē böl] **229**–14, **231**–3

Volume [väl/yəm, –yōōm] **75**, **193**

volunteer [väl/ən tïr/] **121**–17

volunteer [väl/ən tïr/] **41**–Q

vomit [väm/ət] **110**–E

vote [vōt] **140**–A

waffles [wä/fəlz, wö/–] **80**–8

wages [wā/jĭz] **165**–12

wagon [wä/gən] **156**–6

waist [wāst]

waist apron [wāst/ ā/prən] **93**–30

waistband [wāst/bănd/] **100**–5

wait [wāt] **94**–B, **128**–B, **170**–T

waiter [wā/tər] **82**–8

headwaiter [hĕd/wā/tər] **185**–12

waiting area [wā/tĭng ër/ē ə] **182**–16

Waiting Room [wā/tĭng rōōm/] **118**

waitress [wā/trəs] **83**–9

wait staff [wāt/ stăf/] **185** ✦

wake up [wāk/ ŭp/] **38**–A

walk [wök] **53**–2

crosswalk [krös/wök/] **128**–15

walk-in freezer [wök/ĭn frē/zər] **185**–3

walk [wök]

walk a dog [wök ə dög/] **129**–F

walk down [wök/ down/] **153**–D

walk to class [wök/ tə kläs/] **11**–C

walk up [wök/ ŭp/] **153**–C

walk with a friend [wök/ wĭth ə frĕnd/] **143**–A

walker [wö/kər] **113**–11

wall [wöl] **56**–10, **194**–5

drywall [drī/wöl/] **178**–19

wallpaper [wöl/pā/pər] **59**–8

wallet [wä/lət, wö/–] **94**–13

walrus [wöl/rəs] **213**–32

war [wör] **199**–10

Revolutionary War [rĕ/və lōō/shə nër/ē wör/] **198**–8

warehouse [wër/hows/] **175**–7

warm [wörm] **13**–4

warm clothes [wörm/ klöz/] **146**–6

warning label [wör/nĭng lā/bəl] **112**–8

Warnings [wör/nĭngz] **112**

wash [wäsh, wösh]

mouthwash [mowth/wäsh/, –wösh/–] **109**–25

washcloth [wäsh/klöth/, wösh/–] **57**–4

wash [wäsh, wösh]

wash clothes [wäsh/ klöz/, wösh/–] **219**–K

wash hair [wäsh/ hër/, wösh/–] **108**–E

wash the dishes [wäsh/ dhə dĭsh/əz, wösh/–] **60**–M

wash the windows
[wäsh/ dhə wĭn/dōz, wösh/–] **60**–I

washer [wä/shər, wö/–] **50**–12, **101**–3, **180**–37

dishwasher [dĭsh/wäsh/ər, –wö–] **54**–8, **185**–2

Index

washing [wä/shĭng, wö/–] **61**–21

wasp [wäsp, wösp] **214**–17

waste [wāst] **121**–31, **218**–12

  wastebasket [wāst/băs/kət] **57**–26

watch [wäch, wöch] **94**–16

watch [wäch, wöch] **39**–X, **147**–C

water [wö/tər] **209**–3, **225**–1

  body of water [bäd/ē əv wö/tər] **204** ✦

  bottled water [bät/ld wö/tər] **146**–11

  cold water [köld/ wö/tər] **57**–7

  hot water [hät/ wö/tər] **57**–8

  hot water bottle [hät/ wö/tər böt/l] **113**–15

  watercolor [wö/tər kŭl/ər] **233**–21

  waterfall [wä/tər föl/] **204**–2

  water fountain [wö/tər fown/tn] **224**–9

  water glass [wö/tər glăs/] **83**–22

  watermelons [wö/tər mĕl/ənz] **68**–18

  water pollution [wö/tər pə lōō/shən] **218**–14

  water polo [wö/tər pō/lō] **229**–15

  waterskiing [wö/tər skē/ĭng] **227**–7

water [wö/tər] **176**–F

WATER SPORTS [wö/tər spörts/] **227**

wave [wāv] **145**–17, **225**–17

wave [wāv] **2**–F

wavy hair [wā/vē hër/] **33**–10

way [wā]

  hallway [häl/wā/] **184**–18

  one way [wŭn/ wā/] **154**–3

  one-way trip [wŭn/wā/ trĭp/] **152**–16

  two-way radio [tōō/wā/ rā/dē ō] **179**–22

  wrong way [röng/ wā/] **154**–2

Ways to Conserve Energy and Resources
  [wāz/ tə kən sürv/ ĕn/ər jē n rē/sör/səz,
  –rĭ sör/səz] **219**

Ways to Get Well [wāz/ tə gĕt/ wĕl/] **114**

Ways to Pay [wāz/ tə pā/] **27**

Ways to Serve Eggs [wāz/ tə sürv/ ĕgz/] **76**

Ways to Serve Meat and Poultry
  [wāz/ tə sürv/ mēt/ n pōl/trē/] **76**

Ways to Stay Well [wāz/ tə stā/ wĕl/] **114**

Ways to Succeed [wāz/tə sək sēd/] **10**

weak signal [wēk/ sĭg/nəl] **14**–12

WEATHER [wĕdh/ər] **13**

Weather Conditions [wĕdh/ər kən dĭsh/ənz] **13**

Weather Map [wĕdh/ər măp/] **13**

webcam [wĕb/kăm/] **196**–12

Webpage [wĕb/pāg/] **197**

website address [wĕb/sīt ə drĕs/] **197**–4

wedding [wĕ/dĭng] **22**–2

Wednesday [wĕnz/dā, –dē] **20**–11

weed [wēd]

  seaweed [sē/ wēd] **225** ✦

  weed eater [wēd/ ē/tər] **176**–12

  weed whacker [wēd/ wăk/ər] **176**–12

weed [wēd] **176**–G

week [wēk] **20**–15

  last week [lăst/ wēk/] **20**–18

  next week [nĕkst/ wēk/] **20**–20

  once a week [wŭns/ ə wēk/] **20**–22

  this week [dhĭs/ wēk/] **20**–19

  three times a week [thrē/ tīmz/ ə wēk/] **20**–24

  twice a week [twīs/ ə wēk/] **20**–23

weekdays [wēk/dāz/] **20**–16

weekend [wēk/ĕnd/] **20**–17

Week [wēk] **20**

weigh [wā] **75**–B

weight [wāt] **32**–8

Weight [wāt] **32, 75**

weightlifting [wāt/lĭf/tĭng] **228**–16

weights [wāts] **231**–22

WEIGHTS AND MEASUREMENTS
  [wāts/ ən mĕzh/ər mənts] **75**

welder [wĕl/dər] **169**–63

well [wĕl] **42**–14

Well [wĕl] **114**

west [wĕst] **155**–2

western [wĕs/tərn] **237**–15

wet [wĕt] **101**–17

  wet suit [wĕt/ sōōt/] **225**–4

whacker [wăk/ər] **176**–12

whale [wāl] **213**–29

wheat [wēt] **177**–2

wheat bread [wēt/ brĕd/] **71**–19

wheel [wēl] **159**–26

  wheelbarrow [wēl/băr/ō] **176**–3

  wheelchair [wēl/chër/] **113**–9

  wheel cover [wēl/ kŭv/ər] **158**–9

whisk [wĭsk] **78**–21

whiskers [wĭs/kərz] **216**–18

white [wīt] **24**–14

  whiteboard [wīt/börd/] **6**–3

  white bread [wīt/ brĕd/] **71**–18

  White House [wīt/ hows/] **138**–7

whole salmon [hōl/ săm/ən] **71**–3

wide [wīd] **97**–36

widow [wĭd/ō] **41** ✦

widower [wĭd/ō ər] **41** ✦

width [wĭdth, wĭtth] **17**–19

wife [wīf] **34**–12

  ex-wife [ĕks/ wīf/] **35** ✦

  former wife [för/mər wīf/] **35** ✦

wild [wīld] **215** ✦

wildlife [wīld/līf/] **220**–3

willow [wĭl/ō] **210**–13

win [wĭn] **229** ✦

wind [wĭnd]

  windbreaker [wĭnd/brā/kər] **90**–24

  wind power [wĭnd/ pow/ər] **218**–2

  windshield [wĭnd/ shēld/] **158**–1

  windshield wipers [wĭnd/shēld/wī/pərz] **158**–2

  windsurfing [wĭnd/sür/fĭng] **227**–10, **227** ✦

window [wĭn/dō] **47**–11, **56**–17, **136**–7

  drive-thru window [drīv/thrōō/ wĭn/dō] **128**–11

  ticket window [tĭk/ət wĭn/dō] **152**–12

  window pane [wĭn/dō pān/] **178**–16

windy [wĭn/dē] **13**–18

wine glass [wīn/ glăs/] **83**–23

wing [wĭng] **70**–20, **214**–1

winter [wĭn/tər] **21**–40

  winter scarf [wĭn/tər skärf/] **90**–5

WINTER AND WATER SPORTS
  [wĭn/tər ən wö/tər spörts/] **227**

wipe [wīp] **60**–O

wipers [wī/pərz] **158**–2

wipes [wīps] **37**–15, **61**–23

wire [wīr] **181**–13

  wire stripper [wīr/ strĭp/ər] **181**–42

wireless headset [wīr/ləs hĕd/sĕt] **14**–14

wiring [wīr/ĭng] **186**–7

withdraw [wĭdh drö/, wĭth–] **132**–F

witness [wĭt/nəs] **141**–11

wolf [wŏŏlf] **216**–5

woman [wŏŏm/ən] **30**–2

women [wĭ/mən] **30**–3

Women's Socks [wĭ/mənz säks/] **91**

Women's Underwear [wĭ/mənz ŭn/dər wër/] **91**

wood [wŏŏd] **178**–18

  plywood [plī/wŏŏd] **178**–17

  redwood [rĕd/wŏŏd] **210**–18

  wood floor [wŏŏd/ flör/] **58**–21

  woodpecker [wŏŏd/pĕk/ər] **214**–8

  wood screw [wŏŏd/ skrōō/] **180**–33

  wood stain [wŏŏd/ stān/] **181**–24

  woodworking kit [wŏŏd/wür/kĭng kĭt/] **232**–14

wooden spoon [wŏŏd/n spōōn/] **78**–9

Woodwinds [wŏŏd/wĭndz/] **238**

wool [wŏŏl] **61**–5, **98**–3

word [würd] **190**–1

word problem [würd/ prä/bləm] **192**–11

Words [wördz] **8**

work [würk] **121**–30, **154**–16

  workbook [würk/bŏŏk/] **7**–26

  work gloves [würk/ glŭvz/] **92**–17, **179**–17

  work light [würk/ līt/] **181**–44

  work pants [würk/ pănts/] **92**–5

  work shirt [würk/ shürt/] **92**–2

work [würk] **8**–I, **10**–J, **38**–K

WORK [würk] **186**–187

Work Clothes [würk/ klōz/] **88**

worker [wür/kər]

  careful worker [kër/fəl wür/kər] **179**–2

  careless worker [kër/ləs wür/kər] **179**–1

  childcare worker [chīld/kër wür/kər] **166**–16

  construction worker
    [kən strŭk/shən wür/kər] **178**–1

  dockworker [däk/wür/kər] **167**–23

  factory worker [făk/tə rē wür/kər, –trē] **175**–3

  farmworker [färm/wür/kər] **177**–8

  food preparation worker
    [fōōd/ prĕp ə rā/shən wür/kər] **185**–4

  garment worker [gär/mənt wür/kər] **167**–29

  postal worker [pō/stəl wür/kər] **169**–49

  sanitation worker [săn/ə tā/shən wür/kər] **169**–54

  social worker [sō/shəl wür/kər] **169**–57

Worker [wür/kər] **92, 93**

working [wür/kĭng]

  not working [nät/ wür/kĭng] **62**–1

  woodworking kit [wŏŏd/wür/kĭng kĭt/] **232**–14

Working with a Partner [wür/kĭng wĭth ə pärt/nər] **8**

Working with Your Classmates
  [wür/kĭng wĭth yər kläs/māts/] **8**

work out [würk/ owt/] **230**–N

WORKPLACE [würk/ plās/] **164**–165

WORKPLACE CLOTHING
  [würk/ plās/ klō/dhĭng] **92**–93

world [würld]
    world languages [würld/ lăng/gwĭ jəz] **189**–13
    world music [würld/ myōō/zĭk] **237**–32
WORLD MAP [würld/măp/] **202**–**203**
WORLD HISTORY [würld hĭs/tə rē] **199**
worm [würm] **212**–23
worried [wür/ēd] **42**–13
wrap [răp] **72**–24
wrap [răp] **240**–F
wrench [rĕnch] **158**–22, **181**–47, **181**–48
wrestling [rĕs/lĭng] **228**–17
wrinkled [rĭng/kəld] **101**–19
wrist [rĭst] **106**–14
    wristwatch [rĭst/wäch/, –wöch/] **94**–16
write [rīt]
    write a check [rīt/ ə chĕk/] **27**–D
    write a cover letter [rīt/ ə kŭv/ər lĕt/ər] **173**–G
    write a final draft [rīt/ ə fī/nəl drăft/] **191**–L
    write a first draft [rīt/ ə fürst/ drăft/] **191**–H
    write a note [rīt/ ə nōt/] **135**–A
    write a resume [rīt/ ə rĕ/zə mā/] **173**–F
    write a thank-you note
        [rīt/ ə thăngk/ yōō nōt/] **174**–O
    write back [rīt/ băk/] **135**–H
    write on the board [rīt/ ön dhə börd/] **6**–E
writer [rī/tər] **169**–64
Writing and Revising [rī/tĭng ən rĭ vī/ zĭng] **191**
Writing Process [rī/tĭng prä/sĕs] **191**
Writing Rules [rī/tĭng rōōlz] **190**
wrong way [röng/ wā/] **154**–2
xylophone [zī/lə fōn/] **238**–15
yard [yärd]
    courtyard [kört/ yärd/] **51**–21
    yardstick [yärd/stĭk/] **181**–16
YARD [yärd] **53**
yarn [yärn] **233**–22
year [yïr] **20**–4, **31**–9, **31**–10
Year [yïr] **21**
yellow [yĕl/ō] **24**–2
yesterday [yĕs/tər dā/, –dē] **20**–7
yield [yēld] **154**–9
yoga [yō/gə] **122**–4
yogurt [yō/gərt] **72**–22
young [yŭng] **32**–1
Your First License [yər fürst/ lī/səns] **137**
YOUR HEALTH [yər hĕlth/] **114**–**115**
zebra [zē/brə] **217**–33
zero [zïr/ō] **16**
ZIP code [zĭp/ kōd/] **4**–9
zipper [zĭp/ər] **99**–25
Zones [zōnz] **19**
zoo [zōō] **222**–1
zoom lens [zōōm/ lĕnz/] **235**–23
zucchini [zōō kē/nē] **69**–25

Geographical Index

Continents

Africa [ăf/rĭ kə] **202–5**

Antarctica [ănt ärk/tĭ kə, –är/tĭ–] **202–7**

Asia [ā/zhə] **202–4**

Australia [ö strāl/yə] **202–6**

Europe [yŏŏr/əp] **202–3**

North America [nörth/ ə mĕr/ə kə] **200–201, 202–1**

South America [sowth/ ə mĕr/ə kə] **202–2**

Countries and other locations

Afghanistan [ăf găn/ə stăn/] **203**

Albania [ăl bā/nē ə] **203**

Aleutian Islands [ə lōō/shən ī/ləndz] **200, 203**

Algeria [ăl jĭr/ē ə] **203**

American Samoa [ə mĕr/ə kən sə mō/ə] **202**

Andaman Islands [ăn/də mən ī/ləndz] **203**

Angola [ăng gō/lə] **203**

Argentina [är/jən tē/nə] **202**

Armenia [är mē/nē ə] **203**

Austria [ö/strē ə] **203**

Azerbaijan [ăz/ər bī jän/] **203**

Azores [ā/zörz] **202**

Baffin Island [băf/ən ī/lənd] **200**

Bahamas [bə hä/məz] **200, 202**

Bahrain [bä rān/] **203**

Bangladesh [băng/glə dĕsh/, băng/–] **203**

Banks Island [băngks/ ī/lənd] **200**

Belarus [bē/lə rōōs/, byĕl/ə–] **203**

Belgium [bĕl/jəm] **203**

Belize [bə lēz/] **201, 202**

Benin [bə nĭn/, –nēn/] **203**

Bermuda Islands [bər myōō/də ī/ ləndz] **200, 202**

Bhutan [bōō tän/] **203**

Bolivia [bə lĭv/ē ə] **202**

Bosnia [băz/nē ə] **203**

Botswana [bät swä/nə] **203**

Brazil [brə zĭl/] **202**

Brunei [brōō nī/] **203**

Bulgaria [bŭl gĕr/ē ə] **203**

Burkina Faso [bər kē/nə fä/sō] **203**

Burma [bür/mə] **203**

Burundi [bōŏ rōōn/dē] **203**

Cambodia [kăm bō/dē ə] **203**

Cameroon [kăm/ə rōōn/] **203**

Canada [kăn/ə də] **200, 202**

Canary Islands [kə nĕr/ē ī/ ləndz] **203**

Cape Verde [kăp/ vürd/] **202**

Central African Republic
[sĕn/trəl ăf/rĭ kən rĭ pŭb/lĭk] **203**

Chad [chăd] **203**

Chile [chĭl/ē] **202**

China [chī/nə] **203**

Colombia [kə lŭm/bē ə] **202**

Comoros [kăm/ə rōz] **203**

Congo [käng/gō] **203**

Cook Islands [kŏŏk/ ī/ləndz] **202**

Corsica [kör/sĭ kə] **203**

Costa Rica [kōs/tə rē/kə, käs/–] **201, 202**

Croatia [krō ā/shə] **203**

Cuba [kyōō/bə] **201, 202**

Cyprus [sī/prəs] **203**

Czech Republic [chĕk/ rĭ pŭb/lĭk] **203**

Democratic Republic of the Congo
[dĕm/ə krăt/ĭk rĭ pŭb/lĭk əv dhə käng/gō] **203**

Denmark [dĕn/märk] **203**

Devon Island [dĕv/ən ī/lənd] **200**

Djibouti [jĭ bōō/tē] **203**

Dominican Republic [də mĭn/ĭ kən rĭ pŭb/lĭk] **201, 202**

Ecuador [ĕk/wə dör/] **202**

Egypt [ē/jĭpt] **203**

Ellesmere Island [ĕl/əs mĭr/ ī/lənd] **200**

El Salvador [ĕl săl/və dör/] **201, 202**

Equatorial Guinea [ē/kwə tör/ē əl gĭn/ē, ĕk/wə–] **203**

Eritrea [ĕr/ə trē/ə] **203**

Estonia [ĕ stō/nē ə] **203**

Ethiopia [ē/thē ō/pē ə] **203**

Federated States of Micronesia
[fĕ/də rā/təd stāts/ əv mī/krə nē/zhə] **203**

Fiji [fē/jē] **203**

Finland [fĭn/lənd] **203**

France [frăns] **203**

Franz Josef Land [fränz/ yō/səf länd/] **203**

French Guiana [frĕnch/ gē ăn/ə, –ä/nə] **202**

French Polynesia [frĕnch/ păl/ə nē/zhə] **202**

Gabon [gă bōn/] **203**

Galápagos Islands [gə lä pə gōs ī/ləndz] **202**

Gambia [găm/bē ə] **203**

Georgia [jör/jə] **203**

Germany [jür/mə nē] **203**

Ghana [gä/nə] **203**

Greater Antilles [grā/tər ăn tĭl/ēz] **201**

Greece [grēs] **203**

Greenland [grēn/lənd, –lănd/] **200, 202**

Guam [gwäm] **203**

Guatemala [gwä/tə mä/lə] **201, 202**

Guinea [gĭn/ē] **203**

Guinea-Bissau [gĭn/ē bĭ sow/] **203**

Guyana [gī ăn/ə] **202**

Haiti [hā/tē] **201, 202**

Hawaiian Islands [hə wī/ən ī/lənds] **200, 202**

Hispaniola [hĭs/pən yō/lə] **201**

Honduras [hän dŏŏr/əs] **201, 202**

Hong Kong [häng/ käng/] **203**

Hungary [hŭng/gə rē] **203**

Iceland [īs/lənd] **203**

India [ĭn/dē ə] **203**

Indonesia [ĭn/də nē/zhə] **203**

Iran [ĭ răn/, ĭ rän/] **203**

Iraq [ĭ răk/, ĭ räk/] **203**

Ireland [īr/lənd] **203**

Israel [ĭz/rē əl, –rā–] **203**

Italy [ĭt/l ē] **203**

Ivory Coast [īv/rē kōst/] **203**

Jamaica [jə mā/kə] **201, 202**

Japan [jə păn/] **203**

Jordan [jör/dn] **203**

Kazakhstan [kä/zäk stän/] **203**

Kenya [kĕn/yə, kēn/–] **203**

Kiribati [kĭr/ə băs/] **203**

Kuwait [kōō wāt/] **203**

Kyrgyzstan [kĭr/gĭ stän/, –stän/] **203**

Laos [lows, lä/ōs] **203**

Latvia [lăt/vē ə] **203**

Lebanon [lĕb/ə nən, –nän/] **203**

Lesotho [lə sō/tō, –sōō/tōō] **203**

Lesser Antilles [lĕ/sər ăn tĭl/ēz] **201, 202**

Liberia [lī bĭr/ē ə] **203**

Libya [lĭb/ē ə] **203**

Lithuania [lĭth/ōō ā/nē ə] **203**

Luxembourg [lŭk/səm bürg/] **203**

Macedonia [măs/ə dō/nē ə] **203**

Madagascar [măd/ə găs/kər] **203**

Madeira Islands [mə dĭr/ə ī/ləndz] **203**

Malawi [mə lä/wē] **203**

Malaysia [mə lā/zhə] **203**

Maldives [möl/dēvz, măl/–] **203**

Mali [mä/lē] **203**

Malta [möl/tə] **203**

Marshall Islands [mär/shəl ī/ləndz] **203**

Mauritania [mör/ə tā/nē ə] **203**

Mauritius [mö rĭsh/əs] **203**

Mexico [mĕk/sĭ kō/] **200, 201, 202**

Moldova [möl dō/və, mäl–] **203**

Monaco [män/ə kō/] **203**

Mongolia [mäng gō/lē ə] **203**

Montenegro [män/tə nē/grō, –nĕ/–] **203**

Morocco [mə räk/ō] **203**

Mozambique [mō/zəm bēk/] **203**

Namibia [nə mĭb/ē ə] **203**

Nepal [nə pöl/, –päl/] **203**

Netherlands [nĕdh/ər ləndz] **203**

New Caledonia [nōō/ kăl/ə dō/nē ə] **203**

New Zealand [nōō/ zē/lənd] **203**

Nicaragua [nĭk/ə rä/gwə] **201, 202**

Niger [nī/jər, nē zhĕr/] **203**

Nigeria [ni jĭr/ē ə] **203**

Northern Mariana Islands
[nördh/ərn mä/rē ä/nə ī/ləndz] **203**

North Korea [nörth/ kə rē/ə] **203**

Norway [nör/wā] **203**

Oman [ō män/] **203**

Pakistan [păk/ə stăn/] **203**

Palau [pə low/] **203**

Panama [păn/ə mä/] **201, 202**

Papua New Guinea [păp/yōō ə nōō/ gĭn/ē] **203**

Paraguay [păr/ə gwī/, –gwä/] **202**

Peru [pə rōō/] **202**

Philippines [fĭl/ə pēnz/, fĭl/ə pēnz/] **203**

Poland [pō/lənd] **203**

Portugal [pör/chə gəl] **203**

Puerto Rico [pwĕr/tə rē/kō, pör/tə–] **201, 202**

Qatar [kä/tär, kə tär/] **203**

Romania [rō mā/nē ə, rōō–] **203**

Russia [rŭsh/ə] **203**

Rwanda [rōō än/də] **203**

Samoa [sə mō/ə] **202**

Saudi Arabia [sow/dē ə rā/bē ə, sö/dē–] **203**

Senegal [sĕn/ə göl/, –gäl/] **203**

Serbia [sür/bē ə] **203**

Seychelles [sā shĕlz/, –shĕl/] **203**

Sierra Leone [sē ĕr/ə lē ōn/, –lē ō/nē] **203**

Singapore [sĭng/ə pör/] **203**

Slovakia [slō vä/kē ə] **203**

Slovenia [slō vē/nē ə] **203**

Society Islands [sə sī/ə tē ī/ləndz] **202**

Solomon Islands [säl/ə mən ī/ləndz] **203**

Somalia [sə mä⁄lē ə] **203**
South Africa [sowth⁄ ăf⁄rĭ kə] **203**
South Georgia [sowth⁄ jör⁄jə] **202**
South Korea [sowth⁄ kə rē⁄ə] **203**
Spain [spān] **203**
Sri Lanka [srē⁄ läng⁄kə, shrē⁄–] **203**
Sudan [soō dăn⁄] **203**
Suriname [soŏr⁄ə nä⁄mə] **202**
Svalbard [sväl⁄bärd] **203**
Swaziland [swä⁄zē länd⁄] **203**
Sweden [swēd⁄n] **203**
Switzerland [swĭt⁄sər lənd] **203**
Syria [sĭr⁄ē ə] **203**
Tahiti [tə hē⁄tē] **202**
Taiwan [tī⁄wän⁄] **203**
Tajikistan [tä jĭk⁄ə stän⁄, –stän⁄] **203**
Tanzania [tăn⁄zə nē⁄ə] **203**
Tasmania [tăz mā⁄nē ə] **203**
Thailand [tī⁄länd⁄, –lənd] **203**
Togo [tō⁄gō] **203**
Tonga [täng⁄gə] **202**
Tunisia [toō nē⁄zhə] **203**
Turkey [tür⁄kē] **203**
Turkmenistan [türk mĕn⁄ə stän⁄, –stän⁄] **203**
Uganda [yoō găn⁄də] **203**
Ukraine [yoō⁄krān, yoō krān⁄] **203**
United Arab Emirates [yoō nī⁄təd är⁄əb ĕm⁄ər əts] **203**
United Kingdom [yoō nī⁄təd kĭng⁄dəm] **203**
United States of America
   [yoō nī⁄təd stäts⁄ əv ə mĕr⁄ə kə] **200, 202**
Uruguay [yoŏr⁄ə gwī⁄, –gwä⁄] **202**
Uzbekistan [oōz bĕk⁄ə stän⁄, –stän⁄] **203**
Vanuatu [vä⁄noō ä⁄toō] **203**
Venezuela [vĕn⁄ə zwā⁄lə] **202**
Victoria Island [vĭk⁄tör ē ə ī⁄lənd] **200**
Vietnam [vē⁄ĕt näm⁄, –năm⁄] **203**
Wake Island [wāk⁄ ī⁄lənd] **203**
Western Sahara [wĕs⁄tərn sə här⁄ə] **203**
Yemen [yĕm⁄ən] **203**
Zambia [zăm⁄bē ə] **203**
Zanzibar [zăn⁄zə bär] **203**
Zimbabwe [zĭm bäb⁄wä] **203**

Bodies of water
Arctic Ocean [ärk⁄tĭk ō⁄shən] **200, 203**
Atlantic Ocean [ət lăn⁄ tĭk ō⁄shən] **200, 202–203**
Baffin Bay [băf⁄ən bā⁄] **200, 202**
Baltic Sea [böl⁄tĭk sē⁄] **203**
Beaufort Sea [bō⁄fərt sē⁄] **200**
Bering Sea [bĕr⁄ĭng sē⁄, bĭr⁄–] **200**
Black Sea [blăk⁄ sē⁄] **203**
Caribbean Sea [kăr⁄ə bē⁄ən sē⁄, kə rĭb⁄ē ən–] **201**
Caspian Sea [kăs⁄pē ən sē⁄] **203**
Coral Sea [kör⁄əl sē⁄] **203**
Gulf of Alaska [gŭlf⁄ əv ə lăs⁄kə] **200, 202**
Gulf of California [gŭlf⁄ əv kăl⁄ə förn⁄yə] **200**
Gulf of Mexico [gŭlf⁄ əv mĕk⁄sĭ kō⁄] **200, 202**
Hudson Bay [hŭd⁄sən bā⁄] **200, 202**
Indian Ocean [ĭn⁄dē ən ō⁄shən] **203**
Labrador Sea [lăb⁄rə dör⁄ sē⁄] **200**
Mediterranean Sea [mĕd⁄ə tə rā⁄nē ən sē⁄] **203**

North Atlantic Ocean [nörth⁄ ət lăn⁄tĭk ō⁄shən] **202**
North Pacific Ocean [nörth⁄ pə sĭf⁄ĭk ō⁄shən] **202, 203**
North Sea [nörth⁄ sē⁄] **203**
Pacific Ocean [pə sĭf⁄ĭk ō⁄shən] **200, 202, 203**
Philippine Sea [fĭl⁄ə pēn⁄ sē⁄] **203**
Red Sea [rĕd⁄ sē⁄] **203**
South Atlantic Ocean [sowth⁄ ət lăn⁄tĭk ō⁄shən] **203**
Southern Ocean [sŭdh⁄ərn ō⁄shən] **203**
South Pacific Ocean [sowth⁄ pə sĭf⁄ĭk ō⁄shən] **202, 203**

The United States of America
Capital: Washington, D.C. (District of Columbia)
   [wä⁄shĭng tən dē⁄sē⁄, wö⁄–] **200**

Regions of the United States
Mid–Atlantic States [mĭd⁄ət lăn⁄tĭk stāts⁄] **201–10**
Midwest [mĭd⁄wĕst⁄] **201–9**
New England [noō⁄ ĭng⁄glənd] **201–11**
Pacific States [pə sĭf⁄ĭk stāts⁄] **201–7**
Rocky Mountain States [räk⁄ē mown⁄tn stāts⁄] **201–8**
South [sowth] **201–13**
Southeast [sowth⁄ēst⁄] **201–13**
Southwest [sowth⁄wĕst⁄] **201–12**
West Coast [wĕst⁄ kōst⁄] **201–7**

States of the United States
Alabama [ăl⁄ə băm⁄ə] **200**
Alaska [ə lăs⁄kə] **200, 202**
Arizona [ăr⁄ə zō⁄nə] **200**
Arkansas [är⁄kən sö⁄] **200**
California [kăl⁄ə förn⁄yə] **200**
Colorado [kăl⁄ə răd⁄ō, –ra⁄dō] **200**
Connecticut [kə nĕt⁄ĭ kət] **200**
Delaware [dĕl⁄ə wĕr⁄] **200**
Florida [flör⁄ə də, flär⁄–] **200**
Georgia [jör⁄jə] **200**
Hawaii [hə wī⁄ē] **200**
Idaho [ī⁄də hō⁄] **200**
Illinois [ĭl⁄ə noy⁄] **200**
Indiana [ĭn⁄dē ăn⁄ə] **200**
Iowa [ī⁄ə wə] **200**
Kansas [kăn⁄zəs] **200**
Kentucky [kən tŭk⁄ē] **200**
Louisiana [loō ē⁄zē ăn⁄ə] **200**
Maine [mān] **200**
Maryland [mĕr⁄ə lənd] **200**
Massachusetts [măs⁄ə choō⁄səts] **200**
Michigan [mĭsh⁄ĭ gən] **200**
Minnesota [mĭn⁄ə sō⁄tə] **200**
Mississippi [mĭs⁄ə sĭp⁄ē] **200**
Missouri [mə zoŏr⁄ē, –zoōr⁄ə] **200**
Montana [män tăn⁄ə] **200**
Nebraska [nə brăs⁄kə] **200**
Nevada [nə văd⁄ə, –vä⁄də] **200**
New Hampshire [noō⁄ hămp⁄shər] **200**
New Jersey [noō⁄ jür⁄zē] **200**
New Mexico [noō⁄ mĕk⁄sĭ kō⁄] **200**
New York [noō⁄ yörk⁄] **200**
North Carolina [nörth⁄ kăr⁄ə lī⁄nə] **200**
North Dakota [nörth⁄ də kō⁄tə] **200**
Ohio [ō hī⁄ō] **200**
Oklahoma [ō⁄klə hō⁄mə] **200**
Oregon [ör⁄ĭ gən, –găn⁄, är⁄–] **200**

Pennsylvania [pĕn⁄səl vān⁄yə] **200**
Rhode Island [rōd⁄ ī⁄lənd] **200**
South Carolina [sowth⁄ kăr⁄ə lī⁄nə] **200**
South Dakota [sowth⁄ də kō⁄tə] **200**
Tennessee [tĕn⁄ə sē⁄] **200**
Texas [tĕk⁄səs] **200**
Utah [yoō⁄tö, –tä] **200**
Vermont [vər mänt⁄] **200**
Virginia [vər jĭn⁄yə] **200**
Washington [wä⁄shĭng tən, wö⁄–] **200**
West Virginia [wĕst⁄ vər jĭn⁄yə] **200**
Wisconsin [wĭs kän⁄sən] **200**
Wyoming [wī ō⁄mĭng] **200**

Canada
Capital: Ottawa [ät⁄ə wə] **201**

Regions of Canada
British Columbia [brĭt⁄ĭsh kə lŭm⁄bē ə] **201–2**
Maritime Provinces [mĕr⁄ə tīm präv⁄ən səz] **201–6**
Northern Canada [nör⁄dhərn kăn⁄ə də] **201–1**
Ontario [än tĕr⁄ē ō⁄] **201–4**
Prairie Provinces [prĕr⁄ē präv⁄ən səz] **201–3**
Québec [kwĭ bĕk⁄] **201–5**

Provinces of Canada
Alberta [ăl bür⁄tə] **200**
British Columbia [brĭt⁄ĭsh kə lŭm⁄bē ə] **200**
Manitoba [măn⁄ə tō⁄bə] **200**
New Brunswick [noō⁄ brŭnz⁄wĭk] **200**
Newfoundland and Labrador
   [noō⁄fən lənd ən lă⁄brə dör⁄] **200**
Northwest Territories [nörth⁄wĕst⁄ tĕr⁄ə tör⁄ēz] **200**
Nova Scotia [nō⁄və skō⁄shə] **200**
Nunavut [noō⁄nə voōt⁄] **200**
Ontario [än tĕr⁄ē ō⁄] **200**
Prince Edward Island [prĭns⁄ ĕd⁄wərd ī⁄lənd] **200**
Québec [kwĭ bĕk⁄] **200**
Saskatchewan [sä skăch⁄ə wən, –wän⁄] **200**
Yukon [yoō⁄kän] **200**

Mexico
Capital: Mexico (City) [mĕk⁄sĭ kō⁄ (sĭt⁄ē)] **201**

Regions of Mexico
Chiapas Highlands [chē ä⁄pəs hī⁄ləndz] **201–18**
Gulf Coastal Plain [gŭlf⁄ kō⁄stəl plān⁄] **201–16**
Pacific Northwest [pə sĭf⁄ĭk nörth⁄wĕst] **201–14**
Plateau of Mexico [plă tō⁄ əv mĕk⁄sĭ kō⁄] **201–15**
Southern Uplands [sŭdh⁄ərn ŭp⁄ləndz] **201–17**
Yucatan Peninsula
   [yoō⁄kə tän⁄ pə nĭn⁄sə lə, yoō⁄kə tän⁄–] **201–19**

States of Mexico
Aguascalientes [ä⁄gwəs käl yĕn⁄täs] **201**
Baja California Norte [bä⁄hä käl⁄ə förn⁄yə nör⁄tā] **200**
Baja California Sur [bä⁄hä käl⁄ə förn⁄yə soōr⁄] **200**
Campeche [käm pā⁄chā, käm pē⁄chē] **201**
Chiapas [chē ä⁄pəs] **201**
Chihuahua [chĭ wä⁄wä, –wə] **200**
Coahuila [kō⁄ə wē⁄lə] **200**
Colima Michoacán [kə lē⁄mə mē⁄chō ə kän⁄] **201**
Distrito Federal [dĭ strē⁄tō fĕd⁄ə räl⁄] **201**
Durango [doō răng⁄gō, –räng⁄–] **201**

Geographical Index

0 صفر 16
1/4 (ربع) كوب 75
1/2 (نصف) كوب 75
1 سنت 26-1
1 أونصة سائلة 75
1 باينت 75
1 جالون 75
1 كوارت 75
1 كوب 75
1 ملعقة شاي 75
1 ملعقة طعام (سفرة) 75
1 واحد 16
2 اثنان 16
3 ثلاثة 16
4 أربعة 16
5 سنتات 26-2
5 خمسة 16
6 ستة 16
7 سبعة 16
8 ثمانية 16
9 تسعة 16
10 سنتات 26-3
10 بالمائة 17-12
10 عشرة 16
11 أحد عشر 16
12 اثنا عشر 16
13 ثلاثة عشر 16
14 أربعة عشر 16
15 خمسة عشر 16
16 ستة عشر 16
17 سبعة عشر 16
18 ثمانية عشر 16
19 تسعة عشر 16
20 عشرون 16
21 واحد وعشرون 16
22 اثنان وعشرون 16
23 ثلاثة وعشرون 16
24 أربعة وعشرون 16
25 سنتا 26-4
25 بالمائة 17-11
25 خمسة وعشرون 16
30 ثلاثون 16
40 أربعون 16
50 سنتا 26-5
50 بالمائة 17-10
50 خمسون 16
60 ستون 16
70 سبعون 16
75 بالمائة 17-9
80 ثمانون 16
90 تسعون 16
100 بالمائة 17-8
100 مائة 16
101 مائة وواحد 16
1000 ألف 16
10,000 عشرة آلاف 16
100,000 مائة ألف 16

1,000,000 مليون 16
1,000,000,000 بليون (مليار) 16
أب 4-34
أب أعزب 35-23
الآباء المؤسسون 198-7
ابتسم 2-D
ابتعد عن النوافذ 147-I
الإبحار بمركب شراعي 227-8
ابحث عن لافتات الوظائف الشاغرة 173-C
ابحث عن مخبأ وملجأ 147-H
أبحث عن مقعدك 160-F
ابحثي عن كلمة في المعجم 8-A
أبخرة سامة 179-3
ابدئي الحديث 12-A
إبرة 98-17, A-12, 100-10
إبرة / سرنجة 118-12
أبرز بطاقة هويتك 137-C
إبريق شاي 55-16
إبريق شاي 16
أبريل / نيسان 21-28
إبزيم (مشبك) 99-28
إبزيم (مشبك) الحزام 94-20
ابشر الجبن 77-G
أبعاد 17
ابقَ في شوارع جيدة الإنارة 143-B
ابقَ هادئا 147-E
ابن 34-15
ابن الأخ أو الأخت 34-19
ابنة 34-14
ابنة الأخ أو الأخت 34-18
إبهام 106-16
أبو الحناء 214-16
أبو سيف 212-10
أبوسوم 216-4
أبيض 24-14
إتباع الإرشادات 9
اتبع الإرشادات 147-F
اتبع النصيحة الطبية 114-J
اتجاه واحد 154-3
اترك فراغا في سطر أول جملة في فقرة جديدة 190-D
اتركوا الحجرة 11-O
اتصل بمعارفك خارج الولاية 147-L
اتصل واطلب أجازة مرضية 186-A
أثاث للفناء المرصوف 53-19
أثاث وإكسسوارات 59
إثبات التأمين 136-8
أقفل 231-22
الاثنين 20-9
اجتماع أباءومعلمين 22-5
اجتماع المستأجرين 64
اجتماع شمل الأسرة 44
إجراء مكالمة في حالة طارئة 15
إجراء مكالمة هاتفية / تليفونية 15
إجراءات الإسعافات الأولية 117
الإجراءات المتبعة في حالات الطوارئ 147-146
إجراءات طبية 118
أجرة 118
أجرة / تعريفة 152-2

اجري محادثة 11-L
أجزاء الزهرة 211
أجزاء المقال 190
أجزاء ماكينة الخياطة 98
اجلس / اقعد على مقعد 6-F
اجمع 192-A
أجنحة 70-20
أجهزة إلكترونية وأدوات التصوير 234-235
أجور 165-12
أحاسيس 42-43
احتفال 206-6
احتقان في الألف 110-7
احتم 147-J
الأحد 20-8
الأحداث والوثائق الحياتية 40-41
أحذية 87-13
أحذية ذات كعب عال 89-21
أحذية رياضية 86-7
أحذية نسائية بدون كعب 95-27
أحذية وإكسسوارات 94-95
أحرز درجات جيدة 10-H
أحزمة 94-6
احسبي 17-B
احصل على الوظيفة 173-L
احصل على تصريح للمتعلم 137-F
احصل على رأي شخص آخر 191-K
احصل على سند الملكية من البائع 157-E
أحضر معك سيرتك الذاتية وهويتك 174-D
احضني 2-E
أحمر 24-1
أحمر الشفاه 109-38
أحمر خدود 109-37
احمل الكتب 11-F
أحوال الطقس 13
الأحياء البحرية والبرمائيات والزواحف 212-213
الأحياء البرية 220-3
أحيائي (عالم بيولوجيا) 194-2
أخ 34-6
أخ غير شقيق 35-28
أخ من زوجة الأب أو زوج الأم 35-30
اخبز في الفرن 77-H
أخت 34-5
أخت غير شقيقة 35-27
أخت من زوجة الأب أو زوج الأم 35-29
اختر الجواب الصحيح 9-P
اختراع 199-19
اختلف 12-L
أخرج بطاقة ايه تي أم الخاصة بك 132-G
أخرج قطعة ورق 9-Y
أخصائي تجميع 166-7
أخصائي تصليح أجهزة إلكترونية 167-24
أخصائي تصليح أدوات منزلية 166-4
أخصائي تصليح أسقف البيوت 62-8
أخصائي سمع 115-9
أخصائي صحة أسنان 119-3
أخصائي طبي لحالات الطوارئ 121-32
أخصائي علاج طبيعي 115-12

أخصائي في شؤون التغذية 120-15
أخصائية اجتماعية 169-57
أخصائية حضانة أطفال 166-16
أخصائية علاج مهني 168-45
أخضر 24-5
الأخطار على السلامة والمواد الخطرة 179
أخطبوط 212-9
اخف رقمك السري الذي تستخدمه في جهاز الصرف الآلي 143-C
اخل المنطقة 147-K
اخلط المكونات 77-R
أداة إنقاذ 225-20
أداة تحكم في ألعاب الفيديو 232-4
أداة مراقبة الطفل 59-7
إداري 120-13
الإداريون 5
ادخل الحجرة 11-A
أدخل بطاقة ايه تي أم الخاصة بك 132-D
أدخل رقمك السري (رقم PIN) 132-E
أدخل عنوان البريد الإلكتروني للمرسل إليه 197-C
ادعي أحدا 12-H
ادفع رسم تقديم الطلب 137-D
أدوات التنظيف 61
أدوات الخياطة 100
أدوات المطبخ 78
أدوات طعام بلاستيكية 79-19
أدوات للغلق 99
أدوات معالجة الأسنان 119-4
أدوات ومواد البناء 180-181
الأدوية المباعة بدون وصفة طبية 113
أدوية مباعة بدون وصفة طبية 113-18
اذكر الحالة الطارئة 15-G
أذن 105-12
أذن مثقوبة 32-17
اذهب إلى المقابلة الشخصية 173-K
اذهب إلى مكتب أو وكالة توظيف 173-E
اذهب لعمل فحص للغازات الملوثة 157-J
آر في (مركبة ترفيهية) 156-10
اربط حزام المقعد 160-H
الأربعاء 20-11
الأربعون 16
ارتفاع 17-16
ارجعوا إلى الصف 11-M
أرجل 70-21
أرجواني 24-6
أرجوحة 224-16
أرجوحة شبكية للنوم 53-23
أرز 67-10, 81-30, 177-1
إرسال بطاقة / كارت 135
أرسل البريد الإلكتروني 197-I
أرسل سيرتك الذاتية وخطابك التقديمي 173-H
ارسمي صورة 8-F
إرشادات 155
إرشادات وخرائط 155
الأرض 205-3
أرض الملعب 5-2
أرضية زلقة 179-6

أرضية 46-6
أرضية خشبية 58-21
أرغن 238-20
أرض دعوة 12-J
ارفع / التقط الكتب 11-E
ارفع يدك 6-A
أرفق صورة 197-G
أرفق ملفا 197-H
أرقام زوجية 192-4
أرقام فردية 192-3
اركض إلى الصف 11-D
أرنب 215-13
أريكة / كنبة مزدوجة 56-1
أزرق 24-3
أزرق غامق 24-10
أزرق فاتح 24-11
أزرق كحلي 28-5
أزرق لامع 24-12
أزل كل شيء من على مكتبك 10-I
ازميل 181-55
اسأل البائع عن السيارة 157-B
اسأل، "كيف حالك؟" 2-B
أساور 95-9
الاسباتي 233-32
أسبوع 20-15
الأسبوع الحالي 20-19
الأسبوع القادم 20-20
الأسبوع الماضي 20-18
استئجار شقة 48
استاد 126-1
استبدل المساحات 157-K
استخدم علامة الوقف والترقيم 190-C
استراليا 202-6
استردي أمتعتك 160-L
استشاري في شؤون المسارات الوظيفية 172-10
استعارة كتب ذاتيا 133-10
استعد للمقابلة 174-A
الاستعلامات 14-22
استعمال لمبات كهربائية خفيضة الطاقة 219-H
استكشاف 199-8
استمارات بريدية 134-19
استمارة إقرار جمركي 161-16
استمارة التاريخ الصحي 118-4
استمارة تسجيل بالمدرسة 4
استمع إلى قرص مدمج (س دي) 6-C
استمع إليها بعناية 174-K
اسحب النقود 132-F
أسد / سبع 217-36
أسد البحر 213-33
أسد الجبال (الكوغر) 216-2
أسطوانة 193-41
إسعافات أولية 117
إسفنجة 61-19
الأسقلوب 212-19
أسقلوب 71-12
اسلق الدجاج 77-M
الاسم 4-1

الاسم الشخصي 4-2
اسم العائلة 4-4
أسماك 209, 71-14
أسنان 106-7
أسود 24-13
أسورة طوارئ طبية 117-3
آسيا 202-4
إشارة الانعطاف 158-6, 159-34
إشارة ضعيفة 14-12
إشارة قوية 14-11
إشارة مرور 128-8
اشترِ وجبة خفيفة 11-K
أشجار 208-1
أشجار ونباتات 210
اشرب سوائل 114-C
اشرب 11-J
اشرح شينا 12-M
اشطب الكلمة 9-R
إشعاع 218-15
إشعال 159-33
أشعل الأنوار 11-B
الأشكال 193
الأشكال الهندسية المجسمة 193
اشكر الشخص القائم بالمقابلة 174-N
اشكر شخصا 12-E
أشواك القنفذ 216-23
إصبع قدم 105-10
إصبع يد 105-16
اصعد الطائرة 160-E
أصفر 24-2
أصفر باهت / عاجي 24-16
إصلاح الحنفيات المتسربة 219-F
أصلح 33-12
أصمّ / صمّاء 32-12
اصنع / جهّز علبة بمستلزمات الكوارث 146-B
اضرب (اطلب) رقم ٩ ١ ١ 15-E
اضرب 192-C
اضرب الخليط 77-S
أضف الخضروات 77-N
إطار / عجلة 158-5
إطار احتياطي (استبن) 158-23
إطار للصور / برواز 58-4
أطباء أخصائيون 120
اطبخ 76-C
اطبع / أدخل موضوع الرسالة 197-D
اطبع / أدخل نص الرسالة 197-E
اطبع / أدخل كلمة المرور الخاصة بك 197-A
اطرح 192-B
اطرح أسئلة 174-M
اطرح لنفسك أفكارا وتمعن فيها 191-F
اطرحي سؤالا 8-K
أطعمة مخبوزة 73
أطعمة مغلفة 146-10
أطفئ الأنوار 11-P
إطفاء الأنوار 219-G
إطفائي / رجل إطفاء 144-9
إطفائي 167-26

إطفائية 125-12
أطفال مزعجون 23-11
أطفال هادئون 23-12
اطلب (اضرب) رقم الهاتف / التليفون 15-A
اطلب إجراء كشوف طبية منتظمة 114-H
اطلب العناية الطبية 114-A
اطلب المساعدة 10-F
اطلب تحصينك بلقاحات ضد الأمراض 114-I
أطلس 133-8
اطهِ البروكولي على البخار 77-D
اطهِ ببطء (على نار هادئة) 77-P
اطهِ في الميكروويف لمدة 5 دقائق 77-T
أظهر بطاقة الصعود والهوية 160-C
إعادة استعمال أكياس التسوق 219-B
إعادة التصنيع أو التدوير 219-C
اعبر شارع مِئْن 155-E
اعتداء 142-3
اعتداء بهدف السلب 142-11
اعتذر 12-F
الاعتناء بسيارتك 157
الأعداد 16
الأعداد الأصلية 16
الأعداد الترتيبية 16
الأعداد الرومانية 16
الأعداد الصحيحة 192
أعداد صحيحة سالبة 192-1
أعداد صحيحة موجبة 192-2
أعراض مرضية وإصابات 110
اعرض شينا 12-D
أعشاب 84-9
إعصار 145-14
أعضاء الجسم الداخلية والخارجية 106
أعضاء الجسم الداخلية والخارجية 107
أعط اذكر اسمك 15-F
إعلان الاستقلال 198-5
إعلان مبوب في صحيفة 48-2
الأعمال المنزلية 60
الأعمال اليومية الروتينية 38-39
اعمل بمفردك 10-J
اعمل في مجموعة 8-I
أعواد الثقاب (كبريت) 146-16, 226-21
الأعياد 239
الأعياد الرسمية 22
أعياد الميلاد (الكريسماس) 22-18
الأعياد والمناسبات الخاصة 22
أغاني تقليدية للأطفال 37-22
أغسطس / أب 21-32
أغلق كتابك 6-H
أغلق هاتفك / تليفونك المحمول 160-I
أغلق هاتفك / تليفونك المحمول 174-G
افتح كتابك 6-G
افحص الزيت 157-H
أفخاذ / أوراك 70-22
إفريقيا 202-5
افصل 76-B
أفعال متعلقة بالرياضة 230
أفلام كارتون (رسوم متحركة) 236-3

أفوكاته / زُبدية 84-6
أقارب / أقرباء 44-6
أقاليم المكسيك 201
أقاليم الولايات المتحدة 201
أقاليم كندا 201
اقبلي دعوة 12-I
اقتباس 190-9
اقترض / استلف نقودا 26-B
أقحوان 211-21
اقرئي التعريف 8-B
أقراص خبز 80-17
أقراص للبرد أو الزكام 113-27
أقراص للمص ملطفة للحنجرة 113-30
اقرض / سلّف نقودا 26-C
اقسم 192-A, 17-D
اقفل أبوابك 143-E
اقفل السماعة / اكبس مفتاح "انه" "end" 15-D
اقل الفطر بسرعة وفي قليل من الدهن 77-E
إقلاع / مغادرة 160-J
أقلام ألوان شمعية 59-14
اكبس مفتاح "أرسل" "send" 15-B
اكتئاب 115-5
اكتب مسودة أولى 191-H
اكتب اسمك 4-C
اكتب الأسماء بحروف كبيرة 190-A
اكتب الحرف الأول في الجملة بحرف كبير 190-B
اكتب خطابا تقديميا 173-G
اكتب خلاصة عن مهاراتك وانجازاتك 173-F
اكتب رسالة شكر 174-O
اكتب على السبورة 6-E
اكتب مسودة نهائية 191-L
أكتوبر / تشرين الأول 21-34
اكسر بيضتين في سلطانية آمنة الاستعمال في ميكروويف 77-Q
أكل النمل 217-24
أكورديون 238-19
أكياس تخزين بلاستيكية 72-25
أكياس مهملات 61-24
آلات أخرى 238
الآلات الإيقاعية 238
آلات النفخ الخشبية 238
آلات النفخ النحاسية 238
الآلات الوترية 238
البس ملابس مناسبة 174-B
ألبوم صور 235-31
ألبوم صور رقمية (ديجيتال) 235-32
آلة البيع 152-9
آلة تسجيل النقود 27-10
آلة تسجيل نقود 73-15
آلة تصوير وفيديو 235-24
آلة تمزيق الورق 183-24
آلة حاسبة 17-6, 183-25
آلة عرض علوية 7-16
آلة عرض على شاشة بلور سائل (إل سي دي) 6, 235-29
آلة كاسيت نقالة 234-6
التحق بدورة تدريب السائقين 137-G

التحق بدورة لتعليم قيادة السيارات B—137
التقط القلم الرصاص 6—I
التماس / عريضة رسمية 148—5
التهاب الحنجرة 110—6
التهاب في الأذن 111—3
التهاب في الحنجرة 111—4
التهاب مفاصل 111—16
التواء الكاحل 110—18
الزم الفراش B—114
ألعاب رياضية جماعية 229
ألعاب رياضية شتوية ومائية 227
ألعاب رياضية فردية 228
ألعاب نارية 239—7
الألفي 16
ألق القمامة N—11
القوقع 212—22
إلكترون 195—30
ألم 115—3
ألم في الأذن 110—3
ألم في الظهر 110—5
ألم في المعدة 110—4
الألوان 24
الألوان الأساسية 24
الألوان المحايدة 24
ألوان مختلفة 23—16
أم 34—3
أم عزباء 35—22
أماكن للزيارة 222
أماكن مختلفة للسكن 52
إمبراطور 199—3
أمتعة / حقيبة 161—18
أمحُ الخطأ M—10
امرأة 30—2
أمريكا الجنوبية 202—2
أمريكا الشمالية 202—1
أمريكا الشمالية والوسطى 200—201
الأمريكيون الأصليون 198—3
الأمس 20—7
امش مع صديق أو صديقة A—143
أمعاء 107—42
املأ الخانة (الفراغ) O—9
املأ طلب التقدم لوظيفة J—173
أمين مكتبة للمعلومات المرجعية 133—9
أمينة الصندوق 132—1
أمينة صندوق 73—13
أن يتقدم لامتحان الجنسية I—140
أن يكون عمره 18 سنة أو أكبر G—140
أن يكون مقيما في الولايات المتحدة لفترة ٥ سنوات H—140
إناء / قِدْر 78—6
إناء الكعك 78—26
إناء تقديم 55—21
إناء لفرشاة الأسنان 57—24
إناء للحليب 55—15
إناء للسكر 55—14
إناء مزدوج للغلي (غلاية مزدوجة) 78—8
أناناس 68—23

أنبوب (أنابيب) 74—12
أنبوب / ماسورة 181—17
أنبوب اختبار 195—42
أنبوب مدرج 195—38
أنبوب معجون أسنان 74—24
انتبه للتحذيرات العامة D—147
انتخابات 139
الإنترنت (شبكة المعلومات العالمية) 197
انتظر السيارات المارة 154—9
انتظر على الخط H—15
الانتقال إلى المنزل 49
أنثى 4—18
انجح في امتحان قيادة السيارة H—137
انجح في امتحان E—10
الإنجليزية كلغة ثانية / الإنجليزية لمتحدثي اللغات الأخرى 189—14
انحني H—3
اندماج 154—10
أنزل القلم الرصاص 6—J
انزلاق الطين 144—6
إنسان الغاب 217—39
انسخي الكلمة E—8
انسكاب نفطي 218—17
الإنشاء باللغة الإنجليزية 190—191
انصهار 218—10
انضم إلى هيئة أهل الحي لمراقبة الأعمال المشبوهة 143—L
انظر في إعلانات السيارات A—157
انظر مباشرة في عينيها J—174
إنعاش القلب والرئتين 117—17
الانعطاف إلى اليمين فقط 154—7
انعطف يسارا على شارع أوك C—155
انعطف يمينا على شارع باين B—155
ألف 104—6
انفجار 144—4
انفجار بركاني 145—16
انفخ الإطارات بالهواء L—157
أنفلونزا 111—2
أنْفيّة المِجْهَر الدوارة 194—15
انقر زر "تسجيل" "sign in" B—197
الأُنقليس (ثعبان بحري) 212—12
إنه أصغر من اللازم 97—37
إنه أغلى من اللازم 97—44
إنه أكبر من اللازم 97—38
إنه مبقع 97—42
إنه ممزق / مقطوع 97—41
إنه يتمزق / تنحلّ خيوطه 97—43
أنوار عقدية (لتزيين الشجر) 239—18
أنواع الأدوية 113
أنواع الأفلام 237
أنواع البرامج التليفزيونية 236
أنواع التدريب الوظيفي 172
أنواع الخامات 98—99
أنواع الرياضيات 192
أنواع المشاكل الصحية 115
أنواع الموسيقى 237
الأويرا 223—11

أوبو (مزمار) 238—3
أوتوبيس / حافلة 128—9, 151—14
أوتوبيس مدرسة 156—21
أودومتر (عداد المسافة) 159—28
أوراق نشافة 101—5
أورانوس 205—7
أوروبا 202—3
الأوزان 75
الأوزان والمقادير 75
إوزّة (إوزّ) 214—13
أوشحة 95—12
أوقات النهار 18
الأول 16
أول رئيس 198—11
أونتاريو 201—4
أونصة سائلية من الحليب 75—1
أونصة من الجبن 75—11
أيام الأسبوع 20, 20—16
إيداع 132—3
آيس كريم / بوظة / جيلاتي 72—26
آيس كريم في كوز من البسكويت 79—13
الإيصال، الوصل 27—6
إيقاعية حزينة (ريذم آند بلوز) / روحية (صول) 237—28
بظ (بعد الظهر) 18—5
بائع زهور 130—8
بائع في محل البقالة 72—4
بائع متجول 129—29
بائعة أو بائع 94—3
بائعة زهور 167—27
بائعون 84—7
باب 46—3
باب الجراج 53—7
باب أمامي 53—11
باب حاجز (مضاد للعواصف) 53—10
باب خروج في حالات طوارئ 161—14
باب دوار 184—2
باب زجاجي منزلق 53—18
باب منخلي (سلكي) 53—15
بادمنتون (لعبة تشبه كرة المضرب) 228—6
باذنجان 69—23
بارد 13—6
بارد جدا 13—7
باستا (ضرب من المعكرونة) 67—12
باقة زهور 211—28
بالونات 44—4
باوند (رطل) من شرائح لحم البقر 75—12
باي (الرمز الذي يمثل النسبة بين طول محيط الدائرة وقطرها) 193—46
باينت زبادي (لبن مجمد) 75—3
بابايا 68—20
بتلات (تويجات) 211—8
بتولا (شجر القضبان) 210—7
البحث عن منزل 49—48
البحث عن وظيفة 173
البحرية 138—15
بحيرة 204—13

البدالة / السنترال 21—14
بدر 205—12
بدلة 87—11
بدلة أعمال 88—11
بدلة سباحة / بدلة استحمام للنساء (مايوه) 90—26
بدلة سهرة رسمية للرجال 89—17
بدلة غوص 225—4
بدون منفذ / طريق مسدود 154—6
بديل السكر 79—20
بديل لبن الأم (حليب مستحضر) 37—3
بدين(ة) 32—7
بذرة 211—1
برتقال 68—5
برتقالي 24—4
برجمة 106—17
برد 111—1
برطمان / مرطبان 74—2
برطمان مربى 74—14
برعم 211—7
برغوث (براغيث) 63—25
برغي خشب 180—33
برغي ربط ملولب 180—32
برق 13—17
برقوق 68—13
بزْكة (سترة فرائية مقلنسة) 90—9
بركة زهور 204—21
البرمائيات 212
برنامج إخباري 236—1
برنامج أطفال 236—9
برنامج تسوق 236—10
برنامج حياة واقعية 236—6
برنامج رياضي 236—11
برنامج عن الطبيعة 236—7
برنامج كوميدي 236—2
برنامج مقابلات 236—4
برنامج منافسات أو مسابقات 236—8
برنيطة (قبعة) بيسبول 86—5
بروتون 195—31
بروكلي (نوع من القرنبيط) 69—13
بريد إعلامي 134—3
بريد برّي 134—6
بريد جوي 134—5
بريد سريع 134—2
بريد مستعجل 134—1
بريد مسجل 134—4
بساطة أو حصيرة مطاطية 57—5
بستان خضروات 53—27
بستان فاكهة 177—10
بستاني / جنايني 167—28
البستوني 233—30
البسط 192—5
بسطرمة 71—23
بسكويت (كعك رقيق محلى) 73—38
بسلة (بازلا) 69—21
بصل 69—19
بصل أخضر / كرّاث أندلسي 69—20
بصلة 211—2

بصمة إصبع 136-5
بط 70-18, 214-12
بطاريات 146-15
بطارية 158-20
بطاطا / بطاطس 69-17
بطاطا حلوة 69-18
بطاطس مطهوة في الفرن 81-25
بطاطس مقلية 79-2
بطاطس مقلية ومفرومة 80-3
بطاطس مهروسة (بوريه) 81-23
بطاطين 146-7
بطاقات بيسبول 232-2
بطاقة إرشادات للطوارئ 161-26
بطاقة إقامة دائمة / البطاقة الخضراء 40-2
بطاقة الأجرة المدفوعة 152-11
بطاقة السعر 27-1
بطاقة الوصفة الطبية 112-4
بطاقة بريدية (كارت بوستال) 134-16
بطاقة بيانات تغذوية 122-8
بطاقة تأمين صحي 118-3
بطاقة تحذير 112-8
بطاقة تعريف بريدية 183-41
بطاقة جهاز الصرف الآلي (بطاقة إيه تي أم) 132-15
بطاقة صعود 161-20
بطاقة ضمان اجتماعي 40-5
بطاقة عليها الاسم 92-15
بطاقة نادي السيارات 162-4
بطاقة هاتفية / تليفونية (بطاقة مكالمات) 14-15
بطاقة / كارت معايدة 134-15
بطانية 58-11, 225-15, 11
بطريق 214-11
بطن 107-27
بطيخ 68-18
بعد الظهر (العصر) 18-17
بعد حدوث الحالة الطارئة 147
بعوضة (ناموسة) 214-22
بقالة صغيرة 128-3
بقة (بق) 63-24
بقدونس 69-28
بقرة 215-1
بكرات شعر 33-19
بلاتيوس 217-46
بلاط / قيشاني 57-12
بلاط 178-11
البلاط مشقوق 62-4
بلح البحر 212-17
بلح البحر 71-13
بلدة صغيرة / قرية 52-3
بلّغ الشرطة عن الجرائم 143-K
بلّغ الشرطة عن أية علب أو طرود مشبوهة 143-J
بلوزة 87-8
بلوزة سادة (بسيطة) 97-33
بلوزة مُزيّنة (مزركشة) 97-34
بلوط سام 210-24
البلوفر (الكنزة) الفيروزي في / داخل الصندوق 25-6

بلوفر (كنزة) 28-2, 87-14
بلوفر (كنزة) ذو رقبة عالية 96-7
بلوفر (كنزة) ذو رقبة عالية جدا 96-9
بلوفر (كنزة) ذو رقبة على شكل حرف V 96-8
بلوفر (كنزة) ذو رقبة مقوّرة 96-10
بلوفر (كنزة) صوفي يلبس من طريق الرأس 88-3
بلوفر (كنزة) من صوف محبوك 88-2
البلوفر (الكنزة) الأبيض أمام البلوفر (الكنزة) الأسود 25-7
البلوفر (الكنزة) الأخضر بين البلوفرات (الكنزات) الوردية 25-12
البلوفر (الكنزة) الأسود خلف البلوفر (الكنزة) الأبيض 25-8
البلوفر (الكنزة) البرتقالي فوق/على البلوفر (الكنزة) الرمادي 25-9
البلوفر (الكنزة) البنفسجي بجانب البلوفر (الكنزة) الرمادي 25-10
البلوفر (الكنزة) الرمادي تحت البلوفر (الكنزة) البرتقالي 25-11
البلوفر (الكنزة) الفيروزي في/داخل الصندوق 25-6
البلوفرات (الكنزات) البنية على الجهة اليمنى 25-3
البلوفرات (الكنزات) الحمراء فوق البلوفرات (الكنزات) الزرقاء 25-4
البلوفرات (الكنزات) الزرقاء تحت/أسفل البلوفرات (الكنزات) الحمراء 25-5
البلوفرات (الكنزات) الزرقاء في الجهة الوسطى 25-2
البلوفرات (الكنزات) الصفراء على الجهة اليسرى 25-1
بلياردو 228-2
البناء 178
بناية شقق / عمارة سكنية 50-1
بنت عمرها 10 سنوات 31-10
بنت / ابن عم(ة) / خال(ة) 34-9
بنجر / شمندر 69-5
بندة 217-41
البُنْش (معطف شبه عباءة) 90-19
بنطلون / سروال 87-12
بنطلون أطفال سهل الخلع 37-11
بنطلون جينز 86-2, 92-19
بنطلون خاص لموظف الأمن 93-22
بنطلون ضيق 97-29
بنطلون ضيق جدا 91-19
بنطلون عمل (شغل) 92-5
بنطلون قصير (شورت) 89-25
بنطلون كابري (بنطلون ضيق مطّاط) 88-8
بنطلون واسع / فضفاض 97-30
بنفسجي 24-8
البنك / المصرف 132
بنك / مصرف 124-5
بنكرياس 107-45
بني 24-17
بنّي / سِنت واحد 26
البهشية 210-19
البهو 50
بواب 184-1
بوابة 53-9, 161-8

بوابة أمن 50-16
بوب (شعبية) 237-25
بودرة استحمام 108-4
بودرة أطفال 37-14
بودرة للوجه 109-41
بوريتو 79-9
بوصة 17-15
بوفيه / ركن السلطات 79-24
بوفيه / مقصف 55-24
بوفيه 185-10
بوق (كلاكس) 159-32
بوق / نفير (ترومبت) 238-11
بوق فرنسي 238-13
بوك تشوي 69-15
بولينغ (لعبة الكرة الخشبية) 228-3
بوم 214-5
بونسيتة 211-24
بيان الإيداع 132-4
بيانو 238-14
البيت الأبيض 138-7
بيت في مدينة 52-6
بيت للدمى 59-18
بيت للعجزة 52-12
بيت متنقل 52-7
بيتزا 79-10
بيج / أسمر مائل إلى الصفرة 24-18
بيجاما 91-24
بيروكسيد الهيدروجين 117-9
بيسبول 229-9
بيسلي (نسيج مزركش بالرسوم) 96-26
بيض 66-7
بيض أومليت (عجة) 76-12
بيض مسلوق جيدا 76-8
بيض غير تام السلق 76-9
بيض مقلي 76-7
بيض مقلي خفيفا ومقلوب 76-11
بيض مقلي على شكل عيون 76-10
بيع الأشياء الشخصية المستعملة في فناء المنزل 102
بيغل (أقراص من الخبز) 73-40
تؤدّب K-36
تابلو السيارة ولوحة العدادات وأجهزة القياس 159
تاج 119-9
تأخذ (تركب) الأوتوبيس إلى المدرسة 38-H
تأخذ رسالة 171-Q
تأخذ قيلولة 53-A
تاريخ 20-1, 189-12
تاريخ الانتهاء 136-10
تاريخ العالم 199
تاريخ الميلاد 4-13
تاريخ الولايات المتحدة الأمريكية 198
تاريخ انتهاء الصلاحية 112-7
التاسع 16
التاسع عشر 16
تأكدي من فهمك للكلام N-12
تاكو 79-8
تأليف موسيقي / مؤلّفة موسيقية 199-15
تبادلوا الأفكار للوصول إلى حلول / أجوبة H-8

تبسط / تطرح فرضية 195-A
تبكي 206-B
تبلع مادة سامة J-116
تبويب 197-7
تترك رسالة 171-P
تتزلج 230-U
تتسوّق 28-A
تتصل بالمدير / المشرف 48-A
تتظاهر 233-G
تتعطل السيارة 162-D
تتقيأ / يستفرغ - تستفرغ 110-E
تتمدد 230-M
تتمرن / تمارس تمرينات رياضية 230-N
تجربة 195
تجفف / تنشّف الأطباق 60-N
تجفف الشعر 108-H
تجلس الزبون 82-B
تجمع أشياء A-232
التجمع السلمي 140-1
تجهيز سفرة الطعام 83-17
تجهيزات 181-18
تحبك بالصنارة F-233
تحت غطاء المحرك (الكبّوت) 158
تحتفظ لنفسها 28-B
تحتفل 206-C
تحدث عن خبرتك L-174
تحدث في الهاتف / التليفون 15-C
تحدّث مع أصدقاء / كوّن شبكة من الاتصالات 173-A
تحذيرات طبية 112
تحصى / تعُدّ A-84
تحضر E-240
تُحضر الأطفال من المدرسة M-38
تحضّر وجبة الغداء F-38
تحضير الطعام وسلامته 77-76
تحطم طائرة 144-3
تحلّ مسائل رياضيات M-170
تحليل دم 121-30
تحمّي F-36
تحوّل الطالب إلى الانتظار N-171
تحوّل المكالمة O-171
تحوّل المكاييل C-75
تحويل بقايا الطعام إلى سماد M-219
تحيّي الطالب M-171
تختم L-116
تخريب متعمد 142-1
التخطيط لمسار وظيفي 172
تخلع ملابسه E-36
تخليق ضوئي 194-10
تخيط باليد B-98
تخيط بماكينة الخياطة A-98
تخيط ثيابا L-170
تخيم 226-5
تدخل إلى سيارة الأجرة (التاكسي) E-153
تدريب 172-2
تدريب أثناء أداء الوظيفة 172-7
تدريب حرفي 172-5

تدريب داخلي 172—6
تدفع المرجحة B—224
تدفع إيجار الشهرين الأول والأخير E—48
تذكرة 152—15
تذكرة إلكترونية 161—19
تذكرة تحويل 152—5
تذهب (تسير) تحت الجسر A—153
تذهب إلى حجرة الصف J—38
تذهب إلى محل البقالة L—38
تذييل 190—10
تراقب C—195
تربة 208—2
تربط رباط الحذاء A—86
تربية بدنية 189—17
تردي البلوفر B—87
ترتر 99—33
ترجع / ترد H—27
ترجع إلى الوراء C—235
ترجمي الكلمة C—8
الترداد 20
ترسم بالألوان E—233
ترضّع B—36
ترقية 172—4
تركب حول الزاوية D—129
تركض حول الزاوية H—153
ترمي الكرة نحو السلة (تقذف الكرة) H—230
تريّح / تهدّئ I—36
تزرع شجرة E—176
التزلج بمزلج ذي خط دواليب 228—10
التزلج على الثلج 227—2
التزلج على الجليد 227—4
التزلج على الماء 227—7
التزلج على الماء مع استعمال شراع 227—10
التزلج على لوح بعجلات 228—13
التزلج على منحدر 227—1
التزلج في الضاحية 227—3
التزلج مع القيام بسلسلة من الحركات 227—5
تزن الطعام B—75
تزيل R—109
التزيين 99
تسأل عن المميزات B—48
تستحمّ (تأخذ دشا) A—108
تستحمّ C—38
تستخدم آلة تسجيل نقود S—170
تستلم الكارت F—135
تستمع إلى الرسائل R—171
تستمع إلى نبض القلب C—118
تسجل النتائج D—195
التسجيل وإرسال بريد إلكتروني 197
تسحب العربة A—224
تسحب دما F—118
التسعون 16
تسقي الزرع F—176
تسلم رخصة القيادة الخاصة بك I—137
تسلية وترفيه 237—236
تسمم من مبيدات الحشرات 218—16
التسوق 27

تسيء السلوك أو التصرف B—44
تشتري / تدفع حساب G—27
تشتري A—94
تشرف على موظفين O—170
تشطف الشعر F—108
تشعر بالغثيان D—110
تصفح موقع على الإنترنت 197
تصفف الشعر بالفرشاة 108—I
تصفيف الشعر 33
تصفيق B—148
تصل إلى خلاصة E—195
تصوّر بكاميرا فيديو A—240
تضع P—109
تضع الغسيل في الغسالة C—101
تضع طابع البريد C—135
تضع واقيا من أشعة الشمس D—108
تضفر الشعر على فروة الرأس 33—14
تضيف مسحوق الغسيل B—101
تطبخ العشاء / تحضّر العشاء Q—39
تطبع R—170
تطبع رسالة A—171
تطريز 233—24
تطريز أبليكيه 99—31
تطلع على البريد الإلكتروني W—39
تطلع / تصعد الدرجات مشيا على قدميها C—153
تطلي الأظافر O—109
تطوي الملابس F—101
تعاطَ دواء D—114
تعاير المقادير A—75
تعبر الشارع A—128
تعتني بالأطفال P—170
تعديل الثياب 100
تعزف على آلة A—238
تعلّق الملابس H—101
تعلّم / تدرّس Q—170
تعلّم كلمات جديدة 8
تغسل الشعر E—108
تغسل النوافذ I—60
تغنّي له ترنيمة لتنويمه O—36
تغيّر الحفاض G—36
تغيّر الملاءات P—60
تغيير C—148
تفاح 68—1
التفاضل والتكامل 192—19
تفحص الحنجرة E—118
تفحص العينين D—118
تفحص ضغط الدم A—118
تفحص / تأخذ درجة الحرارة B—118
تفرز الغسيل A—101
تفرّغ مجفف الملابس E—101
تقاسما كتابا M—8
تقاطع طرق 128—129
تقاول على السعر A—102
تقبّل الاعتذار G—12
تقدّم إلى الأمام بسرعة D—235
تقدّم طلبا C—48
التقدم لامتحان 10

تقدم للامتحان التحريري E—137
تقرأ الصحيفة V—39
تقرأ الكارت G—135
تقع O—116
تقفز I—230
تقلّم الأظافر N—109
تقلّم الوشيع (الشجيرات) B—176
تقوم بإجراء تجربة B—195
تقوم بتعبئة الصناديق M—49
تقوم بتفريغ الصناديق N—49
تقوم على خدمة الزبائن T—170
تقوم من السرير B—38
التقويم 20—21
تقويم الأسنان 119
تكتب العنوان على الظرف B—135
تكتب إليها ردا على الكارت H—135
تكتب رسالة في الكارت A—135
تكلّم مع المعلّمة B—6
تكوي الملابس G—101
تلال 204—16
تلبّس H—36
تلسكوب 205—23
تلعب ألعابا B—232
تلعب معه M—36
تلفّ F—240
تلفزيون 56—6
تلفزيون ذو شاشة مسطحة 234—7
تلفزيون نقال 234—8
تلفزيون بشاشة كبيرة 50—14
تلقي الكارت في صندوق البريد D—135
تلقي خطابا 148—A
تلقي محاضرة B—122
تلمّع الأثاث E—60
التلوّث 218
تلوث المياه 218—14
تلوث الهواء (الجو) / ضباب دخاني 218—11
تماثيل أبطال 233—26
تمارس أشغالا يدوية D—232
تمارس التضريب C—232
تمثال (مانيكان) الخياطة 100—2
تمثال صغير 232—1
تمدح J—36
تمر / بلح 68—28
تمرين حيهوائي 122—5
تمساح 213—36
تمسح / تزيل التراب عن الأثاث A—60
تمسح المنضدة O—60
تمشّ إلى الصف C—11
تمشّط (تسرّح) الشعر G—108
تناول الطعام في مطعم 185
تناول قبل ساعة من الأكل B—112
تناول كل الدواء حتى ينتهي C—112
تناول مع أكل أو حليب A—112
تنتقل إلى الشقة F—48
تنجب طفلا L—41
تنحني O—230
تنزه / يقوم (نقوم) بنزهة D—224

التنزه سيرا على الأقدام 226—7
تنسيق المناظر الطبيعية والبستنة 176
تنطط الكرة J—230
تنظّف الحوض بالفرشاة K—60
تنظّف الفرن C—60
تنظّف مكان تجمع النسالة D—101
تنظم المواد L—171
تنفس إنقاذي 117—16
تنورة (جونلا) 87—10
تنورة طويلة 96—18
تنورة قصيرة 96—16
تنورة قصيرة جدا (ميني) 96—15
تنورة متوسطة الطول /
تنورة بطول بطن الساق 96—17
تهجّ اسمك B—4
تهزّ D—36
تواليت / مرحاض 57—21
توأمان 28—1
توبة 238—12
توت 210—20
توت العليق 68—17
توت العنبية 68—16
توت شوكي 68—15
توت مشكّل 81—36
توتر / إجهاد 115—4
توجه / تصوّب Q—230
التوفير في استهلاك الماء E—219
توقّع عقد الإيجار D—48
توقيت ألاسكا 19—28
التوقيت الأطلنطي 19—33
التوقيت الجبلي 19—30
التوقيت الصيفي 19—25
التوقيت القياسي (الشتوي) 19—26
توقيت المحيط الهادئ (الباسيفيكي) 19—29
توقيت الولايات الشرقية 19—32
توقيت الولايات الوسطى 19—31
توقيت نيوفاوندلاند 19—34
توقيت هاواي – ألوشيان 19—27
التوقيع 4—19
التونة (سمك التن) 212—8
التونة 71—7
تي شيرت جاف 101—18
تي شيرت مبلّل 101—17
تي شيرت متسخ 101—15
تي شيرت نظيف 101—16
التيار الكهربائي مقطوع 62—2
تين 68—27
تيهور / جرف ثلجي 145—18
الثالث 16
الثالث عشر 16
الثامن 16
الثامن عشر 16
الثاني 16
الثاني عشر 16
الثانية إلا ثلث 18—12
الثانية إلا ربع 18—13
ثدي 107—26

ثدييات 209–10	جهاز تشغيل أقراص فيديو رقمية	جراج / كراج 47–14	حافة رصيف 129–21
الثدييات 217–216	(دي في دي) 56–7, 234–10	جراج سيارات / موقف سيارات 124–1	حافظ على لياقتك البدنية E–114
الثدييات البحرية 213	جهاز تشغيل أقراص مضغوطة	جراح 121–36	حافظ على محفظتك أو حقيبة يدك D–143
ثعلب 216–15	(سي دي) 234–38, 159–1	جراد البحر (استاكوزة) 71–10	حافظة ملفات / دوسيه 183–50
ثقّابة آلية / آلة حفر بالهواء المضغوط 178–9	جهاز تشغيل دي في دي نقال 234–11	جرّارة (تراكتور) 177–9	حافظة نقود 94–14
نقب الباب / عين سحرية 51–32	جهاز تشغيل س دي شخصي 234–5	جرافة لشق الطرق (بولدوزر) 178–6	الحاكم 139–20
ثلاث عشرة مستعمرة 198–1	جهاز تشغيل ملفات	جرح 110–13	حالات الطوارئ والكوارث الطبيعية 144–145
ثلاث مرات في الأسبوع 20–24	إم بي ٣ الموسيقية (MP3) 234–2	جرد للاهتمامات 172–11	حالات العجز 32
الثلاثاء 20–10	جهاز توليف (أمبليفاير) 234–13	جرد للمهارات 172–12	حالات طبية طارئة 116
الثلاثون 16	جهاز ستريو 56–8	جرد 215–17	حالات طبية وأمراض خطيرة 111
ثلاجة 54–9	جهاز ضد اشتداد التيار 196–1	جرد (جرذان) 63–27	حامل / رف لتعليق الملابس 98–16
ثلث 17–3	جهاز فاكس 183–21	جرس الاستدعاء 121–28	حامل 32–15
الثمانون 16	جهاز فيديو 102–7	جرس الباب 53–14	حامل الحقائب 160–1
ثمن 17–5	جهاز لاسلكي مرسل ومستقبل 179–22	جرعة 112–6	حامل الهاتف / التليفون المحمول (النقال) 94–15
ثنية ساق البنطلون 100–9	جهاز لألعاب الفيديو 232–3	جرو 215–12	حامل ثلاثي القوائم 235–25
ثوان 18–3	جهاز لقياس ضغط الدم 118–9	الجريمة 142	حامل للجرائد والمجلات 56–23
ثوب حمام / برنس 91–29	جهاز هاتف / تليفون للمعوقين سمعيا 15–26	جريمة القتل 142–12	حامل لوحة 233–18
ثوب قماش 98–15	جهة الوصول 162–5	الجزء السفلي من الظهر 107–29	حاويات وتعليب 74
ثوم 69–30	جوارب بارتفاع الركبتين 91–12	جزّار / لَحام 166–13	حاوية / وعاء 74–5
ثياب الجراحون والممرضات 93–31	جوارب بارتفاع الكاحل 91–11	جزازة العشب 176–6	حاوية 160–6
ثياب غرفة العمليات 93–38	جوارب رسمية 91–9	جزر 69–3	حاوية تخزين بلاستيكية 78–4
جائع / جوعان 42–5	جوارب رياضية 91–8	جزمة (حذاء عالي الساق) 95–28	الحبار 212–7
جاروف / لقّاطة الكناسة 61–17	جوارب قصيرة 86–6	جزمة (حذاء عالي الساق) للتسلق 95–31	حبة 113–21
جاروف 176–7, 178–22	جوارب قصيرة الارتفاع 91–10	جزمة عالية الساق ذات مقدّم من الفولاذ 92–6	حبك بصنارة معقوفة (كروشيه) 233–25
جاز 237–24	جوارب قصيرة لكلا الجنسين 91	جزيء 195–27	حبل 226–19
جاكتة (سترة) جلدية 90–4	جوارب كاحلية 91–7	جزيرة 204–8	حبل الوثب 224–4
جاكتة 90–8	جوارب للنساء 91	الجسم 104	حبل مطاطي 181–15
جاكتة ثقيلة 97–27	جواز سفر 41–10	جص 178–15	حبوب (سيريال) ساخنة 80–9
جاكتة خفيفة 97–28	جوبية (سترة يرتديها العمال) 93–24	جغرافيا وبيئات طبيعية 204	الحجاب 194–18
جاكتة خفيفة (بليزر) 92–12	الجودو 228–11	جفاف / قحط 145–11	حجرة التجميد في الثلاجة / فريزر 54–10
جاكتة رئيس الطهاة (الشيف) 93–29	جورب سروالي نسائي 91–18	جفن 106–10	حجرة الصف 6–7
جاكتة سبور / معطف سبور 89–14	جورب نسائي فوق الركبة 91–17	جلد 107–31	حجرة حقائب علوية 161–13
جاكتة طويلة من زغب أو وبر 90–16	جوز الهند 68–24	جلد 98–6	حجرة صف / فصل دراسي 5–7
جالون ماء 75–5	جولف 228–8	جليدي 13–22	الحد من القمامة A–219
جاملي شخصا C–12	جي بي إس (نظام تحديد الموضع عالميا) 155–11	جمبري / ربيان 71–11	الحدائق والمنتزهات العامة الأمريكية 220
جاموس / بيسون 216–6	جيب 100–7, 217–50	جمجمة 107–47	حدبة 217–51
جاوب على السؤال L–8	الجيش 138–14	جمّد / برّد D–76	حدد أهدافا A–10
الجبر 192–16	جيش 199–11	الجمعة 20–13	حدد موعدا لمقابلة شخصية I–173
جبن 66–4	جيل للدش 108–2	جمل 217–38	الحديث اليومي 12
جبن أمريكي 71–26	جيل للشعر 108–16	جملة 190–2	حديثة 199–2
جبن سويسري 71–27	حاجب / ناطور 184–4	جمنازيوم (قاعة الجمباز) 5–19, 126–10	حديقة الحيوانات 222–1
جبن شيدر 71–28	حاجب 106–9, 182–3	جميل(ة) 32–14	حديقة النباتات 222–3
جبن موتساريلا 71–29	حاجب الريح الزجاجي 158–1	جناح 122–3, 184–16, 214–1	حديقة خضروات 177–14
جبهة 106–2	حاجب المحكمة 141–13	جناح خاص 82–4	حديقة على السطح 50–4
جبيرة / جبص 113–20	حاجز أفقي دوار 152–8	جندب 214–24	الحديقة وملعب الأطفال 224
جبيرة لليد 117–14	حاجز منخلي للمستوقد (حاجب النار) 56–12	جندي 169–58	حذاء أكسفورد 95–29
جد 34–2	حادث سيارة / حادث طريق 144–2	جندي بريطاني 198–9	حذاء التزلج على الثلج 231–26
جدار / حائط 56–10	الحادي عشر 16	جندي هوّاري على استعداد للحرب	حذاء تنس (كرة المضرب) 95–32
جدار الخلية 194–5	حار 13–3	بإنذار دقيقة واحدة 198–10	حذاء ذو كعب عالٍ 95–25
جدار داخلي 178–19	حارس 141–3	جنوب 155–3	حذاء شبيه بالموكاسان 95–30
جدة 34–1	حارس أمن 132–5	الجنوب الشرقي / الجنوب 201–13	حذاء عالي الساق (جزمة) للمطر 90–20
جدري الماء (جديري) 111–6	حارسة أمن 169–55	الجنوب الغربي / الجنوب 201–12	حذاء نسائي 95–26
الجدول الدوري 195–26	حاروق / ملهب ببنزن 195–37	جهاز الصرف الآلي 132	حذاء وقاية 179–20
جدول مواعيد 152–4	حاسوب 7–15	جهاز آلي للرد على المكالمات 14–17	حراشف 212–3
جذع 210–4	حاشية (هدب) 100–8	جهاز تحضير المأكولات 54–26	حرب 199–10
جذور 210–5, 211–3	الحاصل 192–9	جهاز تحكم عن بعد (ريموت) شامل 234–9	الحرب الثورية / حرب الاستقلال 198–8
جذوع 211–9	حاضنة أطفال 166–9	جهاز تشغيل أسطوانات 234–12	الحرس الوطني 138–19

الحرف الأول من اسم الأب 4–3
حرف الظنبوب 106–21
حرق متعمد 142–7
حركة سياسية 199–16
حرم المدرسة 5
حروف الجر 25
حروف الجر المتعلقة بالحركة 153
حروف الهجاء 7–13
حرية الدين أو العبادة 140–3
حرية الصحافة 140–4
حرية الكلام 140–2
حرير 98–5
حريق 144–8
حريق غابات 144–7
حزام أدوات 92–3
حزام أمان بالمقعد 159–52
حزام أو نطاق تنورة أو بنطلون 100–5
حزام لدعم الظهر 179–18
حزمة بطاريات 235–26
حزمة ثلج 117–13
حزمة موز 68–29
حزين 43–19
حساب المثلثات 192–18
حساسية 111–8
حشرات 209–11
الحشرات والعنكبوتيات 214
حشو 119–8
حصان 215–4
حصبة 111–5
الحصول على أول رخصة قيادة لك 137
حصيرة حمام 57–28
الحضارات 199
حضانة 188–1
حضّر الحقيبة A–162
حظيرة 177–11
حفاض يلقى بعد الاستعمال 37–10
حفاضات من القماش 37–8
حفلة 64–2
حفلة التخرُج 206
حفلة عيد ميلاد 240
حفلة موسيقى الروك آند رول 222–5
حفلة موسيقى كلاسيكية 223–14
حقائب يد / جزدانات 94–2
حقق تقدما G–10
حقل 177–7
الحقوق 140
الحقوق والواجبات المدنية 140
حقيبة / شنطة يد 87–9
حقيبة أصابع / شنطة سهرة 89–19
حقيبة أوراق 88–13
حقيبة تحمل على الظهر 94–18, 226–15
حقيبة كتف نسائية 94–17
حقيبة مستلزمات الطفل 37–16
حقيبة نقل 94–19
الحكم / القرار 141–14
حكم 229–6
الحكومة الاتحادية (الفدرالية) 138

حكومة المدينة 139
حكومة الولاية 139
الحكومة والخدمة العسكرية 138–139
حل 192–14
حل الكلمات W–9
حلاق 129–19
حلق بمشبك 95–37
حلق لأذن مثقوبة 95–36
حلقات بصل مقلي 79–4
حلقة تسنين 37–25
حلمة زجاجة الرضاعة 37–2
حلوى 239–12
حلويات 84–8
حليب 66–5
حليب خفيض الدسم 81–42
حماة 34–10
حمار 215–3
حمار وحشي 217–33
حمالة أطفال 37–17
حمالة البنطلون 94–1
حمالة الثياب 101–11
حمالة فوط / مناشف 57–15
حمّام 46–4
الحمّام 57
حمامة 214–15
حمل الأمتعة على الظهر 226–6
حملة انتخابية سياسية 139–29
حمو 34–11
حمى / حرارة 110–8
حنجرة 107–35
حنفية 57–8
الحنفية تنقّط / تقطر 63–17
الحواس 106
حوافر 216–17
حوت 213–29
حوش / فناء / صحن الدار 51–21
حوض 54–4, 57–25, 107–50
حوض الاستحمام (بانيو) 57–2
حوض زهور 53–20
الحوض طافح / مسدود 63–18
حول الحرم 5
حوّلي D–17
الحيوانات الأليفة والقوارض 215
الحيوانات البحرية 212
حيوانات المزارع 215
الحيوانات المنزلية 215
حيوانات محشوة 59–15
حيّ الشخص القائم بالمقابلة H–174
حيّ الناس G–3
خائف / متخوف 43–23
خاتم 95–40
خاتم رخيص 23–20
خاتم غالي 23–19
خادم فندق 184–7
خادم لإيقاف السيارات 184–3
خارج القسمة 192–10
خالٍ من السكر 122–7

الخامس 16
الخامس عشر 16
خبز / عيش 67–11
خبز أبيض 71–18
خبز بالثوم 81–28
خبز جاوداري 71–20
خبز قمحي 71–19
خبز محمص (توست) 80–4
خبيزة 211–12
ختام 190–8
ختم 183–47
ختم البريد 134–24
خدمات الضيوف 130–12
خدمات المسبح (حمّام السباحة) 184–21
خدمة تقديم طعام 185
خدمة غرف 184–17
خذ 106–3
خذ استراحة H–11
خذ السيارة إلى ميكانيكي C–157
خرائط 155
خرازة / دباسة 183–28
خرز 95–34, 99–32
خرزات / دبابيس من السلك 183–29
خرسانة 178–10
خرشوف 69–22
خرطوشة حبر 183–45
خرطوم / زلومة 217–47
خرطوم 53–21
خرَق / أقمشة للتنظيف 61–9
خروف 215–6
خريطة 7–12
خريطة أحوال الطقس 13
خريطة العالم 203–202
خريطة إنترنت 155–12
الخريف 21
خزان أكسيجين للغوص 225–5
خزان البنزين 158–10
خزانة 5–11, 54–1
خزانة البوفيه العلوية 55–22
خزانة المؤن 182–1
خزانة ذات أدراج 59–6
خزانة ملابس بمرآة وأدراج 58–1
خزانة ملفات 182–11
خزّن حقيبة اليد الخاصة بك G–160
خزينة 132–6
خس 69–1
خشب 178–17
خشب رقائقي 178–18
الخشبية (زيلوفون) 238–15
خشخيشة 37–26
خصلة 33–8
خصومات 165–13
خضروات 66–8
الخضروات 69
خضروات مجمدة 72–27
خضروات مطبوخة على البخار 81–32
خط الهاتف / التليفون 14–4

خط تجميع 175–6
خط مائل / خط قطري 193–31
خط مستقيم 193–22
خط منحني 193–23
خطاب / جواب 134–13
خطّاف / كلاب 180–39
خطاف عروة 180–40
خطر كهربائي 186–6
خطط للحالة الطارئة A–146
الخطوط 193
خطوط متعامدة 193–24
خطوط متوازية 193–25
خطير 186–1
خفاش / وطواط 216–7
خفر السواحل 138–18
خلاط 54–12
خلاط كهربائي 54–25
خلية 194–4
خمسة دولارات 26
الخمسون 16
خمسون دولارا 26
الخميس 20–12
خنزير 215–2
خنزير البحر 213–30
خنزير هندي 215–14
خنفساء 214–18
خوخ 68–10
خوذة 93–23
خوذة فوتبول (كرة قدم أمريكية) 231–19
خوذة واقية 92–9
خور / شرم 204–9
خيار 69–10
خيار مخلل 80–11
خياط (ترزي) 100–3
خيّاطة 100–1
خياطة 167–29
خيشوم (خياشيم) 212–2
خيط 99–23, 100–11
خيط لتنظيف الأسنان 109–24
خيمة 226–10
دائرة 193–34
دائرة تسجيل المركبات الآلية 124–4, 137–136
داخل السيارة 159
داخل الطائرة 161
داخل العلبة 117
داخل صندوق السيارة 158
دار المحكمة 125–13
دافئ 13–4
دب 216–11
دبابيس (وصلة الفخذ بالكاحل) 70–23
دبابيس أمان 37–9
دبابيس شعر محكمة 108–21
دبة محشوة 37–23
ديوس 95–38
ديوس بمشبك 100–14
ديوس شعر 108–19
ديوس كيسي 183–35

الرعاية الصحية 118	رأس الدش 57–13	دور سفلي / تحتاني (بدروم) 47–13	دبوس مستقيم 100–12
رعشة 110–9	رأس السرير 58–10	دور عرض / سينما 126–6	دجاج 66، 3–70، 16
رغيف (أرغفة) 74–10	رأس خس 69–32	دورات مياه 5–9	دجاج مطهو في الفرن 81–22
رغيف خبز 74–22	راصد قرميد 186–8	دورة مقدمة على الإنترنت 172–8	دجاج مقلي 76–1
رف 54–2	رافعة ذات ذراع طويل 178–5	دولاب / خزانة 58–5	دجاج نيئ 70–24
رف الأجهزة الصوتية والمرئية 56–5	راقب حالة الطقس 147–C	دولاب أدوية 57–22	دجاجة 215–8
رف المستوقد (المدفأة) 56–11	راكب 150–2، 3–152، 15–161	دولار 26	دجاجة مطهوة 70–25
رف أو صفاية صحون 54–5	راكب الأمواج المتكسرة 225–15	دوّن مذكرات 10–C	دراجة 129–22
رف في المجهر 194–17	راكب دراجة 224–2	ديسمبر / كانون الأول 21–36	دراجة / بسكليتة 151–15
رف للكتب 7–10	راكتبول 228–12	ديك 215–7	دراجة بخارية / موتوسيكل 150–4
رفع الأثقال 228–16	راكون 216–13	ديك رومي 70، 17–239، 14	دراجة ثلاثية العجلات 224–12
رفقاء شقة 64–1	رأي 44–3	ديك رومي مدخّن 71–25	الدراسة 8–9
رق (سلحفاة) 213–42	راية / علم 239–8	ديك رومي مطهو في الفرن 76–4	دراما 236–12
رق / دف 238–17	راية 44–1	ذَيْم / 10 سنتات 26	درة (ببغاء صغير) 215–15
رقائق بطاطس مقلية (شيبس) 73–35	رباط الحذاء 94–24	الديناري 233–29	دُرج / جارور 54–23، 2–58، 2
رقبة 104–3	رباط رياضي للجوارب / سروال رياضي 91–6	ذنب 216–5	الدرج مكسور 62–7
رقعة الداما 232–7	رباط للجورب 91–16	ذاكر في المنزل 10–D	درجات 13–8
رقم الحساب الجاري 132–14	ربة أعمال / صاحبة أعمال 166–11	ذاكر الكتب 137–A	درجة الحرارة 13
رقم الشقة 4–6	ربة العمل / رئيسة 164–4	ذبابة 214–28	درجة فهرنهايت 13–1
رقم الهاتف / التليفون 4، 11–15، 30	ربة منزل 168–33	ذراع 105، 14–194، 23	درجة مئوية 13–2
رقم الهاتف / التليفون المحمول (النقال) 4–12	ربع 17–4	ذراع نقل السرعات (فتيس) 159–50	ردار 210–16
رقم الوصفة الطبية 112–5	ربع قمر 205–11	الذراع واليد وأصابع اليد 106	دردش 12–B
رقم الوصول 14–16	ربع كوب من السكر البني 75–8	ذُرة 69–12، 177–4	الدستور 198–12
رقم بطاقة الضمان الاجتماعي 4–15	ربلة أو بطة الساق 106–22	ذُرّة 195–28	دعاية منبثقة 197–9
رقم تعريف السلعة (SKU) 27–5	ربو 111–9	ذقن 106–1	دعسوقة 214–26
رقم حساب التوفير 132–11	الربيان / القريدس (الجمبري) 212–18	ذكر 17–4	دعوة / عزومة 64–9
رقم رخصة القيادة 136–11	الربيع 21–37	ذنب / ذيل 216–22	دفتر بنكي 132–10
ركبة 106–20	رجال 30–4	ذهاب وعودة 152–17	دفتر شيكات 132–12
ركوب الأمواج المتكسرة 227–9	رجل 105–9	ذو مربعات 96–24	دفتر طوابع بريدية 134–18
ركوب الخيل 226–9	رَجُل 30–1	رنة 107–39	دفتر منظّم 183–49
ركوب الدراجات على الجبال 226–8	رجل أعمال / سيدة أعمال 166–12	الرئيس 138–8	دفتر مواعيد 183–48
ركوب الدراجة 228–5	الرجل والقدم 106	رئيس 199–5	دفع الحساب ذاتيا 73–10
ركوب الزوارق 226–1	رحلة ذهاب فقط 152–16	رئيس البلدية (العمدة) 139–26	دقائق 18–2
ركوب الكانو (الصندل) 226–3	رحلة متأخرة 161–30	رئيس الجرسونات / رئيس النوادل 185–12	دقيق 73–29
ركوب المزلجة 227–6	رخصة تاكسي 152–22	رئيس الطهاة (شيف) 83، 16–185، 7	دكة / مقعد طويل 224–10
رمادي 24–15	رخصة قيادة سيارة 40–4، 9–136	رئيس القضاة / رئيس المحكمة 138–13	دكتاتور 199–6
رماية السهام 228–1	رداء التخرج 206–8	رئيس مستخدمي حمل الأمتعة 184–6	دلفين 213–31
رمز مفتاح المنطقة 4، 10–15، 29	رداء الجراح 93–37	رئيس وزراء 199–7	دلو / جردل 61–7، 225–8
رمز 155–5	رداء غرفة العمليات 121–38	رائد فضاء 205–17	دلو الحفاضات 37–7
الرمز البريدي 4–9	رداء مستشفى 121–19	رابط بعقيفة وحلقة 99–29	دليل / بينة 141–9
رمز البلد 15–33	رزمة (رزم) 74–8	رابطات / وصلات 197–10	الدليل 131–24
رمز المدينة 15–34	رزمة بسكويت 74–20	رابطة عنق (كرافتة) 88–12، 92–13	دمىّ ورقية 233–28
رمل 225–23	رسالة صوتية 14–18	رابطة عنق (كرافتة) رفيعة 97–35	دمية 59–21
رموش 106–11	رسالة نصية 14–19	رابطة عنق (كرافتة) عريضة 97–36	دنتلة 99–9
رئان 51–31	رسغ 106–14	الرابع 16	الدنيم (قماش قطني متين) 99–7
رواق 5، 10–184، 18	رسوم أو نقوش على الجدران 148–1	الرابع عشر 16	دهّان (منازل) 168–46
الرواق 51	رشاش النشا 101–12	راجع الإعلانات المبوبة في الصحف 173–B	دهان / طلاء 181–25
رواية 133–16	رشاش للألف 113–32	راجع عملك 10–L	دهان أكريليك 232–10
رواية إثارة / رواية مغامرات 237–19	الرصيد 132–17	راجع مواقع الإنترنت للبحث عن الوظائف	دهان زيتي 233–19
رواية بوليسية / تشويق 237–20	رصيف 129–24، 152–7	الشاغرة 173–D	دواء 121–20
رواية حب (رومانسي) 237–16	رصيف تحميل 175–15	راجع هجاءك 197–F	دواء موصوف طبيا 112–3
رواية خيال علمي 237–18	رصيف ممتد داخل البحر 225–18	راجع / أعد الكتابة 191–J	الدواجن 70
رواية مرعبة (فيلم رعب) 237–17	رضيع 31–6	راجعي النطق 8–D	دواسة البنزين 159–46
الرياضة الجمبازية 228–9	رطب 13–15	راديو (مشعاع) 158–19	دواسة الفرملة 159–45
رياضة ركوب الرمث 226–2	رعاة البقر (كاوبوي) 237–15	راديو 159–37	دود معوي 111–13
رياضيات 189–10	رعاية الأسنان 119	راديو بساعة 102–6	دودة 212–23
الرياضيات 192–193	رعاية الأطفال ودور الوالدين 36–37	رأس 104–1	الدور السفلي / التحتاني (البدروم) 50

ريش (ضلوع) لحم بقري 70–5
ريش (ضلوع) مشوية / مشوية على الفحم 76–2
ريشة 214–4
ريشة تنظيف 61–1
الريف / منطقة ريفية 52–4
ريفية 237–27
زاوية / ناصية 128–7
زاوية حادة 193–28
زاوية مستقيمة / زاوية 90 درجة 193–26
زاوية منفرجة 193–27
زبادي / لبن 72–22
زبد 66–6
زبون / شخص يتناول الطعام 82–6
زبون / عميل 132–2
زبون 72–1, 94–4, 164–2
زبونة 185–9
زبيب 68–25
زجاجات ماء 146–11
زجاجة 74–1
زجاجة رضاعة 37–1
زجاجة ماء 74–13
زحل 205–6
زر 99–24
زر التقدم إلى الليلة 197–3
زر الرجوع إلى البقعة 197–2
الزراعة وتربية المواشي 177
زرافة 217–32
زردية 180–7
زرع شجرة 219–N
زريبة 177–17
زعانف 225–7
زعفران 211–17
زعنفة (زعانف) 212–1
زقاق 51–24
زلاجة 231–24
زلاقة 224–13
زلزال 144–5
الزمام المنزلق (السوستة) مكسور 97–39
زمام منزلق (سوستة) 99–25
الزمخر (بسون) 238–4
زنبق 211–26
زنبقة 211–11
زنبور 214–17
زهر الطاولة / النرد 232–6
زهرة الربيع 211–14
زهرية 55–23
زهور 208–7, 211
الزواحف 213
الزوايا 193
زوبعة 145–15
زوج 34–13
زوج الأم 35–25
زوجان 239–4
زوجة 34–12
زوجة الأب 35–26
زورق شراعي 225–3
زي مُوحّد 88–10, 231–16

زيارة لعيادة أسنان 119
زيت 73–31
زينة 239–15
زينة / زواق 240–1
سائق بطيء 23–4
سائق سيارة أجرة / تاكسي 152–21
سائق شاحنة 169–61
سائق مسرع 23–3
سائل تصحيح 183–36
سائل تغذية يعطى في الوريد 121–25
سائل غسل الأطباق 61–21
السابع 16
السابع عشر 16
ساحة الطعام 131–15
ساحل 204–12
سادة / مصمت 96–19
السادس 16
السادس عشر 16
ساعة (يد) 94–16
ساعة 7–9, 18–1
ساعة الدوام 165–7
الساعة الواحدة 18
ساعة توقيت للمطبخ 78–18
ساعد 106–13
ساعد الناس المعوقين 147–G
ساعدي أحد زملائك في الصف 8–J
ساعي 185–15
ساعي البريد / حامل البريد 134–20
ساق حمل 70–13
السباحة مع استعمال أنبوب التنفس 227–11
سباق الخيول 228–19
سباق المضمار والميدان 228–18
سبّاك / سمكري 63–20
سبانخ 69–11
السبت 20–14
سبتمبر / أيلول 21–33
السبعون 16
سبلات 216–18
السبلة الخدية (سوالف) 33–7
سبورة 6–1
سبورة بيضاء 6–3
ستائر 56–16, 58–7
ستائر معدنية أو خشبية صغيرة 58–8
ستار الدش 57–14
سترة المختبر 93–33
سترة داخلية بطول كامل 91–22
سترة داخلية بنصف طول 91–23
سترة رياضية 88–4
سترة صوفية تريكو 88–7
سترة قصيرة واقية من الرياح 90–24
الستون 16
سجادة 56–24, 58–22
سجق (نقانق) 80–2
سجق (هوت دوج) 79–6
سجق / نقانق 70–12
سجّل السيارة 157–F
سحلبية 211–19

سحلية 213–40
سخان الماء لا يعمل 62–1
سخّن الفرن مسبقًا 77–A
سدادة أذن 179–15
سدّد النقود (الدين) 26–D
سر باتجاه مستقيم على شارع إلم 155–A
سر مسافة ناصية إلى شارع فيرست 155–F
سرطان 111–10
سرطان البحر (كابوريا) 71–9
السرعة القصوى 154–4
سرقة معروضات المتجر 142–8
سرقة هويات الغير 142–9
سروال تحتاني قصير 91–5
سروال تحتي قصير رجالي / سروال تحتي 91–14
سروال تحتي قصير نسائي / كيلوت بيكيني 91–13
سروال فضفاض / بنطلون رياضة 89–23
سرير / فراش 58–9
سرير طفل رضيع 59–3
سرير مستشفى 121–22
سرير واحد كبير 184–15
سطو 142–2
سعدان إفريقي 217–31
السعر / التكلفة 27–7
سعر التنزيلات (المخفض) 27–3
السعر العادي 27–2
سعيد / مسرور 43–31
سعيدتان 28–6
السفر في رحلة 162
السفر في رحلة جوية 160
سفعة (ضربة) شمس 110–14
سقالة 178–4
سقف 46–1
السقف يسرب / يرشح 62–3
سكة 152–14
سكر 73–30
السكسية (ساكسفون) 238–5
سكين 55–4, 83–30
سكين تقشير 78–16
سكين لتقطيع اللحوم 78–12
سكين لقطع اللحم 83–29
سكين متعدد الاستعمالات 226–20
سل 111–15
سلاح مشاة البحرية (المارينز) 138–17
سلاطة الشيف / سلاطة رئيس الطهاة 80–14
سلاطة بطاطس 80–19
سلاطة سبانخ 80–13
سلاطة فواكه 80–21
سلاطة كرنب (كولسلو) 80–18
سلاطة معكرونة (باستا) 80–20
سلاطة وجبة العشاء 80–15
سلام / دَرَج 50–10, 53–3
سلامة الطعام 76
السلامة العامة 143
السلامة في مكان العمل 179
سلة 56–3
سلة التسوق 73–9
سلة الخبز 83–11

سلة الملابس (سبت للغسيل) 57–1
سلة الغسيل 101–2
سلة للمهملات الطبية 121–31
سلة مهملات 57–26
سلحفاة 213–43
سلسلة 95–33, 180–41
سلسلة أمان للباب 51–33
سلسلة جبال 204–15
سلطانية (وعاء) خلط 78–31
سلطانية الشوربة 83–21
السلطة التشريعية 138
السلطة التنفيذية 138
السلطة القضائية 138
السلطعون (سرطان البحر) 212–20
سلف (أخو الزوج أو الزوجة / زوج الأخت) 34–17
سلفة (أخت الزوج أو الزوجة / زوجة الأخ) 34–16
سلك 181–13
سلك الطاقة 196–2
سلك الهاتف / التليفون 14–2
سلك تالف 179–5
سلك تمديد 181–14
سلم 178–2
سلّم الكتب 11–G
سلّم النجاة من الحريق 50–2
سلم درجي 61–13
سلم متحرك 131–23
سلّم ورقة امتحانك 10–O
سلّم ورقتك 191–M
سلمون كامل 71–3
سلّي الحقائب 160–B
سلّمي وودعي ملوّحة بيدك 2–F
سمّ الصورة 9–V
سماء 209–9
سماعات رأس 6–8, 234–4
سماعات ستريو 234–14
سماعة أذن 115–10
سماعة الهاتف / التليفون 14–1
سماعة رأس بميكروفون 14–13
سماعة رأس لاسلكية بميكروفون 14–14
سماعة طبية 118–10
سماق سام 210–23
سَمَق 93–26
سمك 66–1
سمك أبو سيف 71–5
سمك التروتة المرقّط 71–1
سمك الصلور 71–2
سمك القد (بكلاه) 71–8
السمك المفلطح 212–15
السمك الهلالي (قنديل البحر) 212–14
سمك ذهبي 215–16
سمك طازج 71–16
سمك مجمد 71–17
سمك مشوي على الفحم 81–29
سمندر 212–27
سمندل الماء 212–26
سمُور 216–9
السن 32

سنة 20-4
سنتيمتر [سم] 17-14
سنجاب 215-21
سندوتش النادي (كلوب سندوتش) 80-12
سندوتش جبن مشوي 80-10
سندوتش دجاج 79-5
سندوتش همبورجر (لحم البقر) 79-1
سندوتش همبورجر مع الجبن 79-3
سندان 210-17
سهم 231-8
سهول 204-19
سهول ساحل الخليج 201-16
سوائل قابلة للاشتعال 179-8
سوسن 211-16
سوق المزارعين 84
سوق المقايضة أو الخردوات 222-6
السويد (جلد أو قماش مزأبر) 99-8
سياج 177-19
سيارات وشاحنات 156
سيارة 150-1
سيارة أجرة / تاكسي 150-3
سيارة إسعاف 116-1, 121-34
سيارة إطفاء 144-10
سيارة النفايات 127-22
سيارة ذات ٤ أبواب / سيارة صالون 156-1
سيارة ذات بابين / سيارة كوب 156-2
سيارة رياضية متعددة الاستعمالات (إس يو في) 156-7
سيارة سبور (رياضية) 156-4
سيارة ستايشن 156-6
سيارة صالون فاخرة / سيارة ليموزين 152-20
سيارة فان صغيرة (ميني فان) 156-8
سيارة فان للنقل 156-18
سيارة قطر أو سحب 156-14
سيارة ليموزين 156-11
سيارة مكشوفة (كابريوليه) 156-5
سيارة هييريد (تعمل بالبنزين والكهرباء) 156-3
سير الأمتعة المتحرك 161-23
سير ناقل 175-9
سيرة ذاتية 133-13
السينما 222-2
شاحن 14-10, 234-17
شاحن البطارية 235-27
شاحنة / لوري 150-6
شاحنة بيك اب 156-12
شاحنة صهريجية 156-20
شاحنة قاطرة 156-15
شاحنة نفايات 156-19
شارب / شنب 33-5
شارة 93-21
شارع 150-5, 155-8
شارك في الصف B-10
شاش 117-8
شاشات الوصول والمغادرة 161-7
شاشة 196-11, 235-30
شاشة للعرض 6-2
الشاطئ 225

شاطئ رملي 204-10
شاعر بالبرد / بردان 42-4
شاعر بالحرّ / حرّان 42-1
شامبو 108-10
شامة / خال 32-16
شاهد 141-11
شاي 81-39
شاي أعشاب 81-40
شاي مثلج 79-12
شباك تذاكر 152-12
شبشب / خف 91-26
شبكة صيد أسماك 226-17
شبكة للشعر 93-25
شبكة للشوي 78-14
شبه جزيرة 204-7
شبه جزيرة اليوكاتان 201-19
الشتاء 21-40
الشجر الأحمر (صنوبر حرجي) 210-18
شجر الصنوبر 210-9
شجرة أعياد الميلاد (الكريسماس) 239-16
شحّم طنجرة / طاسة خبز B-77
شخص متخصص في إبادة الحشرات 63-21
شخصان متزوجان 35-20
شخصان مطلقان 35-21
شديد الرياح 13-18
شراء المنزل 49
شراء سيارة مستعملة 157
شراء منتجات معاد تصنيعها D-219
شراء وصيانة سيارة 157
شرائح لحم حمل 70-15
شرائح لحم خنزير 70-10
شرائح لحم عجل (بتلو) 70-6
شراب للسعال 113-29
شرطة 190-20
شرطية / ضابطة شرطة 168-48
الشرفة (الفراندة) الأمامية 53
شرفة / بلكونة 51-20
شرق 155-4
شروق الشمس 18-14
شريان 107-36
شريحة (فيليه) سلمون 71-4
شريحة (فيليه) هلبوت 71-6
شريحة 194-3
شريحة لحم (بفتيك) 70-2
شريحة لحم بقري مشوي (ستيك) 81-24
شريحة لحم مشوي 76-3
شريط 99-30
شريط التمرير 197-15
شريط القوائم 197-1
شريط تصحيح 183-37
شريط حزم لاصق 183-32
شريط شديد اللصق 181-49
شريط فيديو 133-18
شريط قياس (مازورة) 100-17
شريط قياس 181-45
شريط لاصق بدون لون 183-30
شريط لاصق للأسلاك الكهربائية 181-43

شريط لاصق للتغطية 181-53
شريط للرأس 90-3
شريط معقم 117-7
شطرنج 232-8
شعبية فولكلورية 237-29
شعر 104-2
شعر أحمر 33-15
شعر أسود 33-16
شعر أشقر 33-17
شعر بني 33-18
شعر شائب (أبيض) 33-13
شعر طويل 33-3
شعر قصير 33-1
شعر مجعد 33-11
شعر مموج 33-10
شعر ناعم 33-9
شعر واصل للكتف 33-2
الشعور بخيبة أمل 28-4
شفّاطة / ماصّة 79-18
شفة 106-5
شفرة تعريف المنتج 27-4
شفنين بحري 212-11
شقة تمليك 52-5
شقة غير مفروشة 48-4
شقة مفروشة 48-3
الشقق 50-51
شقيق البحر 212-24
شلال 204-2
شمال 155-1
الشمال الغربي الباسيفيكي (المحيط الهادئ) 201-14
شمال كندا 201-1
شمام 68-19
شمبانزي 217-27
شمس 209-8
شمسية 90-17
شمعة 56-20
شهادة جامعية 41-7
شهادة جنسية 40-6
شهادة دبلوم 40-3
شهادة ميلاد 40-1
شهادة وفاة 41-11
شهر 20-3
شهور السنة 21
شوارع المدينة 126-127
شوّاية 53-17
شوربة / حساء 72-18, 80-16
شوربة دجاج سهلة 77
شورت داخلي (شورت ملاكمين) 91-4
شورت للسباحة للرجال (مايوه) 90-22
شوكة 55-3, 211-29
شوكة السلاطة 83-27
شوكة طعام 83-28
الشّيئيّة (عدسة المجهر) 194-16
شيك 132-13
شيك الراتب 165-14
شيهم / نيص 216-10

صابون 57-4, 108-3
صاحب المصنع 175-1
صاحب الملك 51-27
صافح J-3
صافحها باليد I-174
صالة الطعام 82-1
صالون حلاقة 131-18
صالون لتجميل الأظافر 130-3
صانع قهوة كهربائي 54-11
الصباح 18-15
صبار 210-21
صبغة للخشب 181-24
صبغي (كروموسوم) 194-8
صحّح الخطأ N-10
صحراء 204-4
صحن الخبز والزبدة 83-19
صحن ساتليت 53-6
صحن صابون 57-3
صحن طعام مفلطح 83-18
صحن للفنجان 83-25
صحيفة 133-6
صخرة 208-6
صداع 110-1
صدر 104-4, 107-25
صدرة 89-15
صدرة ثقيلة 90-14
صدف البطلنيوس 71-15
صدفة بحرية 225-24
صدور 70-19
صديرية النجاة 161-25, 226-14
صديرية أمان يمكن رؤيتها عن بعد 92-4
صديرية للثديين (سوتيان) 91-20
صرار الليل 214-23
صرّاف / أمين صندوق 166-15
صرصور (صراصير) 63-26
صغير 96-2
صغير جدا 96-1
صغير(ة) 32-1
صف / طابور 73-11
صفصاف 210-13
صفيحة معدنية للإبرة 98-18
صقر / نسر 214-9
صك ملكية 41-9
الصل (كوبرا) 213-41
صل في الموعد المحدد F-174
صلصة خردل (موستردة) 79-22
صلصة طماطم (كاتشب) 79-21
صمام غلق الغاز 146-4
صمغ 183-33
صمولة 180-36
صناديق للبريد 50-11
صنارة صيد سمك 226-18
صندل 88-9
صندوق البريد 128-13
صندوق السيارة 158-11
صندوق اللعب 59-16
صندوق المصاهر الكهربائية (الفيوزات) 62-13

صندوق المهملات 53—24
صندوق بريد (ص. ب) 135—9
صندوق تبريد 225—9
صندوق ثقيل 23—13
صندوق حفظ الودائع 132—7
صندوق خفيف 23—14
صندوق رمل 224—15
صندوق زنبركي تحت السرير 58—19
صندوق قفازات 159—44
صندوق لإلقاء البريد 135—12
صندوق للبريد 53—1
صندوق معروضات زجاجي 94—5
صندوق وحدة المعالجة المركزية 196—3
صندوق / خانة البحث 197—5
صنع الملابس 98—99
صور فوتوغرافية 58—3
صورة جادة 206—3
صورة زائدة التعريض للضوء 235—34
صورة غير واضحة 235—33
صورة فوتوغرافية 136—4
صورة مضحكة 206—2
صورة ناقصة التعريض للضوء 235—35
صوف 98—3
صوفتبول (لعبة شبيهة بالبيسبول) 229—10
صياد سمك تجاري 167—17
صيانة 184—23
صيد الأسماك 226—4
صيدلي 112—1
صيدلية 112—113، 128—4
صيدناني (سنجاب أمريكي صغير مخطط) 215—20
الصيف 21—38
صينية 55—17
صينية أطباق الحلو 83—10
صينية حاملة 161—21
صينية طلاء 181—51
صينية فطائر 78—28
صينية لخبز الحلوى (البسكويت) 78—27
ضابط شرطة / شرطي 141—1
الضاحية (الضواحي) 52—2
ضباب محمّل بدخان 13—14
ضبابي 13—20
ضبط منظّم الحرارة (الترموستات) 219—J
ضبع 217—30
ضجيج 64—5
ضحية / مجني عليه 142—10
ضريبة مبيعات 27—8
ضرير(ة) 32—11
ضع الجمل في ترتيبها الصحيح 9—X
ضع خطا تحت الكلمة 9—S
ضع دائرة حول الجواب 9—Q
ضع سائل التبريد 157—I
ضع صلصة بالملعقة على السطح 77—F
ضع علامة صح في المربعات الصحيحة 9—U
ضع كتبك في مكانها المعتاد 9—Z
ضغط دم عال / ارتفاع ضغط الدم 111—14
ضفدع 212—25
ضفيرة أسلاك 186—7

ضمادة لاصقة 117—5
ضمادة مطاطية 117—12
ضوء الوقوف للطوارئ 159—36
ضوء عمل (بلادوس) 181—44
ضوء ليلي (نور سهاري) 37—27
ضوء مثبت / تركيبة إنارة 55—18
ضيفة الشرف المتحدثة 206—4
طائر 208—4
طائرة 150—8
طائرة عمودية / هليكوبتر 151—9
طابع بريد 134—23
طابعة 196—17
طابعة ليزر 183—19
طابعة نفاثة للحبر 183—18
طابق الكلمات مع بعضها 9—T
الطاقة الريحية 218—2
الطاقة الشمسية 218—1
طاقة الكتلة الإحيائية / الطاقة الإحيائية 218—9
طاقة حرارية أرضية 218—7
طاقة كهربائية 218—5
طاقة نووية 218—8
الطاقة وحفظ الموارد الطبيعية 218—219
طاقم أسنان اصطناعية 119—10
طاقم الإسعاف 116—2
طاقم البستنة 176—1
طالبة 6—5
طاولة العملية الجراحية 121—40
طاولة الكشف 118—7
طاولة الكي 101—14
طاولة بلياردو 50—15
طاولة جانبية / كومودينو 58—23
طاولة حجرة الطعام / سفرة 55—9
طاولة سرير 121—21
طاولة طرفية أو جانبية 56—14
طاولة طويلة / منضدة 54—22
طاولة قابلة للطي لألعاب الورق أو الشدة 102—4
طاولة قهوة 56—19
طاولة لتغيير ملابس الطفل 59—1
طاولة نزهة 224—8
طاووس 214—14
طب الأسنان 119
طباخ الطعام السريع 185—1
طباشير 7—18
طب أمراض نفسية 120—8
طبق / صحن 55—1
طبق السلاطة 83—20
طبق كبير / طبق كسرولة 78—10
طبق كبير مسطح 55—20
طبل (طبول) 238—16
طبيب 118—5
طبيب أشعة 120—6
طبيب أطفال 120—4
طبيب أورام 120—5
طبيب باطني 120—1
طبيب تخدير 121—35
طبيب تقويم الأسنان 119—5
طبيب عيون 120—7

طبيب قلب 120—3
طبيب ولادة 120—2
طبيب / طبيبة أسنان 119—1
طبيبة بيطرية 169—62
طرد 134—17
طرق الدفع 27
طرق الشفاء 114
طرق المحافظة على صحتك 114
طرق لتحضير البيض 76
طرق لتحضير اللحوم والدواجن 76
طريق بين ولايات / علامة طريق سريع 154—17
طريق سريع 155—9
طريق سير الأوتوبيس 152—1
طريق للإخلاء 146—5
طريق للهرب / مهرب 146—3
طريقة هيمليك لمعالجة الاختناق 117—18
طعام الحيوانات المنزلية 72—5
طعم الوجبات السريعة 79
طفح جلدي 110—10
طفل 31—7
طفل ضائع 144—1
طفل في أول مراحل المشي 31—8
الطقس 13
طلاء الأظافر 109—33
طماطم / قوطة / بندورة 69—6
الطمّاق / كساء للساق 90—12
الطنان 214—10
طنجرة / إناء للشوي 78—13
طنجرة / مقلاة 54—24، 78—5
طوق (شريط) مطاطي 183—34
طوق لتقويم الأسنان 119—6
طول 17—17
الطول 32
طويل(ة) 32—4
طيار 161—11
طيارة من الورق والبوص 225—2
الطيور والحشرات والعنكبوتيات 214
ظامئ / عطشان 42—2
ظبي 217—35
ظربان 216—12
ظرف / مغلف 134—14، 183—43
ظفر 106—18
ظل 225—13
ظلال الإجابة الصحيحة 10—K
ظهر 104—5
الظهر 18—16
العائلات 34—35
عاجز(ة) 32—10
عارضة 178—3
عارضة أزياء 168—41
العاشر 16
عاصفة ترابية 13—19
عاصفة ثلجية / عاصفة ثلجية شديدة 13—23
عاصفة ثلجية شديدة 145—13
عاصفة رعدية 13—16
عاصفة من البَرَد 13—21
عاصفة الولاية 139—22

عامل المنضدة (الكاونتر) 79—17
عامل بالمصنع 175—3
عامل بناء 178—1
عامل تحضير الطعام 185—4
عامل تعبئة 175—8
عامل توصيل 167—21
عامل جرد مخازن 169—59
عامل طباعة 169—50
عامل غير محترس 179—1
عامل محترس 179—2
عامل محطة البنزين 162—3
عامل مراكب 167—23
عامل مزرعة 177—8
عامل نظافة 169—54
عامل نقليات 168—42
عامل(ة) ماكينة الخياطة 98—14
عاملة تجهيز وتنظيف الغرف 184—20
عاملة ماكينات 168—37
العاملون بالمستشفى 120
عامود إنارة الشارع 148—3
عبّى خزان البنزين 157—G
عباد الشمس 211—10
عبّارة 220—4
عبد 198—4
عبور المشاة 154—13
عبور سكة حديد (مزلقان) 154—14
عبور مدرسة 154—15
عثة 214—21
عجلة القيادة 159—26
عجوز / مسنّ(ة) 32—3
عدّاد 152—23
عداد السرعة 159—27
عداد الغاز 62—14
عداد موقف السيارة 129—25
عدة لتركيب نماذج 232—9
عدة لصنع دمية 232—13
عدة نجارة 232—14
عدسات لاصقة 115—8
عدسة مقربة (زوم) 235—23
عربة أطفال 37—18
عربة أطفال 37—20
عربة تجهيز وتنظيف الغرف 184—19
عربة تسوق 72—7
عربة ذات منصة 239—2
عربة قطار نفقي 152—6
عربة لنقل الأمتعة 184—8
عربة مقطورة 156—17
عربة النقل السريع / مكوك 152—19
عربة نقل يدوية 175—11
عربة يد 129—28
عربة يد ذات عجلة واحدة 176—3
عرض / تجربة حية 122—6
عرض 17—19، 182—6
عرض المنزل للبيع على الإنترنت 48—1
عرّف / قدّم نفسك 2—C
عرف 217—49
عش 209—12

295

عشرة دولارات 26
العشرون 16
عشرون دولارا 26
عصا 113–16
عصا التزلج على الثلج 231–25
عصا الحلوى 239–17
عصا اليردة 181–16
عصا هوكي 231–11
عصفور / دُوري 214–7
عصير تفاح 73–32
عصير ليمون (ليمونادة) 84–3
عضّاضة 37–24
عضلة 107–32
عضو المجلس التشريعي 139–24
عضو كونجرس 138–4
عضو مجلس المدينة 139–28
عضو مجلس شيوخ / سناتور 138–6
عضو مجلس شيوخ الولاية 139–25
عطارد 205–1
عطلة / أجازة 22–6
عظم 107–33
عقد الإيجار 51–28
عقد زواج 41–8
عقد لؤلؤ 95–39
عقرب 214–30
عقيفة وعروة (مشبك وفتحة) 99–27
عكاز 113–10
علاج بالإبر الصينية 122–2
علاج بالتكلم 115–13
علاج طبيعي 115–11
علامات اقتباس 190–15
علامات الوقف والترقيم 190
علامات مدرسية 10–4
علامة استفهام 190–12
علامة تعجب 190–13
علبة (علب) معدنية 74–3
علبة / صندوق (صناديق) 74–6
علبة إسعافات أولية 117–1، 146–18
علبة الكاميرا 235–28
علبة حاوية ست زجاجات أو علب 74–9
علبة حاوية ست زجاجات صودا 74–21
علبة حبوب (سيريال) 74–18
علبة سمك التونة 72–19
علبة فول 74–15
علبة كرتون (كراتين) 74–4
علبة لأخذ الطعام إلى المنزل 82–5
علجوم 212–28
العلل الشائعة وأمراض الطفولة 111
علل وحالات طبية 111
علم الأحياء (بيولوجيا) 194
علم الطبيعة (الفيزياء) 195
علوم 189–11
العلوم 195–194
علّية 47–8
عم / خال 34–8
عمة / خالة 34–7
عمق 17–18

العمل مع رفيق 8
العمل مع زملائك في الصف 8
العملة 26
عملة دولار فضي / دولار واحد 26
عملة رمزية 152–10
عمليات رياضية 192
عملية الكتابة 191
عمود فقري 107–49
العناية بصحتك 114–115
عنب 68–3
عند البوابة 161
عند الجمرك 161
عند الميكانيكي 158
عند نقطة تفتيش الأمن 160
عند وكالة السيارات (معرض السيارات) 158
عنزة / ماعز 215–5
عنف عصابات 142–4
عنكبوت 214–29
عنوان 133–14، 190–5
العنوان 4–5
عنوان المرسل 134–21
عنوان المرسل إليه 134–22
عنوان رئيسي (مانشت) 133–7
العودة من السوق 66
العون في المشاكل الصحية 115
عيادة 186–2
عيد الذكرى 22–12
عيد الرؤساء 22–11
عيد الرابع من يوليو / عيد الاستقلال 22–13
عيد الشكر 22–17
عيد العمال 22–14
عيد المحاربين القدامى 22–16
عيد ديني 22–7
عيد رأس السنة 22–9
عيد رسمي 22–8
عيد سنوي 22–3
عيد كولومبس 22–15
عيد مارتن لوثر كنغ جونيور 22–10
عيد ميلاد 22–1
عين 105–11
العين 106
عيّنات 84–5
عيّنّة المجهَر 194–14
غائم 13–10
غابات المطر 204–1
غابة 204–11
غار 220–6
الغاز الطبيعي 218–3
غاسل الصحون 185–2
الغد (غدا) 20–6
غذاء الأطفال 37–4
غرب 155–2
الغرب الأوسط 201–9
غردينيا 211–18
غرز / دروز 117–15
الغرطر 213–39
غرفة الجلوس (الصالة) 47–12، 56

غرفة الصحون 83–13
غرفة الطعام 46–7
غرفة الطفل الرضيع 47–10
غرفة العمليات 121
غرفة النوم 58
غرفة بالمستشفى 121
غرفة بسريرين 184–14
غرفة تخزين 185–5
غرفة طعام 55
غرفة مؤتمرات 182–4
غرفة نزيل 184–13
غرفة نوم 46–2
غرفة نوم الأطفال 47–9، 59
غروب الشمس 18–18
غزال 216–14
غسّال الصحون 83–14
غسالة 50–12
غسالة صحون 54–8
غسالة ملابس 101–3
غسل الملابس 101
غسل الملابس في ماء بارد 219–K
غسول أطفال 37–13
غشاء الخلية 194–6
غصن 210–2
غصن كبير / فرع 210–3
غصين 210–1
غضبان 43–29
غطاء 78–24
غطاء خارجي 90–25
غطاء شعر للحمام 108–1
غطاء مأخذ التيار الكهربائي 181–46
غطاء محرك السيارة (كبّوت) 158–4
غطاء محور العجلة 158–9
غلاية / برّاد شاي 54–17
غوريلا 217–29
الغوص مع خزان التنفس 227–12
غوفر (سنجاب أمريكي) 215–19
غير مرتاح 42–9
فاتورة الهاتف / التليفون 15–28
فأر (فئران) 63–28
فأر 215–18
فأرة (ماوس) 196–15
فأس 180–3
فاصلة 190–14
فاصلة عشرية 17–7
فاصلة عليا 190–16
فاصلة منقوطة 190–18
فاصوليا 69–8
فاكهة 67–9
الفاكهة 68
فان بضائع 156–13
فانلا قطن أو تريكو 92–14
فانوس 226–22
فاوض على سعر 157–D
فبراير / شباط 21–26
فتّاحة علب 78–1، 146–8
فتّاحة علب كهربائية 54–14

فتح حساب 132
فتحة أنبوب النفايات 51–26
فترة الاستعمار 198
فتّش على المرافق 147–N
فجل 69–4
فحم 218–4
فخذ 106–19
فخذة حمل 70–14
فخورة 43–21
فراشة 214–19
فرّانة / خبّازة 166–10
فراولة / فريز 68–14
فرح / عرس 22–2
فرس البحر 212–13
فرس النهر 217–43
فرشاة 33–22، 108–14
فرشاة أسنان 57–23، 109–22
فرشاة التواليت 57–20
فرشاة رسم 233–20
فرشاة طلاء 181–22
فرشاة طلاء أسطوانية 181–23
فرشاة مسح وحك 61–20
فرشة من الإسفنج 226–13
فرع البنزين 162–E
الفرق 192–8
فرق الشعر 33–4
فرملة اليد 159–48
فرن 54–20
فرن لتحميص الخبز 54–15
فرن ميكروويف 54–13
الفرن / التنور متعطل 63–15
فروة 216–19
فريق 229–3
فريق البحث والإنقاذ 145–20
فستان 86–3
فستان سهرة 89–18
فستان شبه رسمي 89–20
فستان للحوامل 88–5
فصّاد 121–29
فصفصة 177–5
فصول السنة 21
فطر (عيش غراب) 69–27
فطير الوافل 80–8
فطيرة 81–35
فطيرة بسكويت 80–6
فطيرة محلاة (بانكيك) 80–7
فطيرة مدورة (موفينية) 79–16
الفظ (فيل البحر) 213–32
فقاريات 194–12
فقدان السمع 115–2
فقدان القوى العقلية (خبل) 111–18
فقرة 190–3
فقمة 213–34
فك 106–4
فك نقودا 26–A
فكّر في المهمة 191–E
فتل 211–20

فلفل حار 69-29
فلفل رومي / فلفل حلو 69-7
فلكة 180-37
فلكي / عالم فلكي 205-22
فلوت 238-1
فم 104-7
الفم 106
الفناء الأمامي والمنزل 53
الفناء الخلفي 53
فناء مربع 5-1
فناء مرصوف في الهواء الطلق 53-16
فنّانة 166-6
فنجان 83-24
فنجان قهوة كبير 55-7
فنجان للشاي 55-6
فندق 124، 3-184
فنون 189-15
فنون اللغات 189-9
فني كمبيوتر (حاسوب) 182-12
فني كمبيوترات (حواسيب) 167-19
فنية سجلات طبية 168-39
فهد 217-34
فوط صغيرة رطبة 146-12
فوطة / منشفة صغيرة 57-6
فوطة صدرية 37-5
فوطة يد 57-17
فول 72-17
فول الصويا 177-3
في أثناء الحالة الطارئة 147
في الموعد المحدد 19-23، 161-29
في صالة المطار 160
في غرفة الانتظار 118
في غرفة الكشف 118
فيتامينات 113-17
فيروزي / تركواز 24-9
فيروس نقص المناعة البشرية 111-17
فيزيائي (عالم طبيعة) 195-33
فيضان 145-19
فيل 217-42
فيلم 235-22
فينوس 205-2
فيولونسيل (كمنجة كبيرة) 238-7
ق.ظ. (قبل الظهر) 18-4
قائمة التسوق 67-14
قائمة الطعام 82-7
قائمة الطعام في مقهى 80-81
قائمة منسدلة 197-8
قابس 234-16
القابض (الدوبرياج) 159-49
القارات 202
القارة المتجمدة الجنوبية (انتاركتيكا) 202-7
القاروس 212-6
قاضي 141-6
قاطع التذاكر / كمسري 152-13
قاطع العشب / آكل العشب 176-12
قاطع دوار 232-16

قاطعة أوراق 183-22
قاطور (تمساح أمريكي) 213-37
قاعة اجتماعات 184-25
قاعة المحكمة 141-7
قاعة الولائم 185-14
قاعة حفلات 184-26
قاعة محاضرات 5-18
قاعدة 193، 45، 194-20، 3-234
قاعدة السرير 58-18
قاعدة الشمعة 56-21
قامطة تثبيت 180-6
قبضة (أكرة) الباب 53-12
قبعات 95-11
قبعة 90-1
قبعة التخرج 206-7
قبعة التزحلق على الجليد 90-11
قبعة الجراح 93-35
قبعة أو شمسية المصباح 58-26
قبعة رئيس الطهاة (الشيف) 93-28
قبعة راعي البقر 92-18
قبعة صلبة 92-1، 179-9
قبعة من القش 90-23
قبل حدوث الحالة الطارئة 146
قبلي K-3
القد 212-5
قدر صغير 78-25
قدر طبخ 54-16
قدم 104-8
قدم ضاغط 98-19
قدَمي صديقا I-3
قديمة 199-1
قراءة الوقت بالنظر إلى الساعة 18
قراءة فاتورة الهاتف / التليفون 15
قرادة 214-27
قراصيا (برقوق مجفف) 68-26
قرانيا 210-15
قرحة (كلْو) 110-15
قرد 217-26
القرش 212-4
قرص 113-22
قرص طائر 231-27
قرص فيديو رقمي (دي في دي) 133-19
قرع 69-24
قرميد / طوب 178-12
قرن 216-21
قرنبيط 69-14
قرون الوعل 216-16
قِن C-17
قسائم (كوبونات) 67-15
قسم الأحذية 95-7
قسم المجوهرات 95-8
قسم المنتجات الزراعية 72-2
قش / برسيم 177-18
قشارة خضروات 78-15
قشدة (كريمة) حامضة 72-21
قشدة / قشدة حليب 81-41
قشّر الجزر K-77

قصاصات النثار الورقية 239-3
قصيرة(ة) 32-6
قضاة 138-12
قضاعة (كلب الماء) 213-35
قضبان تسلق 224-14
قضيب أمان 59-10
قضيب مسك مانع للانزلاق 57-11
قطار 150-7
قطار نفقي / مترو أنفاق 151-12
قطارات لعب نموذجية 233-27
قطارة 195-45
قطر 193-37
قطرة للعين 113-31
قطع (قرّط) البصل L-77
قطع 175-5
قطع التوفو في شرائح C-77
قطّع الدجاج إلى قطع صغيرة I-77
قطّع الكرفس إلى مكعبات J-77
قطع سلك للتنظيف 61-5
قطع غيار سيارة 158-159
قطعة قماش مخرمة توضع تحت الطبق 55-11
قطعة لحم بقري مشوي (روزبيف) 71-21
قطعة من الحلوى 73-37
قطن 98-1، 177-6
قطيفة 99-10، 211-13
قطيفة مضلّعة 99-11
قف 6-D، 154-1
قف عند الزاوية / الناصية D-155
قفاز 231-17
قفازات 90-6
قفازات تلقى بعد الاستعمال 93-27
قفازات صوفية بلا أصابع 90-10
قفازات عمل 92-17، 179-17
قفازات غرفة العمليات 121-39
قفازات مطاطية 61-4
قفازات من اللثى 93-34
قفص صدري 107-48
قفل الباب 159-25
قفل بمزلاج ثابت 51-34
القفل مكسور 62-6
قل اسمك A-4
قل، "أهلا وسهلا" A-2
قلائد / عقود 95-10
قلب 107-38، 239-6
قلْب O-77
قلعة من الرمل 225-12
قلق(ة) 42-13
قلم تخطيط 24-7
قلم تخطيط العين 109-36
قلم جاف للتخطيط قابل للمحو 17-7
قلم حبر جاف 22-7
قلم حواجب 109-34
قلم رصاص 7-20
قلم صمغ 232-11
قلم كحل 109-35
قلنسوة / برنيطة 88-1
قلنسوة غرفة العمليات 121-37

قم بالتسجيل إلكترونيا 160-A
قماش قنب 233-17
قماش من القنب لوقاية الأثاث والأرضية 181-54
قمة جبل 204-14
قمح 177-2
قمر صناعي / سائل 205-20
قمع 195-40
قميص 86-1
قميص بدون أكمام 96-11
قميص تي شيرت 86-4
قميص خاص لموظف الأمن 93-20
قميص داخلي (فانيلا) 91-1
قميص داخلي حراري 91-2
قميص ذو 3/4 (ثلاثة أرباع) كم 96-13
قميص ذو أكمام طويلة 96-14
قميص ذو أكمام قصيرة (نصف كم) 96-12
قميص طويل للنوم 91-28
قميص عمل / قميص شغل 92-2
قميص قصير بدون أكمام وبفتحات كبيرة للذراعين (قميص داخلي) 89-24
قميص متجعد (متكرمش) 101-19
قميص مكوي 101-20
قميص نوم للنساء 91-25
قميصول (سترة نسائية قصيرة) 91-21
قناع 239-9
قناع أكسجين 161-24
قناع التزحلق على الجليد 90-15
قناع الجراح 93-36
قناع الغطس 225-6
قناع الوجه 93-32
قناع تهوية وتنفس 92-7
قناع لاقف الكرة 231-15
قناع واقٍ 179-12
قناع واقٍ من الجسيمات 179-14
قنفذ البحر 212-21
قهوة 73-81، 33، 37
قهوة بدون كافيين 81-38
القوات الجوية 138-16
القوات المسلحة 138
القوارض 215
قواعد 64-7
قواعد الكتابة 190
قوس 231-6
قوسان 190-19
قولي، "مع السلامة" L-3
قومي بإملاء جملة N-8
قيادة سيارة تحت تأثير الخمر 142-5
قياس المساحة والحجم 193
قياسات 17
قيثار (جيتار) 238-9
القيق الأزرق / الزرياب 214-6
قيب 210-12
قيود / كلبشات 141-2
قيوط (ذئب أمريكي) 216-3
كائنات حية 194-1
الكابيتول (مقر الكونجرس الأمريكي في واشنطن) 138-1

كيميائي (عالم كيمياء) 195—25
كيوي 68—22
لا تتأخر عن الميعاد E—174
لا تتسوّق إلا على مواقع إنترنت مؤمنة H—143
لا تتناوله مع منتجات ألبان D—112
لا تدخّن G—114
لا تشرب الخمر وتقود سيارة G—143
لا تشرب مشروبات كحولية F—112
لا تفتح بابك للغرباء F—143
لا تقود سيارة أو تشغّل آلات ثقيلة E—112
لا تلق القمامة في غير مكانها L—219
لا يستطيع التنفس N—116
لاصق / لصيقة التسجيل 136—13
لاصق 102—3
لاعب 229—5
لافتات المرور 154
لافتة شارع 129—26
لافتة شقة خالية 50—7
لافقاريات 194—13
لاما 217—25
لانشون السلامي 71—24
لبادات للركب 179—19
لبادة تحبير / مختمة 183—46
لبادة تدفئة 113—13
لبادة كتف 231—20
لبادة لتغيير حفاض الطفل 59—2
لبادة معقمة 117—6
لبادة وقائية للطفل 59—4
لباس تنكري 239—11
لبلاب سام 210—25
لبن / حليب مخفوق 79—14
لثة 106—6
لحاف 58—16
لخام 169—63
لحم 66—2
لحم الحمل (الضأن) 70
لحم الخنزير 70
لحم بقر 70
لحم بقري مقلي بالتقليب 76—6
لحم بقري مملح (بلوبيف) 71—22
لحم خنزير مملح (بيكون) 70، 11، 80—1
لحم فخذ خنزير 70—9
لحم فخذ خنزير مسلوق 76—5
لحم للسلق (لحم معدّ للخنة) 70—3
لحم معد للشواء (روستو) 70—1
لحم مفروم 70—4
لحم مفروم مطبوخ في قالب 81—31
اللحوم والدواجن 70
لحية 33—6
لخبطة / خربطة 64—8
لسان 106—8
لسعة حشرة 110—11
لعب وألعاب 59
لعبة دوارة بزنبرك 59—5
لعبة لوحية 232—5
لغات العالم 189—13
لغز 59—17

كلب إمداد / قضيب إمداد 20—98
كلب غير مطيع 23—18
كلب مطيع 23—17
كلمة 190—1
كلْي 11—I
كلية / جامعة 188—7
كلية 107—43
كلية أهلية 127—17، 188—6
كُم 100—6
كمامة ضد الغازات السامة 179—13
كمان (كمنجة) 238—6
كمان أجهر (كونتراباص) 238—8
الكمبيوتر (الحاسوب) 196
كمبيوتر (حاسوب) 183—17
الكمبيوتر المكتبي 196
كمبيوتر محمول 196—16
كمثرى 68—4
كن على دراية بالبيئة المحيطة بك I—143
كن مهندما C—174
كناديس (سرير مزدوج) 59—9
كنبة / أريكة 56—18
كنزة فضفاضة / سترة رياضية
بغطاء للرأس 89—22
كنسية 237—30
كنغر 217—44
كنيسة 127—14
كهربائي 62—9
كهوف 220—7
كوارت حليب 75—4
كوارتر (ربع دولار) / ٢٥ سنتا 26—4
كوال 217—45
كوب زيت 75—2
كوب صيدلي 195—39
كوب من الدقيق 75—10
الكوبة 233—31
كوز صنوبر 210—11
كوسا 69—25
كوع 106—12
كولومبيا البريطانية 201—2
كولونيا / عطر 108—6
كولونيا بعد الحلاقة 109—30
كومة سماد طبيعي 53—25
الكون 205
الكونجرس 138—2
الكونجرس القاري الأول 198—6
كويبك 201—5
كيبورد (لوحة أصابع) كهربائي 238—18
كيس (أكياس) 74—7
كيس البقالة 67—13
كيس الماء الساخن 113—15
كيس المكنسة الكهربائية 61—12
كيس أمان هوائي 159—43
كيس خس 69—31
كيس دقيق 74—19
كيس للنوم 226—12
كيس وسادة / مخدة 58—14
الكيمياء 195

كرة القدم الأمريكية (الفوتبول) 229—11
كرة الماء 229—15
كرة المضرب (تنس) 228—15
كرة بيسبول 231—18
كرة قدم 231—12
كرتون(ة) بيض 74—16
كرز 68—11
كرسي 7—11
كرسي أمان لسلامة الأطفال بالسيارة 37—19
كرسي بعجلات 113—9
كرسي حجرة الطعام 55—8
كرسي ذو مسندين / فوتيه 56—22
كرسي قابل للطي 102—5
كرسي للشاطئ 225—22
كرسي مرتفع 37، 82—6, 3
كرسي هزاز 37—21
الكرش (كرشة) 70—8
كرفس 69—9
كركدن (خرتيت) 217—28
كرمة 177، 210—16, 22
كرنب / ملفوف 69—2
كريم / معجون 113—25
كريم أساس 109—40
كريم للجسم / مرطب للجلد 108—9
كريم مضاد للهيستامين 117—10
كستبان 100—15
كسرولة (طبق) خضار بالتوفو الجبني 77
الكسور 192
الكسور والكسور العشرية 17
كسوف الشمس 205—16
كشف الحساب البنكي 132—16
كشف قليل التكلفة 122—1
كشف نظر 136—6
كشك التسجيل 160—2
كشك الهواتف المحمولة (النقالة) 131—22
كشك جرائد 128—12
كشكشة مانعة للأتربة 58—17
كشمير 98—4
كعب 106—24
كعب استلام راتب 165—11
كعب الحذاء 94—22
كعب عالٍ 97—32
كعب واطئ 97—31
كعكة 73—39
كعكة الدونات 79—15
كعكة جبن 81—34
كعكة سريعة وسهلة 77
كعكة من طبقات 81—33
كف 106—15
كف الحيوان ذي البراثن 216—20
كُلْ أطعمة صحية F—114
كل يوم / يوميا 20—21
كلّاب 195—43
كلارينت 238—2
كلاسيكية 237—21
كلب 215—11
كلب البراري 215—22

كابينة الشاحنة 156—16
كابينة الطيارين 161—10
كاتب / موظف مكتبة 133—1
كاتب المحكمة 141—12
كاتبة / مؤلفة 169—64
كاحل 106—23
كارافان 156—9
كارت / بطاقة 239—5
كارت ذاكرة 235—20
كأس فارغ 23—10
كأس للماء 83—22
كأس للنبيذ 83—23
كأس ممتلئ 23—9
كاشف أدخنة 51—29
كافيتيريا 5—14
كاميرا فيلمية / كاميرا ٣٥ مم 235—21
كاميرا رقمية (ديجيتال) 235—19
كاميرا فيديو كمبيوترية 196—12
كاميرا للأمن 50—19
الكبار والأطفال 30
كباس 181—50
كب لحم (كبيبة) 81—27
كبد 107—40
كبدة 70—7
كبسول أو طباقة 99—26
كبسولة 113—23
كبل 196—13
كبل عبور الطاقة 158—21
كبير 96—4
كبير جدا 96—5
كتاب تلوين 59—13
كتاب رقيق (رفيع) 23—8
كتاب سميك (غليظ) 23—7
كتاب صوتي 133—17
كتاب مدرسي 7—25
كتاب مصور 133—12
الكتابة على لوحة المفاتيح 196
كتالوج إلكتروني 133—11
كتّان 98—2
كتف 105—13
كتلة تضريب 232—15
كتيب إسعافات أولية 117—2
كتيب الامتحان 10—1
كتيب دائرة تسجيل المركبات الآلية 136—1
كثيب 204—5
كدمة 110—12
كراسة بسلك 7—29
كراسة تمارين 7—26
كراسة ورق طويل 183—38
كرة 59، 193—12, 42
كرة البولينغ 231—5
كرة السلة 229، 8—231—4
الكرة الطائرة 229—14
كرة الطائرة 231—3
كرة الطاولة 228—14
كرة الفوتبول 231—21
كرة القدم 229—12

لفة (لفافات) 74—11
لفت 69—16
لفة مناديل ورقية 74—23
لفيفة صوف أو قطن 233—22
اللقاء والتحية 2
لقمة ثقب 180—28
لوائح السلامة 164—6
اللوح الأم 196—5
لوح الكتف 107—28
لوح خشب حبيبي 181—20
لوح خشبي لركوب الأمواج المتكسرة 225—16
لوح خشبي مقاس ٢ بوصة × ٤ بوصة 181—19
لوح زجاجي في نافذة 178—16
لوحة الترخيص المعدنية 136—12
لوحة المفاتيح 14—5
لوحة تقطيع 54—27
لوحة رقم السيارة 158—12
لوحة فنية 56—9
لوحة للتزلج على الثلج 231—23
لوحة مفاتيح 196—14
لوحة منشورات 7—14
لون مائي 233—21
لويحات البلاك 119—12
لويحات تسقيف 178—20
الليل 18—20
ليلك 211—23
ليم (ليمون أخضر أو حامض) 68—8
ليمون (ليمون أصفر) 68—7
ليمون الجنة (كريب فروت) 68—6
منزر (ثوب عمل ذو كمين) 92—8
مؤشر سهمي 197—12
مؤشر 197—14
مؤلف 133—15
مؤلف موسيقي / ملحن 199—14
المنوي 16
ماء 209—13
ماء بارد 57—10
ماء ساخن 57—9
مائة دولار 26
مأخذ التيار 58—28
مادة طاردة للحشرات 226—23
مارس / آذار 21—27
ماسحة 183—20
ماسورة العادم 158—15
مأسوي (تراجيديا) 237—14
ماشية 177—21
المأكولات البحرية وأطعمة شهية 71
مأكولات خفيفة 73
مأكولات مجمدة 72
مأكولات معلبة 146—9
ماكينة تصوير مستندات 183—23
ماكينة حلاقة 109—27
ماكينة حلاقة كهربائية 109—26
ماكينة خياطة 98—13
ماكينة سنفرة للتنعيم 180—11
ماكينة طوابع 135—11
مالج 176—10، 178—13

مأمور الحديقة أو المنتزه 220—2
مانجو 68—21
مانع لأشعة الشمس 108—8
مايو / أيار 21—29
مايونيز 79—23
مباراة بيسبول 44—2
مبارزة بالسيف 228—7
مبراة أقلام كهربائية 183—26
مبراة الأقلام الرصاص 7—23
مبرد أظافر 109—32
مبرمجات 196—10
مبشرة 78—2
مبكرا 19—22
مبنى البلدية 124—8
مبنى خاص للمكاتب 124—2
مبيّض 101—8
متأخرا 19—24
متألم(ة) / مصاب(ة) بألم 42—11
متحف الفنون 223—9
المتحكم في حركة السرير 121—27
مترجم شفهي / مترجم تحريري 168—35
المترددة (ترومبون) 238—10
متزوج للمرة الثانية 35—24
متشابهتان ومختلفتان 28
متضايق / منزعج 43—28
متطلبات الحصول على الجنسية 140
متطوع 121—17
متغير 192—12
متهم / مدعى عليه 141—5
متوازي أضلاع 193—33
متوتر(ة) 42—10
متوسط 96—3
متوسط(ة) العمر 32—2
متوسط(ة) الطول 32—5
متوسط(ة) الوزن 32—8
مثار 43—22
مثانة 107—46
مثبّت الشعر 108—12
مثقاب كهربائي 180—8
مثلث 193—32
مجاعة 145—12
المجرّة 205—15
مجرفة خلفية 178—8
مجزة تشذيب 176—9
مجفف شعر بالهواء الساخن
(سيشوار) 33—23، 108—18
مجففة 50—13
مجلة 133—5
المجلجة / ذات الأجراس 213—38
المجلس التشريعي للولاية 139—23
مجلس الشيوخ 138—5
مجلس المدينة / المجلس البلدي 139—27
مجلس النواب 138—3
مجمّع ضخم يمكن السير فيه 185—3
المجموع / الإجمالي 27—9
المجموع 192—7
مجموعة دعم 115—15

مجموعة نجوم متألقة 205—14
مجهر (ميكروسكوب) 194
محار 71
محار رخوي 71—14
محاسبة 166—1
المحاصيل 177
المحافظة على نظافة المجتمع 148
المحاكمة العادلة 140—5
محامي 168—36
محامي دفاع 141—4
محب / عاشق 42—18
محبط 43—27
محتار 43—26
محدد موقع المصدر العالمي / عنوان موقع الإنترنت 197—4
محرج 43—24
محرك / موتور 158—18
محرك أقراص محمول 196—8
محرك القرص الصلب 196—6
محرك بحث 197—6
محرك قرص دي في دي / سي دي روم 196—9
محطة الأوتوبيس 124—7
محطة بنزين 125—10
محطة فضاء 205—18
محطة قطار 152
محطة قطار نفقي / محطة مترو أنفاق 151—11
محطة قطار نفقي 152
محفظة 94—13
المحكمة العليا 138—11
محل أجهزة إلكترونية 131—20
محل أحذية 130—10
محل أدوات لتحسين المنازل 127—20
محل أدوات مكتبية 127—21
محل أقمشة 99
محل الأدوات المعدنية / محل أدوات الحدادة 148—4
محل البقالة 72—73
محل آيس كريم 131—16
محل بطاقات معايدة / محل كروت 130—7
محل بيع الحلوى 131—17
محل بيع كتب 130—4
محل بيع ملابس الحوامل 131—19
محل تعديل الثياب 100
محل سوبرماركت 127—18
محل شرائط فيديو 129—20
محل لبيع الأثاث 126—8
محل لعب 130—5
محل لكعك الدونات 129—17
محل متعدد الأقسام 131—13
محل مجوهرات 130—2
محل منتجات الحيوانات المنزلية 130—6
محل موسيقى 130—1
محل نظارات (نظاراتي) 130—9
محل هدايا 184—5
محمصة الخبز (توستر) 54—6
المحيط / الماء 225—1
محيط 193—36، 204—6
محيط خارجي 193—43

مخ 107—34
مخبز 127—19
المختبر 121
مختبر العلوم 195
مختبر حواسيب 5—15
مخترع 199—18
مخدة دبابيس / مدبسة 100—13
مخدرات ممنوعة 142—6
مخرج للطوارى 51—25
مخروط 193—40
مخزن 50—17
مخضرة 53—26
مخطط (تصميم) طابق في مبنى 186—4
مخطط / مقلّم 96—20
مخطط بياني 192—15
مخفر الشرطة 124—6
مخفف الصدمة 158—8
مخفقة (مضرب) بيض 78—20
مخفقة 78—21
مخلب 214—2
مخمّد الصوت (شكمان) 158—16
مدارس ومواد الدراسة 188
مدان (محكوم عليه) / سجين 141—15
مدبرة منزل 168—34
مدخل 164—1
المدخل 50
مدخل الشقة 51
مدخل غرفة الطوارى 121
مدخنة 53—5
مدرّب 5—20، 229—2
مدرجات 5—3
مدرسة 126—9
المدرسة 5
مدرسة ابتدائية 188—2
مدرسة إعدادية 188—3
مدرسة ثانوية 188—4
مدرسة حرفية / مدرسة تقنية 188—5
مدرسة للكبار 188—8
المدرع 216—8
المدعي العام / وكيل النيابة 141—10
مدفأة 159—40
مُدلاة 95—35
مدمّة / أداة لجمع العشب 176—8
مدير / مشرف 50—8
مدير 72—8
مدير حسابات 132—9
مدير صالة الطعام 185—11
مدير مكتب 182—8
المدينة / منطقة حضرية 52—1
المدينة 4—7
مدينة ملاهي 223—10
مذاق حمضي / مُر 84—4
مذرتا الملح والفلفل 55—13
مذكرات لاصقة 183—39
مذنب 205—24
مر عبر نقطة الأمن D—160
مرآة 57—18

مرآة الرؤية الجانبية 158-3
مرآة كاملة الطول 58-6
مرآة للرؤية الخلفية 159-35
مراجيح 224-11
مرارة 107-44
مراسلة صحفية 169-52
مرافق 48-5
مراهق / من ذوي السنوات بين ١٣ و ١٩
من العمر 31-11
مربع 193-30
مربع نصي 197-13
مربعات ملوّنة 96-22
مربي مواشي 177-22
مرة في الأسبوع 20-22
مُرتاد مكتبة 133-3
مرتان في الأسبوع 20-23
مرتبة / فراش 58-20
المرتفعات الجنوبية 201-17
مرتفعات شياباس 201-18
مَرْج 204-20
المرجان (الشعب المرجانية) 220-5
مرجرين (سمن نباتي) 72-20
المرحاض (التواليت) مسدود 63-19
مرسال / ساعي 168-40
مِرَشّة 53-22, 181-21
مرصد 205-21
مرض السكري 111-12
مرض القلب 111-11
مرض اللثة 119-11
مرطب للهواء 113-12
مرفاع (كوريك) 158-24
مرفاع (ونش) 178-7
مرفاع شوكي 175-12
مراقب الوظائف الحيوية 121-26
مرقاق العجين / شوبك 78-30
مركز الدفع 73-12
مركز الطبيعة 208
مركز بريدي آلي 135-10
مركز تجاري (مول) 130-131
مركز تسوق 126-7
مركز جمباز (جمنازيوم) 184-24
مركز رعاية أطفال 129-30
مركز مؤتمرات 127-24
مركز موارد 172-9
مرهق / تعبان 43-32
مرهم 113-24
مرهم مضاد للجراثيم 117-11
مرهم واقٍ من أشعة الشمس 225-10
مروحة 55-19
المريخ 205-4
مريض 118-6, 121-18
مريض(ة) 42-12
مريلة 92-11
مريلة خصرية 93-30
مريلة نوم للأطفال / بيجاما ذات قدمين 91-27
مزادة (قربة ماء) 226-24
مزارع / فلاح 177-13

مزراب 53-4
مزرعة 52-9
مزرعة كبيرة 52-10
مزلج بخط دواليب 231-10
مزلج جليد 231-9
مَزْلق ذو عجلات 224-7
مزهر (ذو أشكال وردية) 96-25
مزيل التجمد 159-41
مزيل المكياج 109-42
مزيل رائحة العرق 108-5
مزيّن بهداب (شراشيب) 99-34
مزينة أظافر 168-38
مزينة شعر / مصففة شعر 167-31
مسؤول إحضار الطلبات 175-10
المسؤول عن توظيف موظفين جدد 172-14
مسؤول منتخب 139-32
مسؤولة تنفيذية 182-5
المساء 18-19
المسّاحات 158-2
مسّاحة مطاطية (سكويجي) 61-15
مسار 208-3
المسار الوظيفي 172
مساعد النادل (الجرسون) 83-12
مساعد الناظر 5-5
مساعد طبيب 168-47
مساعد طبيب أسنان 119-2
مساعد ممرضة معتمد 120-12
مساعدة إدارية 166-3
مساعدة النادل 185-13
مساعدة رعاية صحية منزلية 167-32
مساعدة طبيب أسنان 167-22
مساكن الطلاب 52-8
مساكن المسنين 52-11
مسألة رياضية 192
مسألة سهلة 23-23
مسألة صعبة 23-24
مسألة كلامية 192-11
مسبح / حمّام سباحة 51-22, 184-22
مستأجر / ساكن 50-6
مستحضر لغسل الفم 109-25
مستخدم مساعد 177-20
المستشفى 121-20
المستشفى 120-121
مستطيل 125-9, 154-18
مستطيل 193-29
المستعمرون 198-2
مستكشف 199-9
مستلزمات المكتب 183
مستودع 175-7
مستوقد / مدفأة 56-13
مسجد 126-5
مسحاج / فأرة النجار 181-57
مسحاج تخديد 180-12
مسحوق الغسيل 101-7
مسدس 142-13
مسرب البولينغ (لعبة الكرة الخشبية) 222-4
مسرح 127-23
مسرحية 223-8

مسرور 44-5
مسطرة 17-13
مَسكرة (مستحضر تجميلي) 109-39
مسكّن للآلام 113-26
مسلات حياكة 233-23
مسلسل تلفيزيوني 236-5
مسمار 180-34
مسمار العقدة 180-38
مسمار ملولب 180-35
مسموح الدوران 154-5
مُبنّة / عجوز 30-5
مسوّق بالهاتف / بالتليفون 169-60
مشاة 128-14
المشاركة مع آخرين في ركوب سيارة واحدة 219-ا
مشاكل الأسنان 119
مشاكل المنزل وإصلاحها 62-63
مشاكل خاصة بالملبوسات 97
مشاكل في النظر 115-1
مشبك الرف 194-21
مشبك الملابس 101-10
مشبك شعر 108-20
مشبك ورق 183-31
مشتاق إلى الوطن / شاعر بالحنين للوطن 43-20
المشتري 205-5
مشجّع 229-4
مشدّ 91-15
مشرف 165-5, 6-8
مشرف على خط التجميع 175-4
مشروب غازي / صودا 79-11
مشروبات 73
مشروبات غازية / صودا 73-34
مشط 33-21, 108-13
مشط مدبب الأسنان 108-15
مشغّل الأسطوانات (دي جاي) 64-4
مشغّل فيديو 197-11
مشمئز(ة) 42-7
مشمس / صافي 13-9
مشمش 68-12
مشواة 54-21
مصاب بالملل / سئم 43-25
مصادر الطاقة 218
مصارعة 228-17
مصباح (أباجورة) 58-25
مصباح أرضي 56-15
مصباح الشرفة (الفراندة) 53-13
مصباح الفرملة 158-14
مصباح أمامي 158-7
مصباح بطارية 146-14
مصباح خلفي 158-13
مصباح يصنع من قرعة 239-10
مصبغة / تنظيف جاف 128-2
مصحّح البصر 115-6
مصدر ضوئي 194-19
مصرف المياه / بلاعة 57-7
مصطلحات تاريخية 199
مصعد 131-21, 184-9
مصفاة (للسوائل) 78-22

مصفاة 78-17
مُصلّح / عامل تصليح 62-10
مُصلّح أقفال 62-11
مصمم 175-2
مصمم فنون تخطيطية 167-30
مصممة تزيين الأراضي 176-5
مصنع 126-3
مصنع 175
مصنع ملابس 98
مصوّر 206-1
مضاد للحموضة 113-28
مضرب بيسبول 231-14
مضرب تنس 231-2
مضرم 54-19
مضمار الجزْئي / السباق 5-21
مضيف / مضيفة طائرة 161-12
مضيفة 82-2
مطابقان 28-3
مطار 151-10, 160-161
مطب هوائي / اضطراب جوي 161-22
مطبخ 46-5, 83-15
المطبخ 54
المطبخ في مطعم 185
مطبعة / محل لتصوير مستندات 129-18
مطر حمضي 218-13
مطرقة 180-1
مطرقة ثقيلة / مرزبة 178-23
مطرقة خشبية 180-2
مطرّي للنسيج 101-6
مطعم 82-83, 125-14
مطعم وجبات سريعة 128-10
مطفئة حريق 129-27
مطفئة حريق 179-21
مظلة للشاطئ 225-14
المظهر 32
معادلة / صيغة 195-34
معادلة 192-13
معارف خارج الولاية 146-2
معافى / معافية 42-14
معالج 115-14
معالج صغير (ميكروبروسيسور) / وحدة المعالجة
المركزية 196-4
معالم 220-1
معاون معلّم 5-16
معبد يهودي 127-16
معتدل 13-5
معجم 7-30
معجم مصوّر 7-31
معجون أسنان 109-23
معجون حلاقة 109-29
معدات السلامة 179
معدات المكتب 183
معدات رياضية 231
معدات مزرعة 177-12
معدات مكسورة 179-4
معدة 107-41
معرض الأحياء المائية 222-7

معرض الصحة 122
معرض سيارات 126—4
معرض فرص العمل 172—13
معصرة ثوم 78—11
معطف (بلطو) مطر 90—18
معطف (خارجي) / بلطو (خارجي) 90—2
معكرونة رفيعة وطويلة (اسباجتي) 81—26
معلاق 113—19
معلبات 72
معلِّم 5—8
معلِّمة / مدرِّسة 6—4
معلومات شخصية 4
معول 178—21
مغرفة 78—7
مغسلة عامة 128—1
مغلف بريد 183—40
مغنطيس 195—36
مغنولية 210—8
مفتاح 155—6
مفتاح 51—30
مفتاح الباوند 14—7
مفتاح الضوء 58—27
مفتاح النجمة 14—6
مفتاح أنابيب 181—47
مفتاح ربط 158—22
مفتاح ربط قابل للضبط 181—48
مفرش الطاولة 55—12
مفرش سرير / شرشف 59—11
مفك براغي 180—30
مفك براغي مصلب الرأس 180—31
مقادير السوائل 75
مقادير المواد الجافة 75
مقارنة الملبوسات 97—96
مقاس واحد للجميع 96—6
المقاطعات البحرية 201—6
مقاطعات البروج (البراري) 201—3
مقال 190—4
المقام 192—6
مقاول 186—5
المقاييس 17
مقبرة 127—15
مقبس الهاتف / التليفون 14—3
مقبض تعديل تقريبي 194—24
مقبض تعديل دقيق 194—22
مقدّم (إصبع قدم) الحذاء 94—23
مقدمة 190—6
مقر سباح الإنقاذ 225—21
مقشة / مكنسة 61—16
مقشرة أسلاك 181—42
مقص 100, 20, 33—16
مقصورة 182—7
مقطع من خط 193—20
مقعد أمامي 159—51
مقعد أمان للطفل 159—53
مقعد جامد (قاسي) 23—5
مقعد خلفي 159—54
مقعد طري (مريح) 23—6

مقعد مائل الظهر 161—27
مقعد مستقيم الظهر 161—28
مقعدة / أرداف 107—30
مقلمة أظافر 109—31
مقلمة الوشيع (الشجيرات) 176—11
مقهى 126—11
مقياس 155—7
مقياس البنزين 159—31
مقياس الحرارة 159—30
مقياس الزيت 159—29
مقياس حرارة (ترمومتر) 118—11
مكالمة خارجية 15—32
مكالمة دولية 15—35
مكالمة محلية 15—31
مكالمة هاتفية / تليفونية على الإنترنت 14—20
مكان إعادة الزجاجات الفارغة 73—16
مكان العمل 164
مكان الميلاد 4—14
مكان تجمع 146—1
مكان لوقوف السيارة 50, 18, 128—5
مكان مخصص للمعوقين لوقوف سياراتهم 128—6
مكتب 6—7, 164—3, 182—9, 183—182
مكتب الإدارة 5—12
مكتب الاستقبال والتسجيل 184—12
مكتب البريد 135—134
مكتب التأجير 51
مكتب بريد 125—11
مكتب تداول 133—2
مكتب سياحة / وكالة سفر 131—14
مكتبة 5—17, 125—15
المكتبة 133
مكسرات 73—36
مكسور الخاطر 42—16
مكشطة 181—52
مكعب 193—38
مكعبات 59—19
مكنسة كهربائية 61—10
مكواة 101—13
مكواة شعر 108—17
مكوك / بكرة 98—21
مكوك الفضاء 205—19
مكياج 109
مكيِّس / معبِّئ أكياس 73—14
مكيف الهواء 159—39
ملء استمارة 4
ملاءة 58—13
ملاءة مفصلة 58—12
الملابس اليومية 86
ملابس التمرينات الرياضية 89
الملابس الداخلية وملابس النوم 91
الملابس الرسمية 89
ملابس العمل 88
الملابس الموسمية 90
ملابس النوم 91
ملابس ثقيلة للتدفئة 146—6
ملابس داخلية طويلة 91—3
ملابس داخلية لكلا الجنسين 91

ملابس داخلية للرجال 91
ملابس داخلية للنساء 91
الملابس غير الرسمية 88
الملابس غير الرسمية والرسمية وملابس العمل 89—88
ملابس للغسل (الغسيل) 101—1
ملابس مستعملة 102—2
ملابس مكان العمل 93—92
ملاحظ طاقم البستنة 176—4
ملاكمة 228—4
ملجأ 52—13
ملحقات المكنسة الكهربائية 61—11
ملعب 50—3
ملعب كرة 224—1
ملعب كرة السلة 229—7
ملعب كرة المضرب (تنس) 224—6
ملعقة 55—5
ملعقة خشبية 78—9
ملعقة شاي 83—31
ملعقة شاي من الملح 75—6
ملعقة شوربة 83—32
ملعقة طعام (سفرة) من السكر 75—7
ملعقة مبسطة 78—19
ملف بطاقات دوار 183—44
ملف ذو ثلاث حلقات / كراسة 7—27
ملفوف حول الرأس 90—7
ملقاط 117—4
ملقط بوتقي 195—44
ملقطة 78—23
ملك 199—4
ملمِّع الأثاث 61—8
ممتلئ / شبعان 42—6
ممثل 166—2
ممحاة (القلم الرصاص) 7—21
ممحاة 7—19
ممر 72—6
ممر الجراج 53—8
ممر المدخل الرئيسي 53—2
ممر المشاة 128—15
ممر دراجات 224—3
ممرض 120—16
ممرضة 168, 8—118, 44—120
ممرضة جراحة 120—9
ممرضة مرخصة 120—10
ممرضة ممارسة مرخصة 120—11
ممزق الدروز (أداة فك الخياطة) 100—18
ممسحة إسفنجية 61—6
ممسكات الآنية الساخنة 78—29
ممشاة (مشّاية) 113—11
الممطر (معطف واقٍ من المطر) 90—21
ممطر 13—11
ممنوع الانعطاف إلى اليسار 154—8
ممنوع الدخول / اتجاه خطأ 154—2
ممنوع الوقوف 154—11
ممونة أطعمة 185—16
مناديل للتنظيف 37—15
مناديل مطهّرة 61—23
مناديل ورق 54—3

مناطق التوقيت 19
المناظر الخلابة 162—2
المنافس / الخصم 139—30
منبّه 58—24
منتجات الألبان 72
منتجات بقالة 72
منتجات للخبز 73
منتجات مزروعة بسماد طبيعي 84—2
منتصف الليل 18—21
منجلة / ملزمة 180—26
مندهش 43—30
مندوب خدمة عملاء 167—20
منديل رأس مزدان بالرسوم 92—16
منديل قماش للمائدة 83—26
منديل مائدة 55—10
المنزل 46
منزل وفناء 53
منشار دائري 180—9
منشار معادن 180—5
منشار منحنيات 180—10
منشار يدوي 180—4
منشر الغسيل 101—9
منشفة للاستحمام 57—16
منشقة 113—33
منشورات دورية 133—4
منصة 206—5
منصة جلوس خارجية 240—2
منصة نقالة 175—13
منطقة الاستقبال 182—15
منطقة الامتحان 136—2
منطقة الانتظار 182—16
منطقة الصعود إلى الطائرة 161—9
منطقة عمل 154—16
منطقة فرز وتفتيش 160—4
منطقة للعب 130—11
منظار واقٍ 179—11
منظر بديع 23—21
منظر قبيح 23—22
منظف الفرن 61—3
منظف زجاج 61—14
منظف مطهّر 61—18
منعّم الشعر 108—11
منفذ الناقل التسلسلي العام (منفذ يو إس بي) 196—7
منفذ طاقة 159—42
منفرج(ة) 42—15
منقّ للهواء 113—14
منقار 214—3
منقذ / سباح الإنقاذ 225—19
منقّط 96—21
منقوش 96—23
مهاجر 199—13
المهارات المطلوبة للمقابلات الشخصية 174
مهارات حرفية 170
مهارات للعمل في مكتب 171
مهارات هاتفية / تليفونية 171
مهتاج / متهيج 64—6
مهد 59—20

هجرة 199—12	نصف دولار / ٥٠ سنتا 26	ميزان بنابين / شلقول 180—29	مهرجان ريفي 223—13
هدف 231—7	نصف قطر 193—35	ميزانية 186—3	مهملات ملقاة في الطرقات العامة 148—2
هدية 240—3	نصف كوب من الزبيب 75—9	ميكانيكي سيارات 166—5	مهندس 167—25
هراوة / مضرب جولف 231—1	نصلة / شفرة 180—27	ميكروفون 234—18	مهندسة مبرمجات كمبيوتر (حاسوب) 167—18
هرة / قطة 215—9	نظارات 115—7	نائب الحاكم 139—21	مهندسة معمارية 166—5
هرم 193—39	نظارات أمان 92—10	نائب الرئيس 138—9	المهيب 234—15
هرمونيكا 238—21	نظارات سلامة 179—10	نائب رئيس الطهاة (سو شيف) 185—6	مؤئل 194—11
هريرة (هرة صغيرة) 215—10	نظارة شمس (واقية من الشمس) 90—27	ناب 217—48	مواد عازلة 178—14
هزلي (كوميدي) 237—13	النظافة الشخصية 108—109	ناتشوز 79—7	مواد مشعة 179—7
هضبة المكسيك 201—15	نظام اتصال داخلي (إنتركوم) 50—5	نادل / جرسون 82—8	المواسير مجمدة 63—16
هلال 205—10	النظام الشمسي والكواكب 205	نادلة 169—56	مواشي 177—15
هلال / قمر أول الشهر 205—9	النظام القانوني 141	نادلة / جرسونة 83—9، 185—8	مواصلات إلى المطار 152
هليون 69—26	نظام الهاتف / التليفون الآلي 14—23	نادي ليلي / ملهى ليلي 223—12	موتيل (فندق صغير) 126—12
هناك زر مفقود 97—40	نظام تحويل هاتفي / تليفوني 182—13	نار المخيم 226—11	موجة 225—17
الهندسة 192—17	نظام حقن الوقود 158—17	ناشط سياسيا 199—17	موجة حارة 13—13
هوائي / إيريال 14—9	نظّف A—76	ناطحة سحاب / بناية عالية الارتفاع 127—13	موجة بحرية مدية / تسونامي 145—17
هوايات وألعاب 232—233	نظّف المكان من الأنقاض M—147	ناظر المدرسة / مدير المدرسة 5—4	موز 68—2
هوكي الجليد 229—13	نظّم أفكارك G—191	نافخ أوراق الشجر 176—2	موز عفن 68—32
هيئة التمريض 120	نعسان 42—3	نافذة / شبّاك 47—11، 56—17، 136—7	موز عير ناضج (نئ) 68—31
هيئة محلفين 141—8	نعل الحذاء 94—21	نافذة تقديم الأطعمة للسيارات 128—11	موز ناضج (مستوي) 68—30
هيب هوب (راقصة) 237—26	نفائس / أشياء ثمينة 132—8	النافذة مكسورة 62—5	موس حلاقة 109—28
هيلولى 194—9	نفايات خطرة 218—12	نافورة 224—5	موسيقى 168—43
الواجبات 140	نفس اللون (ألوان متشابهة) 23—15	نافورة مياه للشرب 224—9	موسيقى 64—3، 189—16، 238
واحد كامل 17—1	النفط / البترول 218—6	ناقشي مشكلة G—8	موسيقى الرجي 237—31
الواحد والعشرون 16	نقار الخشب 214—8	ناقل التروس 159—47	موسيقى الكآبة (بلوز) 237—22
الواحدة وعشرون دقيقة 18—10	نقالة مرضى 121—33	ناقل حركة أوتوماتيكي 159	موسيقى حية 84—1
الواحدة وأربعون دقيقة 18—12	نقّح / دقق I—191	ناقل حركة يدوي 159	موسيقى صاخبة راقصة (روك آند رول) 237—23
الواحدة والثلث 18—10	نقد وعملة 146—17	نايلون 99—12	موسيقى عالمية 237—32
الواحدة والربع 18—9	نقطة 190—11	نبات منزلي 56—4	موشور / منشور زجاجي 195—35
الواحدة والنصف 18—11	نقطة البداية 162—1	نباتات 208—5، 210	موظ 216—1
الواحدة وثلاثون دقيقة 18—11	نقطة نهاية 193—21	نبتة / فرخ 211—5	موظف 165—9، 182—2
الواحدة وخمس دقائق 18—7	نقطتان 190—17	نبتة صغيرة 211—4	موظف استقبال 118—2
الواحدة وخمسة عشر دقيقة 18—9	النقل العام 152	نبتة منزلية 211—27	موظف الإدخال 120—14
الواحدة وخمسة وأربعون دقيقة 18—13	النقود 26	نبتون 205—8	موظف تنظيم الملفات 182—10
الواحدة وعشر دقائق 18—8	نكاف / أبو كعب 111—7	نتائج الانتخابات 139—31	موظف جمارك 161—17
وادي 204—18	نيكل / ٥ سنتات 26	نتيجة المباراة 229—1	موظف دائرة تسجيل المركبات الآلية 136—3
وادي ضيق 204—17	نمر 217—37	النتيجة 10—3	موظف فندق 184—11
وافق K—12	نمر أمريكي 217—40	النجاح في المدرسة 10	موظف مبيعات 169—53
واق من أشعة الشمس 108—7	نملة (نمل) 63—23	نجّار 62—12، 166—14	موظف مسؤول عن الشحن 175—14
واقيات قصبة الرجل 231—13	نموذج للتفصيل (باترون) 99—22	نجم 205—13	موظف / ـة 5—13
واقية الأذان 179—16	نملة بيضاء (نمل أبيض) 63—22	نجم البحر 212—16	موظفة استقبال 164—5، 169—51
وجبة عشاء مجمدة 72—28	نهاية الأسبوع (عطلة نهاية الأسبوع) 20—17	نحلة عسل 214—25	موظفة الاستقبال 182—14
وجع أسنان 110—2	نهر 155—10، 204—3	نحيف(ة) 32—9	موظفة بريد 169—49
وجه 193—44	نواة 194—7، 195—29	نخر / بلى 119—7	موظفة جدول الرواتب 165—10
الوجه 106	النوع 4—16	نخل 210—14	موعد 22—4، 118—1
وحيد 42—17	نوفمبر / تشرين الثاني 21—35	نرجس بري 211—25	موفينية إنجليزية 80—5
وردة 211—15	نونية للأطفال 37—12	نزيف في الأنف 110—17	موقد 54—18
وردة عنق / بمباغ / بابيون 89—16	نيو إنغلاند 201—11	نزيل 184—10	موقع تخييم 226—16
وردي 24—7	نيوترون 195—32	نساء 30—3	موقع إنشاءات 126—2
ورق 211—6	الهاتف / التليفون 14—15	النسب المئوية 17	موقف أوتوبيس 129—16، 152
ورق إنشاء 232—12	هاتف / تليفون بالأجرة (تليفون عمومي)	نسخ مصورة من الأوراق المهمة 146—20	موقف أوتوبيس / موقف حافلات 151—13
ورق تغليف ألمونيوم 72—23	129—15، 25—23	نسخ مصورة من بطاقات الهوية	موقف سيارات أجرة (تاكسي) 152—18
ورق تغليف بلاستيكي 72—24	هاتف / تليفون ذكي 15—27	وبطاقات الانتمان 146—19	موقف للمعاقين 154—12
ورق توايليت 57—19، 146—13	هاتف / تليفون لاسلكي 15—24	نشافة ملابس 101—4	موكب استعراضي 239—1
ورق حائط 59—8	هاتف / تليفون محمول أو خلوي 14—8	نشرة إعلانية 102—1	ميثاق الحقوق 198—13
ورق سنفرة 181—56	هادئ(ة) 42—8	نص 190—7	ميزان 57—27، 72—3، 135—8، 195—41
ورق طبع في رأسه اسم المؤسسة / قرطاسية 183—42	هبوط / وصول K—160	نصف 17—2	ميزان بريدي 183—27

يشتري منزلا M–41	يدخل بيانات B–171	يبحث عن كتاب B–133	ورق مذكرة 7–28
يشحن D–175	يدخل على الطريق السريع I–153	يبرمج كمبيوترات I–170	الورقات 26
يشعر/تشعر بالدوار (دوخة) C–110	يدخل في مناظرة B–139	يبقى على اطلاع بما يجري F–140	ورقة 210–6
يشغّل/يذيع B–235	يدفع الضرائب B–140	يبيع سيارات K–170	ورقة إبرية 210–10
يشغّل آلات ثقيلة H–170	يدفع الفاتورة (الحساب) I–82	يتحدث لغة ثانية N–170	ورقة الإجابات 10–2
يشم C–106	يدفع تقدا A–27	يتخرُج D–40	ورقة بيانات طبية 121–24
يصاب بإصابة / يصاب بأذى C–116	يدفع غرامة تأخير E–133	يتذوق D–106	ورم في الإصبع 110–16
يصاب بصدمة B–116	يدق بالمطرقة D–178	يترك بقشيشا J–82	وريد 107–37
يصاب بصدمة كهربائية F–116	يدهن / يطلي P–49	يتزلج على الثلج V–230	الوزارة (مجلس الوزراء) 138–10
يصاب بنوبة قليلة D–116	يذهب (يسير) فوق الجسر B–153	يتزوّج K–41	الوزرة (أوفرول) 88–6
يصبح مواطنا G–40	يذهب / تذهب للفراش Y–39	يتساقط الثلج 13–12	الوزن 32
يصدر الحكم بمعاقبة المتهم F–141	يرتّب (يسوّي) السرير F–60	يتسلقان القضبان C–224	وسائل الاستجمام في الطبيعة 226
يصرف شيكا سياحيا F–27	يرتّب الأثاث Q–49	يتطوّع Q–41	وسائل النجاح 10
يصرف شيكا A–132	يرتّب أوراقا E–171	يتعلّم قيادة السيارة E–40	وسائل النقل الأساسية 150
يصفف الشعر C–33	يرجع / يصل إلى المنزل R–39	يتغرغر L–109	وسائل للحفاظ على الطاقة والموارد الطبيعية 219
يصل لخط النهاية T–230	يرسل وثيقة بالفاكس G–171	يتفرّج على بيوت H–49	وسادة / مخدة 58–11
يصلح أدوات منزلية J–170	يرشّح نفسه لمنصب عام A–139	يتقابل مع سمسار عقارات G–49	وسادة كنبة للزينة 56–2
يصمم A–175	يرصد القرميد (الطوب) B–178	يتقاعد O–41	وسط المدينة 124
يصنع B–175	يرقانة 214–20	يتمنى / يفكّر في أمنية B–240	وسيم(ة) 32–13
يصنع الأثاث G–170	يرقصون A–64	يتناول كمية مفرطة من الدواء K–116	وشاح شتوي 90–5
يصنع / يصوّر نسخا D–171	يركّب البلاط C–178	يتناولون الإفطار E–38	وشم 32–18
يصوت في الانتخابات A–140	يركّب نظاما لرش المياه H–176	يتناولون العشاء S–39	وصف الأشياء 23
يصير جدا N–41	يركض عبر الشارع G–153	يتوفّى / يموت R–41	وصف الشعر 33
يضحك A–44	يركل E–230	يتولى / يحصُل على الملكية K–49	وصف الملابس 96–97
يضرب B–230	يرمي A–230	يتولى منصبه D–139	وصف الناس 32
يضع اللعب في مكانها G–60	يرى A–106	يجري أعمالا بنكية على الإنترنت C–132	وصفة طبية (روشتة) 112–2
يضلّ الطريق / يتوه B–162	يزرع A–177	يجز المرجة A–176	وظائف ومهن 166–169
يضيّق البنطلون D–100	يزيل الأطباق من على الطاولة / يُنظّف الطاولة G–82	يجمّع C–175	وظيفة جديدة 172–3
يطبخ C–170		يجمع أوراق الشجر بالمدمّة C–176	وظيفة لمبتدئ 172–1
يطبع A–196	يسابق S–230	يجمع / تجمع القطع A–170	وعاء الطهي بالبخار 78–3
يطبع وثيقة على طابعة I–171	يساعد المرضى B–170	يحاكم / يخضع للمحاكمة D–141	وعاء / إناء 55–2
يُطعم C–36	يساعد زبونا D–95	يحدد موعدا لاجتماع J–171	وعاء / إناء للخلط 54–28
يطفئ الشمع C–240	يسافر P–41	يحرر شيكا (شخصيا) D–27	وعاء لتصريف النفايات 54–7
يطلب تسجيل المنافع العامة باسمه O–49	يسبح L–230	يحرق نفسه H–116	وعاء للسرير / نونية 121–23
يطلب من قائمة الطعام D–82	يستبدل I–27	يحزّم / يربط حزام الأمان L–36	وعاء للمهملات المعاد تدويرها 61–2
يطلي / يدهن A–178	يستخدم بطاقة ائتمان B–27	يحصد B–177	وعاء مهملات / صفيحة زبالة 51–23
يطوّل البنطلون A–100	يستخدم بطاقة إهداء E–27	يحصل على بطاقة مكتبة A–133	وعاء مهملات 53–24
يطير طائرة F–170	يستخدم بطاقة خصم من الحساب C–27	يحصل على قرض J–49	وعاء / حاوية جبن حلوم 74–17
يطيع القانون C–140	يسترخي U–39	يحصل على وظيفة F–40	وقاء للأذن من البرد 90–13
يعاني من حساسية E–116	يستعرض السلع المعروضة للبيع B–102	يحضّر الطاولة A–82	الوقت 18–19
يعبر الطريق في غير المكان المخصص لذلك C–128	يستعمل مزيل رائحة العرق C–108	يحفر السن D–119	وقّع اسمك D–4
يعد الصحف للاستعمال ثانية B–60	يستعير كتابا C–133	يحكم بإدانة المتهم E–141	وكيل تذاكر 160–3
يعطس B–110	يستنسخ ملاحظات C–171	يحلب C–177	وكيل تي إن إيه / مفتش أمن 160–5
يعلف / يقدم العلف D–177	يستل ضرب الكرة P–230	يحلق M–109	ولايات المحيط الهادي / الساحل الغربي 201–7
يعمل K–38	يستيقظ A–38	يحمل الصينية H–82	ولايات جبال الروكي 201–8
يعمل الواجب المدرسي T–39	يسجّل A–235	يحمل الطفل A–36	ولايات منطقة الأطلنطي الوسطى 201–10
يعمل في الحديقة B–53	يسجل اسمه في الخدمة الانتقائية D–140	يختبئ D–240	الولاية 4–8
يعيد كتابا D–133	يسجّل الطلب E–82	يخدّر الفم C–119	ولد عمره ٦ سنوات 31–9
يغادر العمل N–38	يسجن / يودع السجن G–141	يخرج من الطريق السريع J–153	وليمة 239–13
يغرق I–116	يسدد دفعة الرهن العقاري L–49	يخرج من سيارة الأجرة (التاكسي) F–153	يؤدي الخدمة في هيئة محلفين E–140
يغسل الأطباق أو الصحون M–60	يسعل A–110	يخرز / يدبّس F–171	يأخذ أشعة سينية B–119
يغطس K–230	يسكب الماء C–82	يخطب حبيبته J–41	يأخذ حماما / يستحمّ B–108
يغنّي أغنية B–238	يسمّد / يغذّي النباتات D–176	يخلو إطار السيارة من الهواء / تنام العجلة F–162	يأخذ مذكرات بالإملاء K–171
يفحص النبض A–122	يسمع B–106	يد 105–15	يأخذ/يحصل على مخالفة لتجاوز السرعة القصوى C–162
يفرَج عنه / يطلق سراحه H–141	يسوق شاحنة E–170	يد صغيرة 23–1	ياسمين 211–22
يفرّغ سلة المهملات L–60	يسوق عبر النفق K–153	يد كبيرة 23–2	ياقة 100–4
	يشاهد التلفزيون X–39	يدخل المدرسة B–40	

يودع نقدا أو شيكا B-132
يوسّع البنطلون C-100
يوسفي 9-68
يوصّل (يأخذ) الأطفال إلى المدرسة / ينزّل الأطفال
عند باب المدرسة G-38
يوصّل البريد E-135
يوقف سيارة E-129
يوقف مؤقتا E-235
يوكّل محاميا B-141
يولد A-40
يوليو / تموز 31-21
يوم 2-20
اليوم 5-20
اليوم المدرسي 11
يوم سيء في العمل 186
يونيو / حزيران 30-21

يفقد الوعي A-116
يفوز في الانتخابات C-139
يقابل / تقابل الجيران R-49
يقبّله متمنيا له نوما مريحا P-36
يقتلع (يخلع) السن F-119
يقتلع العشب من أحواض الزهور G-176
يقدّم الوجبة F-82
يقدّم عرضا I-49
يقرأ له N-36
يقرسها الصقيع G-116
يقص الشعر A-33
يقصّر البنطلون B-100
يقع في غرام فتاة H-40
يقود السيارة إلى مكان العمل / يذهب إلى العمل I-38
يقود أوركسترا C-238
يقوم بأعمال يدوية D-170
يقومون بجولة سياحية A-220
يكسر عظمة من عظامه P-116
يكنس الأرضية بالمقشة J-60
يكنس السجاد بالمكنسة الكهربائية H-60
يلبس الحذاء لقياسها C-95
يلبس ثيابه D-38
يلتحق بالجامعة I-41
يلتقط صورة فوتوغرافية A-206
يلعب في فرقة روك آند رول D-238
يلعبان الشدة H-233
يلقف D-230
يلقي C-230
يلقي القبض على شخص مشتبه فيه A-141
يلقي القمامة Q-60
يلمس (يحس باللمس) E-106
يلوّن (يصبغ) الشعر D-33
يمارس رياضة P-39
يمثل أمام القضاء C-141
يمحو C-196
يمرر G-230
يمسح الأرضية D-60
يمسك بالخصم لإيقافه F-230
يمشّي كلبا F-129
يملأ النخر E-119
يموّج الشعر B-33
ينام / تنام Z-39
يناير / كانون الثاني 25-21
ينتظر (يقف) في الطابور B-94
ينتظر الإشارة الضوئية B-128
ينتقل إلى السطر التالي D-196
ينتقي B-196
ينزف M-116
ينزل / يهبط الدرجات مشيا على قدميه D-153
ينسخ وثيقة بماسحة H-171
ينطلق R-230
ينظّف الأسنان A-119
ينظّف الأسنان بالخيط K-109
ينظّف الأسنان بالفرشاة J-109
ينظّفون المنزل O-39
يهاجر / يهاجرون C-40
اليوجا 4-122

Research Bibliography

The authors and publisher wish to acknowledge the contribution of the following educators for their research on vocabulary development, which has helped inform the principals underlying OPD.

Burt, M., J. K. Peyton, and R. Adams. *Reading and Adult English Language Learners: A Review of the Research*. Washington, D.C.: Center for Applied Linguistics, 2003.

Coady, J. "Research on ESL/EFL Vocabulary Acquisition: Putting it in Context." In *Second Language Reading and Vocabulary Learning*, edited by T. Huckin, M. Haynes, and J. Coady. Norwood, NJ: Ablex, 1993.

de la Fuente, M. J. "Negotiation and Oral Acquisition of L2 Vocabulary: The Roles of Input and Output in the Receptive and Productive Acquisition of Words." *Studies in Second Language Acquisition* 24 (2002): 81–112.

DeCarrico, J. "Vocabulary learning and teaching." In *Teaching English as a Second or Foreign Language,* edited by M. Celcia-Murcia. 3rd ed. Boston: Heinle & Heinle, 2001.

Ellis, R. *The Study of Second Language Acquisition*. Oxford: Oxford University Press, 1994.

Folse, K. *Vocabulary Myths: Applying Second Language Research to Classroom Teaching*. Ann Arbor, MI: University of Michigan Press, 2004.

Gairns, R. and S. Redman. *Working with Words: A Guide to Teaching and Learning Vocabulary*. Cambridge: Cambridge University Press, 1986.

Gass, S. M. and M.J.A. Torres. "Attention When?: An Investigation Of The Ordering Effect Of Input And Interaction." *Studies in Second Language Acquisition* 27 (Mar 2005): 1–31.

Henriksen, Birgit. "Three Dimensions of Vocabulary Development." *Studies in Second Language Acquisition* 21 (1999): 303–317.

Koprowski, Mark. "Investigating the Usefulness of Lexical Phrases in Contemporary Coursebooks." *Oxford ELT Journal* 59(4) (2005): 322–32.

McCrostie, James. "Examining Learner Vocabulary Notebooks." *Oxford ELT Journal* 61 (July 2007): 246–55.

Nation, P. *Learning Vocabulary in Another Language*. Cambridge: Cambridge University Press, 2001.

National Center for ESL Literacy Education Staff. *Adult English Language Instruction in the 21st Century*. Washington, D.C.: Center for Applied Linguistics, 2003.

National Reading Panel. *Teaching Children to Read: An Evidenced-Based Assessment of the Scientific Research Literature on Reading and its Implications on Reading Instruction*. 2000. http://www.nationalreadingpanel.org/Publications/summary.htm/.

Newton, J. "Options for Vocabulary Learning Through Communication Tasks." *Oxford ELT Journal* 55(1) (2001): 30–37.

Prince, P. "Second Language Vocabulary Learning: The Role of Context Versus Translations as a Function of Proficiency." *Modern Language Journal* 80(4) (1996): 478-93.

Savage, K. L., ed. *Teacher Training Through Video - ESL Techniques: Early Production*. White Plains, NY: Longman Publishing Group, 1992.

Schmitt, N. *Vocabulary in Language Teaching*. Cambridge: Cambridge University Press, 2000.

Smith, C. B. *Vocabulary Instruction and Reading Comprehension*. Bloomington, IN: ERIC Clearinghouse on Reading English and Communication, 1997.

Wood, K. and J. Josefina Tinajero. "Using Pictures to Teach Content to Second Language Learners." *Middle School Journal* 33 (2002): 47–51.